THE DEFINITIVE BIOGRAPHY

BOB CRANE
The Definitive Biography

Carol M. Ford

with Dee Young and Linda J. Groundwater

Copyright © 2015 Carol M. Ford

All Rights Reserved

ISBN: 978-1-943201-04-4

Library of Congress Control Number: 2015903933

Cover Credits:
Graphic Design by Darin Peters

All rights reserved. No part of this publication may be reproduced or transmitted in any form or by any means, electronic or mechanical, including photocopying, recording, or any information storage and retrieval system without the written permission of the author.

The authors have made every effort to ensure the accuracy of the information within this book was correct at time of publication. The author does not assume and hereby disclaims any liability to any party for any loss, damage, or disruption caused by errors or omissions, whether such errors or omissions result from accident, negligence, or any other cause.

Fron cover photograph:
Bob Crane from his days at KNX-CBS Radio. Image dated March 29, 1962.
Source: © Disney ABC Television Group. Photographer: ABC Photo Archives. Courtesy of Getty Images. Used with permission.

Back cover photograph:
Bob Crane as Colonel Robert E. Hogan from the *Hogan's Heroes* episode, "The Experts." Image dated June 24, 1970.
Source: © CBS/Landov. Used with permission.

First Published by *AuthorMike Ink, 9/17/2015*

www.AuthorMikeInk.com

AuthorMike Ink and its logos are trademarked by *AuthorMike Ink.*

Printed in the United States of America

Dedicated to
Charles A. Zito

Carol Ford and her colleagues have exhaustively researched every conceivable detail of Bob Crane's life. This book shifts the focus from the sensational and the negative to a holistic, factual view of a talented individual whose life ended too soon. Even those who are not fans of Bob Crane will find this book worthwhile reading.

—Cindy Vitto, PhD, Dean, College of Humanities and Social Sciences, Rowan University, Glassboro, New Jersey

If you're a Bob Crane fan, this book is a must. Loved the old pictures of Crane in his WLEA days.

—Kevin Doran, owner, WLEA 1480-AM

The family really appreciates what you're doing for Bobby. We sure do. Bobby was just a big teddy bear..., and everybody loved him, and they didn't want to hear any bad things. Strange, people probably think he walked around with horns sticking out of his head, but he was a good guy.

—Jim Senich, cousin

Bob Crane was a broadcasting pioneer who made landmark contributions to the industry on both coasts, but until now, has never received proper credit for much of it. Ford and her colleagues delve into Crane's radio career like never before. What they have discovered and presented here is nothing short of amazing.

—Danny Lyons, WICC 600-AM and WEBE 108-FM operations manager/ WEBE on-air personality, Bridgeport, Connecticut

Bob Crane: The Definitive Biography *is the most extensive biography I've read about a movie or TV actor... The authors captured fond memories and perspectives from Bob's friends and relatives who knew him best...* Bob Crane: The Definitive Biography *is a must read for anyone who is a fan of his TV show and legendary radio work.*

—Bill Dillane, NHTV, North Haven, Connecticut

Bob Crane's definitive book by Ford, Young, and Groundwater is easily one of the best Hollywood-related books I have seen. The research is fantastic... I would easily place Bob Crane: The Definitive Biography *in a top ten list of performing arts nonfiction.*

—James Zeruk, Jr., Author of *Peg Entwistle and the Hollywood Sign Suicide*

This book sheds light on an addiction that is tragically confined to the shadows, behind closed doors. Sex addicts are subject to immediate moral judgment, when we are ironically more accepting of other addictions. Bob Crane: The Definitive Biography *can serve as an inspiration for anyone seeking to understand the often double world of the sex addict.*
 —Susanne A. Quallich, ANP-BC, NP-C, CUNP, FANNP, University of Michigan Health System; Member, *Urologic Nursing* Journal Editorial Board; and an Expert on Men's Sexual Health

Bob Crane: The Definitive Biography *is an in-depth, well-researched look at a man with an immense talent that has been, since his death, highly underrated. The authors have done an outstanding job. There are many biographies in the world of literature, and this is certainly up there with the best of them.*
 —Dean Mardon, former host, *The Dave Dee Drivetime Show*, Radio Kidnappers, 1431-AM/104.7 FM, Napier, New Zealand

Acknowledgements

This project has been far more than just researching, writing, and publishing a book for me. It has been nearly a life-long journey. I first discovered *Hogan's Heroes* in the mid-1980s when I was just fourteen years old. *Hogan's Heroes* quickly became my favorite television show, and Bob Crane was my favorite among the cast. There was no Internet in 1985, so I didn't discover any details about the life and death of the show's star right away. But soon, I did learn about Bob's unsolved murder, and I was crushed. And my little, fourteen-year-old self made a promise that somehow, some way, I would fix it and make it better. As a kid, I had *no* idea how I was *ever* going to do that. But that didn't stop me.

This inexplicable determination to "fix it" grew. On weekends, other kids went to the movies or to the mall; my parents took me to the county library to "research" Bob Crane. Over the years, I started to *understand* who Bob Crane really was, and the more I understood, the more tenacious I became. When Linda Groundwater, Dee Young, and I crossed paths and began collaborating on this book in 2006, all of the pieces started to come together.

It took a little while, but now, more than thirty years later, I have *finally* made good on that promise.

I didn't travel this path alone. So many people have walked some or all of it with me. They cheered me on when things got exciting, and stood by me and held me up when I was frustrated or at the point of exhaustion. To my loyal family, friends, and colleagues, I owe you so much, and no amount of thanks will ever repay you for your love, friendship, help, and support.

My unending gratitude goes to:

Karen Crane, Robert Scott and Zoe (Taylor) Crane, Jack Crane, Max Crane, Jim Senich, Jane Senich Ryfun, Barbara Senich Trembley, Faye and Reverend Edward Beck, Charlie and Yvonne Zito, Doug Palmer, Arlene Martel, Morgan Kaolian, Carole S., Danny Lyons, Frank Derak, Al Warren, Curt Hanson, Paul Groundwater, Andrew Groundwater, Michael Ambrosini, Raul Moreno, Joe Cosgrove, Leo and Carole McElroy, Stosh Jarecki, Cecilia East, Ed Robertson, Diane and Tom

Thornton, Jack Coomb, Gary Lycan, Pamela and John Thompson, Carol and Dr. Edwin Gordon, Jane Lippoth Golden, Don and Judy Sappern, Wayne Zito, Judy and Brian Zito, Debbie Zito Buzzeo, Ken and Kathy Thomas, Jack Bryant, Kevin Shumaker, Heidi Perret, Joe Tonzelli, Janet D'Alesandro, Katie R. Brownlow, Ryan Rayburn, Cicelia Theresa "Punkin" Krug, Kristina Moran, Bob Taylor, Todd Lockhart, Katie Gallagher, Sharon Hampton, Miriam Perez-Martin, Rebekah Lazar, Linda and Kevin Alexander, Sally and Steve Russell, Jamie and Ryan Curran, Erin and Eric Fisher, Rosaria Mineo, Kathy Pane Miratello, Elise and Ian Turner, Lori Ann and Mike Palma, Laura and Mark Douglas, Lauren McClintock, Noreen Dunn, Melody Edwards, Jane Hokanson Hawks, Beth Ulrich, Judy Rollins, Brian and Donna Dettling, Meredith Smith, Pauline and Gavan Callahan, Melanie Davis, Andrew Davis, Bianca Ellison, Susan Goldring Rubinstein, Angel Rosenthal, Vrinda Rao, Veronica Ochipinti Menard, Corrine Ochipinti, Antoinette Gurden, Robert Scardino, Denise and Joe Centola, Cliff and Wanda Henderson, Marc and Tania Celia, Maria Llull, Zack Llull, Leslie Warner Kohler, Sharon Bain, Stu and Lesley Woolley, Dave Sorensen, LaVerne Cash, Marty Breedlove, Becky Cloud, Ashley Cross, Bill Dillane, John Ramsey, Jude H. Cormier, Kevin P. Doran, Brian O'Neil, Joe Farnham, Bob Cain, Dean Mardon, Angela Caporizzo, Ron Marcus, Mary Witkowski of the Bridgeport Public Library, Don Barrett (Los Angeles Radio People), Louis K. Sherwood, Jr., Texas Wesleyan College (Fort Worth, Texas), Nancy Vaskas, Philippe Spurrell, Le Cinéclub: The Film Society (Montreal, Quebec), Uri Davidov (for Landov), Ashley Dumazer (for Getty Images), Stamford High School, WLEA 1480-AM (Hornell, New York), WICC 600-AM (Bridgeport, Connecticut), Radio Kidnappers (Napier, New Zealand), WKAL 1450 AM (Rome/Utica, New York), the Stamford Historical Society, CBS Columbia Square Alumni Group (Los Angeles, California), the Connecticut Broadcasting History organization, Bridgeport Symphony Orchestra (formerly Connecticut Symphony Orchestra, Bridgeport, Connecticut), and the Stamford High School Class of 1946.

Very special thanks to:

My publisher Mike Aloisi, who saw the potential of this book, and who guided me and also allowed me to do certain things my way. Thank you so much for trusting me, and for understanding this book's importance and believing in it.

Darin Peters, my graphic artist and designer, who gave the pages of this book a creative personal touch, endured my pickiness, and worked tirelessly to make it perfect. You are a true "Miracle Worker" and a dear friend, and you have made this book finally become a reality with a design that is visually stunning.

Dee Young, my investigative "partner in crime," Connecticut radio resource extraordinaire, and dear friend, I couldn't have gotten through this without you. You spent countless days and nights trekking across Connecticut with me by road, rail, and sky to travel in Bob's footsteps and understand *his* Connecticut. We have laughed together and cried together, and without you, this book would not be here. I love you like a sister, always.

Linda Groundwater, the first person to bravely step forward and start this project in 2003 and who I joined forces with in March 2006. We worked literally around the clock, you and I, talking with so many beautiful people from Bob's life. Our roles on the project changed, but the goal never did—to tell Bob's honest, true, and *complete* story, and to put him first before our own egos, always. Thank you for starting this, thank you for caring so much about Bob, and thank you for helping me push it up and over the mountain to the finish line. I will remain forever grateful to you, my "sisterfriend."

And finally, my deepest, heartfelt thanks and love go to my family—my sister Barbara and her husband Jeff Reim, my exceptionally talented nephews Benjamin and Adam Reim, and my parents Robert and Jan Ford. I love you all more than anything and anybody, and hope I have made you proud.

—Carol M. Ford
March 2015

Foreword

I don't know if it was the harmlessness of classic 1960s sitcoms that attracted me, or the memory of that addictive opening title music floating through my childhood home, but I became happily reacquainted with *Hogan's Heroes* in 2003. Watching the episode, I was taken with its cleverness and simple wish to entertain, and I was hooked.

It didn't take long before I remembered that the star, Bob Crane, had been murdered. I was only a pre-teen at the time, and I didn't remember any of the details. But he struck me on screen as a talented and funny man, and so I looked it up on the Internet. And what I found astounded me.

Yes, I found the details of the murder. Yes, I found an overwhelming amount of information about his private sex life (the movie *Auto Focus,* a purported "biopic," had been released in 2002, sending the online world into a frenzy of salaciousness and character assassination). But what really struck me was what was buried beneath the surface, all these things I didn't know: that Bob Crane had been a groundbreaking disc jockey; that he was an excellent and avid drummer; that he was from New England, like me; that he did enormous amounts of charity work. I got more and more fascinated.

And then I got angry.

Why didn't the world know *this* stuff? Why was all anyone knew about Bob connected with his sex life? Why was *this* his legacy?

It didn't seem fair. And it wasn't. Right then and there, I vowed to do something about it. I was a journalist when I was in the U.S., and although I was now ten thousand miles away in Australia, I had the Internet and determination. And so I began. And eventually, I had Carol Ford and Dee Young, who could do things in the U.S. that I couldn't do from here, and the project grew. And the more we learned, the more I was sure that what I had started was the right thing for us to do.

Bob was more than his addiction. He was a man who loved his family, loved his work, loved his country. He gave and gave and gave. And though his judgment wasn't always sound, his heart was always in the right place.

I'm so proud to have been a part of showing the world the flip side of Bob Crane. What we present in this book is what his legacy should be: the truth.

—*Linda J. Groundwater*
March 2015

Contents

Remembering Bob Crane 3

Author's Introduction 15

Preface 21

Chapter 1 – The Spirit of Stamford, Connecticut 25

Chapter 2 – A Star Is Born 53

Chapter 3 – The Idea of Learning 75

Chapter 4 – The Invincible Robert Crane 105

Chapter 5 – The Actor's Actor 147

Chapter 6 – Welcome to Stalag 13, Colonel Hogan 187

Chapter 7 – Among the Stellar Elite 279

Chapter 8 – Masquerade 323

Chapter 9 – Life's Illusions 371

Chapter 10 – Third Act Twist 457

Chapter 11 – Specks on the Parthenon 511

Chapter 12 – Laughing All the Way to the Grave 583

Resources 601

Index 627

Source: Courtesy of Scott Crane. Used with permission.

Remembering Bob Crane

(As told to the authors of this book.)

My first introduction to Bob Crane occurred when he had a morning show on radio. I was his guest for half an hour and found his interview full of interest in me refreshing. I watched his performances on TV, and based on those shows, had no difficulty in recommending him to Norman Barasch for *Beginner's Luck*. Bob was a good-looking guy—a bit rugged in appearance with a brashness that projected a great personality. It was a tragedy that his life was cut down so early.

— *Monty Hall, producer, actor, singer, sportscaster, game show host*

He brought a distinctive style that was unique. There never has been and there never will be another Bob Crane. When I think about Bob Crane, I think about a ray of light. I think about a person of love. That's how I remember Bob Crane, and that's how Bob Crane should be remembered.

— *Joe Cosgrove, KPOL (Los Angeles) staff announcer, and owner, KTHL, Lake Tahoe, CA.*

I called him to do the telethon, and I asked him to come to Connecticut to do the local segment. Bob said, "I'll do it for you for $2,000"—just to cover expenses. National would have paid him almost $20,000 to do it. They couldn't figure out why he did it for me, but he did it.

— *Eliot Dober, friend and former Connecticut State Director for United Cerebral Palsy; Executive Director of the Office of Protection and Advocacy for Persons with Disabilities for the State of Connecticut*

I loved Bob. I worked with him, and we had an awful lot of fun at the WICC Booth Hill stations. I knew Bob as a good musician; a very, very talented morning man on radio; and just a great, all-around fun-type guy.

— *Morgan Kaolian, WICC traffic announcer and Channel 43 television personality*

We're hoping to put this right. I really believe what they did in [*Auto Focus*] was make him look as though he were a sleazy guy, and that's the last thing he was. He was really a gentleman. The sensationalism people go after is just unconscionable.
— *Pam Thompson, actress, "Beginner's Luck," "Send Me No Flowers," and "The Bob Crane Show"*

Disc jockey was really not the term for Bob Crane or myself. Radio personality is probably a better definition because we did more than just give the time and the temperature. We would give anecdotes about people who were friends of ours—Frank Sinatra, Dean Martin, Peggy Lee, Lena Horne, Ella Fitzgerald, [and others].
— *Gary Owens, KMPC radio personality; actor and comedian, "Laugh-In"*

Bob was kind. He was kind to those he worked with. He was kind to those he knew. There were many sides to Bob, and not all were bad.
— *Leo McElroy, KNX radio staff announcer*

Bob was very professional, agreeable, charming, easygoing. He was a wonderful guest. I just can't overuse the word wonderful. He was one of our *best* guests.
— *Anne Kear, talent agent, "Celebrity Cooks"*

I'm happy to set a wrong right. Bob was a well-together, fun gentleman. Full of laughs. A real professional.
— *Derek Smith, owner and producer, "Celebrity Cooks"*

Bob was a great, doting dad and loved his children. It's a part of his life he really wanted to be very important.
— *John Thompson, actor, "Beginner's Luck"*

If Bob could help this screwed up world in some way, he'd try to find a way to fix it. He liked good things. He liked kindness—because he *was* kind. He was trying to heal the world by laughter.
— *Cynthia Lynn, actress, "Hogan's Heroes"*

I think it's wonderful to point out that this is a person who had a huge amount of talent and who everybody loved and who was a decent, loving guy, and charming, and did great things.

— *Diane Thornton, KNX librarian*

Bob was a great friend who always made us laugh. I never remember him being ugly or unfriendly. I couldn't associate those reported stories with my friend Bob. It just didn't fit his character.

— *Neil McGuinness, school friend and classmate*

Bob was very thoughtful, and he cared about people. He wanted to do the right thing. I really believe that. That's why I liked him. You never know *everything* about *anybody*. Even your own family, sometimes they surprise you with things that they've been thinking, and thinking, and thinking about, and suddenly, will pop out. So I think we have to give each other breaks. We do the best we can, that's my motto.

— *Maureen Arthur, actress, "The Wicked Dreams of Paula Schultz"*

He was a good friend and a good listener. He was not a braggart. I think he would have eventually been a more important actor if he had stayed alive. Bob didn't get what he deserved. He was a *star*. Some people have said he was a young Jack Lemmon, and what he was hoping to do was follow in the footsteps of a Jack Lemmon-type and become a serious actor as well. That was his original aim, not just to be a Hogan's Hero, but to be something else. So that's what he was working toward. That's what he would have been doing over the last twenty or thirty years.

— *Harvey Geller, friend and neighbor*
Former Vice President and editor, "Cash Box" (West Coast)
Columnist, feature writer, reviewer, and sales executive, "Variety" and "Billboard" magazines

He was a very loving and caring person, a total professional, and his work was a gift to the industry. *Hogan's Heroes* gave joy to millions, and that was his signature. He was a very talented man, and to lose *that*—he gave a lot to us as an actor and a person.

— *Victoria Berry Wells, actress, "Beginner's Luck"*

He was a proud guy. It wasn't the kind of ego that was nasty. He was the star of the show, and he knew it, but he never threw it around. I think he wanted to be good. He would never settle. If he muffed a line, which was rare, we'd do it again. From the time he did the pilot to the time he did the last show, he was Hogan. *He was Hogan.*

— *Jerry London, associate producer and director, "Hogan's Heroes"*

I would want people to know that Bob Crane was a child of God, and he should be seen in that light. You don't just discard someone because they lost their way.

— *Arlene Martel, actress, "Hogan's Heroes"*

Bob was open and friendly. He should be remembered as a hard-working actor and not a *weirdo*. He should be remembered as a normal guy who strayed. He was such a nice person to me. I never thought he was evil to anybody. At the same time, I can't believe he felt good about what he was doing. I remember the day *The Larry King Show* called after he died. Larry [my brother] got on the phone with Robert Clary and told him. They *all* agreed, "If we can say all that we want to say about Bob, but good things, then we'll go on the show." There were no takers.

— *Tom Davis, brother of Larry Hovis, actor, "Hogan's Heroes"*

I always thought of him as like Skippy. He knew that I called him Skippy, and it was just that attitude of everything's good and going along. I never saw the depression and hangovers that they tried to show in the movie *Auto Focus.* Coming to the show late, I was never aware of that. He was always there. I just thought he was a nice guy to be around and to work with. And he made that character of Hogan great.

— *Bruce Bilson, director, "Hogan's Heroes"*

I'm sorry to hear that negative and exaggerated rumors about Bob's life persist. I am constantly amazed that such [things] are generated about celebrated people and have such an extended lifespan.

— *Nathan Gottfried, school friend and classmate*

I never saw Bob lose his temper or acting like a Big Star. My memories of the six years working with him were always positive. Too bad he had to leave this earth so young.

—*Robert Clary, actor, "Hogan's Heroes"*

Bob Crane was very professional. Low key. He knew what to do and how to do it. This guy was very relaxed. He, of course, came to work prepared. He knew comedy, so getting to the joke was easy for him, as me. I felt we had an immediate chemistry. I also felt he respected me as an artist, and we trusted each other in our finding what made the scene work.

—*Ted Lange, actor and director, "The Love Boat"*

I just remember him being a charming guy. I knew a little about his background, that he worked in radio, and had the charisma and the natural charm and everything to be able to act. He never really did anything different from what his persona was or what his regular character was like, but what he did—he did very well. He seemed very comfortable and relaxed, and he made everyone else feel the same way.

—*Rick Plastina, actor, "Send Me No Flowers"*

He was always on. He was always cracking jokes. He was a very funny man. Had a great sense of humor. And the band liked him. They were skeptical to start with, but once they got into the music, they loved him.

—*Stu Phillips, music producer, "Bob Crane, His Drums and Orchestra Play the Funny Side of TV"*

We could see that Bob was always a star ready to shine, and all it took was a brilliant script like *Hogan's Heroes*. Bob was blessed with being famous in two careers—to be on top in the music business and then suddenly be on top as an actor shows that people all over the world loved him in whatever he did. To sum Bob Crane up, he's the happy-go-lucky guy that if you were to be stranded on a desert island, he'd be the guy you'd like to be with—fun, fun, fun!

—*Richard Addrisi, recording artist*

We were like brothers. There are so many memories; I really couldn't pick out one. I would say every time we were together, it was a fun time. Bob was a many-faceted guy. I would like him to be remembered for the positive things he's done with his life.

—*Charlie Zito, best school friend and classmate*

He was humble, and he didn't have a big ego. Money didn't mean a whole lot to him. He just loved what he was doing, and doing it right and being a success. He had feelings; he had very sensitive feelings. Bobby was just a big teddy bear, and everybody loved him. Strange, people probably think he walked around with horns sticking out of his head, but he was a good guy.

—*Jim Senich, cousin*

I remember Bob as just a wonderful, wonderful person. It's a tragedy that his legacy has to do with the pornography, and all of the things that have come down—the writing, the movies—all deal with this side. Rather than what I think is the real side: the side of a very, very caring man; a man who understood himself as a wonderful father, as a lacking husband, he certainly confessed that, and wanted to change. *Tremendous talent*, in the sense of music, in the sense of drama, in the sense of comedy; any cast that worked with Bob will tell you that he was just an actor's actor.

—*Reverend Edward Beck, addiction counselor, and vice president of operations, Windmill Dinner Theatre Corporation*

I have only really friendly memories. He was an energy source, and Bob was a perfect gentleman with the women around the theatre. You can put things together after the fact and make a false pattern. The facts are the facts, but the facts and the truth aren't exactly the same thing.

—*Donald Freed, director, "Tunnel of Love" (1959) and "Who Was That Lady" (1960), the Valley Playhouse, Woodland Hills, California*

Bob Crane in his signature role of Colonel Robert E. Hogan in *Hogan's Heroes* (circa 1965).

Source: From the author's personal collection.

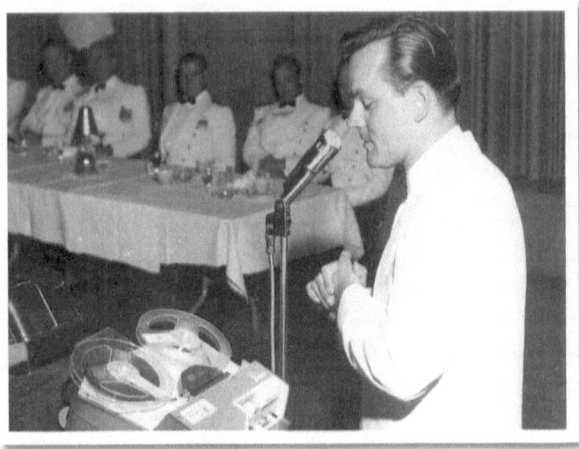

Giving a demonstration performance of his KNX-CBS Radio Show to a military audience (circa 1960).

Source: Courtesy of C.S. and used with permission.

The Crane Family (circa 1944) at their home in Stamford, Connecticut. Bob Crane (back row, second from right) with his parents Alfred and Rosemary at the far left, and older brother Al (center, in uniform), who served in the Navy during World War II. Others in the photo are unidentified but are believed to be relatives of the Cranes.

Source: From the author's personal collection.

Bob Crane performing with a jazz band in Connecticut (circa 1946-1949).

Source: Courtesy of Scott Crane. Used with permission.

Bob Crane as Paul Burnett and Bernard Fox as Scott Marlowe in the stage production of *Beginner's Luck* (circa 1973).

Source: Courtesy of Scott Crane. Used with permission.

Bob Crane with his first wife and childhood sweetheart, Anne Terzian (circa 1968).

Source: Hollywood Press Syndicate. From the author's personal collection. Used with permission from Karen Crane.

Bob Crane with his children—Bobby, Debbie, and Karen—from his first wife, Anne (May 1964).

Source: © Disney ABC Television Group. Photographer: ABC Photo Archives. Courtesy of Getty Images. Used with permission.

Bob Crane with his second wife, Patricia Olson (Sigrid Valdis). Patty portrayed Fräulein Hilda, Colonel Klink's secretary, in seasons two through six on *Hogan's Heroes*.

Source: Courtesy of Scott Crane. Used with permission.

Bob Crane with his infant son, Scott, from his second wife, Patty (circa 1971).

Source: Courtesy of Scott Crane. Used with permission.

Bob Crane smiles at fans during a personal appearance (circa 1967).
Source: Courtesy of Scott Crane. Used with permission.

Author's Introduction

Simply a Human Being

The biography of character should be as intimate as your own.
   –Bob Crane, Summer 1964

When Bob Crane scribbled the above notation in a manila notebook, he had been participating in a summer acting course taught by legendary actress and acclaimed acting teacher Stella Adler. The notebook contained several acting exercises, along with Bob's handwritten notes detailing how he could improve his acting skills.

Determined to become a professional actor, Bob pursued acting as a career from almost the first moment he stepped foot in Hollywood in August 1956, after accepting the offer from KNX-CBS Radio to become the station's morning radio personality. By the summer of 1964, Bob not only commanded the Southern California radio airwaves, he had already done plenty of acting—theatre performances, small movie roles, and television appearances on *The Dick Van Dyke Show, Rod Serling's The Twilight Zone*, *The Alfred Hitchcock Hour*, and most notably, his regular supporting role on *The Donna Reed Show*, with *Hogan's Heroes* on the horizon.

Bob was dedicated to acting, and he never stopped honing his skills. On screen, he made it look easy—so easy, in fact, that when watching *Hogan's Heroes*, critics and audiences alike believed he was just playing himself and not really acting. Yet he *was* acting, having worked very hard at developing and perfecting the character of Colonel Hogan and any character he chose to play. That people believed he was *not* acting is testament to him as an *exceptional* actor.

Many myths exist about Bob Crane, and that he was not a serious actor is only one. Since the time of his death, incomplete research and sensationalism have all but destroyed the reality of who Bob Crane really was. This work aims to do better.

Writing a biography is not easy. In fact, this is probably the most challenging project I have ever done or will ever do in my life—even though after decades of research, I know this subject extraordinarily well. Writing a biography is not to be taken lightly, nor is it something one does quickly or on a whim. Much as the actor develops the character, the author must also develop the subject of the biography's focus. It must be objective and personal, all at once. Just as an actor perfects his acting skills and makes the character his own, so, too, must the author sharpen the mind and embrace the subject as the leading character in the biography.

In my profession as an editor and managing editor of the life sciences publications, I have edited countless scientific manuscripts for scholarly journals. I have discovered that producing a biographical work is really not all that different. From inception, to methods of research, to verifying facts for accuracy, it is a scientific, evidence-based procedure.

However, it is also more than just gathering facts and piecing together a timeline from birth to death. A biography should contain a very human element. To achieve this, you must step directly into the life of your subject, getting as close as you can to it, and eventually, submersing yourself. Your subject's lifeline eventually runs adjacent to your own. The written words become as much your diary as they had been those of your subject, with each word chosen with great care and precision.

The biography of the subject becomes as intimate as your own.

In all, writing a biography is a delicate—not a reckless—process, where the end result, if done properly, is simply the truth revealed. This delicate and intricate research process has never before been done for Bob Crane, a man with a story worth telling.

Dee Young, Linda Groundwater, and I have personally talked with and met nearly two hundred people from all facets of Bob Crane's life and who knew him well. In many instances, their conversations with us were exclusive and shared publicly for the first time. Their overflowing of sentiment reiterated how much they loved and adored him. To them, he was a talented musician. A genius in radio. An actor's actor. A gifted director. A man driven to success. A loving father. A caring friend with a sunny personality. A proud American. A kind, sensitive man who sought warmth and human compassion. A man with a boyish quality that hinted at his naïveté. A man who loved to laugh, as well as make others laugh. A man who loved life.

But they also talked of another side to Bob Crane—a side he kept private, hidden from the public and many of his friends and coworkers:

his proclivity for sex and amateur pornography with numerous consensual women. This side was revealed and his privacy invaded on a grand scale in the days following his June 1978 murder. It has received unprecedented attention that continues to this day, with little understanding.

Bob Crane was a complex man, and he was not proud of this side of his life. Shortly before his murder, he recognized and accepted his behavior as a destructive and powerful addiction, and he began to battle it. Realizing he could not overcome it alone, Bob sought professional help. He reached out to at least two professional counselors, including Reverend Edward Beck, whom he had known as the manager of the Windmill Dinner Theatre Corporation.

Little has been told about Bob's desire to break free of his addiction. Most do not realize that Reverend Beck was assisting him in locating a leading sex addiction therapist in Los Angeles at the time of his murder. It is also not widely known that Bob alluded to destroying his homemade pornography after his play *Beginner's Luck* wrapped in Scottsdale and he returned home to Los Angeles. He had committed himself to making this positive change in his life; being a better father to his children, whom he loved dearly, had been his strongest motivator. However, just as Bob had begun the long and arduous journey toward recovery, someone brought a sudden end to his life, crushing his hopes and dreams of the future.

Most media have not been kind to Bob Crane since his death and have handled his life story poorly. Despite his great professional achievements, his former stature in the Hollywood community, *and* the fact that he was a victim of murder, media focus and public attention remained fixed on scandal and ridicule.

For example, an episode of the popular television series *Frasier*, starring Kelsey Grammer, takes the name Bob Crane and uses it as the butt of a tasteless joke. Niles and Daphne Crane are expecting their first child—a boy. They are having difficulty choosing a name for their unborn son, so they decide to let the Hand of Fate choose for them. Whatever name Niles points to in the phone book will be the baby's name. To Niles' horror, the name "Bob" is the first name he points to, indicating his son's name would be Bob Crane. In a fit of panic, he tears through the phone book with a bottle of White Out™, blotting out every "Bob" he can find. The joke is that even just the *name* Bob Crane is repulsive. A fan of the television series, Bob's first cousin Jim

Senich had tuned in to *Frasier* that night. He watched in sorrow and disbelief at the crassness of the "joke." It was not only an insult to his cousin's memory and to their family, but to everyone else with the name Bob Crane as well.

Actress Victoria Berry Wells, who had worked with Bob on stage in *Beginner's Luck* and who discovered his body following his murder, encountered the same insensitivity. When she appeared in court to testify during the trial of murder suspect John Henry Carpenter (different from the film director and producer), she was shocked by the callous remarks made by some.

"I had to cry when they showed the tripod and that scene with the police there," she said. "Seeing Bob again, I just burst out crying. They took me outside, and the police officer said to me, 'Well, he would have died of AIDS, anyway.'"

This is not the legacy Bob Crane wished to leave his family and this world. It is also not the legacy he deserved.

Based on our extensive research, there is no question that Bob Crane was a good man. He was neither a devil nor a saint, but rather, simply a human being who, like all human beings, was not perfect. Within these pages, the people who knew Bob intimately, and in some instances better than most, speak out on his behalf and help tell his *full* story, a story that has long since been forgotten or ignored. They share details of a man who, up until now, has been terribly misunderstood and misrepresented. They want you to know the man they knew, a man who was far different than how he has been presented since his death.

This is the *true* story of Bob Crane.

Carol M. Ford

Source: Courtesy of Scott Crane. Used with permission.

*"When I was a kid, I fell in love with Spencer Tracy in 'Captains Courageous.' That, to me, was the ideal. A good man, a brave man. What I would want to be.
I'm still in love with that."*

— Bob Crane

Preface

> *"I had been practicing every night with the rock bands waiting for Stan. And I figured, 'He's not going to let me sit in.'*
> *And suddenly, you let a fourteen-year-old...[You let me]!*
> *I've waited thirty-five years to sit in with you!*
> *I've been following Stan's band since 1941, and my biggest ambition was, way back when, for him to stand up and say, 'Shelly Mann is sick.' I've spent all my life waiting. Thank you."*
> – Bob Crane to Stan Kenton and audience after sitting in on drums with The Stan Kenton Orchestra, Columbus, Ohio, June 1976

In the spring of 1976, Bob Crane was in Columbus, Ohio, starring as the lead character in his play *Beginner's Luck*, which he also occasionally produced and directed. The Stan Kenton Orchestra was in town, and one evening, Bob ventured out to the jazz club where the band was performing. During a break between musical "sets," Bob—taking liberty as a fellow musician and celebrity—found his way up on stage. Easing himself comfortably behind the drumset, he began riffing with the band.

After a few minutes, Stan Kenton took notice.

"What do you wanna play?" he asked Bob.

"Anything!" Bob chirped. "I know every one of your damn arrangements!"

And a few moments later, they—with Bob on drums—started playing *Intermission Riff*.

The number concluded; the audience cheered. It had been an impromptu treat to have the *Hogan's Heroes* star entertain them. But the greater thrill had perhaps been for Bob, who, overflowing with euphoria and giddy with excitement, addressed his fans and thanked Kenton.

Bob typically exhibited great confidence on stage, whether he was acting or seated behind a set of drums. Yet on this night, Bob's voice betrayed the spirit of a fourteen-year-old boy—the boy he used to be, the young drummer who had dreamed of the moment when he would finally share the stage with one of his all-time great music idols. His performance with Kenton was not the first nor the last time he sat in and drummed with a music legend. He did so many times, and he also interviewed them on his KNX-CBS Radio show, got to know them, and in some instances, befriended them. And with each instance, it strengthened his resolve to go further and aim just a little higher in his career.

The very first step on Bob's ambitious climb to the top was his love of drums and music. During his school years, Bob would practice and learn every hit of the 1940s, front his own jazz band, organize neighborhood marching bands, teach his friends how to play drums, build upon his skills by taking lessons from Cozy Cole in New York City, and seek to further his talent.

As not just a drummer—but *the* drummer—at Stamford High, Bob learned how to win and hold the attention of his classmates. From behind a bass drum, snare drum, tom toms, and a high hat, he gained confidence, and with that confidence, he succeeded in every venture taken. The more he drummed, the more popular he became. The more his popularity grew, the more his confidence grew in tandem, permitting the occasionally shy and timid teen to become animated, self-assured, and more often than not, very funny. Bob radiated an irresistible charm that seemed to cast a magical spell on those around him—a ray of sunshine that broke through overcast skies during a time when boys were being sent off to war and the future was uncertain.

Young Bob Crane—"Bobby" to his family and school pals—thrived on his friends' and classmates' accolades. Their perception of and reactions to him, whether positive or negative, fed or eroded his self-esteem and inner spirit. More than their attention, he yearned for their acceptance. And he worked very hard to get it and keep it. By the time he graduated from high school, Bob was one of southwestern Connecticut's best-known musicians and Stamford High School's most popular students.

Music pulsed through Bob, always, and his drums were symbolic of his success. A pair of drumsticks and his drumset would accompany him everywhere he went throughout his entire life—from radio, to the set of *Hogan's Heroes*, to his travels across country performing *Beginner's Luck* and other theatre plays, right up to the night he died.

Validation of his talents and achievements was monumental for Bob. When permitted the opportunity to play drums with The Harry James Orchestra in 1975—this time, *Two O'Clock Jump*—Bob beamed in delight as Harry James sang his praises to the audience:

"We have a lot of friends, like Mickey Rooney, who plays the drums, and Mel Tormé, who plays the drums. But they don't *play* the drums. But I'll tell you one thing, Robert. *You* played your butt off!"

But most people don't know about this or about other important aspects of Bob's life. Most people only know small segments of his entire life story.

This is the story—the *complete* story—of Bob Crane. What you will find within these pages is a complete history—a rich history—of a man as told by those who knew him well, and in many instances, better than most. A man who displayed immeasurable talent and kindness; one who was brilliantly lucid and yet undeniably complex, contagiously happy and remarkably humble; a human being with goodness mixed with weaknesses and imperfections no different than anyone else. He was a man who retained a childlike innocence and joyful abandonment despite his sharp wit, fame, and addiction. Bob embraced life and viewed the world around him with wide-eyed wonderment and unbridled ambition. Driven from the outset, he pushed himself in everything he did to achieve his goals—striving for perfection, always seeking to please others, wanting for others to genuinely like and accept him, and craving success.

In 2015, Bob Crane would have turned eighty-seven years old. It has been thirty-seven years since his murder. Tragically, we will never know how brightly his star would have shone had he lived. All we know is what we have lost.

Bob Crane performs on drums with The Tommy Dorsey Orchestra (circa 1976).
Source: Courtesy of Scott Crane. Used with permission.

Source: From the author's personal collection.

Chapter 1
The Spirit of Stamford, Connecticut

I think I was born about twenty-five years too late. I was made for the stage. I know. The stage. The coach is ready in about five minutes. You can get on it, Crane... That's a wild record there. Woody Herman, one of the all-time greats of the dance band business, now working with a quartet because it's cheaper, and a bit of "The Sunny Side of the Street."

— Bob Crane over his KNX-CBS Radio Show, Hollywood, California, March 9, 1962

Bob Crane's high school graduation portrait, Stamford High School Class of 1946, Stamford, Connecticut.

Source: Courtesy of Stamford High School. Used with permission.

Caricature of young Bob Crane by his Uncle Mike Senich (circa 1940).

Source: Courtesy of Scott Crane. Used with permission.

Chapter 1

The Spirit of Stamford, Connecticut

Bob Crane, the tall, well-known drummer of room 226, has been active in all of the popular music assemblies during his three years at Stamford High School. Bob's twinkling brown eyes and boyish smile have won him many friends among his classmates. His 5-foot, 11-inch frame is a familiar sight around S.H.S. In his junior year, Bob was vice president of his homeroom. He served as tympanist for the community symphony orchestra for the Lenten concerts, both last year and this. Through Bob's constant efforts, his successful band has been in the spotlight at several of S.H.S.'s more successful events. His hobbies are being with his girlfriend Anne and collecting records. Bob's ambition is to play with Stan Kenton's orchestra and then be a C.B.S. studio staff artist.

—"The Siren," Stamford High School Newsletter, April 1946

His eyes were fixed on Gene Krupa's hands as the legendary drummer enthralled thousands of spectators at the New York World's Fair. Louder, softer, faster, slower… His own hands moved involuntarily to the cadence and rhythm, copying the movements of the icon before him, his heart beating in time with the music, his soul discovering something it didn't even know it had been missing. He was mesmerized. He could scarcely breathe. The drums, the showmanship, the music, the applause—he was swept up, and he knew, at that moment, that he must be a part of it, forever.

It was September 1939. Eleven-year old Bob Crane had just found his destiny.

Born in Waterbury, Connecticut, in 1928, Bob Crane grew up about sixty miles southwest in Stamford, where his family moved when he was almost two years of age. Waterbury was known for its brass industry, but in a Depression-era world, the Crane family needed to be in "the city that works."

> ### Walking to School in Stamford, Connecticut
> ### Spring 1938
>
> The trees lined both sides of the street, the early morning dew still clinging to the shrubs and spring foliage as Bobby Crane and Jack Ransohoff walked to school together. As was nearly always the case, Bobby sang as they walked. The two fourth graders continued their mile-long trek up Glenbrook Avenue, past Julia Stark Junior High School, to Glenbrook Elementary School on Crescent Road, a stone building constructed in the 1800s. As they walked along, Bob sang, happily passing the time and entertaining his friend.
>
> "Hey Bobby, what song is that?" Jack asked, kicking a stone out of the way.
>
> "*Top Hat, White Tie, and Tails*," Bob answered, grinning. "I'm steppin' out, mah dear, to breathe the at-mos-phere," he continued, his voice still a pure soprano, as they turned into the school lot and hurried around to the back.
>
> There, Bobby and Jack saw their classmates already lining up—girls in one line and boys in another—preparing to enter the two-storey building through separate doors. They scrambled into line and followed the leader into the school. Once inside, the boys and girls merged into their classes, ready to begin the day's lessons.
>
> Jack Ransohoff, younger brother of Hollywood producer Martin Ransohoff, became friends with Bob when they were in third grade. "He was *always* singing," Jack recalled. "I learned more songs from him just walking to school. He was really my main source of a lot of songs I know."

The Stamford of the 1930s and 1940s was everything one might expect in bustling Hometown, America. At the heart of the city was the Town Hall, sitting majestically on the corner of Atlantic and Main Streets, and overlooking a stretch of businesses known as Park Row. Flowering trees sprawled in the courtyard, and cars, trolleys, buses, and townsfolk maneuvered around it at a casual pace. Shops lined Main, Atlantic, and Bedford Streets, and High Ridge Avenue and Strawberry Hill Road stretched into Stamford's outlying suburbs of Belltown, Springdale, and Glenbrook.

A stone's throw by train from Manhattan, 1930s Stamford benefited from New Deal agencies like the Works Progress Administration, which created public works jobs at minimum wage—then about forty cents an hour—for the development of new roads, buildings, bridges, and schools. When the Second World War erupted in the 1940s, Stamford tightened its belt again with rationing, and sent its young men off to fight. Many were lost in battle. When the war was over, the city began to transition. Trading in its industrial hat for a white collar, the city closed many of its factories and lured business tycoons from Manhattan across Long Island Sound to the area. And they kept on coming; Donald Trump's lavish Trump Parc is now a part of the city's legacy. Stamford is old, yet new; modern, while retaining some of its old-town charm; both vintage and sophisticated. Over the years, much has changed, and yet much has stayed the same.

Stamford was the stomping ground of Bob's youth, the place he always called *home*. It's where he attended school; played baseball, football, and other sports with his friends; played in jazz and swing bands; landed his first real job; and met and married his first wife. Stamford was important to Bob, and wherever life's adventures took him, he never forgot his roots.

Between 1930 and 1942, Bob's family moved frequently, living in at least eight different residences during that time. Earliest accounts and public records of Bob's childhood reach back to 1933, when he was in kindergarten at Springdale Elementary School in Stamford. In 1936, Bob's parents moved the family to Poughkeepsie, New York, where Bob's father had taken a job at the Lucky Platt Department Store. City records indicate that the Cranes lived in Poughkeepsie for two years. Later, a local Poughkeepsie newspaper reported that Bob attended the W.W. Smith Elementary School. (Yet none of Bob's classmates could recall him attending anywhere except in the Stamford school district.) Apparently homesick, the Cranes soon returned to Connecticut in 1938, moving into the Glenbrook section of Stamford, where Bob attended Glendale Elementary School from third through sixth grades. In seventh and eighth grades, he attended Julia Stark School, and in ninth grade, students from all schools within Stamford merged into Burdick Junior High for one year.

The Cranes relocated several times within Stamford after returning from Poughkeepsie, but in 1942, they settled into their permanent home on Oaklawn Avenue in the Belltown section. Their home was a short distance from Stamford High School on Strawberry Hill, where Bob attended grades ten through twelve.

Bob's heritage is a rich combination of Irish and Ukrainian ancestry, infused with strict Catholicism. His parents, Alfred and Rosemary, were hard-working, quiet, unassuming people, and their sense of Old World tradition and religious values melded with American determination and innovation, providing a firm and respectable, comfortable, and loving home atmosphere.

Bob's great-grandfather on his father's side was Robert E. Hogan. This was an ironic coincidence with no connection to the naming of the television series that would make Bob an international star. Robert Hogan and his wife, Margret, both of Irish descent, were married in 1875 in Stamford, where they resided for most of their lives. Married for more than fifty years, they were the parents of ten children, including Mary, who married Patrick Crean (as the Crane surname was originally spelled). Patrick had emigrated from Ireland in 1883. Over the course of twenty years, Patrick and Mary would change the spelling of their last name to "Crane," settle in Waterbury, and have six children, including Alfred Thomas Crane, Bob's father, who was born on August 2, 1906.

Bob's mother, Rosemary Senich, was born in Waterbury on February 8, 1906. Rose's parents, Onnifer and Anna Walko Senich, were married in 1895 and had emigrated to America around 1896 from the region known as Galicia in central Europe, what is now Southeast Poland and Western Ukraine. Bordered by the Carpathian Mountains to the east and the Ural Mountain Range to the west, the Ukrainian region over time has encompassed sections of Russia, Poland, and Romania. Anna—called Babba by her grandchildren—and Onnifer raised their family in Waterbury, where they spoke Russian and attended the Russian Orthodox Church.

Al and Rosemary Crane were married in 1925. On May 14, 1926, they welcomed their first child—a son, Alfred John, whom they called Al Junior—into the world. Two years later, on July 13, 1928, Rose gave birth to their second son, Robert Edward.

Michael Senich, brother of Rosemary and uncle to young Al and Bob, was a professional illustrator and cartoonist for King Features Syndicate, whose many works included *Sir Roger* in the 1940s and *The Katzenjammer Kids* from 1974 to 1981. Mike's daughter (and Bob's cousin) Jane Ryfun Senich recalled, "Think of the finest human on the planet. That was my father. A really exceptional human. He had a warm heart. He was incredibly creative."

Mike had a way with children that gained their respect, love, and trust. "Dad talked about wheeling Bobby in a baby carriage up and down Race Street in Waterbury," Jane said. "He would get down on their level, on the floor, eye to eye." Such a connection had influenced Bob, and he idolized and looked up to his Uncle Mike. The affection had been mutual. When Bob was about ten years of age, Mike presented his nephew with a drawing, in which he inscribed, "The Greatest Little Nephew on Earth—'The Invincible' Robert Crane," From Your Uncle Mickey Senich-o."

When Al and Rose moved the family to Stamford in 1929, Al found work in the floor covering business at C.O. Miller's Department Store on Bank Street, where he was employed for several years. After returning to Stamford from Poughkeepsie in 1938, Al accepted a job as a salesman for the Floor Covering Shop on Bedford Street. Later, he was promoted to manager and became a member of The Bedford Street Association.

The owners of The Floor Covering Shop, Frank Karas, and his wife, Marion, knew Al as a "very gentle person who was soft-spoken and very nice." They thought the world of the Cranes, and remembered Rose as being especially lovely.

Rosemary Crane was pretty, sweet, and petite, with dark hair and a kind smile. Her eyes twinkled with the same sparkle and happiness as those of her youngest son. A homemaker, she doted on her family, caring for her husband, raising her two sons, and offering them loving kindness and support. In return, her family adored her.

"She was a lovely lady, my Aunt Rose was to me," said Bob's cousin Jim Senich. "She was tops, and she was very pretty and had a great personality."

She also had a great laugh—a laugh Bob had tape-recorded and later used in various on-air skits on his KNX radio show. "I must be honest with you," Bob said over KNX one morning. "Obviously, I played the Frenchman and the Russian. My mother played the laughing [girl]. That *is* my mother! No kidding around! She's got a silly laugh, that's all."

The Cranes attended Catholic Mass regularly, and they instilled in their sons the importance of building good character by working hard and treating others with respect. Further, the large, extended Crane-Senich family was close, and it was a good family atmosphere. Together, meals were shared, holidays were enjoyed, and milestone occasions were celebrated. As a result, the cousins all got to know each other well—they were not just cousins; they were friends.

"My brother and I were younger than Bobby and young Al, but they never shut us out," Jim Senich remembered. "That was a good thing. I was the young guy, the little squirt. But Bobby would never ignore me, and neither would his brother Al. And that's why when we were down there visiting, I'd go up and bang on his drums, and he probably said, 'Oh, Lord,' but we were never mad; we'd go out in the back yard and play ball and all that stuff. It was a good family."

As with any family, tension in the home existed at times. Bob's father could be tough on his sons, and Jim remembered the atmosphere changing from light to anxious when his Uncle Al came home. Bob's school friend, Edwin Gordon, also remembered there being a sense of rigidity inside the house, and he noted that as head of the house, Bob's father could be a "taskmaster." While Bob's brother Al challenged their father, often engaging in heated arguments, Bob remained quiet and stayed out of the way, not wanting to add to the problem and often wanting to keep the peace.

"Bob just played the game," Jim said. "So he'd never get into any arguments. I never saw him argue with his dad."

Occasionally, the arguments between Bob's father and brother would escalate until Al, Jr. ran out of the room, leaving everyone else glancing around uncomfortably at each other. Sometimes Bob would respond by tossing out a joke to lighten the moment. Other times, he would go upstairs to talk with his brother to try and smooth things over.

Jim also recalled that Al did not seem to trust his wife. "He would sneak home at lunch and hide in the bushes. He would spy on my Aunt Rose! He thought she was having an affair with the milkman."

Bob's father was just "very uptight," Jim added, stressing that these moments did not define the family atmosphere as a whole. "He was very *picayune*; everything had to be just right."

Bob focused his attention on his music—even more, perhaps, when times were stressful. Since he had seen and heard Gene Krupa at the World's Fair in 1939, music and drums were as much a part of him as breathing. He was also living in what many consider the greatest music era in history—the Big Band era. Jazz and swing fusion ruled the ballrooms, and their sounds were powerful, loud, intoxicating, *hopeful*. If you weren't performing in a band, you were jitterbugging and Lindy-hopping to Glenn Miller, Duke Ellington, Woody Herman, and Tommy Dorsey. And Bob was still dreaming of being a part of it.

Bob's very first drum was a gift from his father for Christmas in 1938, when he was just ten years old. His father wanted to give Bob a special present that year, and he bought the snare drum at a local store in Stamford for twenty-three dollars. He asked the store's owner, Vito Schigliampaglia, to hold the drum for him until Christmas.

But the drum was sold out from under him by accident to someone else. Furious, his father didn't demand his money back. Instead, he swiped another drum—this one valuing seventy-five dollars—and walked right out of the store with it! Today, that drum would cost more than $1,200.

"I promised my boy a drum for Christmas, and by the holy saints of Ireland, he's goin' to have one!" Al Crane declared.

Schigliampaglia felt bad for the elder Crane, and he looked the other way, knowing Al would return later to pay for it and "make it right."

Many years later, after Bob achieved great fame, Schigliampaglia displayed a photograph of Bob as Colonel Hogan in "a prominent place" in his store. On the image were the words, "I, Vito Schigliampaglia, am responsible for the show business career of Bob Crane, star of TV, radio, and movies!"

During his school years, the youngest of the Crane household would listen to and practice his music for hours on end. He played tympani and snare drum in the Stamford High School orchestra, and snare drum in the school's marching band, and he was a bandleader of the Crane-Catino Jazz Band. Racing home from school, he would bound up the five front steps of the two-story white colonial house; dashing inside, he would greet his mother and retreat to his small bedroom on the second floor, where his drums had been patiently waiting for him. Soon, the house and entire neighborhood would be filled with the sound of cadences, drum rolls, rim shots, and blast beats.

But as time went on, his parents were not as impressed. "Play the drums if it makes you happy," seemed to be their attitude, according to friends Edwin Gordon and Donald Sappern; it was a lot better than engaging in illicit behavior like drugs and drinking and sneaking around. They neither encouraged nor dissuaded their son from his passion, but rather, they "put up with it." To them, his ambition of being a professional musician was a pipe dream.

"They realized he had other talents should his drumming not pan out," Charlie Zito, Bob's best friend from school, remembered. "They realized what charisma he had, and he would always be successful. I think in the back of their minds, they knew that because they never really said, 'Quit the drums.' I guess as long as he was happy, they were happy."

Al, Jr. sang a little, but other than Bob's drumming, there was not much music in the Crane household. Yet music was everywhere, filling the airwaves with the click of a switch and rotation of a dial. Radio brought a select few entertainers into the public spotlight and into the home. With a new medium that could reach the masses, a handful of jazz musicians, such as Benny Goodman and Gene Krupa, attained overnight stardom and a measure of celebrity never before realized. Music and radio went hand-in-glove for Bob, and in his very early teen years, he began to crave both.

Bob dreamed of playing with Big Band and jazz musicians, and he set his sights high. Working after school at odd jobs, regardless of how demeaning he thought they were, he earned money to buy his instruments. Drive and motivation to achieve a goal quickly became his mantra, teaching him very early in life that hard work and determination paid off.

"He worked hard because he had to pay for everything himself," said Charlie. For instance, "he wanted his tri toms, so he had to work a lot of hours for that one."

"I started out," Bob explained, "sweeping the sidewalk and putting boxes together. I'd hate for my friends to see me sweeping, and if anyone was coming along that I knew, I'd duck inside and hide the broom."

And Bob had a *lot* of friends, and he was very popular. Many of his school friends and classmates had nicknames, such as "Rusty," "Alamo," "Smitty," "Lefty," and "Flip." Bob's nickname happened to be "Bottles."

Childhood friend Neil "Corny" McGuinness remembered, "One of our diversions was to go over to Bob's house on our bikes after class, just a couple of us. Bob lived down by the river over toward the east side of Glenbrook almost to the Darien line where a river made its way through pastures and eventually under the Boston Post Road into Long Island Sound. It was quite a journey to get there. And finally, we would reach Bob's house. There, Bob had a pile of bottles that he'd collect, and we'd take them down to the river, toss one in, and commence to try to break it by throwing stones as it bobbed away. From that fun time in our lives, we gave Bob the nickname 'Bottles.' He carried that nickname all the way through high school, at least for some of us."

Friend and classmate Jack Williams remembered Bob from their first and second grade and high school. Bob lived around the corner from Jack and was just a regular neighborhood kid and playmate, with nothing "startling or remarkable" about him in grade school. After second grade, Jack and Bob lost contact with each other until they met up again at Burdick Junior High. In Jack's senior yearbook, Bob wrote, "To my Springdale Playmate."

"When he was playing drums in the band, we were all proud to claim him as a 'Springdalian,'" Jack explained. "I remember him as a 'Personality' at Stamford High School who was always smiling and friendly. Of course, when he showed up as Colonel Hogan, we were all very proud of him and enjoyed the series."

In his early teen years, Bob formed a "pick-up band" with a few of his friends that included Martin Ransohoff. With Bob as the drummer, the band ultimately consisted of a pianist, a trumpet player, a saxophonist, and Martin played accordion. They played for parties and other local events. Not only did Bob organize neighborhood jazz bands, but he also organized neighborhood sporting teams and local marching bands. In junior high school, he led the drum and bugle corps, and he taught others, including Charlie Zito, how to play the drums.

"We used to win prizes when we marched in parades," Charlie recalled. "There were four drummers, and Bob showed us all the marching rhythm. When we marched in our first parade and showed off our drum and bugle corps—we were *so* proud of that. That was one of our happier times. You just couldn't get the smile off our faces with anything."

Bob met Charlie during an intramural baseball game. They were both in seventh grade at the time, and the year was 1940. After the game, they started talking and discovered they shared an interest in music. Charlie, whose family was quite musical, and Bob became "like brothers."

"I used to spend an awful lot of time in his house, and he at mine. I played piano and a little bit of saxophone. My father played so many instruments—the saxophone, guitar, mandolin, and violin. When Bob would be at the house and my father was home, they would get into some terrific discussions."

Charlie also called Bob a "great organizer." Every time they played sports or marched in a parade or did anything "newsworthy" in the community, Bob would write a short article for *The Stamford Advocate*, the local newspaper. Not every event warranted a "press release," however.

"We had a basketball team, and we'd play other schools and other neighborhoods," said Charlie. "And Bob organized the whole thing. He got all the players among our friends, and he would keep a record of everything. We called ourselves the Belltown Commandos. The first season we lost all of our games. Bob, usually with his quip, said, 'I think next year if we do this, we better change our name! Or nobody will show up to play!' I think we won one game that year—and that's because the other team didn't show up! So we changed our name to the Belltown Braves."

During this era, it was common for most kids to play some kind of instrument. According to Charlie, it was also a great way to meet girls, who played in the band as well. However, it was not by playing in the band that Bob met the girl who would become his childhood sweetheart and his first wife, Anne Terzian. Rather, it was on the Belltown baseball field. Bob had had his eye on Anne ever since she was eleven and he only thirteen. But after a fateful moment over the second-base bag, Anne and Bob became inseparable.

"I met Anne when I was fourteen," Bob explained to ABC radio personality Fred Robbins in the late 1960s. "I was playing second base for the baseball team, and she was riding her bicycle and bumped into me." He further punned in an interview with Hollywood columnist Polly Terry, "And boy, did I fall for her!"

"Anne was Bob's first girlfriend," Charlie recalled. "And wherever you saw Bob, Anne was right there, and vice versa. They were together constantly. But *constant*. Even through junior high school and high school, and then after we graduated. She even took up playing the glockenspiel so she could be in the band with him. So they were always together. *Always*. And he would always hold her arm. Up the stairs, down the stairs, walking to different classes. Always held her by the arm. And you could really see she was going to be the girl for him. And she was. By our standards, she was only a kid. We used to tease him a lot about that. But he only had eyes for Anne. That was it."

According to Bob's friends from school, Anne was quiet, reserved, and pretty "in a plain sort of way," with a terrific personality. A Belltown girl, Anne lived only a couple blocks from Bob—about a fifteen-minute walk around to the other side of the baseball field. Anne was friendly with everybody, yet she chose her confidants carefully.

Anne's parents had emigrated to America from the "Old Country"—her father, Alexander, was Armenian and from Turkey, and her mother, Ellen, was from Sweden. Unable to speak no more than a few words of English, Alexander arrived in New York on March 7, 1921. His family had been killed when the Turks destroyed their Armenian village in 1915, after which, he was assimilated into Turkish culture until he found the opportunity to leave in 1921.

The period between 1915 and 1920 was one of extreme horror and suffering in Armenia. On April 24, 1915, what is now known in Armenia as Genocide Day, the Turkish government ordered the arrest of six hundred prominent individuals and leaders in Armenian society who were either deported or executed. Today, those of Armenian heritage in the United States, France, and the Middle East are the direct descendants of survivors of the Armenian Genocide. Anne's father was one of those survivors.

After working as a chauffeur and valet for a wealthy employer in New York City, Alexander Terzian opened his own taxi business. Following that venture, he owned and operated a cleaning service, and then became a furrier and a tailor. While living in New York, he noticed Ellen. The daughter of a shoemaker, Ellen came to America at fifteen years of age. She, too, had trouble with the language, and learned to speak English while working as a governess in New York. After meeting Alexander, she assisted in his tailoring business, and they were later married. On March 20, 1927, the Terzians had their first daughter, Victoria Ellen (called Bunny by her friends); on October 19, 1930, they welcomed Anne Margit into the world.

Friend and classmate Jane Golden described Anne as being the complete opposite of Bob. While Bob was "the most outgoing guy you could find" and "completely everybody's friend," Anne hung back, allowing him to laugh and kid and play his drums—and shine.

"Everybody would just say Annie was a very sweet, nice gal," Jane said. "But maybe he liked her quiet demeanor—she didn't challenge him to any extent. He was always kidding with people, laughing, slapping you on the back. She wasn't that kind, but maybe she complimented him in that way. You can't have two people slapping you on the back all the time, right?"

From the start, Anne made sacrifices; while other girls attended dances with their boyfriends, Anne remained at home so Bob could play drums in various gigs, knowing how important Bob's music was to him. Though together constantly, she maintained a quiet, loyal distance when Bob bounced from job to job during their school days, earning money along the way. It was clear to all that Bob and Anne were made for each other and meant to be together.

In high school, Bob took general education classes, and according to his friends, did fairly well at keeping his grades up. However, like most students, he was eager to just get through and get out into the real world.

Stamford High School was and still is a grand structure, looming above Strawberry Hill Avenue, its horseshoe driveway extending out to the highway like two arms encircling those about to enter. Constructed in 1895, it originally employed ten teachers and had a total enrollment of one hundred seventy-three students. By the 1940s, it housed more than two thousand students and consisted of grades 10, 11, and 12. In 1934, as part of the New Deal's Public Works of Art Project, seven murals were painted and hung in the school's octagonal music auditorium.

Within these decorated walls, students would hear live music performed by their own classmates during in-school assemblies, and it was impossible to miss Stamford High's Drummer Boy, sitting front and center of the Crane-Catino Jazz Band, jamming to the Big Band hits of the 1940s.

Don Sappern played piano in the Crane-Catino Jazz Band ever since Bob asked him during their sophomore year. Playing three times a week in some instances, the band would perform for Stamford High School as well as other area high schools, including Greenwich and Norwalk. The Crane-Catino Jazz Band also played throughout the community, including at Laddin's Terrace (a popular nightclub that boasted the largest dance floor in Connecticut) and for veterans.

"He would front the band one week; I would front it the next," Don said. "We really had a very, very interesting time, and the kids loved it. Our band would always work Friday nights at a different high school. We'd play for dances. And the reason we became close was because I had the car. I could transport his drums. We performed Glenn Miller stuff, like *String of Pearls*. We didn't really feature anybody. We did a lot of Woody Herman stuff that we *butchered* because it was really very tough."

Don's father, also a musician, encouraged his son's interest in music. When Bob and the rest of the band needed a place to rehearse, Don's house was a logical choice. Lugging their instruments over to the Sappern residence, the band would practice in the cellar, which had been outfitted for music and soundproofed.

"My family lived in Glenbrook with a *big* basement, a great sound," Don explained. "We used to bring twelve to thirteen guys in there and set up a band, and it had great, *great* acoustics. And that's where most of the practices took place. We practiced in high school once in a while, but not very often."

After a performance, Don would drive Bob, who was rarely, if ever, permitted to drive the family car, back home. It would be late—around midnight or later—and not wanting to wake Bob's parents, they would quietly unload Bob's drums out of the car and onto the front porch. Then, they would sit in Don's car parked in Bob's driveway and listen in total silence for hours to radio broadcasts out of the Ambassador Hotel in Chicago.

"It was *great!*" Don remembered. "We'd sit and listen to Woody Herman and all the bands that we were very, very up on. I knew at that point in time he *had* to get involved ultimately in some sort of music because he *loved* it. That was his life—*that was his life.*"

Edwin Gordon, who was a year older than Bob and graduated from Stamford High School in 1945, began playing bass in the orchestra and jazz band at age fifteen—during his junior year. Edwin went on to become an acclaimed researcher and expert in the fields of music and music learning theory, and is the founder of the Gordon Institute for Music Learning. Following graduation, Edwin also played bass professionally with Gene Krupa. During their school years, Edwin also transported Bob and his drums to and from different band performances, and during those trips, they often discussed music. Bob had indicated to Edwin that he was growing frustrated trying to learn how to improve his drumming technique on his own and without formal music instruction. He sought to find a teacher, someone who could mentor him and show him additional music skills he so desperately craved.

One day, around the age of sixteen, Bob and Edwin decided to skip school and take the train from Stamford to Manhattan in search of music instructors. Having done some preliminary investigation, Bob discovered that many famous musicians liked to hang out between 48th and 52nd Streets—known as Tin Pan Alley— in between stage time. So the two young aspiring musicians embarked on a quest in search of their idols, and as they approached their target locale, Bob took immediate notice of a legend.

"There's Benny Goodman," he said to Edwin, a jolt of nervous excitement rushing through him.

Goodman, who had been playing "The Seven Lively Arts of Cole Porter," along with Sid Weiss, Teddy Wilson, Cozy Cole, and Red Nichols, among others, was on a break. Bob quickened his pace and marched straight toward the gathering of music greats. Bound and determined, and full of fearless energy, he introduced himself.

"Hi! I'm Bob Crane!" he said with a smile and a touch of courage. "And this is my friend, Ed Gordon. How are you?" His tone was neither shy nor pushy.

Goodman started to put out his hand, but with at least five other musicians standing in close proximity, instead of returning the salutation, he chose to simply walk away. It was obvious that he did not want to be bothered with a couple of kids.

"But the other musicians were just so kind to us," Edwin claimed. "I ended up becoming very, very good friends with Sid Weiss, and Bob was directed toward the Adler Drum Studio."

Because of this meeting, Bob started taking lessons from Cozy Cole, traveling into Manhattan at least once a week by train to do so. The more he played his drums, the more, according to friend Charlie Zito, "he came into his own." It gave him the confidence to develop a multitude of other talents, including a sense of humor, a quick wit, a bubbling personality, a sharp memory, a natural ability to lead, and the skill of organization.

"We had some talented people," Jane Golden recalled, "and it was very popular in those days for five or six guys to get together and do a little band. And these bands were very important. They played at a lot of festivals and gigs around the town. They played for a lot of different things, and if you had a good musician in the middle, like you did with Bob, it just took off. He was very instrumental in keeping the Stamford High School band together."

Some members of the school jazz band were somewhat critical of Bob's drumming abilities. Don Sappern called him a "fair drummer," saying he played with better drummers over the course of his life. However, he was quick to admit that Bob was *very* excited about drumming, and people tended to like him as a good leader—"guys listened to him."

As a professional musician and educator, Edwin Gordon remembered Bob as a "flashy" drummer, and when compared to professional musicians, "not that good." According to Edwin, Bob had the tendency to rush tempo and use a lot of technique.

"He would *love* to hit rim shots. He would get *very* excited, and the tempo would rush."

Bob had always been a musical *entertainer*, and based on popular consensus, he was a *very good* musical entertainer. Moreso, he was fun—fun to listen to and fun to watch.

It has been previously published that Bob dropped out of high school to join the Connecticut Symphony Orchestra. However, Bob did, in fact, graduate, and while he also played for the Connecticut Symphony Orchestra (now the Bridgeport Symphony Orchestra), he did not do so as a paid member. Instead, he played with the orchestra while he was still a student in high school.

In the mid-1940s, the Orchestra was in financial trouble and had been hurting for musicians. As part of an agreement with Stamford High School and other local high schools, students had the opportunity to play as extras with the orchestra. From 1944-1946, Bob played tympani for the Connecticut Symphony Orchestra as well as with the Norwalk Symphony Orchestra, all while still in high school. Stories circulate that he was kicked out of the Connecticut Symphony Orchestra for horsing around—for making a joke that the conductor did not appreciate. One 1967 newspaper published a quick blurb with a little more detail than other accounts: "Bob Crane lost his job as drummer with the Connecticut Symphony Orchestra for interpolating jazz touches in a Bach fugue." However, because he was never employed with the Orchestra, no official records of Bob's time with the orchestra exist, making it difficult to prove.

But interestingly, the rumor about Bob dropping out of school began with Bob himself! According to his school friends, after his success in Hollywood, he used to joke regularly about it, claiming he dropped out to get a reaction. As Bob grew older, he learned the fine art of self-deprecating humor, and unfortunately, his tall tale of being a high school drop out was taken as fact after his death. While it could not be verified, it's also quite possible that Bob invented the story about being kicked out of the Connecticut Symphony Orchestra—all just to get a laugh.

At Stamford High School, Bob was a celebrity. Almost all of the students enjoyed the jazz band performances and Bob's drumming in particular. Neil McGuinness remembered the Crane-Catino Band as exciting and a lot of fun for the kids at school. Bob would often entertain his classmates with a solo on drums. "He was great. Kids would cheer and scream and clap. We all thought he was another Gene Krupa. Because of his marvelous, inspiring drum playing, he became extremely popular. His personality reinforced it, and everyone wanted to be Bob's friend."

Friend and classmate David Dugan remembered, "When Bob was on stage with the band, a lively, deeply involved side of him was revealed. He loved his music, and it showed strongly. He would be smiling big one minute, and as the music changed, so would the expression on his face."

All in all, if you attended Stamford High School from 1943 to 1946, you knew Bob Crane, whether you traveled in his circle of friends or not. When the Crane-Catino Band was on stage, the students loved it—it was "big time," and as the drummer and personality-plus, Bob became one of *the* most popular kids at school.

Alice Jarrell wrote, "I remember Bob Crane sitting in back of me in school with his 'sticks' (fifth grade). He became the 'leader of the band' throughout our Stamford High School years. The best are never forgotten."

"In our senior year, he was in my English class," Aniello Casillo recalled. "He sat right behind me. He kept tapping his drumsticks on the desk! Had those drumsticks *everywhere!* The other classmates didn't mind the tapping. They thought it was funny. Miss Higgens minded, but he kept doing it because it was funny."

In 1940, Audrey Ivanko and her family moved to Stamford, where she began eighth grade at Stark School. She also remembered Bob's drumming throughout his school years. "He was extremely popular and carried drumsticks all the time. He would be playing with them on the desk, chairs, everywhere he could get a sound, and he wanted to be a drummer more than anything."

Patricia Mucci had similar recollections. "Bob was always in the limelight. Everyone knew who he was, even though we didn't know him personally. He always had a smile. He most always had drumsticks in his hands. He would tap on lockers, bannisters, or whatever was around as he passed from class to class. Most students knew his name. We were proud to say he made it."

For someone who seemed so bold and grandiose, Bob was also extremely sensitive, and he worried about what other people thought and felt. Audrey remembered Bob sitting next to her in one of their classes. The other kids teased Bob for having to sit beside her because she was slightly overweight. "But he was nice and never paid attention after the first tease," she said.

David Dugan also recalled Bob as being considerate of others. During one of their art classes in school, the teacher stepped out of the room momentarily. She had a very pronounced lisp, and Bob entertained the class by doing an impersonation of her. He had the teacher's voice, lisp and all, down pat, and his fellow classmates were laughing at how much he sounded like her. The charade continued until a girl in the class scolded Bob for making fun of the teacher. Worried that his impersonation might be considered hurtful, Bob stopped instantly; it had bothered him so much.

"He never did that again when that was brought to his attention," David said. "That revealed a sensitive side to his personality."

During troubled times, we, the Class of 1946, express faith in man… This yearbook has been written with a sincere conviction that man will forsake selfishness and devote himself to one cause, peace—just, lasting, and universal.

"Foreword," *The Spirit of 1946*, Stamford High School Yearbook

World War II was at its peak when Bob was in high school. There was food rationing. No more than two pounds of meat per family. Butter was unheard of. Sugar from Cuba had been cut off for fear of the trade ships being sunk. Three and a half gallons of gasoline per week were permitted unless it was to be used for something pertaining to one's job. The war affected every part of life. For many, it meant enlisting in a branch of the service and going "over there" to fight. For those who stayed on the homefront, it meant volunteering and sacrificing—doing any and all that could be done to support the United States Armed Forces and help the Allies win the war.

At night, windows were heavily draped, with no lights showing through. During air raid drills, Charlie Zito's father, an air raid warden, went around to different neighborhoods ensuring lights were out. With the city of Stamford blacked out, Bob's father would go to the rooftop of Stamford High School, where he and other volunteers would watch the night sky for enemy aircraft. If an enemy plane was suspected, it was reported.

Kids in school during that time had more of a "superman" approach to the war. Charlie explained, "You never really thought about *dying* at that age. If somebody was going to die, it wasn't going to be us."

Nevertheless, it was a very serious time for high school students. Gym class consisted of commando training, push-ups, and according to Charlie, "other more strenuous forms of torture."

"We didn't have gym," Charlie recalled. "We went outside with gym shorts on—ice, snow, mud, whatever—and did calisthenics and ran around the track. They had somebody teaching us hand-to-hand combat. They really were trying to toughen us up."

Families with sons serving overseas on the front lines posted little flags in the shape of a pennant upside down in their windows. If you had one son in the service, you had one pennant or star. Some families had three sons in the service, so there would be three flags. If you lost a son, it was etched in black. Bob's family displayed such a flag, and it came very close to being etched in black.

In August 1943, when Bob was fifteen years old, Al, Jr. joined the Navy, and on August 11, 1944, he reported for duty on the *USS Bunker Hill (CV-17)* aircraft carrier. The *Bunker Hill* saw action in the Pacific Theater, and Al saw at least four major engagements while serving on duty. Al was on board on the morning of May 11, 1945, just three days shy of his nineteenth birthday. While supporting the Okinawa invasion, the carrier was attacked by two kamikazes, severely damaging the ship. Her losses included three hundred forty-six men killed, forty-three missing, and two hundred sixty-four wounded.

When it was learned that the ship had been attacked and badly crippled, the Crane household went into turmoil. "*The waiting and the waiting and the waiting,*" Charlie recalled. "Wondering *did Al survive*? It was just *terrible*."

Communications in 1945 were not as they are today, and nearly three weeks passed before word arrived about Al's fate. During those weeks of not knowing, which Charlie said seemed like an eternity, Bob would go to Charlie's house often.

Bob was devastated by the possibility that his brother might have been killed. He held it together most of the time, but when he was with his closest confidants, he would let his true feelings show.

"I'll tell you," Charlie said, "if you *really* got into it with him, and I didn't like to do that too much—I didn't want to see Bob that way—he would be brought to tears. And so consequentially, when it got to that point, I would change the subject. And then he caught on, and then he would change the subject, and we'd forget about it for awhile. It just wasn't the same. He didn't want to upset his parents. He didn't want his parents to think he was still going on with his life and having all the fun he was having at the time. He thought maybe they would get the wrong impression. He used to bring a drum with him, and he'd play, and I'd play piano, and we'd listen to some of my records. But it wasn't the same."

Al survived the attack, but not without physical and psychological injury. Seeking an escape out of the burning hull, he climbed up a red-hot chain out of the fire to the ship's surface, and he was badly wounded. Later, he learned that his shipmate who had relieved him of his radio post shortly before the attack occurred was killed in the attack. While Al had been very proud to serve in the war and on the *Bunker Hill*, he would carry these scars of guilt with him for the rest of his life.

When word reached Stamford that Al was alive, "it was like Christmas," Charlie recalled. "It had been sad, especially the not knowing. Every time you'd see it—what we used to do to have fun, it was always in the background. There was a war on. Your neighbors were being killed. Brothers were being killed. And not knowing for a long time that Bob's brother did survive was horrible."

The school was preparing to graduate Bob, Charlie, Don, and many of their classmates and friends early so they could enter the war. Their report date was to have been May 20, 1945. With Victory in Europe (VE) Day occurring only a few days prior, on May 8, 1945, they *just* missed their draft date by a mere fraction. Their parents breathed a sigh of relief, and instead of going off to fight a war, their kids continued on with school.

On June 5, 1946, Bob, along with more than five hundred and fifty classmates, graduated from Stamford High School. It was a rainy Wednesday evening, and "dark and threatening skies hung over Boyle Stadium during the exercises, which had already been postponed once, as the graduates, impressive in blue and white caps and gowns, marched to their places at the far end in solemn procession."

In the Stamford High School 1946 yearbook, Bob's graduation picture appears. His big, radiant smile and joyful eyes express his optimism and exuberance, all the while hinting at the sensitive and warm soul dwelling within his lanky frame. Next to his graduation photograph is his official high school statement—how he wanted to be remembered by his classmates: "Bob—Loud ties…drumming…musician of note. Homeroom Vice President 11, Popular Music Assemblies 10, 11, 12; Band, Orchestra 10, 11, 12; Member of Requiem Orchestra. Future—Staff Musician in Studio Orchestra."

The first seventeen years of Bob's life were full and happy, yet not without fear or worry. He graduated from Stamford High School overflowing with hopes, dreams, and ambitions. Driven to succeed at whatever he chose to accomplish, he exited school in pursuit of success. His love of music and drums opened his eyes to a new medium—radio, which had started to take hold during high school.

Yet drumming would remain his outlet, his way of unwinding or relaxing after a busy or stressful day. It was his hobby, his passion, his confidence. It helped mold him, and it never failed him.

"I think people who make waves are frustrated, angry, insecure, or tense," Bob wrote in a 1968 article for *Guideposts* magazine. "I know that in my own case, it helps to have some harmless safety valve for tension. In my dressing room, I keep a set of drums. I used to be a pretty fair drummer; my idol was Gene Krupa. Now, when I feel my nerves begin to stretch (and when the rule of silence on the set isn't in effect), I like to bang out a whole medley of wild rhythms."

As Bob made his way in the world, he would reach back to his growing-up years in Stamford, reconnect often with his relatives, and remain friends with nearly everybody. He attended reunions as often as his hectic schedule would allow, and every time business called him to New York City, he *always* made it a point to visit his friends in Stamford.

"He was just a nice guy, kept in touch with all his friends, and just stayed with where his roots came from," Jane Golden said. "He never lost track of Stamford. Connecticut. *Ever.*"

A great many members of Stamford High School's Class of 1946 remember their classmate and friend "Bobby" Crane fondly. Classmate Doris Sidney Leidecker perhaps best summarizes the impact Bob made on those he knew and encountered during his youth:

"Bob had a way about him that could brighten the darkest day. He made others feel good about themselves with a generosity of spirit rare in a teenager or anyone. And we, the remainder of the class of '46, have remembered our Drummer Boy fondly throughout the years. We could use some of his sunshine now!"

Source: Courtesy of Scott Crane. Used with permission.

"Edwin (Eddy) Gordon (bass), Bob Crane (drums), Frank Duffy, Joe Guiliani, Ed Hlavaty. December 1944 School Assembly" As handwritten by Bob Crane in his photo album.

Source: Courtesy of Scott Crane. Used with permission.

The Spirit of Stamford, Connecticut

Bob (center), with his parents Rose and Al Crane (circa 1933).

Source: Courtesy of Scott Crane. Used with permission.

Bob (left) with his older brother Al, Jr., and his mother (circa 1932).

Source: Courtesy of Scott Crane. Used with permission.

Bob as a toddler (circa 1930).

Source: Courtesy of Scott Crane. Used with permission.

Rose Crane with her two sons, Bob (left) and Al, Jr. (circa 1935).

Source: Courtesy of Scott Crane. Used with permission.

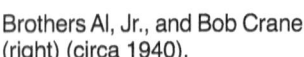

Al Crane with his two sons, Bob (left) and Al, Jr. (circa 1935).

Source: Courtesy of Scott Crane. Used with permission.

Brothers Al, Jr., and Bob Crane (right) (circa 1940).

Source: Courtesy of Scott Crane. Used with permission.

The Spirit of Stamford, Connecticut

Crane-Catino Band

The curtain opened, the auditorium lights were dimmed, the students hushed, and the band on stage was jumping into the well-known "One-O'Clock Jump."

Such was the scene way back in our Sophomore year, when Teddy Catino's orchestra gave their first musical assembly for the students of S.H.S.

In that first assembly, Teddy and Bob Crane were the lone Sophomore representatives. Teddy was the leader, and Bob, the drummer. The remainder of the band was made up of Junior and Senior musicians, who, although older than their leader, respected his ability.

After numerous assembly performances, the band in its Sophomore year, tackled its biggest stage success: that of playing for the well-known Junior "Show Time."

After that, the band was made. It played for assemblies and school dances, at many top social gatherings in this section of the state. It was called upon to play for the Katonah, New York, High School prom; the Darien and Greenwich proms; and last, but not least, our own school proms.

In the Junior year, the band was reduced from twelve pieces to nine. The draft was at last catching up with high school musicians, so much that when the final music assembly of the year came around, the band made its appearance with only six musicians.

During the summer vacation, Teddy Catino joined the Musicians' Union to go with a semi-name band. With its leader gone and its musicians entering the armed forces, the band was dwindling fast.

The lone survivors were Bob Crane, Frank Daly, Jr., and Teddy Martino. With his music library and stands under his arm, Bob started his own band with what was left of Teddy's band. Augmented by some Greenwich musicians, Bob's band was on its own.

This year's first music assembly found the high school jazz trio (Don Sappern, Teddy, and Bob) as its music-makers. This combination was enlarged to the original twelve pieces by the time the second assembly rolled around.

With a grand total of about fifteen assemblies in the last three years, the band closed its books on high school jazz.

With the exception of one or two, all the members are planning on music as a vocation.

Source: Stamford High School Yearbook, *The Spirit of 1946*, page 146. Courtesy of Stamford High School. Used with permission.

"Me in Fairfield Memorial Park. January 1945. I'm standing on the ice of the little fish pond. Ann took it."
As handwritten by Bob in his photo album.

Source: Courtesy of Scott Crane. Used with permission.

"Ann in my backyard. She's helping me cut the lawn. Taken by me on June 16, 1945."
As handwritten by Bob in his photo album.

Source: Courtesy of Scott Crane. Used with permission from Karen Crane and Scott Crane.

"Ann and Bob on Ann's front steps. Ann's not looking at Bob but just in front of him. Bunny took this one in January 1945."
As handwritten by Bob Crane in his photo album.

Source: Courtesy of Scott Crane. Used with permission from Karen Crane and Scott Crane.

Note: Anne prefers her name spelled with an "E." However, in this album, Bob had written it without the "E." It was common for her name to appear with and without the "E" in early printed works.

Chapter 2
A Star Is Born

The first station I started out with was a 250-watt station. I went to a 1,000-watt station, which was the Bridgeport station... And from the 1,000-watt, I went to the 50,000-watt, which is quite a jump, and it has happened to a lot of people. It's a fortunate thing to be in the right place at the right time.

—Bob Crane in a presentation to students at LA College, 1963

Early professional portrait of Bob Crane, circa 1950.

Source: Courtesy of Scott Crane. Used with permission.

Bob Crane behind the microphone at WLEA, Hornell, New York, circa 1950.

Source: Courtesy of Scott Crane. Used with permission.

Chapter 2

A Star Is Born

I had always wanted to be in radio. Once I got into radio, I found out that the man that hired me said that everything I did was funny, including the news. So he said, "You just be a funny guy with the records," and that's how I got into the comedy end of it. So there I was, at twenty-one, in my first radio job, up in Hornell, New York. After about a year up in Hornell, I applied for a job, and I finally found one in Bristol, Connecticut. And I only got that job because the wire recording I sent played back slow—slower than what I recorded it at. So the station that hired me thought they were getting someone like Edward R. Murrow. After about three months, a friend of mine in Bridgeport, Connecticut, who was also a program director, said, "Hey, if you ever hear of a morning man who doesn't drink, let me know. And so I said, "I don't drink," and he said, "We'll hire you. The main thing is, you don't drink." And within a couple of weeks, he said, "Hey, you can be very funny. We're not gonna have you do news or anything in the morning. You just do the funny stuff between the records." And this is the way it all began.

—Bob Crane, August 4, 1972, WCFL 1000 Radio, Chicago, Illinois

One word continues to be used when people talk about Bob Crane's radio work: *genius*. Time and again, industry colleagues and peers reach for that word to describe Bob's off-the-cuff comedy and lightning-fast wit that entertained fans and secured a healthy return on investment for every radio station that employed him. Bob's unique blend of self-deprecating humor, sharp wit, and speedy delivery became his trademark—a marketable brand that was intelligent enough for adults to sit up and listen, and innocuous enough that their children could be with them when they did.

Bob spent more than fifteen consecutive years in radio, with humble and often arduous beginnings on the East Coast before becoming a morning drive-time phenomenon on the West Coast. In a time when radio was still king, Bob cut his teeth in the business and helped transform the medium by doing things that had rarely, if ever, been done before. Further, everything he did on the air—every sound effect, gimmick, joke, skit, and quip—was spontaneous. While he prepared extensively for his show and devoted countless hours of his own time to hone his skill, *nothing* was rehearsed. While he is universally remembered as Colonel Hogan, Bob Crane must be credited for paving the way for radio personalities and disc jockeys for generations to come.

Bob's love of music was the force behind his decision to enter the world of radio. Ever since his school days, he held career ambitions of becoming a studio musician or playing with the Big Bands. But by the time Bob graduated from high school, the Swing era was all but dead, and his dreams of pursuing a career in music died right along with it. He wanted to keep his beloved music close to him, but he was forced to set his sights elsewhere.

Ever since taking an interest in music, Bob enjoyed listening to his favorite bands on the radio. And as he listened to the music, he also heard something else—the man behind the mic, announcing the songs, reading the news, and quite often, making him laugh. Bob's interest was piqued. And so, his interest in radio grew.

Radio was a natural career progression for Bob; music had already become very important to him, and he figured radio would be his *in* to the music world.

"Bob was funny, and he was playing the drums from the get-go," cousin Jim Senich said. "We always heard about him being in school things, he was always involved in that, so I think that was in his mind right from the beginning. It drove him even more than being a drummer. He really wanted radio. Early on, there was no doubt radio was what he wanted to do, and that was it."

As a drummer and a musician, Bob could feel the four-count or eight-count measures leading into a song, and he paid attention to what the radio personalities of the day were doing. He made note of what he liked, what made him laugh, what was effective—*and* what he did not like. The good, he filed away to ultimately be retrieved later; the bad, he remembered but never used. As a kid upstairs in his small bedroom, he wrote skits, commercials, and music. He would then put on make-believe radio shows, acting out his skits and introducing records. His audience was usually his girlfriend Anne, who would sit in Bob's bedroom doing her homework as he prepared radio skits, or his best friend, Charlie Zito.

A Star Is Born

"He would put on a disc jockey show—*just for me!*" Charlie said. "He used to say, 'You got anything to add? How did that sound?' And it was *really* terrific. The guy had *so much* talent. He was just unbelievable."

At the tender age of twelve, Bob performed his very first radio shows in his childhood bedroom. Seated behind his drumset and with his phonograph player nearby, he would flip on a record, find the track, introduce the song, adlib a repertoire, and then, he would happily begin playing his drums along with the record. With a market share of two—Charlie and Anne—Bob began developing the skills that would one day serve him at the highest level in broadcasting. But it would be another ten years before he would have the opportunity to broadcast to the masses. With no experience and little money, it would take some time for Bob to break into radio, and so his first foray into the world of employment after high school was doing something entirely unmusical: working in his hometown jewelry store.

Finlay Straus Jewelers was a chain of jewelry stores with headquarters in New York City; many Finlay Straus stores were located in New York, Connecticut, and northern New Jersey. Milton Schwartz owned and managed the Stamford store, and he was described as a kind, older gentleman who treated his employees well.

Friend and Stamford High School classmate Gloria Rosa also worked at the store, running customer credit applications. She had fond memories of working for Schwartz and found Bob to be quiet and serious when he worked.

"He was very nice and very friendly," Gloria said. "He got along nicely with everyone, and everyone liked him. Most of the time, we talked about the different things in the store, but we never talked about anything personal. We'd sit downstairs in the basement every day having lunch. I'd have a big ham and pepper sandwich, and he had peanut butter and jelly!"

Bob worked a full schedule at Finlay Straus beginning shortly after he graduated from high school. His hours were typically nine o'clock in the morning until five o'clock at night, except for Thursdays, which was Stamford's "late night," when stores were open until nine o'clock.

Mr. Schwartz may have been a good boss, but he could also be considered a good con artist. He was skilled in tricking his loyal customers into purchasing merchandise they might otherwise not want or even need, a selling technique he taught to his staff. Bob's anecdotes about working at Finlay Straus sound as if they originated right out of Stalag 13.

"I was making forty dollars a week at the time," Bob explained. "I was always the guy the manager called to sell clocks. 'Mr. Crane, front please,' he'd say. I was never allowed to sell the bigger items. The essence of the credit jewelry business is, 'Don't let a customer close his account.' Well, when this lady came in, she wanted to pay off her account. That was in the days when TV was still a novelty; few people had a set. But we had one in the basement that was being repaired. It was one of those old jobs with the two doors in front of the picture screen, and all of the parts had been taken out. The manager sent me downstairs to get ready while he began conning the customer upstairs. Finally, he brought her down to the basement and showed her the TV, telling her things like, 'You'll have to pay only $1.25 for the next one hundred twenty-five years!' As the big selling point, he whipped open the doors of the TV cabinet, pointed at my face in place of the picture tube, and said, 'See what a beautiful picture you get?' Then he slammed the doors shut and took her upstairs again. She did buy the set on time, but only after we'd gotten it fixed. And from then on, whenever she saw me in the store, she looked at me in an awfully funny way.

"I didn't know anything at all about fixing watches," Bob continued. "I was working for a really junky store that didn't specialize in quality. For example, this place, it sold a variety of things, advertised some $9.95 radios, but we were not to sell one under any conditions. We managed this by sticking a pencil through one of the speakers. I used to double as a salesman. If a customer came in and insisted on buying one of these radios, we'd run to the back and get one out with a damaged speaker. 'All right,' we'd say, 'but before you take it, let's hook it up and see how it sounds.' Of course, it sounded terrible. 'Gee,' we'd say, 'that's funny. But of course, we have had some trouble with this model. On the other hand, we have a real bargain here for only $19.95…!'"

While the atmosphere was relaxed and friendly, selling jewelry, clocks and small appliances wasn't what Bob had in mind for his future. He *hated* his job there, feeling confined in the small shop working, as he described it, "the world's most miserable watchmaker." He simply stayed there to earn money while waiting for Anne to graduate. In fact, it was so far away from what he wanted to do, that when Milton Schwartz indicated his desire to leave the store to Bob when he retired, Bob turned him down.

When Bob told his father, Al was furious.

Cousin Jim Senich said. "The guy that owned [the jewelry store] didn't have any children. He said, 'Bob, when I die, this store is yours,' which was worth a great deal. Al berated Bob for not accepting the offer. One time, he really went at it with him. He said, 'You're out of your mind! You want to go into radio? You're not going to make any money.' But Bobby just kind of went off on his own and did what he thought was right. Bob ignored him. He just ignored him."

To the elder Crane, a man who had endured the hardships of the Great Depression and the rationing of war, inheriting Finlay Straus was a terrific opportunity and a solid place to build a career. It offered job security and a steady paycheck, something that was not to be taken lightly.

To Bob, however, it meant agony.

Bob's answer, despite the repercussions, remained a firm no. Torn between flattery and professional stagnation, Bob officially declined Schwartz's offer, and challenging his father, he made a stand.

In June 1948 and within a few short weeks of Anne graduating, Bob proposed to his high school sweetheart. A date was set, and the young couple began preparing for their wedding. Their parents held a party in honor of their engagement, and on Wednesday, June 23, 1948, *The Stamford Advocate* published the Terzian-Crane engagement announcement:

> At a family party at their home on Fairland Street, Mr. and Mrs. Alex Terzian announced the engagement of their daughter, Miss Anne Margit Terzian...to Robert E. Crane, son of Mr. and Mrs. Alfred T. Crane of Oaklawn Avenue. Miss Terzian and Mr. Crane are graduates of Stamford High School.

"From the first," Bob said. "Anne and I didn't care about anyone except each other. When she finished high school, I gave her a ring, and shortly after that, we were married."

At the same time Bob and Anne announced their engagement, on June 21, 1948, Bob met with enlistment officer Lieutenant Raymond C. Ellis and entered the Stamford National Guard. It was a way to volunteer his time in the service without the worry of being drafted. He entered with the rank of private, grade VII, and he served in the 192nd FA Battalion in Stamford. During his two years of service with the National Guard, Bob also participated in field training and eventually achieved the rank of corporal. Later on, he would joke about his time spent in the service as nothing spectacular or even worthy of mention in comparison to what he remembered of his family and friends during World War II. He referred to himself as a "Remington Raider"—an enlisted man with a desk job typing on Remington typewriters. And as with other areas of his life, Bob also often made light of his service, telling tales of his "hardships" to the press.

"Once at Camp Edwards in Massachusetts," he explained, "I got wounded in the office. Spilled a cup of scalding water on my arm. But I showed up every day at the typewriter with my arm in a sling. The war must go on."

Bob and Anne were married on May 21, 1949, in St. Maurice Roman Catholic Church—"The Little Church on the Hill"—on Glenbrook Road in Stamford, with their family and close friends in attendance. Bob was twenty; his bride, just eighteen. Friends Jane Lippoth and her then-fiancé John Golden, and Charlie Zito and his then-fiancée Yvonne, along with family and other friends and classmates, watched Anne glide down the long aisle escorted by her father, her beautiful lace gown simple yet elegant, her veil descending from her sparkling tiara and flowing over her radiant countenance, neck, and shoulders. The handsome groom stood proudly before the altar, his brother as his best man at his side. Across from him stood Anne's sister Ellen as maid of honor and her friend Mary K. McGowan as her bridesmaid. Beaming from ear to ear and dressed in a white tuxedo with black tie and cummerbund, Bob took a deep breath as Anne arrived before him, and he watched as his future father-in-law lifted his daughter's veil and kissed her cheek lightly.

"They were a couple of cute kids, really," Jane Golden remembered of Bob and Anne. "And she was so beautiful in her wedding dress. Absolutely beautiful."

Following the traditional Catholic ceremony, the newlyweds celebrated with a reception held at Chatham Oaks (now Chatham Manor) in Darien, Connecticut, after which, they left on their honeymoon to the Poconos in Stroudsburg, Pennsylvania. The newlyweds traveled with another couple to their honeymoon destination. They had been married just an hour before the Cranes' ceremony in St. Maurice Church and also happened to be honeymooning at the same hotel in the Poconos.

"It worked out just fine," Bob said. "It's sort of nice to have another couple on a honeymoon—up to a point, of course. We had a good time together."

The Pocono Mountain area in Pennsylvania was quaint and charming, not too far from home, and was, at the time, considered the "honeymoon capital" of the Northeast. But Bob also knew of a radio station not far from their hotel, and he planned to pay the station a visit.

WVPO—the "Voice of the Poconos"—is a radio station still in operation that serves the heart of the Poconos: Stroudsburg, East Stroudsburg, Tannersville, Mount Pocono, and Camelback Mountain. Located just off of Main Street in Stroudsburg behind the Presbyterian Church, WVPO brings the news, weather, church services, and classic oldies to its listeners. WVPO initially signed on the air as WHAB-AM in 1947, and one year later, it changed its call letters to WVPO. In 1949, its format was a blend of news and popular music.

Bob was hungry for a big break, and a small station just starting up seemed like the perfect place to get his feet wet. After settling into their hotel room, Bob trekked the short distance from the hotel over to WVPO.

He barely made it in the door before they turned him down flat.

"I couldn't even get an audition. They wouldn't listen to me," Bob confessed.

Back at the hotel, interested staff wanted to know how his audition went, and he was forced to tell them about his failed attempt. They teased and cajoled him for the rest of their stay, chiding Bob with wisecracks about him being "The Voice of the Poconos." He played along, but inwardly, he was *not* laughing. Crushed but not crippled by the rejection, he picked himself up, brushed himself off, and returned with his bride to their new home on Fairland Avenue in Stamford.

He also dragged himself back to the dreaded jewelry store.

Undeterred, he flooded East Coast radio stations with query letters and audition tapes, hoping to be noticed.

"He wanted to work in New York," Jim said. "[And if not, there] he wanted to work at WTIC in Hartford because that was the big one in Connecticut, but he couldn't get in there."

Bob waited patiently but also sought to better prepare himself. In the fall of 1949, he completed a course in station operations/radio techniques taught by Bridgeport's WLIZ personality and program director Wallie Dunlap at the University of Bridgeport. He also continued to play in local jazz bands in Fairfield County, Connecticut (including Stamford and its neighboring towns of Greenwich, Westport, Norfolk, and Darien). In between, he continued his service with the Stamford National Guard, having achieved the rank of full private by July 1949. Yet only dead air answered his avalanche of inquiries, and Bob began to fear radio might turn out to be nothing more than his father suspected—a dream.

But he refused to give up.

In early 1950. Anne and her mother were away in Sweden visiting relatives. Bob and Anne had been living with her parents in the two-storey colonial house on Fairland Avenue in Stamford, and Bob had been holding down the fort with his father-in-law while his wife and mother-in-law were away.

On one cold winter day in March 1950, as Bob was working at Finlay Straus, the store phone rang. Bob answered, and his life changed.

"Bob Crane?" the operator asked. "This is Hornell, New York, calling."

It was the phone call he had been waiting for all his life. WLEA, a radio station in Hornell, was looking for an on-air announcer. It was a young station, having signed on in 1948. While Bob had been hoping for an opportunity closer to home, he also recognized a break when he saw it. Bursting with excitement, Bob decided to abandon Finlay Straus and take the gamble to pursue his dream in radio. It was a monumental decision.

Bob's father was not impressed, still angry at his son for turning down the offer to inherit the store. Al, Sr. believed radio was a dead end and a risk, and he thought Bob was foolish. Further, Bob had a wife to support—Al could not comprehend how his son could even consider risking a steady income when he was just newly married, with the hopes of starting his own family.

Intense debates ensued between Bob and his father about WLEA and Bob's decision to move to Hornell. It was rare for Bob to argue with his father, but in this instance, he held his ground. Bob was *going* to Hornell, with or without his father's blessing or permission. Bob's

A Journey to Destiny

The vehicle sputtered and crawled to a stop on the country road. Bob shivered, this time not with adrenaline but from the frigid air. He was used to the cold temperatures, but the farther north he had driven, the lower the mercury in the thermometer had dropped. And now, his unreliable clunker had just given up the ghost.

Trying the ignition several times without any luck, Bob resigned himself to the fact that he would have to walk. Sliding out of the car, he retrieved his belongings and began hiking up the road. Before long, he heard the sound of a horse-drawn wagon coming up behind him. He watched as the farmer pulled back on the reins and brought his cart to a stop.

"Where are ya headed, son?"

"Hornell. I'm applying for a job, and I'm afraid I've run into bad luck already. My car broke down."

"Mm-hmm. Well, hop in."

"Really? You don't mind?"

"You wanna get there, don't ya?"

With a smile, Bob nodded. "Yes, sir. Thanks!"

Climbing into the back of the wagon, he situated himself in between bales of hay. The rickety carriage jolted as the farmer gave the reins a light snap and the horses came to life.

"So what kind of job?" the farmer yelled over his shoulder.

"Radio!" Bob blurted, his enthusiasm reborn. "At WLEA. I'm applying to be their new announcer!"

The farmer chuckled. "Okay, settle down, radioman."

Bob arrived in Hornell on the back of that farmer's wagon, intact and with bits of hay sticking out of his suit. To his utter amazement and dismay, however, WLEA had other plans for him.

"I'm sorry, but you want me to do—*what*?" Bob asked, dumbfounded.

"Routine maintenance. We need a guy to just clean up and fix things around here. I thought you understood."

"What I understood was that you needed an announcer. That's why I'm here. For the announcer job."

"Yes. Right. Well, can you do *this* job while we continue interviewing?"

"You're kidding."

"Look at it this way, kid. You can still say you're working in radio."

mother, however, supported her son, and she quietly urged him to accept the job at WLEA.

Jim Senich explained, "Rose believed in Bobby. She believed in Bobby all the way. Her feeling was, 'Bob, go for it.' That was *it*; there were no ifs, ands, or buts. None at all."

So after receiving an honorary discharge from the National Guard, Bob packed up his car—"a broken-down jalopy" according to Jim—and began his journey to Hornell.

"Bob couldn't even afford to bring his family up there," Jim said. "He got a ride in on the back of a horse and wagon because his car broke down. He had an old beat up car, and a farmer drove him in."

But when Bob arrived at WLEA, he was in for a shock. "When he got there," Jim said, "he found out the job wasn't going to be an announcer; he was going to be a maintenance man. But he stayed."

Stunned at the misrepresentation, Bob still accepted the maintenance job. It was a fateful move because no sooner had he swept the floor, then WLEA offered him the job as their announcer. Fifty-one radio announcers had applied for the position, Bob included. Out of those fifty-one, forty-nine had been from New York City. WLEA believed the city applicants would not be satisfied with the small-town station, and so, they hired the one person who was not from a big city: Bob Crane.

WLEA also took notice that Bob was enterprising and full of energy. After only two weeks behind the WLEA microphone, Bob had proven early but promising capabilities. Then within a month of Bob being hired, WLEA underwent more changes, and after firing just about everyone at the station, they promoted Bob to program director—with an increase in salary to forty dollars a week.

But Bob didn't care about the money. For Bob, the thrill was just being behind the mic, working his audience, and performing his show—*for real*. Not just *pretending* for Charlie and Anne and his friends, not dreaming about it from behind the counter at a jewelry store, but doing the *real thing*.

At WLEA, the fledgling radioman spread his wings and took flight.

> *The simplest gimmick that I used [was] a little saltshaker that I filled with water. And we had Borden's as a sponsor. This was up in Hornell, New York. And I would take a glass and the saltshaker. And I'd say, "Borden's guarantees fresh milk... Go ahead. Go ahead, now, Bessie." Or no, I think it was Elsie the cow. And I would use the saltshaker as a sound effect with the water coming out going into the glass. And I'd make believe I was milking the cow. And how fresh can the milk be?! ... This is how I got into the gimmicks thing. Then finally I decided [if] I could do it with sound effects, why not <u>voices</u>. Then I started adding voices...*

—Bob Crane, in a presentation to students at LA College, 1963

Bob spent nine months in Hornell working for WLEA, from March through December 1950. Bob also drummed three nights a week at the local Elks Lodge for eleven dollars a night. He continued attending church services, and he served Mass regularly at St. Ann's Catholic Church. Barely scraping by on his meager radio salary and any extra money he made playing drums, he lived at the YMCA for six dollars a week. A can of soup heated up on the radiator was often his dinner.

Meanwhile, Anne stayed behind in Stamford with her mother and ailing father. She found work in a local office as a secretary to help support them.

"We knew it was ridiculous," Bob said, "for her to try and live in Hornell on what I was making, and her father had become ill, fatally ill."

But things were more complicated than the young Cranes were letting on to most people. Not even a full year into their marriage, Anne and Bob were considering a divorce. Bob was also seeing a young lady in Hornell, and he and Anne talked of ending their marriage. But Bob and Anne soon reconciled.

"I think mostly, he wasn't home as much as he should have been. His job kept him away. Anne kind of missed him," Charlie Zito explained. "I met him by chance in one of the stores here in Belltown. I said, 'What's this I hear about you and Annie getting a possible divorce?' And he said, 'I'm not...we're not going to do that. I just can't. We decided that we're not going to get a divorce and get into court

Bob Crane over WLEA
March 1950—December 1950

Unfortunately, no known recordings of Bob's WLEA radio program exist. However, based on his presentation to brodcasting students at LA College in 1963, the following is an example of how a segment of his show in 1950 might have sounded.

"Cluck-cluck-cluck-cluck," the chicken cackled loudly, almost obnoxiously. Bob grinned and stifled a small giggle. The sound of an egg dropping into a bucket filtered through Bob's headset and drifted across the airwaves.

Plop.

"Another!" shouted the giant from Abbott and Costello's kids' record, *Jack and the Beanstalk.*

With a fluid motion, Bob lifted the stylus from the acetate and replaced it gently.

"Cluck-cluck-cluck-cluck," the hen repeated.

"Another!" the giant bellowed.

"Cluck-cluck-cluck-cluck." A brief pause, then, "Cluck-cluck-cluck-cluck." Another pause. "Cluck-cluck-cluck-cluck."

He lifted the stylus, its needle suspended in anticipation of where its operator would place it next.

"Not only is the milk fresh," Bob announced into the microphone. "But the eggs are fresh, too. Borden's gives you the sweetest, freshest, best-tasting milk that you ever poured into a glass. Fun to drink anytime."

With the swiftness and accuracy of a bird of prey, Bob lifted the needle and repositioned it.

"Cluck-cluck-cluck-cluck."

"Another!"

Plop.

"There's just nothing that tastes so good as good Borden's milk. Borden's is the *good, fresh* milk. And here, over at WLEA 1480 on your AM dial, we guarantee fresh milk, fresh eggs, fresh fruit, fresh weather, and fresh tunes. Here's the…"

Bob hesitated, then chuckled into the mic.

"I was about to say fresh."

A sweeping arrangement of strings drifted over the airwaves as Bob placed the stylus onto the record.

"Here's the *lovely* Patti Page with 'Would I Love You,'" he added, his tone calmer and softer, as if he were reading a bedtime story.

> "Oh, for just the chance to love you," Patti crooned. "Would I love you, love you, love you."
> Then out of nowhere…
> "Another!" the giant shouted.
> *Plop.*
> "That darn hen just never quits!" Bob declared, lightly scolding the chicken.

and start lying about each other. It wouldn't do any good for the whole family. It would just be a lot of problems.' And we left it at that. I never pushed him for anything else."

"It was hard on Anne and me to be apart like that for almost a year," Bob admitted. "The station couldn't afford a raise."

Charlie agreed. "It was *very* hard because [in those days], you had to go where the jobs were. And the job in Hornell—that almost wrecked his marriage."

Although tough on his marriage, WLEA had been the perfect location for him to dig in and really learn broadcasting. He was young and inexperienced, but motivated and driven. Here, he could try out different ideas—testing the water and figuring out what worked and what failed. As program director, he also took liberties at doing things on air that he would not have been able to do elsewhere, such as mixing sound effects and comedy routines into paid advertising.

It was—and still is—unprecedented, controversial, and often forbidden to "roast" a paying advertiser on the air. Yet there was something in Bob's delivery that left most advertisers not only shelling out the big bucks for airtime on his show, but also wanting more.

During his youth and as a young adult, Bob had listened to and noted the comedy styles of radio entertainers of his era.

"I know one of Bob's heroes was Arthur Godfrey," Jim Senich said. "He loved Godfrey."

Comedic entertainer Henry Morgan was a prominent radio personality of the 1930s and 1940s. Two of Morgan's gimmicks caught Bob's attention—that he poked fun at advertisers and that he employed the art of self-deprecating humor. Henry Morgan was also known as a cutthroat, and he sometimes pushed the envelope too far with sponsors. This often landed him in trouble. Astute to such nuances, Bob noticed and learned. By combining his own ideas with the styles of those he admired, his own brand of comedy began to emerge and take shape.

As he experimented, Bob also discovered that he could work short stories into his routine. He did this not only by combining sound effects and voices, but also by mixing up the commercials as well. Years later, as he grew adept at his skills, a listener could expect to hear several different commercials, intertwined with a voice impersonation or two (all Bob's own creation and talent) and various sound effects.

Bob's jokes were light and occasionally included a touch of innuendo. They were tame enough to keep the Federal Communications Commission (FCC) happy, innocent enough to be kid-friendly, and dicey enough to keep the adults laughing.

Everything Bob did on his radio show was rhythmic, as if he had rehearsed it a dozen times or more. He had prepared for it, retrieved the album out of his growing stockpile records, located the tracks, and decided which ones to use within a commercial. However, his on-air delivery was unrehearsed and unplanned. He had a natural feel for both music and comedy, and as one joke slid into another, he maneuvered through his show the way a cab driver maneuvers through rush hour traffic.

The job at WLEA was what Bob had been seeking, but not where he had been seeking it. Bob wanted a bigger station, and in the summer of that year, an event occurred that forced him to reconsider moving back to his home state.

On August 11, 1950, Anne's father Alex Terzian passed away in New York City following complications from surgery at only forty-nine years of age. Anne was devastated, and she and her mother supported each other emotionally and financially. But with Anne's small secretarial salary as their main source of income, they struggled to make ends meet. It was very clear to Bob that he was needed back in Connecticut.

"When my father-in-law died after an operation, it was a sad time for all," Bob said. "He was a remarkable man."

While in Hornell, Bob continued to send out audition tapes to radio stations in Connecticut and Northeast. Finally, in December 1950, WBIS in Bristol, Connecticut, responded with an offer. With nine months of experience at WLEA under his belt, Bob packed up his personal belongings and his radio show, and he returned home.

WBIS, a 500-watt station, was located at 183 Main Street in downtown Bristol. Situated above Kresge's Department Store and across from the Bristol Bank and Trust Company, the WBIS facility was composed of the news studios, a control room, offices, and the main studio, which also contained a piano.

Bob was eager to start his new job. Yet when he introduced himself in person, the WBIS managers were stunned. The man standing before them could not possibly be the same man they had heard on the audition tape. No, the young man who called himself Bob Crane talked fast and was quick and hip and glib; he certainly sounded nothing like the Edward R. Murrow-type they thought they were hiring.

After some investigating, it was discovered that the manager's recorder had played Bob's wire tape slower than it should have, thus distorting Bob's voice and making it sound deeper than it actually was.

"My voice was higher then," Bob laughed as he recalled the moment years later. "But on the tape I sent out, I sounded like Smokey the Bear."

WBIS decided to keep Bob, but not because they loved his voice.

"When he heard me speak, he was pretty disappointed," Bob said, explaining the reaction of the WBIS program director. "But he liked my sense of humor, so he kept me on."

Bob accepted the offer. In a very short time, the managers became so impressed with his talents that they promoted him to program director and senior announcer.

While Anne and her mother remained in Stamford, Bob stayed in Bristol during the week, living in a boarding house on Federal Hill, and returned home to Stamford on weekends. He earned forty-five dollars a week, and although he again supplemented his income by playing drums, including regular stints at the Bristol Elks Club on South Street, money was still tight. His room in the boarding house in Bristol had no refrigerator, and Bob would keep his milk on the windowsill outside.

"My biggest problem was if the sun came out because in a day, I'd have sour milk. I used to play a couple of records, then run up the hill to check on my milk."

But he no sooner began work at WBIS, when a call came in from Bridgeport. Wallie Dunlap, Bob's former radio techniques course instructor at the University of Bridgeport, was in need of Bob's help.

Dunlap was looking for a morning announcer for WLIZ in Bridgeport, and he had remembered his former student. He saw promise in the young radio man, and he made Bob an offer. To Bob's surprise, the main stipulation had nothing to do with radio. He simply must not drink! WLIZ had apparently had issues with morning radio announcers showing up for work hung over, and Dunlap was through with the behavior causing trouble at work.

The WLIZ job also came with a ten-dollar increase in salary, pushing Bob up to fifty-five dollars per week. Bridgeport was also closer to home, only thirty miles north of Stamford.

"I've been hired for the strangest reasons," Bob said. "Because I was a small-town boy, because a tape distorted my voice, and because I didn't drink."

He didn't have to think twice. After only three months at WBIS, Bob took a flying leap south into the heart of Fairfield County, Connecticut, and now within earshot of New York City.

In April 1951, Bob began his five-year stint as Southwestern Connecticut's early morning town crier, becoming one of the Northeast's most successful radio personalities of all time.

And a star was born.

A Star Is Born

Bob and Anne Crane on their wedding day — May 21, 1949, St. Maurice Roman Catholic Church, Stamford, Connecticut.

Source: Courtesy of Karen Crane. Used with permission.

Bob and Anne Crane out with friends at Laddin's Terrace in Stamford, Connecticut (circa 1949). Jane (Lippoth) Golden and her husband John are third and fourth from left.

Source: Courtesy of Jane Golden. Used with permission.

A Star Is Born

Bob Crane at WLEA in Hornell, New York (circa 1950).
Source: Courtesy of Scott Crane. Used with permission.

Bob Crane in his radio booth, station unknown (circa 1950-1955).
Source: Courtesy of Scott Crane. Used with permission.

Source: Courtesy of Scott Crane. Used with permission.

Chapter 3
The Idea of Learning

New 'Town Crier'
Bud Thorpe, having left WLIZ, the station has a new "Town Crier" from 6 to 9 a.m. He's Bob Crane, a Stamford lad who went through Wallie Dunlap's first radio course for the University of Bridgeport and has since been gaining experience at Hornell, N.Y., and with WBIS, Bristol. Dunlap considers him "one of the bright young men in radio's future."

—"The Bridgeport Telegram," April 19, 1951

Source: Courtesy of WICC-600 AM Radio, Bridgeport, CT. Used with permission.

TUNE IN ON BOB CRANE
6:00 to 10:15 A.M.
MONDAY THRU FRIDAY
OVER WICC

Bob Crane and Wallie Dunlap at WICC-600 AM Radio, Bridgeport, CT, circa 1953.

Source: Courtesy of WICC-600 AM Radio, Bridgeport, CT, and Eliot Dober. Used with permission.

Chapter 3

The Idea of Learning

Eventually, what you're looking for is gonna happen, and by the time it does happen, you'll be that much better along the way to what you should be. Don't get discouraged, and just keep on plugging along, and what you want will eventually be yours. You know, there's nothing to stop it if you just keep on working hard. And by working hard, I mean doing the best job you possibly can. Everything happens for the best, and I believe it completely.

— Bob Crane in an audio letter to his cousin, Jim Senich, 1962

The May 5, 1951, edition of *Billboard Magazine* reported that at WBIS, Bob Crane's Top-20 Show had "been extended to thirty minutes, nightly." Yet by the time that issue went to press, Bob had already vacated the WBIS booth. Having spent a little more than one year behind the microphone—ten months at WLEA and three short months at WBIS—Bob was primed for taking on the challenges and responsibilities awaiting him at WLIZ in Bridgeport, Connecticut.

At just twenty-two years of age, Bob had traveled a galaxy's distance from a ride in the back of a farmer's hay wagon, and an entire universe from repairing watches and selling jewelry and other novelties from his hometown's emporium just two years prior. Now, nestled comfortably back in his own backyard, Bob would be broadcasting during the morning rush hours to most of Connecticut, as well as to parts of New Jersey, and more importantly, New York.

While Bob may have been happy to return home to Connecticut and his wife Anne, his ambitions reached beyond the Nutmeg State's borders. Connecticut may have been where he needed to be, but New York City was where he desperately *wanted* to be.

Jane Senich Ryfun explained that her father, Mike Senich, an artist working at King Feature Syndicate in Manhattan, had a strong influence on his nephew Bob, both personally and professionally. She suspected that in some aspects of his life, Bob had sought to emulate his Uncle Mike, who was driven toward success in his own career and was a genuinely happy individual.

"My dad was incredibly creative. For my dad to leave Waterbury, it was a big deal. My Aunt Rose, Bob's mom, had left Waterbury, and that was *big*, to leave Waterbury. So I guess he did what Bob was hoping he could do, and I guess that's what my dad and Bob had in common. My dad had a wonderful sense of humor. He would just listen, and he was so accepting and so confident. The glass was *always* half-full! I have had these wonderful aunts who were these incredible influences on me. You have *wonderful* people like that in your life, and I'm sure that my dad was that to Bobby. He was one of these *really* great go-to people. And just so positive."

By many accounts, Bob was, indeed, a positive person. By those same accounts, he was highly driven and passionate about his chosen career in radio. Thus, when Bob received the offer from WLIZ to host the station's morning show, he had been elated.

Things could not have been working out better for young and ambitious Bob Crane. Not only would his own family and friends be able to hear his daily broadcasts, but all of Long Island and Manhattan would as well. WLIZ, then located at 114 State Street in Bridgeport, was only a short walk from the banks of Long Island Sound, and directly across The Sound, the coveted New York City skyline beckoned.

Now strategically positioned, Bob's long-range goal of gaining a foothold in New York City had been neatly placed at his doorstep.

Like many cities in Connecticut during the mid-twentieth century, Bridgeport was an industrial city, and one steeped in history. Founded on October 3, 1836, Bridgeport was home to showman and businessman P.T. Barnum, the H.M.S. Rose Foundation, the first successful helicopter—the model VS-300—designed by Igor Sikorsky, and the Corsair fighter jet. Bridgeport's industry and labor force was not only, as author Lennie Grimaldi described, "the armament center of the nation" during both World Wars I and II; it also "produced an assortment of offbeat and progressive firsts, including model trains, luxury cars, aerosol sprays, and undergarments."

Bridgeport also boasted a variety of entertainment venues. Whether it was theatre, music, or moving pictures, the "Park City"—as it was and still is affectionately known—was a short distance from New York and Boston. As syndicated columnist Arthur "Bugs" Baer observed, "If you're not on Broadway, everything is Bridgeport."

The Idea of Learning

By the spring of 1951, everything was Bridgeport for Bob Crane. While finding his footing at WBIS, Bob's broadcasting mentor and Bridgeport University course instructor Wallie Dunlap had other ideas for his former student.

A life-long reporter with an interest in broadcasting, Wallace B. "Wallie" (sometimes "Wally") Dunlap had gotten his start during his teen years as a cub reporter for the *New Orleans Tribune* in the 1930s. From there, he moved to reading news reports for a New Orleans radio station, which gave him his first taste in broadcasting. Dunlap served in the U.S. Army Air Force during World War II; he directed theatrical shows while serving in the Air Force and continued to do so after the war. Following World War II, he spent time in radio broadcasting in cities such as Philadelphia and New York, before eventually settling at WLIZ in Bridgeport.

As program director and station operations manager for WLIZ, Dunlap sought to fill the void left by Bud Thorpe, who had moved on to other ventures, and he specifically wanted a young, reliable, energetic, and most importantly, sober announcer.

Dunlap was impressed with Bob's work. Further, because he didn't drink and came from a small radio station (and therefore would consider this a step up), Bob was assured the morning timeslot at WLIZ. Taking over the WLIZ microphone in April 1951, Bob slid comfortably into his routine, becoming southwestern Connecticut's morning wake-up call.

Bob had only been with the station for a few months, when then-WLIZ station owner Manning Slater decided he wanted to buy another local radio station, WICC-60 (now WICC-600), also in Bridgeport, which had been in operation since 1926. In late 1951, WLIZ entered into negotiations to purchase WICC, and in early 1952, WICC was turned over to WLIZ for $200,000.

Shortly after the purchase was finalized, WLIZ management took over station operations of WICC. The stronger signal of WICC prevailed, while the weaker WLIZ signal faded into oblivion. Most of WICC's original staff and radio talent were immediately replaced with those of WLIZ. The details of the transfer were described in the March 1, 1953, issue of Bridgeport's *Sunday Herald*:

> On January 17, 1952, the way was cleared by the Federal Communications Commission in Washington for the transfer of the license of WICC, Yankee Net-

work outlet, to the Bridgeport Broadcasting Company [BBC] operators of radio station WLIZ, for $200,000. At 12:30 a.m., January 25, 1952, WICC announcers were notified that they would not be going on the air today, and that the staff at WLIZ would take over. Phillip Merryman, head of the BBC, announced on an 8:00 a.m. broadcast that the station had started operations of WICC. WLIZ did not broadcast that day. Telephone callers to WLIZ were greeted with, "Good Morning, this is WICC, formerly WLIZ." Most of the morning programs of WLIZ were being aired, but those usually carried by WICC, with the exception of Yankee Network commercial programs, were not heard. Executives of WICC were Phillip Merryman, president, Wallace Dunlap, vice-president; Manning Slater, vice-president in charge of sales. Bob Crane became the featured morning disc jockey, as the "Town Crier."

The station transfer from WLIZ to WICC solidified Bob's position in the radio and broadcasting industry. In February 1952, he was promoted to program manager for WICC, and by March 1953, he had risen to the level of WICC operations director.

Climbing the WICC ladder was not the only positive change for Bob. As he grew in his career, so, too, did his radio program. In Bridgeport, Bob continued to experiment and tinker with commercials and gimmicks. He had learned at WBIS how to improvise when a guest failed to show up. He had also discovered that instead of performing all of the voices in his show on his own, he could start "talking back" to other voices on records. He brought this technique with him to Bridgeport, where he began to enhance this skill.

"After all the years of talking to myself," Bob said, "I found that it was better to talk back to records."

This trick further allowed him to interact with the commercials, where a listener was led to believe Bob was engaging in fluid conversation with the sponsor on the recording. In so doing, he was able to streamline his show and jam-pack as many sponsors into his morning program as he possibly could, providing up to ten commercials in as many minutes.

The Idea of Learning

Harvey Geller, former Vice President and Editor for *Cash Box* magazine (West Coast), and a columnist, feature writer, reviewer, and sales executive for *Variety* and *Billboard* magazines, was a close friend of Bob on both coasts. Harvey respected the raw talent Bob brought to radio, and he recalled an incident of Bob's quick wit and ability to think on his feet.

"One day I brought Guy Mitchell up," Harvey said. "Guy Mitchell was a big star at the time, and we were plugging some record, and I said, 'Let's get off the highway here. I want you to meet a friend of mine who's on the air.' So I took Guy Mitchell to see Bob Crane. And at that moment, Bob was playing a record that was a big hit that was called *Cherry Pink and Apple Blossom White*. So Guy immediately took on the voice of the orchestra leader, who was Spanish. And Guy could do a very good Spanish accent. So Bob said, 'Hey, keep that, keep that!' He said to the audience as the record ended, 'Hey, guess what! I'm playing this record, and guy who walks in—the guy who recorded this number just happened to show up!' He interviewed Guy Mitchell for about fifteen minutes, with Guy pretending to be the orchestra leader! Guy and I left; Bob never told the audience that it was Guy Mitchell, who was just as big an artist, or bigger, as the guy he was portraying. And as we drove away, I figured Bob would come on and say, 'I was only kidding, that was Guy Mitchell doing the voice.' But he never said it."

Bob had also come to dislike being referred to as a disc jockey. His show was so much more than just playing records and reading the news and weather. He wanted the distinction of being known as a *radio personality*.

Much attention was gained with his on-air promotions. One promotion ran during the summer of 1953, when each WICC radio personality was given one week to call his own. Bob chose the week of July 12, which included his birthday. He dubbed it Enarc Week.

Retired WICC disc jockey and radio personality Frank Derak recalled another of Bob Crane's radio antics, which shows the immense popularity Bob enjoyed.

"It was two weeks before Valentine's Day, and Bob got on the radio and asked his female audience to send the station Valentine's Day kisses in the mail," Frank explained. "The promotion moved into high gear on the second day, and after that, letters, cards, and all sorts of adoring gifts poured into the station—all with big lipstick kiss marks on them! Thousands of deliveries were made to the WICC studios, so much so, that the Health Department served WICC with a notice to stop the promotion immediately. Evidently, they believed it was unhealthy for their postal carriers to handle packages covered with kisses. No one ever heard of a postal employee complaining, but the promotion ended. That didn't stop the kisses from arriving daily for about a month, well into March!"

Another popular stint Bob did over the air was having a chicken rate new records. The worse the record was, the more eggs it received! Listeners could hear a hen cackle and then eggs being dropped into a basket after the record was played. But there never really was a hen in the studio; it was all done by Bob with pre-recorded sound effects.

Bob flourished at WICC. His radio program was unique, exciting, entertaining, and fun. He pushed the envelope and took chances, then learned to be careful and think twice about how far he could actually take a joke. He often learned the hard way when an advertiser was unhappy with the way Bob enhanced a commercial. In the beginning, sponsors were not entirely certain of his brand of humor, and occasionally, they became upset.

In one instance, his early antics nearly resulted in his termination from the station. A local Bridgeport sandwich shop had purchased advertising during Bob's program, and as usual, Bob began inserting his humorous commentary, listing the ingredients of the shop's specialty sandwiches. According to cousin Jim Senich, the shop owners were baffled and angry when they discovered that in addition to deli meats and cheeses, bits of street, sidewalk, and dirt also comprised their sandwiches. Shortly after the commercial aired, the store owner called the station, and they were *furious*.

Station management tore into Bob, shouting, "Never do that again!"

But then something interesting happened. Around noon that same day, the shop owner called back.

"Never mind what I said!" he exclaimed. Apparently, lunch sales were going through the roof. They had never seen so many people in the store before, all wanting to try his sandwiches, saying things like, "I was curious to see if I was going to get bits of concrete in my sub sandwich!"

Bob was lucky, and it didn't stop him from toying with the radio spots that ran during his show unless the sponsor specifically requested it. If anything, it cemented his decision to do so. But it had been an important lesson—be careful with how far you take the joke. Many years later, when talking to a group of LA College students in 1963, Bob cautioned them about how much might be considered *too* much. He urged the next generation of disc jockeys and radio personalities: "If you're ever in doubt, if you think something is a little bit off-color, you're debating it. If you *have* to debate it, then don't do it. If you reach that point where you're thinking, 'Should I say that?' then don't say it. Because you're gonna offend somebody. If *you* gotta think about it, then *they're* gonna think about it. They're gonna hear it at home and say, *'Ehhhh?'"*

As Bob's ratings increased, so did his salary, which was determined based on the number of commercials he played. By 1956, the rising radio star was capturing sixty-five percent of the audience share and receiving fan mail from as far away as Alaska. He no longer had to worry about heating a can of soup on the radiator at the YMCA or keeping his milk on the windowsill because he could not afford a Frigidaire. Now, he was making five hundred dollars a week (the equivalent of $4,400 a week in 2015). Not bad for a kid who got his start putting on radio shows in his childhood bedroom!

Shortly following Bob's move to WLIZ/WICC, Bob and Anne relocated from Stamford to Bridgeport. The first home Bob secured on his own for his family was a duplex apartment in Bridgeport, where he left for work at five-thirty in the morning. and he returned home at seven o'clock at night.

"Bob told me that he had everything prepared in the afternoon," Jim Senich recalled. "He would never go home when he went off the air. He said, 'I would stay there so that when I came in in the morning, everything was ready to go.'"

Bob Crane had arrived.

And so had a new baby boy. On June 27, 1951, Anne gave birth to a son, affectionately called "Bobby, Jr." by his parents and baptized Robert David Crane at St. Charles Borromeo Parish Church in Bridgeport.

Anne was also working as a receptionist for a doctor's office. Now independently financially stable, Bob and Anne believed it was silly that Anne's mother should reside in Stamford all alone. They suggested she move up to Bridgeport and into the apartment with them. Mrs. Terzian scoffed at the idea initially, thinking she would be a burden.

"She feared she'd be in our way. She was wrong!" Bob said.

Anne's mother decided to move in with her daughter, son-in-law,

BOB CRANE The Definitive Biography

The Bob Crane Show over WICC
Bridgeport, CT

As with WLEA, no known recordings of Bob Crane's WICC radio program exist. Based on his many KNX and KMPC airchecks, as well as firsthand accounts, the following is an example of a typical morning at WICC in Bridgeport, Connecticut.

At 6:12 a.m., the main doors to WICC flew open, and in rushed Bridgeport's number-one radio personality. Hair mussed; tie draped loosely around his neck; folders, records, and drumsticks tucked under one arm; coffee in one hand and a wire recorder in the other, Bob Crane plowed into the studio. There, he deposited his stacks of paraphernalia on the guest chair, placed his cup of brew onto the only clear spot on the control table, and crashed down into his announcer's chair. Characteristically late, he had already heard on his drive into work the smooth sign-off of the WICC radio personality who held the shift before him: "This has been Dick Alexander, here and mighty glad to be." The morning news briefs that ran until 6:05 had also ended, and Patti Page was now crooning her number-one *Billboard* hit, *The Doggie in the Window*, to cover for his tardiness.

"Seven minutes. Getting better, Crane," the man said with a wry smile, his deep intonation resonating through the booth. The first African-American disc jockey in Connecticut, Dick Alexander gathered his own belongings and watched the frenetic radio personality arrange his records and attach his show notes onto the metal stand in front of him. "One of these days, you might just be early and make it in on time. Then I wouldn't have to cover for you."

"Eventually," Bob quipped, pulling the microphone toward him and slapping acetate onto the two turntables. "Maybe I'll get the fly to fill in for me," he added, indicating the station's Pet Fly.

"Would be an improvement," Dick chided.

Bob pulled a face, and with a quick glance at the live turntable, he estimated he had about thirty seconds before the track ended. Sliding beneath the console for a moment, Bob positioned a makeshift floor apparatus to his liking. He tested it once, and when one of the turntables spun to life, he pressed it again, causing it to stop. He climbed back into his chair and checked his watch. Ten more seconds.

"You're one wild man, Crane," Dick laughed.

Grinning and with a twinkle in his eye, Bob lifted the stylus from the record and pulled the microphone in close to him. Pressing the floor contraption with his foot, his opening music cued, and he spoke into the mic, effortlessly replacing the Patti Page record with another on the turntable as he spoke to the thousands of groggy Connecticut and Long Island residents.

"Hello there, and a happy good Monday morning! In case you are just waking up, and you probably are, unlike me, who has been up since four A.M., this is Bob Crane over WICC 60 A.M. on your radio dial, taking over for Dick Alexander – who *was* here, and is mighty glad to be..."

Cue: Slamming door effect.

"...going!"

"So long folks," another voice from the record announced, Bob having found the miniscule track with perfection, as if some sixth sense had told him exactly where the precise sound was located on the vast twelve-inch surface.

"Yes," Bob answered the phantom speaker, holding the stylus steady in the air. "Now, we have quite a show for you lined up—not only today, but for this whole week! Ralph, tell 'em what they've won."

"Huh?" Bob answered himself in a disguised dialect that was two octaves lower than his own.

"Tell our listeners what we're gonna do?"

"Oh. I'm having breakfast. You tell them," "Ralph" said.

"That's our dynamic engineer, folks. Ralph Winquist. Been here since '48. Station couldn't run without him. But I'm driving him away, I think. Anyway, we have quite the event planned for this week. And this is a very special week. Why, do you ask? Even if you didn't ask, you know I'm gonna tell you. Now, get out your calendars and your pencils and...yes, put down your coffee. That's right. This is a very important event. I want you to circle it, block the whole thing out."

A brief round of applause and cheering from the turntable.

"Because this is *my* week here at WICC."

Another round of applause and cheering.

"A big whole week, just for me!"

Another round of applause.

"And I'm calling it..."

Bob slid his chair toward the snare drum and performed a drum roll for five seconds. At its conclusion, he said prominently into the mic: "Enarc Week."

A hen cackled, and an egg dropped into a basket.

"Aw, now c'mon!" Bob laughed. "You're not gonna rate my week already, Henrietta! It's hardly just begun!"

The hen cackled again, followed by another egg plop.

"Folks, we'd better get to a commercial before I get plopped on outta here."

From the engineer's control room, Ralph Winquist took his cue and played the recording for Camel Cigarettes.

"You know," the actor on the ad informed, "if you were to follow a busy doctor as he makes his daily round of calls…,"

"Yes?" Bob answered, now having a conversation with the recording.

"…you'd find yourself having a mighty busy time keeping up with him."

"I'll bet."

"Time out for many men of medicine usually means just long enough to enjoy a cigarette."

"Is that all?"

"And because they know what a pleasure it is to smoke a mild, good-tasting cigarette…"

"Ok, easy there."

"…they're particular about the brand they choose. In a repeated national survey, doctors in all branches of medicine, doctors in all parts of the country were asked, 'What cigarette do you smoke, Doctor?'"

Bob cued his engineer, and Ralph lifted the stylus on his record as Bob placed his down onto his record.

"Uh, lemme think about it….uh…Jane? Jane! What cigarettes do we buy? Uh…hang on….I've got it right here…uh…"

Bob lifted the needle and cued Ralph, who replaced his own, and the sponsor's actor continued with the ad.

"Once again the brand named most was Camel."

Cue: One needle up, the other needle down.

"That's it! That's it! Yeah, that's the answer! I knew it all along!"

Cue again.

"Yes, according to this repeated nationwide survey, more doctors smoked Camels than any other cigarette. Why not change to Camels for the next thirty days and see what a difference it makes to your smoking enjoyment."

Cue: One needle up, the other needle down.

A woman's giddy laughter.

Cue again.

"See how Camels agree with your throat. See how mild and good-tasting a cigarette can be."

"Whew," Bob chuffed into the mic. "No controversy here during Enarc Week, that's for sure. And just in case you were wondering, Enarc is Crane spelled backwards."

The hen cackled and delivered another egg.

"A guy just can't catch a break," he said with a laugh. "How 'bout a little drumming with Leroy Anderson's *Blue Tango*?"

and their new baby. "Nana" to her grandchildren, she looked after Little Bobby while his parents were away at work.

"We had a bedroom for her, enough privacy for each of us," Bob explained. "Soon Nana was reveling in cooking and sewing and crocheting, as well as doting on the baby. We knew how much attention Bobby would receive from Nana, and we wanted to save to buy a house."

Things were working out for the young couple, and they were together again as one family unit. Whatever marital troubles plagued them while Bob had been in Hornell appeared to have worked themselves out.

And Bob was in all his radio glory. It seemed to bother nobody that he was routinely a little late, perhaps because they knew he had already prepared for his next day's show before leaving work the day before and was only late by a few minutes. Bob was also technically savvy. He could work things out in his mind and did not often need to rely on others. If something went wrong, he demonstrated the ability to think quickly and resolve any issues almost immediately, right on the spot.

"He was technically sharp," his cousin Jim recalled. "That was a big, big plus. Most jocks like myself didn't know engineering-wise anything. If you hit the button, and the turntable didn't turn, we didn't know what the hell to do; we screamed. Bobby never went to school for it, but he was technically sharp. He would work on his own car, if anything broke in the house, he would just go over and fix it in ten seconds. So he had a technical background, and that coupled with his creativity enabled him to create that morning show. When he went to Bridgeport, he really took off because they had more equipment and more to work with."

By 1953, Bob had established himself as a leading radio personality in Connecticut and in the Northeast. That same year, the annual issue of *Who's Who in TV and Radio* published a brief biosketch of Bob in the column, "Back in Your Own Back Yard":

> **BOB CRANE** is a likeable chap—even if he does play the drums—as several hundred pieces of mail in a recent "Why I Like Bob Crane" contest will attest. The Connecticut Symphony Orchestra and a few "pop" bands—Louis Prima's for one—would like to sign Crane and his set of drums to a long-term contract, but Bob is busy building a heavy following at WICC,

Bridgeport, Conn., as a disc jockey and humorist. Born July 13, 1928, at Waterbury, Conn., Bob began to feel an urge to work in radio about the time most kids ask Pop for a new bike. Began as a disc jockey.

Jack Coombe, who was then broadcasting out of WNOR in Norwich, Connecticut, recalled how "radio people" in Connecticut would occasionally get together for what they considered a "gab session"—a time to get together for lunch and network with each other about what was going on at their particular station and in the industry in general.

"I remember Bob for his quick wit and exceptional good looks that always caused feminine heads to turn when he was present. I, also like many of my colleagues at the time, liked Bob and enjoyed being with him. He possessed a sort of charisma, if you will, that attracted him to people and they to him."

Bob Crane was in great demand and becoming more popular by the day.

On April 25, 1953, WICC moved its studios from the Cilco Building on State Street in Bridgeport to Booth Hill in Trumbull, Connecticut. Concurrently, WICC maintained a scant office staff and one small studio in the Stratford Hotel in Bridgeport, and thus able to keep their Bridgeport mailing address.

The move was to accommodate both the WICC radio studio and the fledgling UHF station—Channel 43—that Phillip Merryman, then-owner of WICC, had launched on March 15 of that year.

The one-storey, duplex-style building was located in a secluded, wooded area of Trumbull and resembled a warehouse. Its broadcasting tower (the Hi-Ho Tower) dominated the skyline and remains clearly visible above the trees from all directions to this day. On the left side, the radio studio; to the right, Channel 43 television, and where Bob experienced his first time in front of a camera.

In addition to his responsibilities as WICC program manager, station operations director, and on-air personality, Bob took on the job of chief video engineer and performed several television shows live over Channel 43. Bob poured his heart and soul into the new television station, doing everything he could to make Channel 43 successful, all without receiving any extra income.

"When I became program director," Bob explained to a group of LA College students in 1963, "I used to do a television show at night on the UHF station, and I'd do the morning show, and I'd also fill in if one of the guys was sick, and I'd also do the afternoon show. Just give me a mic! I was that much of a ham. Just let me go on! I don't care! The television show I did for nothing. UHF television, nobody was watching. Yet I would go on and knock myself out."

One show in particular was a variety program that Bob performed with Morgan Kaolian, a professional artist and licensed pilot, who was at one time a traffic reporter in southern Connecticut. Affectionately known locally as "Captain Traffic," his Flight 60 reports were famously broadcast over WICC from the 1950s through the late-2000s.

Morgan's recollections of working at WLIZ and WICC and with Bob Crane are vivid, detailed, and amusing.

"I was hired by WLIZ in about 1951 after winning too many of their art contents," Morgan began. "The station had a contest running where you had to draw a representation of a song they had just played and send it in. I created a placard for *Surrey with the Fringe on Top*, from the Broadway musical *Oklahoma!,* and I won a nice set of silverware from the station. I kept entering and kept winning! They figured they had to do something to get me to stop winning, so they hired me as their art director and made it impossible for me to enter their contests anymore."

When WLIZ purchased WICC and took charge of the station's operations, Morgan migrated to WICC as a freelance artist. He also began reporting the traffic, and in March 1953, Morgan became Channel 43's art director.

"I first met Bob when he was working up at Booth Hill," Morgan remembered. "We spent many hours on the air together over Channel 43. We broadcast live in the afternoon, and our programs were improvisation shows. There were some crazy stints that we did, all in the style of Ernie Kovacs."

One of those crazy stints was Angie the Antenna Man. "Angie wore a crazy hat and a raincoat, and carried an umbrella," Morgan explained. "Bob and I were in a scene where he was looking down on something. The audience thinks it is a woman because of what he says. The camera was just on his face as he's talking. 'Honey, I just can't tell ya how much you mean to me. I've fallen in love with ya.' And he's going on and on like this. And then the camera comes on my face—as Angie! And I'm making cross-eyes! You wouldn't expect that!"

The station showed other innovations as well, using film versions of popular music produced specifically for television—the first music videos. "We used Snader Telescriptions at that time," Bob said in a 1963 presentation to LA College broadcasting students. "They were like a record, but they were a movie of the guy doing it. Nat Cole, for instance, singing *Mona Lisa*, was popular at that time. We played Nat Cole's *Mona Lisa* almost every night on that show cuz we had only five or six of these things to put in. And they bridged the comedy stuff. And we had horses come in. Horses that would count [stomps foot] for us. And we had a guy come up. Now it's a gag we use on the show, but it's true. This guy really came up, and he said, 'Go ahead. What's two and two?' And the horse would go [stomp stomp stomp stomp]. And then the guy would say, 'Ok, come on boy. One more.' And *weird* things like that. This same guy also did impersonations. He did Ronald Coleman in *Lost Horizons*, and the great H.B. Warner, who was a great actor of yesterday. And Ronald Coleman would do this great, '*Ahhhh-hhh Great Halamah! Here in this Shangri La! You are an old man! If I take you out of this land, you will suddenly become ancient! I know it will happen! You are young now! By the way, how old are you?'* And H.B. Warner went [stomp stomp stomp stomp]. The guy just couldn't forget his other routine!"

Morgan also recalled the time Bob came riding into the Booth Hill studio on horseback to the sounds of familiar Native American music. "They had a wide studio door because they had to get equipment in and out. And here was Bob on a horse! I don't remember if he was dressed as an American Indian or not, but in the background was Indian music, like you would hear in Westerns. And he comes riding into the studio from the parking lot, right in front of the cameras. We opened the studio doors, and there he was, arms folded across his chest, riding on in like an Indian on this horse! That was funny!"

But the station failed miserably, and by the summer of 1953, Wallie Dunlap and Phillip Merryman were fighting to keep Channel 43 alive.

WICC's television station did not suffer from lack of entertaining programming; rather, it was ahead of its time. But in the 1950s, UHF television was in its infancy, and it was expensive. To be able to receive the UHF signal, installation of a bow-tie antenna on the rooftop and connection to a special converter were required. The new technology was not something most people could afford, averaging about one hundred dollars, and as a result, it was a luxury they did not believe they needed.

The Idea of Learning

Morgan explained, "Manufacturers of television sets had promised that all TV sets would have UHF tuners in subsequent models. It didn't happen until years later. By that time, audiences for Channel 43, 'The Best You Can See,' were very scarce. The station was a failure and a money loser. There was no audience…ever!"

The station floundered. Undeterred, Bob, Morgan, and other WICC staff, including Dick Alexander, Frank Delfino, and Wallie Dunlap, forged ahead. Morgan laughed at the time Bob held up the one-hundred dollar bill on the air and offered it to the first person who called.

"Nobody called," Morgan said. "Not one person! But we had lots of fun. Most of the laughs were from the staff. We were performing mostly for the cameramen and crew, and entertaining ourselves, if nothing else. It's like that one skit we used, where we are talking about different tools and drills. I held up a bit and said, 'You wanna know something? This is a better bit than the one we're doing!'"

Channel 43 eventually ceased broadcasting in December 1960. A few months later, a fire gutted the radio side of the Booth Hill studios, and all WICC airchecks and Channel 43 footage archived in the building—including recordings of Bob Crane's WICC radio and Channel 43 television shows—were lost.

As always, drums remained important to Bob, and he continued to play in local jazz bands in Connecticut. In addition to playing with Ronnie Rommel's Orchestra and Lou Prima's Band, he also played at other Bridgeport venues, including Matt Lucy's Hotel Tap Room at 577 Howard Street, at the Ritz Ballroom on Fairfield Avenue—where the great Big Bands of the 1940s, including Stan Kenton and Duke Ellington still played—and for the crowds that frequented Pleasure Beach, an amusement park island just off the coast of Bridgeport and the neighboring town of Stratford. Some of the Connecticut name bands Bob played with included the Bobby Dukoff, Billy Butterfield, Tony Parenti, Eddie Safranski, and Larry Fotine bands. In addition to playing locally in Bridgeport, he also played at The Westner in Westport, Connecticut, and the Glen Island Casino in New Rochelle, New York.

Salvatore "Tootie" DeBenedetto played in a Connecticut-based band with Bob during the early to mid-1950s. He recalled that he and Bob started a group called Crane and Friends. "We played a lot of nightclubs in Connecticut, Boston, New Jersey, New York—we did many, many clubs. He was a *damn* good drummer, too. Damn good. He was an exciting player. I mean, a lot of times, we gave him the solo…he was good. He was *very* good."

The drums also followed Bob to WICC, where he would beat out a rhythm to accompany the songs he chose to play. And his diverse style and talent were starting to make national headlines. The December 1955 issue of *TV Radio Mirror* dedicated a one-page tribute to Bridgeport's "Man of the Morning":

> A glib-tongued, fast-thinking, pixilated young man joined Bridgeport's Station WICC…and has since been signing on the air at 6:05 A.M., Monday through Saturday, with "The Bob Crane Show." Four hours and ten minutes later—after a program of chatter and music, punctuated by exchanges with the raucous critics and cynics that Bob has assembled on tapes, records, and transcriptions—he signs off… Bob breakfasts and simultaneously presides over three turntables and two tape machines…and the program gives Bob a chance to beat out an occasional passage on his bongo drums ("great") or give out with some baritone singing ("mediocre"). "I'm really a ham at heart," Bob grins, "and live and breathe my four-hour show throughout the twenty-four." He's constantly looking for new voices and gimmicks to spring on his listeners—who, incidentally, comprise 75% of the area's radio audience.

Still, New York eluded him.

WICC has always been an active part of Bridgeport's community, and as program director and an on-air personality, Bob was involved in all aspects of WICC's community service. In addition to making public appearances on a regular basis and acting as master of ceremonies for various events, Bob also served as program advisor for the Junior Achievement program in Bridgeport.

Founded by Horace A. Moses in Springfield, Massachusetts, in 1919, the Junior Achievement program aims to provide young adults with the opportunity to experience our free enterprise system. High school students between fourteen and seventeen years of age organize and operate their own corporations. WICC was one of the longest running sponsors in the history of Junior Achievement in Connecticut.

As a program advisor for WICC's Junior Achievement program, Bob was responsible for teaching students the art and technology of broadcasting. Author and educator William B. Secor, PhD, was involved in Bridgeport's Junior Achievement as a high school student.

"We had a weekly radio program on WICC, and we took turns being presenters," explained Secor. "It was a combination of school news and music. Our Junior Achievement included creating a corporation, electing officers, articles of incorporation, statement of purpose, and so on. Crane was very professional, very organized, and kept us in line. He was in his 20s and a disc jockey at the station, and very energetic. We were under time restraints and had only a half hour. The program aired live on a Saturday. Crane was organized and disciplined; he had to corral a bunch of teenagers! I remember Bob Crane worked very well with teenagers and had a wonderful sense of humor."

Bob enjoyed teaching others about radio, and he was thoughtful, informative, and patient, and he also went "by the book." Eliot Dober, who was born with cerebral palsy, knew Bob because his father owned a percentage of WLIZ and would often visit the station. When Eliot accompanied his father, Bob would entertain him and take him under his wing. Eliot recalled his experience of being on the air with Bob.

"I used to get up there to WICC by six-thirty in the morning. Bob was on until ten o'clock in the morning. And we fooled around on the air. Now you would never think I would be on the radio! I was really overcome. I was appreciative. Bob never said no to me. I think I was the only one he never said no to. Bob went by the book."

WICC also sponsored or managed many contests, including the Barnum Festival Tom Thumb and Lavinia Warren Contest, where two young people competed for the chance to be given the title "Tom Thumb" or "Lavinia Warren" (Tom Thumb's wife) as part of the festival. Bob presided over this contest in 1955, and contestant Deborah Griswold recalled:

"The criteria for the contest at that time was to answer questions on the history of Bridgeport, P.T. Barnum, and so on. Bob was the moderator at the Channel 43 studios. My father and I spent many nights at the Stratford Library, learning as much as we possibly could on the subjects. On the night of the contest, it came down to two final contestants—myself and another girl. The last question came up, and Bob read it: "When a person crosses the street using a long white stick, what does it signify?" Of course, I didn't know the answer, but the other girl, did, and she became Lavinia Warren. I was stunned, my father was pissed, and Bob was embarrassed by the question. He came over to me after and gave me a big hug. He told me how sorry he was that it wasn't a historical question and that I did a great job with my answers. He knew how to handle a bad situation and keep an eleven-year-old from having a major meltdown. I've never forgotten his kindness!"

Bob Crane was successful. He was popular. He was funny. He was kind. He was well known. And while he had become a local celebrity and was occasionally brash with a joke, Jack Coombe claimed that Bob retained a genuine humbleness about him.

"I do recall there was a modicum of modesty in him, in spite of his sometimes brash behavior. Bob did have a positive effect on people, known or unknown. We all knew that his apparent brashness was part of his personality and his struggle to succeed in his chosen career. But in that respect, he was no different than the rest of us. We all suffered from the same dilemma: how can we get ahead in this crazy radio business? Most of us, at least I did, knew that Bob was destined for much greater things."

Yet something was lacking in Bob's universe. Despite his ongoing success in radio and his love of drumming, something was missing, and he was actively searching.

"Bob got along with *everybody* very well," Eliot Dober observed. "And everybody liked Bob. He liked the people at the station. But you know, when he was done with the radio, he would hang around for an hour, and then he was gone. And to be honest with you, I don't know where he went."

While at WICC, Bob continued to contact radio stations from Boston to New York, sending recordings of himself, hoping to move into

The Idea of Learning

a bigger market. In mid-1953, Gene Rayburn, a prominent radio personality in New York City who was known as part of the Rayburn and Finch Show, announced he was leaving radio to go into television. Bob took immediate action. In a letter on WICC letterhead dated September 10, 1953, Bob reached out to program director Dick Pack:

"Being a Program Director myself, I realize the number of applications you must be receiving since the Gene Rayburn announcement appeared in the trade press. However, I do hope you will grant mine extra consideration for what may prove to be our mutual benefit. My four-hour (6AM-10AM) morning show is the highest rated program Monday thru Saturday in this New York area market, with a Hooper and Pulse rating of 55 percent share of audience. Needless to say, the entire four-hour period has been sold out for the past three years. In addition to radio, I also have a two-hour TV show across the board, 5 to 7 PM. I shall be glad to send a tape but would appreciate your listening to my show live, inasmuch as our signal does cover New York City. I plan to be in New York on Thursday, September 17, and would like very much to meet with you. May I hear from you? PS—Because of my position with WICC, I should prefer this letter to remain confidential."

Whether Bob met with Mr. Pack in New York City for consideration is unknown. What *is* known is that they passed him over, as did many other stations on the East Coast, and he remained at WICC, striving for that something more, recognizing in himself what the big stations in New York had yet to see, and growing increasingly frustrated because of it.

"It was a case of really working hard," Bob explained in an audio letter to his cousin Jim Senich. "I didn't just work on my shift. When I first got in the business up in Hornell, I used to work from eight o'clock in the morning until *midnight*, every night. And at that time, Anne was living back in Connecticut, so thus, I *could* devote all those hours to my job. And I used to go back to the station and pick out records and plan shows—shows that never went on, just to be *doing* things, I *loved* radio *that* much. And I was constantly *listening* to guys. When I got to Bridgeport, I was, here again, listening to guys and working like crazy. When I went to WLIZ, I was working the whole day long there, and then WICC was the same thing. I never wanted to go home! I just wanted to work at the station. Then finally, after a few years, enough guys were canned because they were impatient for stardom, and I suddenly found myself as the kingpin at WICC. And then the last *two* years I was there, I was getting offers to go to *bigger* stations, the next step up. I was offered a job in *Boston*, and Cleveland, and Baltimore, and whatnot. But I didn't *want* those jobs. I felt that I wanted *New York*, that eventually New York would ask for me."

New York. It was always New York for Bob, and his friend Harvey Geller remembered that even early on, New York entered the conversation. "I used to drive up to Boston as a song plugger to get my records played, and as I drove along the highway, I would hear this guy in Bridgeport. And I could tell he was very talented. So one day I found out where he was, and I drove over to his building. He was working out of the transmitter station. I drove up there and introduced myself, and no song plugger from New York had ever come to see him. He was trying to get work in New York, but they said he sounded too much like Ted Brown, who was a very talented guy in New York. But he couldn't get into New York."

"He was so much ahead of his time, it was unreal," Jim Senich elaborated. "No one was doing what he was doing. When he went to work in Bridgeport, he had incredible ratings there. His big thing was to work in New York, but he never got the opportunity. He got very little sleep. I know he was always late when he was at WICC. He was *never* on time. He was always late because he'd be out playing drums at night somewhere. Dick Alexander, who did the overnight show, said he was never on time, He'd come running in, hair flying all over the place, and then he would just start his show and sound great."

New York ignored him, but Bob pushed on. In a letter dated August 9, 1954, to his Uncle Mike Senich, Bob explained his climb to his then-current position at WICC. But he longed for a chance in the Big Apple.

"I arrived in radio in 1950 in Hornell, New York, on WLEA as their only disc jockey. After ten months of hard work and ars [sic] kissing, I received an offer to join WBIS in Bristol, Connecticut, as morning diskey jerkey… After hiding in the hills of Connecticut for three months, I again received an offer to join WLIZ, Bridgeport, which later took over WICC, same city. After only one year of terrifying toil on the early morning shift, they made me a program manager of the radio and of WICC. They also increased my hours on the air. They also put me on TV. They also gave me an extra hour on my morning show. They also gave me another extra hour on Saturday and another half on Sunday. They also gave me a broom and told me to shove—but the money is good."

"He had a drive," Jim Senich said. "Anyone who becomes as great as he did, they've got that drive, and nothing is gonna stop them, nothing. Father, mother, owner of a jewelry store, whatever. No one's gonna stop them. Threat of being fired, whatever… it just wouldn't stop him. It wouldn't stop him."

> *A lot of the salesmen were against the way I worked the show when I first started. And…if you get into this business, you'll run into program directors who you think at the time are completely out of their minds! Oh, the guy is a nut! Who eventually, you'll realize, and I know it sounds corny, but you'll think back, he was right. He was right at the time. There's a certain something, like my son says to me now, he's eleven years old and going to school, "Why do I have to do all this homework every night?" And I said, "Because you're learning how to study. Not that you're gonna remember this whatever… I <u>hope</u> you remember and digest what you're reading. But it's the <u>idea of learning</u>."*

– Bob Crane, on his work at WICC and Channel 43, Bridgeport, Connecticut, in a presentation to students at LA College, 1963.

The idea of learning. Bob did not figure out until many years later that what you learn, while important, is perhaps not as significant as the experience of learning itself. Things happen for a reason, and accepting that you always have more to learn—sometimes before you can move up in your life or career—can be difficult, as Bob explained to his cousin Jim in a Spring 1962 audio letter:

"I went to see Bobby play a Little League ball game, and Bobby will be eleven at the end of June. And *he* feels pretty discouraged tonight because he was only up once, and he struck out. He happens to be on a major league team this year; last year he played on the minor league team because he was only nine and a half. Well now he's *ten and a half,* and he's up with the *bigger* kids. So now he is *up* with the major league kids but not capable of playing like a twelve-year old because he's *not*. He feels he *should* be, and he gets awfully discouraged because he doesn't have the experience. In his own mind, he really figures if he is just given a chance, he can really prove it, and he probably *will*, eventually. After he gets more experience."

Bob admitted that while he was at WICC, he thought he was at the top of his game. His local fame, as well as articles published about him in the newspaper and in trade magazines, reinforced his belief and stroked his ego. For example, in 1955, the December issue of *Radio TV Mirror* gushed that Bob Crane was "simply in great demand throughout Connecticut." With such glowing praise fed to him repeatedly, Bob could not understand why New York City was turning him down. It frustrated him.

Bob confided to his cousin, "I was *convinced* working out at WICC in Bridgeport was the greatest thing that ever happened to me, until I had been *there* a couple of years. And then suddenly, I felt there was no other place but New York for me. I just *had* to make New York. Well, I started pounding on doors in New York and sending auditions. And I wanted the job that a lot of other guys were getting. Every time I was turned down for some guy who didn't have what *I* considered at that time, half as good a show as *I* had, it made me feel real bad."

But New York was not Bob's destiny. What he didn't realize was that in addition to his family, friends, and adoring public, someone *else* was, indeed, listening and paying very close attention to the man behind the mic at WICC.

And soon, everything was about to change.

August 17, 1956. The early morning fog had given way to hazy sunshine, and the temperatures would climb to a balmy 88 degrees by the afternoon. Jane Golden, Charlie Zito, Don Sappern, and the rest of Stamford High School's Class of 1946 were getting ready to attend their first milestone Class Reunion—their tenth. Held at Laddin's Terrace in Stamford, one of the premier country clubs in Fairfield County, the weather was cooperating for their big event.

The Idea of Learning

At the reunion, Jane and the rest of the class received a Western Union Telegram. The header of the telegram displayed a drawing of a rose-colored orchid, with "Congratulations" in script on a banner. The note announced:

CLASS OF 1946 REUNION=
POST ROAD LADDINS TERRACE STAMFORD CONN=

SORRY CANT BE THERE ON OUR WAY TO HOLLYWOOD WHERE I START MY MORNING SHOW FOR CBS ON SEPTEMBER 3RD GIVE OUR BEST TO ALL=

BOB AND ANN CRANE=

Stamford High's hometown drummer boy was on his way up.

"Bob, Sr., this spring day, March 24, 1955, Mom and Dad Crane's house." (Handwritten on the back of the photo.)

Source: Courtesy of Scott Crane. Used with permission.

The Idea of Learning

"Installation – The Southern New England Telephone Company, Bridgeport, CT, September 14, 1951." (Typed on the back of the photo.)

Source: Courtesy of Scott Crane and WICC-600 AM, Bridgeport, Connecticut. Used with permission.

Bob Crane on the air in Bridgeport, Connecticut (circa 1951-1952).

Source: Courtesy of WICC-600 AM, Bridgeport, Connecticut, and Eliot Dober. Used with permission.

BOB CRANE The Definitive Biography

"The best you can see is on Channel 43!" Bob Crane and Morgan Kaolian (as Angie the Antenna Man) performing a skit over WICC Channel 43 (circa 1953).

Source: Courtesy of Morgan Kaolian and WICC-600 AM, Bridgeport, CT. Used with permission.

Rating the records! Bob Crane with the infamous chicken that lays the rotten eggs.

Source: Originally published in *TV Radio Mirror*, December 1955.

Promotional WICC postcard featuring Bob with Wallie Dunlap (circa 1953).

Source: Courtesy of Scott Crane and WICC-600 AM, Bridgeport, CT. Used with permission.

The Idea of Learning

WICC Channel 43 Staff—March 1, 1953
Here is the entire staff of Channel 43 who will be working in front of the screen and behind the scenes to bring you top video entertainment. L-R: Seated, Tillie Sakowitz, Lorraine Stacey, Wallie Dunlap, Philip Merryman, Betty Prokop, Manning Slater, Dorothy Maestri, and Judy Stickles. Standing, Barbara Munson, Pat Turner, Morgan Kaolian, Dave Bond, Dave Bodge, Frank Delfino, Bob Crane, Warner Moore, Bill Curikshank, Mike Horn, Mitch Siniawer, Jack Bell, Elliott Weissman, and Ralph Winquist. (As originally published in the *Bridgeport Sunday Herald*, March 1, 1953.)

Source: Courtesy of Scott Crane and WICC-600 AM, Bridgeport, CT. Used with permission.

WICC Junior Achievement (circa 1955).
Bob Crane sits as program director to his WICC JA radio company. Crane served as JA advisor for several years in the early 1950s when he was with WICC. Standing in rear is the administrative advisor, David Kenney, who served as advisor from 1951-1962. (As originally published in the *WICC 1982 Annual Report*.)

Source: Courtesy of WICC-600 AM, Bridgeport, CT. Used with permission.

BOB CRANE The Definitive Biography

WICC 600 ON YOUR DIAL — P. O. BOX 9140 — TELEPHONE 5-1601

BOB CRANE RESUME

Bridgeport, Connecticut

EDUCATION

Stamford High School Graduate - 1946
Radio Course University Of Bridgeport
Night School - 1947

RADIO EXPERIENCE

Announcer-Disc Jockey
March 1950 - December 1950
WLEA, Hornell, New York

Announcer-DJ-Program Director
December 1950 - April 1951
WBIS, Bristol, Connecticut

Announcer-DJ-Morning Personality-Program Manager
April 1951 - February 1952 WLIZ, Bridgeport, Connecticut
February 1952 - WICC, Bridgeport, Connecticut

TV EXPERIENCE

"Bob Crane Show" -45 minutes Monday thru Friday
WICC-TV April - July 1953, extended to two hours
in August 1953

PERSONAL DATA

Age 25. Height 6'. Weight 175 lbs.
Eyes - brown. Hair - black.
Professional Drummer with semi-name bands
for ten years.

Southern New England's Leading Radio Station in the Wealthy Industrial Center of Connecticut

Source: Courtesy of Scott Crane. Used with permission.

Chapter 4
The Invincible Robert Crane

The Bob Crane Show [is] the wildest, funniest morning program in radio. Besides keeping you posted on sigalerts, weather, sports, and the best of the "good" music, Bob Crane pokes fun at just about everybody, including his boss, his sponsors, and his guests. He's the only radio personality who hosts leading film and TV stars for live, unrehearsed interviews daily.

—KNX-CBS Radio Promotional Flyer (circa 1962)

Bob Crane and Gene Krupa engage in a drum battle over KNX-CBS Radio (circa 1962).

Source: Courtesy of Scott Crane. Used with permission.

Bob Crane…Who? This poster was presented to Bob Crane by 20th Century Fox film producer Jerry Wald, who was a fan of Bob's KNX radio show. The poster is a spoof of the 1958 film, *The Fiend Who Walked the West*. Jerry Wald was also the producer of *Return to Peyton Place* (1961), in which Bob later appeared in one of his first acting roles.

Source: Courtesy of C.S. Used with permission.

Chapter 4
The Invincible Robert Crane

If I tell a joke that's not so funny, I have a faster-than-sound plane which shoots it down before it reaches San Francisco.

–Former WICC disc jockey Bob Crane, from his $50,000-yearly perch at KNX in Hollywood, April 7, 1957

Early in the morning, on Monday, September 3, 1956, residents of Southern California awoke to KNX Radio, the Los Angeles flagship radio station of the Columbia Broadcasting System (CBS), as they had been doing since the station first went live on May 4, 1922. Groggy and bleary-eyed, they stumbled around the kitchen for their first cup of brew, fumbling for the paper and used to hearing the familiar and subdued intonation of long-time KNX morning man Ralph Story.

Instead, on this day, they heard something completely different.

"Shattering the tranquility of the dawn hours," like a glass splintering apart on a tile floor, Bob Crane startled his listeners awake and announced himself to Hollywood, Los Angeles County, the Southern California communities, and the world. *The Bob Crane Show* over KNX-CBS Radio had officially debuted, and a radio legend came into his own.

A few weeks earlier, on August 11, Bob had signed off for the last time at WICC in Bridgeport, Connecticut. He had accepted the offer from KNX in Hollywood to move his radio show—and his family—to the West Coast. It was a major, life-altering decision.

New York City had always been Bob's ultimate goal, especially in light of his terrific success at WICC. With his gaze fixed stubbornly on Manhattan, Bob had not only never considered the West Coast, he never expected Hollywood to come looking for him.

It was a dramatic change of pace for Bob and Anne Crane, both born and raised in Catholic households in the ultra-conservative and mostly Republican state of Connecticut. Now, three thousand miles away from family and friends, the young, attractive Cranes traded in snow shovels and winter coats for surfboards and bathing suits. Life in

California was going to be different, indeed, for Bob and Anne, and for their little son Bobby, who had celebrated his fifth birthday in June.

"I remember it like it was yesterday," said Joe Cosgrove, who was the staff announcer for KPOL in Los Angeles, a competing station of KNX that played what was referred to as "beautiful music." He later went on to launch his own radio station, KTHO in Lake Tahoe, California. Very shortly after the Cranes arrived in California, Joe was one of the first to offer his welcome.

"I read in the trades that this guy was coming in from New England," Joe recalled. "And that's where I'm from—Boston. I had done programs at KNX, and so I knew the folks at KNX very well. I drove over, got through security, went up, and I welcomed Bob the first week he was at the station. He had a very bright shirt on, and he had a fantastic smile. And it was like we had known each other forever. He was just that kind of a guy. We spent about half an hour together, and he told me that he was a drummer and that he loved music and dance bands. He was just thrilled to bring his family to California. Bob was a very upbeat person and a very approachable kind of a guy. We had a very nice conversation, and he was an absolutely delightful person to meet. He told me I was the first person to really come over and greet him. Bob was so excited about coming to Los Angeles. He appeared confident, and was very, very, *very* excited about it and felt that this was a turning point in his life."

Bob's goal had always been to make it to one of the big stations—one that could reach a wider audience, and in turn, pay him more money. And as it turned out, that summer, one of those big stations made a move that would send Bob packing for Hollywood.

Bob Crane's advancement to KNX is the stuff of legend.

CBS-owned WEEI in Boston was one of the stations on Bob's radar, and unbeknownst to Bob, he was also on theirs, only not for the reasons he would hope. When CBS polled their stations to find out what competition in each market was giving them trouble, WEEI hollered Bob's name. WICC's signal stretched into the Boston area, and Bob's morning show was taking its toll on the station. CBS needed a solution.

"WEEI had the biggest horror story," recalled former KNX booth announcer Leo McElroy, who worked with Bob at KNX from 1960 to 1963. "[They] had this guy in Bridgeport, Connecticut, who was just killing them."

So CBS tried to remove this problematic personality—by getting him to move to WEEI for seven hundred dollars a week and a three-year contract. Bob gave serious consideration to the tempting offer, only he didn't want to be tied down for a specific length of time. CBS refused to budge on the three-year clause, forcing a stalemate. Despite the chance to move to a bigger market, which was what he wanted, Bob turned them down.

What Bob didn't know was that CBS was facing another problem over on the West Coast. KNX-CBS Radio in Hollywood needed a replacement for their longtime morning drive man Ralph Story, who had recently accepted an offer to host *The $64,000 Question*. His departure left CBS in a worrisome predicament. Morning drive was the most listened-to time of the day in radio, and Story had been both successful and lucrative for KNX. Who could possibly fill the gap?

Program director Robert P. Sutton was intrigued by Bob Crane, and he believed Bob was just the type of personality who could not only replace Story, but become a KNX hallmark, just as Story had been. If Bob didn't want to be at WEEI, CBS was prepared to make him an offer they thought he couldn't refuse: a five-year stint as morning man at KNX Hollywood.

Bob was indeed interested, but it was a lot to consider: uprooting his family and moving three thousand miles away from all that was familiar versus being in the middle of Hollywood, at a *huge* station, and making more money—a *lot* more money. But it wasn't gone to be easy for CBS. If Bob was going to accept, he had one major stipulation of his own.

In the mid-1950s, if you were behind the radio microphone, you were rarely, if ever, permitted to play your own records during airtime. The handling of records was reserved solely for the station engineer, who worked with the on-air personality during the course of the live program. As per union regulations at major market stations across the country, engineers played the records, while DJs/on-air personalities did the talking.

"In those days," explained 1960s KNX advertising salesman Tom Bernstein, "there were no carts, cassettes, or digital files. Everything was on electrical transcriptions. KNX had a large engineering department and a big union contract. Engineers ran the boards, and cued and ran the music and commercials. When a non-union person was in a studio, production or air, he'd better not touch anything (tape, record, etc.) without asking the engineer in charge. The personalities or DJs stayed behind the mic."

Bob had managed to skirt this otherwise stiff regulation by working at stations that were rural and smaller, and/or had fired their management at about the same time of Bob's arrival at the station. At WLEA, WBIS, WLIZ, and WICC, Bob could play records to his liking with little or no rebuff, and he was permitted the creative freedom to play just about every song, gimmick, voice impersonation, and sound effect he could get away with on the air. In so doing, he became accustomed to running his radio program *his* way. It had proven successful in the ratings, and he was not about to let that go—not even for the powerhouse known as *Columbia Broadcasting*.

But Los Angeles was a far cry from Hornell, Bristol, and Bridgeport. KNX was not a rural radio station or a station that had just fired everybody and allowed DJs to do their own thing. It was highly unlikely for anyone to make such demands and insist on a format so vastly different from the norm and outside of union regulation.

Yet Bob did just that. In the spring of 1956, Bob and CBS entered into serious negotiations.

As a general rule, mute communication between on-air talent and engineer needs to be fluid, spontaneous, and clear for the program to succeed. But Bob's show was so unique that only he, and he alone, could know in a moment's notice what track he wanted to play. He knew every groove in every record like the back of his hand, and he was able to grab a record containing a certain sound effect or gimmick with split-second timing. Bob Crane wanted this freedom. And he demanded that CBS get the engineers' union to agree. If KNX wouldn't let him be the architect of his own radio program, then Bob was prepared to decline the offer.

"Bob made it clear a number of times that he really felt he needed to be the designer of what he did and who he was," Leo McElroy explained. "And he just made this point over and over again: 'This is the way I do my show because this is the way I think my show should be done. And don't bring in your consultants to tell me how to do it.'"

Fortunately for Bob, CBS was hungry enough for something fresh that would appeal to their Southern California audience, and they were willing to fight for him. To prove they were serious about their offer,

CBS turned to the Radio & Television Engineers Union (IBEW) and negotiated with them to allow Bob the artistic freedom he desired—a turntable of his own and the capability to play his own records.

"It almost led to a big strike," 1960s KNX advertising salesman Gordon Mason recalled. "But the station prevailed."

IBEW eventually bowed to Columbia Broadcasting, and with the agreement in place between CBS and the union, Bob Crane accepted the job at KNX with a firm five-year contract in place—one he did not balk at—on May 29, 1956. For the first time ever in a major market, an on-air personality had been granted special dispensation by the engineers' union to have artistic control over the records and his program. This event changed the future of radio dramatically. Because of the allowance by IBEW for Bob to play his own records, DJs and radio personalities elsewhere started to do the same.

"Today, talk shows have board ops (non-union trainees who punch up phone calls and 'producers' who screen calls)," Tom Bernstein stated. "DJs do it all themselves. Now, most stations probably have only two engineers on staff—a chief and one for maintenance."

Even more astonishing is that Bob would not only have one turntable of his own, but eventually, he would work as many as six turntables—all at his command—that he could cue at any given moment during his show. Bob could play any number of his thousands of records, while his engineer would play commercials and songs in tandem with the show's pace.

"CBS solved two problems at once," Leo McElroy said. "They solved WEEI's ratings problem, and at the same time, they found KNX a morning guy, and he shows up out of Bridgeport and just takes over."

Bob Crane had big boots to fill at KNX. His predecessor, Ralph Story, had been a station and audience favorite for more than seven years. His strong and melodious voice had filled the Southern California airwaves with stories, tidbits, observations, and anecdotes about everyday life in Los Angeles. Story didn't perform any gimmicks on his show; nor or did he "mess" with the commercials. In fact, Story often felt that he had too many ads to squeeze in, limiting his time for narration.

Bob couldn't have been more different. Something that took the listeners—and sponsors—time to warm up to.

"If you couldn't sell that time with Ralph Story, you couldn't sell, period," Gordon Mason explained. "People were pretty much kind of depressed, really, because it wasn't Ralph Story anymore, and he was such a good talent. We were kind of bland and kind of in limbo, and worried about how we were going to maintain the business that was running on Story after he'd left with the new guy, whoever that would be. It was difficult because we had the highest rates in town, and the ratings were slipping. But we managed. It's always tough when that happens because your competition then goes to the advertisers and says, 'You don't want to be with them anymore because you bought that show, and it's not there anymore.'"

It didn't help that Bob was the polar opposite of Story, and potential advertisers did not initially understand Bob's technique of incorporating commercials into traditional programming. According to 1960s KNX advertising salesman Tom Thornton, "Their immediate reaction was, 'He is making fun of the most important thing in my life,' which is the man's product or business."

"Bob did a whole different thing from Ralph," KTHL station owner Joe Cosgrove said. "I [knew] it would work because no one could be Ralph Story. Ralph was very conventional and had a very unique delivery. And Bob was a totally different kind of guy. I told Bob, 'If you just be yourself, that's what got you here, and that's what'll make it go.' And he did."

While the lack of immediate success did not deter Bob, he later confessed in a letter to his cousin Jim Senich that the first two years in Hollywood at KNX were rough. He had not been concerned about his position because he knew he had a firm contract in place. But adapting to the West Coast audience had been a challenge, and there were many times he felt like throwing the towel in and giving up.

"I was the so-called brash, con type," Bob said later in a 1967 interview. "Many people wouldn't accept that. For the first five years, I batted my head against the wall. Then I began to make public appearances so people could see me and know I wasn't an old ogre."

Personal appearances and charity events had a dynamic effect in boosting Bob's market share ratings. He spent an enormous amount of his personal time out in the community, meeting and greeting his audience, and setting up and performing his show wherever he could. KNX sales manager Gordon Mason explained that radio stations at that time typically discouraged their on-air personalities from making personal appearances because the station could not control the personality or the event. But in Bob's case, KNX actually encouraged it.

"Bob made his show portable, and it had been an incredible amount of work," Mason said. "It was the same show, except it was a different show, tailor-made to each place he went. He went to a lot of organizations, social clubs, almost anywhere they could get more than ten people in a group."

Many of those gatherings were luncheon and dinner events. "He'd be off the air at ten o'clock in the morning, and he'd be busy doing his monologue, and of course, he'd go out in the afternoon," Mason continued. "And sometimes, he'd work in the evening—which is remarkable for a guy who had to get up at four or five o'clock in the morning and face the day, face the radio. He made about two hundred and fifty personal appearances a year for the first two years, and he probably would have made more, but his doctors told him he was going to kill himself. I've never seen anybody with that kind of *energy*, maintain that drive for personal appearances. It really made a difference because the influential people felt a personal involvement with him. You couldn't ever get to know other morning people in LA radio. But they knew Bob Crane, and eventually, after about a year or two, he became a 'must buy' to some agencies."

All of this was Bob's own idea. "They didn't have much of an advertising budget, so they couldn't buy billboards and all the other things you'd buy for advertising," Mason said. "So they blessed the effort. They didn't particularly get behind it or push it. We set Bob up everywhere."

In addition to gaining potential sponsors for KNX, taking his show on the road also gave Bob the opportunity to involve his audience in an improvisational performance.

"He had a very cute little routine," explained Mason. "He had a Wollensac tape machine and himself. For example, we'd go to a food broker because food brokers in Los Angeles have all the big accounts, and we'd be out for a recommendation. We'd want them to recommend Crane to their boss and get him to open the door to *his* boss. And Bob would take the boss aside and say, 'Who's the biggest playboy in the crowd?' 'Oh that would be old Sam.' 'Who's got the reputation for being the smartest guy?' And he'd ask about ten questions all about the people who worked there. He had these wild tracks on a program on his tape, and he had a little cart, and he'd just do a monologue. Like, 'Sam is known for his concern that everybody be treated well here, and just the other day, he said—,' and he'd hit the button, and Mel Blanc would come out saying, '—There's no light in the men's room!' Which was the same technique he did on the air, really, except a little different because he didn't cook up a story to go with it."

While Ralph Story segmented his show, creating definitive breaks, Bob made the *entire* time he was on the air his show, creating one seamless program and breaking away only to allow the newscast. In essence, Bob performed his radio program as one, all-inclusive show. Whether it was a commercial, a song, a commentary about the latest local or world event—Bob spliced everything into one presentation. Commercials bounced back and forth between and within songs and talk and drumming. Listeners, sponsors, KNX staff, and CBS had no idea what to think about their new morning personality, and nobody ever knew what was about to happen next on *The Bob Crane Show*.

Yet by "clustering" his radio spots in such a way instead of just playing three commercials in a row, Bob would more than accommodate each sponsor's paid time slot and also make the commercial more entertaining to the listener. As a result, the commercials became memorable and more valuable to both KNX and the paying sponsor.

Because of his growing popularity in Los Angeles, somewhere along the way, Bob Crane was dubbed "King of the LA Airwaves," a title that has prevailed over the years. However, Gordon Mason laughed at the interesting overuse of this title. "Bob was called a lot of things, but I never heard 'King of the LA Airwaves.' It probably came from the publicity department—out of a promo!"

In Leo McElroy's published memoir, he recalled working alongside Bob, writing, "Being on duty during Crane's show was immensely entertaining. He played records, but interspersed with them were comedy voice tracks and his frequent drum solos. He didn't hesitate to interrupt commercials, and sometimes, a thirty-second ad might take three or four minutes to finish."

Most sponsors embraced the way Bob aired their spots once hearing the way their messages were incorporated. Leary at first, they soon came to realize that Bob was not ridiculing their products, but rather, using them to sculpt a full program, one that was not fragmented but that flowed from one sound bite into the next. In this way, they were actually getting greater exposure, and consumers were more apt to remember what they had heard about their product.

KNX salesman Tom Thornton explained, "Most sponsors knew that when their commercials were going to be in Bob Crane's show, there was the chance that they would be, well, not ridiculed. He never ridiculed the product; nor did he demean the product or the individuals. He made a sport with it, he made a joke out of it, but you *certainly* listened to the commercial *intently* because it became a part of the show. After a couple of years—his first couple of years—we were considering in the sales department putting a premium on that. There was a premium just to be in Bob's show to begin with."

Of course, Bob also incorporated his drumming into his show. According to Gary Owens, KMPC radio personality and television entertainer of *Laugh-In* fame, "Bob and I were of the same era, at that time, where you could use a lot of sound effects and add a little music to it. And he was very good. He was very talented; he had a rhythm. Most drummers have a great comedic rhythm about them. Mel Brooks is a friend of ours. I once asked Mel, 'If you were not Mr. Funnyman in Hollywood, what would you like to have been?' He said, 'I would like to have been a drummer more than anything else.' And Bob was the same way. There was a rhythm within the comedic overtone of drummers."

Since Bob's earliest days experimenting with radio, as far back as his school days when he put on mock radio shows for his best friend Charlie Zito and future wife Anne, he had been honing his craft. Over time, he developed the uncanny ability to locate a groove on an acetate recording in a matter of seconds. He could feel the show, the pace, the music, the timing, the humor—and it *worked*. Further, most of the voices heard on his show were his own. He performed literally thousands of voice impersonations over the air, unbeknownst to his listeners, who perceived a studio filled with random folks with whom Bob carried on a conversation.

In addition to the off-the-cuff and overused title "King of the LA Airwaves," Bob was also officially christened radio's "Man of a Thousand Voices." In 1959, journalist Elmer Gaede was granted a rare, behind-the-scenes look at Bob's show. He described what he saw and heard in an article published in the August 9, 1959, edition of the *Los Angeles Times*:

> The secret undoubtedly wondered at by many of the thousands who are entertained six mornings a week from 6:15 to 10:00 by the energetic Bridgeport

(Conn.) transplant, as they traverse the Los Angeles freeways to work or do their housework, is how [Bob] manages to intersperse—and spoof—his commercials so ingeniously with such pixyish recorded comments. Listeners never know what's coming next. They're continually being surprised and caught off balance by the antics of his 'thousand voices' on recordings—of which he has stacks and stacks. The voices might break into the middle of a commercial with kidding comments which peculiarly fit into the sense of the advertising message, or they might similarly introduce the commercial. The result is that Crane's commercials are probably more closely followed by listeners than the "ordinary" popular music and other entertainment he also provides… On his pledge not to disclose the "big secret," the writer was permitted to observe Crane in action. Secrecy is required by the arrangement which enables the happy-go-lucky pied piper to perform this recorded-voice legerdemain. It may be said, however, that involves the uncanny co-operation and complete understanding between Crane and his engineer—the man who sees that it goes out correctly over the airwaves… And the strange part is that it is done entirely ad-lib, without script—other than the sequence of the musical recordings and commercials—mute testimony to the complete understanding between Crane and his engineers… Bob goes through all the gestures, facial and otherwise, of a real conversation with another persona, answering back, contradicting, arguing, etc.—even facing toward the recording as if it were a live being.

Watching Bob perform his show was *"fascinating,"* described Leo McElroy. "It was a little bit like watching a really skilled athlete do something that you're not sure you totally understand. Because Bob's hands flew. I mean, he is sitting there, he's whamming away on the drums in one second, and then suddenly, he spins around, shuffles through his albums, which were racked up in no particular order, finds

Send Dead Flies

One of Bob Crane's most successful gimmicks, and a story he recounted often while making personal appearances and when acting as a host or master of ceremonies, was the time he asked listeners to "send dead flies" to him in the mail. The following is one of Bob's recorded renditions of "Send Dead Flies":

One day, I got on the air, and I said, "Look. There are 700,000 people out in San Fernando Valley. If *each* person in San Fernando Valley will kill ten flies a day, per person, in no time at all, we'll get rid of all the flies."

So a fella called up at six-thirty, and he says, "Crane, it's a great idea, ten flies a day a person, I got four people in my family, what's my quota?"

And I started giving out quotas, forty flies, fifty flies. And at seven o'clock, some fella called up—and this *really* happened—he said, "Are you serious about this whole *fly thing*?"

And I said, "That's right."

He said, "You *sure* the people are gonna take it serious?"

I said, "Alright. I'll test how effective the campaign is."

And when I got back on the air at seven-fifteen, I said, "Look. So I *know* you're killing the flies, after you kill them, *mail them to me*."

And when I got off the air that day, I received a phone call from the post office department. And this gentleman on the other end says, "What is this *stupid* thing you're doing *now*?" It seemed this gentleman was a listener, and he worked for the post office department.

And I said, "I got people killing the flies and mailing them."

He said, "You can't do that! It's against the law!"

I said, "I didn't realize that."

And he said, "And besides that, do you know what our stamping machine is gonna *do* to those flies?"

So I said, "No, I *didn't* realize that."

And he said, "Well, you better, boy!"

I said, "What do I do now?"

And he said, "You'd better tell your listeners not to mail the flies."

I said, "*You* tell them."

So he said, "Alright, I will."

So the next day, this gentleman came on this show, and I cannot name him now for legal reasons. He's gonna sue me 'cuz it's a true story! He came on the air the next day—a *very* high official at the post office, too. And he read the law! It says, "Don't mail dead flies."

And I didn't know that. He made a big thing about them being diseased.

I said, "Now, let me ask you something. What about if they *boil* them first?"

> And he said, "Oh, I don't know. That's…eh…You mean they'll *sterilize* them?"
>
> I said, "Yes. Yes."
>
> He said, "Well, I'll tell you what. There is no law against mailing sterilized flies."
>
> Now you can imagine some poor, groggy-eyed guy, who has had a real *heck* of a night before, turning on his radio at eight o'clock in the morning and hearing this very high official at the post office and some idiot discussing how do you mail dead flies. And at *that* time, the question was should we raise the postage to four cents? You know…
>
> But I wasn't interested in *that!*
>
> So he said, "I'll tell ya what. There is no law against mailing sterilized flies. The only thing is, your listeners will have to get an affidavit from the Bureau of Animology in Washington saying that the flies they are mailing are sterilized."
>
> So I said, "Alright, just one more question. How do they get the flies to Washington?"
>
> And he says, "*They mail them!* What else?"
>
> **The Bob Crane Show – KNX-CBS Radio (circa 1960)**
> **(Online at http://bit.ly/19Ktt9j)**

the album he's looking for, slaps it on the turntable, slaps the earphone on so he can hear to cue it, cues up the track he wants, signals the engineer, rolls the track into whatever the engineer is playing, and then he turns around, and he's back whamming on his drums again. And this would take place within a matter of seconds. And you would say, 'You know, the average person would take five minutes to find that little voice track that Bob had just found in about ten seconds.' The man had incredible reflexes, and of course, was very practiced at what he was doing. It made it a great visual sport. About a half year along, we actually moved the control room, and I came from the far end of the building around into a control room adjoining Bob's, so I had the glass window between him and me, and I could actually see what was going on. And I mean, it was a fabulous spectator sport. I thought he really was a kind of creative genius in his own way."

Bob's KNX studio was divided into two halves; one side of the room contained his console with four turntables. Behind his seat was his snare drum, and above him was situated a long shelf that housed a wide assortment of records—whichever sound effects, voices, and pre-recorded skits he was going to be using for that particular show or routine. Across from his console sat a long table with two microphones; this is where guests would sit when they were interviewed. In a separate room and behind a glass pane, Bob's engineer (Dave Jarecki first, followed by Jack Chapman) controlled the songs and commercials.

"Bob worked in a large studio for its time," explained Tom Bernstein. "He sat at a console with his mic and three, maybe four turntables and their controls. On the top and sides of the console, Bob had racks of records, which he used for the voices and effects in the commercials. He had a complete drumset that he would play on the air, along with an up-tempo, Big Band recording. He was a good drummer. His engineer sat in a glass-enclosed booth above and facing him so they could communicate with each other while on the air. When Bob was setting up for a commercial, the action was fast and furious. He only had a few minutes to find what he wanted to play and cue them up. Many involved two or three disks. His hands were flying. I guess you could say it was a *performance*."

Gordon Mason recalled that he and other salesmen would bring clients to the station during Bob's program so they could see Bob in action. "Watching him work was *great* entertainment. He was a madman! He was banging on his drums, he was grabbing his wild tracks, he must have had two dozen records with wild tracks on them, and you'd watch him actually make up a story, and make up an intro, and do a spot and make it funny! And he was on the phone, and reading the paper, and he'd come out in the hall and talk to them while the music was playing, then he'd run back inside and do his spot. They never forgot that! That was more effective than taking him out to do a show. Bob never discouraged it, and the advertisers would go out and talk about it. It was great promotion."

Music was also an integral part of his program. KNX was not a music station, but Bob enjoyed music, so it was a part of his show. Bob played what he wanted, and because he was so influential in radio, record promoters sought airtime on his show.

Diane Thornton, wife of Tom Thornton and record librarian at KNX during Bob's time at the station, explained how various records were chosen for airtime. "We picked music for all kinds of things. Bob was so powerful. If you had an album that's new, and you wanted to take it around to the stations, you're going to take it into the library, and you're going to take one to Bob Crane. You're not going to just depend on the record library to say to Bob, 'Oh, this is a good album; you should play it.' If he wanted something, and he didn't have it, he'd send his secretary, or he'd come over himself and find it. It was huge, this library. Bob played what he wanted to play, and that was it. He had his own taste in music. He was more interested in jazz and Big Band sounds and that kind of thing. But he would play a record if he liked the person and he liked the way it sounded. I think he played what he thought was going to be a hit record maybe. He had a good ear and eye for that. But I think he ran his own deal there. It was his show. No one told him what to play. The record promoters courted him because that's their job and because they *needed* that airplay, and Bob was the biggest. If somebody came in and played it for him, and he thought it was fine, he would play it. And that was a big deal. It was a big deal to be played on his show. People listened to and liked the music. But the music was secondary to the humor and the originality of what he was doing."

According to Gordon Mason, Bob settled into his KNX job quickly, and he became accepted and liked by listeners and sponsors. "Once they heard him, they were either shocked or pleased! Most folks at CBS were very conservative in those days, and to think they'd have a guy who said an unkind word about his own advertiser or who'd spoof the president of the advertiser's company was in those days unheard of. But it was very human, and people loved it."

By the late 1950s, Bob was secure in his radio job, and while he was enjoying the rich life that came of his successes, it was a grueling schedule.

"As it is now," Bob said in 1965, "I arise at 5:30 a.m. and leave home at 5:55. By driving 70 on the freeway all the way, I get to the studio at 6:07 a.m. That's after my theme and the first two commercials and just in time to start the second record."

Bob's son, Robert Scott Crane, explained that his father was a workaholic. "I don't understand when he slept or ate. The amount or prep work he did for his shows was just amazing, preparing dozens of sound effects that he would play during the show."

Leo McElroy said, "So much of Bob's show seemed to spring from his brain instantaneously. I think that for many of us, it was hard to tell what was pre-thought and what was something that just suddenly cropped up. He managed to make it appear that it was spontaneous even if it wasn't."

In preparation for his show, Bob would read everything he could get his hands on. He was perhaps one of the most knowledgeable individuals in the entertainment industry of his era.

"He would read the paper," said Gordon Mason. "He would always a have a comment or two on the news. In fact, that was important to him because eventually that became part of his on-air material. So he read the paper quite a bit. He was very well informed on world events, and he was *very* well informed on entertainment events because I think he always had an eye on opportunities, especially if they occurred on TV."

With *The Bob Crane Show* a proven hit with listeners and advertisers, Bob Crane became extremely profitable to KNX and CBS. It was easy for the KNX sales team to sell Bob, and in fact, the station's entire programming to advertisers. Bob Crane was the hook that grabbed advertisers' attention and forced them to spend their money across the board at KNX. Bob's morning drive slot was never sold alone, and his show was bundled with other KNX programming. Bob Crane didn't just make money for KNX. Bob Crane made *a lot* of money for KNX.

"KNX put the highest rate on a spot in morning drive time," explained Gordon Mason. "I think the top was $145, which was enormously expensive then. A lot of that business was on multi-spot schedules, a twelve-plan, a twenty-one-plan, etc. Out of the twenty-one spots, maybe four or five would be in morning drive."

"Let me give you an idea of the impact Bob had," Tom Thornton elaborated. "Stations would base, in those days, their rates strictly on the size of the audience and the efficiency that that audience delivered. Those morning rates were universally the highest rates probably on most radio stations, but with Crane, there was a premium put on top of it that was probably twice as much as what 'Class A' time was worth, and that was from ten o'clock in the morning to three o'clock in the afternoon. It was called *Housewives' Time,* which is kind of funny when you think about it now because there are as many women employed as there are men. It was *very* easy to sell Bob. But one of the things we had to do was package him with something. You couldn't just sell Bob alone. You had to sell Bob with some other programming. *That's* how strong he was. If they bought three on his show, there would be six split/spread somewhere else. And we could get away with it."

Gordon Mason concurred. "It wasn't hard to sell Bob. And it made it easier to sell the station because we had Bob. What we had was the publicity. The morning drive on just about anybody's station would be the most expensive time on the station because your morning tune-in, in this market, which was a huge driving market even then, is golden."

KNX stopped worrying about Bob Crane and his on-air style and sense of humor. "Initially, KNX didn't know what they had," said Tom Thornton. "But they soon did. I could be someplace, and they'd say, 'Where do you work?' And I'd say, 'KNX.' 'Do you know Bob Crane?' 'Yes, I do, very well.' And suddenly, my stock went right up."

"Most clients wanted their spots *enhanced*, which is a better description than *messed*," Tom Bernstein added. "Whatever went over the air was purely Bob's creativity. Nobody told him what to do in that respect. I think he made it all up as he went."

In 1958, CBS decided to add one important component to *The Bob Crane Show*. On September 26, 1958, CBS included an addendum to Bob's current five-year contract. Beginning on October 13, 1958, in addition to his regular show, Bob would conduct live celebrity interviews. These segments would be no more than forty-five minutes in length and air between nine and ten o'clock a.m. Monday through Friday. They would then also be rebroadcast between two and five o'clock p.m. Monday through Friday.

So began Bob Crane's status as Hollywood's premiere celebrity interviewer. During his tenure at KNX, he interviewed thousands of people over the air, most of them notables known around the world—from film, theatre, and television, as well as musicians, singers, composers, and band leaders. Everyone who was anyone in the entertainment business clamored to be a guest on Bob's KNX show, where, according to KNX, Bob reigned as the "only radio personality who hosts leading film and TV stars for live, unrehearsed interviews daily."

"[Bob] was, at the time, kind of all the rage," said Paul Petersen, with whom Bob would later work on *The Donna Reed Show*. "Certainly a bunch of us listened to him on our morning commute. The man was *absolutely* at home in the studio. He could do ten things at once, plus carry on a conversation. A morning drive show has a lot of demands because people are tuning in for traffic and weather and to put a smile on their face."

Celebrities enjoyed being interviewed and often roasted by Bob, and he thoroughly embraced the opportunity to interview them. That he achieved such a remarkable stature in not only radio, but in the heart of the entertainment world—and in such a relatively short period of time—was a pinnacle moment in his career.

Los Angeles radio personality and game show host Geoff Edwards explained, "He was an incredibly good interviewer. So he would get all kinds of people from Hollywood to come over and be on his show. And he did a great job. He was probably one of the best at that. Plus, he didn't repeat himself. There are guys on the radio that are doing stuff between six and seven o'clock in the morning, and they'll repeat it between eight and nine o'clock, thinking the other people had gone to work and hadn't heard it. But he was inventive. He didn't repeat himself. His interviews were *very* good. One of the *best* interviewers. And he was just really a nice guy."

On the air, Bob came across quite personable, but in person, he was careful, and despite his outgoing demeanor, he was also described as being somewhat shy. According to Leo McElroy, the door to his corner office was usually shut, unlike most other KNX staff.

"Bob was not a warm, welcoming guy with everybody," Leo explained. "I mean, he'd be, 'Hey, ol' fellow,' on the air, but he was pretty careful about his acquaintances. When the guys from the front office would want to come down and talk to him, they would have to call. His secretary didn't even sit outside his office. Most of the time, she would be in there working on whatever they were doing. So they would call and say, 'Can I come down and see you?' And the answer usually was no. He was dismissive, but we respected that. This guy was probably the most talked about radio personality in Los Angeles, and as such, they weren't going to offend him. So they just kind of backed off and let him have his way, and talked with him when they could catch him outside his office. There may have been some insecurity to it. He came out of a relatively small market. Bridgeport to Los Angeles in radio terms is a pretty big jump."

KNX librarian Diane Thornton also recalled that Bob tended to keep his family life very private. "He definitely kept his life his business, and probably for not any reason other than that's the way he liked it to be. He and his family lived in Tarzana, and they had a very nice life. But his wife was not around. Record companies invited everybody to cocktail parties and openings and all that kind of thing constantly. He'd go once in awhile, but not a lot. He was a private man, and everybody respected that."

Whether or not Bob had been initially insecure about succeeding in Hollywood is anybody's guess. However, what is indisputable is that Bob was driven to success, and he sought perfection in his work, right from the start.

"Radio drove him even more than being a drummer," explained cousin Jim Senich. "He really wanted radio, and it wasn't until later when he got out to Hollywood that he realized he was going to have the opportunity to do TV and maybe even movies. But early on, there was no doubt radio was what he wanted to do, and that was it. I mean, the things he did with radio were just out of this world. Today, they wouldn't be that exciting, but in those days, when he had six turntables, *nobody* had six turntables, and he had foot pedals, so he could cue them, and he had tracks, where his chair would go up and down. He was so far ahead of himself. He was doing things that guys like Don Imus and others are doing now, making fun of sponsors. He was never dirty or anything like that, but he was funny, and he would nail people."

Richard "Dick" Addrisi and his brother Don of The Addrisi Brothers, who may be best remembered for their hit *Never My Love*, were introduced to Bob in 1959 while they were promoting their record *Cherrystone*. Dick remembered Bob as being "a very dynamic personality, both on the air and in the studio."

Recognizing that Dick and his brother Don were serious musicians and appreciated music, Bob took them under his wing and helped propel them further along in their career. "From the minute we met Bob, our senses of humor gelled, and the three of us hit it off from the beginning," Dick said. "There was a great connection between the disc jockey and the musical acts [in those days]. The DJ was most important in keeping the advertising going with shows at different venues all across the country. Unlike most of the recording acts of that day who were just kids who came up with a song and got lucky with a record, Don and I had been working at a very early age in Las Vegas in 1956, and continued to work variety shows. I think Bob saw our talent as a live act that did more than just come out and sing their record.

"The 1950s, I think, were the most exciting times of radio and records. At this time, Bob Crane was a very prominent figure in radio—that sarcastic sound of his voice and his infectious laugh separated Bob from the rest of the deep-throated boss jocks of other very popular stations. Yes, we talked about the girls in the audience after the show, but never can I remember Bob swearing or relating to women in a derogatory way. Those nights in his car were spent talking about music, our dreams, and how payola would kill radio by playing bad records for big pay. Life was fun then; all my brother and I wanted to do was write and sing our songs. You could tell [he was destined] to become more than just a radio personality. Bob Crane was a major part of our success in the record business. He believed in our talent enough to put us in his car and take us to his shows, giving Don and I a shot at Hollywood's brass ring, which we caught."

Despite his terrific success at KNX, Bob was not number one in the Southern California market share. That honor would go to and remain with KMPC's morning man, Dick Whittinghill. The two professional adversaries ran neck-in-neck, but Whittinghill always edged Bob out. Friend, and *Cash Box* and *Variety* magazine editor Harvey Geller remembered, "The number-one guy was Dick Whittinghill at KMPC, who had the biggest audience. But Crane had the people inside the industry—the movie industry and the record industry—so he had, I think, a better audience."

But not everyone got Bob's sense of humor. His unbridled wit, energy, and enthusiasm sometimes, as he put it, got him into trouble with certain people who simply did not understand where he was coming from. Harvey Geller recalled an incident between Bob and Sonny Bono.

"Sonny was a song plugger like myself, except he represented a lot of rock and roll artists," said Harvey. "In fact, nothing *but* rock and roll artists, and Crane did not play rock and roll on his show. He played Big Band and the middle-of-the-road singers, like Patti Page and Guy Mitchell and Perry Como. So whenever Sonny would show up, Bob would take the records that Sonny brought, and he'd say, 'Are any of these rock and roll?' And Sonny would say, 'Oh, no, these are good records for you to play.' And they were *all* rock and roll! Sonny was working for Phil Spector; that was one of his accounts. So eventually, Bob would try to *lose* Sonny. Whenever he saw Sonny, he would hide. And Sonny would insist that he heard the show, and he knew what kind of record Bob played, and he never would bring that kind of record. One day, Bob and I were heading for lunch, and we were going to the men's room, which was just around the corner from his office in the KNX building. And we spied Sonny sneaking into the office. So we

A Partial List of Celebrities Interviewed by Bob Crane

Marti Allen	Don Collier	John Greene
Steve Allen	Ray Conniff	Lorne Greene
Morey Amsterdam	Bill Cosby	Andy Griffith
Julie Andrews	George Cukor	George Hamilton
John Astin	Bob Cummings	Skitch Henderson
Frankie Avalon	Abby Dalton	Charlton Heston
Harry Babbit	Bobby Darin	Alfred Hitchcock
Diane Baker	Richard Dawson	Bob Hope
Ed Begley	Bette Davis	Robert Horton
Freddy Bell	Dennis Day	"Ronnie" Howard
Ralph Bellamy	Doris Day	Rock Hudson
Carl Betz	Laraine Day	Fran Jeffries
Sidney Blackmer	Olivia de Havilland	George Jessel
Ann Blyth	Andy Devine	January Jones
Ray Bolger	Frank DeVol	Bronislaw Kaper
Pat Boone	Phyllis Diller	Danny Kaye
Barbara Bouchet	Jimmy Durante	Ruby Keeler
Stephen Boyd	Dan Duryea	Stan Kenton
Eddie Bracken	Barbara Eden	Alexander King
Walter Brennan	W.C. Fields	Leonid Kinskey
Francis X. Bushman	Eddie Fisher	Irwin Kostal
Sebastian Cabot	June Foray	Gene Krupa
Mickey Callan	Glenn Ford	Jack Kruschen
Eddie Cantor	Tennessee Ernie Ford	Angela Lansbury
Frankie Carle	John Gary	Joi Lansing
Pat Carroll	Dizzy Gillespie	Carol Lawrence
Richard Chamberlain	Ernest Gold	Gypsy Rose Lee
Ray Charles	Arthur Godfrey	Peter Leeds
Sandra Church	Jerry Goldstein	Jack Lemmon
Dick Clark	Eydie Gorme	Jerry Lewis
Gary Clarke	Robert Goulet	Tiny Little

A Partial List of Celebrities Interviewed by Bob Crane

- Joe Louis
- Alan Ludden
- Roberta Lynn
- Giselle MacKenzie
- Shelley Mann
- Henry Mancini
- Jayne Mansfield
- Rose Marie
- Hugh Marlowe
- Claudia Martin
- Dick Martin
- Ross Martin
- Jackie Mason
- Jane Meadows
- Marvin Miller
- Mitch Miller
- Robert Mitchum
- Mary Ann Mobley
- Marilyn Monroe
- Del Moore
- Mary Tyler Moore
- Jaye P. Morgan
- Russ Morgan
- Ken Murray
- J. Carrol Naish
- Bob Newhart
- Julie Newmar
- Wayne Newton
- Chris Noel
- Louie Nye
- Arthur O'Connell
- Maureen O'Hara
- Patty Page
- Fess Parker
- Barbara Parkins
- George Peppard
- Paul Petersen
- Paul Picerni
- Slim Pickens
- Stephanie Powers
- Otto Preminger
- Paula Prentiss
- Andre Previn
- Juliette Prowse
- Al Rafkin
- Tony Randall
- Martin Ransohoff
- Ronald Reagan
- Julie Redding
- Donna Reed
- Jeannine Riley
- Carl Reiner
- Cliff Robertson
- Jimmy Rodgers
- Cesar Romero
- Mickey Rooney
- Steve Rossi
- Dan Rowan
- Soupy Sales
- Rod Serling
- Omar Sharif
- Arte Shaw
- Jack Shea
- Allan Sherman
- Red Skelton
- Jule Stein
- Connie Stevens
- Inger Stevens
- Barbra Streisand
- Enzo Stuarti
- Terry Thomas
- The Tijuana Brass
- Mel Torme
- Dick Van Dyke
- Jerry Van Dyke
- Robert Vaughn
- Jerry Wald
- Lawrence Welk
- Phil Weston
- Roger Williams
- Jonathan Winters
- Meredith and Remi Wilson
- Natalie Wood
- Pat Woodell
- Jane Wyman
- Keenan Wynn
- Bruce Yarnell
- Alan Young
- Gig Young

went to the bathroom and then came back. And Bob locked the door from the outside, and we went to lunch! And Sonny was there for more than an hour, and when he came back, Bob unlocked the door and Sonny walked out and glared at Bob and never came back. The funny part about it is years later, when Sonny and Cher were very big, Bob was scheduled to be on the show, and Sonny said, 'Nuh-uh, I don't want that guy on my show!' And Bob took it very well. He said, 'If things had been turned around, I would have done the same thing. I deserve not to be on the show!'"

Bob listed Shelley Berman, Jerry Lewis, Johnny Carson, Glenn Ford, and Julie Stein as those whom he had—in some way, shape, or form—insulted, either on air or through his "big mouth." But these were rare occurrences; most knew they could benefit greatly from an interview with Bob. Celebrities weren't the only people Bob interviewed, either. Others gracing Bob's KNX booth included the shoeshine boy down the street; the entity known as the Great Coogamooga; a young man from Napier, New Zealand (Alan Hall), who visited KNX while touring the United States); and some then-unknowns—the up-and-coming talent looking for that big break.

Bob Crane's celebrity interviews provide a rich, historical documentation of the Golden Age of Hollywood. Gary Owens explained, "Disc jockey was really not the term for Bob Crane, or myself. Radio personality is probably a better definition. Because disc jockey became a term back in the 1940s, and I think that Al Jarvis may have created the term *disc jockey*, like a jockey who rides a horse, but the disc jockey would ride the records and play them every day. But radio personality is a better definition because we did more than just give the time and the temperature, and 'Here is,' and 'That was.' We would give anecdotes about people who were friends of ours. Frank Sinatra, Dean Martin, Peggy Lee, Lena Horne, Ella Fitzgerald. All of them were good friends of ours because we had a lot in common. Bob was different because first of all, I don't recall another disc jockey in Los Angeles playing drums as a reverberative signpost. Bob's radio show was an overview of Hollywood in the early 1960s."

A new job. A new city. A new life. As Bob was basking in the glow of all Hollywood was going to offer, Anne may have been a little less certain. Where Bob was outgoing, Anne was more reserved, and according to those who knew the couple, she preferred the serenity of the home.

"You'd see Anne by Bob's side in the press photos," classmate Jane Golden remarked, "and he's got this big grin on his face, and she's standing there next to him, and she's smiling, but you can see she's not as comfortable."

The Cranes had settled into the Los Angeles suburb of Tarzana, eighteen miles northwest of Hollywood and about a half-hour or forty-five-minute drive to KNX depending on traffic. There, Bob, Anne, and Bobby made their home and began adjusting to California life. Bobby was growing up, and he had also begun taking part in his father's radio program. Audiences ate it up, hearing cute, little six-year-old Bobby Crane petitioning for his dad to become the next Dodger Bat Boy, or singing the latest Broadway tune along with his dad's drumming.

The transition from East Coast to West Coast had, indeed, been an adjustment for Bob and his family. But whereas Bob had thrived, Anne seemed to quietly pull back.

"I told Bob that he'd be in for a real culture shock out here," Joe Cosgrove recalled. "I said, 'You're coming from a *very* conservative part of the country. I think you can let it all hang out here and pretty much grow here differently because the West Coast is very liberal-minded in many respects.' I think it was obviously to his liking. It's just a very open society here and much more so than back East. I think that's really what made him blossom out here because the last thing that Ralph Story would do would be to play drums on the air, which Bob loved to do. I remember Bob used to lead people in their cars and say, 'Okay, all you people driving in from the Valley, you join in on this.' And he really connected. I think the West Coast was his cup of tea."

Nevertheless, the Cranes got used to their new life, and on June 19, 1959, Anne gave birth to a daughter, Deborah Ann, and one year later, on November 29, 1960, Karen Leslie was born. Bob and Anne doted on their children, providing for them a safe, secure home. Living next door to the Cranes in Tarzana, Harvey Geller remembered seeing Bob trick-or-treating with the kids and taking Bobby to Little League practice.

"Another reason that Bob and I were close," Harvey explained, "is both his son Bobby and my son were about the same age, and they played Little League together—Tarzana Little League. So Bob and I would go to the ball games on Saturdays and Sundays together, as well as seeing each other all during the week. He was the greatest dad in the world, a much better dad than I was. He was with the children whenever he had a chance, the trick or treating, the Little League, the getting home to be with them for dinner every night. You could see his eyes would light up when the kids were around, sitting around the pool with them, playing games with them."

"Bob and I became very close friends," Gary Owens said. "We lived in Encino, and Bob lived in Tarzana, which are two side-by-side suburbs of Los Angeles. So we would see each other at frequent things. I was the honorary mayor of Encino, and I took over from Tim Conway. Prior to that I had been the honorary mayor of Woodland Hills, which I took over from Buster Keaton, the great comic, in 1961. And then when we came to Encino, and got to know Bob even better because we lived not far from each other. So it's one big happy family all the way around, when you work in television and movies and radio and animated cartoons, you work with the same people frequently. Bob's wife was a wonderful lady—Anne—and we liked her *very*, very much, and the family, the children. We knew his family quite well. His wife, we'd see her quite often. Many times Bob couldn't be there, so Anne would take over as part of the Crane family. And we would see them on occasions. Bob was proud of his children, too, and their great talents. I didn't see his children very often. I'm sorry, I wish I had, but I didn't see them very often. But I know he was proud of his family. Bob was proud of his family, his wife *and* his kids. He was actually quite a family man, as a mainstream kind of person."

In 1956, Bob may have thought he was ready to take on CBS and Hollywood, and in many ways, he was. He had successfully maneuvered his way through contract negotiations and maintained a radio show that became one of the most successful in the history of Los Angeles. After five years, however, he realized just how much he had grown in his career and how much he had learned. Not long after, he began to seek something new.

"Six years ago, when I came out here to KNX, I really wasn't, *truthfully* now as I look back, ready for the step to what I am now in," Bob explained to his cousin Jim in an audio letter. "I developed *into* it, I feel, and for the past *three* years I've been doing what I felt I *was* doing six years ago, but I *wasn't*! In other words, my own *mind* was about

The Art of Self-Deprecating Humor

Bob excelled at self-deprecating humor, and he often told his mishaps in a glib, humorous way. In 1966, he wrote the following about an interview gone wrong:

The incident with Shelley Berman happened when Shelley had only been in the business about a year. He was appearing at a Hollywood nightclub called The Interlude, and he didn't get to bed before four in the morning. The Interlude wanted him on my show (which hit the air at nine a.m.), but I sent word to him that as a special favor, I'd tape his appearance at eleven. I did my interviews live, actually, but I also taped them so I could repeat them on Saturdays.

It happened that when Shelley came in, wearing dark glasses, I was just sitting at a table. As soon as the mic was turned on, I went into my usual spiel. I said, "Hey, Shelley, it's great having you here. Tell me, is it true that all these method actors have to wear tight jeans and T-shirts?"

He looked at me and asked, 'What are you talking about?'

"Well, I read that you studied at the Actor's Studio," I replied. "I see all these kids on the Sunset Strip, and they have the same uniform—tight jeans and sweat shirts."

Shelley almost yelled then, "That's not Actor's Studio." I saw he was getting a little mad.

I knew then that he'd never heard my show, didn't know a damn about me, and had thought he was coming into a studio to have a straight interview. That wasn't the way I ran my show. Knowing he was getting mad, I said, "Well, all these kids wear the same things."

Shelley snapped, "If they're wearing the same things, it's only because they don't have the money to afford any more than that."

"Well, if they don't have the money, how come they can spend sixty cents on a cup of espresso coffee?" I asked.

With that Shelley looked around at his publicity man. "What the hell did I get into here?"

We went into a commercial right then, and when it was over, I said, "Okay, Shelley, let's get back." He was livid at that point.

"No, I don't want to go back," he shouted. I figured that was all on tape, and we'd have a great show for the next day, a guy getting mad. Anyway, we finished about half an hour later. By that time, he wanted to kill me. I walked him to the elevator, and I said, "Shelley, I'll come to see you at The Interlude."

He yelled, "Don't do me any favors." With that, he got into the elevator. Well, come to think of it, I don't believe he waited for the elevator. He just went down the shaft.

About a half hour later, I got a phone call from Chicago. It was his manager, and he said, "Bob, I just happened to be talking to Shelley Berman on the phone."

I said, "Oh, what happened?"

He said, "Shelley's pretty upset by that interview. You taped it, huh? Hey, would you do us a favor and not put it on the air?" Shelley felt it just didn't come off right. He's willing to come back and do it some other time, but this just didn't work right. I said that was O.K. with me.

Soon after that, I got a call from that mighty agency, MCA, who handled both Shelley and me. I told them what happened on the interview and added, "He didn't understand the kind of show I do." They replied that I come on strong when somebody doesn't understand what I'm doing. I said, "Well, that's all part of the game." Then we both hung up.

In another half hour, I got a phone call from some lawyer in Beverly Hills. He said, "Look, this is to make it official. Destroy that tape. Just don't play it. Destroy it." So I said fine, and we never did put it on the air.

More than a year went by, during which Shelley got bigger and more secure. As for me, the episode had taught me never to tape an interview—to do it live or not at all.

Then I got a phone call from Stan Rubin, who was the producer of the *G.E. Theatre*, and he said, "Bob, I've got a small part in one of our shows that you could have fun with. The guy's a boozer, a broad chaser—the kind of thing you just did in *Tunnel of Love*. You play the buddy to the lead in the show."

"Who's the lead?" I asked. When I found out it was Shelley Berman, I almost cracked up. I explained the circumstances of our meeting.

"Look, just don't say anything," he said. "Walk on the set, and it'll be all right. After all, that interview stuff was more than a year ago. No harm can come of it."

So I took the chance. I was at that time determined to prove I could act as well as interview. That was why I kept turning down TV shows that would be just an extension of my radio show. I thought I could be a player rather than just a performer.

I walked on the set of the *G.E. Theatre* play, and Shelley simply said, "Hi."

I said, "Hi, I'm Bob Crane."

He said, "Yeah." So everything went slick until the final day. I didn't play any scenes with him actually because my scenes were all on the phone. Shelley was always calling me his old buddy, asking for advice.

On that final day when we all were being photographed together, Shelley suddenly turned to me and said, "All week I've been trying to figure where I knew you from. Did I do a radio show with you?" I said yeah.

> He said, "Oh, God." All I could think of was that the camera was turning on us, but fortunately, there wasn't any sound on.
> Shelley said, "I'll never forget that one."
> "Well, I'll never forget it either, Shelley; it was pretty disastrous," I said.
> "I was new then," he replied. "I didn't really understand. Now I know that you do wild interviews. But then I thought that you were a guy trying to be smart. I know better now. So let me come on again, will you?" I agreed, me and my big mouth. So he came on, and the interview got TOO wild for me! How about that?

three years ahead of what my actual performance *was*. And the only thing I can say is, comparatively speaking, thinking *back,* now, to when I first began in this business, I've *always* been that way, and I guess we *all* are, and that's why people keep on trying to get ahead because they believe they are capable of doing such-and-such a job, and eventually you *do* become capable, and then the opportunity comes, and you can handle it.

"I used to listen to this Hal Morgan in Cleveland. And I picked up a little device that Morgan was using out in Cleveland of talking over intros to records. I started doing this when I was up in Hornell. I talked over the intro, so rather than have dead air I'd be talking, and as soon as the vocal came in, I would stop talking. Since that time, I've worked on that particular thing. You can pick up a lot of little different things; from the guy who's absolutely the *worst,* you may find him doing something that you can adapt to your own style. These are *all* things that you can use as you go along. You can drop what you feel isn't right, and you pick up *new* things, and eventually, you start developing your own style.

"Hornell, New York, was a *hell* of a lot better for me than Bridgeport when I first started. It took me about two years to get to Bridgeport, so thus, I got two years' experience up in the hills. But I got to do a *lot* of things. I got a lot of experience. You know—the old line about the big fish in a little pond, and it really applies in this particular sense. With three stations in town, WNAB [in Hartford, Connecticut] and WICC were the big kingpins. WLIZ was the *nothing* station, and they were trying all different things to be successful, and thus, when I arrived, they had just *fired* everybody. And I got a lot of experience right off; they allowed me to *do* things that they *wouldn't* have allowed me if it had been a big station. I *grew* with WLIZ. After I'd been there a year, they bought out WICC, and I suddenly found myself the morning man on one of the biggest stations in Connecticut after I'd only been in the business two or three years. But here again, it was the thing of being in the right place at the right time. After I had been *on* the morning show in Bridgeport at WICC for about three years, *then* I really started being worthy of the position. But I happened to be there when they didn't *have* anybody else around.

"And it was a case of really working hard. But when I first got in the business up in Hornell, I used to work from eight o'clock in the morning until *midnight*, every night. And at that time Anne was living back in Connecticut, so thus, I *could* devote all those hours to my job. And I used to go back to the station and pick out records and plan shows—shows that never went on, just to be *doing* things, I *loved* radio that much. And I was constantly *listening* to guys.

"So thus, when I got to Bridgeport, I was here again, listening to guys and working like crazy. I never wanted to go home! I just wanted to work at the station. Then finally, after a few years, enough guys were canned because they were impatient for stardom, and I suddenly found myself as the kingpin at WICC. And then the last *two* years I was there, I was getting offers to go to *bigger* stations, the next step up. I was offered jobs in *Boston*, and Cleveland, and Baltimore, and whatnot. But I didn't *want* those jobs. I felt that I wanted *New York*; that eventually, New York would ask for me.

"And what happened? It was a good thing I *didn't* take these other jobs, and the contracts that would have offered me a lot of money, but they were two- and three-year contracts, and I *didn't* take them, and suddenly in 1956, I got a call from the coast here. Somebody in New York, at WCBS in New York, sent a *tape* of me out here to the coast, they liked it, and I ended up coming out here. And the first two years out *here* were a son of a B. Really, it was *rough*. I don't mean so far as my position goes, because I had a firm contract. But so far as relaxing and adapting myself to this particular market, and there were many times I felt like *chucking* the whole thing.

"But I didn't. Because I loved radio *that much*."

Bob Crane commanded the KNX airwaves for nine years, from September 3, 1956, to August 16, 1965. Innovative, cutting edge, and way ahead of his time, Bob has been called a broadcasting genius by his radio colleagues and superiors. He is one of radio's unsung pioneers, spending fifteen consecutive years behind the mic from one coast to the other and staying close to the broadcasting medium for his entire life.

"Bob's timing was perfect," said Joe Cosgrove. "He couldn't have picked a better time to get out there. He brought a distinctive style. It was unique. There was *no one* like him. That's why he fit in so well—because *he was unique.* There never has been, and there never will be, another Bob Crane."

Grander times were on the horizon for Bob Crane. His reign in Hollywood had only just begun.

Source: Courtesy of Karen Crane. Used with permission.

Alan Hall (center), on the air with Bob Crane and Pat Boone (June 6, 1961). Alan Hall was visiting the United States from his homeland of New Zealand.

Source: Both photos courtesy of Alan Hall. Used with permission.

The Invincible Robert Crane

Source: Courtesy of Scott Crane. Used with permission.

KNX Promotional Albums for Bob Crane

In the early 1960s, KNX-CBS Radio distributed two albums—"Laffter Sweet and Profane" and "The Effervescent Humor of KNXtrovert Bob Crane." "Laffter Sweet and Profane" featured portions of Bob Crane's fifth anniversary show (the flip side features Pat Buttram), while The Effervescent Humor features a Canada Dry radio spot and the "Send Dead Flies" monologue as performed on "The Tonight Show" with Jack Paar. Both albums were distributed to potential KNX advertisers so they could get a taste of how their commercials would be broadcast over KNX. Below are the liner notes of "Laffter Sweet and Profane."

Laffter Sweet and Profane – KNX Promotional Album
(released August 1963)
Liner Notes: Bob Crane

This disc is important for a number of reasons, one of which is that men who make important decisions in advertising are not apt to be alertly up and about and listening to radio when Bob Crane shatters the tranquility of the dawn hours on KNX. Crane comes on at 6:00 a.m. and continues at a crackling pace until 9:55 a.m. Mon.-Fri. and on Saturdays from 8:10 a.m. to 11:55 a.m.—with timeout for the news. It is important that ad men know about Crane. The record constitutes an introduction.

The honor of occupying the flip side goes to Crane because the listener is more apt to flip over Crane's antic ebullience than over the drier humor of the sager Buttram.

Separating the boys now, we give you first, Bob Crane, a Bridgeport (Conn.) boy who was bid come to The Land of the Orange (and the Nut) by KNX radio back in 1957 [Author's Note: incorrect—should be 1956].

The Crane side of the platter opens in confusion with Mike Nichols and Elaine May, a first-string team, discussing Crane and attempting to explain him. They fall flat on their collective faces, of course, because Crane defies definition...and then the sweet boyish voice of Crane himself comes crashing and exploding up out of the ashes of the Nichols-May defeat, so listen and perhaps you can fathom the phenomenon that is Bob Crane.

Crane is completely lacking in respect for all things with the possible exception of The Great Coogamooga, a mythical deity whose acquaintance you are about to make.

The Crane side of the disc purports to be excerpts from our boy's 5th Anniversary Show on KNX, itself made up of material extricated from Crane's five years of non-stop non-conformist morning jubilation.

During the five years, Crane has interviewed three hundred guests, including Miss [Marilyn] Monroe, an ape, Pat Boone, a shine boy, and Mr. [George] Jessel. Without being acerb, or caustic, or anything other than playful, Crane nevertheless is said to be rough on guests, so they crowd to get on his show. This is not because they're given to Masochism but because when a singer has a new album, few things get it launched with the impact produced by a plug on The Crane Show. The same goes for breakfast cereals and tires.

Source: Photograph by Sylvia Norris. From the author's personal collection.

Occasionally, however, a guest will succeed in working Crane over, as you will hear, herewith, wherein Jonathan Winters triumphs.

Crane approaches something close to genius in integrating his commercials with show-stuff. While he sometimes fractures a sponsor's message, he reassembles the pieces and augments and embellishes said message in such a manner as to increase the plug's effectiveness. This is a matter of record. Crane sells. Crane pitches hard. Add to this that he has the area's fastest-expanding morning audience and you have a degree of value that should make time buyers drool.

BOB CRANE The Definitive Biography

Source: All photos courtesy of Scott Crane. Used with permission.

Bob with his engineer Dave Jarecki (circa 1956).
Source: Courtesy of Scott Crane. Used with permission.

Bob with his engineer Jack Chapman (circa 1962).
Source: Courtesy of C.S. Used with permission.

KNX promotional campaign.
Source: Courtesy of Karen Crane. Used with permission.

The Invincible Robert Crane

Bob at work in his KNX office (circa 1962).
Sources: Courtesy of C.S. Used with permission.

Bob giving a demonstration of his radio show (circa 1960).
Source: Both photos courtesy of Scott Crane. Used with permission.

Bob Crane with Jonathan Winters (circa 1960). Winters was one of the few celebrity guests on Bob's KNX Radio Show who got the better of Bob.

Bob Crane with Jack Lemmon (1962). Lemmon was one of Bob's idols.

Source: Both photos courtesy of Scott Crane. Used with permission.

The Invincible Robert Crane

Bob Crane and his KNX engineer Jack Chapman, broadcasting live from the basement of Columbia Square in Hollywood (circa 1960). John Sutton, son of former KNX program director and general manager Robert P. Sutton, believed "they were converting the underground studio for Bob and Jack." The new studio was located under television station KNXT.

Source: Courtesy of Scott Crane. Used with permission.

Chapter 5
The Actor's Actor

What's my ultimate goal? Movies and my own series. The easiest way to define it is to point to Danny Kaye because he's a winner this year. But he was established as an actor and performer; then he got into what he's doing now. That's the way I'd like to do it.

—Bob Crane, June 1964

Bob Crane at KNX (circa 1964). Beginning in 1959, Bob began his acting career, and from 1963 to 1965, he worked full time for both KNX and *The Donna Reed Show*.

Source: Courtesy of Scott Crane. Used with permission.

Chapter 5
The Actor's Actor

For a long time, I was frustrated. No, I wasn't so unhappy I was ready for the psychiatrist's couch. But I did feel the acting game was agin me. Every time I got a break, something happened. It's not that I want to give up being a disc jockey on KNX to be an actor. I just want to act. And now, I'm getting my chance. Who knows…maybe some day, I'll be right up there with Gig Young and Tony Randall. I can sure try.
—Bob Crane, December 1963

By the time Bob Crane arrived in Hollywood with his family in August 1956, he was well accustomed to performing before an audience. He had enjoyed the spotlight ever since gaining attention as the drummer in his high school jazz band, and then later in professional and semi-professional jazz bands on both coasts. Whether it was from behind a set of drums or a radio microphone, he had quickly become an entertainment powerhouse, commanding the attention of his audience and corporate sponsors on both U.S. coasts.

Aside from his intrinsic passions for drumming, music, and radio, Bob had also dabbled in acting early in life. An innate entertainer and performer, he thrived before an audience, so it is not surprising that he appeared in at least one high school play at Stamford High School. Classmate Eric Ericson remembered seeing Bob perform on stage during their school years.

"Bob and I attended Ms. Leonard's English class," Eric explained. "She also taught drama and had a lot to do with class plays. One of the plays was a musical. I believe it was *Oklahoma*. Bob and several other classmates were in it. Bob was personable, friendly, and smart."

School plays may have been fun, but whatever minor acting Bob had done during those early days was perhaps more for his own amusement than it was a serious career pursuit. Any thoughts of acting had given way to his more resolute ambitions of rhythm and radio. Further, while Bob had been granted the otherwise rare opportunity to work in front of a camera at WICC's Channel 43 in Bridgeport, Connecticut, this was far from acting.

"We didn't do any acting on Channel 43," WICC colleague and friend Morgan Kaolian recalled. "What we did was strictly improvisational comedy. There were no scripts. We knew what the skits were going to be about, but we didn't rehearse actual lines. We just got in front of the camera and ad-libbed our routines."

It was only after gaining a foothold in Los Angeles as a formidable radio personality that Bob considered becoming a professional actor, and it all began with the film *Tunnel of Love*.

Tunnel of Love, starring Doris Day, Richard Widmark, and Gig Young, opened in theaters nationwide on November 21, 1958; the story follows the lives of two young couples over the course of one year. One couple, Augie and Isolde Poole (Richard Widmark and Doris Day), are trying—in the worst way—to have a baby. Admitting they might not be able to have children of their own, they seek to adopt a baby. Their friends and neighbors, Dick and Alice Pepper (Gig Young and Elisabeth Fraser) agree to serve as the Pooles' reference. Despite being happily married, Dick is a happy-go-lucky, martini-drinking, womanizing player. He encourages Augie to break his marriage vows to loosen up, claiming Augie is wound too tightly. The story bounces back and forth between Augie's mishaps and pathetic attempts at being a "bad boy," Dick's fun-loving personality yet skewed perception of why straying should be acceptable, and their wives' seeming ignorance or ambivalence to their husbands' wandering eyes.

Around the time the film opened, Bob and Anne learned Anne was expecting their second child, and she was due in the early summer of 1959. It was a time for celebration, so rather than turn in early, as they would have typically done to accommodate Bob's early morning schedule at KNX, they decided to see *Tunnel of Love*.

Later, as they exited the theatre, Anne turned to her husband and said, "You know, I just spent ninety minutes watching you!"

At that moment, a spark ignited in Bob's mind. He saw himself on that screen, playing a role, and realized his own potential. The flame was lit, and from that point on, Bob would turn his attention to acting.

Many elements of *Tunnel of Love* had appealed to Bob and Anne, not least of which was the film's setting—Westport, Connecticut—a neighboring town of their childhood home of Stamford. Further, the film's premise of a young couple trying to become pregnant and finally succeeding would have reflected their own happy news. However, something else stood out in the movie. Anne had been referring to the character of Dick Pepper, portrayed by Gig Young, and how much he had reminded her of her husband.

Bob had the same musings as he sat in the theatre watching the film, thinking to himself, "There, but for Gig Young, go I."

From the time Bob and Anne left the movie theatre, the idea of being the next Gig Young began to grow in Bob's mind, and with it, the possibility of becoming an actor. He studied the film and Gig Young's role in it, Anne's words having resonated deeply with him and reinforcing his own ideas. He soon found himself relating to the character—physically, dramatically, and emotionally. Certainly, *he* could play that part as well!

"I used to have Gig Young on my radio show, so he knew I was contemplating acting, and he was encouraging," Bob said. "We're always kidding about how he gets the parts I should have had. The other day he called up to say, 'Guess what—I'm doing another Bob Crane type!'"

But Bob had never studied acting, nor had he ever really acted. His passions had always been music and radio. This was something completely new and different, something he had touched the fringes of once he arrived in Hollywood but had not ever done himself. How could he learn? What were his options?

Ambitious and determined, Bob was a self-learner and a self-starter. What he had not learned in school, he figured out how to do himself by experimenting, observing, and reading books—nearly every book he could get his hands on about whatever subject interested him at the time. He employed this skill often during his radio career, dating back to his earliest days at WLEA when he had free reign to try new things on the air. At KNX, he discovered that in order to be one step ahead of his guests on his radio show, he had to know the entertainment business inside and out. So he read. He studied. He learned. Continually. For his efforts, the press hailed him as "one of the best informed persons on the world of entertainment, subscribing to and reading all trade publications and reading every book on the market concerned with the entertainment industry." From music to broadcasting to interviewing, Bob's idea of learning through reading and hands-on experience was serving him well so far. Bob was *constantly* reading, listening, and observing.

"I find that the thing that I found wrong with school, and I think it applies and always would apply, is much of what they teach you in school *at that moment* you're not really interested in," Bob said in a 1971 interview. "And years later, you suddenly realize, I *should've* been interested in it. Prime point is English. I couldn't see any sense in grammar and English and literature and whatnot. And when I got out of high school, I realized what I wanted to be was a radio announcer and get into show business somehow. And I had to go and buy all the books on *30 Days to a Better Vocabulary, Self-Taught English, Self-Taught Grammar*, just because in school, I didn't pay attention. My mind wandered. I was thinking about drumming, the job we had that night, or the after-school dance or whatnot. I found the same thing used to happen in church. The priest would be giving the sermon, and the sermon was about the Bible or something. And that didn't particularly interest me. So my mind would wander, and I never paid attention. And years later, you realize, gosh, I wished I had paid attention! Because now it's one of the reasons I like the talk shows because I feel like I'm getting an education through the talk shows. I hear learned men who are authors and scholars talking, and I'm *learning* something."

So well had Bob learned how to educate himself and retain the information he gathered that he brushed aside serious thoughts about taking formal acting classes. With the exception of one college course on radio broadcasting Bob had taken at the University of Bridgeport, everything he had ever learned in radio he had taught himself by reading, engagement, or emulating others. And perhaps most importantly, it had proven successful.

"I made it a point to study the people in the business I admired most," Bob explained of his career in radio. "It wasn't hard, then, either, since in those days, we had such New York radio personalities as John B. Gambling, Rayburn A. Finch, Jack Sterling, Ernie Kovacs, and Bob and Ray. I learned from them all. I watched Bill Cullen. I liked Art Linkletter's way of conducting an interview while still keeping it light, and I even admired Jack Bailey, host of *Queen for a Day*. Particularly fascinating was how he could listen to all those awful tales of woe, then smile and slap someone on the back and declare her *Queen for a Day*. What I admired most, I guess, is how they all got away with it."

It had worked for him in radio. Why not acting?

"When I was a kid," Bob said, "I saw the movie *Young Tom Edison*. In it, there was a piece of advice I took to heart. Mickey Rooney, who was playing young Edison, was told, 'A man can learn anything from books.' That started me reading everything I could find on comedy and on acting. I loved doing the radio show, but I always wanted to be an actor. I don't believe in acting schools, at least not for me, so the only way to learn—was to act. That's why I began working with little theatres at the same time I was doing my show."

The Cranes' Tarzana home was located just a short distance from the Valley Playhouse in Woodland Hills, which had produced stage plays that included *The Moon Is Blue*, *Billy Budd, The Lower Depths, The Country Girl,* and *Cat on a Hot Tin Roof*. Every day, Bob would drive by the theatre, often wondering if he should go in and inquire about taking a part in a play. Then one day, not long after he had seen the film *Tunnel of Love*, he didn't drive by. Instead, he mustered up his courage and decided to turn in. There, he met Donald Freed, a community theatre director and acting instructor, who was casting for the theatre's production of *Tunnel of Love*. After a brief conversation, Don decided to cast him in the role of Dick Pepper.

"I listened to him every day on the radio," Don Freed explained. "It was *compulsive* listening. He lived about two minutes from the theatre, just a street or two over, literally. And he did come over, and probably within seconds, I suggested he make his debut on the stage. I didn't know he would be as good he was. Then I went down and I watched him put his radio show together in the morning. He had a large listenership. He was filled with energy, and he was *restless*. But the rhythm of his restlessness maintained a bright, witty lyric to it. And though he was quick on the uptake, it would not do justice to the speed of his wit. It was filled with double intentions and puns and plays on words, and the lightweight chauvinistic banter of the time—but not in bad taste and not vulgar. There was a lightness to him that was not oppressive at all with his jokes. He was just as gifted as you would ever see. I think he knew his own particular gifts, and it was clear there wasn't much you could teach him. He set his own limitations, but within those parameters, he was a *star*."

In describing Bob, Don used the term "restless" frequently, sensing an ambitious man who was motivated and had to keep moving, climbing, and doing—always reaching upward to harness and master the next challenge. This restlessness had helped propel Bob in his radio career, and now, it fueled his drive to learn to act. It was becoming apparent that once Bob set a goal, he would not stop until he had achieved it. He was a perfectionist, and his toughest critic was himself.

On the stage of the Valley Playhouse, Bob knew he would be safe to explore this new medium of work without the fear of great criticism, much as he had done in radio at WLEA. Here, while on stage, he went out of his way to build confidence with costars Tom Hatten, a friend and colleague at KNX/KTLA; Richard Cleary, who had appeared on Broadway in the 1951-1952 Tony Award-winning production of *Stalag 17*; and Colleen O'Sullivan, a local community actress. He understood that if he wanted to learn, he had to be serious and take the productions and his cast members just as seriously. According to Don, Bob was "the complete professional and absolute gentleman with the women at the theatre."

The Valley Playhouse's production of *Tunnel of Love* opened in September 1959 and ran through October of that year. On the air at KNX, Bob promoted the play ferociously, hoping to fill the theatre with listeners who were eager to catch a glimpse of their favorite radio morning man on stage. He also invited his KNX and CBS coworkers to watch his performance. Cutting critics off at the pass, he employed his perfected self-deprecating humor and turned his own razor-sharp wit on himself, cautioning his listeners to expect the worst of his performance, proclaiming he was "a celebrity in one field about to lay an egg in another."

Yet the critics were kind in their reviews. The production was exactly what this particular generation and community of theatregoers had expected and enjoyed—a film transformed for the stage. To reinforce Bob's newly found enthusiasm for acting, reviews of the production—and his performance in particular—were good.

So good was the response to this production of *Tunnel of Love*, in fact, that the Sherman Oaks Junior Women's Club took advantage of their community talent and bought out the house on October 9, 1959, with proceeds from ticket sales going to charity.

Meanwhile, shortly before the play opened, Anne gave birth to their daughter—Deborah Ann. With a new baby, a young son, long days at KNX, public appearances, and theatre rehearsals and show performances, Bob was spread thin. His schedule was hectic and full, and he permitted no time for socializing or playing. Don remembered Bob as being especially devoted to his family, and the birth of their new baby girl and his grueling work schedule were two obvious reasons he was always on the go.

"He was very friendly but very busy," Don explained. "*Extremely busy, balancing his career and so forth. He was sort of a whirlwind. It was always fun to be with him. He never wasted any time. He was always working. He would be up very early for his radio drive time, and then he'd be rehearsing at night for the play, and then he would be with his family. He talked about his family a lot. They were very much in the picture. He was very close to his son. I would say *devoted*. Devoted father and husband. His real schedule was extremely crowded, but it would have *always* been because he would have always been creative and ambitious and *restless*."

Bob displayed no signs of an inflated ego that Don could see, and although Bob realized his own amplifying fame, he did not show it. Bob sought knowledge, and he immersed himself in the stage productions at the Valley Theatre to gain it.

"He did nothing that would make what he was doing more difficult," Don recalled. "People behave differently when they are doing something for love or fun or for general principal. He wasn't making any money or anything. You use your time and energy in your own interest for making what you're doing better, and without any waste of time in playing and so forth. Now Bob, you could tell, had a high sense of criticism. He was a social critic—used in an absurdist radio style. He had a strong critical faculty of his own. But I never heard him complaining or criticizing anyone else. But then again, that was typical of working with Bob—when you were working with him, you were *working*. He knew *exactly* what he was doing. He was not being opportunistic, as if we're going to do a play like this on Broadway. But he would be ready for it."

Bob had been with KNX for just three years, and in that short time, he had quickly discovered he had a flair for acting and the stage. Yearning for something more than *just* radio, almost immediately following his performance in *Tunnel of Love*, Bob began to focus on acting, all while continuing to work at KNX. In the autumn of 1960, Bob returned to the Valley Playhouse, and he performed in the Norman Krasva comedy play, *Who Was That Lady*, alongside Colleen O'Sullivan and Tom Hatten. Published reviews noted the production of *Who Was That Lady* was "hilarious."

"That was his transition from radio," Don Freed said. "And his brilliant improvisatory powers in radio he was able to translate to stage and then to television. He was a great specimen of his time. Acting was something new for him, and so I was enthusiastically encouraging to him. It was a pleasure to have a talent like that. And these plays are not too challenging, but they are *very* challenging if you haven't the experience. But his technique! Just that pose, with him standing with his hands behind his back. That's an unusual and original, but perfectly natural, kind of activity for someone who is instead of seeming restless or nervous, he is smiling innocently and with his fingers crossed behind his back."

Acting was a natural career progression for Bob. KNX was not just a dynamic move up in radio; it also served as a vehicle to open new doors, permanently altering his career path. Comedians who were also fine actors—Jack Lemmon, Jonathan Winters, Jerry Lewis, and Dick Van Dyke—were frequent guests on his radio show, and they caught his attention and became his new role models. Bob idolized such performers, nearly to the point of worship, as he had done with his music and broadcasting idols. He became determined to follow in their footsteps.

It was not to happen so quickly, however. CBS had predicted Bob's possible eagerness to transition out of radio, and it was a potential threat to their investment in him. The network had witnessed Bob's blatant refusal to be locked into WEEI Boston's three-year contract and his dogged determination in pushing KNX to change the broadcasting union rules for him. Plus, Bob Crane was handsome, talented, smart, and driven—and he was now strategically placed in Hollywood. CBS was concerned Bob might abandon KNX for a different venue, and the station needed an insurance policy.

It had been fairly common for those who began in radio broadcasting to migrate to television, probably more so in California, and KNX had lost other fresh radio talent to television in the past. KNX colleague Leo McElroy explained, "To give you an example, and this is not Bob, but the news director at KNX at one point told me that he knew one of his newscasters was 'going bad' when he got his hair styled. People who got their hair styled were looked at strangely. When you're in radio, at five o'clock in the morning, you don't care what your hair looks like!"

Bob's fast rise in radio, coupled with his boyish good looks and steadfast drive for success, gave CBS cause for concern. To prevent their star radio personality from immediately chasing after an acting career, CBS included a very specific clause in Bob's first KNX contract. Bob may have won the right to spin his own records, but CBS was going to lock him into radio—and *only* radio. His first contract with KNX included a no-acting clause, preventing him from acting professionally for five years—the duration of the terms of the original contract. This meant that until 1961, Bob could not act in any professional capacity and still remain employed at KNX.

So, for five years, Bob was boxed in at KNX. If he chose to do any acting, he would be restricted to community theatre.

But the wheels were turning.

After his positive experiences on stage in *Tunnel of Love* and *Who Was That Lady*, Bob knew he wanted more. The acting bug had officially bitten. Undeterred by the KNX no-acting clause, he forged ahead with the only avenue open to him—local community theatre and Little Theatre in Southern California. Appearing onstage in smaller venues allowed amateur actors the opportunity to get their feet wet and learn the ropes without risk of widespread failure or humiliation. Bob also incorporated this type of entertainment into his KNX radio show, which became known as The Crane Little Theatre Players.

Harvey Geller attended some of Bob's early theatre performances.

"Acting came very naturally to Bob," he said. "It was no work at all for him. He must have done ten different shows in that period when he was on the air—Little Theatre things where he might do five shows and then off to another show, five performances, all around that part of California. He was learning his craft, all before he went on television. When he was doing these early plays, he was learning. He wasn't great, but he was learning."

Despite his contractual restraints, Bob tested KNX's power hold over him. In 1959, he filmed a short segment of a pilot for a potential new television series—*Picture Window*. It is unsure whether KNX knew about this segment and simply didn't care because it did not interfere with his radio work, if Bob had proven his worth by then so they looked the other way, or they just didn't know. Whatever the case, it soon became a non-issue because *Picture Window* was not produced. Though never televised, the pilot episode of *Picture Window* can be credited as Bob Crane's first official television *acting* performance.

Created by Max Shulman (creator of *The Many Loves of Dobie Gillis*), *Picture Window* was to have focused on the lives of young couples and families living in Suburbia as seen through the eyes of the mail-

BOB CRANE The Definitive Biography

The Young, Ambitious Actor and the Hollywood Producer (Adlibbed Skit)
Performed by Bob Crane and Jonathan Winters

By the early 1960s, Bob Crane had become well known all over Southern California as the "fastest-talking" radio personality of the era. Most Hollywood celebrities and other entertainment notables were keenly aware that if they were guests on *The Bob Crane Show*, their devilish host was going to give them a rigorous, albeit good-natured, roasting. As a result, they would gain almost instant publicity for their current television show, film, play, or record. Rare was the time when a guest got the better of Bob, but every so often, someone did. Such was the case with Jonathan Winters, where even KNX boasted that the great Bob Crane had met his match in glib and wit during a skit adlibbed by the two comedians.

An undercurrent of ambition and motivation flows beneath Bob's usual schoolboy charm and giddiness during this exchange. At the time this skit aired and was recorded, Bob was chomping at the bit to act professionally. However, his KNX contract had forbidden him to do so until 1961. While this was an improvisational routine, Bob tips his hand at his desired professional endeavors. He recovers quickly, and at the time, it would not have raised much of an eyebrow—especially with Jonathan Winters' rapid-fire delivery. In retrospect, however, it does provide an interesting glimpse into Bob's mindset at the time and a peek at his ultimate future.

Jonathan: What, what, what is it Bob? What kind of work? What do you want to do here? What are you doing here, by the way? Who's the agent? What's his name? What's his name, Bob? What's your agent's name?
Bob: I'll be honest with you. I never met him before.
Jonathan: How'd he get through the gate?
Bob: I never met him before.
Jonathan: You never met him before.
Bob: Not my agent.
Jonathan. What, he'd find you in the street? Or some discovery over an ice cream cone?
Bob: It's a big—
Jonathan: What, are you talking about the old days, Bob? What do you wanna do, Bob?
Bob: It's a big company, sir.
Jonathan: Sure, it's a big company.
Bob: I mean it's a—

Jonathan: A billion, billion dollar company, kid. We got 'em going here. You trying to tell me my business? Maybe you wanna come behind the desk.
Bob: No, I don't want—
Jonathan: What do you want, sweetheart? What is it, baby?
Bob: Aw, now, see you—
Jonathan: Wanna get up there beside Marlena, is that it?
Bob: You get the wrong—
Jonathan: Play Humphrey Bojest again?
Bob: No—
Jonathan: We're putting Willard Foster in it. Crazy kid. He's fourteen years old, but he memorizes in two seconds.
Bob: My agent told me that I was very good.
Jonathan: Did he?
Bob: Yeah. He said—
Jonathan: What's good about you?
Bob: Well, I—
Jonathan: What have you done?
Bob: You really wanna know?
Jonathan: What have you done? I really wanna know. I'm not interested for ten minutes.
Bob: Well, you talk so fast! I can't—
Jonathan: Of course! Of course I talk fast.
Bob: Why?
Jonathan: It's a fast world. We gotta wrap a series up in twenty-six minutes.
Bob: Oh.
Jonathan: Oh, sure. Burn a kid out and he's through by the time he's thirty.
Bob: Well the agent said to me, "Go in there." You're a very big man, and you could—
Jonathan: That's right. I am.
Bob: And you could help me.
Jonathan: Big physically and mentally.
Bob: Well, he—
Jonathan: I'm overweight, overtaxed, overtired, and I'm over the hill. It's that simple, kid. Seventy-five pills a day and sixteen syringes and five bottles of juice. That's what keeps me going. Fourteen institutions in five years.
Bob: I've done Little Theatre.
Jonathan: Little Theatre?
Bob: Yeah.

> **Jonathan.** Stay with it. What you ought to do is stay in Little Theatre for the rest of your life. Get a little tiny place. Go off the beach. Get your friends to come in in Levis. Let your hair grow long. Play banjos the rest of your life. Don't come out here. It'll drive you crazy, kid. It's a big thing.
>
> **Bob:** But he told me I was right for the picture. He read me a—
>
> **Jonathan:** They're making a housing project out of the whole lot. It's over, kid. For me and you and everybody. It's all going to pay TV. I've got a job for you in radio as a jockey. How'd you like that?
>
> **Bob:** I—
>
> **Jonathan:** Be happy. Go away to Zuma Beach and work out for a day.
>
> **Bob:** Nah, you see, sir, I'm trying to get out of that. Not want to get out of it because it pays well. But I wanna get into the acting thing, and I'd been—you know, the agent told me I'm right for the part. He read the script, and I thought you were producing a picture. That's why I'm here. You start hollering me like you've been doing for the last ten minutes. It's not my fault.
>
> **Jonathan:** I'm sorry kid. I suddenly looked at your face and saw myself. You're it, Bob Crane.
>
> **Bob:** You mean I got the part?
>
> **Jonathan:** You're our next leading man. You'll be bigger than Peck. Bigger than Spencer Tracy. Bigger than any of them out here.
>
> **Bob:** Well, what made you change?
>
> **Jonathan:** I love you.
>
> ***The Bob Crane Show* / KNX-CBS Radio**
> **Interview with Jonathan Winters (circa 1960)**
> **Laffter Sweet and Profane / 5th Anniversary Promotional Record**
> **(Online: http://bit.ly/16iZtfl)**

man (Max Shulman), who delivers the bills and narrates the episode. Bob plays Jerry McEvoy, who has just received the month's household bills. His wife Mildred has purchased load after load of sand for the kids' sandbox—and why so much sand? Because the kids keep throwing it out. Jerry reacts to her explanation, stating, "I don't want to repress anybody! I just want to go quietly bankrupt in this suburban house you talked me into." His wife tells him not to overreact; everybody is in the same boat financially. "That don't make it a good boat, Missus!" Jerry retorts, and the scene ends.

The *Picture Window* segment is short, not even one full minute in length. But it was just enough to give Bob a real taste of acting before a camera. He began to crave it.

Biding his time, Bob continued his celebrity interviews at KNX, but not without planting seeds in the minds of those who could potentially help him. His unique situation at KNX gave him unlimited star access and the opportunity to network with some of the most powerful individuals in the entertainment industry. He allowed his desire to act become known to them, and he was not above begging, turning on his boyish charm when necessary in the hopes of persuading those in positions of power to just give him a chance.

During this time, a handful of voice talent opportunities arose, and Bob took advantage of them. He worked with Mel Blanc on a promo for a new CBS radio series entitled *Superfun*, where Bob voiced an agent making a pitch for various characters. Then, Rod Serling, who was also familiar with Bob's many impersonations, hired Bob for the episode "Static" of *The Twilight Zone*. Heard and not seen as the radio announcer, Bob provides all of the voice talent heard over the radio in this episode. According to his CBS contract for *The Twilight Zone* dated November 17, 1960, Bob recorded his voice-over parts on November 20, 1960, at CBS Studios. The episode aired on March 10, 1961, and Bob was paid $155.00 for his work.

Finally, in the summer of 1961, Bob renegotiated his KNX contract. By that time, the name Bob Crane had earned its own power. In radio, Bob was at the peak of his game, having been described by friend Harvey Geller as "arguably one of the most listened to radio personalities" in Southern California. There was little doubt that KNX was eager to keep their morning drive cash cow.

With the tables now turned, KNX general manager Robert P. Sutton gave Bob what he wanted—the freedom to act professionally. The no-acting clause was lifted, and beginning in 1961, Bob's KNX contract would be renewed on a yearly basis, with substantial increases in salary with each annual commitment. KNX realized that it was only a matter of time for Bob to move from radio to television. Each time Bob signed his contract for the coming year, CBS and KNX expelled a collective sigh of relief. After Bob signed one contract (dated June 6, 1963), KNX's then-program director Harfield Weedin included a note to Bob that read, "You've made Mr. Sutton and me very happy men. Thanks again.—HW."

As he had in the past, Bob Crane got his way—in this case, remaining in radio with the freedom to act. Leo McElroy believed this was how Bob operated to get what he wanted. Just as he had stood his ground with his radio show's format in 1956, he got his way again. In 1961, Bob was able to renegotiate so he could pursue his acting career.

"I don't think it was a case that he was *given* the freedom," Leo surmised. "I think he *took* it. I think this was Bob's definition of 'this is how I operate, and if you want me to do the show, that's fine, because this is the way I do it, this is the way I run my end of the business. And if you don't like it, then I'll go someplace else where they'll let me do it that way.' I think that was sufficient to keep him off their back. Bob probably got less interference than anybody I ever saw in the business because he steadfastly refused to yield to any of it."

Now free to pursue acting professionally, Bob continued his stage work in community theatre and sought small, lesser-paying roles in film and television. At the outset, he was met with disappointment. The offers to act didn't come rolling in as he had hoped or anticipated, and in addition, he received the taste of cruel rejection.

In one instance, he was approached by producers about appearing in a new film. He was exactly what they wanted. Just when he was about to sign, however, another contender with bigger star power edged him out of the running, and he failed to get the part. Another time, producer Joe Pasternak approached Bob to take the role of the disc jockey in *The Courtship of Eddie's Father*. "You're perfect for the part," Pasternak had said. "You'd just be playing yourself!" Bob was delighted, but then they changed their minds. Pasternak did not believe Bob looked enough like the disc jockey type!

"On the other hand," Bob said, "I'm already typecast. 'Radio,' they tell me. 'You do fine at it, boy. Stick to it.' Even the producers who've heard me on radio are skeptical about giving me acting jobs. They just don't believe I can be funny doing something else. And, for the parts they feel I might be good in, they want Gig Young, Tony Randall, or Jack Lemmon."

Bob pushed on. Finally, the tide started to change, and Bob earned small roles in a few feature films. His earliest appearances in film occurred in 1961, when he appeared briefly in *Return to Peyton Place* (released May 5, 1961, and produced by Jerry Wald, a good friend whom Bob interviewed frequently over KNX) and *Man-Trap* (produced and directed by Edmond O'Brien and released on September 20, 1961).

Bob also accepted a role in an episode of the *General Electric Theatre* series, "The $200 Parley," in which Shelley Berman had also been cast as the lead. It had been an awkward situation for Bob, having had an unsuccessful interview with Shelley Berman over his KNX show about a year earlier. But when series producer Stan Rubin called and offered him the role, Bob had wanted so badly to prove he could act that he took the chance. The taping went well, Shelley Berman and Bob had a laugh about the botched KNX interview, and the episode aired on October 15, 1961.

Alfred Hitchcock also enjoyed Bob's KNX program and saw potential in his acting capabilities. Hitchcock cast him a role in an episode of his television series, *The Alfred Hitchcock Hour*. On January 4, 1963, Bob appeared as Charlie Lessing in the episode "The Thirty-First of February." His work must have impressed the eclectic and enigmatic producer and director. In October 2002, Harvey Geller recalled in a "Letter to the Editor" of the *Los Angeles Times*:

"In 1963, for months, a dozen roses (with unsigned cards) mysteriously arrived daily at Crane's KNX office. Finally, CBS staffers discovered they had been sent by a fan, Alfred Hitchcock."

Stubborn is another powerful word used to describe Bob Crane. He held fast to his ideals all throughout his career in radio, and it quickly became apparent in Hollywood that Bob would not accept just anything that came his way. He was choosy to the extreme, and he became even more so as his acting career unfolded.

In the beginning, producers might not have taken Bob seriously as an actor. However, they did believe he would make the perfect television talk show host. Bob began to receive many lucrative offers from television producers to expand upon his radio program and transition it to the viewing audience. Long before Johnny Carson became the iconic host of *The Tonight Show*, Bob was on the brink of becoming a national late night talk show host sensation. Producers inundated him with offers, imploring him to bring his radio program to television.

His answer was always the same: "No." He turned them *all* down, shocking the entertainment community. Rare was the radio disc jockey earning $75,000 a year who chose to spend his time in community theatre or taking bit film and television parts to gain experience as an actor. For his stubbornness, Bob took a great deal of ribbing and backlash.

"I wanted to make it as an actor, which is something the TV personalities can't do," Bob said. "My wife kept looking at the Jack Paar show and telling me that's what I should be doing on television. But I kept telling her she was wrong. A guy like Jack Paar [was] a brilliant host on *The Tonight Show*, but he couldn't go into movies and play different parts. It's almost impossible for anyone, in fact, to do both. I've had loads of opportunities to do a Johnny Carson-Jack Paar-Steve Allen-type show. It's the easiest thing for somebody to say, when they see what I do with guests, 'Let's just stick a camera in the studio,' but I've never wanted to do that. Art Linkletter and a lot of other good friends in broadcasting told me I was a fool not to branch out into the television emcee business and maybe become another Jack Paar or Johnny Carson. But I couldn't see it. Once you become identified as a TV emcee, you're dead as an actor, and actor is what I wanted to be more than anything else."

Bob explained his own worries about breaking into acting to his cousin Jim Senich: "I know right now I'm trying like *hell* to get into the movie end of this business, or into the comedy acting end of it, and nobody will look at me for *beans*! All they want to do is make me an emcee because this is probably the *easiest* thing right now—I'm capable of *being* an emcee on any of these TV shows. But that's not what I *want*. I want to do the comedy/acting thing. Well, maybe three years from now, I *will* be in the comedy acting, and I will have *gotten* enough experience. And right now, I really *don't* have the experience, and that's the reason why they pass me up and hire the guys that *have* been around for a long time, like the Tony Randalls, and the Jack Lemmons and the Gig Youngs and the rest of these guys that do light comedy… I know I've felt [discouraged] many, many times. And then I just swallow my pride and keep on trudging along, and try to do a better job, and keep on improving, and experience is the only thing."

"*Tunnel of Love* was the first acting I'd ever done," Bob later told the press, "and I really got the bug. Some evenings there were five people in the audience, and we were doing it for no money at all, but to me, it was a step above being a television emcee handing out the toasters and the coffee urns."

So rigid was Bob in his decision to not become pigeonholed into the talk show circuit that he even turned down the offer to appear on

The Ed Sullivan Show. Bob considered his rejection to Ed Sullivan to be a shrewd move, but it was a potential career disaster, and it made Hollywood headlines. It was a chance he was willing to take because he firmly believed it wouldn't do his acting career any good.

"My best way of performing," Bob said, "is the Paar, Allen, Carson way. If I represent myself as a funny emcee, that's OK. When Paar went on with Sullivan, he bombed. You walk out on stage and you get introduced, and you can die. I'll do the type of thing that can benefit me. I'll emcee a special or the Hollywood Palace, representative stuff where I appear as a nice guy. The Sullivan thing is so commercial. I'm grateful for the offer, and I would go on if he would let me play drums."

Bob did not reject offers, however, where he could occasionally fill in as guest host for Jack Paar and Johnny Carson, among others. The week of January 22, 1962, was the first time Bob was asked to fill in for Johnny Carson on *Who Do You Trust?* Upon arriving in Carson's office, Bob noticed nothing except one thing: the drumset. He was unable to contain himself.

"At that time, I was doing a morning radio show from Hollywood," Bob said. "It had then run for five years, following a similar show I'd done in Connecticut. I'd caught on in Hollywood in a very pleasant way, and presently, producers who listened to the show (on the way to their studios, I suppose) were saying to me, 'Bob, why don't we put a camera on you doing those interviews and make it a TV show?' That was very flattering, but I didn't snap it up. I was happy right where I was. Among the producers who talked to me, Don Federson was the most persistent. He was producing the show *Who Do You Trust?* that Johnny Carson was doing from New York. Don told me that Johnny was about to take a week off, and he suggested I go to New York and replace him. I said I didn't want to replace anybody for a week. Then Don told me Johnny was going to be doing a new show, *Tonight*, starting in the fall, and they were looking for a replacement for him on *Who Do You Trust?* I seemed a likely candidate. If I went on for a week, that would be a sort of a tryout. That didn't exactly set me on fire, either. Then Don said, 'Well, you don't mind a free trip to New York, do you? Take your wife. Take your children. Make a vacation out of it and be paid besides.' That I dug. We Cranes had all missed friends we'd left behind in Connecticut. It would be nice to go visit them. So a couple of days later, there we were, headed east for a vacation and some work. We arrived on Friday, three days before I was due to take over Johnny's spot. The first thing I did was go over to meet Johnny. He was in his dressing room, and so I entered. The first thing I saw was a set of drums. I'm really gone on the subject of drums; there was even a time when I made my living beating up on them. I said, 'Hi,' to Johnny and made a beeline for the drums. I started banging away on them, but it gradually came to me that Johnny was warm—but not overly friendly. He just sat there until Art Stark, the show's New York producer, came in. Johnny said, 'Art, I'll be gone for a week.' Then he stood up, said goodbye to me, and that was that."

Despite their seemingly rocky start, Johnny Carson "devoutly hoped" Bob would have done so well as a fill-in on *Who Do You Trust?* that ABC would release Carson from his contract, allowing him to make the move to NBC's *Tonight Show*, replacing Jack Paar (which Bob had already turned down). But it was not to be. Bob was not interested, and after returning to Los Angeles from New York, Bob gave Don Federson his answer: *No.*

"Bob wanted to be an actor," Leo McElroy explained. "He wanted to have roles on television and motion pictures. Bob was frequently compared in those days to Jack Paar, who was doing *The Tonight Show*. They both seemed kind of quirky and irreverent. And for some reason, I was being compared to Hugh Downs. A movie company wanted to do a movie in which they were doing a scene of a Jack Paar/Hugh Downs-type nighttime show, and we were approached about being Paar and Hugh Downs. When the verdict came in, Bob was really insulted. I didn't get cast at all, and Bob was going to be cast as the Hugh Downs person. That struck him as pretty ridiculous [because he had routinely been compared to Jack Paar]."

Regular KNX staff were not particularly worried about Bob jumping ship from radio to delve into an acting career. For the time being, they saw it as merely a hobby he was enjoying. Plus, KNX was paying Bob an enormous amount of money—money he needed to support his family.

KNX advertising salesman Gordon Mason explained that television had very little impact on radio listeners in the early 1960s. "We knew the station had him under contract, but we didn't give any daily thought to, 'We're gonna lose Bob.' We knew the television networks were trying to get him. But we didn't watch much TV in those days. We weren't allowed! This was when TV was just really getting started. The joke used to be, 'You can't watch TV in a canoe.' KNX wouldn't accept any TV advertising, and for a long time, TV wouldn't accept any radio advertising."

In between his small roles on film, Bob continued to act in community theatre. In the summer of 1962, the Laguna Beach summer theatre production team was casting for the stage production of Jerry Evans' *Send Me No Flowers*. They had wanted Harold Lloyd, Jr., or Tom Hatten, but both had been unavailable. Tom suggested Bob for the part, and during the week of August 9, 1962, Bob signed on for the leading role. The play opened on August 28 and ran through September 2, 1962. Bob took off a week from KNX to perform in the play. In the production, Bob played the role of a "nice, solid commuter whose hobby is hypochondria. When he overhears his doctor talking about another patient who is ready to pass on with real heart trouble, he thinks the doc is speaking of him. The comedy begins, and the laughs come fast and hard until the final curtain when all ends well."

Bob was still unsure of his footing in his new acting venture, however, and he admitted to being nervous. He also yearned for people to take him seriously as an actor. "During rehearsals," he said, "I could feel those doubtful eyes on me. Then when we opened, we broke attendance records, and everybody was happy."

In reality, critics were beginning to anticipate Bob's move from radio to acting as a good one, reporting that "although his reputation as a humorist and madcap drummer has been gained from his highly rated, early morning KNX-CBS radio show from Hollywood, and his guest appearances on NBC-TV's *Tonight* and other shows, Crane is fast gaining acclaim for his comedy acting talent."

Trying to push his career along, Bob took what he already knew worked for him from radio—selling himself. He made a video recording of himself and friend Tom Hatten performing a scene from *Who Was That Lady*, one they had previously performed onstage. He then took the amateur film to his agent and said, "Sell me. I want to act."

But his agent balked at him for shunning the talk shows and wanting to act, responding, "Come on, Bob, this isn't a professional piece of film. This is little theatre stuff. You're turning down great money for what you know how to do. You're out of your mind!"

While others may have seen his choices as foolish, Bob was carefully selecting the roles he believed would aid in his future career as an actor. He built his new career small role by small role, himself the strictest of critics. Like an architect, he meticulously designed his place in the entertainment industry as *he* wanted it to be. Each part had to be the right fit. Each role had to be perfect. He settled for nothing less.

"I was making enough money to sit and wait for the right offer to come in," Bob said. "During the ten years I spent on radio and television in Los Angeles, I knew I was making more money than most of the actors who were appearing on my show. I was making $75,000 a year for my last five years on that [radio] show. I could wait for just what I wanted."

"Um…One of the kids is sick."

This final line, uttered timidly and with embarrassment, to this day, generates a terrific response from fans of both Bob Crane and *The Dick Van Dyke Show*. On December 26, 1962, Bob made an indelible mark on his early television career with his guest performance on *The Dick Van Dyke Show* in the episode "Somebody Has to Play Cleopatra."

Bob's character, Harry Rogers, is part of a lackluster amateur community theatre ensemble (and also, conveniently, a drummer). Rob Petrie (Dick Van Dyke) leads the theatre group begrudgingly, after having been talked into the ordeal by his wife, Laura (Mary Tyler Moore). The group's acting is far from stellar, and they struggle through their lines. Bob's character Harry, in particular, has a difficult time. Trying to play the part of Marc Antony, Harry fumbles through his part, exclaiming, "I have aromed from Rive!" As time goes on, however, Harry becomes more comfortable in the part, albeit still eager. Problems arise when each husband, including Rob himself, becomes jealous when Harry has to kiss Cleopatra, whose part has been rotated through each of the wives. Finally, one of the single ladies takes the role, and all problems seem to be resolved. That is, until Harry's wife Shirley (Shirley Mitchell) arrives at the Petrie house, and she sees Harry kiss Cleopatra. An argument ensues, and a jealous Shirley drags Harry out of the house. The ensemble cast watches the open door as the screaming match between Harry and Shirley escalates off stage. Defeated, Harry sulks back inside, forced to abandon the play. But instead of admitting his wife has won, he says sheepishly, "Um...One of the kids is sick."

"I was supposed to go back into the living room and deliver an exit line which was perfect for the situation," Bob said. "Well, four fine comedy minds—director John Rich, Sheldon Leonard, Danny Thomas, and Carl Reiner—spent half a week looking for that line, and finally they came up with it. While all the neighbors were sitting stunned and quiet in the living room, I stuck my head through the door and said, 'Gotta go now. One of the kids is sick.' Now that's what I call giving a script a lot of tender, loving care!"

Many affiliated with *The Dick Van Dyke Show* had been guests several times on Bob's KNX radio program, notably Dick Van Dyke, Mary Tyler Moore, Morey Amsterdam, and Carl Reiner, and he had supposedly "bothered Carl Reiner so persistently" that Reiner finally hired Bob for this one episode. "You really *do* want to act, don't you?" he had asked Bob. "Look, there's a *Dick Van Dyke* script where they need a next-door neighbor who's a kook. We'll send you the script."

Bob received the script for the episode "Somebody Has to Play Cleopatra," and according to Bob, he "rehearsed like a son-of-a-gun."

His persistence, motivation, hard work, and talent ultimately paid off. With this one performance, Bob caused heads to turn his way and take notice. John Rich, who directed the "Cleopatra" episode, told Bob, "Within two weeks after this show is aired, something will happen."

John Rich could not have been more right. One special viewer of *The Dick Van Dyke Show* had taken particular notice of Bob Crane's performance on this solitary episode. Donna Reed seemed to have a soft spot for the young, ambitious radio star and up-and-coming actor, and she liked what she saw on *The Dick Van Dyke Show* that night.

On January 7, 1963, less than two weeks after Bob's episode of *The Dick Van Dyke Show* aired, *The Donna Reed Show* contacted Bob and asked if he would be available to guest star on their series.

"He got a call from Donna Reed personally," Bob's cousin Jim Senich explained, "saying that she'd like to have him on her show, and he was really flattered. So he said, 'Okay, I know where your studios are.' She said, 'No, no, no, we'll send somebody over to get you.' Bobby said, 'A big limo pulls up, and two guys got out, and I got in. There was no smiling, no joking.' He just sat in the middle, and there was one on the left and one on the right!' But he loved Donna Reed and told me, 'I had a great time on the show with her.'"

On March 14, 1963, Bob appeared in a guest-starring role as Dr. Dave Blevins on *The Donna Reed Show* in the episode "The Two Doctors Stone." Donna and her husband, Tony Owen, who produced the series, were impressed with Bob's performance. They had been looking for something new for the series, and Bob's offbeat and brash humor was just the spice needed to balance Donna's sugar-infused storylines.

Two new characters were being created—Dr. Dave Kelsey and his wife, Midge—who would be next-door neighbors and friends of Donna and Alex Stone. Bob's comedic talent and personality seemed to fit the bill.

By this time, *The Donna Reed Show* had been on the air for five seasons. Paul Petersen starred as Jeff Stone and was about seventeen years old at the time. Paul explained, "I understood that Donna kind of wanted to expand her adult role on the show. At this point, Shelley Fabres had pretty much slipped away as a regular because she was pursuing a movie career, with Donna's acquiescence. So the family had sort of been recomposed. My baby sister Patty came on the show, she's ten years younger than I, and then there were the next-door neighbors. Everybody had to make accommodations. It was Donna's show, and if that's what she wanted, that's what we were going to do. Any time you start tinkering with the formula, which was Donna, Carl and the kids, and those sort of situations that ended up with a little moral—that we used to call Mother Knows Best—if you start tinkering with that and bringing in more adult themes and situations and start focusing on adult relationships rather than family relationships, it can be complicated. But people accommodated this really rather well. Frankly, it was, I know for Donna, refreshing."

Eddie Foy, III, was the casting director for *The Donna Reed Show* when Bob was cast as a semi-regular. He was unaware of a car being sent to pick Bob up personally for an audition of the first episode, claiming that was unusual, and such requests would have normally gone through him. When it came time to cast for the role of Dr. Dave Kelsey, he remembered that the person chosen to play the new character on the series "had to be funny, he had to be attractive, he had to be somewhat sexy, he had to be a man who women would look at, he had to have an incredibly good sense of humor, and he had to have kind of a wry personality. And Crane had all that."

But Bob was not Eddie Foy's choice for the role. One other actor had actually been considered for the role of the next-door neighbor—Regis Philbin.

"Once the decision was made to look for somebody," Foy explained, "we did not have the time, the inclination, or any other reason but to just look at two guys. There were two guys we talked about. There was the guy I brought in first, Regis, and I *loved* him. The second guy I brought in was Bob Crane. We did it all within a week and a half. I wanted Regis Philbin. But Tony Owen stayed on top of it; he wanted to know about this crazy guy on the radio. He wanted to know about *him*. He *liked* Regis Philbin. In fact, he thought it was a hell of an idea, but he wanted to know what Crane was about because he loved Crane since he knew him. Bob was the number-one guy on radio in the morning. Everybody in the industry would listen to him. The guy could walk into a room, and there'd be nobody in it, but talk into a microphone, and everybody in the building would be listening to him. He had a very, very wonderful approach, and he was very good at what he did. Bob Crane was an *excellent* radio man."

Eddie Foy claimed that the next-door neighbor character could have been anything—a dentist, a lawyer, a businessman. But Dave Kelsey ended up being a doctor. The purpose of the character was to introduce crazy situations into the mix—"I'm into this, how do I get out of it?" Donna Reed would then be the matriarchal problem solver for whatever mishaps occurred. And according to Foy, Bob seemed to be very much for it.

"Bob Crane wanted to be a television star," he said. "The appointment was made at his convenience because he was on the radio. In fact, when he got the job, we had to reschedule our show to shoot it when he was available. He came to my office, we walked up to the back of the building, and I took him in and introduced him to [*The Donna Reed Show* producer] Paul West. We asked him where he got his ideas for his radio show and his banter, and his very edgy way of doing things. Then there was the question of if he got the job, whether or not they would test him or read him. And there was also the possibility of doing what we call a personality test. I don't remember any readings or anything like that. There's a very good possibility that he did, but if he did, he probably read with Donna."

Bob's interview went very well, although he appeared somewhat uncomfortable to Foy. Whereas Regis Philbin had come across like "a big kid," Bob, on the other hand, seemed more nervous.

"I don't think Crane was shy," Foy said. "He was in an arena he didn't understand and was being interviewed for a job that could make him a ton of money. Was he uncomfortable? Yes. Regis Philbin is a Catholic kid from Notre Dame and has that boyish kind of wonderful, white bread, enthusiastic. He's like a kid. I also thought Regis was good. I didn't know how good Crane was, but I knew Regis was good, because he was fast.'"

Despite the push by Eddie Foy for Regis Philbin to take the new role and Bob's uncomfortable demeanor during the interview, Donna Reed and Tony Owen made their decision, perhaps even before the two men were interviewed for the part. Bob was offered the recurring role of Dr. Dave Kelsey.

"They wanted him *desperately,*" Foy said. "It wasn't like, 'Let's look at Bob Crane and see if he's got anything.' They *wanted* Bob Crane, all because of his radio show. But it disrupted things. It wasn't the norm. Usually, when you cast a pilot, you had your people pretty well set, and your recurring people are pretty well set. So this was out of the norm to get him in there. I think Tony went to Harry Ackerman, who was the executive producer of all comedies at Screen Gems, and said, 'This is who I want.' Bob wasn't under contract in those days; he was recurring, which meant he had to keep himself available all the time."

But according to Bob, Donna and Tony liked him so much that they did, in fact, offer him a seven-year contract to play Dave Kelsey. He refused.

"The *Donna Reed* people saw The Dick Van Dyke Show I did," Bob said. "They gave me one short part on *The Donna Reed Show*. They liked it so much, they said, 'We'll give you a contract for seven years.' I told them I didn't want to tie myself down for seven years. I agreed to do seven of thirteen shows—for very good money—but I told them I didn't think at the end of a year or two I would want to be doing the next-door neighbor."

Rather than locking himself into a mammoth seven-year contract, Bob signed a two-year contract with *The Donna Reed Show* to portray Dr. Dave Kelsey as part of the show's main cast, with Ann McCrea signing on to play his wife.

"When he finally went on the *Donna Reed Show,* and began doing regular television acting roles rather than hosting as he had done some in guest shots, he was thrilled," KNX colleague Leo McElroy remembered. "He said to me, 'My God! I'm getting paid as much for doing this half-hour television show as I get for doing a week of radio.' He was just kind of astounded and thrilled at the same time that this had happened and that he was getting a chance to play a running character, which was consistent with the character he portrayed, the wise guy, and that he was getting paid so much for it. He was like, *'Wow.'* It was like, 'You're not gonna believe this. I'm doing a running part on the *Donna Reed Show*, and I'm getting to play *me*.'"

Becoming a *star*—and not just being an actor—was another goal Bob had set for himself in his early climb up the acting ladder. It had been a big factor for him, having watched and talked with others *stars* who had done the same—Jack Lemmon, Gig Young, and Jonathan Winters. He discussed it with Leo McElroy.

"I had scouted a play that I thought we could do in one of the smaller, local theatres because he liked doing plays, and so did I," Leo said. "And I found this play that I thought would be good because it was a departure role for him and a departure role for me. So I told Bob about it, and Bob just shook his head and said, 'You don't understand. You're an actor. You like playing different roles. I want to be a *star*, and stars play themselves.' So with *Donna Reed,* he was getting a chance to play the role that he had constructed for himself. He was getting the chance to be the Bob Crane that he had built."

With the two-year agreement in place, Dr. Dave Kelsey first barged in on Donna Stone and her family on April 4, 1963, in the episode "Friends and Neighbors."

In the middle of the night, Dave Kelsey shows up on the Stones' front doorstep, frustrated. He and his wife, Midge, have been living with her parents, and he's tired of sharing space with his "out-laws." Donna and Alex graciously allow Dave to spend the night in their home, and the next day, Alex has a talk with Dave over a game of golf. He suggests that Dave and Midge purchase the house for sale next door. The Kelseys do just that, and at first, all seems like it will work out. But to the dismay of Donna, Alex, and especially Dave, Midge announces that she does not wish to live in the new house, not when they are already living with "Mommy and Daddy." Dave is crestfallen, Alex is speechless, and it's Donna to the rescue. She talks with Midge, and soon, Dave and Midge move into their new home. To celebrate, Midge (with a little help from Donna) prepares a feast—roasted chicken with prune stuffing—for Dave and their dinner guests, Donna and Alex. The meal is a tasty triumph, and in true Donna Reed fashion, all's well that ends well.

Bob may have been playing himself, as he put it, but he was still acting a part as written in a script. His influence only went so far, and on *The Donna Reed Show*, he was kept in check. But that didn't mean he did not have any input as to how he believed his character should be performed.

"Bob was a pretty racy fellow, and it didn't seem to me, at least from the early scripts, that the whole of Bob's personality was being invested in Dave Kelsey, our neighbor," Paul Petersen explained.

"I think Bob had some influence as to how he played [the character versus] how it was written," Leo McElroy recalled. "Bob was not shy in my experience. In my experience, he wasn't shy about saying, 'You know, my character would say it like this, not like that.' And I think there may have been elements of that in *The Donna Reed Show*, where he played up some of the zanier aspects of his character on that show. But the fact is, the writers are still the writers, and they were obviously looking for somebody to project that image, or they wouldn't have hired Bob. So I don't think there was a vast disparity between the production image of the role and where Bob went. It was a vanilla and jalapeno sundae."

Bob's personality did, indeed, come through in the character, and he may have been a little *too* much jalapeno on a set that was primarily vanilla.

"I'm not in Donna's image," Bob confessed. "I stand in the corner throwing darts."

In his book *In Search of Donna Reed*, author Jay Fultz reported that director Andrew McCullough was unimpressed by Bob. "He was a weird guy, a terrible actor, but he behaved himself on the show." Why McCullough was displeased with Bob is unknown. Foy also felt snubbed by Bob. According to Foy, Bob exhibited disrespect for him and others on the set. Further, Foy had rallied for the part to go to Regis Philbin, and he had never fully approved of Bob being selected for the role because he did not believe Bob was right for the part or the show itself.

"I didn't like him," Foy said. "I thought he was rude. I think he was an egomaniac. I think that he had the talent to back it up. Once we made the deal, and I said, 'Bob, you've got the job,' I don't think he said ten words to me over the next couple years, not even hello. If someone had said, 'We want to do another show with Crane,' I'd say, 'Good luck.'"

However, Bob might have found interacting with Foy rather uncomfortable. Cousin Jim Senich, friend Charlie Zito, and many others have claimed Bob was sensitive to the feelings of others. If he knew Foy had not supported him in the role, Bob may have instinctively avoided him, which would then have only made the situation worse.

Ann McCrea had kinder words to say about her *Donna Reed* costar. She relayed to Fultz that "Bob never came on to me," and explained that there were no sexual overtures present on the set with Bob. She further claimed that Bob expressed a vehement disapproval of the movie *Tom Jones* and its risqué content. According to Fultz, Ann recognized that Bob "did bring a nutty, manic energy to his scenes and helped lift *Donna Reed* to the top ten in the Nielsen ratings."

Ann also discussed her own part in the series with author Jay Fultz. She understood the spicy kick Bob brought to the show and also explained that her character of Midge was written as a flighty airhead to match Dave's off-the-wall, crazy demeanor. After a few episodes, however, Midge and Dave were toned down and written with a bit more realism, although Midge still retained her flightiness to match Dave's kookiness. Ann also realized how much Bob helped propel her in the business. Although director Gene Nelson saw Ann as a better technical performer, Bob was a hit with the viewing audience, which helped boost Ann's career.

While working on the set of *The Donna Reed Show*, Bob maintained his normal schedule at KNX. Dashing back and forth from Columbia Square to Columbia Picture Studios between the two jobs, it was a chaotic time.

According to Bob, "At ten o'clock in the morning, I used to finish the radio show, run across the street, and do *The Donna Reed Show*. I used to get my make-up on during the nine o'clock CBS News at Columbia Studios, across the street from CBS Radio. Then I'd run across the street and do the last hour of my radio show, which I had guests on. The mechanics of the daily routine drove everyone wild. My secretary got an ulcer. Anne [my wife] got an ulcer. I just went nutty."

He stuck with it, however, because he wanted and needed the experience. It also paid handsomely, and during the two years Bob worked simultaneously at KNX and on *The Donna Reed Show*, he earned a combined annual salary of $150,000. Today, after adjusting for inflation, it would be the equivalent of $1,153,272.58 (U.S. dollars).

Eddie Foy claimed Bob's shooting schedule created great demands on cast and crew, but Paul Petersen did not feel that stress. "It really didn't affect me very much, typical of a young person. It was often the case that we got a jump on the day's shooting by starting with the kids. So if it was a show that was heavy with the kids, we could get our stuff done while everybody else sort of drifted in. And if I recall correctly, Bob's show was off at nine o'clock a.m., so it wasn't like we lost a lot of time. It didn't take much more than a half hour to run him through makeup and get him dressed. But sometimes, it was awkward because he had obligations to KNX. But when you have a long-running show that ran at the pace we were on, it was very easy to accommodate things. For example, if Donna had a little extra time in makeup or hair or needed a half hour, it was perfectly normal for us to start our shooting days with the kids. You make television shows in pieces; it doesn't really matter what time of day you do a particular piece. I think it's fair to say he had a settling in period. He was kind of getting the lay of the land, and that's what happens with visiting guest stars, that's how it worked. But once he slipped into the role, then he knew what was expected of him as Dave Kelsey."

A typical day on the set of *The Donna Reed Show* was, according to Paul Petersen, filled with hard work, but fun work, nonetheless. He explained, "Donna and the story editors—usually they're listed as our associate producers—would go over the next week's script during shooting of the previous week. And on Friday morning at ten o'clock, we would sit down at the rehearsal table. That was kind of our fun day because we would go through the script, and there were a couple of readings. And we'd read the script for the first time and make our comments. Generally, they were funny comments, all done in fun because it really was such a formulaic show. We kept it light, and we always knocked off after two readings about lunchtime. Maybe we'd come back and maybe not; it depends on how extensive the light script changes might have been. On Monday, we polished the script and got it up on its feet. We blocked the entire show during Monday rehearsal. That day might last until three-thirty or four o'clock in the afternoon. There was not a lot of latitude for a director to have the camera *zooming* all around. And once that was accomplished, then we went home on Monday, always in time for early dinner, and then came back on Tuesday, Wednesday, and Thursday to actually shoot the show."

Paul said Bob was "always winging it," even in a show as structured as *The Donna Reed Show*. "He'd look for a bit," Paul continued. "That was sometimes pretty funny because Carl Betz was precisely the opposite. Carl Betz wanted to know where the glasses were on the sink so he didn't knock them over. He required a great deal of rehearsal, and Bob did not. I can't say that he ever came to work unprepared. He knew his dialogue for the most part. He'd *change* it a lot, but that was okay. It was difficult for Carl, but Donna was a *thorough* professional, and I rather think that six times out of ten, she enjoyed that spark of spontaneity. Not only was Bob quick on the uptake, he was a fast learner and very quickly became adept at anticipating camera angles and lighting and all the rest. But of course he had a lot of good teachers; he was working with a lot of great people. And all of us, because it made our own life easier, shared with him the—I don't want to call them tricks of the trade—but that *is* what it is. I think Bob would have loved to push the boundaries. But understand, for a man in this situation where the star of the show is a female with much more power and money, there is always some understandable chafing. You have to *really* be comfortable in your own skin to, on a daily basis, go to work in that environment. Remember the era we're talking about—this is *pre*-women's lib."

Bob, however, did more than just accept Donna's role as the star of the show and decision-maker on the set. He saw her as an ally in his newly established line of work, and thus, one of the keys to his future acting success.

Audiences liked the Stones' new neighbors Dave and Midge Kelsey, and ratings for *The Donna Reed Show* climbed. Viewers enjoyed the more mature storylines that focused on adult relationships rather than just what the Stones' kids were up to.

"We've waited five years for him to come along," Donna Reed said shortly after Bob began appearing as a regular. Although the addition of the Kelseys was out of format for the series, Donna claimed, "I believe we picked up more viewers because we brought in Bob Crane and Ann McCrea as neighbors."

Paul Petersen understood that it may have been a necessary shift to alter the show's format in the effort to improve ratings, but he also revealed strong feelings about the lasting impact of the remaining three seasons over the years. "The marketplace has determined that the first five years of the show are the classic version, and the last three years are rarely shown, and that has to do with the market," he said. "At the end of the day, I believe it was an awkward intrusion into what was a rather simple formula show, family sitcom."

Early in his work on *The Donna Reed Show*, Bob recalled a strange event that would eventually broaden his horizons and open a door to better understanding and appreciation of the acting profession.

"I was hired [on *The Donna Reed Show*] because I fit everything they wanted," he said. "That was, until we got into the screening room.

Expecting everyone to comment about my work—I thought I was pretty funny myself—there was nary a word. Heads just swayed from side to side. Then I heard someone mumble, 'Donna's hair looks too bouncy, and isn't Paul Petersen's hair getting too long?' When the lights went on, Tony Owen turned to me and said, 'And I think your hair's too tight! You look like a wise guy with tight hair.' I broke up laughing. No one had said anything about anyone's acting. Only their hair!"

While it may have seemed odd then and perhaps even more today, Donna Reed had an image to maintain, and the appearance of those working on her show was a tremendous concern. If it meant Bob had to change his hairstyle to please Donna Reed and Tony Owen, then so be it. He changed barbers (a crushing blow to his regular barber from Connecticut, who had relocated to California) and then his hairstyle, claiming (tongue-in-cheek) the experience to be quite traumatic for him. To please Donna and Tony, Bob sported a new do, and from his seventeenth episode of the series on, both on screen and in general, Bob went from the slicked-back look to having "fluffier" hair. It was also ironic, as school friend Charlie Zito mentioned Bob had always been self-conscious about his hair—specifically, about his receding hairline.

However, the incident involving Bob's hair on *The Donna Reed Show* developed into something significant. At the same time Bob was changing his looks, Donna Reed quietly but firmly suggested that in addition to his new look, he also take his acting skills to the next level.

Donna noted, "Bob is funny, and he doesn't know it." She liked Bob Crane, and she saw great things for him as an actor if he would only take himself more seriously in the craft. So she took him under her matronly wing and encouraged her young protégé to hone his acting skills.

"Bob, why must you always be a comic?" Donna asked of him. "You could be a leading man."

Strong words. Words foolish to ignore. Bob accepted Donna's powerful advice, seeking to prove to her that he *was* serious about his acting. During the summer of 1964, Bob did something he thought he would never do. He took an acting course, one taught by American actress and acclaimed acting instructor Stella Adler.

"I read in the paper Stella Adler, famous New York drama coach, is coming to town to give lessons for eight weeks," he said, "and I decided to enroll in the advanced workshop."

This was perhaps one of the most challenging decisions Bob made in regard to any of his chosen careers. Having scorned formal acting classes in the past, it was a big step for him, and it was intimidating. Further, although he had already gained some credible acting experience, this course was not for the faint of heart.

"You walk in that class, and Miss Adler looks you over," he said. "She digs in. In high school, my mind wandered all the time. But not here. I am alert. A student gives a monologue, and then Miss Adler and the class take the performance apart. You stand up and get stripped."

Bob fared well in Stella Adler's acting class, and he learned—a lot. Miss Adler proved to be a tough instructor, but she also admired his talents and effort. She paid attention to Bob, who, for his graduation monologue, portrayed a Southern Jewish lawyer. It was far from Bob's typical—and more comfortable—wisecracking comedic role. It was also a step away from his original mentality of desiring to be a star—a star who "just plays himself." It was real acting.

"A good TV performance," she critiqued him. "Now, do it again with your guts out. Get hacked."

"I look over Stella's shoulder," Bob recalled, "and who's behind her but Marlon Brando, a close friend. Oh, am I glad I didn't see him *before* I did the bit."

While enrolled in her class, Bob interviewed Miss Adler for a documentary, *Stella Adler and the Actor*, which aired on July 13, 1964. During the interview, Bob asked Miss Adler about her thoughts on method acting, and footage of her workshop was added. Bob also asked her if she considered herself a teacher.

"The teacher is an actor and a director," she responded.

Following his graduation performance, Bob earned a kiss from Miss Adler and perhaps some respect. He also gained a new perspective on the craft, her messages that the actor must "constantly act" and how to perform challenging roles having been etched into his psyche.

Wondering what Bob would do with what he had learned, Miss Adler prodded him, "I suppose you'll go back to *The Donna Reed Show* and the pool and the radio show and forget all about acting."

Bob did return, but he did not forget what he had learned and had become a bit wiser.

"You think everything is one big joke, don't you, as you go bouncing along," Stella Adler chastised, pushing Bob even further. Bob's response was both candid and sensitive: "I enjoy life. That doesn't mean I don't care."

It is safe to assume that Stella Adler's course humbled Bob Crane to a degree. Bob began to tone down his cavalier attitude toward acting. Adler's lessons helped to show him the importance of taking his acting seriously, which could mold him into the actor he wanted to become. Her course may have also tempered his outward desire to become a *star*, replacing it with the new desire to become an honest actor—*an actor's actor.*

Bob Crane delivered a fine performance as Dr. Dave Kelsey on *The Donna Reed Show*. However, by the autumn of 1964, he had already outgrown the role, and he no longer wished to play the wisecracking next-door neighbor and husband. Instead, sought something else, something different. Something away from the role of a husband with a wife and kids, a concept he by then believed had been overdone.

"At the end of the first year, I said I'd go one more year," Bob explained. "But by about the middle of the second year, I said I wanted to do something else, a little wilder than the next-door neighbor and a nice doctor. I wasn't happy with the role, which called for a nice-type fella who won't make waves. As long as I was just coming in and out saying, 'Tennis anyone?' the enthusiasm wasn't there. You try; you always try, but there was no area where I could give out—here we go again—that little extra something that makes the part fun to play."

Bob had agreed to continue to play Dave Kelsey for two years, but he was looking for a way out. He was also quickly becoming typecast as the next-door neighbor character. He grew restless.

Paul Petersen noticed Bob's boredom with the character. "Bob relished the new-found fame far, *far* too much," he said. "He was what, fifth banana on a long-running successful family sitcom. Now that's a different kind of fame than you get on the radio. Bob *gloried* in it. He wanted more, he wanted more, he wanted more! This was *new* to him and exciting, but he very quickly grew tired of it, of the grind, and what he thought was a lack of a professional challenge."

Bob asked to be released from his contract, and Donna Reed and Tony Owen granted his request. He arranged to leave the series at the end of the second season, and on the day he filmed his last episode reportedly on December 1, 1964, Bob said he "simply walked out." He admitted that *The Donna Reed Show* people were hurt by his departure, but they recovered quickly and explained away his character's absence to viewers. But he was not fired; nor did he quit because he wanted more money. Articles that claim this are incorrect. Bob Crane left *The Donna*

The Actor's Actor

Stella Adler Acting Course – Summer 1964
Notes Taken by Bob Crane

Bob Crane was serious about learning the art of acting, but it wasn't until Donna Reed encouraged him to take an acting class that he ever gave formal acting education a thought. As it turned out, he ended up learning a great deal from both Donna Reed and Stella Adler, and he often credited both for helping him along his path to career success in the field.

Bob remained in touch with Donna Reed long after he left *The Donna Reed Show*, continuing to ask for her advice about his performances—what worked, what didn't, what she liked, what he should change.

"She was marvelous," Bob said of Donna. "I learned everything I know in the business from her."

In Stella Adler's class, Bob kept intricate notes about how to improve his acting skills. Turning the pages of his notebook, one watches the novice become the actor, the ego deflate, and the preparation of his skill develop for things to come:

Notes
Acting is doing – Not showing!
Don't tell me – Show me.
The actor needs to THINK.

Take the rush out of acting.
Justify your actions.
Let happen.

1st Stage Rehearsal – Ignorance – Finding Out
What energy is – It must happen to you.
Must have idea.
Idea conveyed in sequence.

2nd Stage
Do until easy to convey.
Don't go back – Stay until done with ease.
I know something to tell someone.
Effort – Sound – Convey as it deserves to be conveyed.
Never mind feeling.
Respect the text.
Nature of the action.
The biography of character should be as intimate as your own.

Know whom you're talking to.
Where met.
Where he lived and housed in.
Why are you talking to him about this?
Relationship? To partner is important.
Make scene personal.
Other man – Where success? What did it do to him?
Me – Where success – When?
Impossible to act unless you know biography.
What do you like to do when you're not "career" driving?
Write trip of success.
What's the hierarchy of the society in time of play?
What is the political movement? Is there war?

You must think. Know what you're saying.
Always you talk.

Always understand what you're saying.
To study – Don't run away – Have control.
Everything's in sequence.
Analyzing – She takes things – They are held back.
Nervousness caused by studying too fast.
Idea of play is not words.
Talk to people – Don't be afraid.
Never substitute passion for truth.
Don't squeeze words.
Must make audience see what you see.
Know what you're saying simply.
Two ways to act.
Don't put things in that aren't needed.
Know what you are doing.
You can open up the temperament if you have it.

Understand the idea.
Do not try to interpret.
Be free in the play.
Open up without shame.

Reed Show because he was bored with the character and wanted to perform a different type of role.

For the remainder of the series, which aired its final episode on March 19, 1966, the character of Dr. Dave Kelsey was worked into the storyline by having him mentioned but not seen, with the rare exception of an episode that had been held and aired long after Bob left Dr. Dave Kelsey behind. So when Midge visits Donna, she mentions her husband Dave, but the viewer never sees him.

"Donna's husband, Tony Owen, is producer on that show, and he never misses a turn," Bob explained. "He had an article in *TV Guide* saying I quit over money. That wasn't the case, but last spring, we made an episode with me in about 95 percent of it. It's never been shown. The other day, I asked Donna what they were going to do with it. Donna said they've worked it in. For the first four or five episodes this fall, there'll be references to the fact that I'm away—out of town or something. Then they'll throw in that episode. As I said, Tony Owen never misses a turn."

Now liberated from *The Donna Reed Show*, Bob was once again in search of an acting role. This time, however, he was seeking *the* perfect fit. As before, he was highly selective and quite stubborn in making a decision regarding a new series, and now, not only did he want a leading role, he wanted *the* leading role on a series, and he wanted it to be *different*. Again, just as he had been known to do, he turned down offers, all of which were husband/wife/kids premises that he loathed and absolutely did not want.

"In Hollywood, word gets around fast," Bob said. "I started getting offers from TV producers. One had a series called *Living Doll*, but I couldn't see it, and again they thought I was out of my mind, turning down a chance to go from Donna Reed's next-door neighbor to the star of my own show. Then came the offers to do pilots for shows called *Please Don't Eat the Daisies; My Mother, The Car;* and one in which General Custer comes down off the wall. He's a picture. I told them they *had* to be kidding."

Meanwhile, Bob also continued his radio show at KNX and stayed active in community theatre. In addition, he performed a small part in the film the *New Interns*, directed by John Rich, which was released in theaters on June 1, 1964.

Then one day in December 1964, opportunity came knocking. And it was *the perfect* opportunity that would change Bob Crane's life forever.

Bob Crane in the Valley Playhouse production of *Tunnel of Love*. September/October 1960.

Source: Courtesy of Scott Crane. Used with pernission.

Bob Crane at KNX-CBS getting ready to appear for another professional engagement (circa 1964).

Source: Courtesy of Scott Crane. Used with permission.

Chapter 6
Welcome to Stalag 13, Colonel Hogan

Crane's Hogan is a bright, brash young officer with a good dose of mother wit and a twinkle in his eye. He keeps his patriotic band alert and bouncing in the Allied cause by a satisfying combination of idealism, sternness, mischief, Munchausen lies, and practical ingeniousness. Physically, he matches his spirit: He's tall, muscular, and moves with a jaunty confidence. In every way, he's the very model of the casually daring young soldier who laughs in the face of obstacles and tweaks the nose at danger. Hogan is pure Americana.

—Edith Efron, August 3, 1968

Bob Crane as Colonel Hogan (1965).
Source: Courtesy of Kathy Miratello.

The cast of *Hogan's Heroes* Season 1 (January 1965). Standing left to right: Richard Dawson, John Banner, Ivan Dixon. Seated in front left to right: Larry Hovis, Bob Crane, Werner Klemperer, Cynthia Lynn, and Robert Clary. Original photograph preserved in Bob Crane's *Hogan's Heroes* scrapbook.

Source: Courtesy of Scott Crane. Use with permission.

Chapter 6
Welcome to Stalag 13, Colonel Hogan

After the "Reed Show," I began to get other shows offered to me, and I started analyzing again. Would I be happy five years from now—a show can go on that long—playing opposite a robot? Then "Hogan's" came up, and once I got into it, it felt right. We work hard on the scripts so the lines don't sound too hokey. In other words, we try to give "Hogan's" the extra thought which makes "The Dick Van Dyke Show," for instance, so beautiful.

—Bob Crane, November 7, 1965

Tuesday, December 22, 1964. Three days before Christmas, they met and squared off for the first time. One, a thirty-six-year-old, all-American, somewhat mischievous, happy-go-lucky kid from Connecticut. The other, a forty-four-year-old, staunch, Old World, blue-eyed German. As their characters sparred in their first-ever uneven battle of wits, each actor held his own private reservations about the premise of the series for which they were testing and about each other. The series—a comedy set in an Allied prisoner of war camp deep inside Nazi Germany during the height of World War II—already had a cloud of controversy hanging over it. Further, one man considered his counterpart far too stiff and serious to perform comedy adequately; the other believed his opponent was too wild and crazy to be contained. Yet as they performed their screen test and gave their characters life, their chemistry clicked, and soon, their worries dissipated. While neither man could have predicted what the future would hold, on that brisk and sunny day in Los Angeles, television history was made.

The casting of the brash United States Army Air Force officer Colonel Robert E. Hogan and the pompous German Luftwaffe officer Colonel Wilhelm Klink was inspired. For this series—a comedy with the serious backdrop of war—to succeed, the lead players had to be *the* perfect fit. The dynamic portrayal of this military odd couple had to be articulate, accurate, and precise. For the show to work, for the concept to be accepted, for one of the most outlandish premises in television history to be believed, the actors signed to play the two leading characters not only had to bring these extreme individuals to life with broad, fictional strokes, they had to make them *real* in the details.

Bob Crane had been seeking his own perfect fit from almost the moment he began appearing on *The Donna Reed Show*. Although not the type of series he wanted for himself, he was grateful to Donna Reed for all that she did for him in his career.

The experience Bob gained from Donna Reed and her show was tremendous, and his pay during those years even better. Once he had departed from *The Donna Reed Show*, however, his income was sliced in half, and with three young children at home, he was eager to find another acting job quickly to supplement his radio salary.

He didn't know exactly what he *wanted*; he just knew what he *didn't* want—what he had declared was the "you'd be just right opposite [the already-signed femme star]" part. Every single television offer he had received after *The Donna Reed Show* was of this kind, and he had shunned them all, much to the chagrin of producers.

"*Donna Reed* just wasn't my cup of tea," Bob explained. "I decided that if I ever had my own show, I wanted it to be more hip than *Donna Reed*. Trouble was, after starting on that, [those were] the kind of offers I got."

Then one day during the 1964 holiday season, Bob had an impromptu meeting with producer Jerry Thorpe at a Los Angeles Metro station. There, Jerry presented him with an offer to co-star along side Pat Crowley in a new television situation comedy, *Please Don't Eat the Daisies*. It was a fantastic offer, but it was yet another role the up-and-coming actor did not want. As he had done with earlier offers, Bob shot it down.

Jerry Thorpe was frustrated. Bob's rigid stubbornness and his history of rejecting profound and potentially career-boosting offers had become legendary in Hollywood. Producers first met up with Bob's stonewalling when they wanted him to transition his radio show to a television talk show, and he refused. As an actor, Bob was turning down every role that came his way. *Now* what didn't Bob like?

"I had to talk for a long time to explain to the producer why I wasn't right for *Please Don't Eat the Daisies*," Bob said. "I told him I thought it was the father image. I didn't think it was me. That is, in five years, they would be calling me Mr. Pat Crowley. I also had to explain why I didn't want to do *My Living Doll* before Robert Cummings was considered for the role. I had an idea that I wanted a show which would keep me happy for five years. I tried to figure how I'd feel if I had to do the part for five years. *Daisies* was a safe show, but I didn't want that. I had that with *Donna*."

Then what *did* he want?

It wasn't easy for Bob to put into words exactly what he wanted. It seemed there were no words in the English language to describe it— that instinct he had based on what he specifically did not want. Bob tried to explain that whatever it was, it had to be something original. Something different. Something "swingy"—in other words, hip or radical for its time. Something clever that had never been done before but would have wide audience appeal. Something with an ensemble cast, perhaps. But *not* the next-door neighbor/husband.

"Basically, I wanted to swing, and you can't swing when you project mommy, daddy, and the kids—that I had at home," Bob had said.

Jerry Thorpe then remembered another new comedy series in development. Associate producers Edward H. Feldman and Bernard Fein were in search of a cast for the pilot episode, and they wanted an all-American type for their main character—a U.S. Army Air Force colonel imprisoned in a Nazi prisoner-of-war (POW) camp.

The concept of a situation comedy about World War II set on enemy turf was certainly different. It was so atypical of the industry trend that Thorpe believed Bob would be interested. He dropped the Christmas present squarely into Bob's lap.

Still, Bob was not so sure. Hesitant about what could potentially be a disastrous career move, he balked at first. While he indeed wanted something diverse, this idea seemed both ominous and ridiculous.

"I wasn't convinced it was a funny idea myself at first," Bob admitted. "To a lot of people, it doesn't sound funny at all."

A series about Nazis and World War II did not resonate well with Bob on a variety of levels. Aside from the possible negative industry and public response about presenting such a serious subject as a comedy, as with most everyone else of that era, Bob remembered the horrors and sacrifices of World War II. His older brother Al, his Uncle Mike Senich, and many other family members and friends had served in World War II. Plus, with the Korean Conflict lasting from 1950-1953 and the Vietnam War at its height, broaching the subject of war in general was nothing to take lightly.

In 1965, proper medical treatment and psychological counseling were not readily available for what would later become known as post-traumatic stress disorder, or PTSD, and had been referred to simply as battle fatigue. Thus, service men and women who had actively served during wartime sought other, sometimes dangerous, ways to dull the mental anguish caused by the atrocities they had witnessed and could not easily forget. Bob's brother Al had recently relocated from Connecticut to Los Angeles, and he had been battling his own private demons as the result of his wartime experiences on the *USS Bunker Hill*.

Cousin Jim Senich confirmed that Bob did not want to do *Hogan's Heroes* at first. Bob was sensitive to the hardships U.S. troops had endured and the stress-induced issues they were facing, and he did not want to insult them. Further, Bob originally believed the series was making fun of real POWs, many of whom had suffered during their imprisonment.

"Bob had feelings; he had very sensitive feelings," explained Jim. "He said he would only do the series if the company would run the show to veterans' clubs. They did a trailer and showed it to veterans' groups somewhere in the Midwest, and they all thought it was fabulous. They said if they didn't have a sense of humor, they'd have never been able to get through the war. They loved the trailer. Bob was sold, and the rest is history."

Another initial deterrent with *Hogan's Heroes* was that Bob was unsure of its intended genre. Bob wanted a comedy series, not a heavy drama about war. Bob had turned everything else down up to this point. He was not about to sabotage his first starring role by choosing poorly. However, his curiosity was piqued, and he was interested enough to learn more. He contacted Edward Feldman to hear what he had to say.

"Ed Feldman said he was planning a series to be known as *Hogan's Heroes*," Bob said. "Ed told me, 'We understand you want something swingy. Well, we have this character who's an American colonel in a Nazi prisoner-of-war camp...' 'Hell,' I said. 'I'm looking for a comedy!' 'This *is* a comedy,' he answered. I told him I couldn't believe it, so Ed told me to come see for myself. Eddie Feldman explained the plot to me. How I'm constantly getting my guys out of trouble and helping the Allies. How we've got such a great escape system that we can get in and out of the camp, so we're not stuck there in the scripts. So I thought, why not? The basic idea has been around since *Stalag 17*. It's essentially a solid concept. The teens dig the military, and for the adults, it's all reminiscent of World War II. So I went, got tested, and was hired as Hogan."

On December 22, 1964, *The Hollywood Reporter* published that Bob Crane's screen test for the role of Colonel Hogan that day was the only screen test he had ever done. This may be true for television; however, Bob later relayed that he had also tested for a feature film prior to accepting the role of Hogan.

"I'd been suggested for the part of the son in *Never Too Late*, which Warner [Brothers] was about to make…," Bob said. "So I went and got tested… I didn't get the part. Jim Hutton got the part. Which brings up the question of what's a guy to do? Should he go into *Hogan's Heroes*, when he is lucky enough to be approached on it? I went into *Hogan's Heroes*."

Bob reportedly "flipped" over the scenario, and as soon as he signed the contract, he began his work at perfecting the character of Colonel Hogan. He would work so hard at it, in fact, that he made it look easy, and over time, fans and critics alike would claim it was the role he was born to play.

"I met Bob just once in those days," said *Hogan's Heroes* co-creator Albert S. Ruddy. "He came in; he was a fairly well known local radio celebrity. He was very popular, and he was the typical, all-American guy living in the valley with a station wagon and his kids and a pompadour and his penny loafers. I mean, a really *terrific*, smart, bright, wholesome kind of guy. And we were *all* very taken with him."

A few actors were considered for the role of Colonel Hogan prior to Bob, including Van Johnson, who declined the offer, and Walter Matthau, whom Ed Feldman did not believe could perform comedy. Bernard Fein's widow Kay reported to Brenda Scott Royce that her husband and Ed Feldman had entertained the idea of casting Richard Dawson in the leading role, but it was short-lived. According to Kay, Ed Feldman had seen Dawson in the 1965 film *King Rat,* and apparently pleased with his performance, asked him to test for Hogan. Almost immediately, however, Bernard Fein and Ed Feldman believed Dawson's English accent was far too difficult to understand for the American viewing audience. Further, they decided the leading man *had* to be American, or at least sound American. Dawson was neither American nor sounded remotely American, and Bob Crane turned out to be just what the producers wanted.

"He was *exactly* as we had written Hogan!" Al Ruddy declared. "He also had that glint, that slight mischievous quality, that worked. Bob fit the character of Hogan well. He was everything they expected of him. What were the essential qualities that Colonel Hogan had to have? Number one, as always in a television show—must be likeable. Bob Crane—likeable. Hogan—likeable. Absolutely. You embellish it with a guy who was, whatever word you want to use, a fixer, a hustler, a man who gets things done, against *all* odds comes up with the probable solutions and makes them work. He was a great personality in radio, and he was obviously perfect for the part. I was nothing but excited to have him in the show."

Jerry London worked on *Hogan's Heroes* in many capacities over the show's run—as a film editor, assistant producer, associate producer, and director. He recalled, "The first time I met Bob was when we sat down and read the script for the pilot. I came in for the reading originally so I could be involved for the shooting. I was cutting as they shot the first episode. It was pretty quick. Robert Butler was the director—a really nice guy. Bob was weaving his way into the character. The only thing we knew was that the script was very funny. Great script. You hope the network people will understand and see the future of something that has such great material. You never know with the networks."

"*The main currency* is the actors, the characters," elaborated director Robert Butler. "A multiple cast like *Hogan's Heroes* was a little bit unusual then, so I imagine Werner Klemperer and Bob Crane satisfied everybody's desires. The major casting is largely politics and power, but that didn't affect the rehearsals. In rehearsal, everybody is hungry on a pilot. They want to be *right*. They want to be told what the *hell* they are doing, and they want to be reassured."

One by one, the ensemble cast slid into place. Werner Klemperer, who was then better known for his dramatic roles in such films as *Judgment at Nuremburg* and *Operation Eichmann*, was chosen as the inept Colonel Wilhelm Klink after actor Richard Crenna, a close friend of Ed Feldman's, suggested him. In an interview with Brenda Scott Royce, Klemperer said, "They were sitting around Feldman's office going through the *Players Directory*, and they came by my picture, and

Crenna said, 'There's your Klink,' and Feldman said, 'That's ridiculous. He does heavies, he does straight stuff, he doesn't do comedy.' And Crenna repeated, 'That's your Klink.' And they called me."

In the beginning, the son of world-renowned German conductor Otto Klemperer and grandson of author Victor Klemperer (who published a thorough accounting of the Jewish Klemperers' life in Germany pre-Nazi era and subsequent escape from their homeland following Hitler's rise to power: *I Will Bear Witness, 1933-1941; To the Bitter End, 1942-1945;* and *The Lesser Evil, 1945-1959*) believed the role of Klink was going to be another drama, similar to previous roles he had done.

"When I arrived to read the material with the producers, I was stunned," Klemperer said. "Somehow, the creative people failed to inform me that the show was a comedy. But I had no reservations. The monocle and riding crop were my idea. I based Klink on what I had known or read about the German aristocracy. About their pomposity. And their emotional sterility. To a degree, I based him on the crown prince of Kaiser Wilhelm. He was a very pompous, aristocratic stock-type personality."

In making his decision to accept the offer to portray Klink, Werner Klemperer had one important request—that Colonel Klink always remain the fool. He would play the German kommandant "as long as I can be sure to put him in the place he belongs. I wouldn't want to play Klink if he were a hero," he said. "This is not the modern, suave Nazi image. Klink is very much possessed by the old Prussian, aristocratic image. He is not very bright, is vain, pompous, and quite a coward. To play him, I keep thinking arthritic. Then physically and mentally, everything shrinks. He's tragically comical but never completely stupid because he must be a real person, and he must at all times be in the wrong. His vanity and pompousness are his undoing."

When Klemperer explained the series to his father, however, there was some confusion. His father was seemingly happy for his son for obtaining the work, but he did not understand the plot. The elder Klemperer asked, "Who is the author?" Unable to answer without causing further angst, Werner Klemperer abandoned the conversation, admitting later in an interview, "How do you explain?"

John Banner had always been a strong contender for either of the leading German roles, but at first, it was uncertain which role he should play—Colonel Klink or Sergeant Hans Schultz, the sergeant of the guard. Writer Richard M. Powell, who had revised the pilot script for production, gave his opinion to Fein and Feldman, which was for John Banner to play Schultz. After careful consideration and Klemperer's dynamic screen test with Bob, the decision became clear, and Sergeant Schultz was born.

"I adored John Banner," wrote Robert Clary in his autobiography *From the Holocaust to Hogan's Heroes*. "I had lots of scenes with him, and it was a wonderful challenge… He knew how to make his part even better than it was written. Even though I'm quite a scene stealer myself, I learned a lot from him. What a joy it was working with him."

"To my kids," Bob declared, "he's Santa Claus."

Schultz's unwillingness to take sides was part of the character's amorality. Ed Feldman explained that Schultz's neutrality was basically an "instrument of Hitlerism," meaning that while he may not have agreed with Hitler and the Nazi regime, he also did what he personally had to do to stay alive. Schultz was neither stupid nor foolish; he simply had no loyalties except to himself. "You think Schultz is stupid? Notice that he survives," John Banner said.

"Schultz is in the category of those who don't take sides," Feldman said. "But that also means he's not to be considered one of the Heroes."

Bob added, "Schultz is neither stupid nor a traitor. He simply says, 'I see nothing; I know nothing.' He is a type that appears to have been common in Nazi Germany. The camp kommandant isn't stupid, either. He is an egomaniac who can be fooled when he is buttered up, which is what I do to him. It's not that the Germans in the show are stupid. We're just that clever."

Schultz was dubbed the "cuddly Nazi," and his signature line, "I know nothing," became an immortal and enduring catchphrase. Of his character, John Banner said, "There is no such thing as a cuddly Nazi. Maybe Göering was cuddly to his wife; he wasn't cuddly to the city of Rotterdam. I would refuse to play a sympathetic Nazi. Schultz is not a Nazi. I see Schultz as the representation of some kind of good in any generation."

In describing the relationship Hogan had with Schultz, Bob explained that Schultz was "the kind of guy who comes into the barracks and says, 'Colonel Hogan, I am sorry, but it has been reported that you have a radio here. I turn my back, and you give it to me.' I tell him just to take one out of a footlocker. He sighs and does. I then tell him, 'That's twenty-five dollars please,' and when he objects, I tell him it's ten dollars under cost."

Despite his Jewish heritage, John Banner embraced the role of Schultz, with Bob Crane, Richard Dawson, and Robert Clary all claiming Banner could even upstage dogs and small children.

"They can't upstage me," Banner quipped. "It's physically impossible."

French actor, singer, and artist Robert Clary, a Jewish Holocaust survivor, was cast as French prisoner Corporal Louis LeBeau, the chef. As a child, from September 23, 1942, at nine-thirty at night, when the Gestapo rounded up his entire family and took them away, to April 11, 1945, Clary was imprisoned in Nazi concentration camps, including Ottmuth, Blechhammer, Gross Rosen, and Buchenwald. He lost many of his relatives—including most of his immediate family—through Nazi atrocities. He has dedicated the latter part of his life to speaking about his experiences and educating others about the Holocaust.

Clary wrote in his biography, "My mother's last words were, 'Do whatever they tell you to do. Don't fight it.' It wasn't until a year later that I knew my parents had been asphyxiated in the shower rooms at Auschwitz. When the American armies were coming closer, the Germans started to evacuate the camp. First, all the Jews were ordered to Dachau. A Czech named Zak saved my life by hiding me away. Then the SS gave orders to kill everybody that was left, a mass massacre. Suddenly, it was very quiet: no guards, no SS, no Germans, no dogs even. At four o'clock in the afternoon of April 11, 1945, the GIs of the U.S. Third Army arrived at the gates of Buchenwald."

Clary agreed to accept the role of LeBeau, first because it was a job, and second, because he understood it as the parody it was meant to be and a way to fight back using humor.

Richard Dawson, whom cast and crew called Dickie, was cast as British prisoner Corporal Peter Newkirk, a con man adept at slight of hand. A vaudevillian entertainer turned actor and very well known in England, Dawson's career in the United States was just taking off—much like Bob Crane's—at the time *Hogan's Heroes* went into production. Although not the all-American look the producers had sought, Dawson was, indeed, perfect for the sly, rugged, Cockney Englander they desired.

In a rare interview shortly before his death, Dawson explained exactly how he came to be cast as Newkirk. "Suddenly, Mike Dann appeared, who was a big wig at CBS, who was a very nice man. Very good at making suggestions and that would make him popular with artists… He came, and we were all on the set, and he came to my dressing room with Eddie Feldman. And he said, 'We're very pleased…' I said, 'Oh, good. I'm glad.' He said, 'The only thing, no one can understand you.' And I said, 'I don't understand that. When I do that, we often have to do it again because it's crude. People would laugh. I mean, I wouldn't do it deliberately if I thought no one could understand. Otherwise, write me out of the thing.' He said, 'No, no, but where's it from?' And I said, 'Liverpool. You know, they all talk like that.' He said, '*Why* do they talk like that?' I said, 'I don't know. We don't care, you see. We don't ask you how you talk.' And he said, 'Truly, can you pick somebody else. Another dialect?' 'I just can't do that,' I said. So I went around, a Scot, you know. Most films with an English person in an American film, to them, was the Cockney. [In a Cockney accent]: *Get me to the church on time!* So I said to Eddie, 'I can do a Cockney for you.' And he sad, 'Are they, ah, sort of naughty people. Do they pick pockets, and that?' Ha ha! They started it! Are you kidding me? So I'll do that. And I became Newkirk. And everything was fine."

Singer and actor Larry Hovis, who appeared in the pilot as escaping prisoner Lieutenant Carter, was later signed on for the regular role of the naïve American kid and munitions expert, Sergeant Andrew Carter. In show business since seven years of age, Hovis had "toured Texas as a boy soprano until his voice changed," and he also won a contest with the Arthur Godfey Talent Scouts. A jazz and blues vocal artist who reportedly ate only meat and bread (no vegetables, fruits, or dairy), Larry Hovis considered himself a singer on par with Frank Sinatra. Hovis was also a writer for and member of the original cast of *Laugh-In*, which he performed during his 1966 hiatus from *Hogan's Heroes*. He was then forced to choose between the two shows, and he opted for *Hogan's Heroes*, claiming that would prove better for his career.

"I could have stayed with *Laugh-In*," Hovis explained, "but I knew *Hogan's Heroes* was sure to go at least five years, and I felt that was important to my career and my security."

Hovis and Richard Dawson, who became close friends, eventually penned at least two scripted segments for *Hogan's Heroes*, which impressed Ed Feldman enough to use (episodes are unknown). In between takes on the set, Hovis and Dawson would often play cards, and according to a 1965 report, would engage in "non-sequitur conversations, each saying what pops into his head, bouncing off material to while away the hours."

Rounding out the long-term cast of prisoners was Ivan Dixon, a serious African-American actor with ambitions of becoming a director. Dixon would play Sergeant Ivan (sometimes James) Kinchloe, or "Kinch," the communications expert and radioman. Born in Harlem, Ivan Dixon had been the regular "stand-in" man, or screen double, for Sidney Poitier, doubling for him in small roles and "perilous stunt work," such as in the film *The Defiant Ones*. He believed himself to be the only straight man (non-comedic part) on *Hogan's Heroes* and said, "In the past, I've done mostly dramatic shows. I've never had much experience working with comedians. This gang of cut-ups is really teaching me a lot of new acting tricks."

As a black actor trying to find work in the 1960s, Dixon struggled. During this era, black characters were often written as "ditch diggers" or "cop outs."

"The situation is improving," he said in 1969, "in that there are more jobs for black actors—and the parts are better and less [one]-dimensional. I would never take one of those shuffling parts, but I did take a lot of one-dimensional roles and a lot of what I call 'cop-out' parts. Those are the ones where at the very end, the character cops out. There aren't so many of these parts around now. I think most producers are sincere, and they are trying to make up for the injustices of the past. But let's face it, they also recognize the good economics of using Negroes."

Of his work as Kinch on *Hogan's Heroes*, Dixon said, "Every role can't be Hamlet. It's a regular job, and it's income. Maybe it's not as satisfying as some things I have done, but the greatest asset is the producer allows us to do outside jobs, if they come up. But there aren't that many good parts. One year I did the *Final War of Olly Winter* and *The Fugitive*. If it hadn't been for *Hogan's Heroes*, the year would have been a financial disaster."

At the time of Ivan Dixon's death in March 2008, his daughter Nomathande said, "It was a pivotal role as well, because there were not as many blacks in TV series at that time. He did have some personal issues with that role, but it also launched him into directing." As an African American fighting for equal rights, Dixon sought a more complex character in Kinchloe. However, on the set itself, no one spoke of any racial injustice. Bob was, as best school friend Charlie Zito noted, "color blind." It would seem the rest of the cast and crew were as well.

To help increase female sex appeal on a show with nearly an all-male cast, an attractive lady was necessary. So Colonel Klink was given a pretty secretary—Fräulein Helga—played by Cynthia "Cindy" Lynn.

"First, they didn't even want to see me because I was a nobody," Cindy explained. "I did *Bedtime Story* with Marlon Brando, of course, but the girl had to have pretty legs because Bob was going to give her a pair of nylons for the pilot. She had to raise her legs and say, "Oh, Colonel Hogan, I haven't had nylons in *years!*" Then he says, "Don't you know there's a war on?" And my legs had to show. I go into Eddie Feldman's office, I'm sitting there, had my short skirt on, and he's interviewing me. I didn't even *read*. I crossed my legs, and he saw I had pretty legs, so I got the part. Later on he came to me and said, 'You were such a lady that I didn't know how to ask for you to stand up and raise your skirt, but luckily you crossed your legs, so I saw you had pretty legs, so I didn't have to ask you. So, that worked.' I didn't even read for them! They didn't even know if I *could* read! They just wanted my legs."

Leonid Kinskey, a versatile character actor perhaps best known for his appearance in the film *Casablanca* as Sascha, the Russian bartender, won the role of Vladimir Minsk, the Russian prisoner and tailor, in the *Hogan's Heroes* pilot. However, his character was omitted when the series went into production.

Semi-regular members of the predominately male cast would come to include Leon Askin as Luftwaffe General Albert Burkhalter (whose character was known as Colonel Burkhalter in the pilot), Howard Caine as Gestapo Major Wolfgang Hochstetter, Jon Cedar as Wehrmacht Corporal Langenscheidt, and Bernard Fox as British Royal Air Force Colonel Rodney Crittendon. Representing the fairer sex, Arlene Martel was cast to portray French spy Marie Louise Monet (Tiger), and Nita Talbot was cast as Marya, a Russian spy. Two actresses—Kathleen Freeman and Alice Ghostley—would appear in the recurring role of General Burkhalter's sister Gertrude Linkmeyer.

"Ed Feldman cast actors who had backgrounds authentic to their roles," explained Robert Clary. "Richard Dawson was born in England. Banner and Leon Askin were both from Austria; I was born in France. Werner Klemperer was born in 1920 in Cologne, Germany, and spent his childhood in Berlin."

And Connecticut-born Bob Crane was the all-American, quick-witted, and fast-talking radio personality who had kept all of Hollywood on its toes with his on-air interviews. As Bob described, "Hogan is an extension of what I used to do on radio. Say I'd be talking to Eddie Fisher. After a warm-up, I'd say, 'Now Eddie, tell us exactly what did happen in Rome,' then I'd zing into a record. Now I put my arm around the kommandant's shoulder and say, 'I understand you're coming up for a promotion,' then I change the subject. What I do as Hogan is a lot like what I did on the radio. It's having great fun but not out to hurt anyone. It's Peck's bad boy; keep a straight face and put the Nazis on."

With the key players in place, the cast and crew of *Hogan's Heroes* (with earlier working titles of *Hogan's Raiders* and *The Heroes*) reported first to Desilu Cahuenga Studios at 846 N. Cahuenga Boulevard in Hollywood (now Red Studios), and then to the Forty Acres Backlot in Culver City on Thursday, January 7, 1965, to begin work on the pilot, entitled "The Informer."

Robert Butler was commissioned to direct the pilot episode, but he had not been the first choice of the producers. When initial shooting of the pilot began, the first director bowed to the pressure of a controversial series and resigned. But Butler was delighted at the opportunity to direct the pilot episode and readily accepted. He took his time with it, and according to Clary, he was meticulous and sought perfection. Filming the pilot was to have lasted ten days; however, it stretched for several days longer, with production finally wrapping on the evening of Tuesday, January 19.

"Pilots are a complete joy," Butler said, "because a director is *really* directing. Everybody is *hungry*. They have no knowledge of how the show is to be done or how they're to behave or what the reality on the film will be like. *They—know—nothing.* Now directorially, theoretically, *you* know *everything*. You're in the dark, too, because it's a first. But directorially, you are the leader, and you are the one to whom everyone turns for the answers to those questions. What are we doing, how do we play it, how big is it, how realistic, how naturalistic, how farcical, in the case of a comedy? How funny should we be? How real should we be? It is just a general attack that you are able to bring to the project, unblemished, untouched, unpatterned by any previous activity.

It's a *joy*. You're *really* directing. You're really beginning at the ground floor and building the whole thing up."

In directing the pilot episode, Robert Butler explained that he wanted to craft Hogan as "heroic in the extreme." He instructed Bob to play Hogan as such.

"A lot of comedies—and maybe all comedies—have a character in the lead who's beyond growth and change," Butler said. "He leads *everyone*. *Nothing* is a problem. 'Follow me men, I'll get us out of it. LeBeau is gonna be shot at dawn? *No way!* Let's figure it out guys, *right now*. Let's roll up our sleeves.' It's all very cavalier, and it's all kind of one note, in a way. As far as a spark of the character, a development, a growth, I suppose there are individual moments in the *whole* show where Hogan is taught a life lesson. But that's not so important. What's important is that you have this cavalier, bigger-than-life leader who's never really frightened or daunted by anything. That's one of the really good notions."

Jerry London recalled the grueling schedule they all maintained during production of the pilot, and how *Hogan's Heroes* helped him advance in his career. "Edward Feldman, the producer, actually was one of the producers of commercials when we did *I Love Lucy*. I was on *I Love Lucy,* and he worked for one of the agencies making the commercials. I was in the editing department at Desilu. So I got to know him, and eventually, he hired me to cut a few commercials. Then he called me one day and said, 'Hey, I'm doing a pilot. Why don't you come over and edit it for me?' So this was the pilot of *Hogan's Heroes*. I went over, and we did the editing, and it was a real push. I remember I worked ninety hours to get it ready because Ed had to show it to the network. I worked over the weekend and did a whole bunch of stuff. And before you know it, as soon as I finished the edits, two days later, we were on the air. So I started as an editor, worked my way up to assistant producer, then associate producer, and then he gave me a directing break. And that's how I started my directing career."

Changes were coming to the show already, even though it had barely begun. In February 1965, shortly after the series secured a place in the CBS fall lineup, the president of CBS Television, James Aubrey, was fired without explanation.

John A. "Jack" Schneider was appointed president of CBS Television following Aubrey's dismissal. Immediately, *Hogan's Heroes* underwent style and casting changes, some of which may have been politically motivated. One change was that the Russian POW played by Leonid Kinskey was eliminated from the series. It is unclear if Kinskey backed out of the series after learning of Aubrey's dismissal or if Schneider eliminated Kinskey's role. Some affiliated with *Hogan's Heroes* claim the character was deliberately written out of the series.

"I remember Leonid Kinskey, the Russian, was much too old for the part," explained Robert Butler. "But he was a favorite of Jim Aubrey, who ran CBS at the time. So it was forced upon us that Kinskey be placed in the pilot as the mad Russian tailor. He was subsequently taken off the show. He had been in those great comedies in the 1930s and 1940s, and by the time *Hogan's Heroes* came along, he was, I think, too old to be reasonable in the part."

However, Kinskey maintained that it had been his decision to leave, stating that when he saw the German SS uniforms. "Something very ugly rose in me," he sai. "I visualized millions upon millions of bodies of innocent people murdered by Nazis. One can hardly, in good taste, joke about it."

After Kinskey's departure, Stuart Moss, who had played Sergeant Olsen, the "outside man," in the pilot, was approached to remain on the series as a regular. Moss declined, claiming he did not want a long-term commitment to a television series. Moss did, however, return frequently to guest star throughout the show's entire run. At that time, Larry Hovis was asked to join the cast as a regular, and he accepted, agreeing to play Sergeant (formerly Lieutenant) Carter. The main cast came to be Bob Crane, Werner Klemperer, John Banner, Robert Clary, Richard Dawson, Larry Hovis, and Ivan Dixon, all of whom signed a five-year contract with Bing Crosby Productions for their regular roles on *Hogan's Heroes*.

The pilot episode was filmed in black and white, similar to most television shows of the era. Following Aubrey's termination, the unprecedented decision was made to switch *Hogan's Heroes* from a black-and-white production to color. It was an expensive decision, and it would make *Hogan's Heroes* one of the first television series to be filmed in color. Yet Ed Feldman persevered, insisting, correctly, to the new head of CBS that color film would enhance the final production and be more appealing to audiences, thus guaranteeing longevity both during its original run and in syndication.

Having the pilot episode in black and white with the remainder of the series to be filmed in color presented an early problem, but one that did not linger. Bob Crane claimed he was not worried at all about

First Press about *Hogan's Heroes*

Bob Crane kept meticulous notes about how *Hogan's Heroes* fared in the ratings game in his two leather-bound *Hogan's Heroes* scrapbooks. On the second page of the first volume, three clippings are preserved and are included here.

Crane One of Bing's TV Pilot 'Heroes'

Bob Crane has been signed to star in a new CBS-TV series, "Hogan's Heroes," to be filmed at Desilu for Bing Crosby Productions. A regular [these] past two years [on] "The Donna Reed Show," Crane also has conducted a morning show on KNX since 1956. "Heroes" will be produced by Ed Feldman.

—Clipping from trade magazine, January 5, 1965

Bob Crane Finally Captured by TV

An established disc jockey with a safe and secure income of $100,000 a year might be considered out of his cerebral orbit to give it all up for the uncertainty of a television series. Bob Crane, Hollywood's best-known and most successful radio personality, is taking that gamble. But no one who has seen a preview of "Hogan's Heroes," the new CBS-TV comedy series about a prisoner of war camp in which Bob will star this fall, thinks it's a gamble. The predictions are unanimous that the show will be one of the season's big hits, with Crane emerging as one of TV's bright new stars.

—Bill Irvin, "Chicago American," May 11, 1965

Crane Exits KNX for TV: Rege Cordic Replaces Him

Bob Crane is giving up a $70,000-plus annually spot on KNX to devote his time to "Hogan's Heroes," new CBS telefilm series in which he stars and will be replaced shortly by Rege Cordic, from KDKA Radio, Pittsburgh. Crane for the last eight years has presided during the early mornings at KNX, doing 20 hours weekly.

—Friday, June 4, 1965

the supposed dilemma and was merely happy that CBS had greenlighted the series. Werner Klemperer agreed with the decision to film in color, explaining his belief that if one shoots a starkly dramatic work, black and white is suitable to capture the essence of the serious storyline. The opposite would be true for comedies, which are lighter, and a color production compliments the humor. Ed Feldman was also unconcerned, stating that he didn't think anyone would even notice.

The changes were implemented, and production began. The pressure was on for *Hogan's Heroes* to be a hit. *Everyone* yearned for its success. They were excited and enthusiastic about a comedy series that would prove to be both dramatic in its setting and grounded in its character development.

Bob perhaps carried the heaviest public burden. If *Hogan's Heroes* were to succeed, then as its star, Bob would naturally reap some of the greatest public accolades. But if the series faltered, if *he* were not likeable, if *he* were not convincing in his part, if *he* did not bring the viewers in every week, then Bob, as the leading actor in the series, would most likely be singled out as one of the primary targets as the reason for the show's failure.

As if to drive this point home, at 10:04 a.m. on June 22, 1965, the new CBS Television president sent a Western Union Telegram to Bob on the set of *Hogan's Heroes*. It read:

> YOU KNOW HOW IMPORTANT THIS SERIES IS TO
> US AND I KNOW YOU WON'T LET US DOWN.
> GOOD LUCK.
> JACK SCHNEIDER

On the same day, at 4:51 p.m., CBS producer Perry Lafferty also sent Bob a Western Union Telegram that read:

> DEAR BOB
> BEST WISHES AT THE BEGINNING OF WHAT I
> KNOW WILL BE A LONG AND SUCCESSFUL AS-
> SOCIATION.
> PERRY LAFFERTY

CBS had made it quite clear: *Hogan's Heroes* must be a winner. They would accept nothing less. Neither would Bob. But with a starring role on a TV series and his regular job at KNX, Bob's already manic schedule would now be nothing short of insane. Something had to give.

Bob's intention was to continue at KNX while filming *Hogan's Heroes*, working both jobs simultaneously the same way he had done when he worked on *The Donna Reed Show*. On May 6, 1965, Bob entered into another one-year contract with CBS to continue his morning program at KNX from 1965-1966. By this time, the agreements between Bob and KNX were fairly informal, with Bob himself even claiming that they were more or less a handshake deal, even though signed contracts did exist. Bob enjoyed his work in radio, and KNX knew Bob was their top commodity.

However, after filming the first several episodes of *Hogan's Heroes*, the arrangement soon proved to be far more difficult than Bob or anyone else had anticipated. There was a big difference between being part of a supporting cast and carrying the lead role in a series. Nevertheless, Bob struggled to maintain both jobs.

"I did both *The Donna Reed Show* and my radio show for two years," Bob said. "But that was a situation where I wasn't in every scene. I wasn't Donna Reed in other words. But in this series, I *am* Donna Reed."

The dual career arrangement was to be short-lived. By June 1965, Bob had discovered that juggling two full-time and highly prolific careers was irrational—and impossible. He could not perform both jobs well, take care of himself and his family, and remain sane. It became too much.

"People were swarming around me with fresh cups of coffee, foot massages, and soothing words," Bob had said, "and it suddenly hit me what the trouble was—I was just too darned tired. I had pushed it. When we first started the new series, I was falling apart physically. That's when I decided I couldn't do the radio show too. I tried to carry on until January [1966] after my replacement for radio was hired. But one day, I just started forgetting my lines. That was the day I made up my mind to quit the [radio] show. Being on radio and starring in a TV series at the same time means waking up at five-thirty a.m., going to do four hours of radio, then running down to the set and staying there until seven-fifteen at night, then getting my makeup off and going back to the radio station to get my music ready for the next day, getting home at nine-thirty, eating dinner, looking at my lines for a few minutes, and then falling asleep. I got so I was Uncle Daddy to my kids. 'My wife, what's her name' and all those jokes were apropos. When I'd drive in the driveway, the kids would say, 'Hey, here comes Bob Crane.' I got Bob Sutton (general manager of KNX) on the phone and said, 'I've had it, buddy. I'm bugging out early,' and that was that. Fortunately, there is such a great group of guys over there that they understood."

Despite the signed contract, CBS and KNX realized that it was dangerous to Bob's health for him to continue at full capacity in both

Hogan's Heroes and at KNX. So, with the approval of KNX and CBS, Bob bowed out of radio.

It was a pivotal decision for Bob to leave the medium he had always loved and that had made him both wealthy and famous. After more than fifteen consecutive years behind the microphone, from one coast to the other, Bob hosted "The Bob Crane Show" live for the last time over KNX on Monday, August 16, 1965.

Having given up both *The Donna Reed Show* and now KNX, Bob knew *everything* hinged on *Hogan's Heroes* being a success. In addition, he also decided to take part in the show's profit participation, in which actors were given the opportunity to allocate a percentage of their salary to a profit-sharing plan, with the idea that if the series were successful, it would also do well in syndication. During syndication, those who took part in profit participation would see some of the royalties. Thus, Bob and other members of the cast and crew decided to invest in *Hogan's Heroes*. As official profit participants of the series, they comprised the group known as "Hogan's Horde."

However, this did not mean Bob or other profit participants would see an immediate windfall—or any windfall, for that matter. The profits would come only after the series became successful, ran for an extended period of time, and was then eventually cancelled and pushed into syndication. It was a risk Bob was willing to take. As part of his initial five-year *Hogan's Heroes* contract, Bob agreed to give back a hefty 17.5% of his salary to Bing Crosby Productions in the hopes the show would be a hit, ensuring a steady income while it ran in syndication during the years following its cancellation. Later, after the five-year contracts had expired, each profit participant could renegotiate their percentage. In 1970, during Bob's contract renegotiation, he increased his percentage from 17.5% to 25% for seasons six and seven (had a seventh season been produced). As a primary profit participant, Bob established an entity to officially represent his legal share of *Hogan's Heroes*—Bob Crane Enterprises.

"It won't mean a damn moneywise till we're off the network," Bob said. "We just keep investing the profits over and over. Until it goes off, I'm just a paid employee like everybody else."

But the show had to be a success first, and that meant a lot more work. Bob promoted the series heavily. Every *Hogan's Heroes* photo shoot was without remuneration, all in the effort to help sell the series to the viewing audience and sponsors. In 1965, thousands of promotional photographs were taken of Bob and the cast and released to the media. Within a year, Colonel Hogan was suddenly everywhere—in magazines and newspapers, on a school lunchbox and Thermos®, on the covers of Dell comic books, on a set of Fleer Trading Cards, on a school writing tablet, and in the *Hogan's Heroes* Bluff Out Game. One promotional photograph shows Bob in his standard Hogan uniform munching on an apple while reading a *Hogan's Heroes* comic book, his *Hogan's Heroes* lunchbox resting on the bench beside him. For that photo shoot and all others, Bob received nothing. They were all done to sell the series so that profits would come later.

Members of the cast also made public appearances to promote the series. During those times, the cast would perform routines in costume. In June 1966, Bob Crane and Werner Klemperer journeyed to Venezuela to promote the series, which was to air on a Caracas television station. The Venezuelan station paid for their entire trip and "entertained them lavishly." They also stopped at several Caribbean islands where *Hogan's Heroes* was shown.

"Except for Canada, this was my first promotion trip outside the U.S. for *Hogan's Heroes*," Bob said. "Even in our country, everybody was asking, 'How can you be funny about the Nazis?' They were disappointed that we didn't bring John Banner, who plays Schultz, the guard, whom they love. Apparently his sympathy for the American prisoners strikes a chord for them. He would have been mobbed in Caracas by the Germans there."

While in Venezuela, Bob also discovered that the voiceover actor who dubbed his voice sounded "just like Marcello Mastroianni," an Italian film actor with "a deep, resonant voice." Bob was reportedly slightly embarrassed when he read his cue cards and the Venezuelan people heard him speak for the first time, his "high-pitched, piping voice" not at all being what they were used to hearing. Bob and Klemperer had been scheduled to continue on to Australia and New Zealand, but Australia cancelled their tour. The Australians were "miffed" that Bob and Werner were going to take a short detour to New Zealand to attend an ex-POW convention. "They wanted me for the whole three weeks, or not at all," Bob said. "So I guess I'll have to do that one later."

In other promotions, John Banner appeared at state fairs and performed in a rock and roll band in his Schultz uniform. A cast party was held in Ocotillo Lodge in Palm Springs, California, where the lodge was made over to resemble a POW camp. By orders of CBS, Bob was obliged

Welcome to Stalag 13, Colonel Hogan

The King of the LA Airwaves Resigns from Radio for Prison Life

The following are two trade magazine clippings preserved in Bob Crane's "Hogan's Heroes" scrapbooks.

The Los Angeles Times
Sunday, June 13, 1965
Excerpt from "The Radio Beat: 'Farewell (Sob!) to Bob Crane'"
by Don Page

Last week, Bob Crane told a quivering radio industry that he will bid adieu to his morning following on KNX… Crane has served KNX nobly. His ratings have been admirable, his salary remarkable, and his work unique. No shrinking violet, he created the image of an ultra self-confident performer who pleases himself more than anybody. His radio interviews with show folk were controversial, egotistical, and almost always entertaining. His feuds were contrived and stabbing (from personal experience). And we thank him for the 50,000-watt publicity.

Crane hopes to get out before [Rege] Cordic enters, perhaps by mid-summer. "I'm not going to make a big deal out of it," he said. "I'm just going to say it's been nice, we've all made money, and goodbye. No testimonials, no memory lane, no nothing."

Crane has been considering his own TV series for years, turning down numerous offers, he claims. Consequently, he was working under a handshake contract with KNX while he perused series ideas and scripts. Meanwhile, he'd approach KNX with, "Well, let's try it (radio) again for another year." Crane felt it wasn't fair to continue with this flimsy agreement…

Candidly, he says he'll miss radio because "I won't have a place to say what's on my mind every day. I have a lot on my mind, and I've got to express myself. I'll miss radio for that."

The Hollywood Reporter
Tuesday, August 17, 1965
Excerpt from "Rambling Reporter"
by Mike Connolly

Bob Crane had everyone except Haya Harareet on his close-out KNX caper yesterday. He re-ran the best of his taped interviews with the likes of Gypsy Rose Lee, Jerry Lewis, Shelley Berman, Dick Van Dyke, Fred Astaire, Dick Whittinghill, and the little old newslady from 1st and Spring, and there hasn't been such total disintegration since Trimalchio's mad banquet in the "Satyricon." … Save those tapes, Bob. Radio isn't dead yet.

to wear his *Hogan's Heroes* uniform during most of his public appearances. Occasionally, in the early days of promoting the series, Bob was often met with confused looks by present-day soldiers, saluting out of habit but with uncertainty. They would recognize his military attire, but it was obviously the wrong time period. Further, Hogan's uniform, complete with the "50 Mission" crush cap, was considered non-regulation and reserved for the barracks, and was too casual to wear in a public setting, even during the 1940s. Until the series and his character became known, people generally did not know what to make of seeing him at first. "Ye gads! The Flying Tigers are back!" a bystander once said to him.

Some cast members and crew did not believe CBS promoted *Hogan's Heroes* as much as it could or should have. Robert Clary told Brenda Scott Royce, "Shows like *Beverly Hillbillies* and *Gunsmoke* took advantage of their popularity and they went to opening markets and to fairs and everything. We could have done it because the three times we went to the meetings of the affiliates in Washington and Chicago, we did our act. All the *Hogan's Heroes* did something, and it was very entertaining. Therefore, we could have done more; we could have gone to fairs, but we never did."

But Bob pushed himself. As he had done in radio, he made public appearances on his own, wearing the Hogan uniform, so people would see him and get to know him and his new character. One year, he made over two hundred sixty-five personal appearances, to the point where his doctor once again cautioned him to take better care of his health. He ran himself ragged while promoting the series and perfecting his character. *Hogan's Heroes* was a huge risk for Bob, but one that he was willing to take. The die cast, he placed his bets and gambled on the outlandish prison camp.

Hogan's Heroes debuted with "The Informer" on CBS on Friday, September 17, 1965, at eight-thirty in the evening Eastern/Central Time. Supporters rallied around the series and its star. Two Western Union telegrams that Bob received on the day *Hogan's Heroes* premiered are preserved in his *Hogan's Heroes* scrapbook. One was from Donna Reed and her husband Tony Owen; the other was from Jerry Lewis:

> DEAR BOB
> OUR LOSS IS AMERICA'S GAIN – STOP –
> HAVE A LONG HAPPY FRIDAY NIGHT LIFE.
> LOVE
> DONNA AND TONY
> —

> BEST OF LUCK FOR TONIGHT AND FOR THE EN-
> TIRE
> SEASON WHICH I KNOW WILL BE A SUCCESSFUL
> ONE.
> VERY SINCEREST BEST WISHES.
> JERRY LEWIS

Support for Bob and his new series continued into the season. Three weeks later, on September 29, 1965, Bob received another telegram, this one from Lucille Ball, which he also preserved.

> DEAR BOB
> I THINK HOGANS HEROES IS ONE OF THE REAL
> WINNERS THIS SEASON AND I THINK YOU ARE
> JUST GREAT. CONGRATULATIONS.
> PS IF I KNEW YOU BETTER I WOULD SIGN OFF
> LOVE LUCY.
> LUCILLE BALL

On October 6, 1965, another telegram arrived for Bob, this one from Paul West, associate producer of and writer for *The Donna Reed Show*.

> I AM DELIGHTED OVER THE SUCCESS OF YOUR
> NEW SERIES BOB. NO ONE WORKED HARDER TO
> ACHIEVE IT. NO ONE DESERVES IT MORE.
> SINCEREST CONGRATULATIONS.
> PAUL WEST.

Then, Bob received a signed letter in the mail from Jerry Lewis dated October 8, 1965. It read:

> Dear Bob:
> I am completely delighted with *Hogan's Heroes*.
>
> After seeing the show, it is evident that it's going to run a long time, and I intend to be a constant viewer.
>
> Kindest regards,
> Jerry Lewis
> A Fan

Hogan's Heroes was, in fact, going to be a hit. Bob was thrilled with the series and his role in it.

"When I took the step from radio to this," Bob said, "everyone told me, 'My God, what happens if the TV show lasts a few weeks and goes off? You're giving up $75,000 a year.' I just felt confident enough to take the gamble. It paid off."

According to those affiliated with the series, from the outset, the cast and crew of *Hogan's Heroes* "clicked." There was no outward animosity, no hostility, no egomaniacs, no thoughts of entitlement. They worked together as an ensemble—from the producers to the star to the cast to the directors to the writers to the cameramen to the prop men to the gaffer—each with the same goal—the success of the series. According to actor Robert Hogan, for whom the series was named, those on the *Hogan's Heroes* set were *professional*.

"Be professional," Hogan said. "Learn your lines. Hit your marks. Say them and try and do your job. And they were that. If there was slight kidding around, it was in the best of humor. When you're relaxed, you can enjoy that stuff. The banter doesn't hurt, doesn't get you on your toes. It relaxes you. It was that feeling on the set."

"In the case of *Hogan's*, the guys were all very, very nimble; very experienced in comedy, and being virtually an all-male cast, it was very butch and very locker room," Robert Butler added. "The guys were all very funny with each other because nobody could get away with *anything*, namely some ego trip or some grandiosity, or anything like that. So it was kind of pure and a *lot* of fun. And the material was *very, very good*. Richard M. Powell, who rewrote the pilot script, was a very, very well-thought out comedy writer. It was interesting, too, because a lot of his stuff was a *little* quieter on the page than a lot of his cohorts, but better, richer, coming from character. I remember Bob Crane turning to one of Powell's first act curtain lines, which was simply "Let's eat!" Namely, let's forget this *big, heavy drama* that we're in. Life and death and Nazis, the prison camp, all of that stuff. Let's follow LeBeau's menu for today and have lunch and shove everything else. And it was funny! It just was delightfully characteristic of those very *cavalier*, disguised superheroes in a way. In rehearsal, Crane said, 'Listen, what about *Let's eat?*' And it was just *funny*. It was rich and funny, and very much more *the* series."

"It's the wildest comedy series to hit TV in many years, even in the history of TV," Bob declared, giddy with excitement and crediting the ensemble cast for their collective talent. "It's *Stalag 17*, *The Great Escape*, and *Terry and the Pirates*. It's not *Hamlet*. I think the teenagers will dig it. We do James Bond things. My son flipped, he's fourteen. The affiliates flipped. We like to get in a little bit of everything. I've been Doc Dave Kelsey on *The Donna Reed Show* for two years. I've always played the lecherous guy. I'm the lecherous colonel here. I go for the kommandant's secretary. She's Helga. His name's Klink. Schultz is the jailer. Schultz is a comic German name. He's a pussycat, a big walrus with a mustache. You know what the whole idea of this show is? It's a con. We were the last of the pilots to be made and the first to be sold. There are a lot of wonderfully funny guys in the cast. I love it, and I think we will surprise a lot of people."

Several years earlier, in 1961, two young men sat at a table in Santa Monica envisioning an interesting plot. Its location was a prison, where the prisoners were generally considered the good guys. The guards were buffoons, who looked the other way for their own means and uttered lines like, "I see nothing." The two men began drafting their ideas on paper, and before long, original characters began to take shape and emerge. Their work finally completed, they contemplated their options. Like countless other amateur screenwriters, they wondered if their original script would sell.

Friends Albert S. Ruddy and Bernard Fein wrote the first draft of the script that was to become the pilot episode of *Hogan's Heroes* purely for the fun of it. They never, in their wildest imaginations, expected to not only sell their script, but to see it launch a series that would become an overnight success.

A graduate of Southern California University School of Architecture, Al Ruddy took up writing as a hobby. After partnering with Fein on the script, it took the pair about one year to finalize the first draft of the pilot. Bernard Fein had been an actor, appearing in numerous television shows throughout the 1950s and early 1960s, and perhaps most importantly for *Hogan's Heroes*, was his work on *The Phil Silvers Show* as Private Gomez.

Elaborating on the early development of the pilot script, actor Robert Hogan said, "One of my dear friends is Bernie Fein, who's no longer with us. He would tell me the progression of the show. It didn't start off as a prisoner of war camp. Originally, the show was a prison in northwestern United States. It was really written for a guy like Phil Silvers, and he was going to manufacture stuff and then sell it to the

> ### Scrapbooks of a Star
>
> *During the first couple of years that "Hogan's Heroes" aired, Bob Crane kept two scrapbooks of photographs, newspaper clippings, ratings projections, and notations. Burgundy in color, they are leather bound with his name and the series' title embossed in classic gold print on the cover. In the front of the first volume on the reverse side of the January 7, 1965, call sheet and opposite page one of the pilot script, Bob wrote a journal entry. This brief, handwritten paragraph details the first outdoor shoot of the "Hogan's Heroes" pilot episode, "The Informer," and it captures Bob's thoughts about the day's work. It is reproduced here exactly as he wrote it on the evening of January 7, 1965. Unfortunately, this is the only detailed entry in either of his "Hogan's Heroes" scrapbooks.*
>
> Rained early morning, so camp shots postponed. Werner & I did early morning scene which ends show – similar to CBS-TV test scene we did. Came off well. Everyone happy. Had lunch with Feldman & [Fein] at MGM. Afternoon did barracks shot with G.I.'s. Clary looks good. Dawson nervous. Kinskey padding part as in rehearsal but good. Rest adequate to fair. Scene dragged. Had troubles with lines. Went out to 40 Acres at 6PM to film first exterior of Clary, Pitlik, & me plus dogs. Cold as hell. Took 2 hours to stage & shoot. Saw "Donna Reed Show" (guy flirting with Donna) in car on way home. Fair first day. Tomorrow we see rushes.
>
> ***Note:*** *In some regions, "dailies" are referred to as "rushes" or "daily rushes," depending on how quickly the film is developed. The episode of The Donna Reed Show Bob watched in the car on the way home was "Thy Name Is Woman," which originally aired on January 7, 1965.*

people outside the prison. Phil Silvers could do a great con man. They saw the humor in Silvers getting passes out of the cell to help rehabilitate the prisoners, but he would be just trying to make money, not rehabilitate them. Although of course, in the process, they would become rehabilitated. But the idea was to become funny Phil Silvers. So that's how it started."

Yet, the idea of a funny Phil Silvers-type in a U.S. penitentiary did not impress studios or producers. "When it didn't sell," Al Ruddy said, "we just changed the background to a POW camp."

Ruddy explained that there was another inspiration for the *Hogan's Heroes* setting change; he and others in connection with *Hogan's Heroes* had read in the trade papers about *Campo 44*, a situation comedy that was to take place inside an Italian prisoner of war camp during World War II. At the time, *Campo 44* was in its early stages of development.

"We thought the idea was *perfect*," Ruddy said. "We re-wrote our script and set it in a German POW camp in about two days."

Unfortunately for *Campo 44*, it premiered on NBC in 1967, two years after the premier of *Hogan's Heroes*. It did not fare well in the ratings and was criticized for being too slapstick and silly. Further, many believed it was a pathetic imitation of *Hogan's Heroes*.

Shortly after the setting change, other alterations were made—including changing the names of several main characters. It was during this time when the name Hans Schultz was given to the German sergeant of the guard. This decision would plague CBS, Bing Crosby Productions, and the creators and producers of *Hogan's Heroes* for several years. It just so happened that Schultz was the name of the guard in *Stalag 17*.

In 1967, the two writers of the Broadway play *Stalag 17*, Donald Bevan and Edmund Trzcinski, filed a Federal Court lawsuit against CBS and Bing Crosby Productions. The claimant stated that *Hogan's Heroes* was a blatant act of plagiarism of *Stalag 17*, which had been based on Trzcinski's personal experiences in Nazi Germany. They argued that *Hogan's Heroes* "appropriated the locale, background, and situation of *Stalag 17*, as well as specific characters and incidents." Once the suit was filed, Bevan and Trzcinski attempted to stop production of *Hogan's Heroes* until the trial, seeking an injunction against CBS and Bing Crosby Productions to cease broadcasting of the series. The injunction was denied, and the Courts decided to wait until the entire run of *Hogan's Heroes* was completed before bringing the lawsuit to trial.

Edmund Trzcinski had been so upset by the alleged plagiarism and subsequent lawsuit that he told one reporter in 1973 that if he and Bevan did not win the suit, he would commit suicide. On November 1, 1974, it was reported in the press that a financial settlement was finally reached. Bing Crosby Productions was to pay the authors of *Stalag 17* a combined sum of $300,000. The press further reported that "based on the money made from *Hogan's Heroes*, the idea was a steal."

Al Ruddy cited the lawsuit as "ridiculous," given the fact that he and Bernard Fein had initially wrote about a U.S. penitentiary. Although they later admitted using the name "Schultz" for German guard was a poor choice, Ruddy insisted, "Sergeant Schultz was a character I invented. I took the name from the Jack Benny film *To Be or Not to Be*. The Schultz character was important to the sitcom because it felt some sort of go-between was necessary between the prisoners and Klink."

Ruddy further recalled to Brenda Scott Royce his memories of the lawsuit. "I was in New York working on *The Godfather*, and I had to go downtown to appear as one of the witnesses… The jury actually decided in favor of the *Stalag 17* authors. What happened next was a rare occurrence—the judge reversed the jury's decision. It was called a bench reversal… The judge in this case thought it was ludicrous."

Schultz was not the only name change in the series. In early drafts, Colonel Sharp was the name Al Ruddy and Bernard Fein had given to their senior prisoner of war. When deciding on a new name for the wry American colonel, Bernard Fein thought of his dear friend, Robert Hogan.

"When I was talking to Bernie that night, he said, 'Oh, we changed the name of the character,' Robert Hogan explained. "I said, 'Oh, yeah? What?' He said, 'He's going to be Robert Hogan.' I said, 'That's a kick in the butt!' And he said, 'And we're calling the series *Hogan's Heroes*.' And I said, 'Wow! Good!' I didn't care. I just—'Whoopee! Sell the sucker!' It was fun for me, and I was thrilled that he filmed it."

Bernard Fein's widow Kay told Brenda Scott Royce that her husband had also offered the role of Colonel Hogan to Robert Hogan; however, the namesake of the series had a different recollection. According to Robert, he had never been a contender for the leading role of *Hogan's Heroes*, and as for the two guest-starring appearances, he said, "I got hired by begging, I guess." He insisted that even though he and Bernard Fein had been good friends, there was no prearrangement for him to work on the series. "You can't go walking in the casting office doing that," he said. "And Bernie was the kind of guy who wouldn't put any pressure on anybody to use somebody he knew."

Hogan's Heroes was the first deal Al Ruddy had ever secured in show business. He had no real connections at the time, but one of his friends—Mike Levy—was an agent. Levy took the pilot draft to CBS, and after about a two-month wait, Ruddy was called in for a meeting. Ruddy claims it was by chance and good fortune that *Hogan's Heroes* had found its way onto the list of shows under consideration for the 1965 fall lineup. But there was still one major hurdle to overcome—the World War II prison camp setting.

"I go to a meeting, and there I was sitting opposite William S. Paley, who owned the CBS network. All the executives were there, and they were going to decide what shows to do that year," Ruddy explained. "So I walked in, and I shook his hand, and Mike said, 'We're here to discuss the show Mr. Ruddy did called *Hogan's Heroes*.' And Bill Paley looked across the table at Mike and said, 'I find the idea of Nazis as comic characters to be totally reprehensible.' I thought Mike would have a heart attack and faint, but he just quickly said, 'I'll have Al Ruddy explain it to you.' At which point, I acted out the whole script. I did dog barks and machine gun sounds. I got down under the desk and said, 'I know *nothing*!' And Bill Paley started to laugh. I mean, he just literally started to *laugh*. When I got through, he stood up and said, 'I don't know if I could ever buy that show, but that is the funniest presentation I've ever seen.'"

A couple of months later, Al Ruddy received a call from his agent. CBS executives wanted another meeting. The network wanted to pick up the show. Now in the need of a production company, Ruddy and Fein signed the rights of the series over to Bing Crosby Productions in 1963. Both men were asked to remain with the series as producers and writers. Ruddy declined, having been more interested in continuing a career in the film industry rather than television. Fein, on the other hand, accepted, and along with Edward Feldman, became an associate producer on the series.

"I go up there, and they inform us they're going to do the show," Ruddy said. "When they asked if I wanted to stay with the show as one of the producers. I said I wasn't interested. My agent jumped up and asked if we could be excused. We went out into the hall, and he said, 'I don't get it; are your parents rich?' I said, 'No.' He said, 'I can get you on this show and get you some more money, and you tell me you don't want to do it.' I said, 'That's right.' He said 'Why?' I said, 'Mike, I never thought I'd get this money for doing nothing. Now that I have this money to support myself, I want to go do movies.' He said, 'What do you know about movies?' At which point *I* said, 'What do I know about television?' So I worked on the pilot, and I went off a month later, with misgivings about maybe I had been stupid, and in my arrogance in posturing myself like that. Because when *Hogan's Heroes* went on the air, it became an overnight hit. It was in the top ten."

Hogan's Heroes became extraordinarily popular with viewers very quickly. Laughs from a prisoner of war camp had proven worth the risk, and this "United Nations with barbed wire" was rated one of the top

Will the *Real* Robert Hogan Please Stand Up?

When choosing the name of their lead character, Colonel Robert E. Hogan, associate producers Edward H. Feldman and Bernard Fein never realized the ironies that would come with it.

Would *Sharp's Raiders* have been catchy enough to sell to CBS? Ed Feldman and Bernard Fein must not have believed so. Not liking the name Colonel Sharp, which was the original name of the leading character, Fein decided to name the colonel and the series after his good friend, Robert Hogan. An American television actor, Robert Hogan is best known for his work on numerous soap operas, including *Another World, General Hospital, Days of Our Lives,* and *One Life to Live*. Robert Hogan also guest starred in two episodes of *Hogan's Heroes*: "Reservations Are Required" and "Crittendon's Commandos." In June 2011, he guest starred in an episode of *Law & Order: Special Victims Unit*. It was never intended for Robert Hogan to be the star of *Hogan's Heroes*, and he was more overjoyed that his friend had sold the series to CBS than he was about Colonel Hogan being named after him.

Bob Crane is related to a Robert Hogan as well. Ironically, Bob's great-grandfather (on his father's side) was none other than Robert E. Hogan of Stamford, Connecticut, a toolmaker whose family had emigrated from Ireland.

And there is yet another Robert Hogan connected to *Hogan's Heroes*. Dr. Robert Steadham Hogan, an internist specializing in rheumatology, joined the U.S. Army Air Force in 1942, believing "it was his duty" to assist in the war effort. He climbed to the rank of lieutenant and served with the 450th Bombardment Group. As a B-24 Liberator pilot, he flew many missions beginning in November 1944. On January 19, 1945, following a successful bombing mission near Yugoslavia, Lt. Hogan's B-24, the "Daisy Mae," took a direct hit. Before it crashed, Hogan and his flight navigator, Chester Zukowski, were able to parachute to safety—but behind enemy lines. Hogan was taken prisoner and held as a prisoner of war at Stalag 13 in Nüremburg, Germany, where he remained for six months until the camp was liberated by Allied soldiers. Hogan had loved *Hogan's Heroes* and marveled at its striking similarities, claiming that the real kommandant at Stalag 13 wore a monocle just as Colonel Klink had done. However, the conditions at the real Stalag 13 were much harsher than what was seen on television. His son Richard explained that "the ground was so hard, and the men so hungry at Dad's camp, there was no energy to dig a way out like on the TV show." In 1966, and without telling his family, Dr. Hogan wrote a letter to Bob Crane, who was amazed by the story and the remarkable comparisons. CBS arranged for Bob to visit Dr. Hogan and the Hogan family in Birmingham, Alabama. Richard described meeting Bob Crane as one of the highlights in their family history. Lt. Dr. Robert S. Hogan passed away in 1981 at 58 years of age.

new shows for the 1965 Fall Season. It would seem *Hogan's Heroes* had something for almost everybody.

"For one thing," Bob explained, "the kids love Schultz. He's a grandfather image, I suppose. Our mail shows men love it when I give it to the Colonel, when I con him. The kids, especially the little girls, go for Bob Clary. He's short and French. Dick Dawson as Newkirk is getting through to the older girls with his English accent and Beatles haircut. We've even got dogs for animal lovers. Talk about having something for everyone, we've got it."

But not everyone was singing its praises. Despite its appeal, and thus, promising ratings, *Hogan's Heroes* was also controversial, and from the outset, it garnered just as much criticism as it did accolades. There were two points of criticism: first, the mistaken belief that the show was set in a concentration camp—which drew the ire of Jewish viewers; and second, the idea that the prisoners were not really prisoners and the Germans were inept fools, which angered Germans in America.

Most importantly, Stalag 13 was *not* a concentration camp. It was a prisoner of war camp, and while conditions were brutal for Allied servicemen being held in such camps, there was a big difference between a prisoner of war camp and a concentration camp. There was and is no ethical way *anyone* can make fun of the Holocaust and the atrocities brought on by Hitler and his Nazi regime. As for the second complaint, most of the Germans were not inept fools, but pompous egomaniacs who were bested by the Allied prisoners.

It was a question asked often of the *Hogan's Heroes* actors: "How can you play a role in a comedy about the Nazis?" They did it first because it was a job, but they also accepted the job because they understood the series for what it was—a parody and a satire. It was viewed as a way to fight back with the cutting edge of humor while keeping the reality of what the Nazis were and the imminent danger of what they were capable of hovering just around the corner.

Hogan's Heroes was also not the first nor will it be the last work to do so. In 1940, Charlie Chaplin produced and starred in *The Great Dictator*, and later, in 1968, Bob Crane's friend Mel Brooks released *The Producers*. The musical number "Springtime for Hitler" continues to be one of the film's highlights. *The Great Escape* and *Stalag 17* also contained their own brands of humor. In *The Great Escape*, the character of Hendley "The Scrounger," portrayed by James Garner, was often compared to Colonel Hogan during the early days of *Hogan's*

Heroes, and Bob was reportedly not worried about the comparisons. He said, "Hogan, like Garner in the movie, doesn't mind fighting the war so long as he lives well." In 2012, Paramount Pictures released *The Dictator*, directed by Larry Charles, about a dictator who risks his life to ensure that democracy would never come to the country he "so lovingly oppressed." Finally, the 2014 film *The Interview* is perhaps one of the most extreme examples of parody in recent days.

An early promotional tag line for the series did not help matters. Penned by Stan Freberg as part of an early ad campaign, the line "If you liked World War II, you'll love *Hogan's Heroes*," had only served to fuel the growing controversy. Bob also thought it was in bad taste, and during the run of the series, was eager to correct any misunderstanding it created.

"That line has haunted me for years," Bob said. "People expected Dachau and Buchenwald. It's not a concentration camp. It's a POW camp. We're not making light of atrocities. We're just trying to show how darn clever the Americans were. It was easy to see which letter writers *hadn't* watched the program. No one could see *Hogan's Heroes* and think we were making fun of war. Our comedy is done with characterization. It's outsmarting the boss; it's the kid with a snowball when the top hat goes by; it's getting the best of authority."

The cast and crew did not harbor any concerns once its concept as a parody was understood. "Robert Clary was in a concentration camp," said Cynthia Lynn. "My mother's girlfriends were in concentration camps. My mom almost got shot trying to help her Jewish girlfriend bring food. We went through all that. But it was a comedy, and so it really didn't affect anybody."

Richard Dawson further elaborated on the controversy. "Lots of people were cross with us for the wrong reason. You know? We had Jews in the show. Robert Clary came from Dachau! And he wouldn't do something that was making light of a concentration camp! This was a POW camp! So the moment that people saw it, that all fell out."

"People misunderstood," Bob explained. "[But] now that people have seen what we're doing, the opposition has died down."

Of anyone affiliated with *Hogan's Heroes*, Robert Clary perhaps had more right than anyone to be offended and angry—that is, if the series had honestly been guilty of making light of crimes against humanity and wartime atrocities. Yet the series did not, and thus, Clary had no problems with being in it. He wrote in his autobiography,

"When the show went on the air, people asked me if I had any qualms about doing a comedy series dealing with Nazis and concentration camps. I had to explain that it was about prisoners of war in a stalag, not a concentration camp, and although I did not want to diminish what soldiers went through during their internments, it was like night and day from what people endured in concentration camps. Prisoners of war were protected by the Geneva Convention, received Red Cross food packages, and would write and receive letters, even though they were censored. Solders were not forced to work in German factories, they were not guarded by the SS but by the Wehrmacht, and they were not sent to the gas chambers. I was an actor who was asked to play the part of a French corporal prisoner of war and not a little Jew in a concentration camp, and I never felt uncomfortable playing Louis LeBeau."

Bruce Bilson, of Jewish faith, enjoyed directing *Hogan's Heroes*. However, he had to watch the show first to fully understand its concept and setting. After seeing it, he was also not offended by it.

"The prisoner of war camp was really an issue at the beginning, I think, for me, personally," Bilson said. "I had to see the show. I heard about it. Very much it was people heard POW camp and were thinking concentration camp a little bit. That was part of it. Once I started working on the show, I had no problem with it. A very good director friend of mine wouldn't do the show because he had been a POW and thought that was nothing to make a joke about. And that was the only person that really, really objected to it personally. It was an issue, and they got past it."

Werner Klemperer also shared his feelings about the controversy. "In the beginning, there were people who didn't think it was right to give a comical aspect to that part of the war. But those protests died down relatively fast because the show was immediately embraced by the American public. I thought I saw the show for what it was: a satirical comedy. It was all done a little off center and tongue in cheek. It was never meant to be truly believed as something that really happened. I think that's why it was so successful."

The exterior scenes of *Hogan's Heroes* were filmed on what was known as the Forty Acres Backlot. Situated at the foot of the Baldwin Hills mountain range in Culver City, the Forty Acres Backlot had been home to many film and television productions. Today, what was the Forty Acres Backlot is now composed of storage units, offices, and housing developments. Bruce Bilson recalled the first time he reported to the *Hogan's Heroes* set at Forty Acres.

"One day a week was usually at the camp, which was not at the studio," Bilson said. "It's not there anymore, the piece of landscape that was called the Forty Acres. It was attached to what was once Selznick Studios. On that Forty Acres were Mayberry, Stalag 13, *Gomer Pyle's* Marine Corps base, and the remains of Tara from *Gone With The Wind* when it burned down, as well as the remains of the Atlanta train station. For the first episode I did, I had never been to the exterior location to really lay it out. So Friday, late afternoon, I drove there, and suddenly, there this nice Jewish boy was standing at this Nazi guard base as the sun was going down, all by myself, on this place. It was kind of a weird moment."

Cindy Lynn, born Zinta Valda Zimilis in Riga, Latvia, in 1936, fled Europe with her family during World War II. She had an experience on the series similar to that of Bruce Bilson. "The whole cast all got along so well. I got along great with everybody. The very first time, when we went into rehearsal, we all met around the table. But in the rehearsal, all of a sudden, it was so weird to see the German uniforms walk in. I freaked. My heart started racing. It was like, 'I'm back in Germany in the war.' It felt *really*, really weird. Because the Germans helped us because my mom was a singer, and we were running away from the Russians because we didn't want to be with the Russians, and it was kind of weird."

The series also took its fair share of abuse from other television producers. Al Ruddy recalled, "There were double-page ads in the *Los Angeles Times* and *New York Times* of a cargo ship submerged—half sinking and submarines, saying, 'For those who don't think World War II was funny, watch *Convoy*.' They were on opposite *Hogan's Heroes*. We made a joke of World War II, and this show was serious, they were trying to demean us by putting serious stuff on there."

The producers, cast, and crew were quick to defend the show's premise and explain its locale, but perhaps none more so than Bob Crane. As the network's "Johnny on the Spot," he advocated strongly for the series, addressing countless groups across the country, including former prisoners of war and World War II veterans. He discussed the basic principle of the series—for the Allies to win with the help of humor.

"There were some complaints in the beginning, but the real opposition stopped after we got on the air," Bob said. "A lot of groups that were really prepared to hate it—the Jewish organizations, for instance—suddenly saw that we were showing how damned clever the Allies were, not what patsies the Germans are—of course, that's all part of the plot that we make them look like patsies. The ex-POWs in Albuquerque, New Mexico, have an association. They had a convention and invited me. A lot of POWs are hooked on *Hogan's Heroes*. They're our biggest rooters—along with New York Jewish delicatessen owners! We're not on in Germany, but sometimes Germans who're visiting the set will say they've seen the show here. They'll say, 'We're not that stupid,' but they'll take it with a grain of salt. No one's uptight about it."

Bob was also quick to explain the difference between a prisoner of war camp and concentration camp. *Hogan's Heroes* would never broach the serious subject of the Holocaust, but it did touch on the hardships of prison life and the dangers of war.

"Jokes about rough trips on airplanes are funny—except right after a bad plane crash," Bob said. "To quote Steve Allen, tragedy becomes comedy after a period of time has passed. It's fantasy. I think the kids know that it's fantasy. And of course it couldn't be done using Vietnam or even Korea—it's still too close."

"Eventually, it changed," said Cindy Lynn of the negative response. "It all turned around and went away when they started seeing what it was all about. I got one letter saying, 'Well, at least you were with the Americans, and you were helping the Americans as Fräulein Helga'— that I was not on the Germans' side. I got fan mail because I was helping the good guys."

Despite the controversy, the majority of the viewing audience accepted the far-fetched prison camp scenario, and it reflected in the Nielsen ratings, ranking at number 7 in its opening week, and consistently holding in the top ten during its first season. In fact, the series held consistently high ratings during its entire run. Early ratings also hailed *Hogan's Heroes* as "TV's Top New Show!" during the week of October 12, 1965, when it ranked number one of all shows debuting during the 1965 fall season and fifth overall—behind *Bonanza, Bewitched, Gomer Pyle,* and *The Dick Van Dyke Show,* respectively. By December of that year, it was still in the top ten, closing out the year as seventh out of ninety-five shows on television.

Writers and producers were careful to keep the series light but also maintain realism. There had to be an element of danger, or the series would come off as being campy and completely unbelievable. Bob confessed that he did not agree with the large number of gimmicks in the pilot, feeling they had been too overdone and not necessary. After a few episodes, however, the series became more adventurous, and the element of danger became essential.

"It was a *terrific* equation for a show, in spite of the people who are offended by a comedy in a prison camp," said Robert Butler. "They have a point; if you're a serious philosopher, you can criticize it. But we're not serious philosophers. *Hogan's Heroes* is a war movie. You've got a hero who's Cary Grant or Humphrey Bogart or Bob Crane, with life and death, war and decapitation at every turn. It just works. Sadly, war works in drama. It just works like hell because there's just so much at stake, always. I'm battling, but that's part of the *click* because everything matters. It's not frivolous. It *matters*. You don't want people to *die*."

"I think on our show, we use taste," Bob explained. "Sure, we use a little slap-stick, but we're not a bunch of clods. We're not *Bilko*. We have adventure, but we're not *I Spy*. We have tension in our stories—if you lose that tension, we turn into *McHale's Navy*. Mainly, we use an old comedy technique—being brought down to size, and that's as old as time. Everybody likes to see the braggart get his comeuppance. Take Klink—he's such an egomaniac. Everybody likes to see Klink get bamboozled. Klink and Schultz may be jerks, but let me point out that the guys who come from headquarters in Berlin, these guys aren't jerks. If they were—down goes the tension, and we blow it all. If we sacrifice touches of reality for cheap laughs, we're dead. If Stalag 13 comes off as a country club, we've had it. The bit about the steam room in the stalag—we can't have too many gimmicks. We've got to go to character trait comedy, not one-joke concepts."

Of his own character, Bob said, "He is a gung-ho type, almost like a John Wayne. He can be flip in his relations with the camp kommandant, but in most situations, he is serious. When the heroes get too wild, he says, 'All right, knock it off!' I keep a close eye on the character, and if anything doesn't sound right in the script, I speak up about it. Series can be badly damaged when characterizations get out of hand. The whole concept of *Hogan's Heroes* is walking a thin wire. We got sharpsides, but we don't fall off. I walked on my own kind of wire for nine years on a radio show. People would say, 'No, he isn't a disc jockey. He's not a comic. What is he?' The only answer was, you've got to listen. *Hogan's Heroes* is no easier to pin down. People shouldn't be swayed by what they *think* the show's going to be like. They should see it, and I think they'll like it."

Many who worked on the set of *Hogan's Heroes* claimed that filming the series ran like a "well-oiled machine." The average workday lasted from seven o'clock in the morning until seven o'clock at night, with the exception of Thursday, which was usually the "short day" for most of the cast and crew. Jerry London explained that only one episode was filmed per week, stating they never filmed more than one episode at a time.

Work on each new episode began on Thursday morning, when the cast along with the main guest actor(s) and production crew—including props, wardrobe, director, and assistant director—would convene in Ed Feldman's office, where they would read through the script. According to director Bruce Bilson, because the scripts were written and props finalized so far in advance, there were very few problems by the time they reached this stage.

"Basically, the prop man would go to Ed Feldman and say, 'Is this what a gonculator should look like?'" Bilson said. "And he would approve it or change it, and by the time that Thursday morning meeting, it was just to finalize everything. Ed Feldman and Larry Marks, who was the story editor, would be there, and we'd read the script and discuss suggestions. If there were some thoughts about it, they were discussed at that table and changes were made, or not—usually not."

Cindy Lynn explained that there were usually very few changes to the script because the "writers were so great." Seated around the table, they would try and visualize how each scene would play out and whether or not certain jokes would click. If they worked, they stayed in; otherwise, they would "change a word here and there to make it a little funnier." Occasionally, if the female guest star were unavailable for the reading, Cindy would fill in and read for the guest in her place.

At the time of the script readings, Bob would express his opinions about the dialogue and offer suggestions on how to make certain lines better. Cindy recalled vividly that he also made everybody laugh. "He cracked jokes," she said. "He was a jokester. Joking. We cracked up! He always made everybody laugh. He made it very, very easy on the set."

Following the reading on Thursday, the actors would go home, leaving the director to take the remainder of the day to review the sets and props, and prepare himself for Friday's rehearsal. On Friday, the cast and crew, under the supervision of Feldman, met at Desilu Studios in Hollywood, at which time, they blocked the scenes and offered any last-minute suggestions about the dialogue. Everyone had the weekend off. Then filming began on Monday.

Bruce Bilson explained, "When we were rehearsing was the time for people to make suggestions. Suggestions for jokes. Suggestions for maybe a new line in the scene or a new ending to a scene, whatever. So what we would do is rehearse what was written, and if we had an idea that we all thought might be better, we would rehearse what we would like to present. At the end of rehearsing everything, Ed Feldman would come down, and we would do a run through for him. And we would say, 'Hey, for this scene, we have two versions.' And he'd say, 'Ok, well let me see my version first.' And we would show him what we were suggesting. And he would say, 'Good idea,' or 'No, leave it the way it is.' Or he would find the road down the middle. But his was the final verdict, and there were no arguments about it."

"We had a great schedule," Werner Klemperer said. "We shot Monday, Tuesday, Wednesday, three days. Usually from seven to seven, but sometimes later, eight, nine, ten. Pretty strenuous, but wonderful. When you're having a good time, nothing is strenuous. When you're having a bad time, it takes forever."

On Tuesday, if the weather permitted, everyone would meet at the Forty Acres Backlot to film the exterior scenes. On Wednesday, any remaining interior scenes would be filmed back at Desilu. By this time, it would also be important to ensure that scenes of any of the guest actors were complete.

Jerry London explained some of the set designs at Forty Acres, and he also elaborated on the research that was done to strive for accuracy. "They had a pit dug, and I guess you could put six guys in there. Well, they had to have a hole to get them out of there. You'd have either raised or lowered sets as well for inside or outside the barracks. When they came up through the bed, that was a set. So they had to figure out a way to put a hole in one of the sets so they could put the guys underneath so they could come up through the bed. There was another set piece, where they'd just climb up, and we'd cut to the next level of the barracks. It's all pieces. Everything else was done on stage. A lot of times, Eddie [Feldman] would tell me, 'I'm writing a script and I need a Messerschmidt chasing this or I'll need a ship doing this,' and he'd say, 'Can you get me a shot somewhere and put it into the show?' So I'd go down to the library of the Army or the Air Force, and I'd go into their libraries, and they were very cooperative about giving us stock footage. So they'd come up with the shot and then they'd write the scene for whatever it was around the shot. And if I couldn't find the shot, he'd change it to something else. So we kind of did that work ahead of time."

"That's how it was done every week," Bruce Bilson said. "And it was a wonderful system."

Hogan's Heroes was a series that not only provided great comedic entertainment, but it touched on the basic human need of survival. The harsh element of war played beautifully to the sympathies of the viewers, who came to care about the characters and their plight during the war. Sure, they had a network of tunnels and an escape route, but what *if* Hogan and his heroes were discovered? Fans of the series bought the far-fetched premise hook, line, and sinker, and even though at the end of each episode, all was right within Stalag 13 once again, for twenty-two minutes, through the laughter, there was also an underlying worry. *What if one of the characters died?* And the way to tap into the viewer's anxiety even further, Robert Butler explained, was to add romance.

"You don't have to do scenes, you do *moments*," Butler said. "You do exchanges. Any of these guys can get drilled at any moment. I mean, death is right next to every one of them all the time, so the stakes, the drama, is really heightened. So if a young woman winds up with those guys, instantly it starts to play. The guy among the men who does her the biggest service, does her the biggest favor, is usually Hogan, but if it becomes one of the other guys, it's a *killer*. It's an absolute killer. You've got a capsulized love story where life and death lurk imminently right outside the window. Those moments were not difficult at all. And the wisdom in the experience of the comedy in an ultra-dangerous circumstance, those moments just play wonderfully. And Bob was a smart enough guy to know all of that without any thinking or discussion or anything. So they were easy. I don't remember much directing. I remember working the physical side of everything and keeping the guys in line because they were often crazy and everything. But I don't remember much character work with Bob."

Some reports have alluded to the theory that Bob was routinely unable to perform his lines adequately. A *TV Guide* article claimed that Bob often had trouble with his lines but that nobody seemed to mind. In another 1967 article, Dick Kleiner reported witnessing Howard Morris trying to film a scene in which Bob and John Banner were muffing their lines. After a few takes of not getting it right, Bob became afflicted with a case of the giggles. Unaffected, Morris joked, "This will bring comedy to its knees!" Ivan Dixon added that once an actor "gets in one of these line-muffing streaks, it's awful… The harder you try to get it right, the worse it gets."

Bob being unable to perform his lines adequately on a regular basis was not witnessed by cast and crew. In fact, they recalled just the opposite. Robert Clary said Bob was usually accurate with his lines and rarely had trouble with his performances.

"What was remarkable about him," Clary said, "[was that] on most episodes, he had a big percentage of the dialogue to deliver and was in at least eighty percent on film. It was rare when he fluffed his lines. He would have his script with him, look at the lines before shooting the scene, and most of the time, he was letter perfect. He really was a pleasure to work with."

Tom Davis would occasionally visit his older brother Larry Hovis on the set of *Hogan's Heroes*. Tom described that unlike Larry, Bob could switch in and out of character quickly. He recalled observing Bob prepare for a scene.

"I used to watch him," Tom said. "He'd throw his head back a little bit when he was thinking about a scene, and you could see him kind of getting ready for it. Larry would kind of stare through you. I don't think it was that hard for Bob, in my opinion. When he would blow a line, he would get mad and say, 'Damn it, let's do it again.' He'd kind of back off, go drink a cup of water, and someone would put a hand on his shoulder. Then he [would say], 'Okay guys, I'm sorry. Let's do it again.' That kind of thing. I think he could turn it on and off."

As Hogan, Bob occasionally had to impersonate a German officer, and as part of that charade, he needed to speak with a German accent. Most of the *Hogan's Heroes* actors would often employ a distinguished German accent as part of the episode's storyline, and some of their German accents were exceptional. Bob's German accent, on the other hand, has been criticized as being one of the worst German accents ever heard.

Reaching back to his days in radio as the one-time "Man of 1,000 Voices," Bob could impersonate anyone and imitate anything, and he was often praised for that talent. On *Hogan's Heroes*, Larry Hovis, Richard Dawson, and Ivan Dixon all performed some of the greatest

German accents heard on the series. Why, then, did this seem to be so difficult for Bob?

In truth, it was not difficult at all. He was *directed* to have a terrible German accent to make the show funnier. He adopted a horrible German accent because that was how the producers had wanted it done. "He wasn't *supposed* to do it well!" Jerry London declared. "That was the comedy of it!"

It was also typical for Bob to allow other actors to take the spotlight—to let them have their moment to shine. Paul Petersen, who had worked with Bob on *The Donna Reed Show*, noticed that this translated on film. He said, "As a personality, [Bob was] straightforward. And I think *Hogan's Heroes*—he captured that character and allowed all those wonderful characters around him to take their time in the sun. And that, I believe, he learned *directly* from Donna Reed. A show's success is so much a *mystery* that *whenever* you see a success, you've *got* to celebrate it. I mean, the show made a mark. It was *very* funny! There's just no doubt about that. But I never thought that Bob—and I don't think even *Bob* thought—that *he* carried the show. I mean, I know the name was *Hogan's Heroes*, but he was surrounded by some *wonderful* character actors, my *goodness*."

"It was fun to act with him," Arlene Martel said. "He took from what you were doing and played with that moment. Which is what a good actor does. He played *with* you. Not *at* you. Acting should appear effortless. If it looks like you're straining and trying then you're not a very good actor! I think he had the makings of a very fine actor. He just needed roles that challenged him. He was very attentive, and he gave another actor a lot to play with—to work with. You know, some actors aren't there. They might as well not even be on the set; you could phone your lines in. But he kind of bounced off whatever you were doing. It was really very nice."

Actress Ruta Lee, who had previously acted alongside Werner Klemperer in *Operation Eichman,* remembered working with Bob on the set of *Hogan's Heroes* fondly. "I really liked him a lot! I did *Hogan's Heroes* many times and enjoyed the camaraderie of the entire cast, happily led by Bob Crane! Bob loved to joke around, as did I. Sometimes it was difficult to stop laughing long enough to shoot a scene. He was a generous and concerned leading man, who treated me beautifully when I guest-starred on his show."

"You can't forget the lines," Cindy Lynn said of her time on the show. "I remember my lines from *Hogan's Heroes*! I remember my first kissing scene with Bob. I was *so shy*, and my first scene was a kissing scene with him. And I went like *smack* really fast, and Eddie Feldman said, 'Cut! Cindy, honey, this is a *love* scene… Hold it longer. You know? Hold it…longer.' So I held it a little longer. 'Cut! Cindy… Kiss… You know, *love… Kiss*.' So Bob whispered in my ear, 'Honey, I'll help ya.' So what happened was that he helped me so much that when they said 'Cut!' we didn't hear it, and we were still kissing till we heard them laughing. That was my introduction to my first screen kiss."

Each actor on a series brings to the show a bit of his or her own persona. How much of that persona is used depends on both the actor and director. "What matters to the actor is, who am I, what do I want, where do I come from, where do I fit in this ensemble, and how am I to behave? What's my performance going to be like?" said director Robert Butler. "They answer a lot of those questions in the readings in casting ahead of time. They bring in much of that, but then as you put it all together, and you work to sculpt the various elements into a single whole; people add and detract and sculpt themselves to fit that whole."

Robert Butler added that he had heavily tapped into Bob's own persona and followed his lead in the creation of Colonel Hogan. Bob didn't have a long acting resume, but he did have a glib personality that had served him well in radio. Butler considered that a strength of Bob's persona, and he focused on those qualities when directing to help Bob bring Hogan to life.

"In the extreme, in the real, naked, raw beginning, you've got a radio disc jockey who doesn't have a lot of score, a lot of mileage, in anything else," Butler explained. "You've got a funny guy, a clever guy, a smart guy. A good-looking radio disc jockey and talk show host. How is that going to work? The director isn't primary. The set cast is primary. Who is going to be that person that we're going to wrap that whole show around? And that's the major question. There was no acting discussion, behavioral discussion of Hogan. That wasn't what his experience was, so we didn't do that. If he had been a method actor who had done a lot of *drama*, it would have been difficult because he would have not been comfortable. I was aware that Bob wasn't experienced, but he *was* very clever and charming. I think it might have been my instinct to follow *him* secretly. I undoubtedly decided to follow his strengths. You use the things he does well, and you play to those—charming, fearless, never ruffled, never rattled, on top of *everything all the time*. That's part of what his charm was on his radio show. So you play to *that* in the Bob Crane persona and fit it to the Hogan persona, and off you go. I don't remember much work with Bob. I remember him waltzing through the whole thing *wonderfully*. *And* we mustn't forget Werner's complication to this whole thing. *He* makes it work. I've often thought that the size of the villain determines the size of your whole piece. And if you've got a *really* threatening villain, and in this case, this guy was *truly* dangerous. I mean, he was *so* dumb and paranoid that he could go over the edge at any time! So you had to be very, very careful of him as a hero. And of course, that's what Hogan was. That's the bedrock of the whole thing. How do you handle Klink? He's a ticking time bomb. In the performing and in the structuring of the material, you can't take him for granted. I mean, he'd wipe out the whole thing! I don't care if the audience examines the validity of the thing. That's not my interest. I just want to carry them like crazy. And the way to carry them is to have these two guys in front of them always. Crane being fearless, and Klink being dangerous. I mean, that's a great serum to the whole show."

In terms of directing Bob, Jerry London said, "It wasn't like a struggle. His character was really cemented in with the writing. That was him. The writers were so great that they wrote for the actors so beautifully. They played themselves basically. Bob was a take-charge guy. Had a great personality. There never seemed to be any struggle of who the character was. He was eager to please. Easy going. That was him. He was great. If you want another take, you got it. He liked to finish his work and do whatever he was doing personally, as far as interview or whatever. But I never heard any bad feeling coming out of him at all. *Ever*. Never any temper tantrums. I don't even remember one. He was a straight man. He didn't have that problem. I think he wanted to look good. He cared about his make up, and the wardrobe looked great. And he always had a feeling of leadership. That was all in the character. He was great with lines. He had good instincts as far as what the material interpreted his role as. In other words, he was the leader. He was always the leader. And he was most of the time the guy who came up with the answers. He was the smart guy. I think there were several scripts where, I don't know, something happened, and LeBeau or one of the other characters came up with something. It was probably one of the easiest shows I ever worked on as far as personalities, good writing, production, budget. Everything worked. It was a dream show. On that show, everybody worked for six years. Straight through."

Bruce Bilson did not begin work as a director on *Hogan's Heroes* until the third season. By that time, the actors had established their characters, and directing had moved into a more advanced phase for the series. Bilson said, "The directing is story telling. It's to tell the story well or to make the joke work right. It's not 'Your character wouldn't do that.' Or 'Make your character tougher because in the next scene, this happens.' So it's only for the situation. Bob knew who his character was, so I never said to him, 'No, no. Don't do it that way.' We were mostly on the same wavelength about what the show was, what we were trying to do, and what the scenes were about. And that's why I came back time after time and did twenty-five of them. Bob was no problem at all to direct. There was none of that. There was none of that from any of them. Bob just did that part. He was Hogan, you know? And that was it. I can't remember a time when he just came at it from left field and it didn't make sense for Hogan. So that was it. I don't think he had problems with it at all."

Robert Butler agreed that experiences with Bob on the set were never difficult. "Bob was the kind of guy who wore joy. He was always having a good time. It would behoove me never to defy that, *never* to not believe that. It would behoove me to play with *that*. 'Listen Bob, that's great. It's terrific. Here's another idea.' That's the way you work. You let the person be the person. You let the actor express himself/herself. And then you sculpt the edges a little bit. You try and fix, if necessary, the shading, the edges of the externals. I'm thinking of hitting a home run, I don't know baseball all that well, but I'm told that when you hit a home run, you do it because everything is relaxed. Everything comes together. And the sound of the bat in the hitter's ear isn't a crash or a bang, it's a *click*. That's what the guys feel when they hit a home run. I'm making a point about relaxation and getting everybody to be able to contribute at their most relaxed, efficient level. That's the part of what you do, so when questions about difficulty are asked, I have to think that my responsibility is to *remove* the difficulty. To get that *click*."

The entire cast of *Hogan's Heroes* had not only established, but had maintained, that *click*. And Bob had been in large measure responsible for it. As Ruta Lee observed of Bob's receiving direction, "He took it, did it, and had fun all the way!"

Earlier episodes of season one reveal Colonel Hogan as being much more flippant and cocky, both in his dealings with Klink, Schultz, and the Germans, and with his own men. During the first season, Ed Feldman explained to Bob that he needed to tone down the campy angle of Colonel Hogan and make him more of a leader. Hogan was to be the problem-solver, not the jokester.

"If the audience doesn't believe Hogan, we're dead," Bob said. "Everything bounces off him. If you're Soupy Sales as a colonel, nobody will care. Eddie made it clear to me that I absolutely must not play Hogan as a buffoon. I play him seriously, as a hero, as a leader who can inspire other men to keep fighting, even when behind bars. I originally tried to make the character funny. Eddie convinced me to change. 'You have to be a hero,' he said. The lines dictated heroism. I asked myself: 'What the hell is a hero?' I had a line—a simple line, a kind of understated acceptance of a challenge. I said it in a certain way—almost a dead, flat, guttural tone. Three guys whirled around and yelled, 'That's it! John Wayne!' That's the story. If you want to be a hero—think John Wayne. He'll rescue you every time."

So Bob began to craft his Colonel Hogan who was less Jack Lemmon and more John Wayne, which can be heard in Bob's delivery of the more serious lines. Hogan became more cunning and serious, reserving the slightly more flippant personality for his interactions with Klink and Schultz as part of Hogan's cover act. By season two, Bob had created the hero the writers, producers, and creators wanted.

Actress Victoria Carroll, who guest-starred on several episodes, observed, "I think he retained very much of his same personality. I think what you saw was you got with him. His acting was very natural and very easy. I don't think there was a difference in personalities."

"It came easy because it was very much like him," Cindy Lynn agreed. "That's the way he would have been if he was in a POW camp; he probably would have done the same thing. That's why it came easy to him. He didn't have to struggle. It was *there*. It was him. Bob was more of the flippity Hogan. He was not the in-charge Hogan. He had to work at that. He liked the funny Hogan better. I mean, it was easier for him. He had to work on the slick—the other part. Drama is more difficult because of the timing. If the timing isn't right, then the whole thing is off. It's all in the timing. You can blow it just by one little thing. The serious stuff came harder for him; he had to work on it."

It may have been the role many have claimed he was born to play, but Bob Crane was *not* Colonel Hogan. The directors were wise to play to Bob's strengths to help him create the character, but Hogan was still just a character. Many people saw great similarities in both Hogan and the actor who portrayed him, claiming Bob was just like what you saw on television. However, Charlie Zito, Bob's best friend from school, saw things slightly differently.

"To the extent of him being an organizer and setting up things like he did in *Hogan's Heroes*, that part of it is true," Charlie said. "But he never was very pushy. He was always ready to listen to other people. Like when we used to form our teams and everything, we all had input, but he was the main guy who put it all together. He made sure our names got in the local paper, how many points we scored. And he used to keep all the clippings. He really was a *terrific* organizer. But *not* as a wise guy. He was always interested in your input. *Always.* No matter what he did. I mean, as far as he and I were concerned, anyway. But Hogan—to a point, yes. But not completely. Sometimes he would come off as a *real* wise guy in that series. Let's say the way he handled Colonel Klink, with tongue in cheek. That's him. He was charming, very much so. If you needed him for anything, he would be there. He was that kind of a friend. That kind of a guy. He was always interested in what you were doing."

School friend Donald Sappern agreed. "He wasn't as assertive as Hogan was. The Hogan persona was aggressive. He wasn't. If Bob were a prisoner of war, he wouldn't make waves. That's probably the best way I can sum up. No, he wasn't Hogan."

Harvey Geller, Bob's close friend and neighbor in California, concurred. "As Hogan, he was acting. That was not Crane. He was an actor. But he was not absolutely the quiet guy. So maybe it was in between. But he was not a wise guy as Hogan was."

Actor Jon Cedar, who played Corporal Karl Langenscheidt on *Hogan's Heroes*, stated, "I think that Bob probably was ninety percent Colonel Hogan. But in my book, that's actually very good acting as long as you are really focused on the work and not just 'walking through the part.' And I think the key to his enduring popularity was when you watched him in the role, he was very accessible, and very easy and relaxed. Some of our greatest actors are or were 'just being themselves.' Think about Gary Cooper, Cary Grant, Spencer Tracy, and so many more. Spencer Tracy has been quoted as saying, 'Good acting is simply looking the other guy in the eyes and telling the truth.' So I don't think any actor who 'looks the other guy in the eyes and tells the truth' can be faulted for 'just being themselves.'"

"I think it got easier for him. But it didn't show," Jerry London surmised. "I mean, from the time he did the pilot to the time he did the last show, he was Hogan. *He was Hogan*."

But Bob was frustrated that people did not think he was acting, but instead, thought he was just being himself. He had experienced this response before in radio. The fact was, Bob worked so hard at his job that he just made it *look* easy. He once said, "People say to me, 'Aw, you're just naturally funny. You don't have to work at it.' I don't care if that's what they think. But man, I do work hard at it. *I work hard*."

Actor Monte Markham, who appeared in one episode in season six, explained, "Bear in mind that the actor's instrument is the actor. When you're doing lightweight material and you're doing comedy, that's a hell of a lot of who you are. It's like Johnny Carson was a very quiet man off camera and very, very distant. He didn't really talk to people. He was only on when he was on because he's ultimately playing himself. Bob Crane, his success—which came first? Is he successful because of his personality and the way he was able to handle himself and so then he wanted to act? He wanted to compete and do that. And he found a vehicle that worked. Of course, there's a ton of Bob in Hogan. The question to that is if you're playing a serial murderer, does that mean you're playing yourself? Of course not. If you play a homosexual, and you're not, does that mean you're homosexual? But an actor *always* brings an *enormous* amount of exactly *who—he—is*. The barrel of the character. Whatever you do on film, if it translates to an audience, it becomes successful. *That's* what you're hired for. I mean, you *want* Michael Caine to be Michael Caine. He could play anything and do anything, but he's still basically a star with a pistol. Yeah, Bob was playing himself, but no more than *any* actor plays himself or translates that. Because Hogan was *that* kind of a guy. Happy-go-lucky and on top of it and very cocky and smart and clever, and that's how Bob saw *himself*. He was very quick and very sharp as a personality. He had the whole radio career—carrying a show and talking. I have no idea what Bob turned down or what he was offered or if he was in any great dramatic roles. It's like Robin Williams, who goes a maniacal ninety miles an hour. I saw Robin Williams years before at the Juilliard School for the Performing Arts; he held down some wonderful scenes, it was quite beautiful. Wonderful stuff. And then to see him *act*. Most good comics are damn good actors, dramatically, when they go at it."

For all his efforts, Bob received some of the highest praise in the press. Edith Efron wrote in an article for *TV Guide*, "The stupefaction mostly exists in the minds of those who haven't seen and don't want to see the series because they've been understandably traumatized by what they've heard about it—that it's about a Nazi POW camp with 'funny Nazis'... It is, in fact, a classical black-and-white comedy, with a bunch of admirable guys thoroughly trouncing a bunch of contemptible guys. The good guys are maniacally unstoppable individualists who have burrowed the POW camp into a giant Swiss cheese, through the holes of which they conduct jubilant and successive 'great escapes' in the Allied cause. And the bad guys are Chaplinesque embodiments of authoritarian absurdities—a barking, *heiling*, goose-stepping batch of uniformed robots, pompous asses, bootlickers, toadies, cowards, and dupes. It's a funny, non-offensive show, and its real theme, as Bob Crane sums it up, is: 'Look how clever the Allies are!' Nevertheless, it's still a dubious enterprise to focus laughingly on Nazis at all, and it comes off successfully because of lively scripts, brilliant comedic acting—and Crane."

Hollywood is fraught with tales of woe and scandal from sets that are unfriendly at best and hostile at worst. The *Hogan's Heroes* universe was neither. Rather, the set of *Hogan's Heroes* is reported to have been one of the happiest sets of its own or any era.

Right from the beginning, a strong "male communality," as Robert Butler explained, existed between the cast members. This meant that they kept each other's egos in check. For example, when the cast first read through the pilot script as a group, Robert Clary recalled that Leonid Kinskey had attempted to change the dialogue, "trying very hard to make the show center around a Russian prisoner of war." This type of behavior was usually "squelched" by the group; it just would not be tolerated. Clary also noted that there was an "immediate camaraderie" among the cast, which lasted for the duration of the series.

Werner Klemperer recognized this as well. In an interview with Brenda Scott Royce, Klemperer expressed his sentiments of working with the cast and crew of *Hogan's Heroes*. "We not only got along, we really became kind of friends. We had a fantastic time. We were very much an example of a cast who got along. And I think it shows on the show. We were really a unit, an ensemble. We had a good time, a very good time. We didn't fool around, though. We took it very seriously when we shot [the episodes]."

"Every day was fun on the set of *Hogan's Heroes*," said Cindy Lynn. "We joked around, and there was no drama. Nobody was temperamental, and nobody had an ego. We worked as a team. Great directors. Great writers. Great cameramen. We were a family, all of us. We were a *family*."

"We used to have parties," Bruce Bilson recalled. "I always remember mostly that John Banner liked to dance with my wife, who's five foot two or three. And he was the most graceful dancer you ever saw. He was so light on his feet. He was just fun to watch."

Success starts from the top, and in the case of *Hogan's Heroes*, credit was universally bestowed upon Edward Feldman and how he handled the day-to-day functioning of the set.

"Edward H. Feldman was the main reason for the show's success," wrote Robert Clary. "In a television series, if you don't have a good producer, the show's not going to work. He is the one who hires the cast, the writers, the directors, and the editors. He oversees everything, and Ed was very, very good at it. I have never heard anyone involved with *Hogan's* say anything bad about him. He was kind to everybody. He held the reins. It was his baby, and he made the show what it was: a fun show."

Bruce Bilson agreed. "[Feldman] was the greatest. I will brag about him to anybody who wants to start talking about how to do a show."

Bob concurred, also crediting the success of *Hogan's Heroes* to Ed Feldman. "I don't mean to take anything away from myself or Werner or John, but the real secret is Ed Feldman, the producer. It's the man in the front office that makes the program. There are different writers, different directors, but Ed Feldman pulls it all together. He's the Sheldon Leonard, the Paul Henning, the man with the touch."

"Eddie Feldman was a very sharp leader," Robert Butler said. "That *tone*, that *feeling* has to be laid at his door in great measure. He was smart to run it that way. It was partly survival on part of the guys, too, because they just wouldn't let each other get away with anything. So there was a real *communality*. That male collaboration. When that works, it really is terrific stuff. Whatever you do in this business, you've got to be lucky. That's a part of the deal. And when those guys walked on the set the first day, there was luck going on. They were good guys. They were skilled guys. They were guys who were willing. They just were altogether good guys. To be frank, Dickie Dawson was a *weird* guy, but that character was a weird guy, and everybody let him be who he was and what he was. And we never understood it exactly, and he was always a little out of his mind. But that's okay, because [Newkirk] was a Cockney maniac. And Dickie Dawson was, to some extent, a Cockney maniac. So there was that communality, that *willingness* to find who you are and let everyone else be who they are. That's a part of it all, and it includes a maniac like Dawson, who may not be a maniac at all. That was just my perception at the time. But it didn't hurt anything. And the guys had the strength and the solidity and the roots to not let that stuff hurt them. That's a big part of that hit. I mean, think of those egos and where they could go because you could really get rich if you're on that show as a young guy playing those parts. It *could* have been a snake pit, and it wasn't. Much of that is due to Eddie. Much of it is due to the accidental willingness and collaboration of those guys. It was just a *good, good* thing. And we see it on the film when we look at it these days. It was a different world, too. It was a sweeter, more collaborative world. The show was blessed. It simply was just blessed."

"I think it came naturally," surmised Jerry London. "I have to give credit to Ed Feldman. He was the guy who set the tone for everything. The writing was so great. Everybody was so pleased with their characters. There was no complaining, and everybody was happy. All they wanted to do was have a good time and have a hit show."

Arlene Martel said, "Ed Feldman was a very warm, charming, innocent person as well. He was positive energy. There was a great deal, I felt, of positive energy on that set."

Ed Feldman also made certain that anyone could approach him with questions or ideas, and Ivan Dixon had done so.

"I remember a racial anecdote with Dixon," said Robert Butler. "I must have been thinking in the back of my mind about the French spy who came through, and if all the guys ogle her, they all really dig her, here's Ivan Dixon, the *black* guy. He was kind of digging her, too. So I said to him, 'Ivan, I think you can't covet her the way the rest of the guys do.' And he kind of looked at me funny, and I said, 'Hey, I don't care about the validity of that idea. All I'm saying is that I think we can't do that here.' And he said, 'Well, I don't like that.' And I said, 'I don't like it either, and I don't care that I don't like it; that's what I think we have to do.' He said, 'I won't do that.' It was an interesting argument because neither of us got hot. We were very philosophical about it, both of us, which is a bigger tribute to him than me. But he said, 'Listen, I want to talk to Eddie [Feldman] about that.' Because Eddie was Big Daddy, ultimately. And I said, 'Be my guest, let's go talk to him. Let's get him down here.' So he came down, and I presented the case, and Ivan presented his case. I think I made it clear to Eddie that I didn't care what was true or untrue; I only cared about the fact that this material was being presented to an audience in the best possible way it could be presented for the biggest possible audience result. And I'm sure that Ivan said he didn't care about those statistics, he just thought it was untrue and a big lie. I'm sure those were the positions. And Eddie said, 'Go for it. Be who you are.' Something like that to Ivan. And I said, 'Great, that's good enough for me.' So, I don't think he had any lines. I don't think he had a moment with the actress, but it was just a general attitude in the group. So I said, 'Good enough for me, Ivan.' On we go. And we did. That's good honesty by both Ivan and myself, and great leadership by Eddie in that instance."

As well as portraying the leader of a group of Allied servicemen on *Hogan's Heroes*, Bob mirrored that behavior on the set as well. As the star, Bob brought a level of stability to the set that was pleasant. Instead of a demanding and egocentric prima donna, he was instead an actor who came to work and did his job and did it well.

"The guys got along," Robert Hogan confirmed. "It was a happy fit. It was not one of those disgruntled fits. It starts at the top, it seems to me, always, and Bob was. He was an easy guy."

Arlene Martel observed, "I never heard Bob Crane say anything that was shoddy, shabby, or rude. I never saw him throw a little hissy fit, or start doing a diva kind of act. I never saw him fling his ego around that way. He seemed very patient. Like, 'Okay,'—like a shrug. You'd see him kind of shrugging, like, 'Well, we gotta wait till they set up the lights some more,' or whatever. I never saw him throw any kind of tantrum. He didn't use the show, I think, as an opportunity to demonstrate his power in any way. If you had walked on the set, you wouldn't think that he was the star necessarily. It was ensemble acting. I think everyone liked that idea. It seemed that there was good will among everyone. Everyone sort of rooted for everyone else. That's why I always celebrated when they said, 'You're gonna work on *Hogan's* this week.' That was a big celebration to me. That it was so pleasant on the set. And so warm and friendly and *family*. And I loved the character I played, too. I loved playing Tiger because it was so opposite of other roles I played, like Mr. Spock's wife [on *Star Trek*]."

"If Bob had an ego, I never saw it," Ruta Lee added. "He was the cook that always stirred the bubbling pot of humor!"

Ed Feldman gave Bob his share of accolades as well. In a 1968 issue of *TV Guide*, Feldman said of his star performer, "He's the first one on the set in the morning and the last one to leave. He goes into everything with enthusiasm."

Robert Butler further credited Bob for the positive atmosphere on the set. "We all have to be strong in this racket," he said. "The legs have to hold up. We've heard war stories of shows where they've just gotten sick and crazy. That's usually the war story you hear about a successful show five years later. You hear about the strain. None of that happened. In the unit, on the show, that stuff didn't exist. With Bob, work wasn't work; it was play. He was always willing to do it. I don't remember him being late to the stage. I don't remember any of that stuff. Everything comes from the lead guy. That pattern is very much that lead guy on a series. Is he on time? Is he late? Is he arrogant? Is he humble? That's the way it works. And it continued to work well, and we have to lay that at Bob's door as well as Eddie Feldman's, and the luck of the whole thing fitting together just so well."

"Our preparation was so great, and Eddie was such a great producer. That's why the quality of the show was so good," said Jerry London. "It was a dream show to work on. I loved it. I loved it! I loved being on the set because the guys were so funny. As for directing Bob, he knew the character. You didn't have to give him much direction. I mean, I have to tell you, of all the shows I've directed, and I've directed hundreds and hundreds of shows, the scripts were written so *great*. You'd read the script, and maybe there were three or four line changes, and maybe they can make this joke better, and they went and shot it. It wasn't like they were searching to make it better because Eddie would work with the writers way ahead of time. I remember when we first started the show, we'd have ten scripts ready."

Of whether or not Bob had an ego, Jerry London said, "He was a proud guy. But it wasn't the kind of ego that was nasty. He was the star of the show, and he knew it. But he never threw it around. He was still a good guy and easy to talk to and friendly. But you knew he was the star. Werner Klemperer was the guy who had the big ego. He was the Teutonic German. Oh, boy. He kept saying to everybody, '*I'm* the star of the show! *I* have all the good stuff!' All the other guys would kind of put their hand up over their mouth and chuckle a little bit. They'd all laugh about it. The rivalry between John Banner and Werner Klemperer was legendary—because Banner got all the funny lines. And Werner wanted them. It was very funny between the two of them. Always squabbling like *The Bickersons*. It was hilarious. Of course, the rest of the guys were always goading them on and laughing at them. It was a hilarious time to be on the set and to be in the reading. It was funny, funny stuff. All I can tell you is it was one of the greatest experiences of my life, those six years."

Robert Clary also claimed that the years he spent on the set of *Hogan's Heroes* were "delightful," and that it had produced long-lasting friendships. "The mood on the set was always jovial, cordial, and extremely pleasant," he wrote. "We, the regulars, made the guest stars feel part of the family."

Bob was quick to give credit to the writers, an often-uncelebrated component to the success of a production. "Writing is the key to any show. We're very lucky. Our writers have been creating some marvelous situations."

Bob also gave credit to his fellow co-stars regularly, saying that without them, there would be no *Hogan's Heroes*. "Whatever success the show enjoys is the result of the talents of a group. I'm just a part of it. Ivan Dixon, Robert Clary, Dick Dawson, John Banner, Werner Klemperer, and Larry Hovis share the credit. Without them, there wouldn't be any *Hogan's Heroes*. I think, more important than anything we owe ourselves as actors, is what we owe viewers. It's our responsibility to entertain. We all work to give *Hogan's Heroes* fans a half-hour of honest comedy-adventure. Maybe at times we try too hard, but we'd rather be guilty of that than of not giving a damn."

Fans of the series have occasionally wondered about the recurring but unnamed extras, most of whom portrayed additional Luftwaffe prison guards or the handful of silent prisoners who congregated in the barracks or joined the regular cast in the roll call line up. Their names are now known; in his scrapbook, Bob kept a photograph of them with their names handwritten on the photo: "THE REAL HEROES"—Dennis Gray, Walter Smith, Edgar Johnson, Roy Goldman, Sam Haygan, and Dick Ryan.

Wherever Bob went in his life and career, his drums went with him. He had two dressing rooms on the set of *Hogan's Heroes*, and in one he kept his drums, a hi-fi stereo machine, and stacks of jazz records. Playing drums in between the shooting schedule allowed him to relax and prepare mentally for his next scene. Further, everyone always knew where he was—they just had to follow the sound of the drums.

Robert Clary explained that "in between takes, while the crew were setting for the next scene, he would go to that room and play his drums, which he kept there, loudly, probably at the same time learning his next dialogue. The stage manager always knew where to find him when he was needed. I thought it was very clever of the management to let him make his noise at the studios. Instead of looking for him if he left the studio, again, like the other stars from other shows did. No time was wasted."

Bob said, "I knew I wanted to be an entertainer just as soon as I started studying the drums in grade school. The drums were my ticket to the business, and I still enjoy playing them. In my dressing room, I only have a full set of drums augmented by a complete hi-fi outfit boasting the biggest set of speakers this side of the Hollywood Bowl. When visitors to the *Hogan's Heroes* stages comment that my quarters are loud, they're not talking about the wallpaper or draperies."

Accolades from *Hogan's Heroes* cast and crew about the series and of Bob in particular were plentiful.

Jerry London recalled, "We never had a problem where he didn't show or anything. He was always there on the set, and he practiced his drums a lot. That I remember. He was always full of juice. You never had to pump him up. He was great that way."

"It was one of the good shows to work as a non-regular," Robert Hogan said. "When the show is a hit, the actors' haircuts get better, they have bigger trailers to dress in comparison to your trailer. But you didn't get that feeling at all, which is so important. That starts with Bob. When I met him the first time and then when I did the show, he was a regular guy. Wonderful, easy flow of humor without 'look at me, I'm being humorous.' There was no rumbling anger underneath. He was really delightful. He was a good guy, and how he treated the other guys and everything else. It was just an easy flow, which doesn't always make good comedy, but it sure helps. He was thrilled to be doing his job. He just was a very happy guy, happy camper on that set. I didn't notice any disgruntled guy. There's going to be a lot of prima donna going on. The guy at the top or the woman at the top is going to be like that. And it wasn't. It was a nice, nice set to go on. It was comfortable to do your work. I never felt as though eyes were peering through the back of my head. I felt like I was part of the team. It was just wonderful."

"It was a great show to work on. Great show," said Bruce Bilson. "I didn't have a sense of Bob being a problem or difficult or 'Hey, I'm the star.' I had no sense of any of that. We became pretty good working friends. He would often relax between scenes by playing his drums. I specifically remember when *The Producers* came out, and him playing *Springtime for Hitler*, and playing the drums along with it. I always thought of him as like Skippy. I don't know exactly what that means. But he knew it that I called him Skippy. And not a *lot*, but it was just that attitude of everything's good and going along. I never saw the depression and hangovers that they tried to show in [*Auto Focus*]. I just never was aware of that. Coming to the show late, I was never aware of that. He was always there. I don't recall him ever blowing up or any of that stuff. For me, he was Skippy. Happy-go-lucky guy. I never saw depression. I never saw a temper. I just remember it being good."

Ivan Dixon also found the atmosphere to be pleasant, stating, "All of us get along great—everyone helps everyone else—which is hard to believe at times. There seems to be no rivalry between us. Bob, Werner, and John are the stars of the show. The heroes have much smaller parts, but sometimes, one of us is built up in certain episodes. The producers and writers try and see to it that the built up parts are divided equally among us. I guess if someone started getting a lot more to do, there might be some resentment, but that hasn't happened yet."

The regular cast melded together early and quickly, and it is evident in their chemistry when watching the episodes. Richard Dawson explained shortly after the series began how the regular cast had all taken on nicknames. "Bob Crane is the most untempermental actor I've ever met. He takes so much kidding on the show without getting mad. Although he's the star of the show, he clowns right along with us. Our nickname for him is 'The Clown.' We call Werner 'The Hun.' Larry, because he always wants to go around blowing things up, is called

'Dum, Dum.' Robert Clary is nicknamed 'Pepe La Pur.' John Banner is called 'Smokey The Crowd,' and his size makes it obvious why, and Ivan, 'Ivan X.'"

Richard Dawson and Larry Hovis were recognized to have some of the best comedic chemistry, so they were often paired in scenes together. Many remember them pulling pranks and telling jokes on the set. Kathy Miritello, a close friend and colleague of the authors, had the opportunity to meet with Larry Hovis in Austin, Texas, shortly before his death in 2003. She relayed the following story Hovis had told to her: "The tree stump entrance to the tunnel was actually a hole in the ground about six feet deep. For scenes in which they were shown exiting the tunnel, they would all have to climb down there, and it was hot and cramped, and there were spiders and other insects. Larry said they'd play a joke on the 'new guys' and make them go down there first. Then they would close the lid and tell them they'd join them shortly and instead go off and leave them. They'd purposely wait out of sight to see how long it would take. The person would be stuck down there with the spiders crawling around, and you'd begin to see the lid slowly coming up!"

"I think he'd do that, yeah!" Robert Hogan laughed. "Larry was a wonderful, subdued clown." Hogan added that he never fell victim to that particular prank and had hoped they would not have actually done that to any of the guest stars—just the regulars.

Bruce Bilson recalled other funny moments that occurred during filming. "I remember Larry Hovis and Robert Clary climbing up the side of a German castle on the stage. And it's supposed to be this stealthy thing, and Larry's gun dropped out of his pocket, crashed, *boom*! And these guys kept climbing, and the crew was laughing! It was just hysterical! But you took the soundtrack out, and it was okay. And then there was one where the Jeep came into the town square and hit the fountain, and it was all on stage, and the fountain just slid away! Like on wheels! It was just hysterical!"

Cast and crew shared experiences of how Bob helped make the set fun and easy-going. Tom Davis, brother of Larry Hovis, remembered the atmosphere on the set was "very light, depending on who the director was." He said Bob was always nice to him, and from what he could tell, just about to everybody.

"It was just fun," Tom said. "And that's where I met Bob. He was *so* nice to me. Bob was one of those people that if he liked you, you were *it* at that moment, talking to him. You're the one he's talking to, nobody else. I remember he had a phone call from somebody, and it was, 'I'm talking to Larry's brother.' Something like that. And I thought, 'Whoa...I'm just a kid.' I was 18 then. He would tell me things, and I would ask him about LA, where to go, what kinds of places to avoid. He was nice. He didn't avoid me. He was always friendly to talk to whenever he had time, *Everybody* talked to Bob. And I remember he would always go off...people would pair off into conversations, and Bob would go off somewhere else, to his dressing room or use the phone or something like that. He was always busy, but he was always friendly. If he was around, he'd talk to you. If he was about to do a shoot, he would look over his shoulder to see if anyone was yelling at him to do something. He would come back and talk to you later, if you could find him!"

Robert Clary remembered Bob and the rest of the cast occasionally entered into some heated debates and arguments about one thing—politics. "Except for Bob, the rest of the regular cast of *Hogan's*, including me, were Democrats, and when he didn't agree with us (politically), his voice became like a screeching soprano. I would always say to him, 'Bob, changing from baritone to soprano will *not* make your argument right!' And we would laugh about it."

KNX colleague Leo McElroy spent the day with Ivan Dixon on a project Dixon was doing for ABC several years after *Hogan's Heroes* ended. Leo said Ivan told him, "You know, Bob was fun to work with because you really knew where he was coming from. Bob was never going to spring surprises on you. You knew *exactly* how he was going to approach the lines and *exactly* how he was going to approach the scenes. And you knew he was going to come prepared. Very professional. Very enjoyable to work with."

Jon Cedar shared an experience that had put him off at the time, but then later, he came to think he might have been too sensitive to what may have just been Bob's sharp sense of humor. "I was doing a guest star role in that week's show (not Langenscheidt), and I had taken a full page ad in one of the trade papers. I was heading into the commissary, and Bob was going in ahead of me accompanied by a couple of other people and when he saw me, he stopped, and made a semi-derogatory comment (meant for a laugh from his companions, I think). It threw me for a loop. He made me feel as though I didn't have a right to promote myself through my part in his show. After all these many years, it occurs to me that I may have been too sensitive. For all

I know, he may have just been meaning to tease me to get a laugh."

Yet rivalries did exist, and speculation has swirled for decades over the rumored tension between Richard Dawson and Bob Crane. However, despite what could have been viewed by Dawson as a snub by the producers during the casting of the lead character, there was no animosity witnessed between the two actors on the set, attesting to their professionalism regardless of whether there had been any early or ongoing dissent between them. Bob even referred to Dawson as his good friend, and others close to Bob and Dawson also knew a friendship had existed between the two.

"I never heard it," claimed Jerry London of the Crane-Dawson rivalry. "I never saw a problem. I do know that they did become very close later. I know they were always chatting, and they got together. I never saw any problems at all."

Robert Butler concurred with London, saying he did not think the leading role was *ever* really intended for Dawson. He added that even if there had been an underlying jealousy, the culture of the *Hogan's Heroes* set was such that other cast members would have quickly doused any sort of egomania or openly hostile behavior.

"I wouldn't think that it would be true that Dawson thought he was going to get cast or wanted to be cast as Hogan," Butler said. "I can believe that he was envious. I can believe that he wasn't the kind of guy who would just relax and enjoy the success and the money, and that he would continue to covet something that wasn't his own. I can believe that. But that would get so delightfully squelched by the group, who can take them to their bosom and tease him and taunt him and rib him out of the whole thing that it never became a problem that I knew about. Somehow, in that circumstance, everyone's egos got submerged pretty quickly. They got squelched. I remember the general tenor. As soon as anybody started to walk a little tall, en masse, the gang would start cutting him down. The egos couldn't flourish in this environment. Crane developed whatever he developed. And Werner was a pretty sensible good guy anyway. Sure, the egos were there. They have to be there. They develop. But somehow, in this circumstance, with all your mates on whom you depend professionally—the fame and the fortune can't screw it up. I'm reminded of Anthony Hopkins saying that ego is one of your biggest enemies. He has a lot of respect for acting and a lot of knowledge, of course, about it, and as he occasionally lectures or teaches, he makes that point. The ego is really dangerous. And all actors know that, and in the *Hogan's* situation, it's kind of fortunate that the egos were held in check. The ego as a monster is held in check by the equation, by the fact of the male communality. I think Crane and Dawson probably had great love and respect for each other professionally. And that's what matters. What it looks like it is rather than what it is. What it is doesn't really matter so much as long as you can get through that and quell the difficulties."

Cindy Lynn, however, did claim to have witnessed a friendship between Bob and Dawson. "Richard Dawson and Bob were close, as far as I know," she said. "They got along really well on the set and everything."

Victoria Carroll, a regular guest star on *Hogan's Heroes*, provided an insightful rationale as to why there may have been tension between the two actors, but because she never saw it, she could not confirm it. "It's possible that they didn't get along. I never saw it," she said. "It must have been frustrating for Richard because he was, I believe, a star in England, and he is so funny, and he was really relegated to small parts on *Hogan's Heroes* for the most part. He didn't get a lot of shows where he had a lot to do, and that was probably frustrating. So, for six years, you're playing second fiddle, and I'm sure that got to be a little frustrating. But he handled it well. Always. When you're playing subsidiary characters on any series, and it's running for three, four, five, six years, you want a little bit of the pie. As an actor, you want to *act*. You know, 'Let me do that, give me some more lines.' So that exists on any series. I think, if anything, it would've been a professional jealousy."

According to Bilson, there were rarely issues. "That was a show where there wasn't a lot of tension. The only time I remember—it was a little incident with John [Banner] and Werner, and another time when I think when Ed [Feldman] started to do *The Queen and I,* there was more tension. There was more whiny, bitchy, 'Why is he there; why isn't he with us?' But we got through that, and the show sold, and it didn't affect *Hogan's* at all except for those couple of weeks."

Jerry London further stated, "The guys were so great. It was like a family. After a couple of years and being together, everybody melded together. They all knew their characters. And after six years, God, it was like…I don't remember anything else. We were together for so long doing the show. It was a real family."

Perhaps most telling is a personal letter from Bob to Richard Dawson dated March 10, 1971. In the letter, Bob alludes to at least some professional tension between himself and Dawson, but his tone is hopeful and not unfriendly.

Some argue that Richard Dawson's failure to attend Bob Crane's funeral service lends credence to the supposition that he and Bob did not only not get along, but that they were sworn enemies. However, Dawson may not have attended the service for any number of reasons. This was not the first time he had stepped back from paying tribute to a *Hogan's Heroes* cast member. On January 28, 1973, John Banner passed away suddenly on his sixty-third birthday. A few days later, many members of the cast and crew of *Hogan's Heroes* placed a half-page sympathy ad in *Variety* magazine as a testament to their friend and former colleague. One name is notably absent from the list: Richard Dawson. It is unclear as to why Dawson was not included in the ad.

Regardless, Bob did not seem to want any hostilities. He continually referred to Dawson as his friend, even on the air at KMPC in 1972 and while at KNX prior to *Hogan's Heroes*. Bob also considered Dawson someone of high importance when talking to his family. Bob's cousin Jane Senich Ryfun recalled that Bob made it very clear to her that if she or the family were ever in need of anything, in Bob's absence, Richard Dawson would have been able and willing to step in and help them on Bob's behalf. "He told me if I ever needed help, Richard Dawson would be a good person to call," Jane said.

Other members of Bob's family knew of no open animosity between the two men. Bob's daughter Karen stated, "They were friends on the set, and we attended the boys' [Dawson's sons'] birthday party once. But that's all I know."

Yet Bob's youngest son Scott Crane, as well as Bob's close personal friends John and Pamela Thompson, confirmed that there was some hostility between the two men. Scott said his father tried very hard to be nice to Dawson, but for whatever reason, Dawson did not reciprocate. John and Pam reiterated that Bob mentioned it to them on occasion, but they did not elaborate.

Only Bob Crane and Richard Dawson knew the extent to which they were friends or merely tolerated each other. But in regard to the rumor of tensions caused by Bob being cast as Hogan, Richard Dawson had the final word shortly before his death in June 2012.

"Bob was very easy," Dawson said. "*Very easy.* He played the drums off [stage]. We would be doing a scene, and we'd say, 'Alright, we're gonna rehearse it one more time.' And you'd hear [makes drumming noise]. He'd come in and say, 'That was Dixie.' 'Oh, okay! Thank you, Bob! That's wonderful.'

"The only trouble I ever had with Bob," Dawson continued, "and I told him off once. He was giving a reading off stage to LeBeau. He had a cowlick—a big candy bar on a stick. And he had that in his mouth. We came back after lunch, and he's doing the lines for LeBeau, and [imitates Bob chewing], he was just skimming the lines. He never normally did that. And I saw Robert [Clary] was [doing a close up]—it's a big moment, the close up. And I said to Bob, 'Give him a decent reading!' So he had this cowlick and said, 'What?' And I went, 'Give him a decent reading!' And I saw his jaw [tense up]. And he bit down and took his cowlick out. And he said, 'I *am* giving him a decent reading!' And at the end of this cowlick was his front tooth! It was a cap. And he had bitten down so hard, his cap came off it. They had to rush him to the dentist and get it put back on. And Eddie Feldman came and said to me, 'Never give him acting advice.' And I said, 'Why?' [And he said], 'We run out of cowlicks.' I always remember it. And when I see that show, I always laugh, because you don't see Bob in it. He was just doing lines from some other time.

"We occasionally would adlib…and [in one instance], Robert Clary and myself were on a hill. And Bob had to come in. We were going to go into the barn and see the lady agent. She would give us instructions… And they [producers/writers] came and said Bob was going to go into the barn and he'll do it. And you just look at him *admiringly*. We're really not that mad about it because one of *us* wanted to go into the barn. He [Bob] never demanded those things. Sometimes a writer would think it would be better. And so he came up to us and he said, 'I'm going in the barn, and if she's there, make contact.' And LeBeau had to say, 'Mon Colonel, it could be a trap! There could be Nazis! Soldiers, Gestapo—they could be waiting! We cannot carry on without you, Colonel.' And he said, 'Don't worry about it. Don't worry.' Everything will be fine.' And he gave us a little salute. He started to walk over the hill to where he was going to go into the barn. And I looked at LeBeau, and LeBeau said, "*Ohh, mon Colonel*.' My Colonel. [laughing] And I said to LeBeau, 'Oh, that I had his moral fiber.' And to my surprise, they left that in! I mean, it's not that nasty of a line, but you know, it's really saying, 'He really thinks he's wonderful.' I mean, that's exactly what it means. I always loved the line. 'Oh, that I had his moral fiber.' Of course, that didn't help me. Bob still did the scene. Well, that's show business!"

When Richard Dawson tested for the role of Hogan, his interpretation of the character wasn't what the producers wanted. Dawson clarified, "I played [Hogan] like Bilko. And it was so—it must have been *so horrific*, it *surely* must have been so bad, that if I had *gotten* the [part of Hogan on the] show, we...would have been off in three episodes. I mean, I was *pathetic!* I don't mind telling you! Bob was *wonderful*."

Only one person from the *Hogan's Heroes* set who was approached for this biography held an especially strong opinion against Bob Crane. Stewart Moss, who appeared in the pilot episode as "outside man" Olsen, and then became a recurring guest star, had this to say about Bob: "You do not want to talk to me about Mr. Crane. Bob Crane was the asshole of assholes, the charter member of Assholes of America. I guest-starred along with Mr. Crane on *Quincy M.D.* and appeared in the pilot and six or seven episodes of *Hogan's Heroes*. I did not know him well. He was professional but a wise-cracker. I did not like the man, and I'm sure he knew it. I turned down the offer from the producer Ed Feldman to be a regular on the show." Moss furthered stated that Bob could be quite vulgar on the set. When asked to elaborate further, Moss refused.

Although it is unknown if anyone else heard such vulgarities from Bob, Cynthia Lynn reacted strongly to Moss' account. She said, "Wrong. *Wrong*. Totally wrong. No. Never, *ever* have I heard him say anything, *anything* on the set that was not appropriate, *ever*, when I was there. *No. No.* NO. *Never.* Never. Never. Never. *No* way, no how, never. He did not use foul language. I never heard him say anything that would... If a woman was around... he would mess around with the guys, you know, or whatever, guy talk, that kind of thing. But when there was a woman, he *respected* women. He respected them. He *never* used anything like that if there was a woman around. He was very, very, very careful. Well, not careful—that's the way he *was*! He was considerate of women! He *loved* women. Obviously. Whatever that man said is wrong."

Bruce Bilson was dumbfounded by Moss' harsh response, stating, "I never heard about that. I don't know where that [stemmed from]."

Arlene Martel did not comment on Steward Moss' recollections directly, but she did state that Bob had always treated her and other female guest stars with utmost respect on the set. "We had a lot of love scenes and kissing scenes," she said. "And he never once stepped outside of that or tried to turn it into an uncomfortable situation for me. He was very, very much a gentleman. And by that I mean he was a *gentle man*. I didn't feel any withheld violence. In fact, there seemed to be something romantic about him. I know there was a sweetness there, too, that I felt."

Victoria Carroll also said that she never heard or saw Bob being rude on the set. "No, no, I never saw any inappropriate behavior from him. Ever. He was always very gentlemanly and very professional, but I really didn't have any interaction with him. We had a love scene, and it was very professional. He would go to his dressing room and play his drums between takes. He was reclusive then, but very funny and very charming. He was distant without being rude, if that makes any sense. He was never rude. He was always affable, and as I said, very professional, whether it was running lines, or what he wanted to do in a scene."

Werner Klemperer had also relayed to Brenda Scott Royce that he and Bob were not "particularly friends on a social level," but that they had a "good working relationship." In other interviews, however, he has claimed that he and Bob were friends.

Actress Inger Wegge, who guest-starred in two episodes, had fond memories of working on the *Hogan's Heroes* set. She specifically remembered a promotional photo shoot with Bob. During the photo shoot, he had exhibited a small gesture of affection, which she described as "sweet."

"Bob Crane was absolutely lovely to me and so was John Banner," she said. "I spent the day on the set, and everybody was so nice as they could be. I had a small part, but it was a joy. The still picture was John Banner's idea, and I remember how Bob Crane squeezed my hand extra hard when the picture was taken. About Bob, he never touched me in any way that I found improper. The time the picture was taken, he did squeeze my hand in a very sexy way, but it did not bother me at all. I thought it was sweet and nice, and it must have made an impact as I still remember it. But he never said or did anything he should not do. John Banner, on the other hand, warned me for not going out with Bob. Well, I was never asked. John Banner asked, however, and we met quite often. But Bob never did anything else. He might have winked at me, but most men did. And I am sure he stood close to me. But nothing happened that I felt strange. "

Inger Wegge also noticed that other cast members were somewhat cold toward Bob. She thought it might have been that they had been jealous of Bob, saying, "I didn't get the impression that Bob was always 'on.' Maybe I could feel that the others didn't like him much. I never saw them chum together. Werner Klemperer told me a lot about his father, but he always told people about his father. But I never saw him talk to Bob. As a matter of fact, I didn't see anybody talk to Bob if we were not filming."

Arlene Martel also described Bob as being aloof, stating, "He kind of kept a distance, maybe that was a period in his life when he was not trusting or felt unworthy for whatever his reasons. The other guys would be kind of affectionate and 'pal-sy' with me, and yet he, playing a character who was supposed to be my love interest, he was the most distant. That's the general impression I got. I didn't see him 'Oh ho ho…' you know, and slap on the back. That wasn't his personality. He was—not with anything that I saw—did I see him extend some large gesture of camaraderie with anyone. And I don't know how they felt about him. Nobody gossiped negatively about him. Everyone seemed to respect and enjoy everyone else's talent. You know, there are some sets that are very gossipy and you feel the animosity among actors or their competitiveness. I didn't feel that. I thought that everyone enjoyed everyone else's work on this, that's what made it such a pleasure. But Bob was not very revealing of anything. Maybe if I had been on the show regularly, I would have been able to win his confidence more. It was almost like he wanted to come out but couldn't. He was sealed. Sealed—kind of in prison—*imprisoned*."

Of Bob's distancing himself from others, Bruce Bilson added, "He was very open to becoming a friend and to working together and to chatting and whatever, but he wasn't revealing anything beyond the surface. I don't think most of us do when we're on the set. We come in and this is who we are, and this is who we present ourselves as, and work. Yeah, we talk about hobbies, and 'I've got a boat'…'Oh, ever been sailing?' 'Oh, no'…'Wanna go sometime?' 'Sure.' All of that. You don't expose yourself very much to these people, and they don't expose themselves much to you. It's the working personalities that you bring with you when you come to work. Bob's working personality was fun. It was good. It was a guy with a smile on his face. And playing the drums in the other room. No cameras around the neck that I ever saw. I don't recall that at all."

From the start until the very end, it appears *Hogan's Heroes* was a set that had very little difficulty and where overall, regulars and guest stars alike found it a pleasant and comfortable place to work.

Whatever problems existed were few and far between, and it is a testament to all who worked on the series that they were able to put any personal differences aside while at work to create a very successful show.

Actor Monte Markham appeared in one episode of *Hogan's Heroes* during the last season—"Eight O'Clock and All Is Well." Markham testified that the same good-natured atmosphere that had been present since the beginning of the series existed even by the final season. "Half-hours are difficult—and different," Markham explained. "This was a half-hour comedy. I remember going in now and feeling it's a lightweight show. Bob was a funny guy, very social, and gregarious. I got the call to do [*Hogan's Heroes*], and it was a good five or six days on location with everybody. Werner and I spent many hours just yammering and talking on the set. Werner was great. And Robert Clary was, again, just as charming as you'd expect. It was a very easy shoot. I can see all the guys, and I see the set, where they were all standing around the barrel of fire and keeping warm. They were wearing *very* heavy garments in hot weather. There's nothing quite like a good, *good* series, in other words, it was well run. The guys obviously liked each other. Nobody was a grab-ass. Nobody was bitching and moaning. There are some very *bad* shows to work on. Meaning, it's all falling apart or my trailer's bigger than yours, and complaining all the time. Good sets are good sets, and it's geared off the producer and the star, and they can make it a good set or they can make it a terrible thing to work. It was a well-run show, and for me, it was *very* easy going. It was fun. There were a lot of laughs. They were having a good time. There is *nothing* more pleasant than a successful series when it's running. Then it depends on if it's running well, it's good. I didn't see anything antagonistic with anybody. I wouldn't say Bob was Mr. Golden Boy or Mr. Perfect. We would do the scenes. I will say that this was their sixth year, and they weren't really working hard. I mean, they were all looking to him when they would do their scenes. The guys worked together, and then he would come in. He wasn't working his butt off, no. It was simple stuff to do. And it had really run its course. It was good. The people were good. No big incident happened or anything like that. I remember the laughs, with Werner particularly. He was very funny. Having a good time. In Bob's case, it was like, okay, this is a guy who's a radio personality, and he's got a good personality, and they cast him as this guy, and it's a funny comedy, and it's a slapstick kind of a way and having a good time and make the Germans funny. But *Bob Crane* was not really taken seriously at all."

With his performance on *Hogan's Heroes*, Bob evolved into a professional actor. He went to work, did his job, did it well, and hoped it would translate onto the screen and resonate with audiences. Bob was also his own harshest critic. Throughout at least the first year of *Hogan's Heroes*, Donna Reed would call Bob immediately after the week's episode aired. Together, they would dissect his work in that particular episode, discussing what worked and what didn't. He claimed that she would offer him "words of wisdom and frank evaluation," coaching him on his acting techniques and helping him strengthen his skills.

Yet perhaps it was Bob's own flippant, candid remarks in the press about *Hogan's Heroes* and his character of Hogan that permitted others in the industry to write him off and not consider him a serious actor. "I never take myself seriously as Hogan," he said. "To me, he's not a natural hero, but a natural con man. It's *Terry and the Pirates*, with the hat on the back of his head. I think the pace is beautiful. We try to make the plot premises reasonable, although I grant you the show is pretty far from what actual combat ever was."

Hogan's Heroes ran for six successful seasons on CBS, from September 17, 1965, through April 4, 1971, ending with the episode "Rockets or Romance." Its final prime time broadcast (as a re-run) was on July 4, 1971. *Hogan's Heroes* was considered a dream show for nearly all involved, and during its entire run, key changes would occur that would impact several key members of the cast, including Bob.

The first dynamic change came only one year into the series. Cynthia Lynn, who had won the hearts of her fans as well as the critics for her sweet portrayal of Fräulein Helga, decided abruptly to bow out. Wanting to concentrate on saving her marriage, she left the series right before filming began on season two, and just when *Hogan's Heroes* was beginning to etch itself permanently into television history. She admitted it was a decision she would come to regret for the rest of her life.

Replacing Cindy Lynn as Colonel Klink's secretary from seasons two through six, Patricia "Patty" Olson, who went by the stage name Sigrid Valdis, was cast as Fräulein Hilda. She was equally appealing and sexy in the role of Hilda as Cindy had been as Helga; however,

Hilda appeared a bit less naïve and more cunning than her predecessor. Patty even relayed that when she was hired, the producers had promised her more integral involvement in the prisoners' espionage and schemes. It was also conveyed in the press that Hilda would be Colonel Hogan's primary love interest.

After the fifth season, contracts came up for renewal. Almost all of the regular cast re-negotiated and then re-signed for what they thought would be another two years. Conspicuously absent was Ivan Dixon, who decided he had had enough of prison life, and instead, wished to concentrate on more serious directorial work. In his place, another African-American actor, Kenneth Washington, signed on to play Sergeant Richard Baker, who was also a radioman. Much in the same way Hilda had replaced Helga, both of whom seemed mirror images of the other with their similar blond pigtails and shapely figures, Kinch and Baker were almost interchangeable characters.

Kenneth Washington's prior acting experience included working with David Janssen and Jack Albertson in films, and appearing on such television series as *Petticoat Junction* and *Marcus Welby, M.D. Hogan's Heroes* was the first regular role for Washington. A former law student, he yearned to become an actor, and while working in the courtroom, he decided to take acting classes simultaneously with his law courses.

"I wanted to learn everything I could about acting, so I came to Hollywood," Washington said.

After a few roles in theatre performances, Washington was hooked. His first comedy role was on *Petticoat Junction*. He said, "I was nervous about doing comedy, but it was a great experience, and I only hope the audience had as much fun watching the show as I had in the performance."

For his work on *Hogan's Heroes*, Kenneth Washington should receive credit for trying very hard to replace an actor and a character whom audiences had come to know and love, and expected to see, but then was suddenly missing, with no explanation given. Kinch's absence was not written into any of the episodes during the sixth and final season; Kinch was merely "replaced" with someone new and similar, yet different, which only caused confusion. Despite Washington's best efforts, however, Sergeant Baker was not Sergeant Kinchloe. Audiences could not understand the replacement, and therefore, never fully embraced Baker. To this day, fans still ask, "What happened to Kinch?"

"Ivan wanted to get off and do other things," said Bruce Bilson. "And then eventually, he became a director. The Directors' Guild honored him as a breakthrough for African Americans. He ended up going to Hawaii and started a radio station. But I thought we lost something when we lost Ivan."

During its run, *Hogan's Heroes* was nominated for numerous awards and several Emmys. The series never won for Outstanding Comedy Series, although it was nominated three times by the Academy for the seasons 1965-1966 (lost to *The Dick Van Dyke Show*), 1966-1967 (lost to *The Monkees*), and 1967-1968 (lost to *Get Smart*). Bob Crane was nominated twice for Outstanding Continued Performance by an Actor in a Leading Role in a Comedy Series twice—for the seasons 1965-1966 (lost to Dick Van Dyke) and 1967-1968 (lost to Don Adams). Nita Talbot was nominated for the 1967-1968 season for Outstanding Performance by an Actress in a Supporting Role in a Comedy Series for the episode "The Hostage." She lost to Marion Lorne for her work on *Bewitched*.

The only *Hogan's Heroes* actor to win an Emmy was Werner Klemperer. With the exception of season six, he was nominated consistently each season for Outstanding Performance by an Actor in a Supporting Role in a Comedy Series, and he won for seasons 1967-1968 and 1968-1969.

The Emmy nominations for the 1965-1966 season were announced the week of April 30, 1966. The press continued to hail *Hogan's Heroes*, with one report stating, "One non-rerun was *Hogan's Heroes*, which along with *Get Smart*, is the best new comedy of the year. It's got class, style, pace, and a rousing good cast led by the fine new funnyman Bob Crane."

No one from *Hogan's Heroes* took home a statue at the 18th Annual Emmy Awards on the evening of May 22, 1966. Bob shrugged it off, and in front of the cameras and with *Dick Van Dyke Show* writer Bill Persky and Eva Gabor at his side, quipped "I won't let them know, but I would rather have Eva than Emmy."

It would seem that for the 1965-1966 Emmys, the reward for all *Hogan's Heroes* nominees was perhaps not so much in winning the actual award, but rather, having been nominated at all following their first year on the air. One report stated, "The major complaints about the new system concerned not singling out 'new' programs and people for recognition apart from having to compete with the established ones. Bob Crane and his *Hogan's Heroes*, for example, couldn't really be expected to have a chance against the seasoned and talented Dick Van Dyke and his program, whereas he and the program might have been regarded as one of the best new ones."

The National Academy of Television and Science never recognized Bob Crane with an Emmy for his work on *Hogan's Heroes*. Reports claim Bob resented Werner Klemperer for his dual Emmy winnings. Bob's cousin Jane Senich Ryfun also hinted there was a stab of professional jealousy Bob felt toward Klemperer after having been routinely overlooked by the Academy. Yet Bob remained professional, always.

In March 1971, CBS announced the fall season, and *Hogan's Heroes*, which had lost ground in the ratings war ever since moving to Sunday night, was missing from the schedule.

"Renewals happen generally when you're on hiatus," said Bruce Bilson. "In other words, you finish a season, hope you get renewed, and then the schedule comes out, and if you're on it, you're renewed. If you're off it, you're not. So what happens is everybody goes their way, and if you don't get back together, you're gone. It's not like we're having a going away party. Did you ever expect to work with these people again?"

Bob had been irritated with the decision to move the series at the start of season six. Over the course of its six-year run, *Hogan's Heroes* moved several times: seasons one and two—Fridays at eight-thirty p.m.; seasons three and four—Saturdays at nine o'clock p.m.; season five—Fridays at eight-thirty p.m.; and season six—Sundays at seven-thirty p.m. (all Eastern Time). He was certain the Sunday time slot was at least partly to blame for the cancellation. But Bob, as well as others, had also grown weary of the series. After six seasons, perhaps there were just no more bridges to blow up, secret plans to smuggle out, or jokes to pull.

"The series was canceled for two reasons," Bob said. "One, CBS had enough films to put it into syndication as a five-time-a-week show. Two, *Hogan's Heroes* had been the network's 'utility' series; the time slot had been changed five times in six years. Even with that handicap, we were always in the top 40. Once we made it to the top 10, but I think that was because the other networks were showing a news documentary and the flag salute. Finally, CBS put us opposite Disney on Sunday night, and that did it."

In recent times, television historians have revealed that *Hogan's Heroes* was part of what is now referred to as "The Rural Purge." Between 1969 and 1972, networks, and in particular CBS, went on a cancellation streak in which they axed any television series that had "demographically skewed audiences," despite still strong ratings of those shows. CBS decided that *Hogan's Heroes* would not appeal to the masses, and so was considered "rural." As a result, it fell victim to the network's purge. Other series that were cancelled at this time included *Mayberry R.F.D., Gomer Pyle U.S.M.C., Lassie, The Red Skelton Hour, The Beverly Hillbillies,* and *Family Affair*, to name a few.

Once the decision was made, Bob took it upon himself to contact each of his costars and some crew directly. He sent personal letters to Werner Klemperer, John Banner, Robert Clary, Richard Dawson, Larry Hovis, Ivan Dixon, and Kenneth Washington, as well as writer Bill Davenport, wherein he expressed his heartfelt thanks to each for their part in the success of the series and hoped they remained in contact.

It seems as if I went from a radio station, walked across the street, and became a so-called TV star. It really didn't happen that way. I spent fifteen years in radio before I got to "Hogan's Heroes." I love [acting]. People ask, "Would you go back to radio?" and I've said, "Not really, because this is a step in the right direction—great training—learning to think on your feet, learning to communicate with an audience. It's satisfying. ["Hogan's Heroes"] is so successful because of] the chemistry—the people in it.
—Bob Crane, December 1968

Colonel Robert E. Hogan will always be considered by fans and critics the role Bob Crane was born to play. Of anything he had done before and everything he would ever do after, none would compare to his signature role as the senior prisoner of war, "con man to the Wehrmacht," and underground spy. He breathed life into that character as nobody else ever could and possibly ever will. The years from 1965 to 1971 truly were, from his perspective, the best years of his life.

They were also some of the most tumultuous years of his life. During the course of *Hogan's Heroes*, Bob's life changed dramatically. Cynthia Lynn and Patty Olson became more than just co-stars to Bob, proving dramatically influential in his personal life. Before *Hogan's Heroes* broadcast its final episode, Bob had had two very serious affairs—one with Cynthia Lynn, which lasted from the very start of the series in January 1965 through the spring of 1966 when Cindy left the show, and another with Patty Olson, beginning soon after Cindy's departure from the series. Bob and Anne would separate—permanently this time, and their marriage would end in divorce in 1970. Finally, Bob and Patty would marry in October 1970, and Patty would become pregnant, giving birth to their son Robert Scott Crane in June 1971.

With his international stardom borne from his work on *Hogan's Heroes*, Bob would also come to be recognized as Colonel Hogan wherever he went. People would see him, and they would not shout for Bob Crane; they shouted for Hogan. The series that bestowed upon him the star status he coveted for so long would also do something else, something a little more harmful. Colonel Hogan became the one and only role the viewers would ever associate with Bob Crane, and whatever other role he played, Hogan's shadow was in the way. The very thing he had always wanted would become a roadblock to the future, and his typecasting would pigeonhole him into a prison from which he would never fully escape.

In 1965, when the series was young and Bob had been hopeful, he could not have anticipated any of it. He had welcomed the recognition as Hogan. And as always, his twinkling eyes were ever set on the future.

"I do not think I would ever go back to radio, even should this series fail," he said. "I was in it [almost] sixteen years. I started at $37.50 a week and was near the six-figure mark when I quit. But never did I consider radio as a money-making thing. I did it because it was fun. But fun is one thing and progress another. During my radio days, I'd see a producer for a movie role. He'd look at me and say, 'Oh, yes. Crane. You're the local disc jockey.' I wouldn't get the job. It took me all these years to defeat that image. Nobody knew me. But now, after only three episodes of Hogan, people recognize me at the market or on the street. You know, like, 'How you doin' Hogan?' Hence, I hopefully feel that even should the series not go, I will have established myself as an actor, and this time, producers will give me more of their time."

Bob once proclaimed what he believed defined a true hero: "A hero is someone you realize is perfect—someone you associate with yourself." It is an extraordinarily powerful statement. Bob Crane was a perfectionist, and he worked himself almost to death trying to achieve perfection in all he did.

Colonel Hogan was a larger-than-life character who rarely stumbled and never fell. Hogan was perfect in every way, and audiences of every generation would come to adore him, making him timeless. Hogan became the alter ego of Bob Crane—a hero whom Bob saw as the epitome of perfect. Hogan was the hero that *he* brought to life; a hero so perfect he could counterbalance Bob's own private demons that were quickly starting to escalate and take control.

As the curtain closed on *Hogan's Heroes*, Bob would once again begin to seek another perfect fit; another perfect role that would be tailor-made to his liking.

But he was about to discover that Colonel Hogan was a tough act to follow.

Welcome to Stalag 13, Colonel Hogan

Source: From the author's personal collection.

Original drawing by Mike Senich, uncle of Bob Crane.
Source: Courtesy of Jane Senich Ryfun. Used with permission.

Welcome to Stalag 13, Colonel Hogan

Bob Crane and Werner Klemperer sparring as Hogan and Klink.

Source: Courtesy of Scott Crane. Used with permission.

Bob Crane and John Banner as Hogan and Schultz.

Source: From the author's personal collection.

Richard Dawson, Leon Askin, and Bob Crane clowning around on the set.

Source: From the author's personal collection.

Hogan and his heroes: (left to right) Richard Dawson (Newkirk), Ivan Dixon (Kinchloe), Bob Crane (Hogan), Larry Hovis (Carter), and Robert Clary (LeBeau).

Source: Courtesy of Scott Crane. Used with permission.

Bob Crane and Inger Wegge. Inger remembered that Bob gave her hand a little squeeze during this photo shoot, and she thought it was "sweet."

Source: From the author's personal collection.

Welcome to Stalag 13, Colonel Hogan

Bob Crane and director Jerry London. "From the time Bob did the pilot to the time he did the last show, he was Hogan. He was Hogan."

Source: Courtesy of Jerry London. Used with permission.

The cast of *Hogan's Heroes* season two (circa 1967).
Bob Crane, Sigrid Valdis (Patricia Olson), Director Bruce Bilson, Robert Clary, Ivan Dixon, Larry Hovis, John Banner, and Werner Klemerper.
"It was a great show to work on," Bruce said. "I always thought of Bob like Skippy… just that attitude that everything's good."

Source: Courtesy of Bruce Bilson. Used with permission.

Welcome to Stalag 13, Colonel Hogan

The "REAL HEROES" (Left to Right)—Dennis Gray, Walter Smith, Edgar Johnson, Roy Goldman, Sam Haygan, and Dick Ryan.

As preserved in Bob's *Hogan's Heroes* scrapbook.

Source: Courtesy of Scott Crane. Used with permission.

The cast of *Hogan's Heroes* Season 6. Standing (left to right): John Banner, Richard Dawson, Bob Crane, Werner Klemperer. Seated (left to right): Robert Clary, Kenneth Washington, and Larry Hovis.

Source: Courtesy of Scott Crane. Use with permission.

Welcome to Stalag 13, Colonel Hogan

Top and bottom photos: Bob Crane, Werner Klemperer, and John Banner making personal appearances.

Source: Both photos courtesy of Scott Crane. Used with permission.

Bob Crane greets Richard Hogan, son of Dr. Colonel Robert Hogan (1966).
Source: Courtesy of Richard Hogan. Used with permission.

Bob Crane as Colonel Hogan meets the *real* Dr. Colonel Robert Hogan (1966).
Source: Courtesy of Richard Hogan. Used with permission.

Welcome to Stalag 13, Colonel Hogan

All photos: Bob Crane making personal appearances. Top—with John Banner and Werner Klemperer

Source: All photos courtesy of Scott Crane. Used with permission.

Continuity sequence photographs of Bob Crane in character on *Hogan's Heroes*.

Source: All photos courtesy of Scott Crane. Used with permission.

Welcome to Stalag 13, Colonel Hogan

Bob Crane and Robert Clary having fun on the set of *Hogan's Heroes*.
Source: Courtesy of Scott Crane. Used with permission.

Bob Crane's Letters to the Cast of *Hogan's Heroes* Following Cancellation of the Series

The following are the letters that Bob Crane wrote and sent to the cast of "Hogan's Heroes," thanking them for their work, and where applicable, their friendship. Other letters may have been sent; however, these are the only copies of letters located in Bob's personal files. It is clear that Bob did, indeed, consider the six years he worked on "Hogan's Heroes" the best six years of his life.

Letter to John Banner

March 10, 1971

Dear John:

Well, from the looks of the new fall schedule, our time together on *Hogan's* has ended, but not without a bit of sorrow on my part.

It's been a ball working with you for six years, but above all, Patty and I prize our friendship with you and Christine, and we hope our relationship won't come to an end with the show.

If I can be of any assistance in any way whatsoever, please call on me. Once again, thanks so much for six of the best years of my life.
Bob

Letter to Robert Clary

March 10, 1971

Dear Robert:

With the fall schedule pretty well definite, I just wanted to thank you in writing for all your help during the past six years.

The Vegas situation is dead for June, but there's a good possibility something will happen this fall. If so, and you are available, I certainly hope we will be able to get together again.

Patty and I leave for Australia Wednesday, and when we get back, I'll take off for Illinois for a month. Then we will be staying around for the birth of the baby at the end of May or June.

We would like to have you and Natalie, and perhaps Ed and his wife over for dinner at that time, so stay loose.

Once again, thanks for everything.
Bob

Letter to Richard Dawson

March 10, 1971

Dear Dick:

It looks like *Hogan's* has come to an end and we won't be working together for the next 24 weeks or whatever.

I do want to take this opportunity to thank you for all your help during the past six years. I know we've had our differences, but I do believe it was only because of our individual desires to do the best job possible as we saw it.

As I mentioned to you on the phone, the Vegas situation dissolved along with Frank Sennes and the current economic situation in Vegas, so it's just as well we didn't expend any more effort than we did.

Needless to say, I think you are one of the most talented guys I know, and your recent Merv Griffin appearance was a gas.

I hope sometime in the near future, we can work together again, and I hope on friendlier conditions, but in the meantime, thank you for all your help for the past six years.

Bob

Letter to Ivan Dixon

March 10, 1971

Dear Ivan:

Although you weren't physically a part of *Hogan's* for the sixth and final year, I do want to tell you that your presence was never forgotten.

I hope your career has flourished and above all, I do hope we can work together sometime in the future.

During the five years you were on the show, you made it a hell of a lot easier to face the sameness of the plots and situations by being so damned cooperative, and above all, talented.

Once again, thanks for all your help in the past, and the best to your and your family.

Bob

Letter to Larry Hovis

March 10, 1971

Dear Larry:

Well, it looks like we won't be waiting for you to arrive on Monday anymore. Frankly, I had given up on Fridays, anyway.

I am certainly going to miss working with you, as you have helped to make the past six years the best time of my life.

As you may have read, our Vegas deal fell through, but there's still a possibility it might be revived after I get back from summer stock, so I still have hopes that we can work together again.

If I can be of any help to you in any way, please call upon me.

Again, thanks for all your help.

Bob

Letter to Werner Klemperer

March 10, 1971

Dear Werner:

Even though it's not official, it sure as hell looks like we're not going to be donning the blue, grey, and brown for the coming season.

It's been the best six years of my life, and I hope you feel the same.

I'm sorry the Vegas situation did not work out for June. You probably read that our "friend" Frank Sennes got the ax.

As I told you, I'm doing a play starting the end of June, which will take me up to Labor Day, but I'm still working on a couple of possibilities for our nightclub act. If you are available, I hope you will be part of it.

Patty and I leave for Australia Wednesday, and will only be back for a week (April 4-11) before I take off for Illinois for a month, so if I don't get to see you before they shove us the hell off the lot, please take our new address.

Once again, thanks for everything.

Bob

Letter to Kenneth Washington

March 10, 1971

Dear Ken:

If I forgot to do it before, let me thank you so much for the beautiful Christmas gift.

As you may have heard, we are not renewed for the coming season, and I would like to take this opportunity to thank you for all your help and enthusiasm during the sixth year of our show.

I am sorry we didn't get to work together longer, but it's been a relationship I will always remember fondly.

If I can be of any help in any way, please contact me.

Thanks again for all your help, and best wishes for your future career.

Bob

Letter to Bill Davenport

March 16, 1971

Dear Bill:

Well, the day has finally arrived when we'll no longer be doing the nutty things you dreamt up for us for the past six years.

Although we all knew what would happen eventually, there's a bit of sadness when you realize what a great group we had, and how proud we all were to be doing material we enjoyed.

I am going to be on the road for a month or so with the new Barasch play "Beginner's Luck," but if I can be of any help in any way, please get in touch at our new address.

You have made the last six years the greatest time of my life. For that, many many thanks.

Bob

PS – Vegas is out until at least Fall! So what else is new.

Chapter 7
Among the Stellar Elite

Don't think I don't shake over the idea. But you've got to take a chance sometime, or you never progress.

—Bob Crane on wanting to become an actor, 1965

Source: From the author's personal collection.

Source: Courtesy of Scott Crane. Used with permission.

Chapter 7
Among the Stellar Elite

As far as I know, nobody has followed the line of succession from radio-to-television-to movies as I have in the past ten years or so. It's a long process, but I knew what I wanted and where I hoped to go.
—Bob Crane, 1967

If there was one thing Bob Crane had learned well in his climb to success, it was patience. And having achieved his fame, he felt very comfortable talking about it.

"I got started in radio as the main thing and gradually worked into television," Bob told a reporter in 1970. "It took seventeen years to do it. Nothing happens overnight. And if nothing else can be learned from what I learned, it's *that*. Don't be impatient. It doesn't happen overnight. It took me many, many, many, *many* years. It took me three-and-a-half years to get my first radio job. I was drumming for five years before I ever worked my first job, mainly because I started drumming when I was about eight or nine. But I was fourteen, and I was suddenly playing in clubs. And you know, it takes *time*. That's the trouble, I think, if you want to name one thing that's wrong with most everybody today. Everybody's in a hurry. Everybody says, 'Now! It's gotta happen now! Now, baby, now!' And it *can't* happen now. It just isn't within the power of anybody to make things happen [snaps fingers] overnight like that. Make everybody rich. Everybody beautiful. Everybody happy. As a scientist said on one of these talk shows the other night, he says, 'Okay, everybody's rich. Everybody's healthy. Everybody's got everything they want. Then what?' And this other scientist said, 'There'll still be wars. There'll still be arguments. They'll find something else to fight about.' That's the human nature of people."

Bob had been patient almost to a fault prior to selecting *Hogan's Heroes* as his star vehicle, and he had chosen wisely. As the direct result of the success of *Hogan's Heroes*, by the end of 1965, Bob Crane was a household name, and *Hogan's Heroes* was on its way to becoming a timeless classic, fifty years into the future and beyond.

By season two, *Hogan's Heroes* expanded its viewing audience to include several countries worldwide: England, Argentina, Australia, the Philippines, Thailand, Venezuela, Uruguay, and even Japan; although, in the Far East, it was billed as a drama rather than a comedy. While intrigued, the Japanese were not quite yet ready to laugh at World War II. Unremarkably, Germany was not interested in broadcasting the series. But it hardly seemed to matter. As Colonel Hogan, Bob had gained an international stardom that propelled him to heights that he had never before attained, but for which he had always yearned. Bob Crane had become one of the era's "stellar elite," and his career flourished.

Back home in Connecticut, Bob's family and friends cheered. They were proud to know him and thrilled he had made it in the entertainment business; yet, many were not surprised by his fame. They remembered his outgoing and amicable, albeit humble, personality. His success, they believed, was rightfully deserved.

"When he got his big deal with *Hogan's Heroes*, I sent him a note of congratulations," said Stamford High School friend David Dugan. "He quickly replied with an eight-by-ten glossy in his Hogan uniform and several comments about high school days."

"I remember him as a *personality* at Stamford High School who was always smiling and friendly," recalled classmate Jack Williams. "Of course, when he showed up as Colonel Hogan, we all were very proud of him and enjoyed the series."

Boyhood friend Neil McGuinness said, "Bob was a great friend. He always made us laugh. I never remember him being ugly or unfriendly. He was always good to be around. In that era, to me, Bob was just another fabulous kid from our small neighborhood. When I saw him on television later, I was so glad that he made it big. He was so very much like that character he played in that show—a happy friend that everyone wanted to know."

Janice Marzano, daughter of Bob's school friend and classmate Arnold Poller, who passed away in 2001, wrote, "Growing up, we *had* to watch *Hogan's Heroes* every night it was on—and repeatedly were told, 'I went to school with Bob. I played football with Bob.' My Dad would have *loved* to be part of [this book]!!"

Connecticut radio personality Jack Coombe further expressed his joy at learning of Bob's success. "None of us dreamed he would attain star stature in a short time. When he did with the TV series *Hogan's Heroes*, we were all proud of him and agreed that he deserved the fame."

KNX friend and colleague Leo McElroy said, "I actually celebrated hugely when I heard he had it. My first thought, quite honestly, was, 'This show isn't going to get thirteen weeks. There's no way you can be funny about prisoners of war in a [POW] camp. It's not gonna work. But God, I'm glad Bob got a lead in something.' And that was my reaction. What amazed me was they actually made the bloody concept work! It just astounds me that they somehow pulled it together and got it to fly. A really unlikely comedy setting. I actually read about it in the trades to begin with, and then as I remember, I called Bob and said, 'Wow!' And he said, 'Yeah, I'm *really* excited.' He was being him. He was absolutely being him. It was Bob all the way. It was the same wisecracking Bob. I didn't see a great deal of difference. I think he was getting even better at articulating it, even better at being clear with who he was and what he was doing. It was right on the money. I watched it, and it was one of the few shows that I watched that my kids were willing to watch, which was pretty rare, I have to tell you."

Adored by millions of fans, Bob received scores of letters from around the world, and to say that Bob also adored his fans is an understatement. To his credit, he did his very best to read and personally answer as much of his own fan mail as he possibly could, although it would have been a daunting task. Fans who wrote to Bob in care of the *Hogan's Heroes* studios would receive either an autographed 8"x10" glossy portrait on which he would often inscribe a short note above his signature, or a picture postcard with a pre-printed note in his handwriting on the reverse thanking the letter writer for watching the show, which he would then also personally autograph.

Accolades came from everywhere. Bob was a star, and he was in great demand. It seemed everyone wanted a piece of Bob Crane, who had quickly become a larger-than-life celebrity. Bob had worked hard to achieve it, but he was also nearly working himself to death to maintain it.

Fame and fortune did not come without worry or consequence. Overzealous and obsessed fans can cause distress to public figures and their families. Cousin Jim Senich remembered that following the success of *Hogan's Heroes*, one of Bob's greatest fears was that someone would break into his home and kidnap his children.

"He loved being onstage, he loved being in front of a camera, and there was nothing else he wanted to do," Jim said. "It wasn't that he had the ego, but he *loved that*. But he was concerned about being a celebrity, telling me, 'I have to have a fence around my whole property that they electrify because there's that fear of kidnapping—somebody grabbing one of my kids. I don't enjoy that part of it.' He *worried* about the fear of them being kidnapped."

Bob also often worried about exposing his younger cousins to the other side of fame, a side laced with hidden dangers and fears for one's safety. Jim continued, "Bob said, 'It's the way you gotta live out here.' Annie used to say to me, 'Jimmy, you don't know how much he's wanted to bring you out to Hollywood, but he said, 'I don't want to bring him out to this kind of lifestyle.'"

The Cranes and Seniches—and Bob's father in particular—were exceptionally proud. Al, Sr. had perhaps been toughest on Bob, especially when his younger son had snubbed inheriting the jewelry store in lieu of pursuing a career in radio. Bob had happily been able to prove his father wrong, and now that Bob was a celebrity, Al was just as quick to allow him to do so.

"Bob believed in himself," said Jim. "He really believed it. He was gonna make it, and fortunately, his mom was behind him. Then when he started to branch out and grow, his dad became his biggest fan. You know—'That's my Bob.'"

When Al and Rose Crane migrated west to be closer to Bob and Anne and the kids, they settled nearby, joining Anne's mother, who had been living with Bob and Anne in their home in Tarzana. Tarzana was, at the time, a small yet prestigious community where many stars found private sanctuary away from the bright lights of downtown Los Angeles or Hollywood. It was close enough to Hollywood to commute rather easily in LA traffic, yet exclusive enough to keep prying reporters and fans at bay. On February 24, 1960, Bob gave his wit-laden description of Tarzana over KNX, when, at the time, he had only been living in California for a few years.

"I have *only* been out here on the West Coast for about three-and-a-half years. We did a [radio] show back east, and we were sent out here, we moved out. 'We' being my family—my wife and son and my mother-in-law—it was the usual package deal when you come to California. And you know, living back there is a completely different way of life. Unless you have lived in California, you don't know what it's like out here. For instance, Beverly Hills, you've *all* heard, this is where the stars live. I live in Tarzana, which is right alongside of Beverly Hills. It's just as exclusive, just as exclusive as Beverly Hills! But it's *not* Beverly Hills, you see. To give you an idea of how exclusive Tarzana is, and this is no joke, we actually have a fire department with an unlisted phone number. How exclusive can you get?"

In addition to Bob and Anne's friends Harvey Geller and his wife, the Cranes counted Doris Day, Leonard Nimoy, and Clayton Moore as their neighbors. As much as it most likely excited Bob to have finally been counted among Hollywood royalty, to those around him, he never seemed to be in awe of himself or any other celebrity.

"I think he would just kid about it," said Jim. "He said, 'When I look to the left, I see Doris Day. When I look to the right, I see the Lone Ranger.' I don't think Bob was the kind of guy who was in awe of *anybody*. That's why he could interview them and hit them with a tough question."

Bob's relatives back home in Connecticut were elated to have a star in the family. Some vied for his attention when he returned to visit, occasionally causing friction, much to Bob's discomfort. Bob wanted to please everybody. But that was impossible.

"Whenever he came into New York, he always came up to Connecticut, I'd say maybe three, four, five times a year," Jim explained. "And everybody would get excited, as well we should, but then you'd run into that thing of, 'Who's house is he going to stay at? Where is he going to eat? Well, he can't go to Jim's mom and dad because they don't own a house.' We lived in a first floor rent, very nice rent, but he never went there for dinner; it was always the ones that had the big house. I think it hurt my mom and dad, but they never said it. Every time he came to Waterbury, the family wanted a piece of him, and it got to the point where he'd be at [my relatives' house], but I wouldn't even go up. I felt embarrassed. It was a tough time for me. And again, the relatives were all over him. I wasn't going to play that. I did it once. He was at [my relatives' house]; we went up to their house, and they had Bob and Annie there. They invited us to come up, and they all sat in the other room eating, while we sat out in the parlor. My mother, tough heart that she was, said, 'Let's get the hell out of here; I'm not kissing his ass.' And it wasn't Bobby; it was my relatives. I mean, why invite you to have you sit there while they're eating? And we ran into that. But Bobby didn't want that; he really didn't want that. That wasn't Bobby. Thinking back, maybe Bobby could have said something, too. Maybe Bobby could have said, 'I want to go up to Jim's mom and dad's house.' Maybe he did, and they said something like, 'You couldn't [go there].' But we always had a good relationship, and my dad loved him. When my dad was on his deathbed, and the word got to Bobby, he flew out from California and came up here just to see my dad. He went up and sat with him and held him in his arms. He was a good nephew. The nurses went nuts when they heard he was there. My dad got a kick out of that."

Bob also told Jim that once he achieved his celebrity status in Hollywood, he felt he was deeply indebted to many in the entertainment community. When they would call on him for favors, he never believed he could turn them down.

"He said he *owed* people who helped him to get where he got," Jim said. "And they would say, 'It's payback time.' What I mean is, to make a public appearance or something, or do a small part in a movie. He said, 'One day, we were having a barbecue on the back patio, and I was just ready to give everybody their food, and Annie came out and said, 'Art Linkletter's on the phone.' It was Father's Day or something like that. He had said to him, 'Bob, I need you right now. I was going to do a show, and I'm sick as a dog; you've gotta go for me.' 'What am I gonna say? No? I went.' He said, 'That part of it bothered me; I couldn't really spend the time I wanted to with my family.'"

There were steep prices to pay, but overall, Bob was in his glory. He relished his fame and used it to his advantage. And as he had done with radio, his drums were never far from reach. Bob had an idea, and it was an idea he had dreamed of doing since he was a little boy, when he first laid eyes on Gene Krupa at the 1939 World's Fair.

A little known fact is that Bob Crane provided the percussion talent for the official *Hogan's Heroes* theme song that is heard during both the opening and end credits of the series. Every time the credits roll at the start and conclusion of each episode, it is to the rhythm of Bob's drumming. In addition, Bob's drumming had been incorporated into two *Hogan's Heroes* episodes—"Flight of the Valkyrie" in season one and "Look at the Pretty Snowflakes" in season six, also the last episode of the series to be filmed. But seeing Bob play the timpani or a full drum set had *only* been permitted on two episodes. While it was no doubt fun for Bob to show off his musical abilities on his show, he had also been outspokenly opposed to it from the outset.

"There were a lot of gimmicks in the pilot," Bob explained. "Fun, but unnecessary. And there were a few shows [during the first season] when we became silly—like *McHale's Navy*. But we try to skirt that, and we have enough adventure going to do it. The element of danger is essential. I used to be a drummer, and everyone always asks, 'Why don't you do a show where you drum?' Because it has no basis in the show, that's why. Robert Clary's a fine singer, but he's never sung on the show for the same reason.

"If you'll notice," he continued, "we don't have any real out-and-out jokes on *Hogan*. Basically, the program is drama. We, the 'Heroes,' are pro-American, pro-heroic, and we're always involved in some sort of scheme that's really dramatic. Then the comedy takes off from there. We play *against* funny situations and people. For instance, Colonel Klink's great ego is a big plus for us, as we diabolically set about to tear it down."

While Robert Clary and the rest of the cast did show off their musical talents in a handful of episodes, and there was very little of Bob's drumming on the series, the constant sound of drumming coming from his dressing room eventually led to something more exciting for Bob.

Record producer and television and film composer Stu Phillips could not recall if he had initially called Bob or if Bob had called him, but at some point in 1966, they connected.

"I knew Bob from *The Donna Reed Show*," Stu explained. "I had met him, and I knew he was a disc jockey. And of course, I was in the record business also, and I tried to be friendly so he would play some of my records on the air. And as far as I knew, nobody ever seemed to have a bad word for Bob in those days. I was *extremely* friendly with Paul Petersen and Shelley Fabares then because I was their A&R (Artist and Repertoire) man and produced their records, and they worked with him on a daily basis."

With Shelley Fabares' number-one hit single *Johnny Angel*, Stu became what he considered an "overnight success." He went on to achieve great stature as a television and film composer and record producer in the entertainment industry, where over the period of forty years, amassed a list of formidable credits to his name.

Shortly after season one of *Hogan's Heroes* came to a close, Stu Phillips and Bob Crane began discussing the possibility of an album. Bob may not have wanted his drumming to take away from the drama of the series, but the prospect of recording an album where he could truly showcase his musical talents appealed to him greatly.

"Bob Crane, His Drums and Orchestra Play the Funny Side of TV"
Themes from Television's Great Comedy Series – Liner Notes

In December 1966, Epic Records released "Bob Crane, His Drums and Orchestra Play the Funny Side of TV." It would be the only album that Bob Crane would ever release. Of Bob's work on the album, producer Stu Phillips wrote in his autobiography "Stu Who?" that Bob was "a joy to work with… Any time spent with him always included a lot of jokes and one-liners. He loved to entertain and was always 'on.' Bob's ability as a drummer was professional enough to give us the idea of producing an album of TV themes, with him playing the drums. Bob suggested that he also add a few comedy routines to the overall conception. For three recording sessions, the musicians and I had a ball being entertained by Crane. He was, as far as I was concerned, a great guy." The following are the liner notes from the album.

What is a "Bob Crane?" Well, to begin with, he's a successful actor (star of *Hogan's Heroes*), he was also successful as a disc jockey interviewer (on KNX-CBS Radio in Los Angeles); he's a comedian (though he won't admit it); he writes a little, thinks a lot…and plays drums. (*Plays drums??!!* Yes, he's also a musician, and a good one.)

I first heard Bob play drums several years ago on *The Donna Reed Show*. Most stars usually sing or recite on records, but here was a chance to sign a star who could do everything. And play *drums*!

At the recording sessions, Bob was always "on." Jokes flew thick, fast, and funny. The most talented studio musicians were his audience, and Bob had them enjoying every session.

If you like your music with a sense of humor, then this album is it. The best of TV's comedy shows provides the themes and Bob Crane provides the sense of humor, some of the voices…and the *drums*.

Sit back and laugh with *Thursday Night At The Movies*. (If you don't laugh, we promise we'll never do it again.) Tap your feet to the themes from *The Danny Kaye Show* and *The Andy Griffith Show* (no jokes). Chuckle to *F Troop*, the themes from *The Jackie Gleason Show, Hogan's Heroes, Get Smart,* and *The Green Hornet*. Roar with laughter (we hope) at *Candid Camera*. And just relax to *My Three Sons*.

—Stu Phillips (Producer)

"We connected and just thought of this idea of him doing an instrumental album. Since he was involved in TV, on *Hogan's Heroes* at that time, we thought it would be a cute idea to do themes from television shows, which nobody had really done before to any great extent. Aside from just an album of the actual themes, nobody had bothered to go do arrangements of them. And obviously it appealed to both of us, and we took it from there."

The partnership between Stu Phillips and Bob Crane lasted approximately ten days, on and off, over the course of several weeks, as they collaborated on the album *Bob Crane, His Drums and Orchestra Play the Funny Side of TV*, which would be produced under the Epic recording label. Bob and Stu would meet and discuss ideas about which songs to include, how they would be arranged, and what different types of comedy would accompany the music. As the pair brainstormed ideas, they eventually came up with a list of about seventeen or eighteen numbers.

A total of eleven songs were eventually recorded, with ten making the final cut on the album. These included: 1) *Theme from "Hogan's Heroes,"* 2) *Theme from "Thursday Night at the Movies"* (including *Strangers in the Night*), 3) *Theme from "Get Smart,"* 4) *Theme from "My Three Sons,"* 5) *Theme from "F Troop,"* 6) *Smile You're on Candid Camera ("Candid Camera")*, 7) *"Green Hornet Theme,"* 8) *Theme for Andy Griffith ("The Andy Griffith Show")*, 9) *Melancholy Serenade (Theme from "The Jackie Gleason Show")*, and 10) *Life Could Not Better Be (Theme from "The Danny Kaye Show")*. An eleventh number, *Happy Feet*, from the film *Walk, Don't Run,* was recorded but not included on this album. It later was released as a 45 single on the B side of the *Theme from "Get Smart."*

Prominent composers and arrangers were hired to work with Stu and Bob on the new arrangements of the beloved television themes. Bob had indicated to Stu his strong desire to work with Sid Feller, who had co-arranged numbers with Ray Charles, such as *Georgia on My Mind*. Stu was easily able to accommodate Bob's request. Ernie Freeman, a rhythm and blues arranger who had worked with many singers and musicians, including Dean Martin (*Everybody Loves Somebody, Somewhere There's a Someone*), Frank Sinatra (*That's Life, Strangers in the Night*), and Connie Francis (*Jealous Heart*), had been Stu's choice because he had worked with him previously and because Freeman had been available.

"Basically, we tried to keep the themes so the audience would know exactly what each was," said Stu. "We didn't want to change anything too drastically. Somehow one of them, whether it was *F Troop* or one of the others, we came up with and thought we might change it a bit because some of these themes were so short, we had to make them longer. It was a little difficult to make them longer. So I think at times we discussed what we would do to extend it. But it's the usual thing you would do with any artist. If it was a singer or something else, you'd sit down and go through the material and say maybe we should do this or do you want to go back to the bridge or do two choruses."

Comedy pieces and jokes were also included in many of the arrangements. Stu explained, "Bob wrote *all of that*. For one of them, I said, 'Oh wouldn't that be funny?' And he said, 'Oh, yeah. Let me take a crack at that.' But the others were basically Bob's ideas to do. A couple of them had to be prepared ahead of time because the arrangements were written around what he was doing."

The comedy piece for *Smile You're on Candid Camera* was as follows:

> *(Sounds of construction in the background)*
> *Builder One: We're having a little trouble with this construction job. Maybe you can help us out. When you're building a house, do you start from the roof down or the foundation up?"*
> *Builder Two: Well, that's silly. Anybody would know you start from the foundation up!"*
> *Builder One (shouting): Hey fellas! Come on down!"*

When friend and WICC colleague Morgan Kaolian heard *Smile You're on Candid Camera* on the album, he was amazed to hear the joke. Morgan and Bob had collaborated on the same joke on WICC's Channel 43 in the early 1950s.

"How do you like that?" Morgan laughed. "Bob has immortalized me on his record!"

Once the arrangements and comedy skits were finalized, the musicians who would comprise the full orchestra were hired. Bob was always going to perform on the album as the drummer, but when the hired orchestra first learned of this, they were doubtful.

"The contractor said to me, 'Well, who should I hire on drums?'" Stu explained. "And I said, 'Bob Crane is playing drums.' And he said,

'Oh, you're *kidding*. The guys aren't going to like this.' And I said, 'Well, wait and see.' He said, 'Can he do this?' And I said, 'As far as I know he can. So let's do it.' And we did it."

As it turned out, it became one of the happiest recording sessions Stu could remember. He said, "The orchestra had been skeptical until we played through the first [number], and they said, 'Hey, great guys! It works!' They were very surprised. They felt he was *very* capable. And he was lovely to the musicians. I had a top-notch orchestra, the best guys in town playing, and it was a real love fest. *Everybody*! He loved them; they loved him. He was the perfect star as you can see in that picture. If you look at him, he looks like, '*Wow, I like everybody!*' I mean, the smile on his face is like, '*Hey! Life's good!*' He was thoroughly enjoying himself. *Absolutely*. It was a big high point of his life doing this album because he'd always felt like he could do as good as the guys he admired and played on the air. And he did. He did his job just like any professional drummer I would have hired."

Bob had done very well keeping up with some of the best musicians in the industry. "Compared to a top professional, he was an amateur," Stu said. "Compared to most amateurs, he was very good. As an amateur, non-professional drummer, he was *excellent*. Very good. Compared to Hal Blaine or Earl Palmer or any other names I could mention, he was definitely secondary. But as a guy, as an actor, disc jockey, whatever you want, a person who played drums, he was very good. Sammy Davis played drums; he was very good. But I wouldn't hire him in lieu of Earl Palmer. So—he was good. He was adequate. He did the job. The musicians applauded him at the end of the sessions, and he loved that. That is what he was looking for. Making this album was one of his more exciting things that he did musically in his career. Unfortunately, it wasn't a big seller."

It took three recording sessions to record the numbers for the album. Stu remembered that he and the orchestra "had a ball being entertained by Crane."

"You know, he was always on," Stu said. "He was always cracking jokes. He was a very funny man. Had a great sense of humor. And the band liked him. He didn't come off as a *Bob Almighty*. He didn't try to belittle the musicians. He did just the opposite. Like, 'Hey guys, how am I doing? Hope I don't throw you off.' He was *very* humble. He wanted them to like him an *awful* lot. He was such a good guy; he entertained them. Every time they'd take a break, instead of walking out and doing anything, Bob would sit there and start telling jokes and break them up. They were having a ball! It was a very, *very* friendly, happy three sessions."

But not everyone seemed pleased with Bob's efforts to record an album tied to *Hogan's Heroes*, which could have been viewed as a promotional vehicle to propel his own stardom. The cover photograph of the album features an elated Bob Crane dressed as Colonel Hogan seated behind his drumset, with Werner Klemperer, John Banner, and Patricia Olson (Sigrid Valdis) in their *Hogan's Heroes* costumes alongside of him. Nobody else from the cast is present.

"There was a problem with the cover and getting people from the show and the show itself to give permission for them to appear on the album," Stu explained. "The problem was, to begin with, some of them didn't want to do it. It seems that they wanted money, I think. And the show itself did not say to the cast, 'I want you to do this.' So if they did it, they were kind of doing it on their own to be on the cover. And I think they wanted money, and there was no budget to pay these people. It was a big show, and these people felt that this was their way of making another buck. And so it was a little difficult. I've never bothered to find out if there were any other reasons. But I know that I simply said to Bob, 'Can we get all the people for the cover?' And he said, 'No, no, I'm having trouble. Some of them don't want to do it. The show doesn't want to clear it.' There were a whole bunch of things, and that's how we ended up with what you see on the cover there. He would have loved to have had the whole thing."

Stu recalled that John Banner had come with Bob once to one of the sessions, and Stu said he could tell John and Bob were friends. To Stu, it was clear that John Banner, along with Werner Klemperer and Patty Olson, agreed to be part of the cover photograph primarily as a favor to Bob.

One year later, in 1967, Robert Clary, Richard Dawson, Ivan Dixon, and Larry Hovis released their own album, *"Hogan's Heroes" Sing the Best of World War II*. This album consisted of only the group's individual and collective singing talents, with an orchestra to support them. Notably absent from their record were Bob Crane, Werner Klemperer, John Banner, and Patricia Olson. Whatever the issues may have been, those affiliated with the series either did not know of them or did not wish to speak of them, now dismissing any issues surrounding the records as inconsequential. The two albums simply became promotional items that had been produced during that period of time.

Bob Crane, His Drums and Orchestra Play the Funny Side of TV was released in December 1966. In an ad that ran in *Variety* magazine to promote the album, it was noted, "Epic's musical surprise is Bob Crane, with some good music, but good music with a sense of humor. A guaranteed laugh and guaranteed sales from actor-drummer-disc jockey-comedian-writer-thinker, Bob Crane." Sales were never strong, but it hardly seemed to matter. It was indeed a high point in his life and career. For years, Bob had dreamed of performing with a real studio orchestra, even announcing it as one of his career goals in the Stamford High School newsletter shortly before he graduated and in his high school yearbook. The album may not have been a huge success, but for Bob personally, it was a major life goal achieved, and he thoroughly enjoyed the experience.

"In my lifetime, I've done a little over a thousand recording sessions," Stu surmised, "and I remember it as a pleasant album with no aggravation. And I can remember a lot of albums as unpleasant with a *lot* of aggravation!"

It is astonishing that from 1965 to 1971, Bob not only worked on *Hogan's Heroes*, which consisted of long, ten- or twelve-hour days during each season's production schedule, but in that same time period, he also volunteered and worked in other venues. During this time, he broadcast for the United States Armed Forces Radio Network; appeared regularly on television talk shows, game shows, and variety shows; made two motion pictures; performed on stage in theatre productions; traveled to military bases to meet and talk with veterans and former POWs, as well as to entertain American troops; continued to play in jazz bands; and produced a record. It makes one stop and wonder when he had time to eat or sleep, spend quality time with family and friends, allow leisure time for himself, or frankly, do anything else. Yet he did manage, and he managed quite well.

Bob was an active man, constantly on the move, and hardly able to sit still long enough to do his work or wolf down dinner. With Anne at home minding the house and children, Bob was free to immerse himself in his career.

Almost immediately following the initial success of *Hogan's Heroes*, Bob began receiving requests to appear on talk shows, variety shows, and game shows. Bing Crosby, eager to promote his production company's hit new series, slated the entire cast of *Hogan's Heroes* to perform on the Christmas special of *The Hollywood Palace*, which aired on December 25, 1965. Bob and the cast, donning their *Hogan's* attire, sang musical numbers and acted out comedy routines. Other guests on this episode were Fred Waring and His Pennsylvanians, as well as Dorothy Collins.

From there came a long string of television guest appearances starting in mid-January 1966. Bob appeared on dozens of television shows from 1965 to 1971, including *The Danny Kaye Show, The Lucy Show, The Smothers Brothers Comedy Hour, The Pat Boone Show, The Joan Rivers Show, The Match Game, The Merv Griffin Show, The Red Skelton Hour, What's My Line?, Hollywood Squares,* and *The Tonight Show with Johnny Carson,* to name only a few. While some episodes were taped during Bob's hiatus from *Hogan's Heroes*, many were also filmed concurrently with the production of the series.

But even with the success of *Hogan's Heroes*, Bob was still not satisfied. In the spring of 1966, Bob met and spoke with Eva Gabor, and he explained how badly he wanted to quickly advance in his acting career and break out of the radio stereotype. He also realized he was being stereotyped for television, and it worried him.

"What I'd love to do," he said, "is change my whole image. People used to say to me, 'This is what you do. You do radio.' So I got out of radio and into *Hogan's Heroes*, and now they say to me, 'You do TV comedy.'"

It was becoming quite clear that Bob was not going to be satisfied with just doing "TV comedy." He wanted *more*, and the next step for him on his career trajectory was to transition from television to the big screen.

With the security of *Hogan's Heroes* safely in his pocket by the second season, Bob once again began to plan for the future. As a television celebrity, he had new doors opened to him, and he believed he was on the right track to achieve his new goal of starring in feature films.

Moving through the entertainment industry with meteoric speed, tireless Bob Crane soon found himself standing at the pinnacle of his acting career. Mid-way through the second season of *Hogan's Heroes*, offers to star in motion pictures began to come his way, and the moment to leap from television to film was upon him.

By February 1967, Bob had signed on for his first motion picture:

a Cold War comedy set in East Berlin that co-starred the beautiful German-born actress, entertainer, and artist Elke Sommer. Bob was on the brink of movie stardom, and with the film *The Wicked Dreams of Paula Schultz*, he believed he was ready to hold his own as an actor next to his screen idols Jack Lemmon and Gig Young.

Directed by George Marshall, *The Wicked Dreams of Paula Schultz* starred Bob Crane in the title role of Bill Mason, a con man who pedals his illegal Black Market wares between East and West Berlin during the height of the Cold War. Mason has made a few enemies along the way, and while outrunning his pursuers, he runs right into Paula Schultz (Elke Sommer), an East German Gold Medal Olympian who wants to defect to the West. Mason is only too eager to assist, and after ninety minutes of slapstick hijinks, Paula Schultz manages to gain her freedom by pole-vaulting over the Berlin Wall.

Right from the start, Bob identified with the character of Bill Mason, who was quite similar to Colonel Hogan. In fact, many aspects about the film would mirror *Hogan's Heroes*, not least of all the supporting cast. Three major actors from *Hogan's Heroes* joined Bob in *Wicked Dreams*—Werner Klemperer, John Banner, and Leon Askin. Joey Forman and Maureen Arthur completed the ensemble cast. With such combined comedic talent, the audience expected mild intrigue and generous laughs. So committed was Bob to the film that he even offered his musical talents, playing drums along with the Jimmie Haskell Orchestra for *The Love Theme to "The Wicked Dreams of Paula Schultz."*

Werner Klemperer also felt connected to his role as an evil-minded East German Communist. In a January 1968 article published shortly after the film's release, Werner Klemperer said, "If there are anti-heroes, there have to be anti-villains. According to my last two roles, who's a sweeter villain than I?…It's such a zany farce that our director, George Marshall, allowed me to play the role of an East German bureaucrat as broad as I liked. The character fancies himself to be a great lover—a veritable devil with the women. They gave me all the props—a silken dressing gown, long cigarette holder, and even a mirrored ceiling in my bachelor quarters. I go on the make for Elke Sommer and don't even consider it a rebuff when she pole vaults over the Berlin Wall to avoid me."

Interestingly, it had been Bob's idea to bring other actors from *Hogan's Heroes* into the film. "I'm getting some of the *Hogan's Heroes* people parts in it," Bob declared. "Werner Klemperer and John Banner

Bob Crane's Known Television Appearances while also Starring on *Hogan's Heroes* (1965-1971)

Bob Crane did not confine his work to "Hogan's Heroes" during the show's prime time run. He kept himself extraordinarily busy, appearing on numerous television shows from 1965 to 1971. Further, this is not a comprehensive listing of Bob's entire television career and includes only the time period 1965-1971.

The Linkletter Show – October 27, 1965; December 28, 1966; February 5, 1969

The Hollywood Palace (with the cast of *Hogan's Heroes*) – December 25, 1965

The Danny Kaye Show – January 19, 1966

The Lucy Show – February 21, 1966

The Face Is Familiar – May 7, 1966

Hollywood Talent Scouts – March 7, 1966; August 1, 1966

The John Gary Show – June 29, 1966; September 15, 1968

The Merv Griffin Show – August 8, 1966; June 26, 1967; January 24, 1969; March 31, 1969

Password All-Stars – October 10, 1966

What's My Line? – December 11, 1966

The Red Skelton Hour – January 10, 1967

P.D.Q. – February 8, 1967

The Ed Sullivan Show – February 26, 1967

The Smothers Brothers Comedy Hour – February 26, 1967

Keene at Noon – May 28, 1967

Dateline: Hollywood – July 25, 1967; August 8, 1967

The Woody Woodbury Show – August 31, 1967

Password – May 8-12, 1967; October 15, 1967; October 16, 1967; October 19, 1967; December 2, 1968; February 17, 1969

Everybody's Talking – November 2, 1967

The Pat Boone Show – January 16, 1968

It's Happening '68 – June 14, 1968

The Donald O'Connor Show – September 24, 1968

The Steve Allen Show – October 24, 1968; January 14, 1969; September 18, 1969; November 11, 1969

Operation Entertainment – November 1, 1968

Funny You Should Ask – November 11, 1968; May 26-27, 1969

Here Come the Stars – March 8, 1969

The Match Game – May 5, 1969

You Don't Say! – June 2, 1969

It's Happening '69 – June 22, 1969

> *The Joan Rivers Show* – July 11, 1969
> *Allen Ludden's Gallery* – July 16, 1969
> *The Della Reese Show* – July 25, 1969
> *The Leslie Uggams Show* – October 11, 1969
> *Letters to Laugh-In* – October 22, 1969
> *Love American Style* – October 27, 1969; February 19, 1971
> *The Rosey Grier Show* – November 29, 1969; July 4, 1970
> *The Barbara McNair Show* – December 13, 1969; March 15, 1970
> *Can You Top This?* – April 8-10, 1970; May 7, 1970; October 19-23, 1970
> *The Real Tom Kennedy Show* – August 10, 1970
> *The Virginia Graham Show* – November 15, 1970
> *The Thirteenth Annual TV Week Logie Awards* (Australia) – March 26, 1971
> *The Hollywood Squares* – October 24-28, 1966; December 30-31, 1968; January 3, 1969; July 13, 1970
> *The Tonight Show Starring Johnny Carson* – October 9, 1968; November 18, 1968; July 2, 1969
> *The Mike Douglas Show* – March 19, 1970

and Leon Askin—they'll all be in it, too. It's obvious that [*Wicked Dreams* writer Nat Perrin] watches our show—my character is just like Hogan."

And just like on *Hogan's Heroes* and films like *Some Like it Hot*, which featured the leading men in drag, *The Wicked Dreams of Paula Schultz* would also feature a male cross-dressing scene, with Bob donning a female gym outfit toward the end of the film. Unlike *Hogan's Heroes* and *Some Like it Hot*, however, it did not resonate as well with moviegoers.

Further, the presence of the leading *Hogan's Heroes* actors together in a film set in 1960s Germany only served to mildly confuse viewers and mar audience acceptance of the film. *Wicked Dreams* did not fare well at the box office after it opened in United States theatres on January 3, 1968, with critics finding little to like about it. When reporter Dick Kleiner visited the set in April 1967, he was so baffled by the premise and taken aback by the scantily clad actresses running around in the scene being shot that he dubbed *Wicked Dreams* as "a family film for adults only."

Critic Frank Daley provided a scathing review of the film, stating in February 1968, "Director George Marshall has obviously figured that since he has an unfunny script and untalented actors he had better just liven up the proceedings with a lot of 'high' comedy. Consequently, whenever he can, he has people pulling the clothes off Elke Sommer or anybody else who happens to be handy. It's funny the first time, but by the time you realize that the only thing that isn't going to come off is the movie, it's too late to do much about it except leave. Which is what I did."

The film was not to be the goldmine its producers and cast had hoped it would be. Instead, it proved to be the first taste of typecasting the stars of *Hogan's Heroes* experienced. Moviegoers lined up to see Hogan, Klink, and Schultz, not this Bill Mason fellow, and his East German pursuers Klaus and Weber. Later, both Bob Crane and Werner Klemperer were admittedly embarrassed by the final cut of the film. Klemperer literally begged people not to watch it, and Bob Crane applied his ever-present self-deprecating humor to atone for the box office bomb.

In an interview with reporter Dick Strout in December 1973, Bob said, "I was in that so-called co-starring role with Elke Sommer called *The Wicked Dreams of Paula Schultz*, which hasn't even made it to television yet. Now, for a picture that's five or six years old not having been on television yet, it wasn't that successful in the theaters. I don't know. They're holding it up as a jazz re-issue, I think. Someday they're gonna bring it out in a symposium." Further, during a 1972 KMPC Thanksgiving Day radio special, Bob dubbed *Wicked Dreams* as one of his "turkeys."

Yet, making the movie was a different story, and during production, the mood on the set was reportedly jovial and pleasant. Maureen Arthur, who portrayed Barbara Sweeney, the outspoken and boisterous wife of Joey Forman's character Herbert Sweeney, recalled that making the film was a whole lot of fun.

"It was a good cast—a happy cast," Maureen said. "Everyone seemed to have a good time. We did a lot of outdoor work. I can't really recall how long it took to do it, but I know I enjoyed all of it. We must have been having a good time. I think they [the producers] were very conscious of what it was costing at that time. But we had lovely weather, so we didn't have to stop and wait because of rain."

Production took place during the spring and summer months of 1967, with outdoor scenes filmed on the campus of UCLA. Elke Sommer trained rigorously for her part, insisting that she perform her own stunts and athletic maneuvers.

In a 1968 interview, director George Marshall explained that he abhorred the use of laugh tracks on television, and if a show were to employ the use of a laugh track, then he facetiously argued why not other audience responses, such as a "groan track" or a "cry track," a "boo track" (for villains), a "sigh track" (for love scenes), and a "burp track" (for banquet scenes). Marshall believed that in order to ensure audience engagement in films, more slapstick comedy was needed. Therefore, in *Wicked Dreams*, he would purposely stop filming to insert such physical comedy bits into a scene.

According to Marshall, "If this had been TV, I'd have to get permission from ten vice presidents and five sponsors. Then they'd make me put in a laugh track so as not to take a chance on whether or not the viewers would see the humor. In movies, we are allowed to take calculated risks. I'd hate to think how many times I've had to guess whether or not a scene in one of my four-hundred twenty movies would play. Fortunately, I've been right more often than I've been wrong."

Maureen Arthur found Bob conscientious about his role and very easy to work with. "We got along very well from the beginning," she said. "Bob was lovely to work with. Always knew his lines. You can sense right away if another actor is for himself or if he's for everybody. And those [the ones who are for everybody] are the ones that you hang with and get laughs with and do your best work with."

Bob had been playing a lead character on *Hogan's Heroes* for two years by the time they started filming *Wicked Dreams*. He was professional, knew his lines, and allowed other actors their moment in a scene. He was able to step into his character of cunning and sly Bill Mason, and when filming stopped, he became his easy-going self once again.

"Bob was a real gentleman as far as working with fellow actors," co-star Maureen declared. "He did not upstage, which is a joy. And I'll tell you—Bob *always* knew his lines. There were no pauses. You didn't have to wait and then forget *your* [lines]. As soon as the camera went off, then he was just delightful and very easy to get along with. And that's *always* wonderful. Working on a film is delightful, and you respect one another. You just have to. I have always loved being on a set. And then you get sad when it's all over, and then you go back and do it again with someone else. And you're all a big family. When we stopped and sat down under a tree to get our breath, then we just immediately became who we were, and it was just like a family sitting just there and talking and what happened the night before. It was very easy. It was an easy ride."

It became so much like family, in fact, that Bob was reported to have been quite protective of his leading co-star Elke Sommer. In December 1967, he told *Pageant* magazine that he worried about her "all the time." He further stated, "I won't even let her husband on the set," even though Elke countered by adding she did not need or want anyone's protection, saying, "Somehow, my finishing kick always dashes their hopes."

At the time *Wicked Dreams* was being filmed, those involved with the motion picture enjoyed the script and did not feel it was being done in bad taste. It was a film typical of the era, a light, risqué comedy gentle enough to amuse while providing enough sexual innuendo to elicit knowing glances and snickers from adult viewers. It was meant to be fun for the audience, but it was perhaps more fun for the actors.

"I think we just did it because we liked the script and we all got along together and it's make believe," Maureen said. "I think it was a project, but I think that this was something that Bob really was proud to be a part of. That's always important. We live in a land of make believe, so we don't have to get involved with our emotions on our own level. So that's the way I look at it, and that's the way Bob looked at it—as a bit of fun. I think there should be more of [these types of films]—to have fun and enjoy life. Enjoy the joy in life. I must say as far as anybody who's in our business, it's a joy. And I think we all really understand that, and we're all very grateful for that. Life can be tough, and it can be sad. You can go through all those things when you're acting, but you know that it's not for real. Maybe that's why we all get into this business—we can do things that are outrageous."

According to Maureen, Bob did not adlib any of the dialogue during the film, but she did describe him as spontaneous in his acting delivery, and Maureen enjoyed her scenes with him. "I think it happened quite naturally," she said. "I think we hooked into each other very easily as far as the acting goes. I think we were both very open in how we did our acting. He knew I wasn't trying to out-do him, and I knew he wasn't trying to out-do me. So it came very natural and trusting, which I think makes for the best scenes. If you trust each other, then you know it will even out. I could *never* work with anyone if it was one-upmanship. It just drove me nuts. It doesn't work, and it makes the audience feel very uncomfortable. *Very* uncomfortable. You go to films and movies and you want to feel good!

"He was easy to approach," Maureen continued. "I don't know with everybody, but he certainly was with me. I think we're all different. I think because different people remind us of different experiences in our life. It reminds us and all of a sudden, you stiffen up. I think he was very serious, but I think he was charming. And I think he was very knowledgeable about things, so he was very interesting to sit and talk with. He wasn't trying to change your point of view. He was just expressing himself as we all feel we need to do. I guess that's why we become what we are. So we can express ourselves. I think he was interested in sharing thoughts and how he felt about things. I think that was part of his character. I think he was a very thoughtful person. He would feel one way one day, I don't mean changing his mind about things, but I'm sure he had periods when he was quieter than others, and probably all of his thinking was within himself. But I think when you're on the set, you can almost look at someone and know that either they're learning their lines or they're really thinking about something that's very important to them. So you kind of learn when to talk and when to just kind of back off and get a drink of water or whatever. I think there were days where he probably thought he was just making sure his lines were perfect, and he was thinking within there. And then I think there were times when he was probably thinking of something that had happened overnight on the news and was trying to deal with it. Because he was thoughtful. So he could be very quiet also. But he was always on top of what he had to do and always a pleasure to be around. And *very* good-looking!"

As with his behavior on other sets, Maureen recalled that Bob's sense of ego was primarily healthy, although he was prone to having a bit of an inflated ego from time to time. Yet she did not find it offensive, and in fact, believes it is actually typical of all actors, if they are going to survive in the entertainment business.

"I don't think an actor could work if they didn't have ego," Maureen explained. "I think if they didn't have an ego, I think they could be smashed easily! But I think he had both an ordinary ego and a detrimental ego, actually. I think, as we all are, we are different people at different times."

Bob was a gentleman during the filming of *Wicked Dreams*, and Maureen had nothing negative to say of her experience with him. "He absolutely did not [let his private life interfere with his work]. That's why an actor becomes an actor. Because they act. So I think probably there were days when he wanted to be doing or was thinking about certain things. I don't mean to *become* that character, but you're off on another point of what you're interested in that day. I knew he would be confident, but I felt in him there was a serious side. There were times when he seemed to be thinking of something but then when he got into a scene, that was over, and he got back into the scene."

Bob remained optimistic despite the film's poor results. It had given him his first starring role in a motion picture, and he believed he could only continue to advance. As time went on, he would continue to be offered roles, and one by one, he would turn them down, especially those of a similar nature to *Wicked Dreams*. He did not want to become what he called a "Cold War comedian." Bob viewed his part in *The Wicked Dreams of Paula Schultz* as a credible acting opportunity and another chance to learn. In a February 1, 1968, article, Bob stated, "Being quite honest, I don't think it [*The Wicked Dreams of Paula Schultz*] will defeat TV snobbery. It will help as far as credit goes. I got my feet wet in the movie business, and I'm itching for more."

As with radio and television, Bob gave serious consideration to his film offers. And as he had always done, he was selective, turning down offers that he did not think were right for him. This included a role in a film with Paul Newman and Joanne Woodward, which he declined.

"The timing was perfect, and it is an important picture," Bob said in March 1969. "But I'm wrong for the part. The guy they want should be [six-foot-three], sixty, smoke cigars, and be Mr. Big. Someone like Forrest Tucker. There was a role I could play in the picture—a schnook. But I decided against it. I don't want to be typed at this stage in my career."

At the same time, he was offered the leading role in a film ABC was producing for an upcoming "Movie of the Week"—*Arsenic and Old Lace*. This adaptation appealed to Bob, and he accepted.

Arsenic and Old Lace, originally written in 1939 for the stage by Joseph Kesselring, depicts a day in the life of television critic Mortimer Brewster, who has just become engaged to Elaine Harper. Eager to share this happy news with his somewhat off-beat (and unbeknownst to him, occasionally murderous) family, he introduces Elaine to them.

Trouble begins for poor Mortimer from almost the moment he steps into the old, Victorian-style, eerie but outwardly cheery New England house, where his two spinster aunts reside with his psychologically challenged uncle. Before all is said and done, Mortimer discovers his aunts' macabre secret, attempts to cover it up, and is held hostage and almost killed by his brother, all while trying to protect and control these wildly eccentric and often dangerous people. If Mortimer has any advice for the world, it's "Don't look in the window seat," and "Don't drink the Elderberry wine."

The 1944 movie adaptation directed by Frank Capra and starring Cary Grant and Priscilla Lane was a smash hit with audiences. The 1969 version, directed by Robert Scheerer, starred Bob in the role of Mortimer, the increasingly confused nephew of the sweet but lethal Aunts Abby and Martha, played by Hollywood screen legends Helen Hayes and Lillian Gish. Sue Lyon costarred as Mortimer's pretty fiancée, Elaine, and Fred Gwynne (of *The Munsters* fame) was cast as the criminal brother, Jonathan Brewster, who enjoys dabbling in the art of human butchery. Jack Gilford portrayed Jonathan's sidekick, Dr. Jonas Salk (renamed in this adaptation), and David Wayne appeared as Uncle Teddy, who believes he is Teddy Roosevelt.

Unlike the 1944 major motion picture, the 1969 version was performed as a theatre production and filmed almost entirely onstage. Produced in New York, there were two main sets in the remake: the grand living room and the kitchen, with only a handful of scenes filmed outside and off-stage. Following the production, there is a curtain call by the cast, and the camera pans the applauding audience as the actors take their bow as they would after any theatre performance.

Arsenic and Old Lace producer and writer Luther Davis made several updates to Kesselring's script, much to the chagrin of critics. For example, Mortimer Brewster was no longer a drama critic, but rather, a television critic, while his fiancée Elaine went from being the minister's daughter to a television series actress in a series called *Homicide*. "In the television adaptation of this classical farce," Davis explained in 1969, "I have tried to bring together a star-studded cast and retain the many strengths of the play while making the references topical for today instead of [1944]."

Bob also apparently brought with him some ideas about how to improve the production. Of working with Bob on *Arsenic and Old Lace*, director Robert Scheerer stated, "My only recollection of Bob

Crane was a piece of business he wanted to use in *Arsenic*. It was a "freeze" take after realizing there was a body in the window box."

Interestingly, Bob is billed as "Robert Crane" in the credits of the film. It may be the one and only time his formal birth name is ever used in a production, and one report speculated that the reason may have been network competition. At the time, Bob was contracted with CBS for *Hogan's Heroes*, and he may have been listed as Robert Crane "because one network hates to plug the star of another," the report claimed.

This later film was met with ugly reviews. It seemed impossible to review this version without comparing it to the classic motion picture starring screen giant Cary Grant. Today's critics further claim it bears too much of an ominous foreshadowing to be enjoyed. Further, the opening scene, set in a flashy dance club, written in as a way to update the plot to modern times, instead completely missed its mark with critics and audiences. The final cut of the film also employed the use of a laugh track, a gimmick that critics believed added nothing but more fodder to ridicule.

However, the general dislike of the film by critics may be a bit harsh. When looking past these surface flaws and study the performance itself, a hidden gem is revealed. This 1969 film is not a late-night, made-for-TV flop; it is archived footage of these actors performing live, on stage, in front of a theatre audience—as they would have performed had they been on stage in any theatre production.

Bob Crane was no stranger to the theatre, and from his first performance in 1959 to his last in 1978, he earned high critical praise for his performances. Bob boasted about his work in *Arsenic and Old Lace*, stating that he was "hopeful it will serve as a springboard on Broadway." Watching Bob in this performance of *Arsenic and Old Lace* provides a glimpse of his stage talents, of which hardly any footage exists.

Throughout the film, Bob's performance is strong. His reactions to his crazy and dangerous family allow the viewer to see a vulnerable side not often witnessed in *Hogan's Heroes*. He switches from comedy to drama to a touch of horror effortlessly, and it shows how far he could have taken his dramatic acting had he lived.

Bob was overjoyed he had won the part in *Arsenic and Old Lace* and was humbled at the prospect of working with legends Hayes and Gish. In a *TV Guide* article, he said, "If someone had said to me, before it happened, would you like to work with Helen Hayes and Lillian Gish, I'd have said they were joking!" Bob also took the advice of Helen

Hayes, who had encouraged him to expand his acting style by appearing in more movies and stage plays during his summer hiatus from *Hogan's Heroes*. Hayes, who thought very highly of Bob, stated in the same *TV Guide* article, "I watch *Hogan's Heroes* regularly. This young man, Bob Crane, is a wonderful farçeur, and there are almost none of them around anymore. He's habit-forming."

As elated as he may have been at the time to work with such legends, later on, Bob admitted to hating the production, describing it as "a miserable experience." He claimed in 1970 that *Arsenic* suffered from substandard camera and film quality that caused the final movie to appear purplish in color, lack of time to prepare for the part, and the decision to air what Bob considered the worst performance of the cast.

Bob summed up the experience he had making *Arsenic and Old Lace* by saying it was similar to being Elizabeth Taylor's next husband. "I knew what I was supposed to do," he said. "The problem was how to make it interesting."

"Acting was meant for me and vice versa," Bob told a reporter in April 1970. "I remember Jerry Lewis said once that when small, he was the nutty kid in his neighborhood—and I was the same way. Now I'm in the business for good. I love it. The stage is my favorite; this spring, I'm going to do a two-month run in Chicago with a play, and I'm relishing the idea."

Bob loved acting, and he spent nearly every waking moment from 1965 to 1971 concentrating on furthering his career. At the time, he could not have foreseen the longevity of *Hogan's Heroes*, so he was constantly strategizing for his next role, his next project, and his next move.

Always on the go. Almost never resting. Constantly striving for success.

And as Bob transitioned from television to film, his goal shifted yet again. No longer was he going to be satisfied with just making movies. His quest for advancement was insatiable, and his new goal became to perform in both movies and television—simultaneously, to follow in the footsteps of his screen and television idols. And during his time on *Hogan's Heroes*, Bob was, indeed, doing it all: radio, television, theatre, film, music, and charity work.

"The ideal is what Bob Hope and Dean Martin are doing," Bob stated well into his second year of *Hogan's Heroes* and just before he began filming *The Wicked Dreams of Paula Schultz*. "To have the best of two worlds. Not many other performers can do it. The trick is to be yourself on television and play a role in movies. I'd like to do *both*. It would be nice if *Hogan* ran another couple of years. Then I'd like to concentrate on movies and later star in a variety show. It won't be easy. But then, nothing worthwhile is."

Bob was *restless*. He wanted *more, more, more.* Perhaps most telling is a statement he made in his 1966 interview with Eva Gabor: "I want to be so accepted that I can do anything at all."

Anything at all.

Bob was on a mission. He didn't just want to be a leading radio personality, a television actor, or even a movie star. He yearned to be each of those, synchronizing his acting career so that television and film did not overlap, but instead, *blended*.

As Bob had done with radio, he studied his idols in television and film, striving to ameliorate his own talents and emulate theirs. In August 1966, Bob commented, "How does the future look? I'd love to do movies and more television. If it's possible, I'd very much like to do Jack Lemmon-type roles; I've already been approached about it. In an interview recently, I said I've been waiting for Jack Lemmon to break his leg so that I could get some of the roles he's been getting. Jack sent me a letter which said, in part, 'Bob, I'm having enough trouble without a broken leg; stop wishing.'

Although he had reaped the benefits of patience and career acuity, he also craved acceptance. His restlessness was giving way to something else: an addictive personality that demanded nourishment. Bob desired to succeed at anything—*anything at all*—and everything. He had yet to fail, and it fueled his ambition and drove him onward. This inner motivation toward success and perfection kept him advancing and climbing to the point of near exhaustion. He had something to prove—that Bob Crane was somebody of importance, somebody with great talent, somebody with enormous power, somebody to be respected and admired.

But with the cancellation of *Hogan's Heroes* in 1971, Bob was about to encounter an unforgiving obstacle, and that which had brought him the greatest fortune and glory would become the prison from which he would never live long enough to fully escape.

Lending a Helping Hand

"Bob did many things for charity. I don't know that he ever gets credit for that. But he appeared frequently at various charities, just giving of his time. That's what you do, specifically in broadcasting. You're not paid for it; you just do it! And you raise money for very worthwhile charities. So there are two sides to everything."

—Gary Owens to the authors, July 14, 2008

Bob Crane was a tireless volunteer. He did much for charity and the community while starring on *Hogan's Heroes*, but his devotion to this work started well before and continued long after it.

It began with his service in the United States National Guard from 1947 to 1949 in Stamford, Connecticut. Later, at WICC in Bridgeport, Connecticut, he served as program advisor for the Bridgeport Junior Achievement and participated in other community events, such as judging talent contests and serving as master of ceremonies for various organizations. Later, at KNX in Los Angeles, Bob was constantly on the move, participating in Auxiliary lunches, Kiwanis Club meetings, and telethons; making appearances at grocery or department stores to promote local events; and acting as master of ceremonies for countless organizations. Further, Bob held the title of Honorary Mayor of Tarzana, CA; was a member of the Tarzana Chamber of Commerce; and was the Tarzana Senior Ambassador of Good Will.

After he moved from radio to television, Bob continued his charity work, volunteering with the U.S. Armed Forces Radio Network; Operation Entertainment; the Cystic Fibrosis Fund Drive; the Easter Seals, the Arthritis Foundation, Rheumatism Foundation Telethons; as well as hosting the United Cerebral Palsy Telethon on a regular basis. He also made regular appearances for different fund drives, including "Mesa's Heroes" in Mesa, Arizona, which recognized leading citizens of the community; and promoting the American Lung Association Christmas Seals program.

In October 1967, the *Valley News* publication of Van Nuys, California wrote:

> *Hogan's Heroes* own Colonel Hogan, Bob Crane, is one man who answers the call of civic groups, charities, and worthy organizations, no matter where they might be. Up to one-third of his free time is spent assisting and appearing in behalf of such groups. For instance, during his recent "HH" hiatus, he volunteered more than thirteen hours worth of Armed Forces Radio material. He brought laughs to the ex-POW conven-

tion in New Mexico. Pending is a grand marshal stint at the Richmond Tobacco Festival and full participation in the current Cystic Fibrosis Drive. And there's more, much more. This "Hogan" is a real hero.

The following are only a few of the organizations to which he gave his time.

United States Armed Forces Radio Network
1967-1969

Bob Crane donated his time with the U.S. Armed Forces Radio Network, where he conducted and recorded many more celebrity interviews for broadcast to American troops serving overseas. Many of these historic recordings are also available to the public through the U.S. Library of Congress in Washington, D.C., by appointment.

Operation Entertainment
Eglin Air Force Base, Fort Walton Beach, Florida
ABC-TV / Bob Crane, Host

Bob made many visits to military bases, where he entertained troops and met with veterans and former prisoners of war. *Operation Entertainment* was a program produced by Chuck Barris and Bill Carruthers for ABC that ran in 1968. As part of this series, actors, musicians, and other celebrities traveled across the country and around the world to entertain U.S. troops serving in the military. The entertainers performed on location at Navy, Army, and Air Force bases. In addition to Bob, other hosts included Rich Little, George Carlin, Dick Cavett, Dean Jones, Dick Shawn, Tim Conway, Jimmy Dean, Roger Miller, Norm Crosby, Ed Ames, Flip Wilson, Don Rickles, Jim Lange, Phil Harris, and Dale Robertson. Among the entertainers were Vikki Carr, Donna Jean Young, Roy Clark, Louis Armstrong, Richard Pryor, Barbara McNair, Allen & Rossi, Minnie Pearl, Paul Lynde, Florence Henderson, Martha and the Vandellas, Shelley Berman, the Righteous Brothers, the Lennon Sisters, Aretha Franklin, Ray Charles and the Rayettes, Patti Page, Pat Buttram, Rodney Dangerfield, Kenny Rogers, Larry Storch, Stephanie Powers, and many more.

Bob Crane was the host of the November 1, 1968, episode, which was performed and recorded for servicemen and women stationed at Eglin Air Force Base in Fort Walton Beach, Florida. Performers included Teddy Neeley and his Band, comedian Pat Paulsen, singer Fran Jeffries, and the Lennon Sisters, among others.

Davis Monthan Air Force Base
(Near Tucson, Arizona)
July 1967

When an actor prepares for a role, it is imperative that he or she gets into the character and really feels and understands the part. Without question, Bob did fit the part of Colonel Hogan very well. The character of Hogan was that of an officer in the U.S. Army Air Force, and several scenes from *Hogan's Heroes* show Hogan piloting an aircraft, including a U.S Army Air Force P-51 Mustang. Bob prepared rigorously for his role as Hogan, and when the opportunity arose for him to climb aboard a real jet fighter as a passenger courtesy of the U.S. Air Force, he jumped at the chance.

Bob had been invited by the U.S. Air Force in July 1967 to speak at an officers' dinner at the Davis Monthan Air Force Base near Tucson, Arizona. His flight from Los Angeles was not aboard a commercial jet liner, however. Bob arrived at the Air Force Base via a T-33 jet fighter, piloted by then-Captain Jerry Chipman (now Colonel) of the 4080th Strategic Reconnaissance Wing.

Colonel Chipman stated, "I remember the occasion very well. I was a General's Aide and instructor pilot in the T-33 at that time and was probably selected to pick Bob Crane up at LAX because of my experience in the aircraft. I believe his visit to Davis Monthan AFB (Tucson), was to speak at a 'Dining In,' which is a formal function at the Officers Club. He came across as a very personable guy and did not seem to be overly impressed with himself. I had taken a flying helmet and oxygen mask for Bob to use on the return trip from LAX. The helmet was slightly small, which caused some discomfort. However, Bob endured the flight and presented a great talk to his military audience."

According to press releases of the event, Bob was given every flight maneuver possible, and after landing, he emerged "with butterflies in the stomach and a grin on the face." It had been his first ride in the cockpit of a jet fighter.

Meeting with Veterans and
Former Prisoners of War

While he was starring in *Hogan's Heroes*, Bob entertained many veterans' organizations and former POWs, and he was always received warmly by both groups. Further, they were never short on stories to entertain him!

In 1970, Bob explained, "When the show is on hiatus, I entertain for a lot of veterans' groups and ex-POW organizations. The men tell me a lot of things that happened to them when they were in POW camps, and I pass the stories along to our writers."

The episodes "Cuisine á La Stalag 13" and "Eight O'Clock and All Is Well" are based on real stories told by former POWs. Other episodes also incorporated such real-life tales. Many, if not most, former prisoners of war did not resent *Hogan's Heroes*, and according to Bob, "They know it's strictly for laughs. We walk a thin line, of course. We could do something in bad taste, but our executive producer Ed Feldman has guided us right so far."

Public Service Announcements and Promotional Films

Throughout the 1960s and 1970s, Bob worked closely with several groups on public service announcements (PSAs) and promotional films, including for the United States Coast Guard, United States Air Force, and the Holy Childhood Association (on a Christmas PSA).

Bob and other members of the *Hogan's Heroes* cast, including Werner Klemperer and Robert Clary, worked with Leo Finkelstein, Jr., PhD, to produce several military films for the U.S. Air Force. In return for their help, Leo recalled offering his assistance to them on their work with *Hogan's Heroes*.

Leo stated, "I did indeed direct Bob Crane, but not in Hollywood. I was an Air Force film writer/producer/director back in the late 1960s and early 1970s, and Bob (along with some other members of the *Hogan's Heroes* cast) came out to Norton Air Force Base at San Bernardino and did some work for me for military films I was producing and directing. I found both Bob Crane and Werner Klemperer very enjoyable to work with—easy to direct and readily able to understand the rhetorical strategies I was using."

Later, in 1970, Bob hosted an episode from the U.S. Air Force's *Propaganda Film Series – Volume 3: Vietnam/1965-1971*. The episode, entitled "Friends and Neighbors – People You Know," provides an overview of the work and importance of the United States Air National Guard in Vietnam. Bob hosted this half-hour long episode, filmed at Lowry Air Force Base in Denver, Colorado.

Bob also made several PSAs for the military—one was a television commercial for the U.S. Air Force, where he encouraged young adults to join the Air Force and enter officer training. Another was an audio PSA for the U.S. Coast Guard Academy urging young men to consider an officer's career in the Coast Guard.

Another audio PSA not affiliated with the military was for the Holy

Childhood Association, helping to sell Holy Childhood Christmas Seals to provide food and clothing to mission children around the world.

Patriotism

In 1972, Bob participated in the educational film *Patriotism*, in which he explained to children the importance of being patriotic. Produced by Art Evans, this film was one of several educational productions Evans made for Oxford Films. Bob himself was extremely patriotic, often citing his appreciation for the U.S. military and his love for America. In an interview on August 3, 1968, Bob said, "I believe in independence, individualism, courage, patriotism—the traditional American values. People call me a flag waver. That's right—I *am* a flag waver."

Grand Marshal – Chrysanthemum Festival
Bristol, Connecticut
September 19, 1976

On Sunday, September 19, 1976, the 15th Annual Chrysanthemum Festival took place in Bristol, Connecticut. The festival, launched in 1962 as the Fall Festival and now affectionately known as the "Mum Fest," highlights Bristol's achievements and proud accomplishments. Bob worked at radio station WBIS in Bristol in 1951, and the city honored him as Grand Marshal of the 1976 Mum Festival Parade. He also took part in the opening ceremonies.

The previous day, the city of Bristol held a reception in Bob's honor, during which the native Connecticut radio personality recalled his time at WBIS. "I worked right about where I'm standing now," he said. "WBIS radio was on the second floor, and a department store, Kresge's, was below, and I ate at Kresge's lunch counter."

It is a common belief that Bob was a lot like his character Colonel Hogan on *Hogan's Heroes*. During the Mum Festival reception held in his honor, Bob stated, "I am a lot like the Hogan that is fun-loving, but I'm nothing like the Hogan that's a hero. I faint at the sight of a hangnail."

As part of his role as Grand Marshal, Bob was presented with "a key to the city, three giant yellow mums from Mayor Henry J. Wojtusik, a clock from the Mum Fest Committee, and a hard time from a garland of mums he cut through to open the 15th annual festival." Bob had such difficulty cutting through the garland, that Parade Master of Ceremonies Val McCormack joked, "You'd never escape from *that* prison."

The 50th Anniversary of the Mum Festival was held on Sunday, September 25, 2011, in Bristol. Bill Schwab, who was the chairman of the 1976 festival, served as one of the 2011 parade's marshals and happily recalled meeting Bob Crane, describing him as "charming" and "delightful."

Mum Fest Parade goers in 1976 would agree. Smiling broadly, Bob Crane received enthusiastic applause as he led the parade through his one-time home streets of Bristol, Connecticut.

Arthritis Foundation Telethons

Bob performed with the "Novel Orchestra" that featured some of the era's top stars during the finale of the 1967 Arthritis Foundation Telethon. In addition to Bob performing drums in the orchestra, Morey Amsterdam performed on cello, Jack Bailey on trombone, and Herb Shriner on harmonica. Bob was a regular participant in annual Arthritis Foundation telethons throughout the 1960s and 1970s.

"Funds for Dinah"
Chatham, Ohio
November 23, 1977

In late 1977, Bob Crane traveled to Chatham, Ohio, to host a local fund drive—"Funds for Dinah"—in support of an eleven-year-old Medina County girl who had renal disease. Dinah Brooks required surgery to remove both of her kidneys in her fight against the disease, and she needed to travel three times per week to receive dialysis at the Rainbow Babies and Children's Hospital in Cleveland. After two years of making the long trips multiple times a week, the family's car had broken down. The fund drive was to raise money to purchase a new car for the family, and funds that exceeded the Brooks' family's need were to be donated to other families facing similar circumstances.

Mitzi and a Hundred Guys
March 24, 1975

Actress Mitzi Gaynor assembled one hundred of the leading male movie and television celebrities in Hollywood to be part of a chorus for her television special. Bob was one of the first to sign on for the event, for which none of the stars would be paid. Instead, Mitzi made a sizable donation to the Motion Picture and Television Relief Fund in all of their names. Among the stars who participated with Bob Crane were Tom Bosley, Mike Connors, Telly Savalas, Peter Marshall, Dick Martin, Greg Morris, Vince Edwards, Marty Allen, Jack Lemmon, James Farentino, Ross Martin, Donald O'Connor, Bill Bixby, and Dean Jones.

**United Cerebral Palsy Telethon
Hartford, Connecticut
1970-1978**

Bob was especially dedicated to United Cerebral Palsy. He had close ties to the organization because his friend Eliot Dober from Bridgeport, Connecticut, had cerebral palsy.

Eliot's family owned a portion of WLIZ radio when Bob began working at the station in April 1951. At that time, Eliot was fifteen years of age, and according to Eliot, "I was in and out then, hanging around. And was a real pest!" Eliot remembered Bob being very patient with him during that time, and Bob had even given Eliot the opportunity to go on the air with him. They remained friends after Bob left Bridgeport and moved to Los Angeles in 1956, and Eliot took several trips out to the West Coast to visit him.

Throughout his life, Eliot was a strong advocate for individuals with disabilities. In 1977, he was appointed by the governor of Connecticut to the position of Executive Director of the Office of Protection and Advocacy for Persons with Disabilities for the State of Connecticut, and he served in this role until 1994. In addition, he also acted as the Connecticut State Director for United Cerebral Palsy.

As State Director for the United Cerebral Palsy Foundation, Eliot asked Bob if he could host the local Connecticut edition of the United Cerebral Palsy Telethon, and Bob always agreed. Generally, a celebrity would be paid handsomely to host a telethon *nationally,* and in 1970 and throughout the 1970s, Bob was offered $20,000 to host the national United Cerebral Palsy Telethon. Yet Bob turned down all of the national offers *and* the large sums of money, and instead, he flew back east to Hartford, Connecticut, where he hosted the local segment. He accepted only $2,000—just enough to cover travel expenses. In 1976, Eliot reported that Bob raised $97,000 for the Greater Hartford United Cerebral Palsy campaign, which equated to more than $400,000 in 2015.

Eliot passed away on July 30, 2010, at 74 years of age. Before his passing, he remembered Bob this way: "He got along with everybody very well. And everybody liked Bob. I want people to remember the good things about Bob. He gave of himself, and he was a good person. A positive person. He wasn't a bad guy. Bob was just Bob. And nobody is all good or all bad."

Bob with music producer Stu Phillips (circa 1966).
Source: Courtesy of Stu Phillips. Used with permission.

Source: Courtesy of Scott Crane. Used with permission.

Bob Crane with Art Linkletter on *The Linkletter Show* (circa 1965).
Source: Courtesy of Scott Crane. Used with permission.

Bob returns from a speaking engagement at Davis Monthan Airforce Base (near Tuscon, Arizona) aboard a T-33 U.S. Air Force jet piloted by then Captain (now Colonel) Jerry Chipman (circa 1967).

Source: Wide World Photo. From the author's personal collection.

Among the Stellar Elite

Bob with then-Captain Jerry Chipman of the U.S. Air Force following his first flight in a jet fighter.
Source: Courtesy of Colonel Jerry Chipman (pilot). Used with permission.

Bob Crane hosting the 1976 United Cerebral Palsy Telethon in Hartford, Connecticut.

Source: Courtesy of Eliot Dober. Used with permission.

Bob Crane hosting the 1978 United Cerebral Palsy Telethon in Hartford, Connecticut.

Source: From the author's personal collection.

Bob Crane hosting an episode of *Operation Entertainment,* November 1, 1968. Eglin Air Force Base, Fort Walton Beach, Florida

Source: From the author's personal collection.

Bob Crane, Grand Marshal of the 15th Annual Chrysanthemum Festival, Bristol, Connecticut (September 19, 1976). Bristol Hospital employees wanted to surprise Bob along the parade route, and they pulled in line behind him dressed as guards from *Hogan's Heroes*. David Hartley was dressed as Sergeant Schultz.

Source: Courtesy of David Hartley. Used with permission.

Bob at the Marine Corps Base, Camp Pendleton, California. D.L. Dodson, photographer (circa April 1972).

Source: Official U.S. Marine Corps Photograph. Used with permission. Courtesy of Scott Crane.

Among the Stellar Elite

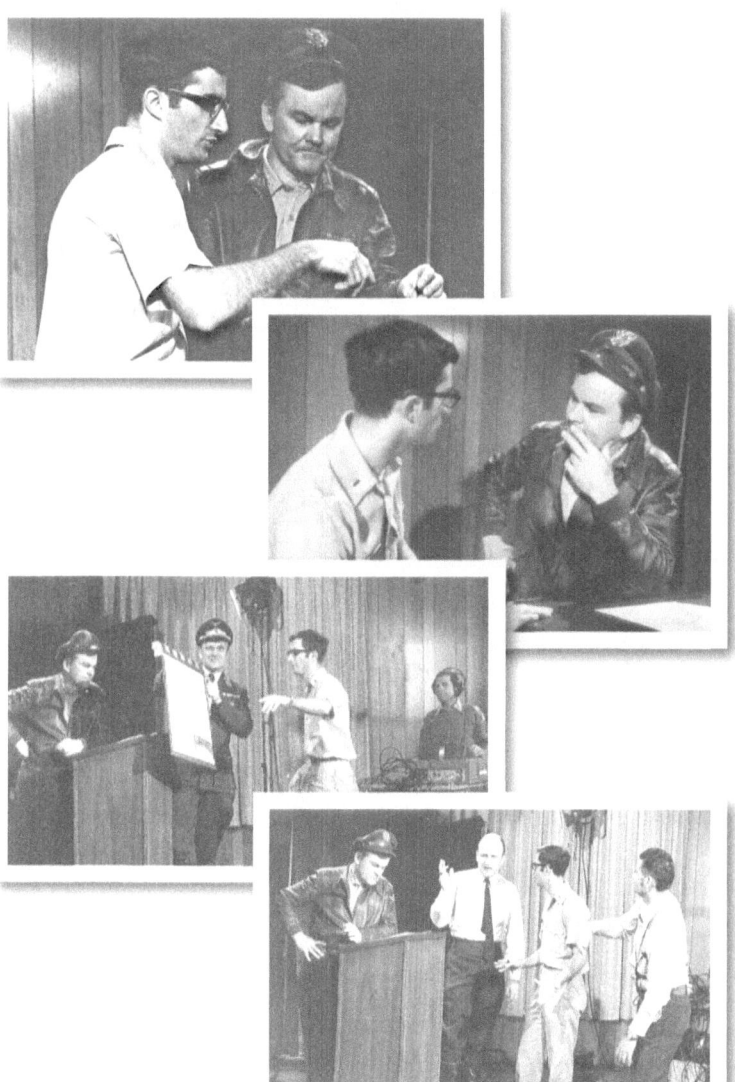

Bob Crane and Werner Klemperer, along with other members of the *Hogan's Heroes* cast, meet with Leo Finkelstein to produce a military film for the United States Air Force.

Source: All photos courtesy of Leo Finkelstein, Jr., PhD, College of Engineering and Computer Science, Wright State University, Dayton, Ohio.

Chapter 8
Masquerade

There are really only two important things in my life: my family and my work—and I work for my family. Fame, success, popularity, money, and all those goodies are great as long as you can share them with those you love and those who love you. The unhappiest man in the world is the quote, star, unquote, who at the end of the day must return to a lonely house.

—Bob Crane, 1966

Bob and Anne Crane (circa 1967). Bob and Anne were married from 1949 to 1970.

Source: Courtesy of Karen Crane. Used with permission.

Bob with Cynthia Lynn (Fräulein Helga, *Hogan's Heroes*, Season 1) (circa 1965).

Source: © George R. Lindblade, photographer. Used with permission.

Bob with Patricia Olson (Sigrid Valdis), (Fräulein Hilda, *Hogan's Hereos*, Seasons 2 through 6) (circa 1968). Bob and Patty were married from 1970 until the time of his death in 1978.

Source: Courtesy of Scott Crane. Used with permission.

Chapter 8

Masquerade

> *You know what happens to the men. They have to pay so much alimony…My own feeling about divorce where children are concerned—and I've got three kids—I'm in love with those kids, and with my wife…Even the thought that I might upset that home relationship, well, I could never really get to the point of gambling with it.*
>
> —Bob Crane to Eva Gabor, June 1966

She sat upright with a start, grasping at the night air and clutching the bed sheets, a familiar wave of terror rippling through her. Barely able to breathe, Anne Crane climbed out of bed and stumbled down the hallway and into the living room, where she lowered herself into a chair. Fighting desperately for air to fill her lungs, she pulled her knees to her chin and sobbed uncontrollably. Her pain was unbearable and very real. Shaking with cold and from fear, she watched her husband cross the room and join her by her side. He was as helpless as she was to ease her pain.

A year earlier, in 1963, Anne's doctor had diagnosed her with hepatitis. In subsequent visits, he had explained that the ongoing symptoms of shortness of breath, nausea, and generalized pain were typical lingering effects of the illness. "Don't worry," her doctor said repeatedly. "What you're experiencing is normal."

But Anne could not believe it. Her symptoms were not subsiding; in fact, her overall condition was worsening. The only person who seemed to understand her pain was her husband—the man she had known for nearly all of her life and to whom she had been married for fifteen years. Bob had talked with nearly everyone they knew about her ailments, and they all agreed with her doctor and said the same thing—all this suffering was supposedly normal. Yet with every traumatic attack that Anne endured, she could not understand why no one else believed the intensity of her pain, and she slowly began to believe the worst: that she was dying.

As he comforted his wife, Bob was grief-stricken and mortified at the thought of losing Anne to an incurable and mysterious illness, one that had yet to be identified. At the time, Bob was in the process of transitioning his career from radio to television and was on the brink of leaving *The Donna Reed Show* in search of his own television series. Plus, their two daughters were still so very young—just three and four years of age—and Bobby was just becoming a teenager. How would he and the children manage if the worst were to happen? What would become of all of them? Later, in 1966, Bob would reveal in two separate interviews how distraught he had been throughout the entire ordeal.

He was on the brink of international stardom. But life at home was turbulent, indeed.

With the success of *Hogan's Heroes*, Bob Crane was basking in the glow of fame and fortune. He appeared to have it all: a dynamic career that was continually evolving and improving; a loving wife and beautiful family; a legion of fans; respect among his peers. A tireless, nervous energy pulsated through him, and by all outward appearances, Bob was as levelheaded and self-assured as Colonel Hogan. And in many ways, he was. But the foundation upon which he had built his entire existence was trembling.

The first significant crack in the façade occurred in 1963, when Anne became gravely ill. At about the same time Bob's character Dr. Dave Kelsey was moving in next door to Donna and Alex Stone on *The Donna Reed Show*, Anne was beginning a battle with hepatitis. It was a horrifying time for Anne, Bob, and their family as she struggled with debilitating symptoms that only seemed to worsen over time.

"She'd wake in the middle of the night, sobbing with terror as she fought desperately for breath," Bob recounted in 1966. "I'd awaken and find her in some dark corner of the house, racked with pain and trying to fight back the tears."

Hardly able to breathe and in excruciating pain, Anne believed she was dying. Despite her pain and fears, her doctor was less worried and did not take her complaints seriously, sending Anne home with little relief or medical advice. His nonchalance baffled and frustrated both Anne and Bob. To them, her pain was very real, not a figment of her imagination.

"For almost a year, a doctor was treating Anne for hepatitis," Bob said. "At first we had no reason to doubt his diagnosis, but as time went on, we began to wonder if it was possible for anyone to suffer so acutely from that disease. It got to the point where only Anne and I had any doubts, any real worries about what was bothering her."

Bob even discussed Anne's condition with Donna Reed's husband Tony Owen while at work on the set of *The Donna Reed Show*. According to Bob, Owen also brushed off Anne's complaints, stating that her symptoms were typical of someone recovering from hepatitis and that she was simply "naturally depressed." Both Owen and the doctor concurred that this depression period was normal and to simply ride it out.

Bob knew that Anne had never been the type to complain, so against everyone's advice, they sought out a second medical opinion.

"His diagnosis was almost immediate," Bob explained. "Anne had a tumor growing inside her which had grown so rapidly during a year's time that it was by then threatening to kill her. It was so huge that it could burst at any moment!"

It took one week for Anne to get an appointment with the surgeon to have the tumor removed, and according to Bob, those seven days of waiting were "absolute hell" for them both. The worry and concern they had experienced prior to the tumor's discovery, Bob claimed, were nothing compared to what they felt during the week leading up to Anne's surgery. In addition to the operation itself, they did not know if the tumor was malignant or benign, and a biopsy of the tumor would be required to check for cancer.

"We were filled with the terrible dread that the tumor might be malignant," Bob told reporter Marjorie Wolfe. "If it was, and with the way it had been allowed to grow…"

Bob was unable to say the words, and he genuinely feared Anne might have terminal cancer. Marjorie Wolfe described Bob's expression of dread. "He left the horrifying conclusion of his sentence unspoken, closed his eyes tight, and shook his head to rid himself of the unspeakable thought."

Bob remained at the hospital for the entire duration of Anne's surgery. After a three-hour operation, the surgeon told Bob the good news. The tumor was benign. Anne was going to be fine, and Bob was flooded with relief.

"Thank God, it wasn't malignant," Bob said. "Thank God, the operation was successful and everything turned out all right. Those were the worst seven days of my life. The very worst. We were terrified. When I think how lucky we are, how close Anne came to dying... Everything's all right now. Anne's fine, and the family is back to normal."

Yet just beneath the surface, everything was far from normal, and the very thing that could have brought a couple closer together—the fight for Anne's life—was likely to be at least part of the reason why Bob and Anne were drifting apart. Even though Bob had genuinely feared for Anne's life, her illness had put a certain strain on their marriage. But for the moment, with Anne's health reaffirmed, life in the Crane household settled down.

As Bob went on to star in *Hogan's Heroes* and become an international celebrity, Anne remained at home. After making a full recovery over a period of several months, Anne resumed her duties as mother and homemaker, allowing Bob the freedom to follow his career, and she silently supporting him from the sidelines.

Anne reportedly never nagged or complained that Bob had to be constantly on the go—every waking minute. He had always been driven toward the spotlight and running from one job or public event to another. Bob survived on a natural high that kept him a blur of motion and able to function well even on very minimal amounts of sleep. He *had* to stay busy. She knew and accepted this from the moment they first met, with no known complaints. As one reporter later would speculate, maybe Anne *should* have complained.

In 1967, *TV Guide* featured the "widows" of prime time television stars, which in addition to Anne, also included the wives of Jim Backus, Buddy Ebsen, Guy Williams, Dale Robertson, Don Adams, Larry Casey, and Fess Parker. *TV Guide* deemed them all "widows" because their husbands were always working and hardly ever home. In the article, Anne was described as often acting as the "community taxi service" during the day.

"I spend a good half of my time driving," she explained. "I drive the kids to school and pick them up. After school, there are music lessons and dentist appointments. Or I'll drive the girls to the ice-skating rink and Bobby and his friends to Griffith Park. Bobby plays drums in a band, and I have to get him and his drums over to some other boy's house for rehearsals. Now I have to start a half earlier in the morning. I'm sitting in other people's driveways, motor running, horn honking, wondering why *their* kids aren't ready."

Meanwhile, Bobby was growing older, and he had been taking on some of the same interests as his father. When he was around five years of age, Bobby started going to work with Bob. Often at KNX, Bob would have little Bobby on the air, singing tunes or giving his dad a plug to be the next Dodger Bat Boy. As Bob moved from radio to television, so did Bobby, who expressed the desire to learn the entertainment business as well. Once *Hogan's Heroes* had earned its place in the CBS line up, Bob also began bringing Bobby to the set when school was not in session.

"He stands on the set, absorbing all the action, and when work is over for the day, we stop at a restaurant together for dinner and then go home where Anne and the girls are waiting," Bob said.

In an interview with reporter Erskine Johnson, little Bobby said that while on the set of *Hogan's Heroes*, he had the title of "go-pher," and that his father kept him running. "I go-for cigarettes. I go-for new pages in the script. I go-for gum. I go-for candy. I go-for coffee," he said.

Debbie and Karen—who in 1966 were ages six and five, respectively—were just starting elementary school. While Debbie had been eager to attend school, just as her older brother had been, Karen, on the other hand, was not all that excited at first. Recognizing that Karen was a shy child, Bob and Anne took great care to prepare her for kindergarten. This had helped dramatically, and soon, Karen was enjoying school just as her parents told her she would.

Karen adored her father, and she treasures the times she spent with him. In a 2013 interview with *TV Confidential,* she explained to host Ed Robertson that her father was attentive to her and her siblings. She also talked about how important music and his drumming were to him.

"[Drumming] was a part of him," Karen said. "He could adapt to any kind of music because he was just focused in on the beat. He could pick up a beat, whatever kind of style it was. He could drum to anything. He was the Benny Goodman lover. Or Dorsey. He became good friends with Buddy Rich, and they would actually do duets together. They would play the Carnation Stage at Disneyland [just off Main Street]; that's where the ice cream was. I think that was part of his love for playing at the Carnation Stage—he was an ice cream lover. We would go to Disneyland purposely so he could meet up with Buddy Rich at the Carnation Stage. They had their two drum sets there, and they would play, and it was awesome. This would be around 1973-1974. He was right out of *Hogan's*, when that ended in 1971, so people still knew him from that. He was kind of a hot property. 'Oh my God, Bob Crane is here!' And people would just jam-pack the whole area there at Disneyland. Buddy Rich and him—they were awesome."

Those who knew Bob agree that it did not take much to make him happy. Simple and straightforward, Bob often wondered why other celebrities in Hollywood were often so complicated.

"Our idea of a great dinner is shrimp cocktail, steak, fresh asparagus, a green salad, and ice cream," Bob told reporter Johna Blinn. "Our entertaining consists of having a few good friends in, and we cook outdoors in an informal setting. The people who 'go Hollywood' are only a small minority. We just look at them and laugh and think, 'Why can't they be normal?'"

In a different interview, Bob said, "Anne and I…go out together, or we don't go. And when we do go,…our idea of a wild time is to go to a movie and have a lemonade or a milk shake afterwards. I just don't relate to some of the things that are going on right now. I don't understand how actresses like Joanne Pettet and Vanessa Redgrave can announce blandly that they are pregnant long before they announce they're thinking of getting married…if they do get married at all! To me, marriage is…well, my own marriage has been so wonderful that I can only say that marriage is not dead. Anne and I are trying to bring up our own children so that they know what's right and what's wrong when they get into moral situations, such as balancing marriages against having affairs. They're our kids, and we're trying our best to do what's right for them, Anne and I."

It was not unusual for Bob to return home after a long day's work on the set of *Hogan's Heroes* after seven o'clock at night. The family would have already eaten dinner, so he would eat alone, usually with the latest issue of *Variety* propped up against a milk bottle. "He's a very plain eater," Anne said. "Give him a steak and a potato, and he's happy."

But was Anne happy? Friends of Bob and Anne said that they had strong suspicions that life was not as rosy as Bob had been painting it to the media.

"Bob always looked the same," Stamford High School friend Jane Golden recalled. "I never saw any face on him other than the one I saw on *Hogan's Heroes* and in the pictures I have of him. He smiled all the time—just a happy guy. Anne was friendly and happy. We all liked Anne. You would not *not* like her. She was very sweet and very nice. She had like a half smile, a little nervous smile. You know, 'I think I'm supposed to smile for this picture.'"

Best school friend Charlie Zito claimed that the life of a Hollywood wife—or "widow"—was not something Anne enjoyed. Once Bob became famous, women continually vied for his attention, and it became increasingly difficult for her to cope. Charlie said, "One time, Anne was here visiting [relatives]. Any time she was in town, she always stopped in to see my wife. And Yve said to her, 'How is your lifestyle in California?' She said, 'Not so good. We're really not happy at all. *I'm* not happy. Bob is happy. But for instance, we'd go to a party, and somebody is trying to take your husband away right in front of you. And they don't give a damn whether the wife is there or not.' She found that awfully hard to bear."

Bob and Anne's daughter Karen also remembered the intrusion by fans into their personal lives. In her 2013 interview with *TV Confidential*, she explained that anytime they were out in public, no matter where it was, fans would swarm around them get a chance to meet her father.

"My dad would take my sister and me all the time to either Tarzana Park or Balboa Park, and we wanted time with Dad and him pushing us on the swing," Karen remembered. "I was six or seven. Kids would be coming up to him to get his autograph and always interrupting our swing time or sleigh time. And so my sister and I got kind of annoyed. We wanted our dad to start wearing that face disguise with the glasses so that people wouldn't recognize him so we could have him to ourselves."

Bob and Anne's privacy was also compromised at home. Even though Bob never complained about it to the media, it had to be difficult for him and Anne to be living with Anne's mother for nearly all of their married life. Despite Bob's public claims that Mrs. Terzian was not any trouble, and that her support with household chores and raising the kids was welcomed, it was inevitable that his mother-in-law's constant presence in their home would have eroded Bob and Anne's privacy to some degree. And as a parent, Mrs. Terzian may not have been able to view her daughter and son-in-law fully as adults. Bob's cousin Jim Senich recalled an incident where Anne's mother had been particularly harsh with Bob, scolding him as if he were a child.

"Bobby came home one day from work, and it was raining out, and his feet were muddy," Jim explained. "They had a gorgeous white

School and the Shy Child
by Bob Crane

There is no denying that Bob loved and adored his children, and they were without question his anchor in times of uncertainty in his own life. In 1966, Bob wrote an article that was published in the August issue of "TV Radio Mirror," describing his and Anne's efforts to acclimate Karen to school and ease her fears.

Most adults look back upon their kindergarten days as a happy playtime period. But to some children, the thought of leaving their own homes to go into a new environment can be frightening.

My wife and I never had this problem with our two older children, Bobby (who's now 14) and Debbie (our 6-year-old), for both are very outgoing. From the beginning, they were bursting with eagerness to start school. It was different with Karen, who is a year younger than Debbie and inclined to be shy. My wife Anne and I had noticed this shyness when Karen went to parties. She loved going, but she usually sat around quietly, barely joining in the conversation.

Getting Karen used to the idea of kindergarten started the first day Debbie went. On the previous night, my wife and I decided that the best plan would be for Anne to take both girls along that day. After that, whenever my wife drove Debbie to school, she always took Karen with her. Occasionally, she visited Debbie's class with Karen, so that our youngest child would get to know what kindergarten work is like.

My wife and I wanted Karen to look forward to school. When Debbie would bring home a watercolor she had painted or a drawing she had made, we would tell Karen, "When you're five, you'll be able to go to kindergarten, and then you'll be able to bring home pictures like these."

When Karen did become five, my wife and I reminded her that it was now time to start school. We told her, "You'll love it. You'll have interesting things to do, and it will be great fun." But we could tell by the way she clutched my wife's arm that she was still a little frightened. "I'm not sure that I really want to go," she said. Her eyes seemed to beg us for reassurance.

We gave it to her. "You'll like the first day of school," I told her. "You and your mother will go to the auditorium, just the way Debbie did. Your name will be called, and you'll get in line with the other children behind your new teacher. She will take you to your classroom."

Anne added, "I'll come to the class, too. You and I will be there just a little while. Then I'll drive you home."

> That first day, the auditorium was full of frightened, crying children. Anne said to Karen, "Those children don't know anything about kindergarten; that's why they're scared."
>
> Karen didn't shed a tear. The more she saw the other children crying, the more determined she was not to cry.
>
> Sometimes Karen's shyness caused her to have problems at school. One day, she came home looking downcast. It was one of the few days I had off from *Hogan's Heroes*. I asked her, "What's the matter, Karen?" She said, "I dropped my nickel and it rolled under the teacher's desk, so I couldn't buy any milk."
>
> "Why didn't you tell the teacher?" I asked her. "I'm sure she would have been glad to pick up the nickel."
>
> Karen said, "I didn't want to disturb her."
>
> "Honey," I told her, "she would have been much more disturbed if she had known that you went without milk because you were afraid to speak up."
>
> Shyness continued to plague Karen for a while. There were times when she should have raised her hand to ask to leave the room but didn't feel like bothering the teacher. When she would confess this to us later, my wife and I would say, "How can the teacher know unless you tell her? She would feel bad if she knew that you hesitated to raise your hand."
>
> Gradually, we convinced Karen that there are times when a child should speak up.
>
> Kindergarten has been a wonderful experience for her. She loves her teacher, she loves the work—and you can be sure that when she brought home her first watercolor, we made a big fuss about it. Karen is now so mad about kindergarten that even when she's running a little temperature, she wants to go to school. We have to persuade her to stay home!
>
> **Source:** *TV Radio Mirror,* 66(3), p. 4.

carpet, and he came in and stepped on it and got mud all over it. Then Annie's mother just was all over him, screaming at him, and he just wouldn't argue back. He would just take it. Annie said, 'I couldn't believe it; he would just take it.' 'Sorry, I'm sorry I did that.' And Annie said, 'Mom, Bob bought that carpet; everything we've got here is Bob's.' And Bob would say, 'No, no, no, Annie, I was wrong, I was wrong.' That's the kind of guy he was. He was really just a good guy, and it took a lot to get him to lose his temper. I never saw him angry. I never saw him angry."

Bob may not have been angry, but he was frustrated. Bob truly did love Anne and cared about her dearly, and he loved and adored his children beyond measure. But Bob was discontented, and tensions were mounting—on both sides.

Bob neither smoked nor drank. In public or at professional events, if he felt he had to consume alcohol, he would sometimes order one drink and nurse it for the duration of the event. Other times, he would pre-arrange the type of drink he would noticeably be served, not wanting others to know it was non-alcoholic. In this way, he could deflect any embarrassing questions as to why he was not drinking or not actually consuming much liquor.

"Bob would meet with the bartender when he would arrive," his cousin Jim said. "And he would explain to him, 'I'll be seated down there, and I want a non-alcoholic drink. But make sure it looks like booze, and I'll milk it for the night.'"

In fact, Bob was a kid at heart, preferring cookies, candy, and ice cream to alcohol or nicotine. On the set of *Hogan's Heroes*, he was known for snacking on junk food, and at home, he was never without a candy, cookie, and ice cream stash.

"I'm a non-drinker and a non-smoker, but I sure love to eat," he told reporter Johna Blinn. "I cook an occasional steak, but Anne or my mother-in-law does all the cooking in our house. One year, I gained over twenty-five pounds. I swear I had gravy on everything, even the cornflakes. My doctor told me to join the 'Y' and knock off the weight, which I finally did. My wife laughs at me because I have skim milk in coffee, bypass the potatoes, and then I'll have a chocolate and nut sundae. I'm crazy about sweets. In our home in California, we have a cookie drawer."

As an actor, however, Bob was sometimes required to smoke or appear to drink alcohol to stay in character. Anne and the kids would react strongly if he, as Hogan, smoked or drank on television, but if he kissed another woman on screen, the room was silent. It seemed as if kissing another woman as part of the plot did not bother anyone.

"We were all watching the show," he said in 1966. "When I started to smoke, the whole family, led by Anne, howled in protest. But my kissing dolls all the time, no one says a word."

Bob made it very clear in the press that he was not at all interested in the women with whom he worked. To him, an actress was someone who, at the end of the day, was just like the men who worked all day—on the phone with her agent, making deals, and taking off her shoes and massaging her aching feet. There was no attraction in that for him.

It is important to note that Bob's professionalism and his attitude toward his female costars as he expressed it to the media and to Anne need to be considered separately from the behaviors of his addiction. One of the facets of his addiction was his inability to understand it as an illness until shortly before his death. In the effort to focus on other elements of Bob's life—his work, family, career, ambitions, and his true belief system—we have chosen to deal with his addiction separately, apart from his timeline of birth to death. Bob's addiction is discussed in Chapter 11, "Specks on the Parthenon."

"The hardest job I have," he said in 1968 of his role on *Hogan's Heroes* and in *The Wicked Dreams of Paula Schultz*, "is to convince Anne that all the glamorous girls I work with after awhile seem just like men. And they do. For a girl to be an actress, she must be like a man, competitive, hard, unfeminine. The only temptation for an actor is from the extras, not the stars. On a set, the extras come around, wiggling their bottoms, and they have nothing to lose and everything to gain to get a male star worked up. All you have to do is say to one of them, 'Will you have lunch with me?' and you're in big trouble. So you stay away from them—and you get a reputation for coldness."

Many actresses, including Arlene Martel, Inger Wegge, Victoria Carroll, and others who worked with Bob, explained he did not pursue them romantically or make them feel uncomfortable. However, Paul Petersen also recalled that Bob had taken notice of some of the female extras hired for *The Donna Reed Show*, much to Paul's discomfort. In Bob's early acting career, he may have shown less restraint when it came to actresses, and realizing this type of behavior would hinder his advancement as an actor, he opted to view most actresses as business partners. He chose to distance himself emotionally from them, which may have led to his reputation of sometimes being cold and aloof.

When it came to work, Bob remained professional with his female actors. That is, with two very distinct exceptions.

During *Hogan's Heroes* and while still married to Anne, Bob became romantically involved with two actresses. It was his first affair with Cynthia "Cindy" Lynn, Colonel Klink's first secretary Helga, that caused heads to turn and jaws to drop, paving the way for a popular but false notion that Bob had been loyal to Anne until he achieved great success on *Hogan's Heroes,* and that he had been incapable of handling the fame that accompanied it.

Following Cindy's departure from the series shortly after the conclusion of season one, Bob and Cindy ended their affair. Patricia "Patty" Olson, who used the stage name Sigrid Valdis, was hired as her replacement as Colonel Klink's second secretary Hilda, and she would remain for the duration of *Hogan's Heroes*. Bob then began dating Patty, and this time, his relationship with Klink's secretary would be for the long-term.

Both Cindy and Patty were beautiful, strong-willed, feminine women. Regardless of how Bob felt about other actresses working alongside of him and his comparison of them to male business partners, Bob was immediately attracted to Cindy and Patty on many levels, and they, in turn, to him. Each would come to play a dynamic role in Bob's life.

Bob's affair with Cynthia Lynn began in early 1965 and lasted through April 1966. It was not Bob's first affair, nor was it exclusive. But his relationship with Cindy was one of his most serious.

While Cindy remembered her actual entry date differently in her autobiography *Escape to Freedom*, official United States immigration records indicate that on December 17, 1949, the passenger ship *General J.H. McRae* carrying Cindy, her mother Alisa Ziemelis, and her grandmother Anna Bisa, arrived in New York. A refugee from war-ravaged Europe, Cindy would flourish in America, first becoming a model and a dancer, ultimately leading to her working as an actress.

Cindy was born Zinta Ziemelis on April 2, 1936, in the capital city of Riga, Latvia. Her birth father had been an alcoholic, and her mother divorced him one night when he was so drunk that he unknowingly signed divorce papers. On July 10, 1941, Nazi forces invaded Latvia, and Germany controlled the small country until August 19, 1944, when Russian troops liberated Latvia and reclaimed it as Soviet land.

During the German occupation of her homeland, Cindy was kept safe from atrocities because her mother, an operatic soprano, agreed to entertain high-ranking German officers in the theatre. In a shrewd move, Alisa Ziemelis also bargained with the Germans that in lieu of being paid for her talents, she, her mother, and Cindy would receive protection from the Germans should Russia invade.

To escape the Russian occupation, when the bombings began in August 1944, Cindy, her mother, and grandmother evacuated Latvia with other Latvians and wounded German soldiers. They traveled across Europe for the next six years, until they finally reached Bremerhaven, Germany, where they boarded a vessel bound for America. While on the move throughout Europe, Cindy's mother dated two men, a Latvian Army soldier named Visvalds Uritis, who had become Alisa's fiancé following the war, and Captain Fred Rivers of the United States Army Air Force, who had arranged the deportation out of Germany for Cindy and her family.

Once in America, Cindy and her family settled in Long Island, where Cindy attended school. Around 1952 or 1953, Cindy's mother decided to take work in Bridgeport, Connecticut, at the Howard Hotel and Café owned by Matt Lucy. There, Alisa Ziemelis—who had changed her name to Alisa Lind—performed a nightclub act, and sometimes, Cindy accompanied her.

While the audience watched her mother sing, Cindy's eyes were elsewhere. "I think I was sweet sixteen, and I had such a crush on the drummer," Cindy said. "I didn't know who he was. He didn't even pay any attention to me! He would say, 'Hi!' and wave and smile, and that's about it."

Cindy had just laid eyes on Bob Crane. It would be more than a decade before she would see him again.

In the meantime, she made her television debut on *The Jackie Gleason Show* as one of the June Taylor Dancers, and then work for Johnny Carson on *Who Do You Trust?*, escorting contestants in and out of the glass booth. Cindy married Jeff Shipley, a fiberglass curtain salesman (Matt Lucey stood in as her father figure at the ceremony held in Bridgeport). But not long after they tied the knot, Cindy decided she would have better luck finding acting work in Hollywood. With Jeff's support, she left New York and her new husband behind, and arrived in California in 1960.

Cindy's agent wasted no time finding her work, which included appearing on shows with Bob Hope, Jimmy Durante, and Steve Allen, as well as on *The Odd Couple* and *Mission Impossible*. She also worked with Marlon Brando on the film *Bedtime Story*. In 1961, she met Lee Sands, who convinced her to divorce her first husband to marry him. Cindy and Lee were married shortly after her divorce from Jeff.

On September 29, 1962, Cindy gave birth to a daughter, Lisa, also the daughter of Marlon Brando. However, Lee embraced the new baby girl and raised her as his own.

Bedtime Story paved the way for Cindy to audition for other television roles, including that of Helga on *Hogan's Heroes*, which she was offered and accepted readily. To her surprise, the star of the series was none other than the drummer she had quietly gazed upon from afar at Matt Lucey's nightclub in Bridgeport.

Cindy remembered, "When I told Bob about my mom singing at Matt Lucey's in Bridgeport, he said, '*What?* I played drums there!' I said, 'Are you kidding? I had such a crush on you! You didn't even *look* at me!' And he said, 'Oh, my *God*! How *weird* is that?'"

Once the main cast of *Hogan's Heroes* was finalized, they traveled to New York in early 1965 to perform a skit for network affiliates in the effort to help sell the series.

"We had confidence," Cindy said. "Bob had to recite some kind of stupid poem, and I had to do a striptease type thing behind him so people would laugh at his jokes, which were not funny. The glove got stuck; I couldn't get the glove off, and then the zipper got stuck—it was a disaster. But at the end the zipper came off, and I dropped the dress and went out, and that was it. Then, we sat around with all the affiliates and VIPs, and one said, 'You know, we're glad you didn't do a perfect job with your little dance over there or we'd have thought you were a professional.' They liked me from the beginning, the whole group, the whole cast. We knew we had it, and they kept the whole original cast, all of us."

As filming of season one continued throughout the spring of 1965, Bob and Cindy became comfortable with the show and even more so with each other. Bob offered her relaxation tips for her first screen kiss, to the delight of the production team, and when aired, of the audiences as well. The screen romance between Hogan and Helga was so greatly embraced that writers wrote in more kissing scenes in the earlier episodes, until, according to Cindy, CBS believed the show was becoming *too* sexy, and the writers stopped including so many romantic scenes.

It was also becoming very sexy for Cindy personally. She wrote in her autobiography, "When I kissed Bob Crane on the show, I started to feel something for him, but I was confused. I said to myself this is work, and I mustn't mix it up with real life. I thought that Bob had feelings for me, but I really couldn't be sure of that, either." She told us, "You can be the greatest actor in the world, but the vibes—there has to be a special connection there. There has to be *something* there. You can pretend, but there has to be *something* you like about the person."

About midway through filming season one, the cast made a trip to Washington, D.C., to promote the series. While in the nation's capitol, Bob and Cindy admitted to each other that they were both in marriages they believed were not healthy for either of them. Soon after, they confessed their attraction to one other and gave in to it.

In her autobiography, Cindy said she told Bob, "My husband and I are separated. It's very hard trying to keep a family and a career going at the same time. I hardly ever see him, and he's mostly away gambling somewhere."

Cindy also wrote about Bob's admission to her, saying, "Somehow he wanted me to know that there was trouble in his marriage. 'We haven't slept together in years. It's a marriage in name only. We have separate beds. We're just temporarily holding it together because of the children.'"

"How it happened," Cindy told us, "was that he called me the first time we were in [the hotel in] Washington, and he said, 'I've got this big basket of fruit and champagne. Can I bring it up to you?' I said, 'I don't think so because I have my own. And besides that, you're married, and *I'm* married.' He said, 'But I'm not *married*-married.' And I said, 'Well, I'm not *married*-married either, but it still doesn't make it right. So, I'll eat my own fruit, thanks. Go to sleep now. Night-night.' So the next evening, we all went out and had some champagne, and champagne does something to me. I'd just come out of the bathtub. The phone rang, and I answered it. Of course, it's Bob. 'Uh, hi. Um… Let's have a glass of champagne together, that's all, okay? Let's just talk, nothing serious, okay? I just want to see you for just a few minutes.' So I said, 'Well, okay.' And I had nothing to wear because I forgot to bring my nightie; all I had was my raincoat that I wore in the show one time. I had my wardrobe with me, and I had a raincoat. I didn't feel like getting dressed all over again—because I *knew* it was going to happen. I *knew*. So I put that raincoat on, and I answered the door! '*What* are you doing in a *raincoat*?' I said, 'Well, I had nothing to wear!' And so, he spent the night, and that's how it started. Then we would send notes to each other, like little kids, on the set, trying to pretend like nothing's happening. And one day I went to the makeup man, and he said,

'Hmmm you look a little different.' And I said, 'I do?' And he said, 'Yeah, you've got this certain look in your eyes. You look a little different.' But I didn't want to. I didn't. I tried so hard; I tried so hard. But not hard enough. I gave in."

Cindy said Bob made it clear to her that his marriage was beyond repair, and because hers was as well, it was easier for both of them to enter into the affair. "His marriage was on the rocks. He had a hard time in his marriage, and they stayed together because of the children. He said that they're together, but they're not together. They have two separate lives, and because of the children, they tried to be as civil as possible to each other. But there was no marriage."

Whether on the set or alone with her, Cindy said Bob didn't change. "He was the same. He was the same Bob. Same! When we went out to eat or anything, or we were together alone, same. Cracking jokes, laughing. He was an 'up' person, not a depressed person. Definitely not depressed. A social person. He could be serious about [current events] and the news. Of course, he had his serious side to him, but nothing depressing. I never saw him really depressed. He did not keep to himself. He was very open with everybody. He was *Bob*. He was not a quiet guy. He was a comedian in person, too. He cracked jokes all the time. He would be quiet once in awhile, depending on what kind of day he had, or depending on if he had a lot of dialogue or something, he would be quiet and try to do his job, but as far as being open, he was very open to everybody. Accessible. Whoever needed him, unless he was really tied up with something, he'd say 'I'm sorry,' in a nice way he would excuse himself: 'I'm busy right now; maybe later.' He did carry a camera around his neck most of the time. He was a camera bug. He *loved* to shoot pictures. Of all the new actors at work coming in, of everybody, he just kept shooting pictures.

"He had drums backstage, and during lunchtime or whenever, he went and played his drums. Then when we became intimately involved, we'd spend a lot of time in his main, big dressing room, and he didn't play the drums then! We made *our* own rhythm. The only thing he did is, he chewed gum a lot. He always had gum in his mouth. Once in awhile he forgot to take the gum out when we were shooting. 'Drop the gum! Drop the gum!' With men he was more—like a guy. Guys are guys. Guy talk. With women he was a gentleman. He was very gentlemanly. And he was not gay—definitely not gay! And Bob did *not* fool around! I mean, I went with him. Maybe that's why. But he didn't fool around. He made all the women feel comfortable and relaxed, and treated them like women should be treated. I mean, he was great!"

As season one progressed, so did Bob's and Cindy's affair. "We kept it secret," Cindy explained. "Everybody knew, but we pretended nobody knew. We were just like an ostrich. 'Nobody knows; we'll play it real, real cool.' Of course everybody knew when I'd disappear for an hour in his dressing room. I mean, gimme a break! 'We were rehearsing our lines!' Once in awhile, we met at our makeup man's house in Beverly Glen. He knew. Of course, everybody knew. It was just silly. Everybody knew, and they'd crack some jokes and stuff. It was fine. Everybody accepted it."

Cindy said at first, their romance had been based on sexual attraction. They would meet at the makeup man's house two or three days a week, and on weekends, if it could be managed.

"Bob would usually be waiting for me when I got there," Cindy wrote in her autobiography. "We drove up there separately, and I remember how nervous I was the very first time. We'd sit on the sofa and talk for a few minutes, usually about our families, but soon the talk would get personal, and he would start kissing me and undressing me. We always ended up making love on the sofa. It was a very romantic and dangerous situation."

As their relationship advanced, it became more certain and genuine. They would say to each other, "I think I'm falling in love with you." They wondered how long they were going to be able to carry on the façade, or when or if they should open up about it.

During that time, Cindy said Bob shared a very loving, soft side of himself to her. According to Cindy, Bob wanted to divorce Anne, and he urged her to wait a little longer. Meanwhile, he continued to confide his feelings to Cindy, and she believed he loved her.

"He expressed [his love] by saying 'I love you,' 'You're beautiful,' 'I love being with you,' and 'I wish we could spend more time together,'" Cindy said to us. "Beautiful, loving things. A little gift now and then, little gifts, little tokens, nothing expensive, just thoughtful. Thoughtfulness. Or even just *one* flower. Just one little flower. And not even a rose, just a flower. That got to me *all* the time. Just like how Hogan and Helga interacted—their winks and kisses—it was innocent. And that's how I felt—that's how I felt with Bob. It was innocent, it was sweet, it was beautiful. And that's all."

She wrote in her autobiography, "The funny thing about the whole affair is that Bob didn't smoke or consume alcohol. That champagne in Washington was an exception. We usually drank either Coke or 7-Up. That was one of the reasons I felt that I really loved him. During the whole affair, outside of Washington, no alcoholic beverages were consumed. It seemed that when I made most of the bad decisions of my life, champagne was involved. I love it, but somehow, it doesn't love me or it clouds my judgment. Since there was no alcohol involved in my affair with Bob Crane, I thought that this could be it."

They also connected intellectually, and they discussed the current state of events in the country and in the world. Cindy explained to us that they talked about "why there are wars, why people fall out of love—a lot of *whys*. We talked about all different subjects, all different things. Why this and why that? We talked about our hopes and dreams. If we could eventually get together. Have a happy ending. But we were so confused that we were in the middle of a whirlwind, and we wanted it to stop and have a normal life."

Cindy also provided a rare glimpse into the deep psyche of Bob Crane, and an insightful rationale as to one of the reasons his marriage suffered. Bob had married his childhood sweetheart, and his friends from school agree that from the moment he started going with Anne—when he was fourteen and she was twelve—she was going to be the girl for him. Bob and Anne had been inseparable during their high school days, and their apparent storybook relationship and eventual marriage was not without psychological burden.

"He married his childhood sweetheart," Cindy said, "but he said that after she gave birth, he couldn't look at her the same way anymore because she was a mother. For some reason, it just threw him. How can I say this? He loved her, but not in the sexual way. He loved her, but he couldn't *make love* to her because of the kids. She was a mother all of a sudden, and it threw him somehow. He could not make love to a mother. He tried to explain it to me, but I couldn't quite understand. It changed him. It just wasn't the same anymore. He couldn't make love to her anymore."

Cindy also hinted at suspecting there had to be something dark in his life reaching way back into his childhood that he kept hidden from the world, never wishing to discuss it. "He never really wanted to talk about his childhood," Cindy said. "He didn't want to go there. I don't really know why. He didn't want to talk about his childhood. He would change the subject or something. He never really talked about home. The subject never really came up. We were too involved in ourselves. We talked about my childhood, growing up during the war and stuff. But we didn't really talk about that all that much either. When we were together, we were together. Nothing else existed. Our universe for that moment was just him and me. Maybe our being together was an escape from that past. Everything else was forgotten. Nothing else existed."

Some who knew Bob well, including Arlene Martel, described him as someone who required feminine understanding. Cindy agreed with this. "He needed a woman to just be able to accept him for what he was. See, he was gentle, and he needed gentleness. He needed to be treated lovingly. That's how I can explain it. He needed a lot of hugs. He was lacking love! That's what it was, he was lacking—*love*. Just regular hugs. I mean, not even sex, just holding. Just holding. Sometimes, when we were together, it was just being together and just holding each other. That's all, just talking about nothing or about silly things, or serious, or whatever—wherever our brains led us. We just went with the flow. I never saw weakness in him. Just lovingness. No weakness. He had a lot of strength in him, but he was needy. Needy, *just* to be held. Needy, like a baby. In an innocent way. As a matter of fact, very innocent. Like a child. Very childlike a lot of times. I am very sensitive to other people's feeling. With me, he was himself at all times. I've seen him only one way: himself. I've never seen another side of him. Never."

It is unknown if Anne was aware of the affair. Cindy didn't ask, and Bob didn't tell her, but she believed they managed to keep it a secret. And even though she was having an affair with Bob, Cindy spoke highly of his wife and youngest daughter, and cared deeply about what they thought of her.

"Anne is a sweetheart," Cindy said. "I met her, way in the beginning, when we all got together for a party. She's a sweetheart. She's sweet. I like her, a lot. And then later on, I felt weird because I had met her. Many years later, I met Karen, his daughter, in her antique shop. I went in there and said, 'Hi, I'm Cindy—Fräulein Helga,' and she said, 'Hi!' And she gave me the biggest hug and apparently she did like me!"

Season one was coming to a close, and *Hogan's Heroes* had won over audiences and critics. The cast and crew were riding a high, knowing that they would be back on the air for season two. Toward the end of filming season one, the cast and crew went on a brief hiatus. Cindy was at home, and while standing in her kitchen, she heard a knock on the window.

"One afternoon, I went in the kitchen to get some water, and there's a knock on the window. And there's Bob! I said, '*Bob!* Oh my God!' I was so excited to see him! I went outside. I said, 'Oh, my God.' He gave me the *biggest kiss*. 'Oh my God, you're here! Come on inside!' He said, 'No, no, no, no. I can't come inside, and see your mom and everybody there. I'll talk to you later.' And it never happened."

Cindy was unable to keep their affair secret any longer. Soon after this encounter with Bob at her home, she opened up and told a close friend that she was in love with Bob, and he with her, and that they had been carrying on an affair for more than a year. Her trust in her friend had been a terrible mistake. Her friend told Cindy's estranged husband Lee, who suddenly decided he wanted Cindy back. With a bottle of champagne in hand, Lee re-entered Cindy's life on the last day of shooting the final episode of season one. It had also been Cindy's birthday—April 2, 1966.

"My husband came home on my birthday," Cindy explained, "He was a macho Italian and had a lot of jealousy. Even if somebody *looked* at me, he'd freak out. He said he wanted to try to patch up the marriage again and see if we could try. He said he still loved me, and we'd have a bottle of champagne."

Cindy was hesitant at first, but Lee was persistent. She agreed to try and work on the marriage. Lee then admitted he knew of her affair and demanded that she resign from *Hogan's Heroes*. He could not handle watching her screen kisses with Bob. If she was serious about saving their marriage, she had no choice but to resign.

Despite the champagne clouding her judgment, Cindy also wanted to regain a sense of normalcy, and as she put it, regain a "normal life." Cindy complied with Lee's wishes, but when she offered to explain it to Bob, Lee would not hear of it.

Instead, Lee visited producer Edward Feldman directly and explained the situation to him. Both Feldman and Cindy's agent were against her decision to leave the show, telling her she was making a "big mistake." There were other actresses who would give anything for her role on the series, and Feldman and her agent both begged her to reconsider. As Cindy relayed in her autobiography, Ed Feldman also warned her, "You know we all love you and don't want to get tough about this situation. You have a five-year contract, and we could hold you to it."

As Feldman talked with Cindy on the phone, her husband was in Feldman's office. Since it did not appear she was going to change her mind, Feldman had no choice but to release her from her contract, which he did without penalty. "You know how we all feel about you, and we want you to be happy. I could sue you, but I won't. I just couldn't do that to you. I suppose we should be more careful in the future and make sure your replacement isn't married. I'll let your husband into your dressing room to pick up your things. Good luck to you, dear. Goodbye."

Not fifteen minutes later, Bob called Cindy. "What's going on? Eddie called me and told me you're leaving the show. How can this be true? What about us?"

Cindy explained to him that despite their feelings, they were both still married, and she was choosing to save her marriage. She wrote that he said, "Okay, Cindy. I'm sorry it has to end this way," and she answered, "So am I."

With that, Bob Crane was out of Cynthia Lynn's life forever. But when Lee came home with Cindy's belongings from her dressing room, one important item was missing.

"When he came back with my wardrobe, I didn't see that raincoat there. I said, '*Oh my God*, what did I do?' The raincoat, the raincoat! It wasn't there, and I knew right then and there I made the *biggest* mistake in my life."

Cindy would come to regret her decision to leave *Hogan's Heroes* for the rest of her life—both because of her part in the series and because of her love for Bob.

"I never talked to him after that," Cindy said. "I just quit the series, left. I would not have been able to handle it. If I saw him, I wouldn't have left the series. If I would have gone there myself and seen Bob, forget it. I wouldn't leave. No way. I would have stayed. I had to let go completely. The last time I saw Bob [during the affair] was the last kiss in my back yard. He thought I was coming back to the show. There was never any ending to us, except in my backyard, that last kiss. It wasn't intended to be an ending. And I have huge regrets. I *still* haven't forgiven myself. I ruined my career. At the time, it was the right thing to do. I wanted the white picket fence, the family, the whole thing. Unfortunately, I married a gambler. So I was not very lucky in love. That's the biggest mistake I ever made in my entire life. But I never had discussed ending the relationship with Bob because we thought that it would lead somewhere. That's why we were trying to be together as much as possible. Never ending it. The way it ended, it was weird. It was just—that's it. It's over. Done. That part of my life is gone."

Three months later, having had enough of Lee's gambling and spending her money, Cindy filed for divorce. No longer married and free to do as she pleased, she called Ed Feldman back and asked to salvage her role on *Hogan's Heroes*. She was hopeful that they had not yet filled the role.

But *Hogan's Heroes* had moved on, and Cindy's replacement had already been hired. Sigrid Valdis, who had appeared in one episode of *Hogan's Heroes* in season one and was familiar with the premise and the cast, had just signed on as Fräulein Hilda. And she had signed her contract only one day before Cindy called.

"Just one day," Cindy said. "*Everything* happens for a reason. It wasn't meant to be. So it's Fate. Kismet."

The first episode of *Hogan's Heroes* season two, "Hogan Gives a Birthday Party," premiered on September 16, 1966. With the start of the new season, viewers would notice several changes. The series was not as gimmick-ridden as season one had been. The steam room in the tunnel was long gone, and Hogan and his band of prisoners were no longer manufacturing cigarette lighters in the shape of German Lugers in the tunnel. The characters were becoming more developed, and the element of danger was heightened. And most notably, Colonel Klink had employed a new secretary—Fräulein Hilda. The whereabouts of Helga and the reasons behind her departure from Stalag 13 were left to the imagination of viewers. In her place seated comfortably outside Klink's office, Hilda had made herself at home.

Patricia Annette Olson was born on September 21, 1935, in Bakersfield, California. Of Swedish descent, Patty resided in Europe for a short time following high school graduation. Upon returning to America, she lived in New York, where she worked as a designer's, showroom, and runway model. One of her earliest jobs was showing and selling sports cars at an agency on Park Avenue.

"They hadn't sold a car for six months before they hired me, just for the novelty of having a girl salesman," she said in August 1967. "Within three months, I was the manager and selling cars like I was giving them away. Six months after I quit, the agency went out of business."

While living in New York, Patty met George Gilbert Ateyeh, and on November 5, 1958, they were married in Los Angeles. Together they had one daughter, Melissa (also called "Mitsu" or "Mits").

"When I'm not working, I'm a full-time mother," Patty explained in 1967. "[Mits and I] go every place together when I'm not working and she's not in school."

Shortly after Melissa was born, Patty's focus turned to acting. With the money she had earned at the car agency, she enrolled at the Stella Adler Studio of Acting in New York. She had attended twenty-three schools throughout her life by that point, changing schools seventeen times just while in high school alone because her family traveled frequently.

Patty filed for legal separation from George in 1964, and soon after, she returned home to Los Angeles. They were never formally divorced, and George remained in New York for the rest of his life, passing away in November 1967.

On the West Coast, Patty sought work as a character actress but had difficulty finding roles. Producers wanted actresses to drastically change their looks to match the character, and Patty resisted at first. It was only after she agreed to conform to the demands of producers that she began to land acting jobs.

To ensure that she would be memorable in an industry saturated with plenty of female talent, Patty decided one other professional alteration was necessary. She changed her name from Patricia Olson to Sigrid Valdis, and she would be credited as such in all of her film, television, and stage performances.

"I had decided to change my name even before I decided to be an actress," Patty said. "Sigrid can make it, but Pat never could." She further explained in a 1967 interview with Bob Crane for the United States Armed Forces Radio Network that she chose the name because it was Swedish, and thus, represented her heritage.

Patty's early film and television credits include, among others, *Marriage on the Rocks* with Dean Martin and Frank Sinatra, and *Our Man Flint* with James Coburn and Lee J. Cobb. In 1965, she worked with Robert Conrad and Ross Martin in *The Wild, Wild West*; and later, in 1967 she appeared with Robert Vaughn in *The Venetian*. Perhaps most influential to her being cast as Hilda was her season one guest appearance as Gretchen in the *Hogan's Heroes* episode "Top Hat, White Tie and Bomb Sight." Her brief yet notable episodic work on the series impressed producer Edward Feldman, and he remembered Patty when the time came to replace Cynthia Lynn.

Bob was also reportedly quite happy with Feldman's decision to hire Patty. While producers searched for a replacement following Cindy's departure, Bob petitioned strongly for Patty to be chosen. As the star of the show, Bob most likely had some influence in Feldman's selection; however, he neither made the final decision nor used his star power to force it.

Once hired, Patty explained to the press in 1966 that her character was necessary because "with seven guys in prisoner-of-war uniforms, the show needed a female. Here's a bunch of guys in POW fatigues and there's a blonde girl in a low-cut peasant blouse—who is the audience going to watch?"

Male appeal was important, and originally, Patty's wardrobe consisted only of peasant blouses, which Patty found humorous. "It was the first tailored peasant blouse I ever heard of," she said. "It's tightened and low cut." After a few episodes, however, producers became nervous that the blouses may have been a bit *too* low-cut and distracting. So they altered Hilda's attire to loose-fitting, high-knit sweaters instead. "All the things they hired me for, they try to cover up," she said.

In 2005, Patty explained that she actually wore most of her own clothing for the show, joking that the budget for Hilda's wardrobe was next to nothing. "About a dollar a week for me," she said. "They just didn't have many women on the show, so I ended up going out and buying almost my entire wardrobe. My wardrobe was basically a red sweater and a black skirt."

A typical work week for Patty consisted of two or three days a week, and she was contracted to appear in about seven of every thirteen episodes. "When I go to work, the street lights are just going off," she said in 1967. "And by the time I head home, they're just being turned on."

"I basically did my own make up because so many make-up people I dealt with on other shows made me up the way they thought I should look," she said in 2005. "I just got tired of it, so I just said, 'Armand, *please* just put on my base coat, my shadow, and everything, and I'll go to my room, and I'll do the rest of my make up—eyelashes, eyebrows, lipstick."

A natural brunette with short hair, Patty was also not too fond of Hilda's blonde pigtails. In season two, she bleached her hair blonde and added braided extensions. In later seasons, to cover up her naturally dark tresses, she wore a full wig.

"Those pigtails look so phony, I can't believe it," Patty said in 2005. "They look like they are growing out of the back of my neck!"

At the start of the second season, Patty said she was excited about her new role as Hilda on *Hogan's Heroes*. She was initially led to believe that her character would engage in some espionage, and thus, become a more significant character in the series. However, this did not occur. Much like Helga, Hilda was relegated to her secretarial duties, sitting outside Klink's office and announcing, "Colonel Hogan to see you, Herr Kommandant." Only occasionally did Hilda assist Hogan with his schemes, but she usually had her own interests in mind—typically a pair of nylons in exchange for her help. Other times, Hilda assisted Hogan unknowingly and was easily persuaded with a kiss on her cheek from the American colonel.

Yet this did not seem to bother Patty so much. She had studied and prepared to become a leading actress, but while working on *Hogan's Heroes*, her attention and focus shifted to becoming the main interest of her leading man.

Shortly after season two began filming, Bob and Patty started dating, and it was the second love affair Bob would have while working on *Hogan's Heroes* under the noses of those around him. Bob also took Patty under his wing, helping her advance in her acting career; in later seasons of *Hogan's Heroes*, he vied for more screen time for her. In 1969, Bob signed Patty on to act in his summer theatre production of *Cactus Flower*, which also starred Abby Dalton. The play ran for six weeks through the end of June of that year in various parts of Ohio as part of the Kenley Players theatre group. Bob and Patty returned to Hollywood in early July when *Hogan's Heroes* began filming its fifth season.

Bob and Anne had welcomed Patty into their home, and Anne considered her a friend, But something was very, very wrong in the Crane household, and by early 1969, Bob and Anne's marriage was beyond repair.

"We knew something was happening because sometimes Bob would come alone to visit us," school friend Charlie Zito said. "Like if he was in New York, and he wanted to come up to Connecticut and see a couple of his friends, he always stopped here. Whenever he was nearby, he never failed to stop in. But toward the end, he and Anne came separately. They were here together a couple of times when we were having our reunions. After that, she would come, and he would come. But we just didn't ask questions. It was embarrassing for both of us, especially my wife. She didn't want to push that."

The very last trip Bob and Anne made to Connecticut together was in the late winter of 1969, when they visited Charlie and his wife Yve in Stamford. It was an impromptu visit, and Charlie remembered that despite whatever troubles Bob and Anne may have been experiencing, they all had a very nice time that evening. Neither Charlie nor Yve expected that it would also be the last time they would ever see Bob and Anne together as husband and wife. But their suspicions were growing.

Sunday, April 6, 1969. Little Karen Crane had just started to doze off to sleep when she awoke to the sound of her parents arguing. She slid out of bed and shuffled down the hall toward the noise. Peering around the corner of the stairwell, she watched in silent horror at the scene unfolding in the family den. Her father sat quietly, his face buried in his hands, as her mother threw family photographs, still in their frames, into the trash. Her parents were separating, but she could not comprehend it.

In her 2013 interview with *TV Confidential*, Karen described the moment. "Do you remember the scene in *Fatal Attraction* when Michael Douglas is finally coming clean to his wife after they've come back home and found their little girl's rabbit boiling on the stove? The scene after that—once they've put their little girl to bed and soothed her and now they're together in this room, and she's looking at him like…'It's time to come clean.' When he starts admitting to his wife about who he knows did this, they cut to the doorway of the little girl standing in her nightclothes, and she's holding her little stuffed animal. And she's standing there with tears coming down her face because she's just overheard her parents fighting. I remember that both of them finally notice her standing there and realize, 'Oh my God, she heard us.' That was exactly how it happened for me. That's how I found out my parents were splitting up. They had just put my sister and me to bed. We slept in the same room; we had twin beds. Both of us heard my mom and dad arguing in the den, and I never heard them argue, at all. So it woke me up, and I got up out of bed and same thing—I was standing there at the top of the stairs looking down into the den, and I can remember what I saw like it were yesterday. My dad was sitting at our den table with his head in his hands, and my mom was standing next to him where we had a cabinet full of all the family photos. And I remember that my mom was taking every family photo and making a pile of all the photos, and she was slamming each frame down on top of each other as if to say, 'That's it—the family is done.' I don't remember what she was saying to him, and I don't remember what he was saying to her. I just remember the action and noise of those frames being piled up. They finally turned around and noticed that I was standing there, and my dad rushed over to me and brought me back to bed. He put me back in bed, and he was kneeling in between the twin beds of my sister and me, and he was actually holding our hands in between the beds and saying to us, 'Don't worry, it's going to be okay.' And of course, it was never okay. He moved out of the house while we were at school, so we came home to find he was already gone, but we didn't know what was happening. We didn't understand. We figured, 'He'll be back. We don't know where he went, but he'll be back.' We probably figured he was down at the park or something. But of course, he didn't come back. That's how I found out. So, that scene in *Fatal Attraction* was very difficult for me to watch. I was that little girl. I even kind of looked like her at that age, too. I didn't know what divorce was at nine years old. You know, it was all about, 'When's the next Barbie coming out?' We literally had what I considered a fairytale life. We had the perfect house for kids, and it was like our own little Disneyland oasis-type of yard with a pool and a long driveway where we rode our bikes and roller-skated. My life, up until nine, was just wonderful."

Bob had just returned from a ten-week engagement in Chicago performing in the theatre production of *Send Me No Flowers*, which ran from February 12 through April 4, 1969. He had been away from home and his family for more than two months, and he was already planning his next theatre tour, *Cactus Flower*, which would begin in Warren, Ohio, in mid-May. When he came back home following his final performance of *Send Me No Flowers*, whatever had been festering between Bob and Anne over the past several years suddenly escalated and then ruptured.

"Anne wrote to my wife," Charlie Zito explained. "And she said Anne told her, 'You know I told you a lot on our last visit or a few visits past that things were happening here that I didn't like? Well, it all finally came to a head.'"

On April 7, 1969, the beloved *Hogan's Heroes* star made headlines across the country when Anne filed for legal separation. Bob then moved out of the house in Tarzana and into an apartment closer to Desilu Studios where *Hogan's Heroes* was being filmed. Rumors among the tight Hollywood community had been circulating about his affair with Patty, but nobody wanted to believe it. A little more than a month later, on May 13, 1969, Anne filed for divorce, and everyone was stunned. The "perfect" family—the one thing that Bob had so openly adored, hugged close to his heart, and fiercely protected from outsiders—was done.

In a rare interview for a celebrity magazine in October 1969, Anne shared her feelings exclusively with reporter Joanne Sisul. "Are you shocked that Bob and I are separated? Well, you're not as shocked as I am, as the children are."

When Sisul suggested that nothing or no one can break up a happy marriage, Anne responded, "Not true! You've heard the stories, but you'd have to live them to realize how bad it could be. The times when I would be right beside Bob and be literally pushed away by women wanting to make advances. It never worried me, though. I knew my husband too well; his values, his adoration of our relationship, of the children."

Anne pinpointed the problem: they had become too close to Patty, who enjoyed suppers and other family occasions with the Cranes. What disturbed Anne was Bob's eagerness to help Patty by going above and beyond to get her an acting part in *Send Me No Flowers*. It irritated her. But according to Anne, he still called her every day, relieving her of any worry. But then, the bottom dropped out.

When Bob returned home from Chicago, he didn't go home to the house. Instead, he moved into the apartment near the studio, claiming he wanted no more of marriage.

Anne said he told her that they could still be friends.

"I don't need an ex-husband for a friend," she exclaimed. "He'll never marry again. He'd told me that. Why should he? For love? He had that here. Why leave one marriage just to jump into another?"

If Anne was distressed, apparently, Bob was equally so. Anne said, "He tells me, 'Please, just leave me alone. Don't tell me what to do until I straighten myself out.'"

Sisul added in her article, "Like a man beset by a terrible illness that has made him not responsible for his deeds or actions."

Anne explained that she thought her husband was different and that he "wouldn't fall victim to advances from a Hollywood chick." But there

What Price Freedom?

More than once, Bob Crane gambled on his career, upping the ante with each promising career venture, and it paid off. However, the one thing he had said he refused to gamble on was his family—Anne and their three children—Bobby, Debbie, and Karen. So adamant was he in this regard that one of his closest friends, Tom Hatten, declared in 1966, "That's Bob's way... He is the opposite of what you anticipate. When I first met Bob, I expected to find a mile-long line of chicks standing around waiting for him to crook his finger. Everyone who has heard or seen Crane professionally thinks he's the biggest swinger in town. Instead, you discover a man who is a solid citizen. He is devoted to his family."

This is almost all true. *Almost*. Bob *was* devoted to his family. He provided for them and cared for them. He loved and adored his children. He was a solid citizen. He never wanted to insult or offend anyone with his humor. He was sensitive to the feelings of others, and he was his own harshest critic.

Yet all the career success in the world could not change the fact that Bob was terribly unhappy in his first marriage, and he had been for a long time. It did not mean he did not love Anne or his children. He did, very much. He—and Anne as well—both individually struggled with unhappiness throughout most of their marriage, all while keeping a stoic front not only to their children, but also to the prying eyes of the media and public, and their family and friends. The sad truth was that childhood sweethearts Bob and Anne Crane had fallen out of love, and Bob's affair with Patty was the straw that broke the camel's back.

As Bob's first marriage fell apart and eventually dissolved, his privacy began to erode as well. The public started to become unsure of the man behind the Hogan façade, and over the course of the next nine years, Bob would struggle—and ultimately fail—to maintain the image he had worked so long to create and uphold.

Bob and Anne filed for legal separation on April 7, 1969. On May 13, 1969, just eight days before what would have been their milestone 20th anniversary, Anne filed for divorce. Reporter Jim Shaw was present for the court hearing, and he published a lengthy summary of the account, outlining the grim breakdown of finances between the estranged couple. Portions of his article are reprinted below:

> The Los Angeles County Superior Court complaint merely listed the standard charge of mental cruelty and gave no details other than to say that "the defendant Robert Edward Crane has treated plaintiff with extreme cruelty and has wrongfully and without reasonable excuse, cause, provocation, or justification inflicted

upon plaintiff grievous mental suffering, which has impaired her health and destroyed her happiness."

In an accompanying document, however, she stated that it was Bob who asked for the divorce. Because this was so, according to the charges, his visits to the family home since their separation caused "severe emotional upset and trauma" for Anne and their three children. She said that Bob's "unplanned and unwanted" visits to the Tarzana house at any time he so desired upset the peace and quiet of the home.

Anne asked for and obtained a restraining order, keeping Bob from entering upon the home premises except at such times as he would be there to visit the children. He was also restrained from "annoying, molesting, or harassing" his wife in any way, pending the first hearing in the case. Another restraining order tied up community property and assets, estimated to be worth $280,000.

In her application for temporary support, Anne said she would need $3,500 per month alimony and $1,500 monthly for the children.

Bob countered that he had been giving her $800 per month spending money through his business managers, which took care of all household and other bills, including various charge accounts. He submitted a statement to the court, revealing that his net "take-home" pay from Bing Crosby Enterprises, producer of *Hogan's Heroes*, was $7,500 per month. In addition, he said there was $468 per month coming from assorted investments.

On the other hand, the actor listed his own monthly expenses at $5,088.95. The list included such items as $350 a month for rent, $750 monthly for food (including business entertainment), $336 payments on the Tarzana home, $416 for insurance premiums, $560 monthly for travel expenses (he was planning his summer stock tour with the stage play *Cactus Flower*). He cited other expenses: $220 a month for "gratuities" (tips), $200 monthly for clothes, including those needed for business purposes, and $60 each month for a "hair stylist."

Anne requested that a receiver be named to take charge of various assets, including real estate holdings, on the grounds that Bob was leaving the jurisdiction of the court. He resisted this, pointing out that competent managers were capable of administering the properties and were likewise able to pay out any necessary sums for the needs of his wife and children.

It was disclosed at a pre-divorce hearing that negotiations were pending for a renewal of [*Hogan's Heroes*] for another season. The hearing was conducted by Los Angeles Superior Court Commissioner Huey Shepard, who heard financial testimony in connection with Anne's request for temporary alimony and child support, as well as further restraining orders and the receivership pending trial of the divorce case. The commissioner took under submission the temporary petition.

Meantime, both sides agreed that custody of the children should remain with Anne, with rights of reasonable visitation reserved to Bob, including certain weekends.

At the hearing, there was no sign that Bob would contest the divorce. Indications were that there would be long negotiations in the hope of reaching an amicable financial settlement. An offer by the commissioner to set the case for an early trial was turned down.

Whether there was any other romantic interest in the background of the divorce picture was a matter of some Hollywood conjecture after news of the Cranes' separation became public. The eyebrow-raisers were somewhat agog when it was revealed that the only female in the *Hogan's Heroes* show, Sigrid Valdis, was going to be a part of the same summer stock company with Bob, in the production of *Cactus Flower*.

At the commissioner's hearing, most of the time was taken up with the introduction of testimony based on books and records of the Cranes' financial interests, including extensive real estate holdings, television and recording contracts, stocks, and investments. Anne alleged that her husband's monthly income totaled $17,500, and that he therefore could well afford to pay her what she requested.

She said she did not really know her exact needs, due to the fact that bills were being paid by the business managers, who also sent her the monthly allowance of $800. However, in support of her request for $5,000 per month, the court was informed of an affidavit:

"...she has resided in a spacious home in Tarzana for years, with a swimming pool, gardener, etc. She drives her own automobile, and her son has no automobile for his own use. This has been her reasonable standard of living for years."

She charged that Bob placed some property in the names of other persons for the purpose of defeating her "rights and claims" as his wife and to "embarrass, hinder, and delay" any judgment in her favor.

> At the conclusion of the temporary hearing, Bob spoke to his wife for the first time during the proceedings. He asked if he could see the children during the following weekend. Her reply gave some support to suggestions that the divorce case might never come to trial, that there was still a chance for a reconciliation.
>
> She was not brusque in her response to Bob's request. Rather, she smiled cordially, and there was warmth in her voice as she answered, "Call me, and we will talk about it."
>
> Commissioner Shepard awarded Anne $1,500 per month alimony and $200 a month for each of the children, for a total of $2,100 per month until the time of trial.
>
> Bob was directed to keep up payments on the home, plus insurance and taxes, and to pay all "outstanding obligations" of the couple. However, Anne was restrained from making further use of credit cards chargeable to Bob.
>
> Costs of the divorce, including a fee for an accountant to audit the financial records, will be borne by Bob. In addition, he was ordered to pay $3,500 to his wife's counsel "on account," any further fee to be fixed at the trial.

was more to the story, and Bob knew it. Yet he remained quiet about it, never once wanting to bring his childhood sweetheart and the mother of his children into the line of fire. He kept it to himself.

Instead, very shortly before Bob and Anne separated, a reporter interviewed Bob about his career successes and supposed solid family life. Possibly knowing what was about to happen, Bob warned the reporter, "Don't rock the boat—just don't rock the boat!" This reporter did not heed his advice, and the article praising Bob and Anne as the model couple was published, only months before the news hit of Bob and Anne's breakup.

This article and others before it perpetuated the myth that before *Hogan's Heroes*, Bob Crane was loyal to Anne, and after his success on *Hogan's Heroes*, he decided to "go Hollywood" by carrying on two affairs and divorcing his first wife. This misperception was also likely exacerbated when, soon after his divorce to Anne was final, he proposed to Patty.

In August 1967, Patty told *TV Guide* that she had been "hunting for the brass ring," stating that the first man who offered to buy her a merry-go-round, she would marry. Having dated officially since Bob's separation from Anne, Patty and Bob discussed marriage in February 1970. At first, reports stated that they wanted to wait and not rush into matrimony. But it didn't take long for the news to circulate that they were planning to get married as soon as Bob and Anne's divorce became final. Bob may not have had a carrousel, but he did present her with a gold ring, and she accepted.

Bob and Patty were married on October 16, 1970, on a soundstage next door to the *Hogan's Heroes* set. Patty's sister Dale Gudegast and her husband Eric Braeden served as witnesses. Theirs was the first wedding to ever be performed on a studio soundstage. Ed Feldman arranged for a Supreme Court judge to marry them. The ceremony was funded by Bing Crosby Productions and Ed Feldman, which helped the couple keep their expenses for the event down, especially with Bob's steep alimony and child support payments. There was a catch, however. Bob and Patty had no control over any aspect of their wedding.

"Since we met on the show, we wanted to celebrate our marriage [with the people from the show]," Patty explained in 2005. "[We] worked with these people almost daily. We considered the show a family. *Everyone*. From, you know, a gopher to the cameraman to whatever, and invite their families. And this would involve about three hundred and fifty to four hundred people. Bob was broke when I married him because he had just come out of a divorce. In fact, he was in debt. He had to borrow money from his lawyer to get through the divorce. So we couldn't afford to get married in that type of wedding. So Eddie Feldman generously, with Bing Crosby Productions who owned *Hogan's Heroes*, put on this huge wedding. And they just took over... I didn't even see my bridal bouquet until it was handed to me when I walked in the room. Bob thought he was going to get married as Hogan. I think the reason [Bing Crosby Productions] actually put this wedding on was for publicity for the show. Hence, it was a write off for them, basically. My wedding was a write off! We had no control over the guest list at all except we could invite family members or friends. [Eddie Feldman and Bing Crosby Productions] controlled the guest list and invites from the press and CBS executives and all those people. And they invited a lot of the gossip columnists. When we got there, Rona Barrett wasn't there, and she was a very good friend of ours. The next day after the wedding, she called and was furious with Bob—why she wasn't invited? And he had to explain to her that he was actually furious with Eddie Feldman for *not* inviting her. Because she

BOB CRANE The Definitive Biography

Isn't It Romantic?

Bob Crane was a romantic at heart. Among his saved personal belongs were many love letters he had written to Patty and that she saved. Below is just one of those letters, providing a glimpse into not only his feelings for Patty, but also the grueling work schedule he maintained throughout his entire life.

April 29, 1971
Dear Sweetheart—

I love you so. It's now almost 11 PM and I just finished talking to you on the phone. Thank God we at least have the phone. The house just isn't the same without you. I miss you darling and the baby too. I hope the doctor has a good report for you tomorrow.

It was a long ride today to Champagne [California]. I did 3 radio interviews & 3 TV guest shots and was pretty exhausted by the time I got back home. Business last night as I told you was pretty bad. Tonight was better, but I can partly blame the Wm. Morris Office for screwing up our arrival last Sunday. If we had arrived during the day, at least we would have had the newspapers announce our arrival, and perhaps the business would be better now. Guy & Dee seem to think so.

I miss you darling. Hope you like the enclosed. Please save them.

I love you always,
Bob

---

had always been very, very generous to us and very kind to us. She took the explanation very well when she realized we hadn't personally excluded her. They had decorated this whole sound stage very beautifully. They had a gazebo there that we were married in, and they had a 1940s band so Bob could sit in and drum. And people were dancing. It was a happy, happy day. We had been together about four years, and we were deliriously happy."

Bob did not wear his Hogan costume for his wedding; however, Patty *was* made to wear her Hilda wig. "I got married in a Hilda wig!" she said, laughing about it later in 2005. "The next day, we got on a United plane to fly to New York. Under the wig, I was a brunette…

When the flight took off, the stewardess came up and asked if she could speak to Bob privately in the back. And he followed her, and he came back laughing, and I said, 'What was that all about?' And he said, 'They read that he'd married the blonde from the show, and they had gotten a little wedding cake to present to him, and they don't know what to do with it because he's sitting with a brunette!'"

Members of the press reported on the event in papers and magazines. But it was not the big splash Ed Feldman and Bing Crosby Productions might have wanted. Instead, a small blurb appeared in the papers detailing one thing: that Bob had flubbed one of his vows. "The star of television's *Hogan's Heroes* is a bridegroom, but Bob Crane wasn't quite as smooth at the wedding ceremony—conducted on the set—as he is in the program. When it came to the ring giving part of the ceremony, Crane had to ask Municipal Judge James Harvey Brown to repeat one line: 'In token and in pledge…'"

Patty explained the moment in 2005. "I don't know if [Bob] wasn't listening or nervous or what, but…when they ask him to 'repeat after me,' he does this like, 'What? huh?' type of thing and cracked him up. He joked later about, you know, 'A great time to blow your lines!'"

Following the ceremony, Bob and Patty embarked on a "mini" honeymoon to New York City. Their main honeymoon plans were postponed until shooting ended for the season. They officially honeymooned at a tropical resort, and their suite number at the hotel was 647-646. Bob had these numbers engraved on a gold bracelet for Patty, and he also inscribed them on a photo of himself as Hogan that he gave to her. It read "I adore you Patty. 647-646. Your Bob."

Meanwhile, Cynthia Lynn, still remorseful over her decision to abandon *Hogan's Heroes* to save a marriage that was already doomed, sought to return to the series in some capacity. Struggling financially, she called upon Ed Feldman to inquire if he could use her in any future episodes of *Hogan's Heroes*. Feldman accepted her offer, and there were two occasions where Cindy guest starred in later seasons—once in 1967 in the episode "Will the Blue Baron Strike Again?" and again in 1971 in the episode "Easy Come, Easy Go."

It was another mistake. When she returned the first time, Bob and Patty were well into their love affair. The second time Cindy returned, Bob and Patty were married. Cindy recalled her encounters with Bob both times were "friendly, close. Kind of shy. Awkward, a little. The feeling was still there, but you have to let go. You *need* to let go."

During her two appearances later in the series, Bob never talked about anything personal with Cindy. He never said a word to her about his relationship with Patty or his divorce from Anne; nor did he speak of his past affair with her.

"I knew that Sigrid was there, and I heard some things already that he kind of was seeing her," Cindy said. "As a matter of fact, that's why it felt so uncomfortable for me. And I'm sure for him, too. For all three of us. And it hurt. It hurt a *lot*."

Cindy sensed that Bob had changed somewhat when she saw him on the set on these last two occasions.

"I don't know. He was just different," she said. "He was different. I can't explain how, but he was different. He didn't seem happy. That's the only way I can explain it. He didn't have that spark, that sparkle that he always had. The joking, the funniness. Something was missing. He lost something; something wasn't there. It wasn't like the old Bob that I knew. They called me back one more time, but I didn't go. And that's why, I think."

Cindy never saw or spoke with Bob again after her last appearance on *Hogan's Heroes* in 1971. She never followed up to ask him about anything, whether it was about his new marriage with Patty or to talk about their own failed relationship.

"It was gone, over, done," she said. "It was something that could not be fixed."

Although Bob was experiencing major changes in his private life, he appeared to be holding it together. To the public and with the press, he hardly skipped a beat. The fifth season of *Hogan's Heroes* continued on without a hitch. His coworkers on the set never saw him flinch under the pressure of his separation from Anne and the divorce that followed, and his professionalism translates on screen. Bob portrayed Colonel Hogan with the same level of energy and dedication as he had when the character was born in season one.

Bob navigated the tumultuous waters of balancing his private life and his public persona well, even if at the time, he seemed to have missed the joys and excitement his earlier career days had brought him. Yet, in August 1969, at the height of his divorce proceedings, entertainment columnist Peer J. Oppenheimer observed, "There's still something irrepressible in Bob Crane—the trait that has won him more fans than his wisecracks has. It breaks through the temporary gloom, and you feel that he'll set his sights on some new goal and achieve it."

As the sun set on *Hogan's Heroes* in March 1971, it was just rising on Bob and Patty's new married life together. Their financial situation began to improve, and they were residing in Patty's a spacious Tudor-style estate on Tilden Avenue in the Westwood section of Hollywood. Patty was also pregnant, and she was expecting the couple's first child in June.

Bob was planning for the future as well. He was making seemingly endless public appearances on both radio and television, but he was also searching for a new series, and none of the offers were to his liking. Bob was always moving and never stagnant, and his sights were set on finding his own television series and starring in motion pictures—simultaneously.

Patty gave birth to the couple's only child together—Robert Scott Crane—on June 4, 1971. Scott, as he would be called, was Bob and Patty's pride and joy. They chose to name Bob's second son Robert, just as his first son had been named, with their middle names being different. When Bob's friend Harvey Geller asked why Bob has named both of his sons Robert, Bob replied, "I like that name!"

It also seemed that life was settling down for Anne. She became engaged to Charles Sloan, the realtor who sold the house she and Bob had owned in Tarzana, and they were about to be married. Bobby, Debbie, and Karen accepted their new family life, and in time, they would all celebrate major holidays and other life events together as one big combined family. It appeared that life was starting to turn around again for Bob.

The 1970s were to be a transitional time for Bob, and with *Hogan's Heroes* and his first marriage in the past, he was going to reinvent himself—both at home and in his career.

As always, Bob was busy making plans for the future. But the best laid plans often go awry.

Bob and Anne Crane at the 1967 Emmy Awards.
Source: From the author's personal collection.

Bob and Anne and their family on vacation in Lake Arrowhead, California (circa 1966).

Source: From the author's personal collection. Used with permission from Karen Crane.

Bob, Mrs. Terzian, and Bob's daughters Karen (left) and Debbie (circa 1965).

Source: From the author's personal collection. Used with permission from Karen Crane.

"Quiet, Dad!" Daughters Debbie (left) and Karen are "entertained" by their dad's drumming (circa 1967).

Source: Courtesy of Karen Crane. Used with permission.

Bob and Anne Crane visit with best school friends Charlie and Yvonne Zito (early 1969).

Source: Courtesy of Charlie Zito. Used with permission.

Masquerade

Professional portrait of Patricia Olson (Sigrid Valdis) (circa 1964).

Source: Courtesy of Scott Crane. Used with permission.

Bob and Patty on the set of *Hogan's Heroes* (circa 1967).

Source: Courtesy of Scott Crane. Used with permission.

Bob and Patty on their wedding day – October 16, 1970.
Source: Courtesy of Scott Crane. Used with permission.

Bob and Patty on their wedding day – October 16, 1970.

Source: Courtesy of Scott Crane. Used with permission.

Bob drumming with a 1940s band during his wedding reception – October 16, 1970.

Source: Courtesy of Scott Crane. Used with permission.

Bob and Patty (circa 1972).
Source: Courtesy of Scott Crane. Used with permission.

Bob and Patty in their home in Westwood, California (circa 1972).
Source: Courtesy of Scott Crane. Used with permission.

Bob Crane loved animals and owned many dogs and cats throughout his life. Bob and Patty cherished their shih tzu, Star

Source: Courtesy of Scott Crane. Used with permission.

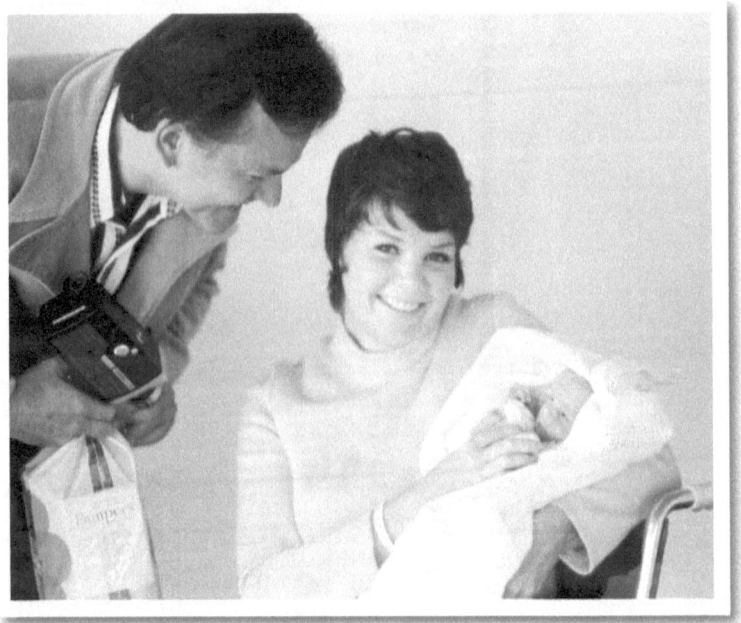

Bob and Patty with their newborn son, Robert Scott Crane (born June 4, 1971).

Source: Courtesy of Scott Crane. Used with permission.

Chapter 9
Life's Illusions

Always, in a new series, you begin by asking that one word—why? You ask all the different variations of why? When the answers indicate there's some plausibility involved, then maybe you've got a series.

—Bob Crane, May 1, 1976

Bob Crane with Dick Whittinghill, KMPC Radio, Los Angeles, California (July 1972).

Source: Courtesy of Scott Crane. Used with permission of KMPC.

A professional portrait of Bob Crane (circa 1975).

Source: Courtesy of Scott Crane. Used with permission.

Chapter 9

Life's Illusions

It seems like old times as I drive to work this week. Coming over my car radio is the friendly patter of none other than Bob Crane. Bob is filling in for his former arch rival, Dick Whittinghill, while Dick is on vacation. He will fill Whittinghill's spot from 6:05 until 9 in the morning on KMPC. Crane possesses a fine sense of humor and a relaxed easygoing manner of speaking—and also plays good music. Radio could use more personalities like him, but now that Bob has hit it big as a TV star, it is not likely he'll be back on radio full time.

— Bob Martin, TV-Radio Editor, *Independent Press-Telegram*, Long Beach, California, July 6, 1972

That '70s decade. Often referred to as a "pivot of change," it was a transitional and often confusing time for America and the world.

The Vietnam War raged until 1975, with fierce opposition across the country and anti-war protests escalating from every corner of America. No more were American soldiers welcomed home from the front lines; they returned to a country that shunned them and called them "baby killers."

Drug and alcohol abuse reached new heights as Vietnam veterans tried to dull their post-traumatic stress stemming from their memories of wartime service in Vietnam; as a result, many became dependent on substances or behaviors.

The term *addiction* grew in use, but it was a much different, less empathetic era than today. During the 1970s, addicts were not understood, and to be deemed an addict or to acknowledge that one *was* an addict was about the lowest point a person could reach. In the public eye, and to family and friends, it would have been considered the ultimate failure. It was almost better to continue one's destructive pattern—the easy path—than to combat it, both from an internal and external point of view.

It was an unsettled time. In addition to America's involvement in the Vietnam War, the Cold War grew more ominous, and women actively engaged in the feminist movement to gain full equality. Beginning in 1973, the energy crisis would grip the nation, and in the wake of the Watergate scandal, President Nixon resigned as President in 1974.

Artists expressed themselves through varying types of music, each wanting to make a statement of the era. This included soft rock/adult contemporary, a hard rock/heavy metal sound that included Kiss and AC/DC, the psychedelic rock of Janis Joplin and Jimmy Hendrix, and the latest rage—Disco—all replaced the 1960s sound of bands like The Beatles. Meanwhile, moviegoers were entertained, enthralled, and/or frightened by *The Godfather Parts I* and *II, One Flew Over the Cuckoo's Nest, The Sting,* and *Jaws*.

Television programs began to explore more sensitive issues and test their boundaries, with the focus shifting from the light parody or sugary domestic life toward realism—tapping into the never-before explored "social consciousness" of the American population. Programs such as *All in the Family, Police Woman, Sanford and Son*, and *The Mary Tyler Moore Show*, among others, would analyze the delicate themes of sexuality, abortion, equal rights, race, religion, and politics, leaving the innocence of the 1950s and 1960s long in the past.

In particular, a new military situation comedy set during the Korean Conflict, *M*A*S*H*, premiered in 1972, not long after the film by the same name opened in movie theaters in 1970. Considered the younger cousin of *Hogan's Heroes,* and even employing many who had gotten their start on the World War II sitcom, *M*A*S*H* would begin as a comedy, but as it matured during its eleven-year run, it would break new ground as a half-hour drama with traces of comedy—or a "dramedy"—focusing on the horrors of war rather than making light of it. This was something *Hogan's Heroes* had never been able to do—or had been *allowed* to do given the restrictions of 1960s television—despite its own serious backdrop of war.

Technology was also breaking new ground, and the 1977 film *Star Wars* proved special effects could literally transform a moviegoer's experience. And with technology came video cameras and recorders, as well as computers—with a whopping storage of 64K of memory space—which were now available to the public. Also debuting were Atari home video games, which caught the attention of young and old, beginning in 1972.

As the world and the nation shifted from a Donna Reed mentality to that of Hawkeye Pierce or Archie Bunker, Bob Crane did as well.

The 1970s had also been a transitional time for Bob, personally and professionally. Throughout the earlier decades and up until 1971, he had enjoyed a long reign of success in both radio and television, excelling in every aspect of his career. However, with *Hogan's Heroes* fading into the past, he soon found himself asking, "Is there life after Hogan?"

By the summer of 1971, nearly seven years had elapsed since Bob said his first lines as the senior prisoner of war at Stalag 13, and during that time, he had experienced tremendous life changes. In addition to becoming an international celebrity, he had divorced and remarried, and along with his new wife, a new baby boy, a teenage son, two middle school daughters, a stepdaughter, and an adopted teenage daughter comprised his immediate family.

Anne had also moved on and was romantically involved with Charles W. "Chuck" Sloan, whom she would marry in Los Angeles on June 23, 1973. Bobby, Debbie, and Karen resided with Anne and Chuck, while Mits and Scotty lived with Bob and Patty.

Bob and Patty also employed a housekeeper, Ana Marie, a teenager of Mexican descent who assisted Patty with cooking, household chores, and caring for Scott. Because she lived with Cranes, was a Mexican citizen, and was still considered a minor at around seventeen years of age, Bob and Patty made the decision to legally adopt her. Adopting teenagers who emigrated from Mexico and took up employment as house servants was a common practice in California at the time.

Bob and Anne, however, remained remarkably cordial with one another. Bob continued to financially support Anne until she remarried, as well as provide for their three children until they became self-supporting adults. He also maintained a strong presence in the lives of his children. As time began to heal old wounds, Bob and Anne grew more receptive toward each other and their new families, to the point of enjoying combined holiday gatherings and other family functions together. Their redefined relationship and ability to put the past behind them seemed to have helped Bobby, Debbie, and Karen transition from the once-smaller nuclear family to one that had doubled in size. While difficult, Bob and Anne's divorce had not been impossible, and it appeared as though their personal lives had settled down and resumed without much further conflict.

Bob's parents, Rose and Al, tolerated the changes in their son's life fairly well, even though Anne had been considered part of the family since school days. Bob's father took to his new grandson Scotty. Rose, however, who continued to dote on both of her sons even as adults, was not as enthusiastic in her acceptance of Bob's new family. As with Bob's earlier ventures, she accepted Bob's new life merely perhaps because these changes were what he wanted. Yet according to family members, Rose seemed only reluctantly supportive.

Bob's extended family back in Connecticut was neither receptive nor forgiving, and his break up with and subsequent divorce from Anne came as a cold shock. It was unfathomable to them that Bob and Anne's marriage could possibly end, and Bob's aunts, uncles, and cousins fell into sharp denial. They simply could not understand how this could be. In fact, Bob's split with Anne and his new life with Patty were so badly received by Bob's extended family that they became taboo subjects during any and all conversations they had with Bob.

Bob's cousin Jim Senich said, "I really don't remember how we heard about it. That would have crushed Bob's parents because Annie was like their daughter. And no one liked Patty. So it was never brought up. *Never. Brought. Up.* Everybody loved Anne, but it was never said to him, 'How could you do that?' But everybody back here was *shocked* because Annie was like one of the family. Really close. I know Anne's mother was kind of tough and gave Bobby a rough time."

Jim also claimed Bob did not change much following his marriage to Patty—that he was still the same as he had always been. But it was evident that Patty was not embraced by the Crane-Senich extended family. From the beginning of their marriage, Patty was an outcast, and Jim admitted that it must have caused Bob some inner turmoil even though he never showed it.

"Bobby was married to someone that nobody back here liked," Jim said. "It had to affect him, but I didn't see it. One of my uncles went out to California and met Patty, and [he didn't like her]. Nobody liked Patty right away. Bobby came to Hartford for something, and a couple of members of the family—I wasn't with him—went up to Hartford to have dinner with them, and she never came down from the hotel."

That Bob's family did not accept Patty with open arms would have been difficult for both Bob and Patty, and most uncomfortable for Patty especially. After that one occasion in Hartford, Patty typically opted to remain in California any time Bob returned to Connecticut to visit family and friends.

Jim added, "It didn't make seeing him more awkward because Patty was never with him, except for that one time."

Others were taken aback regarding Bob's new wife because Bob had simply not told them. School friend Don Sappern was on a business trip in Los Angeles shortly after Bob and Patty had married, and he decided to look up his old friend and have dinner together. When Bob entered the restaurant, instead of Anne by his side, he was with Patty. Don was surprised, but he was not bothered by it. Rather than ostracize Patty, Don accepted Bob's new wife.

"The night we had dinner in LA, he was with Colonel Klink's secretary," Don recalled. "She was a knockout! Wow! I think he probably brought her along just to intimidate me! But he had never told me he and Anne had divorced and remarried. Up until then, I never knew it at all."

Jane Golden had been Stamford High School's Class of 1946 secretary, and as such, she and Bob corresponded when class reunions were being planned. She learned of his divorce and remarriage during the planning of their 30th Class Reunion in the spring of 1976.

"He contacted me all the time for information about upcoming reunions," Jane said. "We sent the usual letter if a reunion was coming up, and then we'd correspond back and forth. It was just idle chatter, though. He'd tell me about Anne, how he was divorced and then was remarried to Patty, and that she was on *Hogan's Heroes*. For the 30th reunion, he wrote to say he was coming to the reunion, but he wasn't coming with Patty because she had to stay home with the kids. The only time he ever explained Patty in the letters, he just said, 'You know, my wife Patty, she was Sigrid on *Hogan's Heroes*. She won't be with me; she's running our house and taking care of our youngest, Scotty, who's having a birthday.' But he talked about how he was doing, and how Annie was doing. And about the people here in Stamford that he was happy to see."

Bob seemed content with Patty, and their life was described in the press as a "happy, noisy household full of laughter, fun, and drum rolls."

"One of the things I tell [my son Bobby]," Bob said in 1972, "is not to get married too young. My first wife was twelve and I was fourteen when I started seeing her, and we were married when I was twenty. I appreciated her and our children, but I was too busy then trying to get ahead. Now, I'm no longer in such a hurry, and I do have time to enjoy my second wife and my new baby. [Patty] and I get along very well together. I never wanted to marry an actress, and I didn't want to get involved with a strong-willed and opinionated woman, which [Patty] is. Yet I've come to love her and even learned to respect her business sense."

And whereas most members of Bob's family disapproved of Patty, one important person was quite fond of her—Bob's father, Al. Scott Crane said that as a young child, he remembered his grandfather as a warm, caring person, and much different than his memories of his grandmother.

"My grandpa [Bob's father] was such a nice, sweet guy," Scott recalled. "I have so many fond memories of Grandpa. He spent a lot of time with us. But my grandmom, Rose, was cold and very distant. If you just looked at pictures of her, maybe she's smiling, but it almost seemed fake. She was always kind of off from the group in the pictures and in the home movies, and would just kind of wave at the camera and smile, but not really join the group. From what I understand, she really liked Anne. And she was really mad at my dad for leaving Anne and marrying my mom. So Rose never liked my mom. But Al loved my mom and thought she was great. He loved having a grandson like me. So Grandpa Al always wanted to be around."

Bob's cousin Jane Senich Ryfun also recalled that after Bob's parents moved to the west coast, and especially after Bob and Anne divorced and Bob married Patty, she had seen a change in her Aunt Rose. Jane remembered how in one instance, Rose brushed off her brother (Jane's father) Mike Senich when he and the family came to Los Angeles, claiming she could not make time to visit with them.

"It crushed my father," Jane recalled. "Absolutely crushed him that Rose would respond to him and us this way. Aunt Rose thoroughly enjoyed Bobby's fame and basically 'went Hollywood.'"

Bob and Patty made their home in a Tudor-style house located near the UCLA campus in the Westwood section of Los Angeles, where they counted their neighbors as Leonard Nimoy, John Astin and Patty Duke, and Carroll O'Connor. Their home also contained an old bomb shelter where Bob kept his drumset and could drum away to his heart's content. Also in the home—a collection of more than five thousand record albums, mostly from the Big Band era, that Bob had amassed over the years, many while working in radio. His collection of records prior to his marriage to Patty had capped out at approximately twenty-one thousand albums; however, he said he gave sixteen thousand of them away when Patty complained their home had become more like a warehouse.

"I couldn't play all those records if I live to be a hundred," Bob admitted in 1975. "But how can you throw out Glen Miller, the Dorseys, Goodman, and Artie Shaw?"

The ground floor of their home was devoted to Bob's audio and video recording equipment, and one area became an editing studio. Ever since his teenage years, Bob had delighted in taking pictures, and from early on, he had been known to carry a camera wherever he went. In 1971, Sony introduced the first video tape recorder, and Bob was one of the first to own such a device.

His video recordings and still photographs were not exclusive; they were of everything that happened in his life. Bob made home movies of vacations, family life, his kids, on the set of *Hogan's Heroes*, and theatre rehearsals. He also enjoyed the newly found capability of recording television shows to watch at his convenience, claiming he and Patty refused to watch television shows when they originally aired, saying, for example, they enjoyed watching Johnny Carson's *The Tonight Show* while eating breakfast.

Bob was in the habit of carrying an audio tape recorder with him at all times as well. In 1964, a brief article in the press read, "Bob Crane of *The Donna Reed Show* feels somewhat lost away from a tape recorder. Even on the set, he keeps a recorder at the ready in his dressing room. He explains, 'I've captured some unexpected material at the oddest times.'"

Instead of handwriting long letters to family and friends back in Connecticut, Bob often recorded and sent audio letters. He also spent hours upon hours making recordings of his record albums for his friends. In one instance, he painstakingly sifted through his thousands of records, selecting with great care several songs from the 1940s. Then, he transferred these songs into a compilation on three audiocassette tapes, filling each tape to capacity on both sides. In between numbers, he announced the next song and the artist as if he were live on the radio. When finished, he sent these recordings to his friend Charlie Zito back home in Stamford.

On another tape Bob sent to Charlie were several recordings of himself sitting in on drums and playing with bands that included The Harry James Orchestra The Stan Kenton Orchestra, and The New Tommy Dorsey Orchestra. It was commonplace for Bob to carry his audiotape recorder with him when he drummed with bands. When not drumming, he also recorded the musical numbers of live shows where he was simply an audience member—just to have them to revisit and enjoy later. He even taped the dinner conversations at the table.

As if that were not enough, Bob also regularly audiotaped his radio programs, whether he was interviewing a celebrity or just going through a regular broadcast without a guest. Following his radio interviews, he wrote to several of his guests personally and asked for their transfer of copyright for his exclusive use of their interview, which they usually granted. Then, he compulsively archived all interviews by celebrity and date aired/recorded, and each with its own corresponding card catalog, as if in a library. This system of easy access and retrieval would prove useful for him later on.

Rare was the time when Bob was without some sort of recording device in his hand. *Every single facet of Bob's life was recorded*, important or otherwise, and the great majority of it was innocuous.

The Crane estate was lavishly decorated, and Patty filled their home with exquisite furnishings, which included an Old English stove that had been refurbished as a table in the living room. Patty loved antiques, and she even designed some of their furniture.

Always the animal lover, Bob owned pets—primarily dogs—throughout his entire life. While married to Anne, the family had owned two dogs—a French Poodle named Candy and a German Shepherd named Penny.

"They're watch dogs," Bob said in 1965. "Candy, the little poodle, wakes up Penny, who then barks at any intruders."

Bob and Patty owned a shih tzu named Star, as well as three cats, including a Persian named Jasper. The backyard contained an in-ground swimming pool, and weekends were spent with family—and especially, his children. Bob loved his children more than anything.

"One of my favorite times with my dad," Scott Crane said, "was him setting me up with his four-track recorder and a microphone and a turntable, and teaching me how to make a radio show. I was really young—maybe four or five. He sat there and taught me how to work the recorder, work the turntable, work the microphone, and basically taught me how to do my own little radio show, which pretty much featured the music of Kiss and me introducing the songs and me talking. I have the tapes somewhere, and you can hear him coaching me. It was a father and son hobby thing to do—to sit together and do this type of project together and make a radio show. I was really proud of it.

"And he got me into music. He bought me a little drum set, and he taught me how to play drums. He would let me play his drums and showed me, basically, the rudiments of drumming. He encouraged me a lot in both—to be a radio DJ, and a drummer or a guitar player. He bought me a little toy guitar. He was very supportive of my interest in music. I know a lot of people seemed to think he was a Big Band aficionado, which he was, but that he was kind of closed off to other music. He really wasn't. Like all parents, you act like you like what your kids like. He acted enthusiastic and excited about new Kiss records.

"The downstairs of our house was filled with—it was a kind of family den, except it was where he kept all his recording equipment and reel-to-reel tape recorders and video equipment and a film projector. We'd actually go down there and watch 16 mm copies of Disney movies, and he'd play them for the family down there because he had a projector set up, and there were a bunch of couches set up and all that. So that's where we'd do the recording for the radio show we produced. We spent a lot of time down there. I'm pretty sure [doing the radio show] was his idea—to pass on something he loved to do.

"Right off that little family-like theater room was the backyard and swimming pool. When you watch our home movies, if they were filmed at home, they're either about Christmas or Thanksgiving or being in the pool. Every time a guest came over, there'd be filming of us—the whole family in the pool. Everyone hung out in the pool in the backyard. We lived on a really quiet street in LA, and we'd play stick baseball with the neighbor kids out on the street. Just, literally, a good-sized stick—not even a bat—and a ball.

"The other thing he used to do: there's a hardware store in LA called Anawalt, and my dad used to take me there, and we made about three go-karts. So we'd go there and buy a piece of plywood, two 2x4s, and a couple of wheelbarrow wheels, and kind of nail it all together—and a rope to steer. And we'd make go-karts and race them down the hill in the neighborhood.

"All the memories I have of him are really good. The one kind of funny memory—you know, he liked to spoil his kids. I had a pretty restricted diet when I was a kid. I was pretty hyperactive, so one of his ways of spoiling me was giving me a caramel apple or cotton candy. [My mom would] want to kill him. He'd say, 'I'm going to take him out for the day to the park.' But he'd end up taking me to the UCLA Mardi Gras Festival or Santa Monica Pier and get me cotton candy and caramel apples and whatever I wanted. And I would come home, and then the huge sugar crash.

"When he was around, he was very hands-on and very fun. He was a big kid at heart. I think there was an interview where he described himself: he said he was a kid in a candy store—a total big kid at heart. And my mom described him that way. She always kind of had to be the parent.

"He never spoke about religion," Scott continued. "He never mentioned it. He seemed more interested in passing on to me his talent for radio and music and his record collecting—things like that. And I became a real avid record collector, too. He was really interested in imparting his love of entertainment and music to me. At holidays, he really liked being with the family. We always went to this place called Vacation Village in San Diego, where I was conceived, actually. They rented a room for Karen, Debbie, and Bobby, and they rented a room for my mom and my mom's daughter. I remember taking vacations to a place called Paradise Point. We always went on family vacations together with the other kids. He had a silver Cadillac, but what he drove was a Ford station wagon. He didn't have a pretense about him. My uncle, who is Eric Braeden, on *The Young and the Restless*—he always liked the new BMW or the new whatever. My dad never got into the showy part of Hollywood. He always drove a family car, except for the silver Cadillac.

"I remember in about 1975 or 1976, he wasn't working very much that year, and money was pretty tight. And there was a new stereo equalizer. He was a huge technological freak; he loved it. And a new stereo equalizer came out. He read a review for it in *High Fidelity* or *Audiophile Magazine* or something. It was $500, which in 1975, was a lot of money. And he spent $500 on it. And my mom was so mad at him for that. It was like spending $5,000."

Money had indeed been tight in the Crane household, but family was important. So after a few small acting roles in the early 1970s, Patty decided to give up—or at least postpone—her career to concentrate on raising Scott and tending to the family. With her free time, she maintained the bills and all expenditures. Bob also claimed he would consult Patty in decisions regarding his career.

"After my divorce, I had ended up with almost nothing," Bob said in 1974. "So Patty jumped right in and sold her house so we could buy the home we now live in. She came to the marriage with financially as much, if not more, than I. So I entrusted everything to her. When I was about to sign a deal, or if I was dickering with a producer, I said I was going to bring my wife in. Now that's the difference between what I am now and what I used to be. Before, when I saw other guys consulting their wives in business, I said, 'Oh, come on, what can a woman know?' And I found out I was totally wrong. It would be safe to say that thanks to Patty, I am no longer a male chauvinist pig. I entrust her with everything. She's a good organizer and perfectionist. For instance, I might say, 'A few rough edges aren't so bad.' But Patty will say, 'Let's round out the rough edges.' But thank God she doesn't make her perfectionism an obsession. She doesn't say, 'Unless you are perfect, I don't want you.' She accepts me as I am. Every now and then, Patty talks about taking up her career again. I think if the right role came, she'd take it. But in the meantime, she really seems to be enjoying our life together, as I am. She loved designing the new house. She enjoys antiquing furniture. She hires the bricklayers, plumbers, electricians, and painters—a full-time job, and she loves it. I hate to sound like a one-man fan club for Patty, but she is so valuable to me in so many ways."

By the mid-1970s, Bob was starting to climb out of the financial pit into which he had landed. But following the cancellation of *Hogan's Heroes*, he struggled to find his professional niche again.

Bob always planned ahead, and long before the cancellation of *Hogan's Heroes*, he was preparing for his future. He had remained active while the show was on hiatus, appearing on various television talk shows and game shows, and had completed two feature-length films. As with the changing times, Bob also wanted to explore situations in his works that were deeper and more realistic.

Bob, always known for his comedy performances and glib personality, yearned to take on more challenging roles. One part he envisioned was that of a young priest who struggled with a very human element denied him—falling in love. Bob wanted to explore the pain and suffering that went along with the priest having to separate himself from the church in order to be with the woman he loved.

"I am a Catholic, and I know what this struggle can mean," Bob said in December 1969. "In a different way, it happened to me when I went through the agony of my wife and I breaking up our marriage after twenty years. There's no conveying the pain of breaks from convictions like these for a priest—or a husband."

The concept never got past the planning stage, but Bob's cousin Jim Senich, who had at one time contemplated becoming a priest, noted, "I think he could have done drama very well. I think today Bobby would have gone on to play those kind of roles."

In 1965, Bob hoped *Hogan's Heroes* would last maybe one or two seasons, just long enough to grant him the desired exposure to advance in his acting career. Once the series had proven to be a hit with audiences and critics, however, Bob was certain it would go beyond the first five seasons and through its contractual seventh season. With the extended two-year contract in place in 1970, no one had anticipated that the sixth season would become its last. It gave Bob and producers cause for concern in one very specific area. The health of a leading cast member was deteriorating.

As *Hogan's Heroes* entered its sixth season, news began circulating among series insiders that John Banner was ill and had been diagnosed with a heart condition. Should something terrible happen, or if he became incapable of performing, it would have a dramatic impact on *Hogan's Heroes*. Would the lovable Schultz be able to be replaced? And if so, who would replace him? Would the series even survive if Banner were not a part of it?

In an effort to salvage the series, Bob took it upon himself to find someone not to replace Schultz, but instead, become a new character, a new sergeant of the guard. Bob consulted his good friend, John Thompson.

Bob met John in Chicago during the first run of the stage play, *Beginner's Luck*. Eventually, he played Cupid for John and *Beginner's Luck* co-star Pamela Hayes, and the couple got married. Bob remained a lifelong friend of John and Pam, who today, perform magic as The Great Tomsoni, and provide ongoing consultation for illusionists such a Penn & Teller and Criss Angel.

"He brought in the producer of *Hogan's Heroes*, Eddie Feldman, to see me," John Thompson said. "The gentleman who had played Schultz, John Banner, had a heart condition, and they were looking for someone to kind of have a back up. Bob's idea was to have an underling to show in case something happened to John. Eddie thought I looked a lot like Alan Alda at the time, and that was a plus. But they were considering me for that backup role when the series ended."

Sadly, less than two years after the show ended, John Banner passed away suddenly in his Austria homeland on January 28, 1973, from an abdominal hemorrhage.

But Bob was thinking ahead in other ways, and when *Hogan's Heroes* was well into its sixth season, he decided to capitalize on his fame and the show's success before it was too late. So he began writing.

It was not unusual for Bob to put his thoughts to paper. As a man with a wealth of knowledge about the entertainment and broadcasting industries, as well as strong views about politics, Bob would often write guest columns in newspapers and trade magazines. He also wrote his own jokes for his radio broadcasts and group presentations, and skits he performed as part of his radio shows.

In 1971, Bob had been toying with an idea about how he believed *Hogan's Heroes* should end and what should happen to the characters following their release from Stalag 13. He started writing, and as his ideas developed, he came to the conclusion that his production, called *"Hogan's Heroes" Revue*, would be a variety show for the stage. And he relished the idea. Performing *Hogan's Heroes* before a live studio audience was something he had dreamed of doing even before the series premiered.

"I hate a laugh machine," he said in August 1965. "The first time I saw the pilot of *Hogan's Heroes*, it upset me. But without it, people are not sure whether it's comedy or straight. I would like to do it in front of a live audience, but this is impossible."

Bob realized it *was* possible to perform *Hogan's Heroes* in front of a live audience, and if done correctly, it could work out quite well. Building upon his inspiration, he combined his love of Big Band music and drums, along with his knowledge of World War II, and created a variety show for the stage based on *Hogan's Heroes*. This time, Bob would write, direct, and produce, as well as perform in the show.

Set in post-World War II America, the plot of *"Hogan's Heroes" Revue* involved Colonel Hogan returning home to the United States after the war. It was common for distinguished United States military officers to have difficulty finding work and fitting in as civilians once the war ended, and it was an issue addressed in such notable films as *The Best Years of Our Lives* (1946) and *White Christmas* (1954), among others. This idea may have influenced Bob's vision of Hogan's post-war life.

Hogan's Heroes cast members Werner Klemperer and Robert Clary were both officially on board to perform in character for *"Hogan's Heroes" Revue*, while Larry Hovis and Richard Dawson were considering it. Bob actually wanted the entire cast to be a part of the production, including John Banner; however, the expense was too great.

"Truth of the matter is, we can't afford it," Bob said. "The actors on the show draw high salaries. And, to be honest, I'd like to go on by myself. But I'm known as Hogan, and that's the place to start. In addition to our big *Hogan's Heroes* sketch, we'll have a classic magician and a chorus line. Most of the show, though, will be based on the nostalgia of post-World War II. We'll start out with the end of the war and Hogan going back to the big band business, with Colonel Klink as his manager. As part of the show, I play the drums, while Werner and [Robert Clary] sing."

In addition to Klemperer and Clary, Bob also enlisted the help of John Thompson. He had been anxious to perform a show in Las Vegas, believing a Vegas act was necessary for anyone in the entertainment business. He also saw the character of Hogan as a draw for audiences. John Thompson remembered precisely how Bob had envisioned the show and was going to execute his concept for *"Hogan's Heroes" Revue*.

"The *Hogan's Heroes* variety show storyline was supposedly on a boat coming home," John explained. "Bob shot some additional footage, and it was to show him coming back from Germany. They were interviewing him, and his storyline was that he was going become a Big Band drummer, go back to playing as a musician. And he said, 'Well I'm bringing a fellow with me,' and he introduced Robert Clary in the character he played as LeBeau, who was going to also join in and sing in with the band. Then, in the background, you heard, 'Ho-gannnn!' And it was, of course, Colonel Klink, whom they smuggled out secretly. He wore a slouch hat, and he was their agent. He was their manager. And this was the set up for a show Bob was going to do in Las Vegas. He wanted me to join the show; I worked as a Polish magician in character with an accent, so they were going to use me as a Polish refugee in the show that they brought along that did a magic act. And it was a great show he had planned because it would start with that television footage, and then all of a sudden, they would pick the screen up and there would be Bob playing with a Big Band. The show was quite well designed. They were going to do a 'Last Days of Hitler and Germany,' and so forth."

With John also committed to providing his talent as the magician for "*Hogan's Heroes*" *Revue*, and two main cast members from the series signed on, Bob set out to finalize the deal in Las Vegas. He met with the entertainment director at the Desert Inn Casino and Hotel, Frank Sennes, who was also the founder of Hollywood's Moulin Rouge. "*Hogan's Heroes*" *Revue* was scheduled to open on June 1, 1971. Then, in March 1971, "*Hogan's Heroes*" *Revue* was abruptly cancelled for reasons never disclosed to the public until now.

Remarkably, the decision to cancel was Bob's.

"The entertainment director in Vegas who was going to do it wanted to get a ten percent piece of the pie under the table," John Thompson explained, "and Bob refused to do it. So it never came about."

Around this time, CBS also pulled the plug on *Hogan's Heroes*. In his personal thank you letters to Werner Klemperer, Robert Clary, Richard Dawson, and Larry Hovis following the cancellation of the series, Bob specifically mentions the Las Vegas act. He expresses his disgust at Sennes, as well as his hope that the show might still be performed at a later date at another venue. But it would never come to pass.

With the demise of the variety show and the cancellation of the series, *Hogan's Heroes* became television history and fully entered the world of syndication. Although the plots ran somewhat stale in the program's later years and cast members were seeking to expand their careers, it was still difficult for Bob to surrender Colonel Hogan to the ages when the time finally came.

John Thompson said. "He felt they would be able to do a couple more seasons. I don't think he was happy about losing it. I'm sure he had a hard time giving up Hogan."

But an apparent silver lining promised to help ease the pain of cancellation. Bob and others who bought into the profit participation program knew that with syndication came royalties, and they began to eagerly await their seemingly assured residuals. Bob had even increased the amount withheld from his paycheck to twenty-five percent for season six (and season seven, had there been one), so he felt confident that he would continue to receive a healthy income in *Hogan's Heroes* royalties.

But there was a problem. According to accountants for CBS and Bing Crosby Productions, by November 1972, *Hogan's Heroes* had still not turned a profit and was struggling to pay off its debtors. This left nothing for profit participants, and therefore, no monies were being awarded to participants. Bob was both frustrated and outraged. The press went so far as to call him "bitter."

"I haven't seen a cent," Bob said. "The other guys keep the books. CBS and Bing Crosby Productions own the show. I'm just a minor percentage owner. They tell me the series is still in the red."

Two years later, in 1974, the story was the same. None of those who entered the profit participation program had seen so much as a penny—even though *Hogan's Heroes* was receiving a strong viewer response in syndication.

"The reruns began while the originals were still being shown," Bob said in 1974. "After three years on CBS prime time and six years of syndication, I'm still waiting to see my twenty-five percent of the *Hogan's Heroes* profits."

And he wasn't alone. Others in the industry lost out due to their investment in the profit participation program. Perry Como, Brian Donlevy, and Walter Winchell also had not received any income following the cancellation of their respective television series.

Bob was justified in his anger. He had sacrificed large sums of money from his paycheck, buying into the series to help make it successful while also hoping to prepare for his future. Further, as the show's star, he had helped make *Hogan's Heroes* the network triumph it had become. But instead, throughout the 1970s, he received very little monetary return on that investment.

"I remember him saying to me, 'You know, we make money on residuals, but we don't make *that* much,'" cousin Jim Senich said. "I know a lot people think you make a lot of money on residuals, but he said you don't make that much money—at that time, anyway. Maybe now you do. But he said, 'You really don't make a whole lot of money.' He was really concerned about keeping his show afloat. That's the only time he ever talked about money. He said, 'People think I'm making a lot of money. But I've got bills to pay and the divorce…I've got the kids growing up. I'm doing this theatre thing, but I've *gotta* make more money than that.'"

"He floundered a little after *Hogan's*, trying to figure out what to do," John Thompson added. "There was an agency that only had two clients, and one of their clients was John Wayne. They decided to take on a third client, which was Bob. They felt they could do big things with him."

With the negative experiences he had with the *Hogan's Heroes* profit participation program, as well as the failed production of *"Hogan's Heroes" Revue*, Bob had become increasingly wary. As it turned out, the agent who wanted to sign Bob insisted upon a commission on his play *Beginner's Luck*, and that was a deal-breaker.

Bob had been performing *Beginner's Luck* across the United States since it opened in Chicago on March 24, 1970, and over time, he had also secured production rights from play owners Norman Barasch and Carroll Moore. Although Bob starred in many stage plays throughout his life, *Beginner's Luck* in fact, became Bob's signature theatre production. In addition to starring in every performance of *Beginner's Luck*, Bob also directed numerous performances. In the 1970s, *Beginner's Luck* was Bob's baby, and it had always been a lucrative production for him. At a time when he needed money the most, he was not about to hand over *any* of his profits from it. He became overly protective of *Beginner's Luck* and refused the agent's demand for commission. The decision cost Bob dearly; the agent walked away.

"This would have been the biggest move for his career," John said, "and he held out over *Beginner's Luck*."

Pam Thompson added that due to Bob's alimony and child support payments to Anne, as well as his own family's expenses, Bob was, "in all fairness, a little pressed."

Bob was indeed *more* than a little pressed. Alimony and child support notwithstanding, Bob and Patty had also purchased a grand half-million dollar estate in Beverly Hills shortly after they were married, only to find that they could not sell their home in Westwood.

"We bought a house in Beverly Hills without getting around to selling the house we're still living in," Bob said in 1975. "I never wanted to move from this house. [Patty] thought we ought to be on the flat land in Beverly Hills because of the kids; we're in a hilly area, and the house has all sorts of staircases the kids were hurting themselves on. So we bought the Beverly Hills house, then decided that we really didn't want to move. But by that time, the economy had turned bad, the interest rates were up, and we haven't been able to sell the Beverly Hills house."

In addition to regular home maintenance, they had to pay taxes for both properties. In May 1975, they eventually found a buyer for the

Beverly Hills estate, allowing them to breathe a little easier financially. They remained in their Westwood home, which Bob claimed made him happy, having preferred it to the more lavish Beverly Hills estate.

"He needed the money *now*," John reiterated. "And he blew it because he didn't want to give up commission on *Beginner's Luck*."

Bob Crane is not the only actor to have experienced trouble finding success following the end of a major hit television series. It often takes a long time, especially if the actor has become so strongly associated with the character from the first series. For lightning to strike twice in television is rare. It does not mean those actors who are unable to find immediate success after their hit series ends are bad actors. It often means they have become typecast, with their fans unable to see them as anything more than a recreation of what they have previously been.

Television is and always has been a powerful medium. It can be an actor's best friend, and it can be his or her worst enemy. Before television, people went to the movies—they went out of their homes to a theatre to watch their favorite actors perform for ninety minutes on a large screen. Whereas with television, a strange phenomenon occurs—the actors are right in one's living room. From week to week, beloved characters flicker to life on a screen, just inches from the viewer. These characters and the actors who portray them will be there for dinner, when we are home sick, during parties and dates, and all with a click of a switch. And, it is free. Television saturated the medium of acting and often, according to Bob, "muddled" the actor's progression into film.

Bob was well aware that *Hogan's Heroes* was been one lightning strike for him. When *Hogan's Heroes* wrapped in 1971, his hopes were high that he would make the leap from television to the movies. When that did not happen immediately, he began to grow concerned.

One project Bob had set his sights on and was eager to be cast in was the 1972 Francis Ford Coppola film *The Godfather*. It was just the sort of dramatic work he wanted, and as a bonus, he knew the producer—*Hogan's Heroes* co-creator Albert S. Ruddy. However, the call from Al Ruddy never came. Bob was terribly offended by what he considered a professional slight, and while in New York at the same time the filming of *The Godfather* was taking place, Bob made his feelings known.

"The last time I saw Bob," Al remembered, "I was producing *The Godfather* in New York. There were big crowds around us all, every place we shot. We were the big flavor of the month in New York. We had cops with us and crowds and so forth. Suddenly, working his way through the crowd. I saw this sorry looking character, a guy almost talking to himself, saying, 'Al, Al Ruddy, it's me, Bob Crane.' I was like, *'What?'* And then he said, 'After all I've done for you, you'd think you would have called me up and offered me a part in *The Godfather*.' I swear to God, I hadn't seen him in years. I was stunned for a moment because we were in the middle of shooting. I said, 'Bob, stand over there; hold on for a second. I'll come talk to you.' So I went back for about five minutes to what we were doing. I turned around, but he was gone. I never saw him again. It was kind of sad; it was kind of *frightening* for a second. He was like some kind of apparition when I saw him. I never forgot it."

It is unlikely that when casting for *The Godfather*, Al Ruddy would have even considered Bob. There are many reasons. First, Bob was then seen as a comedian and not a dramatic actor. Second, casting for the film took place while *Hogan's Heroes* was still in production, with at least the sixth and a potential seventh season to go. *Hogan's Heroes* was a lifetime ago for Al Ruddy, and remembering Bob Crane for a part in a heavy, dramatic film was nowhere on his radar. Yet, the slight offended Bob.

Bob remained active, however, in every avenue of the entertainment business in the years following *Hogan's Heroes*. On television, he performed small guest roles on such programs as Rod Serling's *Night Gallery* (with *Hogan's Heroes* colleague and friend Bernard Fox), *The Doris Day Show* (with John Dehner, who had also guest-starred on *Hogan's Heroes*), and several episodes of *Love, American Style*. He also continued to fill in for Johnny Carson on *The Tonight Show* and made appearances on *Hollywood Squares, The Honeymoon Game, Can You Top This, The Virginia Graham Show,* and *Pet Set* (with Betty White—he brought his shih tzu Star on her program). He also appeared in the pilot episode of *The Delphi Bureau*, which aired on March 6, 1972, and on January 2, 1974, Bob guest-starred in the short-lived television series *Tenafly*.

He later guest-starred on *Police Woman* with Angie Dickenson in the episode "Requiem for Bored Wives," airing on November 29, 1974, in which he revisited his former career in radio by playing a disc jockey. Other episodic work on television included *Spencer's Pilots* (1976), *Joe*

Forrester (1976), *Ellery Queen* (1976), *Gibbsville* (1976), *Quincy, M.E.* (1977), *The Hardy Boys/Nancy Drew Mysteries* (1977), and *The Love Boat* (1978).

Bob also made two films during the 1970s—both by Walt Disney Productions. The first, *Superdad*, opened in theaters on December 14, 1973, and co-starred Barbara Rush, Kurt Russell, Kathleen Cody, Joe Flynn, and Dick Van Patten. In 1976, Bob appeared briefly in the film *Gus*, starring Don Knotts, Tim Conway, and Edward Asner, in the underrated role of the sports announcer "Pepper."

None of the roles were dynamic or what Bob had truly enjoyed doing. Yet it kept him rooted in the acting field, which was extremely important for him.

Bob's cousin Jim Senich recalled that despite the downward swing of his career, Bob believed strongly that he would rebound.

"Bob had absolutely no doubts about his career," Jim said. "He was driven. But he got kidded a lot by some really talented actors, like Jack Nicholson—who was pretty good buddies with Bob. Nicholson, being the actor's actor, didn't consider Bobby an actor. And he would kid him a lot. He'd ask him, 'What's your next dramatic part?' It didn't bother Bob; it didn't bother him at all."

Meanwhile, Bob looked out for others. It had been typical for him to quietly help whenever he could, whether it be for friends, actors just starting out, or even his family. For example, in February 1968, Bob had been at a party and bumped into a character actor looking for work. Bob made him an offer to appear on *Hogan's Heroes*, which the actor accepted gratefully. Prepared to forget all about it, the actor left the party unconvinced that Bob would follow through. Yet two days later, the phone rang, and it was the *Hogan's Heroes* casting director telling the actor to report for work.

In another instance, Bob assisted his cousin Jim Senich, who at the time had been trying to break into broadcasting, in securing a position at WICC. Jim remembered, "Bob did things for me that I didn't even know until later, like the job at WICC. I mean, WICC in Connecticut was the ultimate, along with WTIC in Harford, Connecticut. Suddenly one day the phone rings, and it's Frank Delfino, program director, and he said, 'Jimmy, how would you like to work down here?' Oh my *God*, I hardly had any experience! That was Bob. It *had* to be Bob. So I went down there, and they had me working weekends; then they put me in full time and changed my name to Jim *Dane*, so it sounds like *Crane*, so they called me the Great Dane when I went on the air."

Bob and his brother Al remained close, and after becoming successful in Hollywood, Bob tried to help his brother financially. Al had some singing capabilities, so Bob steered him toward individuals in the music industry who might be capable of helping his brother launch a career. However, despite Bob's efforts, nothing materialized.

Cousin Jim explained, "As the years went on, and Bobby became the great success, young Al moved out to LA and got a place out there, right near UCLA. He was a handsome guy, and he had a good singing voice. Al was more outgoing, but he didn't have the talent that his brother had. But I don't think there was ever any jealousy. I never saw that; never saw that. Right to the end, when young Al died. Never saw that jealousy. Bob would help him as much as he could with contacts, and to be honest, money. Al wound up with Bob's credit card coming across country. Bob was getting outrageous bills—and he realized he had given his credit card to Al. Al enjoyed life, if you know what I mean."

KNX colleague Leo McElroy also recalled a similar experience during the mid-1960s when he and Bob had worked together at the station. "I never saw Bob other than as the Bob that we knew. This was the guy, even in relatively serious moments; Bob was *always* that personality. When I was laid off because we had too many announcers all of a sudden, I started getting calls from other stations. I was really surprised. I was putting the word out rather quietly, and all of a sudden, I'm getting a bunch of calls. I wasn't sure of it. I mentioned it to Bob's secretary, and she said, 'Don't you know what happened? Bob has called every station that has tried to hire him away from here and told them that you were the guy who could beat him in the ratings. That's why you're getting the calls.' So I went to Bob, and I was really touched. I really, honestly, was. I just couldn't think why he would do that. I went to thank him, and in typical Bob fashion, he told me where I could put it. He just didn't want to hear it. It was done, and that was it, and 'Ah, get outta here!'"

Bob was also keenly involved in his oldest son Bobby's life. He tried to help his son in the industry whenever he could, from Bobby's earliest years—when Bobby would accompany his father to work at WICC and KNX and go on the air; to guest appearances on television (such as *Art Linkletter's House Party,* where Bobby made his television debut in 1963 in the "Kids' Spot" interview segment and told Art Linkletter he wanted to be a sports announcer, while Bob reportedly was so proud he "hovered in the front row of the audience, snapping pictures")—to *Hogan's Heroes,* where Bobby, then going by Bob, Jr., would serve as a "go-fer" on the set. Later, Bobby would take an even greater role in his father's professional life.

Scott Crane agreed that his father always wanted to help others, even people who made it clear that they did not even like him. Interestingly enough, one of these people was Richard Dawson.

Bob was selective in his acting career, and he continued to turn down offers to host talk shows and game shows following the end of *Hogan's Heroes*. Bob hated the idea of hosting a game show most of all, and one game show in particular could have made Bob extremely wealthy. But he refused that one as well. Instead of leaving it at that, however, he thought of a person he believed would be perfect for the job—his former *Hogan's Heroes* colleague, Richard Dawson.

"He had helped Richard Dawson tremendously throughout his entire career before *Hogan's* started," Scott said. "Richard was often a guest on his radio show on KNX, and he would promote Richard's comedy act and all that. When *Hogan's* ended, my dad was offered the spot on *Family Feud*. He didn't want to do a game show, so he turned the producers of *Family Feud* on to Richard Dawson, which made him a multi-multi-multi-millionaire. More money than my dad ever made in his career. It made him a huge star and ridiculous amounts of money. And that was after the fact that Richard had made it really well known, including to my dad, that he didn't even like my dad. But my dad continued to help him by saying, 'I don't want to do a game show; give it to Richard.' And he didn't have to do that, but he did. So he helped a lot of people with their careers, even people who didn't like him, which is a strange thing—to be such an open book, to let anyone into your life without any judgment, and continue to help people who don't like you—for no reason at all other than to be nice. I think that's probably what got killed him—being *too* nice and *too* open, and having no judgment on other people, which is a horrible thing. It's a horrible comment on our society that we have to be more careful."

But for all his effort, the Hollywood community never really took Bob seriously as an actor, especially following the cancellation of *Hogan's Heroes*. As Monte Markham observed, they would always view him as the radio personality who ventured into acting and made it big on one television series. This was becoming more evident once *Hogan's Heroes* wrapped. Many years later, in March 1976, the ghost

Walt Disney's *Superdad*

On December 14, 1973, the Walt Disney Productions movie *Superdad* was released in theaters. Directed by Vincent McEveety and originally titled *A Son-in-Law for Charlie McCready*, *Superdad* is a campy, comedic film in the same vein as other 1970s Disney flicks, such as *Escape to Witch Mountain*, *The Apple Dumpling Gang*, *Herbie the Love Bug*, and *The Shaggy DA*. The premise is simple: Dad doesn't like the surfer his daughter likes, so he tries to "fit in" with the gang to keep an eye on her. While it did not receive rave reviews at the box office, it is a fun family film. Bob portrayed the lead character, Charlie McCready, who is consumed with worry over his daughter's selection of a boyfriend, Bart, played by Kurt Russell in one of his earliest roles. Also starring in the film are Barbara Rush, Dick Van Patten, Joe Flynn, and Kathleen Cody.

Bob was not the first choice for the role of Charlie McCready. Gig Young had been signed on as the lead character, but on the first day of shooting, Young and Disney split over artistic differences, as reported in the press. Disney needed an immediate replacement, and Bob was hired for the part. He learned his lines quickly, and shooting began without much delay.

The film was not well received by audiences or critics, however. Bob himself had also hated the new title. He believed *Superdad* sounded like a fantasy-comedy, where the father takes a secret ingredient, allowing him to be able to fly through the air. He recalled that his son Scott, who was four years of age when he first saw his dad in the film, believed *Superdad* was a rip-off of *Superman*. Bob said Scott asked him, "When do you put your cape on?"

"That's not the kind of picture it is," Bob said in January 1974. "But the Disney people say they researched the picture, and it's a great title. But what the hell does it have to do with the picture? It's a warm, Americana comedy. The perfect title would be the song from the picture. It's called *The Best of Times*, and Bobby Goldsboro is going to record it. That tells what the hell the movie's about."

Bob's daughter Karen further remembered, "They really made him a doofus dad on that," she said. "The movie was cute. And I know my dad always hated the word 'cute' as a review because he knew that always means *[throat-cut sound]*. It was an easy role for him to play because it was part of the father. But he wasn't a doofus in real life."

Dick Van Patten, who had co-starred with Bob in the film, shared his memories of working with Bob on the set of *Superdad*. He explained that Bob was "very down to earth and very friendly. He was a natural, and he made it look easy. He never showed any temperament. He did what they told him. He was easy to talk to and a dream to work with. He treated acting like a job." Dick Van Patten never saw Bob again after *Superdad*. He considered Bob "a real pro" in his work, and if there was one thing he wanted people to know, it was that "Bob Crane was A REAL MAN."

An Interview with Bob Crane
by Dick Strout

Recently, we had the pleasure to speak with *Superdad*, Mr. Natural Wit himself, Bob Crane. Our conversation began by commenting that this role as a contemporary lawyer and overly concerned father was a bit detached and unusual from his part as Colonel Hogan.

Bob – Not unusual in the sense that I was doing something out of the ordinary because I have five children, in fact, three daughters who are in their teen years now. So in doing Charlie McCready, I was basically playing the father of a teenage daughter growing up, and the problems that go along with it. And those are the problems that I experience every day.

Dick – Do you consider *Superdad* a little over-anxious, say, in its approach to parental guidance?

Bob – Well, you see, the script in the picture calls for me to be a fumbling father who's trying to do well by his daughter. He's trying to keep up with the daughter and her crowd. And for that reason, teenage kids are involved with surfing, football, volleyball, basketball—many things that a fellow, or a father my age, wouldn't be involved with. And to keep up with the daughter, I do get involved with them, and that's what makes the fun. I mean, I'm Charlie Oaf. You know, here comes Daddy the Dimwit. But in *making* the movie, I had a great deal of fun. In fact, on the set, we ad-libbed. Vince McEveety who directed the picture and his brother Joe wrote it; we had the advantage of – there was a good chemistry between Vince and myself so we got to ad-lib a lot of things. For instance, in the football game that we play on the beach that we shot down in Balboa, I actually was injured, and this wasn't part of the film, and we had to ad-lib out of that. I mean, I was walking around for a couple of weeks in fact with a *limp*! And people thought, "Boy, the guy's really taking this role to heart!" I hurt myself! And I kept screaming to people, "I'm hurt!" And they said, "C'mon, you're doing a role, Charlie!" And I said, "I'm not Charlie! I'm Bob Crane!"

Dick – In addition to football, I understand you exert your prowess at surfing, is that right, Bob?

Bob – And waterskiing. Those are two things that I have tried in real life and failed at, and I know my limitations. In the picture, I had to try them and fail at them again, but in a comedic way. And as I said, I almost got killed doing them. At a couple of spots, Vince even said to me, "Bob, you know, take it easy. You're not a kid anymore." And I said, "Oh, you're doing the script now! What is this? You sound like my daughter." She's saying, "Oh, c'mon Dad. You know, this isn't for you." And I'm saying, "I'm gonna have a good time with you kids! I'm gonna *show* you I'm one of the gang!"

Dick – Why do you disapprove of Kathleen's beaus?

Bob – Well, I think every father thinks that his daughter should marry somebody in his own image. Kathy Cody's boyfriends are not in my image. And they're not *bad* boys, they're just not *me*! [Laughs] And so I immediately say, *wrong*. This one's a surfer. I ask him what he wants to do in life, and he said, "Surf." Well, now, how can my daughter marry a guy who surfs as a profession? That's the fun of the picture, is I'm asking a five-year-old kid, "What do you wanna be when [you] grow up?" Well, the kid says, "A fireman." Who *knows* what he's gonna be? So it's tough to pin anybody down. I have always felt, in my own career, in the years that I was in radio, and on *The Donna Reed Show*, and on *Hogan's Heroes*, and now doing the Disney film and doing plays on the road, it's a matter of being in the right place at the right time and having a little talent to go along with it *and* experience. And all of these things are not done overnight. And in the picture, I also try to convince my daughter, "Take your time. Don't be in a hurry." But that's tough to tell a teenage girl *or* boy. There's plenty of time. You've got your whole life to live. They don't wanna hear that.

I know that in my own life, when I was in my teens, you know, when you're prior to sixteen, you just think when you turn sixteen, that's gonna be the *end all. Boy*, at sixteen, *life* is gonna begin! And you get to sixteen, and you suddenly find out, wait a minute. Nothing's happening. Maybe it's eighteen. Then you get to eighteen, and you said, no, not much is happening. Maybe it's twenty-one. And each…I was in my *thirties*. I was still doing radio, trying to be an actor, and I was thinking, "When does it finally happen? When does somebody come along and say, 'You have *now* arrived as an adult. This is your career.'"

Dick – Has it happened, Bob? I mean, in your opinion, have you arrived?

Bob – This Disney picture is my first real starring role. I did one other motion picture that I was in, that so-called co-starring role with Elke Sommer called *The Wicked Dreams of Paula Schultz*, which hasn't even made it to television yet. Now, for a picture that's five or six years old not having been on television yet, it wasn't that successful in the theaters. I don't know. They're holding it up as a jazz re-issue, I think. Someday they're gonna bring it out in a symposium.

> **Dick –** I imagine what pleasantly confirms stardom is recognition in the public everywhere. Is that right?
>
> **Bob –** This isn't bad. It's a better identification than having somebody come up and say, "Aren't you Whatshisname?" I had a woman in the market the other day that stood next to me and pointed a finger and said, "Don't tell me, don't tell me, don't tell me!" And after about a minute of embarrassment, nobody telling her, and she's standing there, "Don't tell me, don't tell me," finally I volunteered, "Bob Crane." And she says, "No, that's not it." And I said, "Well, I'm sorry. That *is* it." "No, that's not it!" [Laughs] And she walked away convinced I wasn't Bob Crane. I don't know who she thought I was!
>
> **Dick –** [Laughs] Well, *Superdad* will certainly make her remember. Thanks Bob again, it's always a pleasure to talk with you, and I want to thank you for this look at Walt Disney's latest achievement in family entertainment.
>
> **Bob –** Thank you so much for inviting me to be on the show.
>
> **Note:** Page 109 of the revised *Auto Focus* script (dated December 4, 2001) claims that Walt Disney Productions shelved the film *Superdad* for two years. However, Bob Crane accepted the role in October 1972, and the film opened on December 14, 1973. Thus, this and other claims that it was shelved for one or two years after production are erroneous proven by the physical timeline of pre-production filming and subsequent post-production of the project.

of Hogan was still present. Bob was appearing on *Ellery Queen* in the episode "The Adventures of the Hard-Hearted Huckster." In this episode, Bob played a villain, a role that was very different for him. Director Edward Abroms specifically recalled that Bob was a true professional on the set. As was usually the case in his work, Bob displayed no ego and worked well with the cast, and Abroms recognized Bob was still at the top of his game. However, in playing the villain, Bob was less-than-convincing. He hit his marks and did his job well, but it was as if Colonel Hogan, not Bob Crane, was playing the part.

"It would be as if you took the leather jacket and the cap off Hogan and put Hogan in that role and told him to play a bad guy," Abroms said. "Bob did well, but he played a bad guy with a bit of a smile."

It was something that started to erode Bob's ambitions as an actor long before *Hogan's Heroes* ended, and it was turning into a monumental problem. Whatever project Bob set out to do, the good Colonel was suddenly in his way, and no matter which way Bob tried to run,

Hogan turned with him. The very character that had brought him international fame had also come to hinder his advancement in the entertainment industry. This phenomenon could be fatal to even the most gifted actor, and Bob had fallen victim to it.

Bob Crane had become typecast.

> *I used to be asked if I minded playing the straight man for so many people. I don't mind at all. I always told Werner Klemperer the number-one guy doesn't have to be the funny one. Just look at Jack Benny's lengthy career. He never worried about having the punch line. The point is to have the number-one guy likable. If he isn't, forget the show. Likability is the key.*
>
> —Bob Crane, on his role of Bob Wilcox on *The Bob Crane Show*, February 1975

After the tremendous success of *Hogan's Heroes*, Bob yearned for a similar hit. He had been offered other television roles, as well as talk shows—including the offer to host ABC's new morning program *Good Morning America*—that he turned down. Then, one writer approached Bob about a prospective series that did catch his attention—that of a glib television talk show host. It was a role he desired, but the series was never produced.

"It sounded great," Bob said in 1972. "Just the ticket. We had the format all worked out and then something happened. That something was Dick Van Dyke deciding to come out of retirement, and what does he decide to do? What else? He starts a new series in which he plays a talk show host. And so back we went to the old drawing board."

The New Dick Van Dyke Show, in which Richard Dawson also appeared, was short-lived, and ran on CBS from 1971 to 1974, but it was just at the wrong time for Bob. He turned to Paul Henning, creator of *The Beverly Hillbillies* and other comedies that took place in rural settings, for ideas, and together, they began to conceptualize a series. However, as with other attempted blueprints, this project never came to fruition, either.

Other offers came flooding in as well, and as before, Bob snubbed them. "One offer was for me to be head of stewardess training for a swinging airline," Bob said in 1975. "I read the script and said, 'This is

Bob Cummings 1953.' Another script was about the sheriff in a small country town. 'Andy Griffith has already done it,' I said."

Then, in 1974, NBC contacted Bob with an offer, and they were adamant that he accept. But at the time, Bob had something else in the works. In January 1971, Bob, along with Patty and Bobby, had idealized, collaborated on, and written a synopsis for a new series. This work would undergo several name changes during its creation; however, the premise was the same—a television field reporter (intended as Bob's character) would be partnered with his mobile sidekick. In its earliest drafts, it was called *Grimm and Barrett* and then *I Witness*, before Bob settled on *The Bob Crane Show*. In 1973, the final draft of the synopsis was registered with the Writer's Guild of America-West.

Bob pitched the Crane-collaboration script to ABC, and the network liked the concept enough to order a pilot. Bob believed he was perfect for the role; however, he had to choose. Should he continue forward with *I Witness* or sign with NBC on the new comedy?

Bob opted to sign with NBC.

With *I Witness* sold and Bob no longer in control, ABC and the show's production company, Mark VII, Ltd., and Universal TV changed the name and reworked the premise. Now called *Mobile One*, the series starred Jackie Cooper in the leading role. The ninety-minute pilot for the series, *Mobile Two*, aired on September 2, 1975, and the series premiered over ABC on September 12, 1975.

Ratings for *Mobile One*, however, were poor. ABC had slated *Mobile One* on Friday nights, opposite NBC's popular *Sanford and Son* and CBS' *M*A*S*H*. After only eleven episodes, *Mobile One* was cancelled.

But Bob's focus had shifted from *Mobile One* to the new series he had just signed on to. And despite concerns about the concept's ability to fly, he was hoping NBC's star vehicle for him would be his next big hit.

Mary Tyler Moore (MTM) Productions added a half-hour situation comedy to its stable that focused on a successful, middle-aged businessman who decides to quit his day job and go to medical school. The lead character, Bob Wilcox, is a 40-year-old insurance vice president who, once a leader at home and work, becomes faced with having to keep up with college "kids" who are 20 years his junior, do his homework, rely on his wife as the breadwinner, and be a supportive and good father to his teenage daughter. To complicate matters, Wilcox experiences an epiphany and changes his mind about the whole thing. However, when he returns to reclaim his old job, he discovers he has already been replaced. Now committed to a new life, Bob Wilcox finds himself in uncomfortable situations and vulnerable more often than not, which was supposed to set the stage for comedy. Produced by Grant Tinker for MTM Productions and created by Martin Cohan and Norman S. Powell, the series underwent many changes during its short network life.

Bob Crane starred as Bob Wilcox opposite Tricia Hart (also known as Patricia Harty) as his wife, Ellie. Regular cast members included Harold Gould (who appeared several times on *Hogan's Heroes*), John Hillerman (later, known for his role as Higgins on *Magnum, P.I.*), James Sutorius, Todd Susman (one of the P.A. announcers on *M*A*S*H*), Jack Fletcher, Ronny Graham (a friend of Bob's whom Bob had helped earn a part on the series), Bruce Kimmel, and Wil Seltzer. Filming began on Halloween night in 1974, and the series premiered over NBC on Thursday, March 6, 1975, with the episode "Mid-Term Blues." NBC originally ordered twenty-two episodes from MTM Productions; however, only fifteen episodes (including the pilot) were ever filmed. Considered an immediate failure, NBC cancelled *The Bob Crane Show* abruptly after its first season—a season that had survived only a brief half-life.

The Bob Crane Show does have its moments. Take, for instance, the episode "Son of Campus Capers," featuring a very young John Ritter (later Jack Tripper of *Three's Company* fame) in one of his first television roles as a student who enjoys playing practical jokes on others. But the tables are eventually turned, with Bob and his classmates finally getting their revenge with a practical joke of their own. There are other shining moments during the series as well, leading to the belief that if it had been given a chance, *The Bob Crane Show* might have moved past its awkward "early childhood" phase and developed into a mature, smart comedy rather than remain what Bob later described as "silliness." A longer run might have also given the audience the opportunity to accept Bob in a role other than Colonel Hogan—which was proving increasingly difficult for Bob to break.

Norman Powell remembered how he and Marty Cohen conceptualized the series, originally titled *Second Chance* before changing to *Second Start*.

"There was an article in *Life* magazine, which was talking about a mid-life career change," Powell explained. "People who had, for all of their lives, done one thing and then decided they weren't happy at it and made the switch. I thought it might be an interesting concept for a comedy show. I wrote something down and got in touch with Marty. Marty, being a writer and a producer, liked the concept, and because he was working for MTM at the time, we were able to sell the concept to Grant Tinker, who was running MTM. We pitched it to CBS, which picked up a script commitment. So Marty wrote the script, but CBS passed on it."

According to Powell, *Second Start* "languished for a time." However, he and writing partner Marty Cohen urged Grant Tinker to try pitching it to another network. Tinker agreed, and they reached out to NBC. After reading the script, NBC agreed to a pilot commitment.

"The original pilot was conceived as a single-camera light comedy drama about a guy who's been selling insurance—a boring job—all of his life," Powell said. "Since he was a little kid, he wanted to be a doctor. He had some money put aside, so he talked to his wife and kids, and said, 'Would you support me if I go back to medical school at age forty?' And so we sold that concept to NBC, and we hired Jackie Cooper to direct this pilot. We shot the pilot, and it was single camera. We laid in a laugh track, but it was a very, very light laugh track. It was basically a 'dramedy'—a *real* fish out of water. Here's a guy, forty years old, he's back competing with kids half his age in medical school. It was a nice little pilot, and NBC picked it up as a series. We had a good cast. MTM had a very good casting director who was known for quality. This was a quality production house that was known for doing things the right way. So the production values and the care with which we cast these roles—that was what we did. We had some *really* good actors."

But what seemed like a promising new situation comedy/"dramedy" was plagued with setbacks and problems from the outset. As soon as it was picked up by NBC, the network insisted on Bob Crane as its star—a decision Norman Powell had not embraced. NBC wanted Bob because they believed his earlier success on *Hogan's Heroes* would automatically ensure high ratings for the new series. However, Bob was not Powell's first choice.

"I remember I resisted," Powell recalled. "I don't think Bob was right [for the part]. My first choice was Larry Hagman. Larry briefly considered doing it, but then he got an offer to do another pilot, which didn't sell, but it was an hour pilot, and they offered him more money. And then there were other candidates I favored before Bob. But finally

Grant came to me and said, 'Norman, I respect the fact that you don't want Bob to do this. But if you truly refuse him, pass on him, NBC is going to walk away. They want Bob Crane to do it.' And that rolled me right over. He had a proven track record as being a serious lead, and they thought he was, obviously, the strongest choice we could have."

At first, Bob seemed pleased with the premise of *Second Start* and NBC's support of him in the leading role. Further, the character of Bob Wilcox mirrored Bob's own life to some degree. Wilcox, who had suddenly found himself in unfamiliar waters, was symbolic of Bob Crane's overwhelming success in radio only to branch out into the unfamiliar territory of acting, reach the top, and then begin to flounder as he searched for a new series. Bob had also undergone drastic mid-life changes following his divorce from Anne and the start of his new life with Patty in his second marriage. Therefore, he could relate to the struggles of a man who had experienced a whiplash effect of terrific change. He was also excited about the prospect of finally gaining a new series—one that might help him put Colonel Hogan firmly in the past.

"I'd been hunting for the right concept ever since *Hogan's* went off the air," Bob said. "The format looked like it might work."

NBC liked the pilot enough to add *Second Start* to its 1974 fall lineup, a major hurdle to overcome considering some of the competition.

"I had seen their lineup of pilots, and they had a pretty formidable line up of pilots at that point," Powell stated. "I felt *really, really* good about the fact that we had cracked into that inner circle of what I considered quite good pilots."

But then, an unfortunate obstacle loomed in their path. *Second Start* was shelved, falling victim to the Federal Communications Commission's (FCC's) new Prime Time Access Rule.

Announced in May 1970 and implemented on September 1, 1971, the Prime Time Access Rule reduced the number of prime time hours from four to three, restricting network affiliates in the top fifty markets from airing programs for more than three hours in the evening—thus, the new prime time hours were reduced to eight to eleven o'clock p.m. in the Eastern and Pacific time zones, and seven to ten o'clock p.m. in the Central and Mountain time zones. The idea behind the new ruling was to permit local programming more time, forcing the networks to give time back to local affiliates. Over the next several years, the three networks—ABC, CBS, and NBC—voiced their concerns, and in January 1974, the FCC relaxed the ruling, returning an additional half hour to the networks' prime time slot. This meant that prime time could begin one half hour earlier—at seven-thirty p.m. Eastern and Pacific, and six-thirty p.m. Central and Mountain.

But it was not enough to save *Second Start* from the chopping block, and it became one of many new programs NBC cut from its fall 1974 lineup. Other shows affected that year included *Hec Ramsey, The Girl with Something Extra, Lotsa Luck, Chase, Little House on the Prairie, Born Free, Lucas Tanner, In Tandem* (renamed *Movin' On*), *The Rangers* (renamed *Sierra*), *The Rockford Files, Petrocelli, Police Woman*, and *Chico and the Man*.

As the scaled-down fall 1974 season progressed, new programs that did not fare well were cancelled and replaced by those on hold. *Second Start* was given a second chance when NBC rescheduled it for a January 1975 premiere, only to rescind the decision, suspending it yet again in favor of an experimental musical series, *The Mac Davis Show*. As the wisecracks about *Second Start* not even being able to get beyond its own second start circulated, Bob and others began to worry that the series would never air. Finally, the word came that *Second Start* would premiere in March, and Bob was less than exuberant.

"There were rumors in the trades we wouldn't start at all," Bob said. "Grant Tinker, the boss of Mary Tyler Moore Enterprises, who's doing the show, called me and said, 'Don't blow your top, but we're going on in March.' I said, 'March! Nobody goes on in March! You change your anchorman in March! You don't start a show in March.' Grant said to call the NBC boss Larry White; he wanted to talk to me. I call Larry and tell him this is the best news since the Hindenburg disaster. But he says, 'It's okay, you'll be opposite reruns.' I said, 'What night?' He says, 'Thursday, Opposite *The Waltons*.' I said, 'Keep telling me more good news!'"

Norman Powell concurred. "Theoretically, there's less competition, so if you've got a decent show, it's got a better shot than it does in September. There have been a lot of shows that have come on after the prime time onslaught, after everything goes on the air and have been successful. I don't think that mitigated that much against us at that point in time. Maybe it did. I think what really mitigated most against us was that it didn't come on mid-season. It came on *post*-mid-season. It came on in March, whereas mid-season, normally those shows have failed and you're on in January. It wasn't good for the show, that's for sure."

NBC managed to convince Bob that the March premiere could be considered favorable. "We'll have a chance to get more publicity and general attention with a new series in March," Bob said, albeit with a touch of uncertainty, to the press.

The early setbacks *Second Start* experienced no doubt foreshadowed its dismal future, with the press claiming that *Second Start* was doomed before it even got off the ground. However, as it waited for its extraordinarily late premiere date, word got out that significant changes in format were being made. Journalist Marilyn Beck wrote in August 1974, "One of the MTM productions knocked off the fall lineup by the recent prime time access ruling now is rescheduled for shooting in September. From the way things are working out, the delayed debut could be the best thing that ever happened to *Second Start*. The Bob Crane starrer, which gave every indication of being a video flop, now is being revamped, restructured, and rewritten."

With the series postponed, Bob took action, wanting to quell industry rumors that the show was a disaster and to do what he believed was in the best interest of the program and all involved. He began to make demands—and plenty of them. As reporter Robert L. Rose wrote in February 1975, "The thing is, if Bob Crane asks you for something, you might as well do it. Otherwise, you'll get jawboned to death, or the fates will intervene and you'll have to give in anyway. Crane, if anything, is a persistent cuss."

First, Bob challenged Grant Tinker about how the series was filmed. The pilot of *Second Start* was done in one-camera format, similar to how *Hogan's Heroes* had been filmed. But Bob had other ideas, and he fought to have the format changed to a three-camera production in front of a live audience. He pointed out that with the exception of *M*A*S*H*, the hit comedy programs of that era were being performed before a live studio audience rather than rely on a laugh track, and he wanted *Second Start* to do the same.

Norman Powell wasn't so sure. "The very nature of the multiple-camera set up is, in the live performance, you really have to galvanize an audience and make them laugh," he said. "That process is a process of significant rewriting and 'punch the show up' and motivate people who are sitting there on the stage deck to laugh and to become engaged. I had done three years of *The Dick Van Dyke Show*—the *master* of that was Dick Van Dyke. I mean, my *God*, he was brilliant at it—performing before a live audience. Bob was kind of just brash and crass and vulgar, which wasn't his character at all. The character had an innate sweetness as opposed to the brashness that Bob brought to it."

But Bob won out. "I respond to crowds," he said. "I've also been on the road with the play *Beginner's Luck*. I *need* a live audience now. I work better."

That challenge overcome, next on Bob's radar was the concept. He didn't like it from the outset, feeling that it was like "*Donna Reed* time" again. "It was originally designed as a nice, warm, family show, with some nice, warm smiles," Bob said. "I felt that wasn't what I wanted and wasn't what my fans expected of me. I didn't think a show with nice, warm smiles would go very far in the competitive market. The original idea was a nice, soft, warm, human comedy, something like *Apple's Way*, following up on the success of *The Waltons*. That's what all the networks were looking for a year ago. But after it didn't get on, ...I told Grant [Tinker] that now that we have the time, what we need is another MTM product like *Mary Tyler Moore, Bob Newhart, Rhoda*.... You go for belly laughs, not titters and smiles."

Tinker was convinced—and the tone of the show changed.

"Hard comedy goes for the jugular," Bob explained. "Hard comedy is basic. It's what Bob Hope has done for years—Hope and Berle and Benny. But even more important, it's what television audiences want today. Hard comedy is what's on the Top 20 shows. Hard comedy, in other words, is *All in the Family* and *Sanford and Son* and *The Mary Tyler Moor Show* and *The Bob Newhart Show* and *Rhoda* and *Chico and the Man* and *Maude*. Sometimes *Maude* may hit you the wrong way, but when it works, it works extremely well. Hard comedy goes for the fences. It's also what you might call take-a-risk comedy because if you don't hit a home run, you might strike out. It's either a belly laugh or it's no go and no show. I like Johnny Carson because he doesn't hold anything back when he's going for a laugh. Johnny will do anything, say anything, to get his laugh. Some people wonder why Johnny has lasted all these years. The reason is simple—he makes people laugh. He's funny, he's professional, he doesn't tiptoe around. He's out for big laughs and he gets them. He's not interested in smiles and knowledgeable nods, and I'm not, either."

Powell was a strong believer in the one-camera format, *and* the original tone of the show, and when those changed, so did their set. "The permanent sets we had constructed—all of that had to go," he said. "None of that worked for the multiple camera format. MTM threw a *lot* of money at reformatting the show. And in that three-camera format, the show, in my opinion, lost a significant amount of the easygoing charm and certainly the cinematic impact of shooting. We shot the exteriors at USC; it's a beautiful campus. It had its own charm. In a single-camera show, you shoot it more like a movie, so it's got interesting camera angles and coverage, and then it's edited entirely differently. It's designed to be certainly cinematic, whereas with a multiple-camera set-up, three or four cameras on the floor, that's pretty predictable coverage. And NBC was good at it—they were doing *Rhoda*, *The Mary Tyler Moore Show*, and *Newhart*. They had a whole litany of successful comedies. This just turned into a rather broad comedy featuring Bob, who I think in the three-camera format was not as effective as he certainly was in the single-camera show."

As filming continued in the fall of 1974, Bob petitioned for one more change. "How about calling it *The Bob Crane Show*?" he asked NBC programming executive Larry White. "I mean, *Second Start* now really has a bad connotation. Now it's third start or fourth start. The critics will have a field day. And he said, 'Okay, why not?' Just like that."

It was an unprecedented decision because it broke NBC's policy up until that time of never naming a new series after its star. NBC would occasionally change the name of a series after one or two seasons to reflect the star's name if the show became a success, but it was unusual, and never done at the outset.

Bob was thrilled. "I think it's good to have an identity with either the star or the character he plays," he said. "Shows like *Mary Tyler Moore*, *Bob Newhart*, *Rhoda*, and *Kojak* bring immediate recognition. But you don't know who the star is of *Good Times*."

But his excitement was tempered with pragmatism. "If the show doesn't succeed, then what do you do the next time?" Bob hypothesized. "For instance, Dick Van Dyke. He has done *The Dick Van Dyke Show*, then *The New Dick Van Dyke Show*. Now he's preparing a new series. What on earth can he call it?"

"The truth is, the show was not as strong a show as the show they bought—a single-camera show," Powell said. "It wasn't. The show they picked up was different and I think a much better show than the ultimate show. I'm sure Bob felt that being in that role he could manipulate the show more to his liking as time went by. And then when the postponement came down, he jumped on that opportunity right away. He wouldn't have been able to do it had we not been delayed; we were set to go in its original format. All of these adjustments were major mid-course corrections based on a set of circumstances nobody could have anticipated. We did our best to try and make the show something he could be comfortable with, and he was always very respectful. We didn't have that kind of conflict with him at all. *The Bob Crane Show* was basically an interesting, funny, classic fish-out-of-water concept. Where you could explore something that was very real at that point in time when people who were dissatisfied with their lives [saying], 'Can we go on?' 'Can I make a change at mid-life and be successful and happy?' 'Did I do the right thing?' You take a middle-aged guy, with a family, with all of those pressures, and with a brain that's forty years old trying to compete with eighteen- to twenty-year-old kids, playing softball games and being 'one of the guys.' It could have been extraordinary. But as a multiple-camera show, it turned much more burlesque—a much *broader* comedy. You couldn't deal with what I had seen as the nuance of 'emotional change'—what impact does it have on a family? On an adolescent kid whose dad has brought home all kinds of money as an insurance executive, all of a sudden they're living in a funky house where the plumbing doesn't work? It's a whole different lifestyle. So a lot of those qualities vanished in the three-camera concept in the search for broader, laugh-out-loud comedy as opposed to having quiet, tender moments."

Norman Powell pointed to casting as the primary problem. Bob, he said, wasn't the right actor for the role of the vulnerable, sweet Bob Wilcox. "Basically, Bob was a burlesque comedian," Powell explained. "That wasn't my concept for the series, but that's what happened to it. My instinct was that he was the wrong guy, and that's why I resisted hiring him for it. And I was right. I don't know if there was anything we could have done that would have made him work in that particular show. He wasn't meant for that show. He was what he was. He was best in *Hogan's Heroes*. But I think Bob never gelled as that character.... What started out as a dream come true was sort of a nightmare by the time we got through with it. But how much of that was Bob's fault? I don't know. Had it been Larry Hagman in that show, would it have been a success? I don't know. Who knows?"

Viewers no doubt had difficulty separating Bob Crane from Colonel Hogan. Again, Bob could not escape the typecast of the all-American, invulnerable, rugged Air Force officer who was always in control and never off the mark, a vision of himself that even Bob seemed to struggle to let go of. "He didn't bring the humanity to it, the vulnerability," Powell observed. "He was uncomfortable being vulnerable, which I think was part and parcel of this character. The character of Hogan was *so* on top of his game even though he was the prisoner. He was *absolutely* invulnerable. I think Bob had some problems associating with what the character in *Second Start* was.... He liked to pitch *that boy*—the guy who's middle aged but is really just a kid at heart and full of that brashness that kids have, or some kids have. We tried to make what we were doing funnier, but it really lapsed into a much broader comedy. The ability to bring quiet, softer moments into it became more problematic because Bob couldn't handle it very well.

"Everything is judged by how much laughter you're evoking out of the audience that's sitting right there in front of you. It's a type of media. It's sitting right there in front of your face. It was just something he wasn't comfortable with—the softer, quieter moments, the vulnerable moments. We obviously couldn't push him. I tried to reassure him, [co-creator] Marty (Cohan) tried to reassure him, he would get it twisted up, and it wouldn't work. He would say, 'It's not me, fellas. I'm doing my best. I know you guys are working with me. We just disagree on this. I just can't do that. I'll try it, but it won't work.' And he'd *prove* it didn't work. We tried to play to his strengths, or what he felt his strengths were, which was dealing with the bigger, broader comedy, and what we felt he was stronger at—instead of delivering the laugh line, it was being the foil to people like Jack Fletcher or Harold Gould who were really astute about comedy. But it all worked itself out so it became broader and broader to try to evoke the laughter. Sometimes I think we did some stuff that was funny. But by and large to me it was disappointing. It was trying to push the show into a direction that Bob felt comfortable with, but obviously, the audience wasn't buying it."

"They didn't know what to do with me," Bob said later. "They were looking for a leading man who was acceptable to the network. Okay, I was, but they wanted a Bob Crane who could play warmth and charm. I don't play warmth and charm. I play fun, and I said to the producers, 'If it doesn't look like fun, the audience isn't going to buy it.'"

"I think Bob perceived himself inaccurately as a charming Tex badboy, and he pulled a *lot* of slightly off-color jokes, a *lot* of innuendo, a *lot* of stuff like that," Powell said. "He would warm up the audience. He would play the drums, and tell off-color jokes and stuff like that. It was embarrassing. Grant Tinker always came to those shows. I remember him with Bob doing a run of his off-color stuff, and Grant was way down on the floor in the booth. He said, 'I may have to listen to this, but I don't have to watch it.' You know, he was embarrassed."

Bob found the pace of the series exhausting. "On *Hogan's*, you could always take a break while the cameras were being set up for the next shot. But here, I go straight through on my feet all day long. I get tired. And besides, I'm older than I was during *Hogan*."

Disheartened though he was, Bob continued to be generous with his fellow actors, both for their benefit and for the good of the show. "The important thing is to develop people around the central character, which you have to do for a comedy series to make it," he explained. "I often suggest giving my punch lines to other characters. It's better for them to be funny, not me. I wasn't the funny one in *Hogan's Heroes*."

"He was a very pleasant guy," Powell remembered. "I had *no* problems with him. Aside from the fact I didn't think he was very good in the role, he wasn't directly a problem to me as the producer. He was pretty cooperative.... He was a pleasant enough guy to be around. I considered him kind of a pain in the ass, but not to the point to which there was any real conflict between us, between he and I, or between he and Marty. But he was *very* self-centered—a *very* self-centered kind of guy. The young actors were very respectful of him, but there wasn't a closeness there."

As the debut date of *The Bob Crane Show* dragged on, a wary press waited to see how the changes would translate to the screen. Journalists Buck Biggers and Chet Stover wrote in November 1974, "Those well-acquainted with *Hogan's Heroes* give the lion's share of credit for that series' amazingly long run to the star, Bob Crane. Having an instinctive feel for sophisticated comedy, Crane understood precisely how far the stories could go in slapstick without losing believability. Unfortunately, Bob's judgments, right though they were, often led him into arguments with both producers and directors. This, plus Crane's brash exterior, has made it virtually impossible for him to get TV work since the demise of *Hogan's Heroes*. Now, finally, Bob Crane has a new half-hour sitcom... But when do you think the series will begin? In mid-March! Thus, the show not only missed a regular season launch, it won't even get a mid-season send off! And if it fails to earn a decent rating, who do you think will get the blame? Bob Crane, of course."

They were right. *The Bob Crane Show* failed miserably, and, exactly as predicted, Bob shouldered the lion's share of the blame in the reviews. The critics shredded the program, calling it one of the worst television series to air that year. Gary Deeb of *The Chicago Tribune* wrote, "*The Bob Crane Show* features Bob as a forty-two-year-old insurance exec and family breadwinner who drops out of the rat race to go to medical school… For a guy who got into acting—and television—rather late in life, Crane nevertheless isn't one of those timid souls who genuflect at the mere mention of one of the networks. He's a supremely self-confident, rugged individualist with a machine gun, [and a] whiz kid conversation style that honors no sacred cows. [But] you get the feeling that Crane, one of the finest and most underrated comedy actors in the business, is bitter. After [six] popular and profitable seasons as the impish, cocky POW who tormented his Nazi captors in *Hogan's Heroes*, Bob now finds himself imprisoned in a turkey—and the experience, while somewhat novel, isn't pleasant."

The writing was on the wall in big, bold neon letters. Only two weeks into its run, NBC cancelled *The Bob Crane Show*. With the remaining episodes still being aired throughout the spring of 1975, Bob was so embarrassed watching his own show that he changed the channel. He also changed his tune, claiming he had never liked the show's concept, and although in its earliest production days, Bob had expressed hope for the series, he soon began displaying an unabashed and very open dislike of the premise and his character.

"I wasn't all that fascinated by the idea of *Second Start*, the premise of the forty-year-old guy going back to college," Bob said in 1976. "I wasn't that sure. NBC wasn't that sure. The big problem, outside of the story, was that there was no chemistry with the characters. I had nobody to talk to. I wanted comedy, not silliness. I wanted stuff like you see in Mary's show, truth and not just jokes. I was looking for what's in *Barney Miller*, believable people with some kind of conflict going and nothing contrived."

Friend Pam Thompson said Bob didn't embrace the series at all, and it didn't take long for him to stop caring about it. "It was a dreadful show because Bob was not happy," she said. "When he wasn't happy, he just wasn't able to give as much as he normally would have."

"My wife says I'm as readable as a book," Bob said. "When I'm not happy with what I'm doing, that shows. People can see if you're having a good time as an actor. When you're not happy with the script, the audience knows. And they did know."

Another big reason for Bob's discontent, according to friend John Thompson, was pilot episode director Jackie Cooper. "I remember [Bob] wanted to get us involved in television," John said. "He wanted Pam to read for the female lead in *The Bob Crane Show*, and he wanted me to play one of the other roles on it, the second or third male banana on the show, a recurring role. But he had such a problem with Jackie Cooper at the time. He spent all of his time trying to get Jackie removed as director. Jackie Cooper made Bob feel rather inadequate as an actor. Cooper would say things like, 'Oh Bob, the greatest single episodic comedian in our business...is Alan Alda.' And it would bother Bob. He was the star of the show, and [Jackie] kept raving about Alan Alda *constantly*. Bob went way out of his way to finally have Jackie removed from the show as the director because he just felt so insecure constantly. So when it came time for Pam to read, he did not have the juice to push her into the leading role."

"The chemistry was not quite right at first," Bob said. "Our cast of Todd Susman, Ronny Graham, Jack Fletcher, and Trisha Hart is first-rate, but it took time to get used to one another. On *Hogan's* we had the chemistry in the very first show. That almost never happens. We meshed perfectly from the beginning.

"I watch *Barney Miller*," Bob confessed in May 1975. "It's a damn good show. It's got a good chemistry, a marvelous 'gang' feel, just like *M*A*S*H* and *Hogan's Heroes*. It is everything our show ought to be but isn't. Barney Miller is my kind of character. When I saw the show on the other night, I said to my wife, 'There but for Hal Linden go I.' It's not easy after the tremendous success of *Hogan* to be involved in a project that frankly I didn't believe in from the very beginning....*[Second Start]* was a soft show. When NBC bought it, I couldn't believe it."

Bob also pointed a finger at the network. "You can get awfully paranoid in this business," he admitted, "but I truly believe NBC gave up on the show before it went on the air. When I saw the episode NBC decided to use as the premiere, I died. How the hell could NBC say that was representative of our show? None of us were proud of it. It was the very first show we shot. I was embarrassed by parts of it. Hell, I didn't even know my wife's name in the first show. I simply didn't know Trisha Hart. Nothing seemed to work right. But by God, that's the one they led off with! You almost get the feeling they delayed those until they make the official announcement that they're not renewing the show. That way, if they get complaints about those episodes, they can say, 'Look, folks—the show's been cancelled.' That's the feeling I have in my heart."

So what actually happened?

It was a perfect storm. The FCC ruling that created ongoing delays, poor reports in the trade papers, Bob not liking the premise or his character (and going against his better judgment to accept the role out of financial necessity), and Bob's star power that allowed changes that made the show almost unrecognizable as the one that had been sold to NBC in the first place—all of it put the show on a trajectory that would end in disaster.

"It was very tough because I knew the show was failing," Powell said. "And you work harder on a failure than you do on a success because you can see it happening. We knew it wasn't working. The first thing you see the next morning are the overnights—the ratings. We knew it was over. Working in the writers' room doing the rewrites, that grind where you're still working at four o'clock or five o'clock in the morning and you've been in there since eight o'clock the previous morning. That was very difficult. We were killing ourselves trying to make that show work, and it wasn't going to work. I didn't dislike Bob; he frustrated me. I just thought he was kind of crude and not very talented.

"I never look back and say we didn't try too hard. Maybe we didn't try hard *enough*. I just think the original concept and Bob Crane were mismatched. Bob was who he was; the show was what it was. And it wasn't a good fit. So the hybrid that it became didn't fit either."

"Maybe realistically, in a career, you have only one hit series," Bob philosophized in May 1976. "Maybe *Hogan's* was mine."

True to form, throughout the 1970s, Bob filled his resume to capacity in every medium, striving to get his acting career back to where it was during *Hogan's Heroes*. He was a busy actor, never letting the grass grow under his feet. But money was tight. In 1972, he found himself back in a familiar setting, much to the surprise of many, including himself.

When Bob bowed out of his KNX contract in 1965 to concentrate on *Hogan's Heroes*, he admitted he missed being on the air, saying he needed a place to air his opinions on a daily basis. But there weren't enough hours in the day. He returned for a couple of years while also working on *Hogan's Heroes*, when he volunteered many hours for the Armed Forced Radio Network in 1968 and 1969. But outside of that, radio was in his past, and he had made it quite clear to everyone that he would *never* return to radio.

Never say never.

With a new family, bills, alimony, and child support all vying for his cash, doing a radio show would put some much-needed money in his pockets while allowing him to do something he enjoyed.

But KNX did not receive the benefit of Bob's resurrection over the airwaves; instead, he filled in for his old adversary, Dick Whittinghill, at KMPC.

To the broadcasting community and the Southern California listening area, Bob's return to radio was magnificent. The 1956 to 1965 radio ratings war between Bob Crane and Dick Whittinghill was legendary on the West Coast. This was Snoopy and the Red Baron's Christmas truce, and it would last longer than one night. And with Bob's new television star status, KMPC knew his ratings would be strong.

After he spent a week substituting for Whittinghill in July 1972, KMPC approached Bob about becoming involved in radio more regularly, and so they negotiated for him to host a series of specials. The bargaining was a success. "I asked for the sun and the moon," Bob said in November of that year. "They gave me the sun and the moon, and that at least takes care of my alimony to my first wife!"

The first special Bob did that September had a back-to-school theme. A week earlier, he had taped the Timex special, *Make Mine Red, White, and Blue* with Fred Astaire, Michele Lee, and the Fifth Dimension, a salute providing a "music portrait of America and its people."

"It's easy," Bob said. "I was just at NBC taping the Fred Astaire special, and I took a cassette along and got Rowan and Martin and asked for their favorite funny recollections of school. It's much easier for me to handle it this way, instead of calling for an appointment. That way, I'm an out-of-work-actor-returning-to-radio. This way, I'm a working actor doing something on the side."

Former KMPC engineer Bob Maryon was Dick Whittinghill's primary engineer during the 1970s. When Bob substituted for Whittinghill, Maryon worked with Bob the same way as Bob's on-air engineers had at KNX.

"I was Whittinghill's engineer for fifteen years," Maryon said. "Every time Whittinghill would go on vacation, they would hire somebody to come in and fill in for him. And because he was a big personality in Los Angeles, they would hire people who the listeners would know, such as Mickey Rooney and Phyllis Diller. A lot of times, we'd have another DJ working with them. They had a big ad in the paper, and it showed them back-to-back, and talked about him filling in for Whittinghill and things like that. It was kind of exciting for me because I obviously knew who Bob Crane was. In addition to *Hogan's Heroes*, he had a great radio show. He had a lot of interviews and stuff, and he was a top man. He was strong competition. He was a very talented man and a very *nice* man."

Though Bob could have considered a return to radio as a step backward now that he had become a successful actor, Maryon believed Bob may have actually had something else in mind. "When Bob came back to KMPC," Maryon said, "he hadn't been on radio for many years, and he was a big TV star, and he had been a big radio star. In my mind—he never said this to me—but my *feeling* was this was like a big comeback for him. I think this was kind of like somebody who'd been away for awhile and now, 'I've come back and I'm really gonna do it right, and I'm really gonna lay everything out there.' And it was actually a big thing for KMPC, I think, because he was a very well-known personality on radio and television. I think Bob tried to do his show like he used to do when he was on KNX, but I don't remember him doing any interviews when he was at KMPC. But he was very dedicated to what he was doing. I mean, he wasn't coasting. It wasn't, 'I'm Bob Crane, and I can come back and coast here.' It wasn't that at all. It was very dedicated, very intense. It was a challenge for me because he really worked hard at the show, and I think he really wanted to do a comeback. He was probably more relaxed at KNX. But because I think this was sort of a comeback for him, I think it was very intense for him."

As had been the case with KNX, KMPC also granted Bob a waiver to perform his show to his liking, with his engineer handling the commercials and songs, and Bob having special dispensation to play other records throughout the show to enhance the performance. He was both prepared and off-the-cuff, producing his radio show as he had done so fluidly in the past.

"There was a lot of spontaneity," Maryon said. "We didn't sit at the beginning of the show and say 'We're gonna do this, do this, do this…

' It was spontaneous in the respect that his mind worked very fast, and he would decide at one moment, 'Let's do this or let's do that.' I think most of the things that we did, he pretty much decided at the spur of the moment to do."

Maryon recalled that Bob wanted his radio program to be run a certain way, and Maryon, as Bob's engineer, did as Bob requested. As he had done throughout his entire radio career, Bob performed his show the way he believed it should be performed to be successful, and that included integrating commercials into the show. More or less, it was the same type of program he had done at all of the stations before, which came as a little bit of a shock to the KMPC sales team. Yet according to Maryon, KMPC put no restrictions on Bob and did not interfere with how he ran his program.

"We did all kinds of things," Maryon explained. "He had me stopping commercials in the middle so he could lay a voice track in. The sales department wasn't too crazy about that. They used to say to me, 'You can't be stopping those commercials!' And I'd say to them, 'Well, he's the personality, and if that's what he wants, that's what I do.' I don't think you hire somebody like Bob and then say you can't do this and you can't do that. He does what he does. I think it was a little bit overdone because we did *so much*; he *wanted* so much. I don't think he crossed that line as far as getting in trouble with the FCC or anything like that. The only thing I got nervous about was the commercials. I think Bob wanted *so much* to make this a really successful, memorable week, that maybe he did a little bit too much, as far as voice tracks, and stopping commercials. I got the feeling that he was going to throw everything he had or could think of into this week. But again, I think it was a comeback for him to radio, and I think he really wanted to be dramatic and do a lot of stuff. It was different for me but it *worked*. I did what he wanted to do. I wasn't going to fight *him*, I was working *with* him. It was a different mindset, and it was more difficult because it was different from what I was used to doing. But it worked fine."

Bob's radio program was vastly different from Dick Whittinghill's show. With Whittinghill, Maryon said there was no schedule and no formal set up. Whittinghill would say something, and Maryon would react to it. He had the cartridges and lines prepared to feed to Whittinghill, but it was more laid back.

"In *Bob's* case, Bob had *very* specific ideas about *what* he wanted to do and *when* he wanted to do it, and *how* he wanted to do it," Maryon explained. "At KNX, he had referred to his booth and all four to six of his turntables as a *horseshoe*. And it looked like a horseshoe, basically. The reason they did that was because there was really no engineer that could keep up doing what he wanted them to do when he wanted it. So they brought [the horseshoe he had at KNX] to KMPC. They put it in the booth where he worked, and *I* played some of the stuff, and *he* played some of the stuff. There was an announcer's booth on one side, there was glass, and then there was the engineering booth. I had turntables and cartridge machines and tape machines. Then on the other side, we had put Bob's horseshoe, and we just put that in front, and we had a built-in microphone. But he had a lot of stuff in there he was playing, too. We were three feet away from each other. There was glass in between us, but we had an intercom system so we could talk back and forth. When I worked with Bob Crane, it was like I reacted to what he was doing."

Maryon said Bob wasn't nervous, even though he had been away from it for so long. As a radio veteran, he slid right back into it with both ease and intensity, although quite some time had passed and his status in the industry had changed. "I just saw an intensity to really go crazy," Maryon said. "To make this good."

According to Maryon, Bob was a "fascinating, hard-working, and *nice man*. I've worked with some people who have really big egos, and because of that they're not really pleasant to work with. I never found that with Bob. Bob just wanted to do a good show. He wanted to do it right. I think he wanted to recreate some of what he had done at KNX, and I think he wanted people to remember him, and he worked hard at it. I didn't find a great big ego there. I've certainly worked with people where it's very obvious. I didn't see that with Bob. I think he thought we were working together and we were doing things. I didn't see any, 'I'm God, and you're a little angel' or something. I never felt that. I wouldn't consider him guarded. He was just on. I didn't find him to be shy and inhibited when he was off the air. I found him good to work with. It was fun to work with him. It was more difficult because it was so *different* from what I had normally done. But it was *nice*. I looked forward to working with him. It was a challenge. He didn't give me any problems. He wasn't a guy who you thought, '[Sigh]…I gotta work with *him* again.' I *never* felt that way. I admired what he had done in radio; I admired what he did on *Hogan's Heroes*. So it was fun for me, it was a challenge for me, and I thought he was a nice person."

Occasionally, Bob would bring Bobby to work with him, as he had routinely done at WICC, KNX, *Hogan's Heroes*, and even *The Bob Crane Show,* where Bobby worked as assistant to the producer. As Bobby was growing older, Bob made the effort to include his son in all elements of the entertainment industry. Maryon recalled, "His son Bob used to come to visit sometimes, and we worked together for a week. And I can't remember the answer, but I remember when he first came in to me, he said, 'Well, I don't know what to call you,' because my name was Bob, too. He said, 'I don't know what to call you; that's really going to be confusing, if I call you Bob, and I'm Bob.' He ended up calling me something else! But it worked."

At the time, it appeared as though Bob was making a radio comeback. But later, in January 1977, he admitted to his former WICC boss, Manning Slater, that this was not the case. "As much as I loved radio, as hard as I worked at it, you can't go back," Bob said. "At least not now. I want to play down the radio stuff. I did a syndication special for radio [at KMPC]—I got $3,000 for it—and I know the guys on the air weren't earning a thousand a day. But the trade papers headlined it 'Crane Goes Back to Radio.' That hurt me."

But Bob continued to go back after KMPC, only never again as a paid employee of a station. Instead, he was an often-invited guest. Over the course of the 1970s, he entertained listeners over various radio stations across the country, often planned, sometimes by surprise. From July 18 to August 13, 1972, Bob was in Elk Grove Village, Illinois, outside of Chicago, performing in the stage production of *Who Was That Lady I Saw You With?* at the Pheasant Run Dinner Playhouse. As he drove around town on August 4 in a sports car convertible, he found himself at WCFL-1000 Radio, where he popped in for a Coca Cola. While he was there, he asked if they would like to interview him to promote his play. WCFL was happy to oblige, and Bob not only plugged his play, he also gave a historical account of his climb in the entertainment business.

In another instance, Bob was in Seattle, Washington, in 1977, performing his play *Beginner's Luck*. Country radio station KAYO-1150 AM called and asked Bob to come on the air as a guest for an hour. Bob brought with him segments from his celebrity interviews he conducted over KNX, including Jerry Lewis, Soupy Sales, Tennessee Ernie Ford, and Bob Hope, and played them over the air.

The Bob Crane Show
KMPC, Los Angeles, California – 1972-1973

July 5-10, 1972

Bob Crane, one of Southern California's top-rated radio personalities before his successful long run as star of *Hogan's Heroes*, made a return to radio July 5-10 on KMPC (710), taking over the 6:00 to 9:00 a.m. show for vacationing Dick Whittinghill. In previous years, Mayor Sam Yorty, astronaut Walter Cunningham, and Los Angeles Rams coach Tommy Prothro had filled in for Whittinghill.

September 15, 1972 – Back-To-School Special

Bob Crane presented interviews with celebrities who provided humorous stories about their school days (from 6:00 a.m. to 9:00 a.m.). Among the celebrities interviewed were Richard Dawson, Rowan and Martin, and Jerry Lewis.

November 23, 1972 – Thanksgiving Day Special

Bob Crane hosted the third of his six holiday specials on KMPC on Thanksgiving Day from 9:00 a.m. to 12:00 noon. The show was entitled "The Bob Crane Turkey Special" and featured celebrities providing examples of some of their biggest "bombs," including Mary Tyler Moore and Jerry Lewis.

December 31, 1972 – New Year's Eve Special

Bob Crane presented a five-hour New Year's Eve Big Band Special, and during the show, Bob featured more than sixty bands in a "live party sound" from his own personal record library. Bob divided the special into five, one-hour segments, not counting Guy Lombardo's midnight announcement:

9:00 p.m. – 10:00 p.m. – Tommy Dorsey, Glenn Miller, Benny Goodman, Count Basie

10:00 p.m. – 11:00 p.m. – Artie Shaw, Claude Thornhill, Lionel Hampton, Ray Anthony, Les Brown, Gene Krupa

11:00 p.m. – 12:00 a.m. – Duke Ellington, Harry James, Stan Kenton, Jimmy Dorsey, Jimmy Lanceford, Charlie Barnett

12:00 a.m. – Times Square, New York City, Guy Lombardo

12:05 a.m. – 1:00 a.m. – Woody Herman; Blood, Sweat, and Tears; Ted Heath; Don Ellis; Buddy Rich; Maynard Ferguson

1:00 a.m. – 2:00 a.m. – 40 Big Band themes from A to Z, from Herb Alpert to Si Zentner

February 9, 1973 – Valentine's Day Special

Bob Crane provided a medley of Frank Sinatra love songs, along with celebrity interviews about romance (6:00 a.m. – 9:00 a.m.).

April 13, 1973 – KMPC Spring Special

Bob Crane returned to KMPC to present a comedy KMPC Spring Special on Friday from 6:00 a.m. to 9:00 a.m. He promised "a guest list a mile long," including Chicago Mayor James Daley and John Wayne.

One of Bob's final radio broadcasts, occurred when he was in Connecticut from January 29 to February 1, 1976, to host the local portion of the United Cerebral Palsy Telethon in Hartford for his friend Eliot Dober. WICC was just kicking off its 50th anniversary celebration in January 1976, and Bob was more than happy to swing by Bridgeport and help the station celebrate by joining then-WICC on-air personality Al Warren for a live broadcast. Along with Al Warren, who was and still is a dear friend of Bob's cousin Jim Senich, others welcoming Bob to the station included WICC director of sales David Bodge, vice president and general manager Ray Colonari, and executive secretary Martha Gross.

Biography co-researcher and WICC assistant business manager Dee Young had been with WICC for only ten days when Bob visited the studios. She remembered greeting him in the lobby and shaking his hand as he got off the elevator.

"I always remember his smile," Dee said. "He had the greatest, *greatest* smile. He was so nice and pleasant to everybody, and he seemed very happy to be back in Bridgeport and visiting WICC."

WICC has always embraced and honored its former radio personality. When Bob went on the air on the afternoon of January 29, 1976, Al Warren introduced Bob to listeners as "a living legend." It had been almost twenty years since Bob had done last his WICC show before moving to Los Angeles, and he slid behind the mic as though no time at all had passed, sounding as comfortable as ever and giddy like a child.

"Invariably, whenever anybody mentions WICC," Al said during the 1976 broadcast, "they mention Bob Crane, still. You are, what you call, a living legend."

To that, Bob responded, "Let me just say, without WICC and being on this station in my early days in show business, nothing else would have happened for me along the line. The story goes, who's the one who gave you your start, or what helped you along the way. It was the fact that WICC has such a tremendous listening audience and a powerful signal. I don't know whether the antenna ground wires are still laying in Long Island Sound, but people used to say to me, 'Why is the station so popular?' I said, 'It's a good spot on the dial—600; and they've got their ground wires out in the water! And the water goes up and down the coast. So being in this town, you never know who's listening."

When Al asked Bob if the rumor was true, that he may go back to *Hogan's Heroes*, Bob quipped, "I may go back to WICC!"

Bob Crane: WICC's Legend

A January 30, 1976, article in *The Bridgeport Post* written by Tim Holley further exemplifies WICC's adoration of Bob, which still holds true today at WICC.

> Personality plus—that's Bob Crane, the former WICC disc jockey (now movie star) who was in town yesterday to help the Bridgeport radio station launch its 50th anniversary season.
>
> "I always had acting in the back of my mind," he told me at WICC. "Believe it or not, Jack Lemmon was my inspiration. I saw him in *Mr. Roberts* at the Stratford Theatre. I was just twenty-one or twenty-two at the time, and I thought some day, I would like to be an actor. What I saw in Jack Lemmon was a lot of what I was or am, but I tabled it and stuck to what I was doing and I became good. But because of this station and the advertising people who were listening to me, I got to Hollywood," he explained.
>
> "I don't want to sound conceited," Bob continued, "but people were intrigued with me and thought I was crazy and the word got around about this wacky disc jockey who could do ten commercials in ten minutes—what I did was make fun of the commercials."
>
> "So the word got around about this guy from Bridgeport who did something different. And I did. What I really wanted back then was to go to WNEW in New York. It was the Big Apple or nothing. But I got an offer for CBS in Boston for $700 a week, but I turned it down because they were not willing to transfer me to New York after my three year contract expired."
>
> "Then," Bob said, "KNX, the CBS station in Hollywood, heard about this guy who turned down $700 in Boston, and they just lost their morning person, and I got the job."
>
> "So I started out in Bridgeport for $55 a week, left earning $300 a week, and went on to $1,500 a week in Hollywood," the actor recalled.
>
> What's up for Bob? Well, possibly another military comedy series, which NBC is mulling over for next season. Right now, he's in Connecticut to host a Cerebral Palsy telethon this weekend in Hartford at the request of Eliot Dober of Bridgeport, also a former WICC employee.
>
> As I said, Bob is a super personality who is really Bridgeport's personal loss but the nation's gain.

"The *National Enquirer* had an article—a column item—a couple of weeks ago that *Hogan's Heroes* was going to be reactivated, but that was a misunderstanding," Bob declared. "I'm working with the producer of *Hogan's Heroes* right now, Ed Feldman. We're getting together a military show that involves the second World War but is *not Hogan's Heroes*. But the newspaper thought we were reviving it because it's the same initial people—it's the producer and the star of *Hogan's Heroes* getting together again. But we're not gonna do *Hogan's Heroes*."

Bob and Al then bantered back and forth on the air, reminiscing about Bob's days at WICC and reiterating with overflowing sentiment how much WICC treasured him as part of its radio station history.

Following his broadcast on WICC, Bob, along with wife Patty and son Scotty, continued on to Hartford, where Bob hosted the telethon. On February 1, 1976, after the live broadcast of the telethon, Bob received a phone call from back home in Los Angeles. His father, who had suffered a heart attack a few days prior, died unexpectedly.

It was crushing news, and Bob was devastated. Despite his father's heart attack, Bob had opted to stay in Connecticut to fulfill his obligations for the telethon. He was overcome with grief. As soon as they could, he and his family packed up and rushed home. But inclement weather stalled their trip, delaying them in Chicago.

"I remember my dad getting the phone call," Scott Crane said. "It was one of the worst winter storms Chicago ever had—they closed O'Hare for about two weeks. We couldn't get a plane out to get back to LA when he died of a heart attack. And I remember seeing my dad so broken up—just really, really destroyed and crying about the loss of his father."

"You've no idea how bad everyone felt, especially after he did such a wonderful job for us on the telethon," said Eliot Dober, who had driven Bob and his family to Bradley Airport in Windsor Locks, Connecticut, for their flight home.

The death of Bob's father marked the beginning of a time when Bob started to re-evaluate his life and career. It was a turbulent period marked with both extreme highs and lows as he sought an inner peace he was not sure how to find. But Bob turned the harsh magnifying glass of introspection on himself and searched deep within his soul to find the answer, hoping to rebuild his life and career. And he was confident that he would succeed.

December 19, 1977. Six days before Christmas, Bob stepped off a plane in Los Angeles, coming home for the holidays after a stint in Ohio performing what had by now become his signature play, *Beginner's Luck*. Waiting for him was an early and bitter Christmas present: divorce papers from Patty's lawyer.

Two months earlier, on October 19, 1977, and just three days after their seventh wedding anniversary, Patty retained legal counsel and began preparing to end their marriage. By the time Bob got home, she was ready to act. Bob and Patty had been having problems since the death of his father, and their arguments had escalated, to the point where both of them had, at one time or another, threatened to call it quits.

Still, Bob was shattered when the threat became reality.

Beginner's Luck cast member Victoria Berry Wells was with Bob when the papers were served. "He was *so* upset," Victoria explained. "That crippled him. And he was so concerned about his son, Scotty. That's all he talked about. He went through a hard time when he was handed the divorce papers—it upset him *tremendously.*"

Bob was shaken to the core, and very soon, this upsetting splash of cold water would become a strong motivator in his quest for change and renewal. But in the meantime, he needed to work, so he drove himself onward.

In early 1978, Bob accepted three distinct job offers, two of which would come to define the end of his career. The other was a lesser-known series to be filmed entirely on location in Hawaii.

In February 1978, Bob agreed to host a new half-hour television series called *The Hawaii Experience*. The format was relatively new at that time—a reality show. Bob would serve as the host, going behind the scenes of some of the most exquisite resorts on the islands, talking the viewers through places that most of them would never have a chance to see for themselves.

Producer and director John Orland explained, "Wally Sherwin came up with an idea about doing an updated travelogue on videotape as opposed to most of the travelogues and travel shows that had been photographed on film. But videotape for location for small projects was just coming into vogue. We spoke about it, and I really liked the idea of filming something that had an immediate, live look, although the show was not going to be live, it would have that live look, like reality television does now. So we decided to go ahead with the project. The plan for the show was to go all over all of the Hawaiian Islands. The very fact that it was called *The Hawaii Experience* meant it was going to be a show that took in aspects and facets of *all* the islands."

Orland said that *The Hawaii Experience* was going to be a star vehicle for Bob. Some local personalities who were very well known in Hawaii were also going to take part. But this was a show that Bob was going to carry entirely on his own. Orland had only known Bob from his work on *Hogan's Heroes* and considered it a privilege to work with him.

"It really is about formulating the questions and keeping the host on track as to how you want them to adhere to the questions and not deviate too much from what the goals are of the interview, and also just making him comfortable with the facts that he was given about a particular environment or setting or the people he was going to be dealing with. You have to have the cameras on the right people, the group, and whoever's speaking. You don't want it to be on someone else. It's very instantaneous how you have to manage that."

The entire pilot was filmed off the cuff—a "run and gun shoot," Orland explained. Without major studio financial support, the pilot worked from a shoestring budget. The equipment truck had no air conditioning, and with the humidity, the videotape machines kept jamming.

"We had a person with a hair dryer that had to sit inside the truck and keep blowing air on the video tape recorder so they wouldn't condense with moisture and stop," Orland said.

When Bob traveled to Oahu to film the pilot, his son Bobby joined him, which had become the norm rather than the exception. "As I recall, the son was very quiet," Orland said. "It almost seemed like how you would look at a golfer and a caddy. His son always seemed to be there, but just was quiet and just sort of acted like a security blanket for Bob."

This type of show also broke Bob's vow of never playing host on a television program. His singular goal had always been fixed on acting, and he had turned down countless offers to host a talk show. In a letter he wrote to a business associate in 1977, he said, "I'd prefer to continue acting. But after a six-year wait since *Hogan's Heroes*, not forgetting *The Bob Crane Show* for NBC three years ago, I really have to face the realities of the situation." In other words, Bob needed the money, and hosting came naturally to him. According to Orland, however, Bob was quite receptive to this new reality show concept and embraced the novel format.

"He was very, very at ease, and there was no resistance to doing it," Orland said. "In fact, it was almost the opposite. This opened up a new dimension for him. And I think partly because of the technology of doing a show on location—a remote show—using videotape in the manner that we were using it, it was sort of a new concept at the time. Here we were going to be doing a series with just a few people who were just sort of going to the locations and doing the interviews and doing it in a much more freeform, spontaneous atmosphere. So I think he saw it as sort of technology opening up a door for him to maybe go back and do something that he resisted in the past. It was that kind of shoot that I think attracted Bob Crane because it was not a typical studio shoot. It was going to be like a news show. It was going to be about Hawaii and all of the tourist spots and in-depth stories about the various things, some of which the public would be able to see and other things the public would not really be readily exposed to."

This had not been the only talk show in the 1970s that Bob decided to host. In February 1977, Bob explored a new idea for a talk show. According to the press, his concept was to turn "has-beens and once-weres into a television rage," and he hoped his recognition of Colonel Hogan would allow him to capitalize on nostalgia. The series, with the working title *Whatever Became Of?*, would feature Bob in an interview format, talking with celebrities and other public figures of a bygone era that had faded into oblivion.

It was, Bob claimed, the first television program that he ever agreed to host, he had liked the concept *that* much. It made sense in that it was very similar to what Bob had done at KNX, and most likely, some of the people he would have wanted to interview were the very same celebrities he had talked to over the KNX airwaves.

"The problem would be to keep it from being downbeat," Bob explained. "For every one who continues, there are 120,000 who sink into oblivion. A lot depends on the way you do the interview. I try to keep it light, yet get the information. We try to strike a balance. I think it works. There are people who do have a successful 1977 frame of reference. They are not all driving garbage trucks somewhere."

But it seemed that despite Bob's wit and humor, not everyone cared to be interviewed or wanted to promote themselves as has-beens.

"One interview was with the man who played Buckwheat as a child in the old *Our Gang* films," Bob explained. "I could tell he was uncomfortable. I tried to make him feel better by saying people weren't just wondering what happened to Buckwheat, but also what ever became of Bob Crane. He said, 'Yeah, I was wondering that myself.'"

The show never took off, even though Bob believed it in. "I saw in it an appeal and human interest—talking to characters who were part of people's lives in the movies or politicians or whatever. There is an endless array of names or semi-names who would have a heck of a story."

The Hawaii Experience had a much different angle and was more positive. Plus, what better way for Bob to recreate himself and make a come back than as a traveling host who brought his audience with him into the otherwise public-restricted areas of restaurants and resorts of the Hawaiian Islands?

"Bob got involved with *The Hawaii Experience* I believe because of his relationship with Wally Sherwin," John Orland recalled. "Wally had been news director of KHJ television and also general manager of KHJ television, and I believe also had a radio background. So somehow through all of that, Bob and Wally Sherwin got together."

Bob also wasn't above getting a little wild and crazy as the host. One segment was filmed at Sea Life Park on the island of Oahu. There, Bob interviewed the person in charge of the park and discussed how the attendants dealt with the various sea creatures. As part of the interview, Bob ended up climbing in the tank and riding on the back of a whale.

"He was hanging on for dear life!" Orland remembered. "He was, he was! I mean, it was a wild animal, and somehow, Bob got on and rode it! But he was very willing to do it. It wasn't something that we had to push him into doing. I didn't get a sense of any ego whatsoever, I mean, you always run into crowd control issues when you're with someone. And you look at them as just another human being and a work associate, but then people all over Hawaii, 'Oh, that's Bob Crane.' They would ask him for his autograph and prove to be a little bit disruptive. But he seemed to be very willing to sign autographs and basically played the role of who he was."

It should come as no surprise that in the role of host, Bob found himself at home and extremely comfortable. According to Orland, "He was very instinctual. In fact, that part of it with Bob was quite easy. He was a natural interviewer, and he was also a good listener. Part of being a good interviewer is being a good listener, so that when the person is speaking, the interviewer is listening, and that just opens up the interviewee. It allows them to continue speaking about whatever the subject is. If the interviewer doesn't seem to be interested or jumps in too many times and makes it about them, then the interview doesn't succeed. Bob was very, very cooperative. Always pleasant."

But not everything had been pleasant. While filming on location, Bob complained to Orland about his personal life and dissolving marriage. He mentioned that "things were totally out of hand, and he was unhappy about that."

The pilot sold and was to be produced for syndication on what was the dawn of cable television. Yet *The Hawaii Experience* would never see production, and this time, the reasons were not poor ratings or lack of interest. Instead, the reason was grave and unthinkable.

The 1977-1978 television season was rich with innovative programs that stretched the boundaries of the medium like never before. One of these new programs looked at the misadventures of people confined in a luxury cruise ship. *The Love Boat* premiered on May 5, 1977. Starring Gavin MacLeod, Bernie Kopell, Fred Grandy, Ted Lange, and Lauren Tewes, the *Pacific Princess* set sail for love, exciting and new, and traveled the seas with nearly every celebrity imaginable for the next ten years.

Bob Crane appeared on the show's thirteenth episode in the segment, entitled "Family Reunion." The last time he worked with lead actor Gavin MacLeod, MacLeod had been a guest on *Hogan's Heroes,* and Bob had been the star. Now, the roles were reversed.

But that wasn't the only big difference; this time, Bob took on a very serious, emotionally charged role.

In the segment, Bob portrays ship steward Edward "Teddy" Anderson, who is more interested in having a good time than working, causing Captain Steubing much grief in the process. As Teddy goes about his work, he comes across a photograph of his daughter, with whom he has lost touch. Overcome with emotion, he seeks advice from his boss. Bob's scenes are dramatic and very emotional, and soon, his work on this episode would become extraordinarily difficult to watch for his family, friends, and fans.

Coming to terms with his bad behavior and lost relationship with his adult daughter, Bob's character breaks down in tears. And the tears Bob shed while playing the role were real.

Bob's daughter Karen noted in her interview with Ed Robertson for *TV Confidential*, "I do remember asking my dad how he got himself to cry after that episode. I was on the set when they were taping it, and my dad was going through his divorce from his second wife at the time. Things got really heated while going through that divorce, and that's what was going on in his head at this time when he had to dig up these tears in his eyes."

It had its desired effect. For maybe the first time, Bob had pushed himself to achieve the heightened drama, something that had always been out of his comfort zone. It was also an indication of how he was not only pushing his limits in acting, but how he was coming to terms with the problems in his life.

His demeanor on the set, however, was typical of him as an actor and as a person. Ted Lange, who played bartender Isaac Washington on the series, said he was comfortable working with Bob and enjoyed the experience.

"As I remember it, he was very professional," Lange explained. "Professional and fun. Low key. I remember in between set ups, we talked. He knew what to do and how to do it. This guy was very relaxed. He of course came to work prepared. He knew comedy, so getting to the joke was easy for him, as me. I felt we had an immediate chemistry. I also felt he respected me as an artist, and we trusted each other in our finding what made the scene work. I did notice that he listened intently to the director, but somehow made the words his own, while making sure he incorporated what the director wanted. We did not talk about any of his future projects. I do remember we laughed a lot."

Bob also gave Lange advice on his career, which Lange remembered with great fondness.

"I got a chance to tell him about my other ambitions as a talent in Hollywood. One of the things I wanted to do was to be a TV director. I told him how hard it was being black and trying to get producers to take me seriously about my branching out. He said he understood, which I thought was odd. He is a white guy; how could he understand? Then he reminded me that on his show, *Hogan's Heroes*, was an actor named Ivan Dixon. He was black and had similar ambitions. He was able to convince the producers that he was serious and capable. 'Hang in there, it will happen,' Bob said to me. I smiled and thought to myself, 'Yeah, but you don't know these guys; this stuff ain't easy.' The break was over, and we went back to filming the close ups in our scene. But within the fifth year of *The*

Love Boat, I was given a directing assignment on the show. I got into the Directors Guild of America (DGA) and have directed other TV shows since. When I think back on how positive Bob was that it would happen, I have to smile. Because he was right!"

Actress Victoria Carroll, who had also worked with Bob on *Hogan's Heroes* as a guest star, shared a few scenes with Bob in this episode of *The Love Boat* as his character Teddy's girlfriend. She noted that he still seemed to be the same.

"There wasn't that much difference, actually," Victoria said. "He was still very professional. Very nice. There was really no interaction. We didn't talk and say, 'How's the family? How are you? What's new?' between takes. I would see him when we hit our marks, and we'd do the scene, and 'Good to see you,' and that was it. But I didn't see any difference at all. He was his very personable self."

Up until this point, Bob had been defined solely as a comedic actor. But his ability to dig deep down and effectively portray a vulnerable character showed a seismic shift in his abilities since his struggles to play it straight in *The Bob Crane Show* a few years earlier. In spite of his "method, schmethod" attitude, where he proclaimed in 1976, "I've studied the Method, [and] all things you do on television are an offshoot of your own personality or something you find yourself comfortable doing," Bob had *finally* done what Stella Adler drilled into his head—and that he had written down—so long ago: "Open up without shame."

And it worked.

Bob's potential as a dramatic actor was finally realized. But airing only six months before he was killed, his journey on *The Love Boat* came, in hindsight, to be seen as representative of his state of mind, instead of his expanding abilities as a performer. Again, people thought it was Bob playing *himself*. Again, ignoring the *fact* that Bob *could* act.

One other television appearance in early 1978 made an indelible—and inaccurate—impression on Bob's life and career. But this time, it had nothing to do with Bob's work and everything to do with one man's interpretation.

Celebrity Cooks was a Canadian cooking program produced and filmed in Vancouver, British Columbia. Host Bruno Gerussi invited celebrities to join him on the show, where together, they prepared a meal the guest considered a favorite.

Gerussi described it as, "Good food, good wine, good conversation, good music, shared with good people is my idea of a good time. Put this on television, and things will start cooking."

Derek Smith produced the series under his flagship company Initiative Productions Limited. He wrote the following in *The New "Celebrity Cooks" Cookbook*: "Our idea was to provide an entertaining half-hour of frivolous kitchen capers. We stayed well away from the rigid "how-to-do-it" format common to cooking shows. While many of our guests assured us that they could prepare wonderful creations in their homes, they were often hopelessly inept at displaying their culinary talents to a nationwide TV audience. Yet, the results were always entertaining, and more often, hilarious. And that, after all, is what *Celebrity Cooks* is all about."

Anne Kear was the talent agent for *Celebrity Cooks* on January 25, 1978, when Bob's show was taped.

"We taped three shows per evening," she said. "Bob did one show. The other guest that evening was the legendary Julia Child. It was just the most wonderful afternoon and evening. She did two shows. She did one, Bob was in the middle—he was the second guest. And Julia changed clothes and came back. We started at seven o'clock p.m. for the first shoot. So Bob Crane was on about eight o'clock p.m. We taped his show around eight o'clock p.m., and then Julia Child taped her show next. Bob had met Julia Child. He was so nice, and he was thrilled to meet Julia Child. He had watched her first show on the monitor in the green room while waiting for his episode."

The episodes were aired quickly following their taping. Derek Smith said that Bob's episode would have aired at least five times, maybe six, in Canada over the CBC network. Anne Kear concurred, saying that the first air date would likely have been the following week or early February.

Bob prepared Chicken á la *Hogan's Heroes* with Bruno Gerussi. Derek Smith, Anne Kear, and stage manager Roger Packer, all present on the day of taping, declared that Bob had been one of the *best* guests to ever appear on their show. However, within a few months, the truth about Bob's appearance on *Celebrity Cooks* would be analyzed by one lone network spokesman, and as a result, distorted beyond recognition.

He stood by the rail of the ship, looking down at the crowd below on the docks in San Pedro, California. They were waving at him, smiling, and cheering. They loved him—adored him, even—and they wanted him to respond.

Only he didn't feel like responding. He respected, appreciated, and loved his fans, but at that moment, he was angry with them.

Far above the crowd, safely behind the ship's rail, he heard them shouting, "Hogan! Hey, Hogan!" He cringed, resenting their chant. Pursing his lips, he shook his head, almost as if in defeat. Under his breath, and with only one reporter able to hear him, Bob mumbled, "Crane, you bastards; the name is *Bob Crane*."

Hogan's Heroes was still in production at the time this incident occurred, but it was a premonition of things to come—that Bob's own identity was eroding and being slowly overtaken by his on-screen persona. It did not help that CBS forced Bob to appear in the Hogan uniform, jacket, and crush cap for almost all public appearances in the effort to promote the series. And while he had enjoyed the series and the role, he also recognized the damage the ongoing association with Hogan could do, and was doing, to his career. Typecasting worried him.

According to his cousin Jim Senich, Bob often asked: "Is there a world after *Hogan's Heroes*?" Bob spent most of the 1970s trying to find out.

It was a problem not exclusive to Bob. Even Werner Klemperer reached out to Bob in 1977 with the idea of revisiting *Hogan's Heroes* as a new vehicle for them both. But Bob would not hear of it, and the idea was abandoned before it even began.

"Bob was a talented guy," Jim said. "He would have landed something. Something would have happened. He was too good. But he worried about it. He was upbeat except in letters to me where he would say he was really having a rough time moving on in his career. He would say, 'Only you in the family would understand. I can't get a break, Jim. I'm Colonel Hogan to everybody.' He worried about being typecast after *Hogan's Heroes*. He worried about that. He said to me, 'I'm gonna be Colonel Hogan for the rest of my life, Jimmy. I'm trying to get movie parts, more TV shows, but they say, 'You're Colonel Hogan; you're Colonel Hogan.'"

But he was trying. *Always, he tried.*

In 1966, Bob observed: "There just isn't enough greatness available anywhere to insure great television for sixteen or seventeen hours a day, seven days a week, week after week, and year after year. And it might be worth remembering, neither has there ever been enough greatness around to provide that much great literature, that much great painting, that much great sculpture, that much great music, nor, for that matter, that much great bricklaying or bookkeeping or bartending or pole-vaulting.

"Television programming is no different than automobiles or footwear or any other product intended for consumption by the masses. There are enough different qualities, styles, sizes, and materials to satisfy everybody, but in order to find the best—or whatever it is that you as an individual want—you have to be selective. I've yet to hear anyone complain because every pitcher isn't a Sandy Koufax, because every car isn't a Rolls Royce, because every college boy isn't a Rhodes Scholar or because every day isn't Christmas. That kind of impossible perfection is expected, it seems, only of television.

"Another of those awkward little hitches to performing in a television series such as *Hogan's Heroes* is that some of the people who see you on their screens every week let you know what they think is wrong with your show. 'The trouble with your show is that it's giving my kids the idea that World War II was nothing but a load of laughs.' If you're depending on your kids getting their history lesson solely from a television comedy show, it's you—not we—who are going wrong. Entertainment is what we're presenting. We can't purport to be educational."

Bob viewed himself as an entertainer first and foremost. He yearned for greatness, and in the face of setbacks, he picked himself up, brushed himself off, and tried again. He would never stop trying.

Grander things were on the horizon for Bob Crane. A new military comedy series. A new reality show. Cutting his teeth in more serious, dramatic parts from which he had previously shied away. Bob was *finally* on the brink of breaking free of the grip Colonel Hogan had on him, and not only was he striving to reinvent himself as an actor, but he was also working at bettering himself as a person.

He just never lived long enough to accomplish any of it.

Bob Crane's *Celebrity Cooks* Appearance
Fact vs. Fiction

When Bob Crane was brutally murdered on June 29, 1978, it was a little more than one week before the CBS affiliate station in New York had slated Bob's episode of *Celebrity Cooks* to air. As a knee-jerk reaction to Bob's untimely and gruesome death, CBS spokesman Jeff Erdel made the executive decision to scrap the episode, which had been scheduled to air on July 10, 1978, in the United States.

"Things about death kept cropping up all through the show," Erdel said in an interview on July 5. "It struck me as so ironic when I heard he was dead. I don't know if there were serious overtones in the death jokes. I'm no psychologist, but there were just so many that involved death."

Erdel also claimed that Bob had talked about the death of "at least one, maybe two, of the characters" on *Hogan's Heroes*. Erdel added that Bob's conversation was loaded with innuendo and jokes about sex, and that Bob whiplashed from despair about his separation and impending divorce from Patty to enthusiasm about his swinging sex life.

In stark opposition to these claims, those affiliated with *Celebrity Cooks*—producer Derek Smith, talent agent Anne Kear, and stage manager Roger Packer, all of whom were present on the day Bob's episode taped—claim *emphatically* that not only was Bob a terrific guest, he was perhaps one of their *best* guests to ever appear on the show. They were appalled that Erdel's version of events has been accepted as the truth, insisting that nothing Erdel claimed ever actually happened. In fact, they said that *if* Bob acted inappropriately in any way, or *if* he had broken down on the set, they would have either stopped tape and started over, or cancelled the episode altogether. Instead, Bob's episode taped without any problems, and it went on to air in Canada as planned in early 1978.

To the best of our research, film footage of this episode no longer exists, either with the CBC, Global Entertainment, or the people involved with the show who we contacted; therefore, it is impossible for us to provide a conclusive report. We will, however, provide both Erdel's claims as reported by Will Tusher in 1978 and the complete interviews done for this book with those on the set the day Bob's episode was filmed. It is important to note that Erdel's account is secondhand—presented by a reporter and accepted as truth with no verification by anyone connected with the show, whereas the accounts by Smith, Kear, and Packer are firsthand—given by people *who were there*. The episode in question that Erdel pulled because *he* was uncomfortable with it actually aired in Canada several times without a hint of opposition from the networks or audiences. And no one present at the taping considered Bob's behavior odd, inappropriate, or unable to be shown to daytime television audiences—a time when even children might be watching.

While we cannot prove that what Erdel claims in the article is incorrect, the behavior he described would have been extremely out of character for Bob, who—as we have shown—was very capable in keeping his personal life separate from his work. Therefore, it seems more likely that Erdel's version of events *never happened*, and that his story, left unchecked and published at a time when the public was grasping for any information to make sense of Bob's murder, forced a footnote on to Bob's life that was completely false.

Jeff Erdel, CBS Spokesman
(Excerpt Reprinted from Hollywood Reporter Will Tusher's Article, "Who Really Murdered Bob Crane?" – 1978)

Even more prophetic, perhaps, were the words that came out of Bob Crane's own mouth when he went to Vancouver, British Columbia, to tape a guest appearance on a syndicated half-hour TV show called *Celebrity Cooks*. In the almost three years he was doing the show, host Bruno Gerussi probably never had a more voluble, entertaining, unsettling, and revealing guest.

The first U.S. station to buy the series for daytime airing Monday through Friday was WCBS-TV Channel 2, in New York City. The show was scheduled to premiere with the Crane segment. But then murder intervened, and the station withdrew the Crane episode in the interest of good taste. Airing the show was considered even more questionable in light of Crane's behavior on it.

Station press manager Jeff Erdel had screened the show several times—at least once after the murder—and he was so struck by the relevance of what Crane said at the time to his murder two months later that he had virtually committed Crane's remarks to memory. He found Crane's own revelations and insights so eerie, so revealing, that he was surprised that the Scottsdale police had failed to contact him.

At the time, WCBS-TV was the only station in the U.S. that had bought the *Celebrity Cooks* series.

If he had to strike a balance, Erdel said that Crane was slightly more obsessed with death than sex in his remarks, but he could not escape the feeling that the two somehow were interlocked. Crane joked about death as he quipped about sex, and he dwelled on both compulsively.

Says Erdel, "It was one of the most amazing things I've ever seen in my ten years in the business... I still get this weird feeling... Crane was a very funny, warm, sensitive individual—but there was something eerie about the show. A lot of jokes told in the double-entendre style and a heck of a lot of them had to do with death... He talked about the death of some people who were on *Hogan's Heroes*. It seemed to have an effect on him."

Before Crane was murdered, Erdel relates, the actor was struck by an uncanny sense of déjà vu.

"There was an air of death about the whole show," he notes, "and then it really happened," he added solemnly.

"I don't know which there was more of—jokes about death or jokes about sex," Erdel muses. "They all seemed to hinge on the fact that his marriage came down around his ears. He was obviously very distraught about this. He loved his second wife very much, evidently. And he seemed obsessed by the fact that he was separated and she was suing for divorce. There was an awful lot of this. It was, in total, a rather tragic portrait which stuck in my mind."

Remember the old Sinatra song about love and marriage going together? In Crane's case, as he let it all hang out on *Celebrity Cooks*, love and marriage and sexual freedom and death were all enigmatically and prophetically intermingled.

"Now that I think about it," Erdel reflects, "there were more references to sex than there were to death. He went on at great length about his marriage. At this point, he was very anxious to put his life back together again and to carry on and to meet other women."

The seeming contradiction was inescapable. Also inescapable was the fact that the troubled Bob Crane was torn with contradictions. In one and the same breath he mourned the break up of his marriage and yet seemed to welcome the separation as license to be up willy nilly with other women.

"There were some suggestive remarks," Erdel recalls. "There were remarks which could be construed as implying infidelity."

He cannot come up with specific instances, but Erdel stands by his insistence that that was definitely his impression in the screenings of the Crane segment.

"There were an awful lot of comments about young women, about meeting young women, particularly well-proportioned young women," Erdel recounts. "About some of the women who appeared on *Hogan's Heroes* (Pat [Olson] was playing Hilda on *Hogan's Heroes* when Bob Crane fell in love with her. He divorced his first wife, Anne Terzian, in 1970 and married Pat the same year.)

"He said a lot of things that would indicate he was very sorry his marriage was going to pot. There would seem to be a contradiction, wouldn't there? But, like [Bob] said, he was somewhat distraught."

In one illuminating episode, Crane confessed that the dish he had chosen to cook on the show—Chicken á la *Hogan's Heroes*—was his estranged wife's recipe.

"It seemed to sort of stick in his throat, not to make a bad pun," Erdel said.

"Crane said that was one of the things he was going to miss about his wife—the cooking," Erdel remembers. "Then quickly, with very good comedic timing, he added that was not the most important thing he'll miss."

The sexual allusion was not lost on the alert-as-usual studio audience.

"Of course," Erdel nods, "that drew a big laugh."

The big contradiction refused to go away. Bob Crane kept yearning for his wife while at the same time thirsting for sexual encounters with other ladies.

"In addition to going back constantly (to his ambivalent feeling about his wife), he was very preoccupied with going to discos and meeting people at disco—particularly well-endowed young women," says Erdel.

Disco was code for women, and Crane kept stressing the connection. Discos were where the action was. That was where bosomy bedroom companions were to be found.

Crane also could not resist sharing a ribald story illustrating hardships of a touring actor.

"He was saying," Erdel states, "that actors frequently wear special shorts which have the fly sewn over to avoid accidents on stage."

Are there any viable clues in Bob Crane's prophetic appearance on *Celebrity Cooks*—or merely revealing insights? Death and sex. Like love and marriage, they sometimes go together.

The following are three interviews by people with *Celebrity Cooks*, conducted by Linda J. Groundwater (LG) and Carol M. Ford (CF) for the sole purpose of this book. Derek Smith, Anne Kear, and Roger Packer were each present on the day Bob's episode taped. These are their first-hand recollections.

Derek Smith
Owner and Producer, *Celebrity Cooks*
Interview – June 19, 2009

Derek Smith (DS): I'm happy to set a wrong right because I don't like what I've been hearing. We had no such experience whatsoever like that.

LG/CF: We have an article from a magazine that discusses *Celebrity Cooks*, and the whole impression that the world has of Bob's appearance is from someone who supposedly simply watched the tape. Because of this article—and this article was then quoted in the book by Robert Graysmith and depicted in the film *Auto Focus*—the taping of this episode of *Celebrity Cooks* was always regarded as Bob's life beginning to completely unravel. That he couldn't hide his lifestyle, that he was upset when he was on the air, that his marriage was falling apart, that he was very distraught about it and visibly distressed on the air, and that he was obsessed with death and with sex. Is that the experience you had?

DS: No, not at all. *Not at all.* Quite the opposite. Quite the opposite. A well-together, fun gentleman. Full of laughs. A real professional. The most well-adjusted person you'd ever want to meet.

LG/CF: Now, what the CBS spokesman said he got out of what he watched was that the show was loaded with jokes about death, jokes about sex, discussion of Bob's marriage that was breaking down, the whole idea of him going on at great length about his marriage and trying to bring it all back together. My experience of watching celebrity cooking shows is that they are not in-depth discussions of the guest's or star's personal life.

DS: Not really. The show was broken down into three portions. There was an interview portion off the top, a cooking portion in the second segment that kind of went over into the third, and then they ate the food at the end. I was there; I was standing not ten feet away from them watching the show being taped. Roger Packer was even closer than I was, and none of us got any of that impression whatsoever. It's interesting that fellow from WCBS—the only American station that did play that show was WCBS. And I'm talking not just about that show, but we sold them sixty-five shows to play over the summer season. So I'm not surprised that this man would've seen the show. However, I don't know how he got that impression at all.

LG/CF: If you could see this show from your memory of being there without any knowledge of Bob's lifestyle, his coming death, would there be anything to the casual observer to indicate that there was something

either preoccupying him, unusual happening in his life...something? Was there anything that would have made that show stand out to you?

DS: I can't say yay or nay one way or another. I certainly can't think of something specific at all. The only thing I remember specifically from the show—he says to Bruno, "There are two cannibals talking, and one says the other, 'I can't stand my mother-in-law,' and the other cannibal says, 'Well, just eat the peas.'" That was the only joke about anything having to do with death.

And then at the end, the food wasn't cooked, so they had a laugh about that, too. That's all I recall from that show. I've got a awful memory, unfortunately, and I *could've* missed something, but by and large—I'm the owner of the show, and Anne Kear worked for me, and so did Roger, and I used to tell Anne to book comedians or funny people because I like to laugh, and so she did. And I remember that show made me laugh, from beginning to end. And if there were any off-color jokes, we would've stopped tape. And I don't recall any death references, unless they were in a joking fashion, but they certainly couldn't have been anything serious enough for me to stop tape.

So to really answer your questions is very, very difficult.

I do remember what he said to me at the end. When we were going back to the hotel, he said to me, "Where can I get some action?" And I said, "Well, I don't really have any numbers, but if you wanna go over there, you might find something you were looking for."

LG/CF: But it wasn't something that came up during work—like, he stopped work to go disappear?

DS: No. No, no, no, no. And, the action he was looking for was probably just companionship, as we say. It's difficult for people out of town.

LG/CF: How did you end up meeting him? Did you meet him when he came out or had you already met him before when Anne had booked him?

DS: I don't remember that day, but generally, I would meet [the guests] in the afternoon, just to say hello. And then they would go away to do their thing, and we didn't tape till the evening, so we brought the audience in around seven o'clock p.m., and we would have our lunch around that time. At seven-thirty, we would roll tape, and we'd shoot three shows. Bob was just one of the three. We shot three shows in an evening. I don't remember what number Bob was, but we shot the show, and went onto the next one, and the next one, and then we all went home. But nothing stands out in my mind at all—nothing unusual.

LG/CF: How was he on set? Did he understand easily how it was all to work? Was he relaxed?

DS: Oh, very relaxed, absolutely. He was very professional about what he was doing. He knew precisely what he was going to do, as much as anyone else—because most of them weren't cooks. They came on and cooked something for the first time. He probably went through that checklist to see if everything was there. And then we had our lunch. Actually, the guests had their lunch with the production crew upstairs; the technical crew had a lunch somewhere else. And usually I was a part of that lunch, but I don't remember being part of it that day. But Anne would remember. She was kind of a shepherd.

LG/CF: I think the taping of what was ultimately an innocent show somehow had its reputation changed due to the fact that Bob was going through some very personal stuff at that time.

DS: I got a call from the *National Enquirer* when [he was murdered], and of course, I just refused to speak to them. But that show was *never* pulled from the airdate.

LG/CF: It must've aired very shortly after his death.

DS: I don't know. I do know I would've known when the show was pulled, because we only had one show that was ever pulled, and that's because one of the guests said something libelous, and the lawyers wouldn't allow us to air the show. But that was the only show that ever did *not* air, so I know that the show aired, and it aired in its sequence. Again, when, I don't know.

LG/CF: Was there a long timeframe between the original taping and the air date?

DS: Sometimes there would be; sometimes not very often. The host of the show, Bruno Gerussi, did another series concurrent with this one, so we'd sort of shoot a month on, month off, kind of thing. So it's possible there was quite a bit of time between, other times not. In general, there's no rule.

LG/CF: This article I am looking at said the first U.S. station to buy the series was supposed to show the episode that Bob was in the [week] after he died—and they pulled it—but that doesn't mean it never aired originally in Canada.

DS: It certainly aired in Canada. It would've aired in Canada at least five times. They might've pulled it in CBS New York, that's possible, but it certainly aired in Canada, for sure. And each show had at least five or six air shows in Canada.

LG/CF: [To sum up], the WCBS fellow who watched the show said Bob was obsessed with sex and with death, and that has turned that whole episode into such a big false indicator of his life.

DS: Just not true. *Absolutely* not true.

Roger Packer
Stage Manager, *Celebrity Cooks*
Interview – June 19, 2009

LG/CF: Tell us your story.

Roger Packer (RP): I was an employee of the Canadian Broadcasting Corporation (CBC). I worked for them for thirty-three years. I moved up the ranks—I eventually directed and produced, but I was brought up as a floor manager and an audience warm-up person. On *Celebrity Cooks*, I was assigned by CBC to Derek Smith, the producer, and I worked for him as floor manager, meaning I would cue the action—stop and start and cut and all that—and also I would warm up the audience before the show and get them ready to bring the host out, who would do a little warm up, too. So that was my function. And I used to plug the *Celebrity Cooks* cookbooks, too, in the intermission. I worked for them for about three seasons/years. We must've done over sixty programs before it was cancelled, and they had already done a lot of them in Ottawa before it came to Vancouver.

We had many guests come in. Most were met at the airport by Anne Kear—she was the talent coordinator. She would arrange for these people through various agencies and things in Hollywood and New York and Toronto to get these people to come. Lots of them came from California—Bob came from California—and we used to have them come on Canadian-specific airlines. And they would arrive and be brought to the studio and made comfortable in a reception room, like a little dressing room, and they would come in and do their rehearsal. I would meet them and we would walk through what they were going to do, and then we usually did two [or three] shows a night, so we had two guests, some guests did two shows, some did one, whatever.

Then around dinnertime, the chefs, who were actually preparing the finished dish to the guest's recipe because the guest would bring their own recipe—[they] would send it in—and the cooks would cook a finished product, and the guests would actually demonstrate doing the thing on-air. Then they would cook us dinner, and the production staff and the guests and friends and wife, or whoever—we'd all go up to a special boardroom upstairs and we'd have dinner with glasses of wine and everything, and we would sit and chat a little. Then after that, I would go downstairs and warm up the audience, and we would move on to tape the show.

On the day that *he* came, I don't remember exactly what happened, but my impressions of him were that he was an easy-going person to work with, he was very polite, very professional, and on camera he was quite funny. He wasn't just a "talk-to-me"-type guy. He did some things, and he was amusing, and he was no problem at all. No sort of hysterical star quality: "I want this" or "I won't do that" or any of that. *None of that.* He was just very pleasant, very professional. I didn't see or recognize anything in him—he made no demands that were off-key or weird or anything else. He was just a nice television personality that we had all seen on *Hogan's Heroes*. He was just the same kind of a guy when we met him. After the show was finished—if it was a flight back to LA, they would go back on that plane, and Anne would take them to the airport. If the show finished late, we put them in a hotel for the night, and they went back the next morning. They all came on for scale—that was the deal, no matter how big they were—they got scale, plus expenses.

LG/CF: What are your memories of what it was like during the taping? Was there anything to indicate there was something distracting him?

RP: The way we did the show was live-to-tape. I don't remember ever having to stop tape to redo a sequence. I think we redid a song a couple of times because something weird happened with the song, I remember that, but I don't remember us doing a cooking or eating or interview segment a second time on a second tape. It was like live tape. If weird things happened, like if mistakes were made in the cooking process, or things fell on the floor, or something broke, it was all part of the fun of the show because it was supposed to be spontaneous. These people were not professional cooks. They were famous in their own right—they were a comedian, or a singer, or actor, or politician—and they simply had a favorite recipe that they liked to do at home, or their mother gave them, and everyone who isn't a cook has a favorite recipe, and that's what we wanted them to bring forward.

LG/CF: When you talk about there being a rehearsal time, was that really more just to give the guest an idea on how things were going to run, or was it completely off-the-cuff otherwise?

RP: If we had a guest who was a performer, and they were going to do a stand-up comedy routine, or do a song, or play a piano, we would rehearse that with cameras so we could be sure of what we were going to be doing. We may run through that a couple of times. Then to get them familiar with the set, we'd have them behind the counter, and we would block some of it. We had cameras on it because the cameras had their own variety of shots used for every cooking show. You had the mirror shot and all the things, so you didn't have to do anything different for any particular guest. But you brought them in, and he would talk to Bruno, and they would discuss what he was going to do, and discuss if he was going to do something weird, like clambake something. That would all be noted at that time. We didn't actually rehearse the cooking segment, like doing everything we were going to do that night, no; we just made sure he was comfortable, he knew where he was standing, he knew where to look, he knew where the audience was—all that kind of thing, so there were no surprises that night. So he would be comfortable.

LG/CF: In Bob's case, would it have been an interview, or did he do something else?

RP: He was interviewed. Bruno would introduce the guests and say, "Tonight, we have blah blah blah," and in Bob's case, "He was the star of *Hogan's Heroes* for many years, we all know and loved him, here he is, Bob Crane." And he would walk out and join Bruno to applause. And Bruno would ask him what he was doing lately, and had the fame of his previous show he was on helped his career, or not—those kind of questions. Is he on the stage now, what he's doing, is he guesting on other TV shows? That kind of thing—Bruno would sit down and have a chat, not on camera, before they had dinner, so Bruno could have some questions to ask him that he would be comfortable with. So he wasn't firing things out of left field that the guests wouldn't even know where it was coming from.

They would have certain questions that were cleared with the guests: "I want to ask you about your career after *Hogan's Heroes*; I want to ask you about what it was like on *Hogan's Heroes;* I want to ask you if you're doing any movies;" so they would be there. Then maybe there would be a couple of questions thrown in that weren't on the list, but it was to give a rough idea to Bruno of what to ask him to get the best responses. So that's what that was about. He wasn't going to be grilled or have questions come out of left field.

LG/CF: Do you remember what topic Bob spoke about that night, especially pertaining to his private life?

RP: I don't remember anything being talked about his private life. No talking about divorce, or marriage, or kids. That would stand out in my mind because nobody did. The one thing where that was different from was we had a husband and wife team on back-to-back shows and one was a movie actor and was very gorgeous, I remember, but he wasn't a great talent; and his wife was a Broadway actress—they both came, and he did one show and she did one show, and obviously there was some reference to the fact that they were married, but apart from that, we never got into that. We mainly talked about—they were all famous for something, and that's what the public wants to hear about. They want to hear about their star, or their comic, or their politician, their author—whoever it is, they want know about *them*, about what they're doing, and where their career is going.

I didn't know he had an addiction. If we had a guest come to us who had a problem of one kind or another, we were warned by the agency. For example, we had [one guest who] was an alcoholic. And we had to keep him away from the bottle. And on *Celebrity Cooks*, you had all the booze you could ever want because all the liquor companies gave us booze, so we could put the odd bottle out as an appetizing product placement. And we had cases and cases of wine from the BC wine company, and they always had lots of wine, and they were always cooking with wine, and they were always having glasses of wine. Well, when [this guest] came, there was no liquor available. None in the board room, none for the dinner—nothing. So, he came, he was a charming, lovely man—we just had to baby him a little bit.

LG/CF: Did Bob seem delicate at all, as in sensitive to anything, or was he pretty open to whatever was going on?

RP: Yeah, he didn't make any demands. He was taken into the kitchen so that he could see how his product was going to look at night. He wanted to see—I forget what he made, but he wasn't just satisfied with the walk-through. As we said, this is where we will bring in all your products—the finished product will be in the kitchen, and we'll hide it in the stove and bring it out at the magic moment. He wanted to see how that was coming, and he went into the kitchen, which was close to the studio, so he could see what they were up to—if it looked lovely, and he wouldn't be surprised by something that wasn't what he was thinking it was going to be. He did go in the kitchen, and I think they gave him a cup of soup—they always had a big pot of soup for the crew from the leftover food from the night before. If we were shooting for three weeks, the pot of soup was going for three weeks, and it kept getting stuff added to it all the time. And I think he had a cup of soup, from the cook in the kitchen.

He didn't seem delicate or different from anyone else. We had the odd delicate guest who was maybe frail because of age, but Bob was easy to work with.

LG/CF: I am holding an entire magazine article here that directly quotes Jeff Erdel, which has been used to basically hold the show up as an example of Bob's life falling apart. *[Reads article to Roger.]*

RP: I don't see how an eight-hour segment of his life is worth pages and pages and pages.

LG/CF: If that was what was taped, how does that even sound like something that could be considered usable? It doesn't sound like the way *Celebrity Cooks* would work.

RP: Well, no, because we don't get into that. After we have the little chat about, "you're famous," or whatever—in his case, he was famous for *Hogan's Heroes*, "Was it fun doing it? Do you miss not doing it now? Has it affected your career? What are you doing now?" When we get past that, we then talk about his recipe. "Where did you get it? Where did you learn it? Did it come from your mother? Did your wife make it? Why do you like making it?" And then they would actually get down to doing it, and the host, Bruno, would be his assistant. And he would say, "I need some flour, I need this, I need that," and they would have a bit of kit and kaboodle around it, and they might make a mess about it, but that was the fun part.

You have to remember that the show was an afternoon show. We went on at three o'clock for six years. So if there *was* anything a little bit "up"—that would be a ten o'clock show, it wouldn't be a three o'clock show.

There were no diatribes about going off with young women, or breaking up marriages, or wanting to get back to his wife. It wasn't that kind of show; it was a variety show, an entertainment show. Sometimes we had singers or comedians—it was all fun about famous people who were actually cooking for us, which they wouldn't normally do. That is where we were at. It was for fun, it wasn't for in-depth reporting at all.

Anne Kear
Talent Agent, *Celebrity Cooks*
Interview – June 27, 2009

LG/CF: What was your role in *Celebrity Cooks*?

Anne Kear (AK): I was called the talent coordinator, but as the series went on, I really considered myself the associate producer. On paper, I was the talent coordinator, and that was the credit I got on the screen. I had worked on the show for three seasons—we were doing the show out in Vancouver, in British Columbia. The producer felt it was better and easier for the American guests to fly up to Vancouver from Los Angeles. We had originally started the show in Ontario. We taped the first series in Ottawa in a special TV studio in Ottawa the first season. But if any of the American guests that I booked came up from LA, they had to change planes in Toronto, and then fly up to Ottawa and stay overnight. They would do the show in the evening, then they would stay overnight—we would put them up in a first class hotel—and then they would to leave the next morning, again change planes in Toronto, and get back to LA sometime late afternoon or evening. We found that some of the American actors naturally didn't want to take two days out of their schedule to come up to Ottawa. We had no trouble at all getting Canadian celebrities to be on the show, but that's the reason we eventually went out to tape the show in Vancouver—and they were taped at the Canadian Broadcasting Corporation (CBC) Studios in Vancouver.

LG/CF: By the time Bob was booked in, were you the equivalent of the associate producer at that stage?

AK: Oh yes, I was still the "associate producer" and the talent coordinator at that stage. And I remember meeting him very well. One of the perks of the job was to go out in a limousine to the airport and greet all the celebrities off the plane. And of course, we paid for their flights up to Vancouver, and we paid for their rooms at the hotel. We did three shows an afternoon or late evening. And there where two other American celebrities on the plane with him, but I can't remember who they were. I remember just being so delighted to meet him, and of course, I'd seen *Hogan's Heroes*, which was so wonderfully funny, a marvelous TV series. We chatted a lot, and he was awfully nice with the other two celebrities in this big stretch limo that we had laid out for them. I took him to the hotel, and he signed in.

I waited for him in the lobby, and then I took him again in the limo just a few blocks away to the television studio, where he had his own dressing room, and we put his name on the door. We did that for all the celebrities so they would have their name on the door. I just found him so pleasant and charming and agreeable. He was easygoing and chatted with the other celebrities that evening, and chatted with the crew. We had, of course, a professional backstage chef. Part of my job, as soon as I had booked the celebrities usually weeks in advance—[guests] would give me their recipe over the phone, believe it or not. I would take down their recipe in shorthand over the phone and type it out. We didn't have email in the 70s. I think we did have FAX machines.

So I would type out the recipe and give it to our backstage professional chef. She would do the recipe in full. The she would make sure that no ingredients were missing and that it was going to be all right on the show.

Of course I had to give her the recipes as far in advance as I could because she had all kinds of other recipes to prepare. It was a half hour show, or twenty-six minutes I guess, and Bruno would introduce the guest. He would come on through this garden door and then into the kitchen of the studio. It was a wonderfully designed set and a very professional kitchen. And they would chat awhile and talk about his recipe. And then they would start to cook or prepare the dish.

Then there would be the commercial break, as you know, and during that break, Bob would chat very affably with Bruno. When he first walked onto the set, he had a live audience, and they had all recognized him immediately. They had all seen *Hogan's Heroes,* I suppose, so he got a very warm, enthusiastic welcome from the live audience. We weren't prompting them at all—it was just spontaneous welcome. It was Bob Crane!

In the second part of the show, there was more cooking and chatting around with Bruno Gerussi—our host—and at the end, the finished product that our professional chef had prepared would be set on the table with Bob and Bruno, and we always had wine. And I am picturing they had red wine that evening for that episode, and they would carve the chicken and serve it up to each of them and chat a bit more, and then it would end—the episode—on a high note.

LG/CF: Was it really an off-the-cuff program? Aside from obviously needing to know what you were doing when you were cooking, were there parameters around, "This is what we're going to talk about, and this is what you're going to say to me," or was it very natural?

AK: It was very natural. I had gotten Bob's biography from his agent, and I gave that bio to Bruno to read before the show so he would be up on Bob. But there were no set questions ahead of time. It was very informal, and Bruno had done his research about Bob. It was mainly about *Hogan's Heroes*.

LG/CF: And what was Bob like on the air? Was he comfortable doing this live?

AK: Yes! Very comfortable. Very professional. Agreeable, charming, easygoing. He was a *wonderful* guest. I can't just overuse the word wonderful. He was one of our *BEST* guests.

LG/CF: Did you consider him that way because there was no trouble or because he was easy to deal with? What would make one guest stand out from a show perspective?

AK: He wasn't nervous or intimidated by the camera or audience. Some of our celebrities were a little nervous and awkward about cooking, and they'd never met Bruno before until that very day. He would chat in the dressing room with each of the guests before they taped their episode. They didn't know Bruno; he wasn't a big star in the States. He wasn't like Lorne Greene, who was on *Bonanza* and was a comedian. But my point is, a lot of the American actors didn't know him, but that didn't matter because Bruno was a very outgoing, easy guy to talk to, and he knew how to talk to other actors, being one himself.

Bob Crane certainly was [a great talent to be able to work in an informal, unrehearsed show]. It was a very informal, funny show. It was two goofy guys just sort of messing around in the kitchen. And if there was something wrong, or there was an ingredient missing, we just carried on. We didn't stop the tape. And the audience loved it. And there were cue cards with the recipe written out on them. When I said that our chef would bring out the finished product at the end, that wasn't quite accurate. She would, during that last commercial break, put his *Hogan's Heroes* chicken casserole dish in the oven on the set and then when taping resumed, Bruno or Bob would open the oven door, and by magic, there was the finished product. And they would bring it to the table and sit down away from the kitchen set. They would then go into a little garden and sit at a table and have a glass of wine and carve the chicken and eat a little bit and talk some more. Bruno would thank Bob for coming and that would be it. There would be wild applause because the audience loved Bob. It wasn't a big audience like the Letterman show, but it was a very enthusiastic, friendly, live audience.

LG/CF: The taping of this show has always been held out as an example of Bob's life falling apart—that he couldn't hide his lifestyle, that he was visibly upset on stage over things happening in his personal life, that he was obsessed with death and sex. It doesn't sound like any of that was what you experienced.

AK: No! No! Not at all! No!

LG/CF: The person quoted is a station manager from a New York TV station, and he had just seen the show, and says in the show, Bob was obsessed with large, well-endowed ladies, young ladies. He was talking about his marriage breaking up, was in tears. Somebody saying, "This is what I saw," is quite convenient. Because there is no one in the States to say, "No, that's not right." Would there have been anything—to a casual observer—that would kind of stand out and make you say, "Oh, there's something not quite right there."

AK: No. I can say, categorically, *no*. There was nothing—no indication. We didn't know *anything* about his private life. Whatever was in the biography his agent sent us may have mentioned his wife and children, but we didn't know any rumors. Nothing. When Carol first called me and told me about this, I was so shocked that someone would say something like that about Bob Crane. It was just not there.

I was so shocked and saddened to learn that Bob had died. I could hardly believe it, when the news came out about the other side of his life. I could hardly believe it because it was a different person than the Bob Crane who was on the cooking show.

LG/CF: Did anything surprise you about him? After you spent your time with him, did you think, "I didn't think he would be like that or do that?"

AK: No, not at all. After the taping, the limo took him back to his hotel. I didn't see him the next morning, but why would I? He was getting the flight back to LA—whichever flight he was on. I think he even signed some autographs after the taping. More of it's coming back to me now. He didn't immediately rush out of the studio and get into his limo. He signed some autographs, and the people in the audience wanted to shake his hand and chat with him. And then the limo took him back to his hotel, and I didn't see him after that. There were three more shows to be taped that afternoon and evening.

I wish I had the tapes myself. I was there when the show was being taped live, and I saw it again when it was broadcast. I saw all of them on CBC. It was a national network program. *There was nothing!* Whoever this man is who is writing all this salacious stuff, there was no inkling of it at all.

Bob with his son Scott (circa 1971).

Source: Courtesy of Scott Crane. Used with permission.

Bob with his daughter Karen (Christmas 1975).

Source: Courtesy of Karen Crane. Used with permission.

Bob and Patty Crane with their son Scott at their home (circa 1973).
Source: Courtesy of Scott Crane. Used with permission.

Bob with his son Scott (circa 1974).
Source: Courtesy of Scott Crane. Used with permission.

Bob with his friend Eliot Dober, Former President, United Cerebral Palsy Foundation – Connecticut Chapter, at Eliot's birthday party in 1976.

Source: Courtesy of Eliot Dober. Used with permission.

Bob giving a presentation (circa 1973).

Source: Courtesy of Scott Crane. Used with permission.

On March 4, 1973, Bob Crane served as master of ceremonies for the Variety Club of Southern California, a showmen's organization devoted to aiding needy children. Carroll O'Connor received the Humanitarian Plaque from Variety Club president Joseph Sintay during the event, which drew more than 600 attendees to the Century Plaza Hotel in Los Angeles. Monty Hall (far right) was also present.

Source: Courtesy of Scott Crane. Used with permission.

Top and Bottom: Announcement for Bob Crane's KMPC Holiday Special (December 31, 1972).

Source: Courtesy of Scott Crane. Used with permission of KMPC.

Life's Illusions

Bob Crane (back row to the right) with members of the crew of *The Hawaii Experience*.

Bob Crane with Marcia Orland, wife of *The Hawaii Experience* producer and director John Orland.

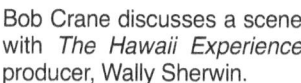

Bob Crane discusses a scene with *The Hawaii Experience* producer, Wally Sherwin.

All photos: Bob Crane on the set of T*he Hawaii Experience* filmed on location on the island of Oahu (February 1978).

Source: All phtos courtesy of John Orland. Used with permission.

Bob seems to be holding on for dear life! During the filming of *The Hawaii Experience* (February 1978), he got a lift from a whale at Sea Life Park, Oahu.

Source: Photo courtesy of John Orland. Used with permission.

Life's Illusions

Bob Crane and Bruno Gerusi on the Canadian television program *Celebrity Cooks* (January 25, 1978).

Source: From the author's personal collection.

Bob Crane prepares to begin filming a public service announcement (location unknown, December 10, 1976).

Source: From the author's personal collection.

Bob Crane visiting his uncles in Waterbury, Connecticut (December 11, 1973). Even after he became famous, Bob always returned home to his roots.

Source: Courtesy of Jim Senich. Used with permission.

Bob Crane with (left to right) WICC Director of Sales Development David Bodge, Executive Secretary Martha Gross, and Station Manager Ray Colonari. (January 29, 1976).

Source: Bridgeport History Center, Bridgeport, CT. Used with permission.

Chapter 10
Third Act Twist

With a wealth of experience behind him, Crane excels in the role of Paul Burnett. This "Beginner's Luck" is a slick, well-oiled machine, which purrs with the effectiveness of a Mercedes Benz. Mr. Crane's performance is quite solid. He makes us forget he was once Hogan…and that isn't an easy thing to do. His character is very human and subject to the same universal human frailties that trip us up in life.

—Ken Williams, Journalist, "The Journal News," Hamilton, Ohio, November 29, 1977

Professional portrait of Bob Crane (circa 1975).

Source: Courtesy of Scott Crane. Used with permission.

Bob with John Thompson and his wife, Pamela Hayes Thompson, following a theatre performance of *Beginner's Luck.* Circa 1975.

Source: Courtesy of Scott Crane. Used with permission.

Chapter 10
Third Act Twist

In "Beginner's Luck," Bob Crane plays Paul Burnett, a nice, average married man whose eye begins to wander. He realizes how much he loves his wife as soon as he loses her. Paul does everything from giving his wife Sally a rubber tree plant to disguising himself as a window washer in his effort to re-woo her. Mr. Crane, a comedian of brilliance and wit, turns in a performance that makes for a charmingly funny evening.

—'Ludington Daily News,' Ludington, Missouri, August 14, 1970

"I was made for the stage," Bob Crane quipped on March 2, 1962. "That's right, the stage. The coach is ready in about five minutes, you can get on it, Crane."

Bob Crane, indeed, had been made for the stage. And when Bob uttered that flippant remark over the Southern California airwaves during his KNX morning show, he had already made his stage debut in *Tunnel of Love* in September 1959, with *Who Was That Lady I Saw You With?* following a year later.

Once he stepped foot on stage and got a taste of the lights and the live audience, Bob was hooked. From that moment when he first experienced the instant gratification of an audience's live response, his heart was with acting, and specifically, the theatre. *Hogan's Heroes* gave him fame, but Bob Crane craved an instant reaction, and he continued performing on stage as often as he could from 1959 through the rest of his life. Other than the few years during the 1960s when *Hogan's Heroes* was his main focus, he devoted an enormous amount of time to theatre productions.

Bob's light shone just as brightly on stage as it did behind a drumset or within the confines of a television prison camp. He excelled as a stage actor and loved every minute of it. He craved the cheers and applause—the raw reactions to his comedy, timing, and delivery received within seconds. It fueled his drive for more.

Bob performed many plays throughout his life—more than thirty productions from 1959 until his very last performance on a fateful night in June 1978.

Most do not realize the degree to which Bob prepared for his stage performances. He kept stringent notes and recorded his performances on both audio and videotape. He also spent countless hours scrutinizing the playbooks and scripts—line by line and page by page—changing the dialogue, restructuring the characters, and providing detailed comments on how to make the next show better than the one before it. Although performing in the theatre provided a steady income when money was tight, it was not something he just did out of necessity. At the start, at the height, and at the end of his acting career, Bob Crane maintained a strong, ongoing presence in theatre. And performing on stage in front of a live theatre audience seemed to be his favorite method of acting and the one he was best at.

The reviews prove it. With the exception of one review that focused on technical difficulties that hampered the performance, none of the reviews found regarding Bob's theatre performances, and specifically *Beginner's Luck*, were poor. In fact, *every single review* praised Bob's performances to the extreme—bestowing upon him and his fellow cast mates accolades of the highest caliber. This does not suggest that every performance was without flaws or weaknesses or that there were *never* any bad reviews; however, in our exhaustive search, we found none.

Whether Hollywood took him seriously as an actor or not, *Bob* certainly took himself seriously. Theatre allowed him to explore new techniques and concentrate on sharpening his skills. Through his work on the stage, he proved he was capable of seeing a production as a whole, not just his part as an actor in it.

Eventually, Bob would transition from actor to director. As an accomplished musician may conduct an orchestra, Bob was able to direct *Beginner's Luck*. According to those who worked under his direction, he was able to see each scene, each character, and each delivery with extraordinary precision, and orchestrate a production that was both entertaining and technically savvy. But it would take a great deal of work and dedication to reach that point.

After years of devoting his energy primarily to *Hogan's Heroes*, Bob decided to return to the stage. By the end of 1968, he had lined up two theatre performances for his 1969 hiatus from *Hogan's Heroes*—

Bob Crane's Known Theatre Performances (1959-1978)
Production Details and Selected Reviews
(in alphabetical order)

6 Rms Riv Vu
Written by Bob Randall

December 7-16, 1973 / Playhouse on the Mall, Paramus, New Jersey
Directed by Dennis Brite
With Nancy Dussault, Francine Beers, Pamela Hayes, Jose Ocasio, Janis Sullivan, Edmund Day, and Robert P. Kaye

Beginner's Luck
Written by Norman Barasch and Carroll Moore

March 25-May 1, 1970 / Drury Lane Theatre, Chicago, Illinois – Premiere
Produced by Anthony DeSantis, Drury Lane Theatre owner
Directed by Vernon Schwartz
With Pamela Hayes, Ann Eggert, Richard Stadelmann, Linda Staab, Tom Elrod, Kenneth Lewis, and Shelly Weiser

August 18-23, 1970 / Cherry Country Playhouse, Traverse City, Michigan
First production of *Beginner's Luck* to also be directed by Bob Crane
With Pamela Hayes, Fawne Harriman, David Whitaker, and William Young

[Unknown dates], 1971 / Off-Broadway Theatre, San Diego, California

April 27-May 9, 1971 / The Little Theatre on The Square, Sullivan, Illinois
Directed by Richard Michaels; Produced by Guy S. Little, Jr.
With Pamela Hayes, David Hull, Vicki Kaywood, and Ken Hamilton

June 22-June 27, 1971 / Canal Fulton Summer Arena, Canal Fulton, Ohio

March 7-April 2, 1972 / Vincent Miranda's Off-Broadway Theatre, San Diego, California
With Abby Dalton, Bernard Fox, and Marvin Kaplan

May 2-20, 1972 / Marquee Theatre-Restaurant, El Paso, Texas
With Pamela Hayes, Bernard Fox, Doug Dudley, and Bea Ramirez
Bob arrived April 29, 1972, and was greeted at the airport by Miss El Paso Bebe Richeson and three members of the El Paso Chapter of the American Ex-POWs.

August 8-26, 1973 / Alhambra Theatre, Jacksonville, Florida
With Pamela Hayes

May 1-June 3, 1973 / Windmill Dinner Theatre, Dallas, Texas
With Pamela Hayes, Jenny Sherman, and Milt Jamin

June 26-August 2, 1973 / Windmill Dinner Theatre, Scottsdale, Arizona
With Pamela Hayes, Pearl Braaten, and John Thompson

[Unknown dates], 1973 / Alhambra Theatre, Jacksonville, Florida

February 20-March ?, 1974 / Don Sherwood's Showboat Dinner Theatre, St. Petersburg, FL
With Pamela Hayes, Ronni Richards, and Richard Stadelmann; Scenic Designer Richard Sharkey.

April 1974 / Windmill Dinner Theatre, Dallas, Texas
With Pamela Hayes, Judy Blye, and Richard Stadelmann

First Week of July 1974 / The Beverly Barn Dinner Theatre, Shreveport, Louisiana

July 16-August 20, 1974 / The Beverly, New Orleans, Louisiana
With Pamela Hayes, John Thompson, and Ronni Richards
Note: Performed one week in Shreveport as a substitution for Frank Sutton (Sergeant Carter on *Gomer Pyle, U.S.M.C.*), who was starring in the production *Luv* at The Beverly Barn Dinner Theatre but passed away suddenly on June 28, 1974. Sutton had been preparing to go on stage for the evening's performance and was in his dressing room when he suffered a heart attack. Bob and his *Beginner's Luck* cast had just arrived in New Orleans for their run at The Beverly. They quickly moved their production to Shreveport to finish out Sutton's week before officially opening in New Orleans.

April 8-May 4, 1975 / Carousel Dinner Theatre, Ravenna, Ohio

May 20-June ?, 1975 / Don Sherwood's Showboat Dinner Theatre, St. Petersburg, FL
With Pamela Hayes

August 6-September 28, 1975 / Drury Lane East Theatre, McCormick Place, Arlington Heights, Illinois
With Bernard Fox, Pamela Hayes, and Ronni Richards.
Note: Richard Stadelmann replaced Bernard Fox as Scott Marlowe after Fox had to leave early for another theatre engagement.

May 25-June 17, 1976 / Country Dinner Playhouse, Reynoldsburg, Ohio
With Bernard Fox, Carol O'Leary, and Ronni Richards

January 4-February 13, 1977 / Cirque Playhouse, Seattle, Washington
With Ronni Richards, Peggy Walton, and Richard Stadelmann

June 28-July 31, 1977 / Country Dinner Playhouse, Austin, Texas

November 22-December 18, 1977 / Beef 'n' Boards Dinner Theatre, Harrison, Ohio
With Victoria Berry Wells, Richard Stadelmann, and Peggy Walton

March 14-April 2, 1978 / La Mirada Civic Theatre, Long Beach, California

May 2, 1978-May 28, 1978 / Windmill Dinner Theatre, Dallas, Texas

June 6-June 28, 1978 / Windmill Dinner Theatre, Scottsdale, Arizona
With Victoria Berry Wells.
Note: Show was scheduled to run through the weekend, with its last performance on Saturday, July 1. The play closes early because of Bob's murder on June 29.

Predictions and Reviews for *Beginner's Luck*

"The star, Bob Crane, seems to have a tremendous personal following, and his performance is really outstanding. *Beginner's Luck* could really find its place in the sun. Bob Crane's performance is near-spectacular. He has the ability to shift stances effortlessly, and at one moment, give out with the whipped-little-cur bit, and then quickly shifts gears and glides into the shifty-eyed-wily-old-fox character. It takes real timing, ability, confidence, and flair for comedy. Bob Crane has all these, and more, safely tucked away in his hip pocket."
—*Traverse City Record-Eagle*, "Bob Crane Sparks Hilarious Funfest at the Playhouse," August 19, 1970

"*Beginner's Luck* is the sort of show that utilizes [Bob's] talents of timing and pacing to the maximum. In addition to starring in the show, Bob also brings his years of experience with comedy to the job of directing."
—*El Paso Herald-Post*, "Riotous Comedy Stars TV's Bob Crane," May 6, 1972

"Mr. Crane [and] Mr. Fox…Their energy, projection, timing, and movement are all a joy to watch. They have mastered the nuance, the little subtlety which makes a funny line funnier by exactly the right pause or lift of the eyebrow. Nothing overdone, nor yet neglected in the doing. Old friends and working companions, they play magnificently to each other, and the scene where they try to fit three people into four separately paired concert seats is a theatrical treasure."
—*El Paso Herald*, "Two of 'Hogan's Heroes' Make Marquee Comedy among the Funniest," May 12, 1972

"This is one of the funniest shows Windmill has staged. Leave your kids at home; it's not that they'll be offended, they just won't appreciate the marital humor."
—*The Arizona Republic*, "Crane Guffaw Producer in *Beginner's Luck*," June 28, 1973

"It looks like another sellout summer for Windmill Dinner Theatre. The final two weeks of Bob Crane's *Beginner's Luck* are SRO [standing room only] except for a few matinee seats."
—*The Arizona Republic*, July 26, 1973

"Crane's easy style on the stage, marked by a sense of timing that can adjust itself to the whims of the audience's laughter, keeps the four-character comedy flowing from one-liner to one-liner. As director, Crane has tossed in a few topical lines and fills the stage with bits of comic business that fattens the slower moments in the script. Crane and company are good at their job. *Beginner's Luck* will make you laugh, no matter where your funny bone lies."
—*The Evening Independent*, "*Beginner's Luck* Is Funny Comedy," February 21, 1974

"Crane puts his *Hogan's Heroes* fame and clownish, animated flair to good use. In addition, as director, he has tightened the play considerably and added a few new lines to keep it fresh... *Beginner's Luck* [is] a summertime sizzler. It won't keep you in stitches, but it will instill a continual smile. Crane, as one might suspect, is relaxed and perfectly at ease. He highlights his performance with a series of cutups and hilarious facial expressions that run a gamut of personalities from little boy mischief maker to outright cad."
—*The Des Plaines Herald*, "Crane Makes *Luck* Summertime Sizzler," August 15, 1975

"There is nothing more appealing than a guy, who has a good time and sweeps all those around him into a general aura of great fun…which is one of the many reasons why Bob Crane has always been a great success. Crane's gift for comedy made him a natural selection for the role of Hogan on the eternally famous TV series *Hogan's Heroes*."
—*The Journal News*, "Bob [Crane] to Star at Beef 'n' Boards," November 10, 1977

"This *Beginner's Luck* is a slick, well-oiled machine which purrs with the effectiveness of a Mercedes Benz. The comedy is clever and witty, rarely though sometimes slipping to cheap sight gags for even cheaper laughs, but for the most part, the laughs are genuine and down to earth. Mr. Crane's performance is quite solid. He makes us forget he was once Hogan in the long-running sitcom, *Hogan's Heroes*, and that isn't an easy thing to do since he has had so much mass exposure on television and in its reruns. Crane gives his character plenty of depth and range, allowing us to laugh with him, at him, and eventually, at our own selves. His character is very human, and subject to the same universal human frailties that trip us up in life.
—*The Journal News*, "Bob Crane Excels in *Beginner's Luck*, November 29, 1977

Cactus Flower
Written by Abe Burrows

May 15-June 29, 1969 / Veterans Memorial, Warren, Ohio
Directed by Leslie B. Cutler
With Abby Dalton, Sigrid Valdis, Woody Romoff, Robert Tananis, Leslie Beard, Casey Walters, and Frederica Minte (The Kenley Players)

Send Me No Flowers
Written by Norman Barasch and Carroll Moore

August 28-September 2, 1962 / Laguna Beach Summer Theatre, Laguna Beach, California
Directed by Jerry Evans
With Betty Ramey, James Martin, Reid Lowden, and Eric Lord

February 12-April 4, 1969 / Drury Lane Theatre, Chicago, Illinois
Directed by Vernon Schwartz
With Edith Wilson, Ken Gilman, Richard Stadelman, Tom Hatten, Frank Loverde, Tim Strasser, Susan Palmer, Dale Benson, Linda Staab, Frank Kress, and Carol Saenz
Note: Rick Plastina replaced Ken Gilman as Vito after Gilman had to leave early for another theatre engagement.

August 31-September 5, 1971 / Cherry County Playhouse, Traverse City, Michigan
With Pamela Hayes, Bob Moak, David Himes, David Brubaker, John Hagan, and Amy Thomson

October 13-November 5, 1972 / Off-Broadway Theatre, San Diego, California
With Robert Kurston

Reviews for *Send Me No Flowers*

"Mr. Crane's comic talents have been widely praised, and *Send Me No Flowers* gives him an opportunity to pull out all the stops. Bob Crane set a new record with his engagement at the Cherry County Playhouse last year and advance sales for *Send Me No Flowers* indicate that he may easily top himself."

—*The Ludington Daily News*, "'Send Me No Flowers' Stars 'Hogan's Heroes' Bob Crane," August 27, 1971

"The role is excellent for Bob Crane. It gives him pretty much full range of his unique talent in the comedy field, employing most effectively a low-key, relaxed, effortless method of portrayal that has won him stardom. A brilliant performance."

—*The Traverse City Record-Eagle,* "Playhouse Capping Banner 17th Year with First-Rate Offening," September 1, 1971

Tunnel of Love
Written by Joseph Fields and Peter DeVries

September-October, 1959 / Valley Playhouse, Woodland Hills, California
Directed by Donald Freed
With Colleen O'Sullivan, Richard Cleary, Anne Pie, Joyce Simmons, and Del Gregory
Note: Bob Crane's first theatre performance.

Review for *Tunnel of Love*

Tunnel of Love—A Mirth-Quaking Must. Jam-packed full of laughs and absolutely one of the best productions from the Valley Playhouse thus far, *Tunnel of Love* chalks up another triumph for director Don Freed. The wonderfully cast starring roles played by Bob Crane, Colleen O'Sullivan, and Richard Cleary do justice to this rapid-fire hit comedy by Joseph Fields and Peter DeVries. Crane, in particular, proves to be most adaptable as humorous bon vivant Dick Pepper. Excellent supporting performances by Anne Pie, Joyce Simmons, and Del Gregory help to make this one of the most entertaining shows we have seen this year.

—Larry Lipson, *Valley News,* September 24, 1959.

Who Was That Lady I Saw You With?
Written by Norman Krasva
October 1960 / Valley Playhouse, Woodland Hills, California
Directed by Donald Freed
With Tom Hatten and Colleen O'Sullivan

July 18-August 13, 1972 / Pheasant Run Playhouse, St. Charles, Illinois
With Pamela Hayes, Sidney Eden, Ralph Foody, John Thompson

another run of *Send Me No Flowers* from February 12 to April 4, 1969, in Chicago; and then immediately following, *Cactus Flower*, from May 15 to June 19, 1969, in Warren, Ohio.

In *Send Me No Flowers*, Bob plays George Kimball, a man who suffers from an assortment of physical ailments. However, George is a hypochondriac, and he has his doctor running in circles performing various tests on him and writing out prescriptions to help make him better—or at least *feel* better. One day, George overhears his doctor talking on the phone to a colleague about test results, and the news isn't good. George panics, believing his doctor is talking about him. And naturally, George thinks he's dying! For the duration of the play, George prepares for his impending death, and part of his planning includes finding an appropriate replacement husband for his wife Judy. The only problem is, George becomes jealous of the potential replacements he has selected for her, resulting in a story full of double entendres and relationship missteps. The doctor, of course, was *not* talking about George, and when George realizes he is *not* dying, he is grateful for his second chance and goes on to live out the rest of his life with his wife.

Actor Rick Plastina worked with Bob in the 1969 stage production of *Send Me No Flowers* at the Drury Lane Theatre in Chicago. A replacement for Ken Gilman, who had to leave early because of a prior theatre engagement, Rick portrayed Vito—a laundry man who poses nothing more than an imagined threat to George's marriage, but who also provides the inspiration for George to move forward with his plans for his not-yet-widowed wife.

Rick remembered that because he was a replacement cast member, he did not have the opportunity to rehearse with the rest of the cast before his first performance. His first meeting with Bob was moments before going on stage.

"Bob couldn't have been more friendly or helpful or welcoming," Rick explained, "and we greeted each other warmly before the play. My rehearsals were always with Vernon Schwartz, who was the director of the production, and with the stage manager. I was interacting with Edith Wilson, who played Bob's wife, and Bob, mainly talking to Edith's character. He's in shock because his character, who he thinks is going to die in the play, starts imagining everything. Whatever negative things can go on, he's imagining these things, and this is one of the dream sequences. My first scene was meeting them, and the second was where

I came down in a tuxedo and started dancing with Edith while he just—open-mouthed—looked at what I was doing in shock, and then went up the aisle. The audience would always laugh at it because Bob was such a wonderful *reactor* as well as actor. After the show, Bob came up to me, and he said, 'Well, I can tell a pro when I work with one, and you're a real pro.' He just made my night because not only was he welcoming and charming, but he paid me a nice compliment, and it was my first professional play, so it was a great way to start."

Rick said that because Vernon Schwartz had been so helpful, and because Bob and Edith were so welcoming, he eased right into the character and the performance with no trouble.

Rick was excited for the opportunity to perform with Bob on stage. As a television star, Bob might have exerted his power over his cast members or displayed an inflated ego; however, Rick explained this was not the case.

"I just remember him being a charming guy," Rick said. "I knew a little about his background, that he worked in radio, and he just had the charisma and the natural charm and everything to be able to act. He never really did anything different from what his persona was—or what his regular character was like, but what he did, he did very well. He seemed very comfortable and relaxed, and he made everyone else feel the same way. So, I was certainly excited about working with him. I worked with a number of other stars after Bob, like Betty Grable and quite a number of others. I only worked with one or two that either were terribly insecure or had an ego problem and would demand that you would do things a certain way so as not to upstage them. Bob was not like that. Bob was just enjoying himself and wanted everyone else to do the same. I didn't see any kind of a star ego with him at all, other than the fact that he looked like a million dollars and seemed like he was really enjoying himself. Of course, me being a kid of twenty-three at the time, I was just thrilled to be on the same stage with him. In that show, he was pretty much like himself. He had all the charm—the normal charm he had as a person—he brought on the stage with him. Then he just played the character and what he had to do. His character was a hypochondriac of the first degree, so he went from being a charming, jovial husband with friends in the play to becoming more and more paranoid. And he played that character beautifully."

According to Rick, there were never any follow-up rehearsals because everything just worked out well. Director Vernon Schwartz was happy with the production. However, live theatre is unpredictable, and Rick recalled one unplanned incident during a performance that Bob managed well.

"Since it was my first show, I would watch as much of the show from the wings as I could," Rick said. "One night, one of the actors in the show, Frank Loverde, was playing Bob's best friend in the play who also thought that he was going to die. So his character has to get progressively drunker as the play went on. Well, one night, the prop person who was preparing the drinks didn't properly clean out the bottles, so the bottle that Frank had to pour into his glass and then get progressively drunk was filled with some kind of—well, it looked like a growth of a plant, which the audience could see—it was that visible! I remember Bob just standing there, and the audience was laughing, as Frank did kind of a double take at this bottle, and he had to keep drinking, and Bob just started laughing. And Frank just turned to him and said, 'Sure, you can laugh, but I'm the one that has to drink the whole bloody thing!' And it got a huge laugh, the audience exploded with laughter that was shared by Bob and with Frank. I think, actually, instead of drinking out of that bottle, Bob just grabbed one of the other bottles that was onstage and started drinking from that one because he wisely realized, 'Hey, maybe it wouldn't be a good idea to drink out of that other one.' Although afterward, when Frank came off, he was not happy with the prop person. Bob didn't say anything to him. He just went along with it. Nothing threw him. Nothing would make him uncomfortable other than, well, Frank's reaction to that one situation. It was an extremely funny moment, even though Frank really lit into the prop person and let him know that that was really unprofessional, and 'I have to drink this, I could get sick doing this.' But Bob just stayed out of the way. He just said, 'Yeah, well, you've got a right,' and 'Yeah, I wouldn't want to drink it, either.'

"Bob came across as very open and easy to talk to when you could ask some questions," Rick continued. "There was never any discomfort or any ill at-ease with him. He just made everyone feel welcome and comfortable. Just the natural osmosis of treating everybody as well as he did. That there was no star ego, that there was no kind of psychosis like the character had. With Bob, it was just kind of a matter of 'You just do your thing, I'll have fun doing my thing, so don't worry about it. You do whatever you can to have fun with the character, and I'll do the same.' So he was totally open that way. There was never anything about Bob that made you feel uncomfortable. He just seemed like everything was easy. 'Let's just take it as it comes and let's enjoy ourselves and have a good time and treat everybody nicely and with respect.' You find the laughs, so you play to them as best you can without trying to beat it over the head. But Bob was just so natural. He was just so relaxed and comfortable. He helped his colleague and at the same time he was letting his colleague upstage him without any problems. He had that quality as being able to just—'I don't have to push it too hard; I just have to react to what you're doing, and the audience will be like me, reacting to the silliness.' And he played the character very well."

Bob's next play, *Cactus Flower*, opened just a couple of weeks after *Send Me No Flowers* closed. Co-starring Abby Dalton, it also featured Sigrid Valdis and provided a rare treat for theatregoers. Not only would they be able to see their Colonel Hogan, but they would also see Colonel Klink's secretary with "Hogan" on stage. Their fans would not have realized that at that very moment, Bob and his first wife Anne had just recently separated and were about to go through a divorce, and that Bob and Patty were in the midst of a serious affair, soon to become engaged and later married.

It would be the only stage performance Bob and Patty ever did together, however. After Scott was born in June 1971, Patty opted to remain at home to tend to their home and family rather than pursue her acting career.

In addition to *Cactus Flower* and *Send Me No Flowers*, Bob also performed stage productions of *6 Rms Riv Vu* and *Who Was that Lady I Saw You With?* on and off throughout the 1970s. However, it would be *Beginner's Luck*, which he would not only star in and direct, but also own the rights to produce, that would become his trademark stage production. He held this particular play close to his heart. He honed it, massaged it, protected it, and perfected it, all up until the very last night he performed it.

During the 1970s, Bob was in the process of a major transition in his career. Aside from the cancellation of *Hogan's Heroes*, he was also going through his divorce from Anne, and by 1971, had six children to care for (four his own). At a time when money was tight, dinner theatre provided Bob with a steady income, even if it meant he had to travel frequently.

However, working in dinner theatre was considered to be a step down in the Hollywood community during the 1970s, and to relegate one's self to such a venue during this time period was a red flag—a signal of a downswing in one's career. Some who worked with Bob in the theatre confirmed he was frustrated that he had been unable to find a hit series following the cancellation of *Hogan's Heroes,* and that dynamic roles in television and film eluded him. They claimed they felt his spirit was a little bit sad about performing in dinner theatre, and that after his split with Patty in December 1977, he was more openly distressed.

In March 1978, he explained to Maggie Daly of *The Chicago Tribune*, "My wife filed suit in Santa Monica Divorce Court, and all she had to say was 'irreconcilable differences,' but she did a character assassination on me, and I don't know why. She called me cold, heartless, and said I neglected the kids and a lot of other untrue things. Anyone who knows me and the kids knows better. I was shocked by those statements but not by the divorce. We had been discussing that for the last six months. It doesn't make sense if she wants to get more money because under California divorce law, everything is divided down the middle. She is asking $4,500 a month and $2,500 a month for our son, Scotty, who will be seven in June. I told her I wish I had that kind of money to give her."

Yet while Bob was troubled about his impending divorce and disheartened by his current career path, he was also making plans. Many claim that even though he was upset, they never saw a depressed, downcast person who was devoid of all hope. Instead, they saw a man who worked very hard at moving forward, trying to make the best of his situation, and seeking ways to better himself and his career.

Bob was not the only actor to turn to dinner theatre as a means to earn money. The 1960s through 1980s marked a time when touring the country and appearing in dinner theatre was typical for actors. Bernard Fox and Abby Dalton both co-starred in *Beginner's Luck* with Bob, and a large number of prominent stars also found regular work in dinner theatres across the country at this time. These included William Shatner, Frank Sutton, Mike Connors, Don Knotts, George Hamilton, Bert Convy, Dick Gautier, Ken Berry, Julie Andrews, Leonard Nimoy, Barry Williams, Ed Ames, Gavin MacLeod, Rip Taylor, Gale Gordon, Dick Van Patten, Dick Van Dyke, Forrest Tucker, Imogene Coco, Meredith McRae, Don Ameche, Bob Cummings, Dorothy Lamour, Sandra Dee, Robert Reed, Gig Young, Betty Grable, Tab Hunter, Mickey Rooney, Artie Johnson,

Bob Denver, Ruta Lee, Elke Sommer, Keith Carradine, Sal Mineo, and Van Johnson, just to name a few.

Bob also kept himself very busy with other work—radio, film, guest-starring on television, and *The Bob Crane Show*—all while he was performing on stage.

The truth is Bob worked *constantly*, even though he wanted a steady role in a series and not just guest work. In 1976, he said, "Thank God I can go on these jobs because guest-starring roles don't come along that often, and when they do, they don't pay too well. People have a weird idea of what happens with a successful series. After it's over, they think we just retire to green pastures. Well, it ain't so. I'd love to get back into an adventure-comedy thing. Critics have long said, 'Bob Crane works best with a gang, like *M*A*S*H* and *Hogan's Heroes*.' I don't like the mama-daddy-and-the-kids shows. There's not much you can do with the wife and the children and the funny dog that hasn't been done."

There was another reason why Bob did not have a proper cash flow, and it had nothing to do with his meager *Hogan's Heroes* profit participation earnings, or his alimony and child support payments. Bob's business manager, Lloyd Vaughan, had been embezzling money from Bob for years, but this did not come to light until after Bob's death. In December 1979, Vaughan missed a payment, and Patty noticed. Represented by A. Lee Blackman, Patty had Vaughan investigated, and when the embezzlement was discovered, she pressed charges. At his trial in March 1981, he pleaded no contest to the lawsuit and was ordered to pay the Crane Estate $108,000 for the $75,000 he had stolen while serving as Bob's business manager. Vaughan served one year in jail for his crime, and he recently called Bob's son Scott and apologized for his actions.

Bob never knew of Vaughan's embezzlement, and he was forced to take jobs he typically passed on earlier in his acting career to help make ends meet. Regardless of his financial situation, Bob *always* took his work seriously. He thoroughly enjoyed performing *Beginner's Luck* before live audiences, and he quickly turned it into his *own* play, crafting a fun and delightful production from an otherwise ordinary storyline. He devoted boundless energy to it, and it was met with resounding success from one side of the country to the other.

KNX colleague and friend Leo McElroy performed in plays with Bob during the early 1960s. Leo said that as with everything Bob did, he sought perfection. He also recalled that from some of his earliest stage performances, Bob searched for ways to enhance the production by altering the dialogue slightly.

"I think Bob's ego, Bob's drive, was caught up in doing it well," Leo said. "I think he would have been absolutely crushed had he felt he was doing a lousy job because that was Bob. Bob may not have ever articulated it, but if you watched him work, whether it was acting or whether it was doing radio, Bob was a *perfectionist*. Bob wanted to be absolutely dead on with what he was doing, and he didn't want to make false steps. He did not want to make mistakes. And he worked *very* hard at not doing that. So with the plays, my understanding of the way Bob worked at every play, whether I was involved or not, was that he was the first guy to be off book and know his lines, and that he expected that he would be dead on with the lines, at least in the manner in which he was going to do them. He was willing to depart from book if he thought his character would be a little more vivid doing the line a little differently. And I never heard of Bob blowing up in a performance or blowing up on his line. He really was into making sure that he had it nailed down and that he was *never* at less than his best."

So it was for Bob in the theatre, and specifically, with *Beginner's Luck*. From its very first curtain until its last, he *owned* it—every performance. He poured himself into it continually, wanting to make it better and ensure its success. In fact, he cared so much about *Beginner's Luck* that producer Norman S. Powell, who had worked with Bob on *The Bob Crane Show*, remarked that Bob seemed to have been more proud of *Beginner's Luck* than he had of the television program.

"He was flush with what he considered his strong points of traveling around doing dinner theatre," Powell said. "We went to Florida to see him doing *Beginner's Luck*. It's *very* broad and burlesque. The pilot for *Second Start* had been picked up, and he didn't like the pilot all that much, even though he knew it had been picked up. We flew down there to screen it for him, and you know, he was prouder of *Beginner's Luck* than he was of *Second Start*. He definitely felt that he should play the straight man, which was reinforced because he had such a warm audience from the dinner theatre group that he traveled around with. They reinforced it. He titillated the audience with double entendres and all that kind of stuff he would do in *Beginner's Luck*."

Beginner's Luck, written by Norman Barasch and Carroll Moore, is a light, romantic comedy set in New York City. Paul and Sally Burnett

BOB CRANE The Definitive Biography

**Bob Crane and Radio Theatre
Rod Serling's 'Zero Hour'/Hollywood Radio Theatre
Jim French's 'The Flaw'/Imagination Theatre/Jim French Productions**

Rod Serling's Zero Hour was a radio mystery/adventure/suspense series produced by Rod Serling that aired from September 3, 1973, to July 26, 1974. Similar to television mystery programs popular at the time, such as *Columbo* and *Ellery Queen, Zero Hour* was a mix of mystery, action, and dry humor. *Zero Hour* was also known as Hollywood Radio Theatre, and the Mutual Broadcasting System ran the series in syndication. Elliott Lewis—a veteran voice actor, writer, producer, and director of radio programs during the 1930s to 1950s, and who later also produced television series, including *The Lucy Show*—directed the series.

Bob Crane had worked with Rod Serling in the past, on *The Twilight Zone* in the 1961 episode "Static" (providing all of the voices heard on the radio), and later in the 1971 *Night Gallery* episode "House – With Ghost." Bob also interviewed Serling over his KNX radio show in the early 1960s. While working in radio, Bob had been known as "The Man of 1,000 Voices," and performing radio drama offered him the chance to use that talent once again. Bob starred in five episodes of Rod Serling's *Zero Hour* for the Hollywood Theatre in July 1974.

"Bend, Spindle, Mutilate" . . . . *July 1, 1974*
"Murder Is a Work of Art". . . . . *July 2, 1974*
"Edwards Tug and Salvage" . . . . *July 3, 1974*
"Larceny on the Lake". . . . . *July 4, 1974*
"On the Lam" . . . . *July 5, 1974*

Bob was a gifted entertainer and voice impersonator, and he was easily able to disguise his voice—as he had done routinely in radio for fifteen consecutive years. In *Zero Hour*, Bob provided the voice talent for several different characters in each of his five episodes.

While in Seattle in early 1977 performing his play *Beginner's Luck* at The Cirque Dinner Theatre, Bob met with writer and radio theatre producer Jim French, brother of playwright Samuel French, the publisher of *Beginner's Luck, Send Me No Flowers*, and other notable plays for the stage.

A disc jockey and a prolific playwright for numerous radio dramas, including the CBS radio *Suspense*, Jim French began writing, directing, and producing plays for Seattle radio listeners in 1965. From 1973 to 1977, he produced a local Seattle radio series called *Crisis*, which consisted of half-hour radio programs focusing on adventure, drama, and comedy, with an occasional western or science fiction episode. The opening of early episodes features French providing a brief overview and introduction of the series: "Sooner or later, when you least expect it, there comes a point of no return. A dead end from which there seems no escape. A moment in time. A moment of *Crisis*!"

While French did not like the name of the series very much, he did enjoy writing and producing the episodes for it. He wrote his episodes around his leading actor, explaining in 2003 that it allowed him to write *for* the cast who would be bringing his characters to life. When Bob was in Seattle in 1977, French approached him about performing an episode.

"He was interested when I asked him if he would record a radio drama I would write for him," French remembered. "I had just finished interviewing him on my radio show—a DJ show, not radio drama. He agreed to do it. I don't think he was the least bit negative. He was gracious enough to accept."

With Bob on board, French penned the script for the episode, "The Flaw." Recorded at Audio Recordings, Inc., Studios in Seattle, "The Flaw" originally aired on February 10, 1977. In addition to Bob, the episode also featured the voice talents of Ronni Richards, Doug Young, John Amendole, Pat French (wife of Jim French), and Phil Harper.

"The Flaw" features Bob as a scriptwriter who is married to a woman he no longer loves. From the official episode description, "A successful writer wants to leave his alcoholic wife, but can't because she's the one who's been secretly fixing all of his deeply flawed scripts." In his attempt to find happiness, Bob's character plots to murder his wife and also enjoys the company of other women.

"Most actors would rather play villains than heroes, they say," French said. "Yes, I wrote the script for Bob to play, but I don't know that I consciously made his character a womanizer because that was Bob's reputation."

A typical day working in the recording studio was "very informal," he continued. "The cast had all received their scripts days in advance. I directed almost all the shows. We would discuss the characters, do a run-through, and then an on-mic rehearsal. Then we were ready to tape.

"Bob was very cooperative, funny, and enjoyable to be around. The session went very fast, as I recall, and I don't remember any unusual number of retakes. Bob was a real pro, and he worked well with the rest of the cast. Working with Bob in the recording studio was thrilling because he was so totally natural. We never heard him 'acting.' His technique was 'invisible,' meaning that if you didn't know he was reading a script, you'd believe he was actually living the part. A few others I've worked with were just as 'invisible,' and all of them were movie stars. Bill Macy, Ruta Lee, Tom Smothers, Keenan Wynn, to name just a few. Bob did a superb job. The radio play I wrote for him remains one of my favorites out of more than five hundred that I've produced so far."

are happily married, living their happily married life without incident or circumstance—until Paul decides he needs to cheat on his wife to save his marriage. He had read that at least one affair in a marriage actually serves to spice things up romantically between husband and wife. Paul has never done such a thing before; nor has he ever considered it. Still, he decides to go through with it and chooses his coworker Monica Rogers for his one-night stand.

Paul is inexperienced at such behavior, and he chickens out—but not before he is caught in the act! One year later, Paul and Sally are divorced. Paul has agonized over his actions and spends his every waking minute regretting his stupidity and is plotting a way to win Sally back. Meanwhile, Sally has been enjoying her freedom, which includes being able to indulge in the company of men—*lots* of men—much to Paul's surprise. One of Sally's acquaintances, Scott Marlowe, happens to drop in on Sally while Paul makes his long-awaited move to win her back. As Paul and Scott vie for Sally's attention and affection, Scott is suave and calm, while Paul fumbles his way through. Paul is clearly the underdog of the two, and nothing goes his way. The more Paul tries, the worse it gets. Yet Sally is touched by Paul's persistence, and she softens. By the end of the play, she and Paul reconcile, to the delight of the audience.

Beginner's Luck may have been the perfect play for Bob Crane, but it had not been written specifically *for* him. Playwright Norman Barasch recalled that he and Carroll Moore had originally asked Monty Hall to play the part of Paul Burnett. Monty, however, believed Bob was a better choice, and he recommended him to Barasch and Moore.

"Crane read the play and loved it," Barasch wrote in a letter to Linda Groundwater. "He subsequently took it on the road and played theatres throughout the county for the next [several] years with great critical and commercial success. I always found Bob to be cooperative, appreciative of the play, and a very upbeat character."

Beginner's Luck opened at the Drury Lane Theatre in Chicago on March 25, 1970, and ran through May 1 of that year. Bob was the original actor to portray Paul Burnett, earning him the honor of being listed in all published copies of the play. Bob accepted the role at a time when he was at the height of his acting career, with *Hogan's Heroes* still going strong, and he had connected with the character instantly. Vernon Schwartz, with whom Bob had previously worked on *Send Me No Flowers* a year earlier, directed the spring 1970 run of the play, but

Bob would soon direct *Beginner's Luck* himself. Eventually, Bob secured rights from Barasch and Moore to tour the country with the play. But Bob did not perform or direct *Beginner's Luck* exclusively. Other productions of *Beginner's Luck* that ran during the 1970s headlined other actors in the starring role of Paul Burnett, most notably DeForest Kelley of *Star Trek* fame. *Beginner's Luck* continues to be performed to this day.

By the time Bob's second run of the play was performed in August 1970 in Traverse City, Michigan, it was being billed as a pre-Broadway run, and Bob's ambitions were to take *Beginner's Luck* all the way to Broadway. Further, he was working with *Hogan's Heroes* associate producer Edward H. Feldman in an attempt to turn *Beginner's Luck* into a feature film. For one reason or another, *Beginner's Luck* never made it to Broadway or was produced as a film. But that did not deter Bob from performing and directing *Beginner's Luck* to the very best of his ability.

Although he loved the basic plot of *Beginner's Luck*, Bob also rewrote and restructured the play *constantly*. He then sent his changes to Norman Barasch for updating the official version of the script. Once Bob started tinkering with the play, ancillary characters that he did not believe propelled the storyline were omitted. He worked on it—almost compulsively—trying to make it better, richer, fuller, and tighter. He streamlined it down to four characters. He was still making changes to the scenes and dialogue as late as its final performance—June 28, 1978.

As with *Hogan's Heroes,* Bob invested a great deal of his heart and soul into *Beginner's Luck*. And he poured all of his energy into perfecting the role of Paul Burnett. Dinner theatre may not have had the glitz and glamor of television and film, but Bob reveled in the opportunity to control the production and perform before an audience.

Pamela Hayes Thompson worked with Bob on the very first run of *Beginner's Luck* in Chicago under the direction of Vernon Schwartz, also earning her a place in the official published script.

"He had stopped doing *Hogan's Heroes* for the summer, and he wanted to do some theatre," Pam recalled. "So he came to Drury Lane, and they auditioned people. The director chose someone [other than me], and Bob said, 'I don't want her. I want the girl that was second.' And that was me. So there we were. I went off to summer stock with Bob in 1970. It was, for me, an *incredible* experience. I had not done very *much* theatre. I was doing modeling and TV commercials and such, and I was *going* to be a famous actress in TV and films. But when we started that show, I learned how to look in his eyes and know what wasn't gonna work! Because he would sometimes cut something and go back. I can tell you he was a *genius* because he could *feel* it, and somehow or other, I could tell from him that we were going somewhere else. And we changed from the moment—from the first time he said, 'Marzipan,' and he said, 'I don't know what that is, so I don't want to say that. Can you give me another *dish*? Like a sundae?' But we had so much fun out there that even though we were cutting and rearranging, people didn't care. And it was so exciting for me. I was young and impressionable, and I thought he was a *magnificent* actor—which I still do. I think *Hogan's Heroes* is a brilliant exhibition of fine comedy timing and work. But he taught me—he taught *me* how to use it, and I'm still using it [in our performances today] to make sure we're doing the right thing."

Pam's husband John Thompson, who occasionally played the role of Scott Marlowe in *Beginner's Luck*, said, "It is a *wonderful* show! And Bob was a *wonderful* character actor as well as a leading man, and he was a *fine* comedian. His big hero, of course, was Jack Benny. And Bob had some of that wonderful—that ability to do those wonderful kind of 'takes' and just wait for the laughs, and he was really a fine comedian. One of the wonderful things of working with him in the play was that *Beginner's Luck* actually became *Bob's* play. He was constantly rewriting it, updating the play and adding humor, and he turned it into something that it originally wasn't. It turned into a marvelous vehicle for him. We'd be standing back stage, and he'd say to [Pam and me], 'Oh in this scene, let's try this,' and he would just run it by us. We all were really good at ad-libbing and such, and we were writing the show as we were doing it. I'm used to adlibbing, and Bob was a great adlibber."

John and Pam agreed that Barasch and Moore were fine with Bob taking the play and changing it to his liking. As long as the money was rolling in, the two playwrights had no qualms about it.

"Bob felt it was *his* play," John continued. "He felt the rewrites that he did through adlibbing and everything else really turned it into *his* show. He's the one who cut it down from a six-character show to a four-character show. He worked at it constantly. It was always a work in progress with Bob. After about two performances, he cut out two of the characters, and it was a four-person play from that moment on. And he combined two suitors for his estranged wife in the show and made it into one, and that was the role that Bernard Fox and I did. Bob taped the show several times. There was so much material that never got written down or chronicled in any way, except we knew the show, and it was always ever-changing. He got bored, so he said, 'Let's do this, let's do this...,' and his writing ability was just *brilliant*. We would just go out and do it, and it would work, instantly. He just had a great sense of what was funny. And it's a shame none of that got chronicled because *that* made the show."

Bob also interacted with the audience after the final curtain call of the show. For fifteen or twenty minutes, he would stand up on stage talking about his days on *Hogan's Heroes* or showing outtakes from the series. And according to John and Pam, he loved it.

"He was charming, and he was kind," Pam remembered. "He used to stand out in the lobby and sign autographs. He made us go out, too, so that's how I know. We all signed autographs for an *hour*. He was kind to *everybody*."

"He was very gregarious," John explained. "One of the most gregarious people I know. Very kind, warm; he loved meeting people. He would stand out there and sign autographs and take pictures and talk. He was a star who really enjoyed his fans. Many times, we'd be having dinner, and someone would come over, and he'd spend fifteen or twenty minutes talking to them, not knowing them at all, just a fan— someone who loved *Hogan's Heroes*."

"And they'd drop cigar ash in his food!" Pam laughed. "I'll never forget that day. He said, 'Oh well, no good deed goes unpunished. Can I have another steak?' But that's the kind of guy he was. And polite, and he cared about his children and his ex-wife. He made sure he paid them every month."

"After the performance and signing autographs, we'd go out," John said. "He'd go drumming, and we'd go with him. For example, at Pheasant Run in Illinois, there was a nightclub lounge, and after work every night, he'd go in and start playing drums. A couple of times, I brought some musicians [I knew along]. And we'd all play. I used to be with a group called the Harmonicats, so I brought out a bass harmonica and played bass with Bob. He just loved playing afterward. That was his other love. Being a drummer. He loved the music business."

By the time Bob brought *Beginner's Luck* to Scottsdale in the summer of 1973, John and Pam had gotten married after dating for several years.

"We were very close, and we both loved Bob very much," John said. "And he kind of played Cupid for us, and he steered me into the direction of—'I think Pam likes you. Why don't you take a shot?' It worked out, thank goodness. He saw something that was wonderful, and it's been great."

John and Pam were very relaxed with Bob, and he was the same with them. The first time John was in *Beginner's Luck* (Scottsdale – 1973), he needed extra rehearsing time.

"It was the first time that I did the show, and it was really interesting because we rehearsed in the swimming pool," John remembered. "So I was just in the pool running lines with them constantly. We would adlib sections of the show, and they worked so well that eventually we would put them in."

They were all so relaxed, in fact, that while on stage, they would try and make each other laugh.

"I thought it was a little bit unprofessional, being the *'actress'* that I am," Pam said with a laugh. "And then I started doing it! I was easily as guilty as they were!"

Pam and John recalled that the practical jokes made for some very funny and memorable moments. In the *Beginner's Luck* storyline, Paul Burnett (Bob) pretends to want to shoot Scott Marlowe (John), but instead of drawing a gun from his pocket, he reveals a banana.

"Oh, the banana!" Pam laughed.

"When we were doing that scene, he would turn his back to the audience as I would burst through the door in the final scene, angry," John said. "He would do some of the damndest things with that banana that people couldn't see. And of course, I would start to—I'm pretty good, but once I lose it, I lose it completely, and he would just enjoy the hell out of that. You can drag that out for ages—and he did. And he enjoyed it so very, very much! I mean, when we would work together, I was waiting in the side stage waiting to go on, and all of a sudden, he would be there. He would be dressed funny, or doing something crazy, just to break me up, just before my entrance. Bob loved practical jokes! My goodness. He was one of the most upbeat people unless he was having problems with Patty or the family. But otherwise, that was about the only thing that ever brought him down."

The funniest scene in the play, John and Pam concurred, was the ticket scene.

"That scene is absolutely brilliant," John said. "It was a really fine comedy."

"Bob made it funny," Pam added. "The ticket scene was brilliant. And he rewrote it. I mean—unbelievable. In the original script book that has the scene in it is not the way it was."

John and Pam were loyal friends to Bob, and vice versa. They watched everything he ever did on television or in film, and they cheered for every success and listened when he needed to share his thoughts and feelings about his troubles.

Pam remembered, "He demanded very little. There was no such thing as, 'We *will* be going out.' It was, 'Hey, c'mon. You wanna go out and drum for a little while?' We're free spirits being in the business. And when we left and went our separate ways between the shows, we seldom called or anything. He was like we are. If you call me and you need something, I'm there. To call me and chat, I don't have it. I don't have the time."

"During the day, we rarely saw Bob," John continued. "It was always at the show, or we'd go back to the house many nights. If he had been filming the show, we'd take a look at it. We'd talk and plan about what we could do to make changes here or to make a scene better or to make a line better. And our friendship was always about the show and the times we were together. Bob was just such a fun-loving guy. It was always great to be in his company. We always had just great, fun times. I remember he was working in Disneyland at one of the attractions that was featuring him. He knew I was going to be on the West Coast, and he called me. He said, 'Open for me. I need an opening act.' So I came in and did my comedy magic act in front of Bob. But it was things like that. He'd just call on the spur of the moment and say, 'Can you come on in and do this with me?' And of course, we always said, 'Of course!' Because it was always just great fun. It wasn't a heavy-duty professional relationship. It was always a fun relationship when we were working together."

John also remembered Bob confiding in him about things that troubled him. "I think in talking to Bob man to man at times, he kind of intimated to me that it was during *Hogan's Heroes* when women started throwing themselves at him, that he was like a kid in a candy store. That's what cost him his first marriage, and I always knew, when he was in a bad mood, it was problems with Patty or problems with the first family, he would sit with me, and he and I would talk about it. He always felt guilty about leaving his first wife—the kids more than his wife. He needed an ear sometimes just to bounce off. He would get very depressed when things were going wrong family-wise for him. It was something that really bothered him a lot. In 1970 when I met Bob and Patty, they hadn't gotten married yet. And they were very much in love. I realized that the very first time we met. And yes, I do remember when—because both Bob and I had vasectomies. Bob was involved with Patty, and all of a sudden, she became pregnant with Scotty. And he said, 'This can't be.' He was ready to leave her over this because he said, 'It's impossible.' He had it done in Japan. In Japan, they don't tie off the vas tubes; they just cauterize them. And when this happens, sometimes they can reconnect. And this is what happened in Bob's case. So he had a paternity test, and he realized it was his son, and that's when they got married."

To corroborate this, Scott Crane provided the authors with official documentation of his father's semen analysis conducted by Richard Peterfy, MD, a urologist practicing in Los Angeles. Dated October 9, 1970, this report proves that Bob's vasectomy had failed and that he could, in fact, father children. This report strongly suggested to Bob that he was the biological father of Patty's then-unborn baby, and it was valid enough proof for him to marry her one week later. Further, in November 1995, Scott consented to a DNA test. This official, notarized lab report was also provided to the authors. The lab (Genelex, Seattle, Washington) took samples of Bob's DNA from the bed sheet where he was murdered (then still in the crime file) and compared it to Scott's DNA. Bob and Scott's DNA markers are a perfect match for father and son. Based on these documents, Bob Crane is the biological father of Robert Scott Crane. Regardless, Bob accepted and raised Scott as his own son.

John continued, "He was a doting dad. He was a great father. Even with his children from the first marriage. He would bring them out all the time. We'd be working in Arizona or Florida. They would always show up. He'd bring them in at one point or another. He tried to foster a relationship with Scotty and his other children."

But the relationship seemed strained to John and Pam. They noticed that it was difficult for Bob's children from his marriage with Anne.

"Unfortunately, fame and money and power do not make for happiness a lot of times," Pam said. "The children seemed a little bit—they were very jealous. I mean, there's the baby coming in, and the father has success."

John added, "I always felt that there was an invisible wall there that the kids really could not [breach]. I think they were there for their father but not for Patty. And Patty had animosity toward the kids. There were problems. That hostility that we never got to see, but we could feel it."

Outside of those few instances, however, Bob remained closed off, and he kept John and Pam at arm's length.

"He really was private," John stated. "But we were as well. You can't get too involved with your leading man or the other way around because it leads to a not fun show."

"Bob and I even discussed that," Pam explained. "Just joking around. He said, 'You're my wife? Are we going somewhere?' And I said, 'No, we're not.' Because frankly, he picked me when he first chose me to work with him because we were *not* attracted to each other. There is such a time when there's just nothing, and that made the relationship so good on stage. There's nothing but trouble if your leading lady is also leading in your sack, and you must cater to her."

John added, "Bob and Pam had a chemistry that I can say is akin to Mary Tyler Moore and Dick Van Dyke. It was a great, great on stage relationship."

"I don't remember ever, ever fighting about anything," Pam said. "I was so overwhelmed, so young. And he taught me *so much*. I'm still working today, and it's because of him. He's taught me so much about timing. And then when John would do the show, I could keep up with them both because I listened. That was my learning time, and he taught me so much."

"Bob and I kind of trained Pam in timing in both physical comedy as well as timing in lines," John elaborated. "And the three of us really did work well together. It really was a great balance. And so was Bernard Fox. Bernard was equally as brilliant. But Bob was a great director, and I remember one of the scenes where I was hit, and he said to me after the first night, 'Oh, you're not getting enough out of that.' I said, 'What do you mean?' And he said, 'Well, just imagine someone…just imagine you just dropped a load in your pants.' That was his direction for me when I got hit! I understood it, and it really works! It was that kind of thing we could say to each other. Bob and I would go right for the best way we could explain it to each other! We could do that. Go right for the meat of the moment, and he was very good at directing. If he saw something that wasn't working, he could find a way to get you to do it."

John and Pam never performed *Beginner's Luck* with anyone else—only with Bob. They continue to hold a fierce loyalty to him to this day, and they could never imagine performing *Beginner's Luck* without him.

"We always said you can't possibly do this show without Bob," Pam said. "It wouldn't be right."

Over the years, other cast members would perform the role of the three characters surrounding Bob in *Beginner's Luck*; however, according to John and Pam, Bob usually rotated the same actors in the roles. Bob believed strongly in the adage that "if it ain't broke, don't fix it." However, it was a young actress named Victoria Berry Wells who, in addition to Bob Crane, would become most notably associated with *Beginner's Luck*.

The Classic Cat, a well-known topless bar in Hollywood featuring beautiful dancers and waitresses, had entertained many of the era's rich and famous. According to their website, it was "the largest, most luxurious topless club of them all. The dancers and the cocktail waitresses were the most beautiful girls in Hollywood. It was packed almost every night of the week with tourists and locals, including many celebrities."

It was here where Victoria Ann Berry, who later married Classic Cat owner Alan Wells, first met Bob Crane. He had been out celebrating his birthday, and the stop at The Classic Cat had been a gift to him from his wife Patty.

"When I met Bob, it was his birthday. He went backstage and videoed all the girls nude and topless, and his wife would let him. I remember thinking how sad that would be for his wife—that she let that happen. I thought there was something desperately wrong and missing. That was my first impression of that situation. But I *loved* him on *Hogan's Heroes*. I thought he was fantastic. And I knew about his radio and that he played the drums. I was very heavy into acting at the time, so I talked to him more about acting. I was on *Starsky and Hutch* on the main title every week, and I had done a lot of television and film work. And I got to know him as a friend. Apparently, the girl that was supposed to go on the road for *Beginner's Luck* [was unable to go]. He talked to me quite extensively about that. Not that much long after [first meeting Bob], I got a phone call. He said he wanted me to do that part of Monica—that he was going to try me out. So I bought the play, and I read it. It was a small part—a cute, dumb blond part."

She found Bob to be pleasant and fun. As an actress, she respected him as an actor, so when Bob offered her the role of Monica in *Beginner's Luck*, she was eager to accept. She traveled with Bob and the cast to Ohio in November 1977, where she performed *Beginner's Luck* for the first time.

"I did the show, and I had very good reviews," Vicky said. "Bob was very proud. I was very sick when I was there, and Bob was absolutely *marvelous* to me. I had a hysterectomy, that's how sick I was, and I still worked. Bob took me to the pharmacy. My doctor bought all my medication for me and checked on me every day to see if I was well. But thankfully, I got better. Bob was so marvelous. I will never forget how marvelous and caring he was with my health. But he was very pleased about my reviews, and I traveled with him on the road a few times after that. There was one special thing I remember—one review I got, Bob came running into the dressing room in Dallas, and he came in very excited. He was very professional. He knew I was very serious about my career. He read the reviews all the time, and he had circled the review. It said, 'Victoria Ann Berry—Her scenes with Crane were the smoothest of the evening.' And Bob thought that was so unbelievable because it's a little part, and to have 'her scenes with Crane were the smoothest of the evening.' He was so impressed with that. He was so excited. There's a lot about Bob that I absolutely loved."

But there was one thing about Bob that she didn't absolutely love. Early on in her tour with *Beginner's Luck*, Bob wanted to film Vicky in a provocative setting. She only ever allowed him to film her once—by the pool. But it made her extremely uncomfortable, and she told him about it. Like a light switch, he turned off any further desires he may have had to film her, and he never approached her again.

"He knew I wasn't into it at all," Vicky said. "He was very protective of me."

Vicky remembered that *Beginner's Luck* was always successful whenever it had been performed, playing to sell-out crowds. The audience response was always wonderful.

"Mondays were dark," Vicky explained. "We performed every Tuesday night, Wednesday night, Thursday night, Friday night, Saturday, and two shows on Sunday. It was *very* popular, and it was *always* crowded. When we first arrived in a new location, the first couple of days were hectic. Everyone would have to get set up in their apartments. Bob would be separate from us. But when we first moved in, when we first got there, he'd come to each one of our apartments and make sure we had everything. Is the apartment working, is everything functioning right? Everything we needed he made sure we had. He'd check up and make sure. He was *marvelous* like that. He didn't just drop us off. And he made sure we had a car between us and that we were totally comfortable with everything. He was *very* good about that. Then we'd have two rehearsals—tech rehearsals, and the blocking and everything. And then we'd take notes. He'd give us notes at the end of performances if things weren't working or if things needed fixing, he'd give a critique to us. What worked or didn't work. I didn't have any problems with him at all."

Vicky further explained how Bob was able to switch from director to actor during the production of *Beginner's Luck*.

"He was in almost every scene," Vicky said. "But he would stand back and say, 'Walk here,' do the blocking, and 'Walk there,' and do the blocking. Every stage is different. You know, theatre in the rounds, you know all different styles. We'd practice our bows, and that was it. The show was smooth, and he'd give critiques, and if things needed addressing, he would address it. Bob gave me a *lot* of freedom. I did a lot of homework on my part, though. I worked hard. I was always trying to work out laughs and make it better. I never got stale with it. I would go over my scene every single night before I went on. And I was always striving to get laughs. Bob and I would work out what worked and what didn't. A lot of it depended on the audience. You'd play to your audience a little bit. You pick it up. It's instinctive. And Bob and I worked well with that. He'd say, 'This audience is this,' and I'd go, 'This is a lousy audience,' and so you play it a little differently. You play the audience. And we worked well with that. We'd bounce back, and we'd improvise and make it longer! A lot of times, we just bounced off each other. He *loved* that. We were getting a lot of laughs. He'd throw in lines. I'd throw in lines. And we'd just feed off each other. And I've never been able to do that with anyone else since."

Vicky explained that as a director, Bob allowed others to shine and to have their moment. "Bob gave me a chance," she said. "He let the light shine on me. He never stole the scene. I've worked with actors who have stolen the scene from me. People tried to steal scenes from Bob. Bob *never* tried to steal a scene from me. I used to watch the show every single night, after my part, and then I'd come back for my bows. Bob was a real pro. He was the star. It was about him. But he gave everyone else their chance *except* with people who would try to take it off him. It was very hurtful. I don't think Bob had an ego at all. I think he wanted the show to work, and to make a show work, a fine director *knows* that *everybody* counts. He was the star of the show. He had the name. The other people were small-time actors. We were blitzed to even get the job."

Not everyone was as respectful or professional as Bob would have liked, however.

"He had problems with egotistical actors, though," Vicky continued. "But I always knew Bob was right. There wasn't a shadow of a doubt in my mind. Not just right, but he was 110% right. He had to deal with a lot of ego. One girl started talking to the audience, making jokes with the audience behind his back. Oh, that was a cardinal sin. Bob was upset about that—he nearly had a *heart attack* over it. And there was another guy who thought he was a top actor, and he kept trying to do things—like wrong direction and wrong turns and wrong ambiance—against Bob. He tried to make it like Bob was stupid. It was a comedy, not a show to make Bob look stupid. Bob was the star. And they had problems over that. But he dealt with it as it came, and he was on top of everything. No matter what else what he was doing, he was always on top of it. He cared very much about his work. I didn't think he was an egotistical man. I'd treat him as an equal. Some other people were very egotistical, and he had to sort of stand his ground. And he was *always* right. I mean, it stood out like a sore thumb how right he was. I have to tell you the truth. I would say if Bob was wrong or out of line. Bob handled it very professionally. He did not lose his cool. He was *right*. And he had to put up with a lot. I respected him immensely. If he said something, I knew it was right. I never questioned it. I put my trust in him, whereas some people didn't, obviously. And they were wrong and stupid."

When Bob wasn't performing on stage, Vicky found him to be very "down to earth." He was older than Vicky, and she respected his experience and enjoyed the fatherly attention he gave to her.

"He gave me his all," Vicky said. "*Professionalism*. I was *so comfortable* with him. I was never nervous, and 'Oh, gee, is he going to yell at me?' and 'Did I do something wrong?' I was free to experiment and improve. I would try different things. He would come in and say, 'That's fantastic!' He would always be positive with me. Only once he corrected me. Only once ever. And I learned to this day how right he was. Bob was right there. Bob was *right there* 110%."

Vicky explained, "A lot of Bob Crane was in that character of

Hogan. But it wasn't Bob. When you would talk to Bob one on one, like I talked to him lots of times, he was not going around like *Hogan's Heroes*. That's ridiculous. He was a person. I think he learned his lines before anyone else ever did. I think he put more into it than anyone else ever did; therefore, it came across effortlessly. He knew his craft. And he knew what worked, he knew what didn't work, and he evolved from that character. Once you get that character down, you play it. It's getting the character that's doing the work, and then you try and improve on your technique and on your work. You're constantly trying to improve on it. I think Bob was like that. But he had the character of Hogan down. That's the hard part. Getting the character and getting the audience's approval and getting a hit show. That's like *gold*. But you have to get the character, and once you get the character, of course, it's part of you."

Recalling when something had not gone quite right on stage during a performance, Vicky said that Bob was able to handle such mishaps effectively and not become distracted by them. He played with the moment, did not get frazzled, and flowed with the performance. In one performance, the champagne bottle had leaked, and instead of faltering, Bob and Vicky improvised.

"We made fun of it," Vicky said. "That would have killed the whole joke that was coming up. So I said, 'Oh, something's leaking in the bag,' and he went, 'Ohhh!' We took the bottle out, and we improvised the whole thing! We made new lines and laughed and joked. We bounced off each other and went on and on. And we were getting a lot of laughs. Sometimes Bob would just add lines when we were really gelling together. And I would just play right off him. I had my character down pat. He had his character down pat. And we just gelled together. Like horse and carriage."

Bob was fond of talking about his theatre mishaps. One particular story became a favorite of his to tell, and it usually garnered a lot of laughs when he told it at presentations. One night during a run of *Beginner's Luck*, he had arrived at the theatre very, very late, which was unusual. He didn't have a lot of time before he went on stage, so he had not had adequate time to change completely. He went out on stage, and he was wearing a pair of shorts, but not regular underwear. He had just thrown on the shorts he needed to be wearing on stage for the first scene, where he runs out of the apartment with the bowling ball. He didn't realize that his pants were unzipped. And someone in the audience noticed, and he very quickly ran off stage. It was not typical for him to arrive to work unprepared, and it had been a lesson for him. From that point on, Bob was never without his special shorts/underwear, and he made a joke of it. This was the same story that he apparently told on *Celebrity Cooks*, offending CBS spokesman Jeff Erdel so much in July 1978 that it aided in Erdel's sole decision to pull Bob's episode from the air. Yet others had not been disturbed by it. For example, Bob told this same story to a group of students at the Texas Wesleyan College on September 6, 1973, as the special guest speaker during the college's special Celebrity Series program. Bob had been so well received that the college dedicated an entire page in its 1974 yearbook to his visit and had even referenced the story in an article in their college newspaper.

Vicky concurred with John and Pam Thompson that the only times she ever saw Bob depressed were the times when he discussed wanting more from his work and the troubles he was experiencing with his family. He was extremely worried about how his impending divorce with Patty was going to affect Scott, and he discussed it occasionally with Vicky. She also recalled him talking about the pilot he had recently filmed in Hawaii (*The Hawaii Experience*). He seemed excited about that prospective new series, and he had even wanted her to take a small part in it.

"He seemed very upbeat," she said. "The only down side that I can remember is he wanted more in his work. That's a definite. I felt that he wanted to get out and do another series. Badly, I'd say. I think he lost a lot when he was on dinner theatre. I think his soul got a little sad. But he had this pilot coming up that he really wanted me in. But with dinner theatre, he felt, 'This is what I have to do for now.' And he made it as professional and as good, and he cared about us, as he could. What was important to him was him was his family and his work. I think he wanted harmony in all areas. And his family—he was worried about little [Scotty] and getting a divorce made him distraught and stressful. He talked about Scotty. That stands out in my mind. He talked about him so much. That was bothering him—his family. I know he wanted more. He wanted another series. But he kept an upper lip. He was fun to be around. I never saw him distressed except about getting the divorce. His family life was tearing him apart. He wasn't in a great place. But he was aware of it. He held it together."

But Vicky also commented that the need for "more" in his acting career was not a problem that Bob had encountered exclusively. She said, "I think most people that are on Bob Crane's level as an actor need to have *more*. Tom Cruise, I've worked with him. He needs it. Don Knotts needed it. I mean, everyone I've worked with. So I don't see why Bob would stand out any more than anyone else. Of course he needed it. It was his life. He gave his life to it. And to lose it and just do dinner theatre, I think that's a very hard thing to do. He wanted to come up. He was *not* quitting. It was very humbling, to have to step down. But I've heard that from Don Knotts and other actors. Not just Bob. So that's nothing unusual there. That's just my opinion."

Victoria Berry Wells loved working with Bob Crane, and she embraced every moment she spent with him performing *Beginner's Luck*. "In a way, I was a little bit like his confidante," she said. "He was very professional. He loved my work, and he was honest. He became very protective and caring with me. I had to earn that. But I won it. And I got it. And I loved it. And I cherished it."

There is no question that Bob excelled in the theatre as both an actor and a director. He was a leader, an organizer, and a star. Yet even while working in dinner theatre, he maintained the mindset of the actor's actor and did his very best to deliver a stage production of the highest quality that would be enjoyed by his fans.

He was also a conscientious performer and director. In July 1974, he and his *Beginner's Luck* troupe traveled to New Orleans for a six-week run of the show at The Beverly. A short distance away, at The Beverly Barn Dinner Theatre in Shreveport, Louisiana, actor Frank Sutton (Sergeant Carter on *Gomer Pyle, U.S.M.C.*) was just opening the play *Luv* when he had a fatal heart attack.

Donna Goobic was the production manager at The Beverly and at The Beverly Barn Dinner Theatre. She remembered, "Frank Sutton was a marvelous guy—a marvelous actor. He passed away back stage in the theatre. Bob brought his show into Shreveport to replace that show and then moved down to New Orleans."

Donna remembered, "He and his cast mates seemed to get along well together. There were never any problems. Sometimes you had stars that are temperamental—they had to have this or that—but he was never like that at all."

Later, Bob sent a note to The Beverly in New Orleans:

Needless to say, my cast & myself, will always consider our stay at The Beverly one of the most enjoyable engagements we've had since starting "Beginner's Luck" over six years ago.

As you may recall—our booking was a substitution for the late Frank Sutton, from "Gomer Pyle." When Frank passed away at your Shreveport Theatre—we opened for his remaining week, then came on to The Beverly. The fact that we were able to do sell-out business and extend our run, even though it was the rainy season (January to December), was a tribute to the type operation you have established. Having a Jazz group that I could drum with every night didn't make me mad, either…
Best from all—
Bob Crane

While Bob may have been struggling to find his professional niche again, he had certainly found success on the stage. His reviews were stellar, and his audiences continued to cheer and applaud his performances. With only rare exceptions, his fellow cast members enjoyed working with him as their director and alongside him as an actor. Despite the professional step back to performing in dinner theatre, his sights were set on a far grander horizon. He wanted Broadway, and he was working diligently in the hope that *Beginner's Luck* would afford him that opportunity. But Broadway, and so many other hopes and dreams Bob had for his future, would never come to be.

Bob Crane and the cast of *Cactus Flower*, performed at the Veterans Memorial, Warren, Ohio, May 15-June 29, 1969. Sigrid Valdis (Patricia Olson) is next to Bob on the right.

Source: Courtesy of Scott Crane. Used with permission.

Bob with Sigrid Valdis (Patricia Olson) in the 1969 theatre production of *Cactus Flower* at the Veterans Memorial, Warren, Ohio, May 15-29, 1969.

Source: Courtesy of Scott Crane. Used with permission.

Members of the cast of *Beginner's Luck* take their bow; from left to right: Bob Crane, Pamela Hayes Thompson, and John Thompson (date and location unknown).

Source: Courtesy of Scott Crane. Used with permission.

Monica Rodgers (Victoria Berry Wells) and Paul Burnett (Bob Crane) did not intend on bowling for the evening! (circa 1978)

Source: Courtesy of Scott Crane. Used with permission.

Bob Crane and Pamela Hayes Thompson as Paul and Sally Burnett in *Beginner's Luck* (1970s). When actor Frank Sutton died suddenly of a heart attack at The Beverly Barn Dinner Theatre in Shreveport, Louisiana, Bob and his Beginner's Luck acting company, who had just arrived in New Orleans to begin their run, moved over to Shreveport to perform. This saved the theatre from losing money during the week following Sutton's death.

Sources: Originally published in *The Beverly* by Nancy Gex. Used with permission.

Third Act Twist

Bob Crane and Pamela Hayes Thompson as Paul and Sally Burnett in *Beginner's Luck* (1970s).

Source: Courtesy of Scott Crane. Used with permission.

A descriptive photograph showing the placement of props for *Beginner's Luck* (date and location unknown).

Source: Courtesy of Scott Crane. Used with permission.

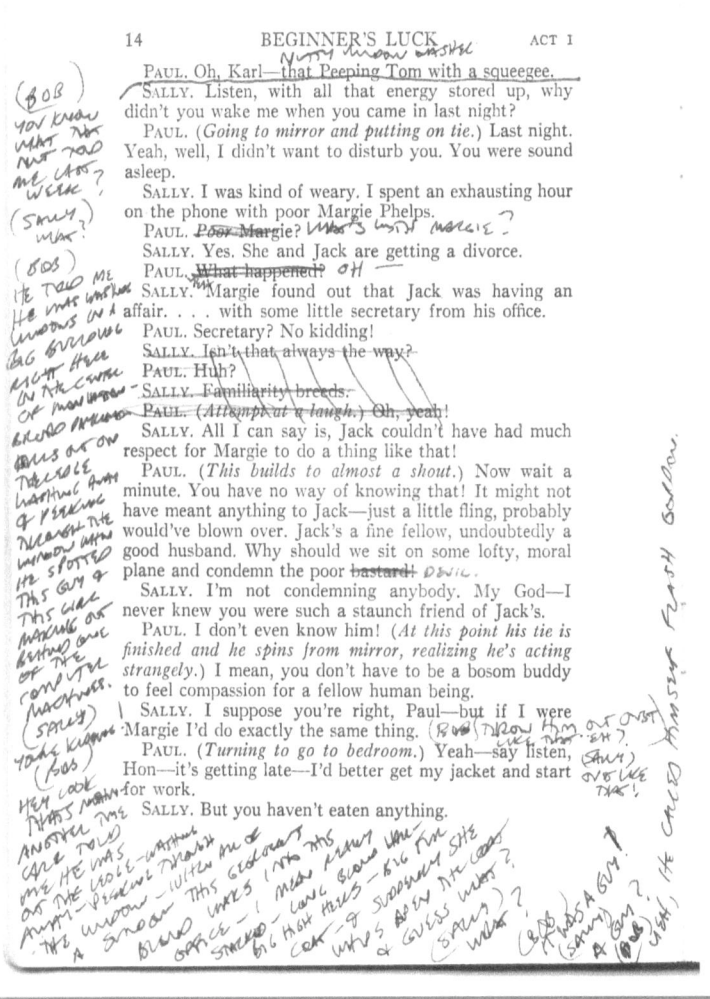

Bob kept meticulous notes in his playbooks and scripts, and he continually reworked the dialogue and scenes for *Beginner's Luck*. He had his playbook for *Beginner's Luck* with him in Scottsdale, Arizona, in June 1978. These are some of those notes he had been making in the days just before his death. Other pages of the playbook are stained with his blood.

Source: Courtesy of Scott Crane. Used with permission.

Hope for the Future

Wednesday, June 28, 1978. 10:30 p.m. Scottsdale, Arizona. Bob Crane, Victoria Berry Wells, and the rest of the cast took their bow, and the final curtain descended on *Beginner's Luck*.

As was typical of any night, following the performance, Bob provided a brief stand-up comedy routine. According to theatregoers that evening, both the play and Bob's routine were well received. Then, as was always the case, Bob greeted his fans in the lobby. He signed playbills, napkins, photographs, and slips of paper, whatever they handed him, enjoying the night and his fans.

But his mind was perhaps elsewhere.

> *Patty's visit on June 18—Father's Day. Could they work it out? Reconcile their marriage? Maybe. It will be difficult. Lots of work involved. Unknown.*
>
> *Scotty's Father's Day present to him—a framed photograph of Scott. A cherished item. To think of it may bring him to tears.*
>
> *Karen's high school graduation, June 22, just a few days ago. So proud of her. Desperate for her to be proud of him.*
>
> *Bobby's birthday, just the day before. His twenty-seventh. Bobby's birthday card is back at his apartment, waiting to be delivered. Might move in with Bobby while he figures things out.*
>
> *Television shows on the horizon. "The Hawaii Experience." Other dramatic works. Putting Hogan to rest once and for all. No more typecasting. "My name's Bob Crane!"*
>
> *Major life changes on the horizon—changes for the better. To be a better actor, a better man, a better father. Things are going to get better! Break free, get back **in control**, and get better. Failure is not an option. Bob Crane is ambitious and driven and a perfectionist, and he can do anything—and succeed.*
>
> *Do "surgery." He has to break off certain friendships. How will he do this? He is a friend. Confrontations are difficult. But he will just come out and say it—**tonight**.*
>
> *Going **HOME**—in a few days, as soon as this run is over. Get out of Scottsdale. He can't wait to go **HOME**. Big, capital letters scrawled in his day planner and underlined several times—**HOME**.*
>
> *New beginnings. A fresh start. Everything is going to be okay.*

Bob gave this photograph to his son Scott a couple of weeks before he died. The note he wrote expresses the love he had for his entire family.

Source: Courtesy of Scott Crane. Used with permission.

And then, the third act twist.

Bob Crane never made it home.

"The last night was like every other show," Victoria Berry Wells said quietly. "I remember it went well. And I remember him driving off with John Carpenter. He left before me, and he was waving. That's all I remember. The show was just a normal show—a good show. And he left with John Carpenter in the car. And that's the last time I ever saw him. *Alive.*"

On Father's Day, June 18, 1978, Bob's estranged wife Patty and their son Scott visited Bob in Scottsdale, Arizona. Although Bob was surprised by their visit, he was touched by the Father's Day present Scotty gave to him. Overcome with emotion, he embraced the gesture and his family. Whatever the future might have held for Bob and Patty (reconciliation or divorce), it is evident that Bob loved his family very much. (Photo taken June 18, 1978.)

Source: Courtesy of Scott Crane. Used with permission.

On June 22, 1978, Bob Crane's youngest daughter Karen graduated from high school. Bob traveled from Scottsdale, Arizona, where he was performing his play *Beginner's Luck,* back home to Los Angeles to attend the ceremony. Bob was very proud of Karen on this special day, and both father and daughter had bright hopes for the future. (Photo taken June 22, 1978.)

Source: Courtesy of Karen Crane. Used with permission.

In the Wake of a Crime: The Death of Bob Crane

The desert at night can be an eerie and foreboding place. Wind swirls and howls through rock formations, and rustles the dry, brittle foliage. In the distance, the sounds of nocturnal creatures—wolves, javelinas, rodents, reptiles, insects—can be heard as they prowl the barren landscape searching for prey or avoiding becoming it. The darkened night sky, pierced with pinholes of light from the stars above, drapes over the vastness of the desert, concealing all that lives and lurks beneath.

In the early morning hours of June 29, 1978, Bob was in his apartment in Scottsdale, Arizona. It was around two o'clock in the morning, and he was sleeping soundly, wearing a pair of boxing shorts and his wristwatch. He was lying on his right side, with his hands tucked comfortably under his pillow and head. Around that time, someone entered his apartment (or may have already been there—no forced entry). As he slept, Bob was bludgeoned twice on his head with a video camera tripod, crushing his skull.

Bob Crane was killed instantly.

The murderer then tied a cord tightly around Bob's neck in a bowtie. It is also presumed that the murderer ejaculated over Bob's body, evidenced by a "white, flaky substance" found on Bob's thigh. This it is unproven because DNA testing was not available in 1978. There was writing on the walls in Bob's blood, and the messages were ritualistic in nature. At some point, the murderer looked outside, leaving a bloody handprint on the draperies. The murderer left the scene of the crime before sunrise, and to this day, the murderer's identity and true motives remain a mystery.

Bob's murder and the events surrounding his death have been scrutinized extensively, and his death has been the subject of many articles, books, television programs, and a feature film over the last several decades. Theories on who may have committed the crime abound and are varied, but without irrefutable proof beyond legal reasonable doubt, it is impossible—and therefore, unethical—to subscribe or commit to any of them. Therefore, no in-depth discussion as to who killed Bob Crane and why is presented here.

Officially, the police believe their prime suspect—Bob's friend John Henry Carpenter (different from the movie producer and director)—committed the crime. They believe Carpenter's motive had been akin to that of a jilted lover. They stated that because Bob wanted to end their friendship, Carpenter was angry and hurt. The police claim that although Bob was not homosexual, Carpenter may have been bisexual and harbored homosexual feelings for Bob. Therefore, because Carpenter was unable to accept that Bob wanted to cut ties, according to police, he murdered Bob Crane.

Police were unable to establish enough physical evidence to connect Carpenter with the crime until June 1992. Their primary piece of evidence was an enlarged photograph showing what they speculated was a piece of Bob's brain matter in Carpenter's car. Carpenter was arrested, and in the fall of 1994, he stood trial. However, the jury was unable to see beyond reasonable doubt, declaring that the evidence the prosecution presented was circumstantial. They could not convict someone based on speculation. Carpenter was acquitted in October 1994 and died only four years later, on September 4, 1998. Whatever secrets he had, he took to his grave.

Bob Crane could never have imagined that his life was about to end. He simply went to bed and went to sleep, as we all do. Only he never woke up. There is some solace in the understanding that because he suffered an immediate and crippling traumatic brain injury, he did not feel a thing following the first blow. Regardless—*Bob Crane was not ready to die, did not want to die, and should not have died in the manner in which did*. He was living a full life—a life he believed was about to get better. His datebook was packed full of life—the names of his children are written all over the pages, not just "Karen's grad," but dates they were getting together and when he would see them. His trip to Hawaii for *The Hawaii Experience* was noted. Plays that ran in Long Beach, California; Dallas, Texas—and, of course, Scottsdale, were marked. Notes to himself about what he thought of performances are included. Also in the pages are all of his public appearances for professional photo shoots and interviews. On another page—a note about marriage counseling, and that the counselor was "not a novice" and "could help." Under that, he had written, "Haven't signed divorce papers," providing a glimpse of hope that he and Patty could have worked through their troubles. From January through June, the datebook is *packed*. Bob's life was being lived—and it was a very full, productive life.

And then, after the first week of July, where he had written the word HOME in big, bold letters and underscored it several times, the datebook is starkly empty. John Carpenter's name does *not* appear after June 29; it is not crossed out on future dates as previously reported. Carpenter's name is just not there at all. Sporadic entries for upcoming theatre engagements appear in July, August, and September, but not much else. One by one, the pages show less and less, until finally, they are all blank.

Bob's life was over.

Bob Crane's untimely death and horrific murder may have shocked the world, but it forever scarred his family, friends, and colleagues. It left a permanent wound, one that will never fully heal, and every so often, it still—without warning—causes great and inexplicable pain for those who loved him. Imagine waking up and learning someone very close to you had not only had died during the night, but had been beaten so savagely that he was unrecognizable.

During the late morning hours of June 29, 1978, Victoria Berry Wells had become increasingly worried. Bob had missed their appointment to tape a voiceover of her for the series he was filming in Hawaii—perhaps for the producers of *The Hawaii Experience*—for their consideration of using her in future episodes. While it is true that he had missed a luncheon appointment, Vicky's primary reason for going to his apartment had been because he had not shown up first to record her voiceover demo, and that was very unlike him.

Since that day, Vicky has experienced nightmarish visions of what she saw inside. In our interview with her in February 2007, we took her to the front door of Bob's apartment and allowed her to turn the knob. But we ended it there. She has worked very hard over the last several decades trying to keep that door closed, and we did not want her to or need her to go inside. This is what she told us during our interview with her:

Vicky: I prayed to be able to…I didn't know what I could add that you didn't have or…

Linda: You've added very, very much. I only have a few things left to ask.

Vicky: Okay.

Linda: I don't need you to go into details about what you found when you went over to Bob's place. Because this story is *not* about that.

Vicky: I get that from you. That's very clear, darling.

Linda: Now, I know you had said you were going over to the condo because you were going to be doing some voiceover with him.

Vicky: Voiceover. For the pilot.

Linda: Now, was he supposed to be somewhere as well that he missed being?

Vicky: Yeah, he had a luncheon. I vaguely remember he had a luncheon thing. It was pretty big.

Linda: Was that with you?

Vicky: No. My appointment was only to do the voiceover.

Linda: Okay. So you didn't go over because he'd missed [the luncheon].

Vicky: No. I went there because I had an exact appointment. And with Bob, no matter what, you had to be on time.

Linda: He was a punctual person.

Vicky: Very punctual. Yeah. Very professional.

Linda: So did it strike you as odd when you got there and the apartment was unlocked?

Vicky: Ohhhhhhh. I didn't know it was unlocked. What surprised me was the newspaper was out in the front and the drapes were closed dark. That never, *EVER* happened. I knocked on the door before I opened it, and I tried, and it was open, and it was completely dark. It was odd from the moment I walked up there. It was dark, and the drapes were closed, and the newspaper was outside the door. That would *NEVER* happen.

Linda: Okay. That's as far as I need to go with that. I had heard that you went over there because he missed a lunch. But the lunch wasn't with you…

Vicky: No. I went over to do the voiceover to send this tape for a pilot he wanted me to be in with him.

Linda: Okay.

Following Vicky's discovery, Bob's loved ones and colleagues had to learn of and come to terms with his death and the fact that he had been murdered. Their reactions ranged from hysteria to guilt to numbness to terror to disbelief. Below are some of their initial reactions.

Karen Crane, Daughter

I was at home in my mom's house, and I had just graduated high school, and I was in my bathroom getting ready to go out with my girlfriends. I was curling my hair. Down the hallway at the other end of the house you could see down into where the kitchen table was. And I saw my mom; she started to shriek. I had no clue what had happened. My grandmother was there at the time—my dad's mom. Even though my parents were divorced, my grandmother would still visit with my mom. I believe everything happens for a reason; and my grandmother was there, and there's my mom. I remember my grandmother's head went down on the kitchen table—it just hit the kitchen table, like she'd just fainted. And I was just thinking, "God, what happened?" [After we learned he had been murdered], it wasn't until some months later when things got quieter that I realized, "Oh my God, Dad's gone. Oh my God, he's not calling me tonight—not checking in to see how I am."

Reverend Edward Beck, Vice President, Windmill Dinner Theatre

Bob's death had tremendous impact. It brought the theatre to a close. The theatre was closed for ten days before we could reopen, that was one impact it had. The second impact was it terrified the cast, when we got the call the next morning or around noon and I went down to identify the body, along with my manager of the theatre, a guy named Bruce. And we were in the apartment for a couple of hours with the police, and identifying him and all of that, television cameras were outside, that kind of thing. But then the whole cast and myself, we went down to the police station, and we were there that evening—well, we were at the police station probably from five o'clock to six o'clock on. The cast was afraid. I mean, they didn't know why he'd been murdered; the police didn't know. I mean, maybe it was some disgruntled patron; they thought maybe they were next on the list. They were terrified. So when we left the police station about ten o'clock that evening, we all went back to a single apartment. It was where the cast was staying. You see, Bob did not stay with the cast; he stayed over at a condominium situation, the cast was in an apartment situation, four to five miles away. We went back to one of the cast's apartment, the biggest apartment, and we sat there *all night long*. I mean, the cast was terrified, the police would *not* let them leave town, and the police told them that they would be able to leave probably the next day, and they were, but *they* were terrified, so they sat up together. I was there I guess till two o'clock or three o'clock in the morning, Finally I left, and then we started the process the next day of getting him to the airport and so forth. I think the guy…, if you'll pardon the vernacular, just beat the shit out of him. Hit him time and time again in the facial areas, and the side of his head. I think Crane was dead with the first blow. But then of course after that, it was sort of ritualistic—very ritualistic, with paintings on the wall with Crane's blood and so forth. But I think, when Bob said, "I'm through. I'm heading—I'm going back home, I'm going back to my family, I'm going back to my career and to hell with you," so to speak, I think this guy just said, "No, you're not," and that was the end of Crane. Such a sad, sad commentary that we sometimes make very, very negative choices which impact us and impact those around us. Bob's children, bless their heart, especially his daughter, will never be able to get over she lost her father in such a tragic way. And of course, people like you, who have been impacted deeply. That's the tragedy of it all. He had so much to give and was unable to give it.

Cynthia Lynn, Actress, *Hogan's Heroes* (Season One)
    What happened was I was thinking about Bob for some reason, I'm thinking, well he's getting his divorce from Sigrid. He's getting his divorce, and he's going to be free. *I'm* free. Maybe we can go out to lunch or something. I saw him on a talk show that they had showed a week later [after taping] or whatever. I called the station, and I said, "Could you get a message to Bob Crane? And tell him that Fräulein Helga called and for him

to call *Fräulein Helga*," and I gave my phone number. That same afternoon I'm watching the news. Bob Crane—Murdered. That's how I found out. Same afternoon. And I just went, *No way*; this cannot be happening. That's a different Bob Crane. It *can't* be him. It just *can't* be him. I didn't go to the funeral or anything. His wife was there, and his ex-wife was there. Who am I? I didn't go. But that hurt. That was pretty painful. I mean, I just left a message to call—but how instinctively it was that I would have called at that time. And a lot of times afterwards, I had dreams about him crying out for help. I saw him in the bed crying out for help.

Jerry London, Director and Associate Producer, *Hogan's Heroes*

It was a real shock to all of us when it [Bob's murder] happened. It was just really no way for anybody to go. Especially a guy like this. It was crazy.

John and Pamela (Hayes)Thompson, Actors and Friends

John: In 1977, Pam and I were headlining in The Folies Bergêres at the Tropicana in Las Vegas, and we got a call from Bob, and he said, "I'm going back into the Windmill Dinner Theatre [in Scottsdale]." I remember there was something that he was definitely afraid of—he was afraid to go back there.

Pam: He said, "I'll match whatever you're making at the Trop."

John: Of course as actors, the money we'd get as performers was in Vegas. He was going to match our salaries. Because we did, unknowingly, keep him out of a lot of trouble. We always were with him; we were very protective of him out in public, and I think that's what he wanted. Unfortunately, we could not get out of our contract, and I always feel guilty—*always*—that if we would have been with him, maybe he would still be alive. He really wanted us to be there, and I really felt that was the reason.

Pam: They called me the Sleaze Queen from *The Enquirer*, which is how I found out about him [being murdered] at all. They hammered us for an hour, trying to get something *awful.*

John: And we knew nothing.

Pam: And we felt like idiots because we said, "No, it can't be; it *cannot* be!"

John Orland, Director, *The Hawaii Experience*

We were in editing for a couple of months. And by the time we had finished the show, it was the end of June. We heard about Bob's death on the news. And of course, I was shocked. We had a distributor for the show—Western International Syndication. It would have been ready to go. It was a show that was going to be in syndication, meaning it was going to be sold to individual television markets rather than aimed at a network. So what happened to it was that we put it together and we started to go out into the marketplace, and Bob was killed. And you know, that was the end of it because the pilot was so much of Bob Crane, we never...I guess maybe we discussed thinking about a possible replacement, but then we really would have to shoot another television pilot because a television pilot for a reality show is very much like a screen test for that person. In other words, a lot of reality shows—you can't imagine anyone else in the part once they've done it. If you did a pilot with a particular star, and it was well received, and something happened, and you didn't have that star anymore, I'm not sure you could just plug in someone else. The dynamics of the show would be totally different. So basically, that ended the show.

Leo McElroy, KNX Colleague and Friend
I will tell you that there were a lot of us after Bob was murdered who would get together in little cells and talk among ourselves about who we thought did it and what we thought had happened and so on. And there was a lot of idle speculation with nothing much going on. But what it was, was a lot of people who just really were concerned that Bob had been killed, and he was getting a bad reputation even as a murder victim. It's a rush to demonize celebrity, and you get that a lot. But it certainly wasn't fun to watch when you had known and worked with Bob. I actually went over to meet with Bob around 1967—over to the studio to talk to him. Geoff Edwards and I both went over because Geoff wanted to get off on Saturdays. He was doing Monday through Saturday show on KFI and wanted Saturdays off. And the idea was if we could swing a deal with Bob to come on and do the Saturday show, that Geoff could get Saturdays off and it would get Bob back on the radio. And so we went over to the studio and talked with Bob, and obviously I was along because I knew Bob a lot better than Geoff did. I can't remember that I ever talked to Bob after that, which really, very honestly, left me feeling really uneasy and guilty when I was told [about his murder]. I was on the road doing some story for ABC television, and they called me in the evening and said, "You were a friend of Bob Crane's." And I said, "What do you mean *were*?" And they said, "Well, he's dead in Phoenix." They didn't give me any details, and my immediate thought was now I know his career has kind of been on a down track since *Hogan's* went off and since *Superdad* did not do real well at the box office. And my God, I haven't been in touch with him in so long. I mean, this is the guy who really tried to help me, and I have not had any contact with him. I have not sought him out. I really felt

guilty. But I didn't sense these dark depths in Bob. Maybe if I had been looking for them, I might have. But I wasn't, and I didn't. I guess I just wasn't looking, really. But there was no indication to look deep within Bob. And so I elected not to do so, whether it was reticence or disinterest or what, I don't know. But I wasn't looking beyond the guy who I had worked with, who was really funny, who had been a help to me, and who I thought was really kind of a genius in his own way.

Robert Clary, Actor, *Hogan's Heroes*
   I was very saddened by the way his life was ended. But my memories of the six years working with him were always positive. Too bad he had to leave this earth so young.

Joe Cosgrove, KPOL Staff Announcer 1956/Founder of KTHO, Lake Tahoe/Welcomed Bob to Los Angeles
   I live by Benjamin Franklin's motto: "He serves God best who serves his fellow man." I've always played that role in my life. And I've worked with some pretty powerful people in America. Not only financially successful, but household names. And I've always found out that no matter how famous they are, they're people. Just like you and me. I hope you hit the human side of Bob. I emailed his family after he died. I mean, years and years later. I emailed his son [Scott] and got a very nice response from him. I know very little about Bob's private life or what happened to him later in life, except that I told his son when I heard about his death, I grieved. I mourned because it's a tragedy. Bob's family was so nice to me, and they came back with such a wonderful email saying thank you. And I said I will always remember Bob as a loving family man who was kind, upbeat, and positive with everybody he met. What can I say? There's an ambiguity to life, right? We don't know…there's a mystery to life. I respect the mystery of everybody's life. I respect their privacy, and I respect who they are. Everybody's a person, and no matter how famous or wealthy they are, they are inhabitants of our planet.

Chapter 11
Specks on the Parthenon

Society looks in on the private world of sexuality and deems something abnormal, while the man does not automatically identify his behavior as illness or disease.

—Susanne A. Quallich, ANP-BC, NP-C, CUNP, FANNP, University of Michigan Health System; Member, *Urologic Nursing* Journal Editorial Board; and an Expert on Men's Sexual Health

A reflective Bob Crane (circa 1970).
Source: Courtesy of Scott Crane. Used with permission.

Chapter 11

Specks on the Parthenon

Bob Crane was a very sensitive and caring and warm human being, with weaknesses and foibles like all the rest of us. Bob's problem was he allowed one of those weaknesses to consume him.

—Reverend Edward Beck, Vice President, Windmill Dinner Theatre Corporation; Protestant Minister; and Addiction Counselor

Bob and Anne Crane had only been married for a few months when something devastating occurred in their lives to cause their young marriage to quake. Joined in matrimony on May 20, 1949, they were separated by early 1950 and were seriously contemplating a divorce. Facing what appeared to be an insurmountable crisis, over the months of February and March 1950, Anne and her mother journeyed to Sweden to visit relatives. While they were away, Bob remained in Stamford, working unhappily at the jewelry store.

But he had not been idle. He had been restless, sending letters to radio stations up and down the East Coast, hoping for his first big break in broadcasting. Then, in March 1950, Bob received the call from WLEA in Hornell, New York. Still wrestling with matrimonial strife and personal turmoil caused by it, he jumped at the offer, which allowed him to focus on his career. He packed his bags and relocated to Hornell, where he worked at WLEA and resided from March through December 1950.

Now living far from Stamford and still reeling from his troubles back home, Bob met a young lady [name withheld for privacy], and they began dating. They dated for most of the time Bob lived in Hornell, and sources say they had been intimate and even discussed the possibility of marriage.

Meanwhile, Bob and Anne prepared to follow through with their divorce. Bob also continued sending out letters to radio stations within the state of New York, and his primary sights at the time were set on Rochester.

But then, the young Cranes had a change of heart. Bob broke off his relationship in Hornell, and by early 1950, he was back in Connecticut and looking toward the future.

It was around this time when best school friend Charlie Zito met up with Bob in Stamford and questioned him about the rumors he and others had been hearing. Was it true? Were Bob and Anne getting a divorce?

"No," Bob answered quickly. "We've decided to work it out."

That was all the two friends ever spoke of it.

Bob and Anne remained together for the next twenty years. By all outward appearances, they seemed to be the perfect couple that went on to have the perfect family, which by the early 1960s also included two young daughters.

"Well, you know…domestic stuff, babies, and all that [got in the way]," Bob explained to a Rochester journalist, discussing why his career path didn't take him through Rochester. "Before I knew it, I was off to Connecticut and eventually to Los Angeles."

But by 1969, headlines were reporting that their perfect family had "cracked apart at the seams." Shortly before their twentieth wedding anniversary, Bob gathered his belongings and moved out, exiting his home and his "first" family forever in silence. Then, just days before their anniversary, Anne filed for divorce, citing mental and emotional cruelty. She was hurt and angry because Bob had asked for the divorce.

After their separation, the public began to learn of Bob's extramarital affairs with both actresses who had played Colonel Klink's secretary on *Hogan's Heroes*—first Cynthia Lynn, and then Patricia Olson, whom he later married. It smacked of inconsistency and contradiction, especially when Bob had been so openly adamant about his devotion to Anne and his family. He had claimed repeatedly that he not only loved them, but he literally *cherished* them and was vehemently protective of them. He could not understand people who "went Hollywood," and wondered, "Why can't they be normal?" Time and again, he told people and the media how much of a family man he was, that he was faithful, that his idea of a good time was going home to his wife or seeing a movie with her. The thought of cheating on his wife was so far-fetched, he would never dream of it.

The seeds for controversy and scandal had been planted. Because Bob had been so forthcoming about his loyalty to Anne, and because he married Patty almost immediately following his divorce, a hungry media and a curious public began to speculate that Bob Crane was unable to handle his fame and had, indeed, "gone Hollywood."

With his first marriage in shambles and his second wedding ceremony conducted on a Hollywood soundstage, many began to wonder, and Bob's public persona began to crumble. He would spend the rest of his life trying to rebuild his image, while at the same time, struggling to escape the typecasting as Colonel Hogan. But he would ultimately fail at both. Following his murder and the discovery of his amateur pornography, Bob went from star to "creep" in one night. Capitalizing on the discovery, the press threw Colonel Hogan into the mix. How could this lovable "character" engage in such a lifestyle? Headlines screamed "This Hogan Is No Hero!" A grand intrusion into and violation of Bob's privacy resulting from his murder developed into a media blitz feeding off of any and all assumptions, each outlet anxious for the next lascivious headline.

For most of their twenty years of marriage, Bob had been disloyal to Anne. Long before he and his family had migrated west to Los Angeles in 1956, and throughout his entire first marriage, Bob hid that side of his life from many of his extended family, his closest friends and colleagues, *and* from the public, while to others, he was immodestly and candidly open about it. He made excuses and lied to himself and everyone around him. And while it is uncertain how much Anne actually knew at the time, sources claim she was aware of at least some of it and was quietly tolerating it.

It is no surprise that the 1958 film *Tunnel of Love* had appealed to Bob and even provided him with a flicker of hope. The character Dick Pepper, played by Gig Young, had it all in the movie—a beautiful wife, children, friends, success—*and* he was having recreational sex with nearly every consensual woman he met. Further, Dick Pepper theorized that not only was his womanizing acceptable, it was *healthy* for his own marriage and well-being. On the screen, to audiences across the country and to Bob Crane, Gig Young confirmed that this lifestyle was nothing to be ashamed of. It was to be *embraced*. And if Bob wanted anything in his life, it was acceptance and approval from all, especially in the face of what he subconsciously knew and ultimately came to realize was unacceptable behavior.

"There but for Gig Young go I," Bob had announced, bestowing his desire to become an actor on Young's performance in *Tunnel of Love*. Perhaps he had meant more than *just* wanting to be an actor.

We will never know exactly what happened between Bob and Anne during the first two years of their marriage. Nor will we ever know the reasons why Bob became drawn into such a serious addiction—one with roots reaching far back to his early life in Connecticut. But whatever the catalyst, it set the shaky foundation for what was to come.

"Sex isn't the answer," Bob declared shortly before he and Anne separated in 1969. "If that's all a couple has, it's not enough. There has to be a lot more than that. There *has* to be, I don't know, a complete sharing. And that's what Anne and I have. We share everything completely. She's a dream. Honestly she is. She never complains. Never nags. She realizes my career is important to me, and she's made all kinds of sacrifices to help me. I can never forget that."

Bob had likely believed such statements. He did, indeed, love Anne, and he often acknowledged her unwavering support of him in his career, drive to success, and his often-grueling schedule. It is evident that he and Anne never stopped loving each other on some level, even following their divorce and after they had both remarried. Although their early court divorce hearings were contentious, they were able to come to terms amicably and settle on the divorce rather quickly. When he requested visits to see their children during the court hearings, Anne was kind, and she told him, "Call me, and we'll talk." Later on, Bob and Anne's daughter Karen also remembered hearing her father tell her mother repeatedly, "I love you, Annie. I never should have left you."

There is also no doubt that Bob loved Patty. The love letters he wrote to her that she saved are passionate and filled with tenderness. Despite their pending divorce and heated arguments, Patty and Bob were reportedly trying to work things out. Their son Scott claims that just before his father was murdered, his parents had been attempting to reconcile. They had talked about relocating to a new home near Seattle, and they had even stayed in the house for a short period of time. It was, as Scott recalled, an effort to try again and start over. A clean slate.

Both Anne and Patty had tried to exist in a marriage where the husband had not only been unfaithful, but was embroiled in a very serious addiction. Regardless of what Anne knew or didn't know, when Bob told her he wanted a divorce, it had been her final straw.

When Bob married again, Patty openly granted him permission to enjoy a lifestyle of consensual sex with other women and engage in amateur pornography. She publicly stated that Bob had "not given up his First Amendment rights" when he marred her. Patty seemed to approve of his behavior—as evidenced by birthday gifts to strip clubs and statements that pardoned him for his trysts with countless women—as long as he came home to her. Yet Patty was also unhappy in her marriage—enough to file for a divorce.

Neither woman would ever have been able to change Bob Crane. Only one person had that power—Bob himself. And the most important thing Bob would ever do in his entire life would be to have the courage to acknowledge his addiction and begin the long, difficult journey toward healing from it. But before that moment of realization, Bob would spend a lifetime traveling a private passage that would leave him unfulfilled and always yearning for more.

> *Nearly all human beings have a deep desire to feel happy and to find peace of mind and soul. At times in our lives, most of us find this wholeness of peace and beauty, but then it slips away only to return at another time. When it leaves us, we feel sadness and even a slight sense of mourning. This is one of the natural cycles of life, and it's not a cycle we can control.*
>
> *To some extent, we can help these cycles along, but for the most part, they're uncontrollable—all of us must go through them.*
>
> *Addiction can be viewed as an attempt to control these uncontrollable cycles. Addiction must be seen as an illness that undergoes continuous development from a definite, though often unclear, beginning toward an end point. No matter what the addiction is, every addict engages in a relationship with an object or event in order to produce a desired mood change, state of intoxication, or trance state.*
>
> —Craig Nakken, *The Addictive Personality*, pp. 1-2

Bob Crane's desire to overcome his addiction to sex was a private battle for him. Outwardly, he seemed to enjoy what some have referred to as his "alternative lifestyle," and there was a part of him—the Addict—that did enjoy it. But privately, inwardly, it was a much different story. Because it was damaging to him both personally and professionally, and because he recognized this and sought help, the correct term to use is addiction.

Each person's situation is unique, and we are not here to judge anyone else's lifestyle or make sweeping statements about "good" versus "bad." The term *addiction* is used here exclusively as it relates to Bob's set of circumstances and his eventual understanding of it.

Those who knew Bob Crane have described him as *restless, driven, a perfectionist, goal-oriented, organized, focused, aloof, a blur of motion, a radio genius, professional, burlesque, a bundle of nervous energy, quick-witted,* and *always wanting more*. He had an insatiable appetite for success, and he was never satisfied with his current career standing. He always wanted to achieve that next goal or take that next step that would propel him to even greater heights. A workaholic, he stopped at nothing to achieve success, and with it, fame. Being rich never really mattered to Bob, but being a star meant the world to him.

As *Donna Reed Show* actor Paul Petersen keenly observed, Bob wanted *more, more, more!*

Working with him on the set of *Hogan's Heroes*, actress Arlene Martel further noted that Bob always appeared to be "*in control.*"

The same can be said of his personal life. Bob was constantly moving, seldom resting, requiring only a few hours of sleep and being able to function extraordinarily well. And along the way, he was obsessively and compulsively *chronicling* every detail of his life.

It has been assumed that Bob's quest for acceptance, the need to be liked, his drive for success, and his powerful addiction to sex were all interconnected. That may very well be true. But what is more telling was his need to document and record every intimate aspect of his life.

Most of us keep momentos, take notes, organize our memorabilia, and save photographs, some of us more than others. We may have a favorite type of item we have chosen to accumulate en masse (for example, comic books, DVDs, or books) or have preserved important documents from historic moments in our lives.

Bob did this to the extreme. He was not a hoarder; he was *not* living under mountains of trash and saving meaningless items that were not important to him. But he *was* a collector, and what he collected and archived were extraordinary details of every facet of his entire life.

Control and organization were important ritualistic traits of Bob.

Dating all the way back to his school days and continuing throughout his life, Bob maintained detailed journals and recorded just about everything. He wrote notes, took pictures, made videos, and created audiotapes not just of milestone events, but of *any and all* events. He also recorded and catalogued his radio shows using a Dewey Decimal-type system, photocopied and archived all of his correspondences, and made scrapbooks containing photographs and newspaper clippings of his work in radio, television appearances in general, *Hogan's Heroes*, and movies. By 1970, he had amassed 21,000 record albums that he managed to reduce to 5,000 (*only* 5,000!) after marrying Patty.

The truth is, Bob archived, noted, recorded, and kept nearly *everything* that served as proof of his stature in his life and career.

"Did you know about him and his watches?" friend Harvey Geller asked. "He had met some people from Timex in Bridgeport. They arranged to send him a new watch every six months, and he would fill out a little form saying how much he enjoyed this particular watch. He saved them. He had *dozens* of watches. He never had to send them back."

At the time of Harvey's interview, this random fact that Bob Crane saved all of his watches, although interesting, did seem rather trivial. But over time, as more of the *real* Bob Crane began to emerge, it provided yet another example of the extent to which he had saved such items. Bob was a compulsive archivist of his life, with bins and bins of documents, letters, scripts, notes, contracts, paystubs, photographs, and audiotapes.

"He was always journaling," Bob's son Scott said. "He was always writing down ideas for plays or direction—so many scripts that I have from him, from his productions, have all of his notes written in pencil about, 'I'm changing this line to this,' or 'Maybe we can do this,' and question marks all over them. The record collection, same thing. He wrote on the back of every record. He would circle the songs he liked, and he would circle the minutes and seconds that he liked of those songs. He was really hyper-organized. I don't know how he did it. I don't know how he had such a big family, such a big career, and kept organized, and slept, and yet had time for this extracurricular life that everyone wants to talk about. It makes no sense to me at all. He kept a really detailed date book, and if an event didn't happen, he would go back and say why it didn't happen. Really ridiculous notes about everything, about every day of his life, no matter what it was or how small it was. He kept notes about it. I don't know where he found the time to do this. When he was doing the radio show in the 1960s, he would get off work in the afternoon. He'd have to wake up at three or four o'clock in the morning to get to get to the radio station on time. He'd get off work around noon and go home or go out, but he would be editing tapes in the meantime for his next radio show, plus lining up guests. Now, me being a radio producer on radio, I'm lining up guests, taking notes, making music samples for the next day—grueling and exhausting.

"He was a workaholic. From what I understand, his brother was an alcoholic, and a pretty bad one. My dad didn't drink or smoke, so his addictions played out in the obsessive-compulsive ways that he worked, took notes, organized everything from his records to his tape library to his card catalog for his radio show. And he filmed everything, too. He developed most of his own film and pictures in his own darkroom, so he was an engineer for sure. That's one of those things where they say John Carpenter was kind of his tech—to set everything up for him. Totally untrue. John was his parts guy. John would get him the parts, and Dad would install them himself. He was a total engineer. He's in the [Paley Center for Media—formerly the Museum of Television and Radio] in New York and Los Angeles for inventing the sampling on radio, which is, you're listening to a DJ talk on the radio and suddenly you hear a crazy sound effect. He was the first guy to do that. And he had to splice all these tapes together. He knew his bits so well that he knew what he was going to say in his five hours the next day that he would literally splice together: 'Here's the first sound effect, here's the second sound effect.' So he really knew his plotline of what he would be talking about for five hours. And he would edit those tapes at night; I don't know where he had the time to do any of that. He was pretty boundless in his energy."

Bob lived his entire life chronicling and recording. He was audio- and videotaping and photographing everything—from birthday parties to nightclub acts to his drumming to his radio shows to family events to random dinner conversations. It made sense to him that—as part of his *entire* life—he would also chronicle his sexual escapades as normally as if they had been his radio show or home movies from the set of *Hogan's Heroes*.

His amateur pornography only *appeared* to be the majority of Bob's life because the media have focused on only that since his death.

In reality, his pornography—while extensive—was merely only a *part* of the *whole* of his chronicling—and by comparison, a miniscule part of it at that.

Although Bob organized and chronicled his life events to the extreme, it was his addiction to sex that became damaging to him personally and professionally. But Bob Crane did not just wake up one day and say, "Today I am going to be a sex addict." Addiction progresses over time, slowly at first, and then escalates. It was no different for Bob.

As Satan in *The Devil's Advocate*, Al Pacino delivers one of the most powerful modern-day film monologues. During Satan's rant to Keanu Reeves' character Kevin Lomax, he says with a grin, "Look but don't touch. Touch, but don't taste. Taste!"

Bob started out by just looking. He talked a good line to the ladies, wanting them to believe he was very capable in the bedroom. But he would only go so far. Then, at some point in his young life, a woman called him on it.

"Put up or shut up," she said.

Embarrassed and longing for acceptance, he took the next step.

The foundation of the addict is found in all people. It's found in a normal desire to make it through life with the least amount of pain and the greatest amount of pleasure possible. It's found in our negativity and our mistrust of others and the world, whether this pessimism is valid or not. There is nothing wrong with this part of us; it's natural to have these beliefs to some degree. However, when these beliefs control one's way of life, as they do in addiction, people get into trouble. Some people are more susceptible to addiction than others; these are people who don't know how to have healthy relationships and have been taught not to trust. They may have been treated badly by others while growing up, and never learned good relationship skills as an adult.
Addiction is an active belief in and a commitment to a negative lifestyle. Addiction begins and grows when a person abandons the natural ways of getting emotional needs met—through connecting with other people, one's community, one's self, and spiritual powers greater than

> *oneself. The repeated abandonment of oneself and one's values in favor of the addictive high causes the addictive personality to develop and gradually gain power.*
>
> —Craig Nakken, *The Addictive Personality*, p. 27

That Bob Crane became addicted to sex and pornography only after he arrived in Hollywood is a myth. In fact, his addiction to sex has its roots in Connecticut.

Best friend Charlie Zito recalled there was nothing remarkable or unusual about Bob's interest in girls while they were still in high school. During the early-to-mid-1940s, the boys from the Stamford High School Class of 1946 were coming of age. They were exploring, experimenting, and discovering. Charlie claimed that he and Bob were no different than the rest of the boys in their class, behaving as any other regular teenage boys of their era or *any* era.

"We were finding out that girls were not just soft boys," Charlie said as he discussed their transition from curious boys to adult men.

Charlie also explained that even though Bob was with Anne—that she "had been the girl for him" and that he was reportedly aloof with other girls who vied for his attention—Bob also observed other girls in their class. One example Charlie gave involved a time when he and Bob were walking home from school one afternoon. As they passed by the house of one of their girl classmates, Bob mentioned that he wanted to "get to know her better."

"But you're with Annie," Charlie told him, a little taken aback.

"Yeah, but she's really cute," Bob answered, referring to the other girl. However, according to Charlie, nothing more became of it.

Charlie claimed that his and Bob's attraction and experiences with girls during high school were normal. He said that he and Bob were just like other regular high school boys their age.

"Bob *really* never went out with anybody else," Charlie said. "Seriously. I mean we had our little escapades. But when they went steady, *that was it*. As we used to call it, they were *going steady*."

However, school friend and band member Edwin Gordon noticed Bob might have been struggling under the weight of some kind of duress.

"The Cranes were *very* strict Catholics," Edwin explained. "And I think that's one of the things that led Bob astray. You know, it's like a minister's son who goes crazy when he gets some freedom. And I know Bob was chomping at the bit because of his father. When we walked from high school down Strawberry Hill, we'd stop in to see Bob's father at The Floor Covering Shop. And his father was always very grim, as I recall. Bob and I were so close. We shared a lot of confidences. He came from this very strict background. Anne also came from a religious background, and they both had a desire to be intimate, but their religion would not allow them to be. We talked about it quite a bit. But he never strayed beyond—he was not of the mind to do that sort of thing. He was a pretty straight arrow at the time when it came to religion. I think he was probably very fearful to go beyond. Of course in those days, sexual relations before marriage was really taboo. It's not like it is today. But he was fighting Catholicism all the way.

"Anne was extremely mature, and he was highly, sexually motivated. I was interested in girls and sex at the time, and so was he, but I was a bit broader. He was very focused on this. He was focused on a getting notoriety and getting sex. And he couldn't wait to have sex, and he couldn't wait for notoriety. He and Anne had some passionate necking parties that I was privy to. I have no reason to believe it went beyond that. I think at that time, *none* of us went beyond that. They used to call it 'going all the way.' And I don't think any of us did. I do remember we went down to a drug store. And we were thinking about buying some contraceptives because we'd met some girls that possibly would be approving. We went into this drug store, and the pharmacist was Catholic. He would *not,* under *any* circumstances, sell contraceptives. He gave us one *hell* of a lecture. But I don't think Bob would have gotten involved unless he could have contraceptives. Pregnancy would have been a terrible thing."

While in high school, Bob was dependent on his friends to drive him to and from jazz band performances. According to his school friends Don Sappern and Edwin Gordon, Bob's father would not allow him to use the family car. And from what Edwin could tell, Bob's parents showed very little, if any, support of his music hobby.

"There was nothing," Edwin said. "His family just didn't approve of what he did. He was a black sheep. I don't know how all the band members all got there, but I know I got there with the car. Bob was *always* dependent on *me*. I don't think his father *ever* took him anywhere. They *didn't* support him in any way. So it was just automatic—expected—that I would drive to Belltown, pick him up, and take him home. And he did what he could. When I would run out of money, he'd peel off dollar bills, and we'd get the gas. So I did the driving."

Edwin further recalled that the atmosphere in Bob's childhood home in Stamford was "*rigid.*" Upon entering Bob's house, it was so bad, that Edwin hated going inside.

"Oh, it was terrible," Edwin explained. "We would just sit there like this [gripping arms of chair, stiffening back]. 'Would…you…like…some…lemonade?' We would talk, and when we would leave, his mother would quiz him, where he was going, when he would expect to be home. It was something I was unaccustomed to because I was always on my own. 'Don't forget you have to do this, and don't forget tomorrow…and don't forget church and don't forget this…' I could see him—he would just *roll* his eyes. I think it was parental power. I don't think it was respect. It was power. I don't think there was a lot of respect there of Bob toward his father. I think his father knew something about Bob and was very aware of it and unhappy, and wanted to do something but didn't know quite what to do. Now whether he thought I was part of the problem, I don't know. But they were never terribly kind toward me. It was just, well, here's one of Bob's friends, and he's driving him, and he's taking him in the car. I never enjoyed going there. And he couldn't *wait* to get away."

Bob had always been interested in music, and Edwin described Bob's drumming as being a release for Bob—a way to work out his frustrations. However, it was not enough. Edwin recalled that when Bob and Anne started seeing each other and then became serious, music was not as important as it once was. Bob began to focus on Anne and their time spent together. Edwin did not know the extent of Bob and Anne's physical relationship, but he did notice that Bob's relationship with Anne took precedence. He also recalled that occasionally, band members would all meet at Anne's house, where the atmosphere was much lighter than it was at Bob's.

"When he met Anne, it was quite different," Edwin said. "They would be alone a lot together. He was *very* interested in her. Before that, he was only interested in his career and where he was going. He was always making plans. *How to get ahead.* Anne wanted a family. She wanted to be happy, and she cared for him a great deal. But she was always concerned if Bob became a professional musician, what would life be like. When we would be unwelcome in his house, we'd go to Terzians' house, and her parents were just lovely. They'd bring us all in, and we'd sit there and have a wonderful time. And her parents liked Bob very much, and they liked all of us. And we had a really good time when we'd go there."

For perhaps the first time, another side of Bob was revealed. It was not as pronounced in high school as it would soon become. Whatever it was, he also kept it very hidden from his classmates and friends, perhaps knowing they would not approve.

"It is my own intuition and pure speculation," Edwin surmised, "but I think Bob had another life. What it was, I don't know, but I know after I graduated, whatever that other life was, he partook of it. I think when I was around, I wouldn't say I governed him, or I was an influence. But I think he knew I would not fit into that other part of life that he had. But there were times I would see him with persons I wouldn't have associated with. And so, there was something going on. Where he got the gas money, I don't know. I don't think he stole money or anything like that. I think he came by it honestly. But there was a part of Bob that was locked up. And as well as I knew him, I don't think anybody knew that part of him. And I think that's what exploded in his more mature years. It finally—*POW!* I think it was always there. It was festering for a long time. He was a square with a long fuse that was ready to blow up at any time. He did what he was supposed to do. Followed the rules. But you could see the volcano taking form. And it was quite obvious that he was going to erupt sometime. I saw that other side of him. He never once told me what was inside of him, what was bothering him. He might have looked like a straight and narrow to many persons, but he wasn't. He *was*, but under duress. Not through choice. He was a show off. He was determined to get out of the house, to get away from his family, to make something of himself, to be recognized, and to be famous. And he wanted very much to be in with the jet set. I guess there was no jet set then. But he wanted to be a part of it. Exciting. He wanted to have an *exciting* life. We had talked about that many times. He wanted a life that was exciting. He didn't want to be bored. He wanted to do things. He just was so sick and tired of the humdrum of boyhood. He was always trying to find an exit. It was like he was in prison trying to break out. He was always experimenting. 'How the hell do you get out of this thing?'"

As time goes on and a person continues to act out, be preoccupied, and remain emotionally distant from others, the Addict side of his or her personality starts to assert more control over the person's internal life. At this stage,

> *the person suffering from addiction will start to feel a "pull" inside. This may come in the form of emotional restlessness or pangs of conscience.*
> *The more addicts seek relief through addiction, t he more shame they'll start to experience, and the more they will feel a need to justify the addictive relationship to themselves.*
> *Shame creates a loss of self-respect, self-esteem, self-confidence, self-discipline, self-determination, self-control, self-importance, and self-love. In the beginning, this shame may be a general uneasiness; it's the first cost an addict pays for the addictive relationship. The addict starts to feel shame about the signs of loss of control that are beginning to appear within... The addict is more apt to feel bad about the internal withdrawal from others, for as addicts slowly start to become more committed to an object or event, they begin to emotionally withdraw from intimate relationships with self, others, and a Higher Power.*

—Craig Nakken, *The Addictive Personality*, pp. 28-29

The first rumors of Bob having a wandering eye and a lust for women began to circulate in the early 1950s, while Bob was working at WICC in Bridgeport, Connecticut. By that time, it was commonly known among WICC staff and fellow jazz band members that Bob was engaging in extramarital sex with multiple women.

"While I was at WNAB, I started hearing stories that Bob kind of had a very active libido at WICC," Bob's cousin Jim Senich said. "I remember hearing stories that he was having extracurricular activities with the young ladies. It hurt me a lot because I just couldn't believe that Bobby would do that. I just couldn't believe that, and I would never, *ever* tell my mom or dad or the family. My wife even. I wouldn't tell anybody, probably more because they wouldn't believe me. But I didn't bring it up because I didn't want to ruin the image of a great guy and a great cousin, a great nephew. But I knew it was true because I heard it from too many people. I remember a sales manager in Greenwich [Connecticut] took me into a record library and said, 'See that wall over there? Oh, Bob was here once visiting, and he had a young secretary, and they were up against the wall.' That kind of stuff. And I heard it so many times I had to believe that it was true. But the guys like Harry Downey and Frank Delfino [at WICC], you never heard a negative word out of those guys because they were professionals. They were pros. Never heard it from them. The people you heard it from were the real creeps in radio. Unfortunately there are a lot of creeps in radio who never did anything to get congratulated for by the public, whereas Bob and these [other on-air] guys were loved by the public. So if they could find out anything, if they could find a word on them, they'd tell everybody."

Jim heard the stories, but he never confronted Bob with any of it. He also reiterated that despite the stories and the knowledge of what Bob was doing, it did not hamper the close relationship he had with Bob and Anne. Nor did it change how Bob treated Jim. This other side of Bob existed, but it was kept quiet. Even Bob's neighbors in Bridgeport never knew of it.

"Oh, God, I would never tell him," Jim said. "No. I'd be frightened of that. I just don't know what he would have said. I don't know. Maybe I should have. We had so many long talks and everything, but we always talked about radio. He would always say, 'Jimmy how's the family? How's it going?' We lived in the apartment in Bridgeport where he had once lived. We didn't know that when we moved in. We didn't know when he worked at WICC, he was living there; he lived in our apartment. That was really ironic. We never heard any stories there about [Bob's extracurricular activities]. He came to see us one day at the apartment, and that was exciting because all the neighbors heard that Bob Crane was there. They were all waiting outside. He came with Annie, and we had a really good time."

Bridgeport radio manager and fellow jazz band member Salvatore "Tootie" DeBenedetto recalled playing in jazz bands with Bob during the early 1950s. According to Tootie, Bob was a "damn good drummer" and a nice guy, and many people—including Tootie—liked Bob very much. Yet there was a side to Bob that Tootie had not liked.

"He was a handsome guy, but he was a womanizer," Tootie said. "It got to the point where I really couldn't take it anymore because he was getting dangerous. He would be trying to hit on a woman while her husband or boyfriend was there. And he'd always laugh it off. He would say, 'You worry too much.' But I was *afraid*. I can't predict where that bullet's going to come from. He was like that even with the girls that worked up at WICC. Some of them were married, and they weren't going to fool around. They said, 'I like Bob, but I'm a married woman.'

Many times I said to him, 'You're going to lose your job.' We played a lot of nightclubs in Connecticut, Boston, New Jersey, New York—maybe a total of sixty clubs. He would be making eyes at these girls and winking at them. I said to him, 'Bob, you gotta be crazy. What are you doing?' We wouldn't let him bring any of the women back with us. We weren't going to do that because we're all going to get in the same truck. No, we're not taking any women, even if they wanted to go, we're not going to do that."

Tootie continued, "It was like he didn't have any fear, and he was no fighter. He didn't think that anything could happen. Many times I had to step between him and a jealous husband or boyfriend and say, 'Hey listen. They guy's only fooling around. He's that kind of a guy who likes to just fool around like this.' And the husband said, 'I don't like that to happen with my wife.' The guy would walk away, and I'd say [to Bob], 'You *gotta* knock it off, man.' He was a beautiful guy. *A beautiful guy.* But you don't get involved in things like that. You just can't keep doing that.

"It was like babysitting. We really had to follow him around. Like a little boy. Don't touch this; don't touch that. It's like when you tell somebody to stop smoking, they say, mind your own business. And that's what he'd say. 'Why don't you knock it off,' he'd say, 'I'm not doing anything.' Well, he *thinks* he's not doing anything, but he's creating problems. And it's dangerous, too. But, he was not a kid. He was a man. Sooner or later, you gotta grow up. But you know, he'd say, 'Okay, Tootie. I'm gonna knock it off. I'm gonna knock it off.' And then go *right* back into it."

Tootie said, "Anne was probably told, 'Your husband is a womanizer.' She probably just shrugged it off like, well, everybody knows he's good looking, and everybody's hugging him, so on. If he would only concentrate on his drumming and the music and the group, I think everything would have been fine. But no. Not him. When a man has a beautiful wife, why do you do that? She had to have known what was going on.

"I used to say to him, 'I thought you had good taste. What are you looking at her for?' But he's looking at the *body*. I'll tell you the truth, they were not good-looking at all. He had an eye for *women*. I think he looked at them from the neck down."

Eliot Dober, who had known and been friends with Bob at WLIZ and WICC since he was a teenager, and for whom Bob had returned to Connecticut to host the United Cerebral Palsy telethons on several occasions, also described this "other side" of Bob.

"When Bob was not on the air, he was entertaining," Eliot said. "But he liked women. He fooled around a lot. His main objectives in life were the radio show, women, and Bob, Jr. I felt Anne knew, although maybe not everything. Bob was pretty much in deep in regard to women. I don't mean to belittle Bob, but he had no real life at that time. He was a loner. But you know, we got along very well. He got along with *everybody* very well. And *everybody* liked Bob. He was a positive person. But when he was done with the radio, he would hang around for an hour and then he was gone. And I don't know where he went. He didn't go home right away. He was private, but he wanted to give the impression that he was very open. But he wasn't. He was private in his own way. Bob was a big kid in a grown up body. All women, any woman, couldn't satisfy Bob. He would go one on one with anyone. Even at the radio station, he had a girlfriend or two. But you know, Bob was Bob. And there are a lot of good things, but he did a lot of crazy things, too. You've got to take Bob in two ways. The good and the bad. Or *was* it bad? In Bob's eyes, it was not bad. Bob was a very complicated person, and as you go on, he became more complicated."

WICC colleague and friend Morgan Kaolian also confirmed that Bob had enjoyed the company of women who worked at WICC, having had affairs on and off during his time at the station. However, friend, neighbor, and record plugger/*Variety* and *Billboard Magazine* editor Harvey Geller, who knew Bob both in Bridgeport and in Los Angeles, recalled something a bit more serious. Bob had confided to Harvey that he wanted a divorce from Anne—and this was not the first time he had considered it. This time, it was during the early 1950s, when Bob and Anne were living in Bridgeport, and Bob was working at WICC.

"I knew he was having affairs," Harvey said. "But he told me that he wanted to leave Anne back in Bridgeport. He decided he would stick it out with her and try to start a new life on the West Coast. I assumed moving to California had helped because they seemed to get along so well. She enjoyed his humor and so did my wife and I. So I think the four of us got along beautifully. So I felt that there was no need to ask him how he was getting along with Anne after he moved to California."

There was a reason why Bob was considering a divorce again, now for at least the second time in his young marriage. He had met someone, and he claimed to have fallen in love with her.

"There was a girl in the local high school who, in about 1956, had interviewed Bob at WICC for an article they were doing in the school paper," Harvey explained. "And they started dating. She was about seventeen years old at the time. And it developed into a relationship. Bob considered marrying her. In fact, he wanted very much to divorce Anne and marry her. She was a very beautiful girl. He didn't talk about it except to tell me that he wanted to marry this girl, but her parents refused to let him because he was Catholic, and she was Jewish. But he continued to see her, even after he went to California, and even after she was married and living in Texas. Once a year, she and Bob would get together. They used to say, 'Same time next year,' just like the movie with the same title. He told me they would get together for a number of years after that."

There were others who remembered similar stories. Eliot Dober also recalled Bob talking of divorce while he was in Bridgeport. "I remember one day Bob said to me, 'Maybe I ought to get a divorce.' And that's the only thing he said. But he never did until he got to LA."

WICC 1950s on-air afternoon personality Wes Hobby was friends with a young lady Bob had been seeing in Bridgeport. Whether this was the same girl that Harvey knew is unknown. Wes also believed Bob had not only talked of divorce, but that he and Anne had actually split up again. "He was separated from his wife at that time and that he was 'dating' a very attractive student at the University of Bridgeport. I know that because while he didn't know it, she was a good friend of mine, and she told me 'all about Bob.' When he moved to the West Coast, I understand he reunited with his wife and son."

Despite Bob's affairs, WICC cared about Bob very much and—at least in his presence and to the public—overlooked his indiscretions and brushed them under the carpet. Those who elaborated on Bob's private life for this book did so with care.

Tootie also made it very clear that although he had been frustrated, and at times, even scared because of Bob's behavior, Bob "was a good guy. A very talented, good-looking guy. I think of Bob quite a bit. I think I've watched *Hogan's Heroes* once since his death because every time I see him, it kind of brings some tears to my eyes. I really loved the guy. I loved him as a friend. When you talked to him, he would always be *there* with you, a nice personality. You know, maybe the music wasn't *all* that important. He just loved being around people, and he thought a lot of people were exciting. I'm pretty proud that I can say, 'I knew Bob Crane.'"

Addiction starts to create pain, the very thing the person is trying to avoid. In creating pain, the process also creates a need for the continuation of the addictive relationship. The addict seeks refuge from the pain of addiction by moving further into the addiction process. The addict seeks happiness and serenity in the high or trance, but because the addict has started to withdraw from himself or herself and others, the addict can't see that the pain he or she feels is created by acting out. Addicts are like kids—if it feels good, they do it. They explore; they follow the emotional impulses that come from the very core of their beings instead of logic… The person may feel uneasy, restless, and guilty. These are early warning signals, but part of the addictive process is learning how to deny these warning signals.

—Craig Nakken, *The Addictive Personality*, pp. 29-30

By the time Bob arrived in Hollywood to take the job at KNX-CBS Radio, he had already had engaged in many short flings—a few of them serious—and was deeply addicted. He had also been romantically involved with two other women during his marriage to Anne, and his relationships with them were serious enough for him to consider divorce at least twice. The new job at KNX and a new life in Hollywood appealed to him both on a personal and professional level. Working at one of the largest radio stations in Hollywood—and in the country—was a dream come true for him professionally. And while he may have always considered Connecticut home, living in California was a thrill. The West Coast culture was more relaxed, more open, and more accepting. Bob fit right in, and he thrived in the laid-back atmosphere of sunny California.

But he had also learned to be more discreet, and the degree and direction to which he projected his interest in women shifted. While some of his colleagues knew of his dalliances, some of his closest friends and family members were shielded from them, many never knowing until after his death. The walls he was constructing around himself were becoming thicker and more difficult to break through. Many of his friends who once believed he had been so open with them were stunned at how little they actually knew of his private life.

"I think if there was anybody at the station who was in Bob's inner circle, it would have been his secretary, and I'm not even sure she was," friend and KNX colleague Leo McElroy said. "But I don't think any of the rest of us were. I was as close to Bob as any on-air staff, and I never pretended that I knew anything about what was going on in Bob's home. I think I knew his wife's name, I think, just from hearing it mentioned, but I never met her, I never met his kids. I never knew anything about what their home life was like or anything beyond that. Our relationship was a working, friendly relationship. I think with anybody who is constantly 'on,' there is always that suspicion there is always something underneath that. I just never got an idea what it was. You can't maintain a personality like that and have people really believe that's all there is to your character. Obviously, there were things about Bob that none of us knew or would have known. But when the revelations came out about Bob's life and addictive issues, I was absolutely shocked. There was never anything that ever made me think that there was something else going on. And maybe it's my own naiveté. Other than the frequent line from Bob, 'I don't drink, and I don't smoke, and two out of three ain't bad,' which I took as a pretty good gag line, I had no idea what he was doing with regard to the *three*. To the best of my knowledge, he was a family guy with a wife and kids, and I was really startled when I found out he was out of that and was getting married to the gal who played on *Hogan's*. That was a little startling, but I didn't know the family, so I kind of just shrugged it off. Yet I didn't see anything that indicated to me that Bob was a sexual addict or that he was voyeuristic. There was a lot of sexual heat, sexual chemistry at CBS. I mean, everybody was aware of everybody else; who looked great and who didn't look great, and who was doing what with whom. But I didn't hear any talk ever about Bob and *anybody* at CBS."

KNX librarian Diane Thornton recalled, "His personal life was so separate and so private. He definitely kept his life his business, and maybe not for any reason other than that's the way he liked it to be. He and his family lived in Tarzana, and they had a very nice life. But she was not a wife who was around. She was not a big socializer. Record companies invited everybody to cocktail parties and openings and all that kind of thing constantly. He'd go once in awhile, but not a lot. But that was business. He was a private man, and everybody respected that. I remember there were a few *Playboy* magazines, which by today's standards were so benign. But that's because it was a guy's office, and as I say, I was twenty years old, I wasn't shocked, but that probably has *nothing* to do or very little to do with what was to come. I'm using the word 'benign' in the true sense of that word. I mean, even *I* wasn't shocked by it! As a girl or a young woman, I had the sense that this wasn't where the girls hung out. But there was no reason for any of the girls to hang out there because it was a whole different situation. He was a man, and it was his office, and he was the star of everything. So who would be hanging out in there anyway? But I never felt that he was a player. I never saw him with a woman. I never saw him in any music department event that we went to—never saw him come on to anyone in today's terms. It was benign. So I think it just came out later.

"He was wonderful. He was a delightful, charming, fun person who really seemed to be enjoying the position he found himself in. Here's a guy from Connecticut, who is in LA, and he had his family, and he's doing well and making a lot of money in those days. And having a great time. Can't beat that. I didn't think that there was anything going on then, but he obviously had this side of him that came out later when there was an outlet for it. And it's very sad because if he had a little more time, no one may have ever known about it, and he may have been able to get past it."

KNX advertising salesman Tom Thornton added, "I never had the impression that he was ever 'on.' He was, to me, very natural. He was just a very ebullient guy. He hit me always as a guy with a pretty good disposition, and if you didn't ask him to do *too* much, didn't put him in a bad situation where he had to stay too long or do too much, and I'm talking about with advertisers, he was pretty good. There was nothing sinister. I never had the feeling of anything like that."

Bob threw himself into his work. He was out the door in the morning before most people were even conscious to arrive at KNX by six o'clock a.m. He would prepare extensively—exhaustively—for his radio shows. He made people laugh, and he loved *making* people laugh.

Cousin Jim Senich said, "I think he would let you only so close. He would be glad to talk about radio, TV, movies, whatever, but that's where it stopped, unless you were really a family member or good friend. You weren't going to get beyond that. Even in his affairs, he would never talk about them; the guys at WICC said they didn't know. I mean they knew after awhile when they heard the stories, but they never brought it up with him because they liked him so much. Bobby was just a big teddy bear. He was a big teddy bear, and everybody loved him, and they didn't want to hear any bad things. Strange, people probably think he walked around with horns sticking out of his head, but he was a good guy. That point about maybe he was hiding something. I never thought of that. I suppose if they put him on a psychiatrist's couch, they might come up with that, but I don't know. Hard as it was with his dad and the tension that was in the house, I never saw him be affected by it, although his friends said he didn't want to go in the house. But I wasn't there day-in and day-out. And humor is healing."

Employing the art of self-deprecation, he could cut the critics off at the pass if he was the first to ridicule himself. It was a technique he had learned to master so well, that even when he was joking in the press, it became fact, even when it was not.

For example, Bob routinely used to tell people that he was not smart or could not tell a "Puccini from pizza." Yet he was very knowledgeable about current events, had studied with Stella Adler, had taken a course at the University of Bridgeport, had taken it upon himself to improve his writing skills, and according to the *Nashua Telegraph's* article published in 1966, was "one of the best informed persons on the world of entertainment, subscribing to and reading all trade publications and reading every book on the market concerned with the entertainment industry."

In another instance, it was reported that Bob had dropped out of high school. Yet it is a false statement, originating from Bob himself. His classmates recalled that just as a joke, Bob used to tell people he dropped out.

Bob had been learning to close people off—engaging in the art of the nonsense conversation. For example, he could talk with someone at great length, but when it really came down to it, he would have divulged nothing of his inner being. However, others in the conversation would leave feeling fulfilled and satisfied, thinking they had just had the best conversation in the world.

KNX advertising salesman Gordon Mason was not surprised that Bob had been promiscuous, and unlike others, he *had* heard rumors at KNX. Gordon also knew of a photo album of naked women Bob carried with him. But Gordon was astonished at the level of Bob's involvement in it.

"I was shocked at the depth of it," Gordon said. "I knew he had a problem, but I was a little surprised that there was that much of a mania with it, and that he became a victim of that appetite. As far as I knew, at the time, he was just a guy, even though he'd carry pictures around, and I thought that was rather strange. And he had a reputation for chasing some of the ladies at the station. But I didn't pay much attention to it. It had not made people dislike him at all. The ladies never worried about him, and the station kept it all very quiet. It *never* affected his work. He had boundless energy. He was a very pleasant guy, always nice to be around, fun to be around."

Radio was a perfect place for Bob to express his opinions about politics, culture, entertainment, and comedy—and he was tucked safely away in a booth. Eventually, he began to want more, and he got it by working to become a professional actor. But as he explored this new career path, he occasionally—although not always—let his guard down, showing some inappropriate behavior toward fellow actresses. Theatre director Donald Freed could not recall Bob being anything but professional while performing in the 1959 Valley Playhouse production of *Tunnel of Love*; however, Paul Petersen had different memories of Bob's demeanor on *The Donna Reed Show*. Paul also had astute observations about radio personalities in general and how that particular profession related to Bob.

"Looking back on all of this, I can put words to what was a gut reaction," Paul Petersen stated. "I didn't like the way he treated Ann McCrea, with the overly friendly placement of hands, and later on, the nibbles on the neck and the tongue in the ear and the kind of sly sexual innuendo. But I didn't have words for recognizing that he, in fact, for *all* the women on the set, not that there were many, exhibited that behavior. I think Ann [McCrea] called him out a couple of times within my direct observations. But it was always playful. It was not like this was a blow up. I don't know what Donna *may* have said to him. As the years went by, I would hear more and more from Donna, but I never, ever heard her say that there was some sort of intervention, although frankly, I wouldn't doubt it. A couple of times, I know Annie [McCrea] was deeply embarrassed, and so was the hairdressing lady, and some other women on the show, as was our publicist. He had sort of different moves for everybody. I had a lot of very attractive young females as my girlfriends who would participate on the show, and Bob was not good to be around. *I* even spoke to him about it. 'Just *lay off* my chicks.' When you're in a scene and all together, there's no such thing as 'an approach.' You're there in the same room together; you're working together in a confined space.

It's just the comments and the pawing and the sudden hugs that were uncalled for, and much too familiar. There was always a funny quip, like 'Oh, don't take this seriously.' But it was inappropriate. At first, I thought he's just being unprofessional, he doesn't know, he's got that radio personality. And of course now that I'm older, I recognize that people who make a success of their life by sitting in a room on their own, talking to the world, they just don't have the social graces. He doesn't have to work *with* anyone when he's all by himself. I think the same can be said of virtually every radio personality I know. It is a very *isolated* profession."

While working on *The Donna Reed Show*, Bob was met with disapproval for his behavior. It may have been what led to his decision to no longer look at other actresses, and instead, treat them as he would if they were men. If he wanted to be successful as an actor, he could not jeopardize that very important goal through recreational sex with his fellow actresses.

"Everybody in the business—all the men, who are proud of *being* men, have an eye for the new, attractive young ingénue," Paul said. "*All* of us do, I do to this day. It's how you *treat* them, that is the difference. *My* training, especially with the role models I had, like Sophia Loren and Donna Reed, and then other women of my acquaintance who were making careers for themselves, like Raquel Welch, for example, for all of their beauty and desirability, were still *professionals*. And you *treated* them that way, particularly in the workplace. Ambition is not a private matter for *men*; nor is making life choices that outsiders may think are rather foolish, confined just to *men*. And when you work in Hollywood, where status is often a very illusory thing, all you really care about is if someone is serious, and when they get to work, they come *prepared*."

Bill Wolff, a writer and producer at KNX, worked with Bob at the station. He remembered, "They hired a hot shot—Bob Crane. He was a big hit, and he was very personable and hard working. I dealt with big egos. He treated me well and on a professional level. It was good. In a way, he was like Hogan: glib and a nice looking guy. Bob had a big ego. He was egotistical—he knew he was the star. He knew who he was. He had the alpha dog role. I don't think he dealt too much with others. Overall, Bob was driven and ambitious, with a bit of charm to him and boyish good looks. Bob was a hard worker and goal-driven. But he was not one you'd pal around with. The sales guys would deal with him as an on-air personality and talk with him about promotions.

He was a 'verbal straight arm.' He'd say, 'Hi,' make idle conversation, and quickly run away. Standoffish. But *always driven*. Bob always used to say, 'If you can reach your goal, then everything would be okay. But if you got what you *think* you wanted, that isn't happiness.' To Bob, success was happiness. 'If I could get *on* a regular series, that would be it for me.' And sure enough, he got it—*The Donna Reed Show*. It was big stuff to all of us. I said, 'Bob you realize that this show is terrific.' He said, 'You know, to tell you the truth, if I could be the *star* of my *own* sitcom, that's all I'd ever ask.' And then later, he got it—*Hogan's Heroes*. The last time I talked to him, he was on *Hogan's Heroes*. Bob mentioned he wanted to be a movie star. 'If I could *only* be a star of a movie, I'd be happy.' And then he got it—*Arsenic and Old Lace*. He was always searching for that next step to happiness."

Slowly over time, addictive logic develops into a belief system—
a delusion system from which the addicted person's life will be directed. The person will fight this and delay it as long as possible, but eventually, the delusion system and the Addict take control.
As the illness progresses, the delusion system will become more complex and rigid. The delusion system is commonly described as a wall surrounding the person, one that has two main functions. First, it keeps one locked inside oneself with only the Addict to relate to. An addicted person's world is a lonely one; his or her focus is directed inward. The second function of the delusion system is to keep away people who would endanger the addictive relationship.

—Craig Nakken, *The Addictive Personality*, p. 35

On *Hogan's Heroes*, Bob Crane portrayed the stoic, fearless, cunning Colonel Hogan, and without question, despite all of his earlier success in radio, it would become Bob's signature performance. Those who worked with him on the set, with only rare exceptions, had nothing but the kindest memories to share. To most, he was pleasant, professional, friendly, charismatic, and focused. He knew he was the star, but he was not nasty, reportedly only having what some called a "healthy ego."

And—he was aloof and distant.

Actress Arlene Martel remembered, "I felt that there was someone very wounded. He wasn't gloomy on the set, but there was something very withdrawn compared to the other fellows—the other actors who were very outgoing. Werner Klemperer, John Banner—everyone had kind of a more cheerful disposition. Whereas Bob was very—kind of sober. Very reflective. He wasn't 'Mr. Look At Me, Look At Me,' like some of the others were. You know, Richard Dawson, show biz personality. I think that was another way of hiding. When you're working with someone, you kind of get to see the more authentic persona. I thought he was really troubled. I didn't know what about. But I had no idea of his personal life. I didn't know if he was seeing someone or not seeing someone. I knew that he was very gentle with me. The only cynical thing he ever said was about my husband. He said, 'Well, where do you think your husband is right now? And who might he be with?' And I was offended. I commented on it. I remember saying, 'You know, that sounds so cynical and bitter,' and he said, 'Well, perhaps.' He kind of dismissed it. Because I think at the core of him, he was not a cruel person or didn't really want to hurt anyone else. Sometimes, you want to strike out when you yourself are so hurt.

"I can see his face so clearly now," Arlene continued. "I can see his eyes. And they were smallish eyes. Small eyes. And they were wary…and *weary* eyes. And I see his mouth, and the lines that went down from it. It was not a mouth that curved up. It was a mouth of disappointment. I'd say he was not revealing anything. Maybe if I had been on the show regularly, I would have been able to win his confidence more. In fact I'm sure I could have because I did feel a connection with him. It was almost like he wanted to come out, but couldn't. He was sealed. Sealed…kind of in prison…imprisoned.

"Religion and spirituality used to come up a lot with me in those days. Anyone who'd listen! It was my way of feeling into where a person was in the universe, if I wanted to. I felt a response in him to that part of me that was interested but isn't necessarily seen outwardly. And I think he had a spiritual nature. In fact, I know that he had…that had been possibly discouraged. I think in the last period of time that I worked on the show, I think he enjoyed my opinions, although he was wary of them. Like 'I could discover more about her if I let myself…I could explore that.' But it never got to the point where he said, 'Tell me more.' It was just that I saw him listen with a real interest. And I was discussing how we bring in things with us to this life that we have to karmically work out and that there is a Higher Power. All of these things I would share because that's what interested me. But I never saw him walk away when I was apostle-tizing. He seemed interested without letting on that he was interested. And I felt that there was something—there was some spark of light in there that was still functioning. But his outward persona, I think, was nothing was going to impress him or get him attached. I think he was seeking, and I guess many people who have addictions are seeking that connection with God. Maybe his was through sex. But he never shared his own ideas on spiritualism and religion with me. I was hoping…hoping… But he also didn't put down my own views. He didn't in any way try to invalidate that. He was respectful, I'd say. He respectfully listened. He was a mystery. But I think I could have been a good influence in some way."

Bob was, by this point, fully immersed in his sexual addiction. And yet, in every job he took, right to the end of his life, he remained professional while he was at work. Work was work, and it remained very separate from the bulk of what was going on in his private life.

"I think he managed to rise above it," Arlene said. "I think that probably saved him, the acting, having the opportunity to play…I think a lot of who he was, was put into Hogan. There was something heavy. Heavy…very weary and tired. And he didn't impose that on anyone else. But there was almost like a wariness in his eyes, that 'I don't trust.' Not the open eyes of, how children's eyes are so trusting and so open. When he was playing drums, that's the time I really felt he was connecting to his healthy, healthy self. It seemed like a wonderful declaration. He was in a whole different world. And he put other people in a whole different world. I think that was a very attractive part of his being. It was a totally positive expression. There was a lot of life and vitality on the set. Well, there was anyway, but he added to it."

Throughout the run of *Hogan's Heroes*, Bob had affairs. His first serious affair was with Cynthia Lynn, who believed he dated her exclusively. While he was with Cindy, he told her he was "not really *married*-married," and that he and Anne were holding it together for the sake of the children. He openly discussed wanting to divorce Anne with Cindy. After Cindy left the series following the conclusion of season one, Patricia Olson took her place—both professionally and romantically.

His relationship with Patty became serious very quickly. It is unknown if Bob dated Cindy exclusively during their affair as she claimed. However, Patty was well aware of Bob's sexual relations with other women and his dabbling in pornography, none of which seemed to bother her at the outset.

Many actresses Bob worked with, and nearly all who contributed to this book, claimed that Bob remained professional on the set with them. However, actress Francine York had a different experience.

"Bob and I were both under contract to Bing Crosby," Francine said. "I was next door doing *Slattery's People* at the same time he was on *Hogan's Heroes*. I thought Bob had a great personality. He was always smiling and laughing when we worked together on *The Red Skelton Hour*. My mom adored him. He gave her a tour of the set, and also gave her and my dad an autographed photo. I didn't have the heart to tell her about his other life, which I saw firsthand. She said, 'Poor man. He's so nice.' And he was. He was a very nice man, and he sparkled. But unfortunately, he had troubles. Too bad because he was a great talent."

Other actresses on the set of *Hogan's Heroes* and elsewhere in his acting career during this time, however, did not find Bob to be lecherous. In fact, he seemed to be exactly the opposite with them.

Actress Inger Wegge stated, "John Banner was the more sex-interested man. He talked a lot about it and would have loved to have me, but we remained only friends long after the show was over. And he wrote me several letters and cards. Still, he always told me to keep away from Bob. When I asked why, he would not tell. Maybe he was jealous of Bob's sex life? Poor Bob, he never did anything at all out of place to me; never said anything, not like John."

Director Bruce Bilson stated, "[Bob and I] became pretty good working friends. I sort of knew that he did some porno kind of videoing. It never came to the set. I never saw any undertones or any issues with any of the women on the set. Honestly. That's something that can happen on any set with any guest actress. You know, there are some very attractive young ladies, and there are a lot of guys. I think we lost power once. I remember we were all walking around outside the set waiting for it to be fixed. But again, there were no histrionics, no hysterics. As far as Patty, everybody had an opinion on whether he should be marrying her or not, but it never came out as any kind of insult or argument or even being mentioned except in the slightest way, and *not* to him."

"His hobby was whatever the latest electronic gadget was," director Jerry London added. "He was into *all* the high-tech stuff at that time. He had all his tape stuff; I'm sure he took a lot of pictures, and everything else. But no one else was really interested in it. He was always up to date on everything. As I remember, he kept kidding, 'Oh, I've got this video tape camera, boy you gotta see it, man; it takes pictures.' Dawson went, 'Oh, well, let me see that.' A couple of months later, Dawson had everything. Either that or Dawson had it first and got Bob interested in it. One or the other. But here's how little of [Bob's addiction came to the set]—I never even knew it. I worked with Bob for six years. I knew he liked ladies. But so what? He's the star of the show. But I never had any inkling of any of the other stuff. Nothing. All I knew was during the show he got a divorce and then got married to Sigrid. But that's really all I ever knew. I just had no idea. All these years later when he died, God, it was a real shock to me. When I saw the movie, it made me very sad. Depressed the hell out of me."

Meanwhile, back home in Connecticut, best friend Charlie Zito began to suspect his friend was starting to become involved in extramarital affairs. "Bob started to do some carousing," Charlie said. "But then, when everything happened, when it all hit the fan, that's when Yve and Anne started to write to each other quite a bit. So actually, my wife knew more about what was going on than I did. My wife wouldn't tell me very much. And some of the things she told me I didn't believe it. She said, 'You don't believe just because you're a friend of Bob's, but something's going on there that really isn't very pleasant.' And I said, 'No. She's exaggerating.' 'Well, why should she exaggerate?' And I said, 'I find it hard to believe.' Then when I started to see it in print and see what's going on, at first I was very disappointed. But I said, 'You know, he's always been a good friend to us,' and I almost looked at it like it's none of our business. I hated to see it. I was a little disappointed. We used to tease him a lot about it. When we were younger—'You know Bob, some day, some women are gonna get you in trouble.' Because some of the things he'd come out with—at the time, we didn't think anything of it because we all talked more or less the same way. Teenagers—we were young teenagers. We used to talk about it. But in a way, it did surprise me. And like I said, I was a little disappointed."

Rick Plastina, who worked with Bob in the 1969 theatre production *Send Me No Flowers* in Chicago, claimed that Bob was professional. He also never noticed anything from this other side of Bob's life.

However, there was one moment that stood out to Rick as a little "interesting."

"Bob Crane threw a cast party for everybody," Rick said. "At the party, Bob greeted everyone when they came in the door, and he looked immaculate. He looked like a movie star. He was tanned, and even though I'd been working with him onstage, I remember him standing there in a blazer, and I think he had an ascot around his neck. And he looked like a star. I came in and introduced him to my then-girlfriend/now-wife, Peggy, and he took her—he greeted her—and then he took her in his arms and gave her a passionate kiss 'hello.' Now, there was nothing lascivious about it, but I was standing there—I was twenty-three at the time, and Peg was about twenty or twenty-one, and I remember going—as Bob took her in his arms and kissed her—I just said, '*Whoa!*' in surprise. And I kinda laughed. I didn't find it offensive or distasteful or anything, I was just like, 'Wow! Welcome to show business!' But there was nothing bad about it. We know all of the stuff that has been written since and in the movie—all of the negative sides of it. But other than *that*—where there was a little indication of, 'Well, yeah, he was a ladies man,' obviously, but it was not like he was doing it in a lascivious way. It was just—it was a passionate type of Clark Gable kiss. He just took her in his arms and gave her the old fashioned kiss. Peggy was stunned, and I think she was flattered. But I remember we both went, 'Whoa! That was interesting!' And like I say, it was in no way offensive or making me feel jealous or angry or anything like that. It was just kind of funny."

However, others were well aware of Bob's growing problem. Tom Davis, younger brother of actor Larry Hovis, remembered that his brother and other members of the *Hogan's Heroes* cast had tried to talk to Bob about his behavior. But Bob simply brushed them off, often making excuses to justify his actions.

"Larry said Bob always felt bad about it," Tom explained. "It was almost like, 'If I don't drink my coffee, I'll be a complete asshole in the morning.' It was kind of like that with Bob. They all [the cast of *Hogan's Heroes*] tried to talk to Bob about it, as far as I know. They all tried."

"It seems to me if a person does the things that allegedly he did," Werner Klemperer stated in 1998 on the *E! True Hollywood Story*, "they don't suddenly happen from Monday to Tuesday that you change. They have to be based on some kind of long-standing difficulties."

"You can't really enjoy an addiction," Arlene Martel declared. "I mean, someone who *has* to drink doesn't enjoy wine the same way as someone who can have it now and then and really love the taste and the feeling and aroma. It's quite different than someone who comes to hate that which he has come to need."

As the illness progresses and the addicted person becomes more and more inwardly directed, others surrounding the person will sense this emotional withdrawal and react to it... Addicts start to manipulate other people and treat them as objects... The Addict is often very self-righteous and self-centered... "Why should I talk with my spouse if she isn't going to believe me?" If family or friends try to connect with the person to find out what is happening, they will be met with some form of resistance—often a lie, silent withdrawal, or even a personal attack.
Friends and especially family want to make sense out of what is happening to the addicted person they deeply care about. In trying to understand, people around the addict label him or her in an effort to cope with the changes. The addicted person may get labeled as "irresponsible," "troubled," "tense," "crazy," "strange," or "weak." What is really being labeled is the presence of the Addict.

—Craig Nakken, *The Addictive Personality*, pp. 46-49

Once he got to Hollywood, Bob's interest in women intensified. So did his interest in photographing them, with their consent, although he also photographed naked women in Connecticut.

"He was the first guy to own a Polaroid camera that I knew, and he started taking pictures of his girlfriends, nude," said Harvey Geller, who knew Bob in both Connecticut and California. "So I went out and bought a Polaroid camera. It didn't help with me! That was amazing. There was one girl that I dreamed about, who worked for Columbia Records in the same building that Bob worked in—in the KNX building. I had had lunch with her a number of times. Just a pretty girl to look at. And Bob hadn't met her. And one day, we walked into the elevator, and there she was in the elevator. I said hi to her, and Bob jumped over to her and grabbed her and kissed her, and he had never met her before. And here I'd been seeing her, taking her to lunch, and *I* never got to kiss her! But she enjoyed it. She knew who he was."

KMPC radio personality and game show host Gary Owens recalled, "We knew his family quite well. His wife, we'd see her quite often. Many times Bob couldn't be there, so Anne would take over as part of the Crane family. He had a bit of a schizophrenic life. Bob grew up Catholic, so he probably spent much of his life with either guilt or shame within the framework of what he was doing. I think it was an obsession with him, being interested in girls all the time and in pornography. He would carry a book of pictures with him all the time, just to show us. Whether we wanted to see it or not was not the question. He'd just say, 'My gosh, look at this!' It was not a delusion as much as it was an obsession. Why? I don't know."

Bob married Patty with the understanding that he could be free to pursue his interests in extramarital sex and amateur pornography—as long as he returned home to her. "He treated other women like the rest of the world treats toilet paper," she told ABC News. "Who's going to be jealous of toilet paper?" But by October 1977, after only seven years of marriage, Patty filed for a divorce. That she filed for divorce did not come as a surprise to Bob; what she accused him of did. Her accusations completely threw him. And according to Harvey Geller, Bob could not understand why Patty believed he had not been faithful to her.

"The last time I talked to him on the phone was about two weeks before he died," Harvey said. "He told me that he was getting a divorce. He said that he had usually lied to Anne when he was fooling around with Patty, saying he was working late. When he was working late on a new show, Patty didn't believe him. She said, 'You tried this routine on Anne when you were fooling around with me, so who are you fooling around with?' And he told me, 'I *wasn't* fooling around. But she wouldn't believe me!' And then he came up with a line that I thought was rather strange under the circumstances, which was, 'I wouldn't cheat on my wife! She has the best body of any woman in Hollywood!' So he *did* lie to me, and maybe to *himself*."

> *There is a point where a person emotionally, mentally, spiritually, and finally, physically breaks down under the stress and pain produced by the addiction.*
> *Acting out no longer produces much pleasure.*
> *The addict's behavior often doesn't even make sense to him or her anymore, so the addict gives up trying to make sense of it and falls into a lifestyle based entirely on addictive ritual.*
> *Unresolved feelings and issues are seen as excuses to act out at any time. People with addictions often start to question their ability to be around others.*
> *They start to feel as if people can see right through them. Sex addicts retreat into a private world often filled only by other sex addicts, if by anyone else at all. The sex addict may be asked to leave a job for unacceptable behavior.*
> *Addicts are afraid of ending up alone. In their desperation, they show a childlike quality; they attempt to connect with others by clinging to family or friends, and often become very upset if it appears that people are withdrawing from them.*
> *The addicted person becomes an emotional pressure cooker whose safety valve is not functioning properly. Soon, something has to give.*

—Craig Nakken, *The Addictive Personality*, pp. 55-61

"He was ridiculously friendly to his fans," Bob's son Scott Crane said. "I don't think there are many stars like that anymore. I think that was more common back then. I mean, there have always been jerks who don't want to talk to their fans, but he was all about his fans. I think that stems from the person he was—his personality—but also from radio. Working in radio, you're always doing public appearance events, so you're used to meet-and-greets with the listeners. So throughout his whole life, he'd been used to being really, really friendly to anyone who came up to him. Some people say it could have easily led to part of his demise—he was too casual, and he didn't have any boundaries with who he would get to know and who he would let into his life because he didn't really seem to judge people. He didn't seem to have that 'You're not worthy of me; I'm better than you; I don't need to spend time with you.' He'd spend time with *anyone* who wanted to spend time with *him*. So he was really open that way—to a fault. Most of us have some kind of a barometer. 'This person seems dangerous or shady or whatever.' He had none of that. He didn't have a protective sixth sense. He was *too* open of a book in that way, and so that got him into trouble. And it got him into trouble with Disney, with bosses, with people—he was just a real open book. I know Victoria Berry has talked about that, how he just let everybody into his life. But be it at Disneyland or the grocery store, he would spend ten minutes talking to a total stranger."

The 1970s was a decade of transition for Bob. As he left the world of *Hogan's Heroes* and attempted to regain success in his career, he struggled to maintain the separation between work and addiction. He had been able to hide his addiction from many for most of his life, but as time went on, he became less careful. It cost him work. It cost him two marriages. It was beginning to cost him his cherished relationship with his children.

And it was about to cost him his life.

On the set of *The Bob Crane Show*, producer Norman Powell recalled that Bob's lifestyle was not visible to him; however, he found Bob's humor to be occasionally off-color, racy, and burlesque.

"The only thing that became really visible on the set was his obvious boastful nature relative to his sexual prowess," Powell stated. "And his wife [Patty] would come to all the shows, and he would introduce her, and she would emphasize her breast size. Turn profile to the audience, and he would make reference to his wife's breasts. It was a little embarrassing. It was nuts. Burlesque. But I didn't get any first-hand insights into what he was doing when he went home."

Bob had learned to keep his sexual impulses very separate from his professional life. When it came time to go to work, it all disappeared. It was almost like it didn't exist. But as time went on, his addiction became much more in control of him instead of the other way around. Whereas Norman Powell had not noticed any improper *behavior* from Bob on the set of *The Bob Crane Show*, actor James Sutorius, who worked on the series, recalled a specific event.

"He did talk about his huge video collections and that it involved girls and such," Sutorius said. "He never got into very much detail as I remember. It's all vague, but he talked about it. I was never invited over. Thank God."

After starring in the Walt Disney Productions film *Superdad*, Walt Disney Studios offered Bob a contract. But it soon fell apart. Not wanting to risk its reputation on someone who was exhibiting what had been termed "unDisneylike" behavior, Disney broke their contract with him.

It started in November 1972, when Bob had just signed on to star in *Superdad* (then still called *A Son-in-Law for Charlie McCready*). In a meeting with a Disney representative and Hollywood reporter Vernon Scott, Bob announced that "I love to sit in with small groups and play the drums [in topless-bottomless bars]. What's wrong with that?" Vernon Scott published the story, and it became one of the first glimpses Disney—and the public—had of Bob's proclivities.

While there were occasional articles Bob contributed to *Playboy* and other adult magazines—not uncommon for celebrities to do—this particular article would be one of only a few times in the mainline press where Bob readily admitted to going to strip clubs. Most glazed over the article until June 1978, when it provided fodder for a growing scandal.

Disney didn't ignore it, however, and they cut ties with Bob. Daughter Karen Crane told Ed Robertson of *TV Confidential*, "When he had finished *Superdad*, Disney did get wind of these rumors that he did have an [interesting pastime]. He loved women—too much. Disney canceled the contract. They originally wanted him to do a number of films for them, but they definitely didn't want that lifestyle connected to them."

Bob appeared in only one other Disney film, *Gus*, which was released in 1976. His role of Pepper was well-performed and under-recognized, but was by no means a starring role. In a time when money was tight, it merely helped pay the bills.

In June 1976, Bob returned to Stamford for his 30th class reunion. It would be the last time Charlie Zito or any of his classmates would ever see their friend again. According to Charlie, Bob was happy and friendly with everyone. He had his camera and took pictures at the reunion, which he then sent to their class secretary Jane Lippoth Golden. He had been exuberant and the life of the party, and everybody loved seeing him, vying for his attention, still proud of their Drummer Boy.

But Charlie could sense something was troubling his friend.

"He was very happy to everybody outwardly," Charlie said. "But there was something bothering him. It was like a nervous energy. Like he was trying to show everybody that he was fine and nothing was bothering him. And the more you try and show that, the more it looks kind of artificial. That's the impression I got. Because I never discussed anything like that with him in-depth. We just skimmed over stuff like that and just let it ride. I never really came out and said, 'Bob, come on. What's your problem?' But I knew he was troubled. We often said Bob never had a chance with any other real relationship in school. He was always with Anne, Anne, Anne. Now he's sowing his wild oats. That's what it usually is with an addiction. Once you have the problem, then you're on your way."

Throughout the 1970s, Bob traveled extensively across the country performing *Beginner's Luck* and other plays in dinner theatres. He took his theatre work seriously, even though he recognized it as a step down in his career. While on the road, he was able to more freely entertain and feed his addiction, which by then was completely in control. Some of his closest friends in theatre, such as John and Pam Thompson, *never* saw this side of Bob. Others witnessed it to varying degrees, and he had made them uncomfortable.

John Thompson recalled, "That hidden, extra life he had, we never, ever saw. We were totally shocked when everything came out. Evaluating it, I think Bob was kind of like a boy in a candy store. When he started doing *Hogan's Heroes*, women started throwing themselves at him."

"We would do the show, and we would go out afterwards to a place that had music because they would let him play drums," Pam added. "So then, of course, John and I being recently together we would go home, say goodnight to Bob, and he would go to his place, and we would go to ours, and so we never knew anything about anything that was going on. I know that sounds ridiculous, but we never saw each other till we went to the show. When I tell you that he had two personalities, no matter what he was doing, I still can't imagine him as anything but a nice guy. He wouldn't hurt anyone. He gave to charity; he did free things all the time. *He was a good person*. And for them to paint him as a sleaze was not fair. He never drank; he never smoked; he never did *any* kind of drugs. Now please understand that we didn't know him really well even though we were with him all the time. When we were home, we didn't get together socially, but when we were on the road, if Patty came with Scotty, we were *all* together. We were close, but it's called, you don't get too close with people you're working with. And I'm sure that's why Bob slipped by us."

"He was very caring with his cast, and I believe very caring with most people," Victoria Berry Wells said. "Except he had his problem, which bothered me. I didn't like it. He'd come back and talk about it, and, 'Guess what we did last night.' Like it was nothing. And everyone would be a little embarrassed. He was like two different people. Like two totally different people. He was loving and caring. He talked about his son Scotty all the time. But I didn't know the depth of how far his sexual problems were. I had no idea until later when I learned it. But I knew there was something wrong. He was great until John Carpenter came in to town; he'd get excited when he was coming in. Bob would come in the dressing room before the show sometimes in front of the other actors and the other actress. And he'd tell us who'd he been with the night before, and we used to just ignore it because it would be embarrassing. He'd talk about his sexual encounters so up and free. He didn't hide anything. But that was all. I didn't pay too much attention to it. I avoided getting into that area and kept on a more one on one. But he was very protective of me.

"And as far as working, he was marvelous. He was a real pro. And kind. And I learned so much from him, and he said I had a great future. For rehearsals and shows, it was his beautiful, kind side. *Only.* The other side was never there. He switched on and off. He was *two different people*. He loved his son. He was *kind*. He was a very lovable man. Very caring. He was always professional. Bob was not boisterous. He was just a normal guy. Normal, down-to-earth, very lovable guy. And not on an ego. I didn't find him to be on an ego trip. And then there was the other side. He had a sickness, which I think helped destroy him a lot more. He would have been able to handle things a lot more. I think that contributed to a lot of his decline."

In early 1978, Bob was in Hawaii filming the pilot episode for *The Hawaii Experience*. By this time, he was struggling with his failing marriage, but this new television program was a bright spot in his career. However, his addiction was so pronounced at this point that it was weaving his way into his professional life as it had never done before. *Hawaii Experience* director John Orland found Bob to be professional, kind—all of the wonderful traits that have been named repeatedly. But in filming the episode, John recalled an incident that angered him slightly, and it was an indication that Bob was beginning to fail at keeping his addiction separate from his work.

"Bob was very, very cooperative," John stated. "Always pleasant. I must say, as a little bit of a negative, when we were shooting on the sidewalk once in downtown Honolulu, there was some gal who was walking down the sidewalk. And in the middle of the interview he was doing—he was actually doing an on-camera promo—he suddenly just turned around and left and started chasing this gal down the street. And my girlfriend, who is now been my wife for thirty-five years, ended up running down the street and dragging him back to the camera. Just following his instincts, he took off, and I was upset because we were in the middle of actually filming. But then we all sort of just laughed about it, and that was it. He didn't say anything.

Now, his son [Bobby] was by his side all the time. He brought him over to Hawaii. I do remember Bob complaining about his personal life and his marriage—that things were just totally out of hand. And he was unhappy about that. But I had *no* idea of anything. No, there was *nothing* at the time as I recall that alluded to anything about that."

School friend Edwin Gordon remembered, "When I heard about his death and the pornography, I would just sit there and watch these TV documentaries. I found it so hard to believe. But then it all came together, and I think it was an explosion. It was just kept inside of him. It was a volcano, and it was ready to go off at any time. It was ready to go off even when we were kids. There was another side of him that I never knew and he didn't want me to know. I don't know that *anybody* did. He was goal-directed for fame, not so much fortune. But he was goal-directed for recognition. He wanted recognition *desperately*. He wanted recognition and an exciting life. He needed that. *Desperately*. That's how I remember him. When I heard he was in Bridgeport on radio, I never thought he ever had that in mind. But he always would talk about disc jockeys, and he would listen to them, and it always fascinated him. But he never told me that's what he had in mind for himself. But he had the personality for it. He had a winning personality to get along with persons very well, happy go lucky, never really made anybody mad. He could turn a difficult situation into a laughing one. He had this ability. He was a goal-directed guy looking for recognition and excitement about ready to explode."

"Bob was a professional actor,' Victoria Berry Wells concluded. "A *lovable, lovable* man. Loved his family. A professional in his work. You couldn't get any more professional to knowing his lines and knowing his work. He'd been on a successful hit sitcom which gave him that. And plus all his background in radio and all that. But *Hogan's Heroes* gave him a lot of confidence, and he evolved out of that. That showed him that he had a successful show and that was part of him. He was tremendously lovable and very professional. And a beautiful man. But he was like two different people. And the other side to me is sad. He needed help. He didn't see that until much later. *But he did see it.*"

*Addicts can't break the addictive process alone. Those who try to break the addiction process find that addiction is all they know, and they return to the addictive lifestyle. To recover, addicts must learn a new lifestyle, slowly exchanging the addictive way of life for a new lifestyle, including relationships with other people.
The addict is helpless and entirely addiction-centered, focused on whatever it is—a drug, a pornographic picture, a drink, another bet, more food—that produces the trance, a momentary and illusionary feeling of well-being.
The process of renewal starts with truth, that most healing of all principles. The potential for recovery has been within us all along.*

—Craig Nakken, *The Addictive Personality*, p. 65

"I felt fine counseling Bob," said Reverend Edward Beck. "I counsel with a lot of people. Bob Crane was just Bob Crane. Happened to be well-known, and happened to have a very, very glaring problem, which at least with me he did not hide from in any way. And I felt him very sincere in his attitude to alleviate and get away from it."

A Private Battle

When Bob performed *Beginner's Luck* throughout the 1970s, he was not aware that the man he knew as Ed Beck was more than an employee of the Windmill Dinner Theatre Corporation. To Bob, as well as to many other visiting actors and entertainers performing for the corporation, Beck was simply the man who oversaw the local housing arrangements, ensured the primary needs of the actors and crew were met, maintained the daily functions of the theatre building, and signed the paychecks after the run of the play had concluded.

For the most part, Beck had very little social interaction with Bob. Once the performance concluded each night, they all went their separate ways for the evening. But he was about to become a man of great importance to Bob. Bob had discreetly talked with another executive of the Windmill Dinner Theatre Corporation, and he was advised to speak with Ed Beck. Only then did Bob find out that Beck was also a member of the clergy—*and* an addiction counselor.

Reverend Beck (a Protestant minister and different from the Roman Catholic Priest and media commentator Reverend Edward L. Beck) became the one person to whom Bob would reveal his deepest, innermost thoughts, beliefs, and troubles in the weeks leading up to his murder. Talking with Reverend Beck, Bob declared that he was, indeed, an addict, and he used the word *addict* to describe himself. He realized that he could no longer control the behavior, and while he did not yet understand it as an illness, Bob was keenly aware that many important aspects of his life were deteriorating because of it.

Both of his marriages had suffered—one had ended and the other was in serious jeopardy—because of it.

His children had suffered because of it.

His career had suffered because of it.

Some of his friendships had ended because of it.

Hollywood executives had lost respect of him because of it.

Bob admitted to Reverend Beck that he had tried several times in the past to break away from the addiction on his own—but that he had failed every time. He also understood that the recovery process would involve a lot of difficult work and mean a great deal of mental and emotional pain for him.

But he was prepared to travel that road. He was ready to heal.

At that moment, Bob Crane took his first baby steps toward recovery. But Bob was not going to heal overnight. There would be setbacks.

He was not going to wake up the next morning and no longer be an addict. He was going to be addicted for the rest of his life, and even if he had lived to be one hundred, he would have been one woman away, *always*, from being a practicing addict again.

Bob knew this, accepted it, and was determined to overcome it. First and foremost, he wanted to change because of his children, who had started asking questions that he could not answer honestly and still call himself a good father. The thought of that alone had crushed him. Second, he sought change to help himself rebuild his career, which had started to crumble because studios and producers were beginning to sever ties with him. And third, he was scared of potential consequences to him physically, hinting to John and Pam Thompson and fully disclosing to Victoria Berry Wells that he was afraid of going to and being in Scottsdale.

Bob confessed his addiction privately to a man of the clergy without telling very many others. It was his *private* battle, and the discussions he had with Reverend Beck were confidential. Bob was a proud man with a healthy ego, and he did not want the masses to know that he was undergoing professional counseling. Had Bob lived, it is possible that the public and media would *never* have known. It would have remained private unless *he* chose to discuss it publicly—as it should have.

Reverend Beck would never have disclosed any of it, and he only did so following Bob's murder to give the media and public a deeper understanding of Bob's inner turmoil. However, the media were not very interested in Bob's desire to seek help and change, usually just glossing over his recognition and acknowledgement of being an addict as a possible motive for his murder.

In Reverend Beck's correspondence to the authors of this book, he warned, "The mountain you seek to climb, though admirable, is formidable. I applaud you for your quest, but the media does not want to hear what you have to say. You know that already, so you will not be disappointed with the response that you receive. The quest is for you, so blessings on you through it all."

Would Bob Crane have been able to beat his addiction? We will never know.

Did he want to? *Yes*. Of that, we are *most* certain.

Reverend Edward Beck's
Professional Background and Credentials

Reverend Edward Beck had been a pastor for more than fifteen years when Bob sought his help. In 1983, he published a memoir, "A Love to Live By," which tells the story of his youth, his involvement in college basketball, and his decision to enter the clergy. Nowhere in his book does he mention Bob Crane. The epilogue, as published in his book, is included in part below to provide Reverend Beck's complete background and professional credentials, which had qualified him to counsel Bob generally regarding addiction and assist him specifically in locating a leading psychologist who specialized in sex addiction to facilitate his recovery.

In 1958, Ed Beck...attended Asbury Theological Seminary at Wilmore, Kentucky, [and the following year] entered Candler Methodist Seminary at Emory.

He was scheduled to graduate from Candler in the summer of 1961. His graduation was delayed six months, however, so that he could accept speaking engagements throughout the nation. He was also invited by World Vision, Inc., to be their college-high school speaker in their Tokyo, Japan, Crusade during the spring of 1960.

In the summer of 1962, he joined the National Headquarters of the Methodist Church in Nashville, becoming a staff evangelist of its General Board of Evangelism. He was one of four men who helped organize the Department of Evangelists, and eighteen months later was selected to direct two separate programs: The Department of Evangelists (later renamed the Department of New Life Ministries) and the S.T.E.M. project (Short-Term Evangelistic Mission). The New Life Ministries helped local churches develop and carry out intensive evangelistic renewal and outreach programs. The S.T.E.M. project was geared to inner city and ghetto areas. For six years, he and a team of fourteen people conducted these missions and trained pastors across the country in similar programs.

In 1967, Ed Beck was selected by the Pentagon to tour European and North African military bases to conduct "Christian Leadership Training Labs" for military personnel.

In 1968, because he found himself away from home and family too much conducting evangelism programs, he happily accepted the pastorate of Warren United Methodist Church in Denver, Colorado.

It was an inner-city congregation, and he felt particularly led to it because of his earlier experiences in the Short-Term Evangelistic Mission, which involved ghetto ministries.

When Ed Beck stepped into the pulpit at Warren United Methodist, he found only 250 weather-beaten, but willing, souls ready to join him in ministering to those around them engulfed in poverty.

But it was a Gideon's Army. Together, the small group went to work, and in six years, they had completed a $3 million apartment complex called Warren Village, designed for single-parent families endeavoring to become self-sustaining. Today, it ranks as a unique ministry in helping single parents in transition to be re-educated and restored.

Looked upon as a model for similar units in other cities, it consists of ninety-six apartment units with a self-contained Day-Care Center able to care for over 125 children. To qualify for residency, applicants must show a sincere desire for self-improvement and sign a covenant that they will live at Warren Village only until they are able to re-enter the world better equipped to maintain themselves and their children and remain off the welfare rolls.

The success of Warren Village is currently an impressive ninety-two percent.

In 1973, Ed Beck was assigned to a post in the United Methodist Church called "Minister to and for Society," an unusual new kind of ministry. In 1974, he became the first Methodist clergyman from Colorado to enter the corporate world as a business executive, still maintaining full clergy credentials. In this new work, he became Vice-President of Operations for the Windmill Dinner Theater Corporation of Dallas, Texas, dedicated to offering the public uplifting family entertainment in a wholesome atmosphere.

In this new work, Ed Beck was the construction overseer of all five theatres located in various parts of the nation. He also supervised their personnel. During this time, he served as a consultant to other theatre corporations, advising and counseling with playwrights, plus working with many actors and actresses concerning the communication of faith in the secular theater.

In April of 1980, Ed Beck was assigned to the post of senior pastor of the First Methodist Church in Pueblo, Colorado, a steel manufacturing city of 100,000 population, located 100 miles south of Denver. After he assumed that pastorate, the church grew from 691 to 937 members.

Colorado's governor, Richard Lamm, proclaimed June 12, 1983, as Ed Beck Sunday in honor of Rev. Beck's dedicated work and service in the United Methodist Church, in his community and for his country—and especially for his work in the organization of Warren Village in Denver.

In-Depth Testimony Provided by Reverend Edward Beck about Bob Crane, His Addiction, and His Desire to Change

The following are Reverend Beck's recollections and views about helping Bob get started on his path to recovery, as told exclusively to the authors of this book.

I was a part of the Windmill Dinner Theatre from 1974 to 1979. I was the executive vice president in charge of building dinner theatres, which we had built a huge one in Louisville, Kentucky. And then I was in the corporate office at Dallas Texas, and then moved the corporate office from Dallas to Scottsdale, Arizona. That was where our corporate office was—just across the parking lot from Windmill Dinner Theatre in Scottsdale. I was already clergy. I have presently [at the time of this interview for this book in 2006] been a clergy for forty-six years. I was United Methodist, and I had served the pastorates throughout the United States but primarily the west, in Colorado. While in Denver, I had built a large complex called Warren Village. It was designed specifically for single-parent families who were in crisis situations. They could come and live there for a period of time. It was not a permanent domicile, but they could be there for a year, two years, three years, for re-vocational training, retraining of whatever kind. We had a daycare center that operated twenty-four hours a day to take care of their children.

Out of that, I met the man who owned the Windmill Dinner Theatre Corporation, and he was very much concerned about what was happening in the art world, especially in dinner theatre. He was looking for a trained person with counseling background to work with playwrights and some of his staff, and to work with some of the actors. Of course, my background lent itself to that, *plus* I brought to it a portfolio of some background in new building development.

So I came to work for him for one year and stayed five. I was assigned by my Bishop to the Windmill Corporation, called to minister to and for society, and that was a very, very prominent thing to do here in the United States in the 1970s. A lot of clergy were going to the corporate world—to *help* the corporate world with their "human" problems. Period. And that was my background and why I went with Windmill.

Well, of course, Bob Crane was a part of a [theatre] circuit. He, along with numerous other actors like himself—Caesar Romero, Van Johnson, people like that—had their different shows, and they went from theatre to theatre. Windmill Dinner Theatre owned five different theatres across the States. And so he was booked into all five over a period of time. I knew Bob from reputation—television work, movie work, that kind of thing. But that did not mean I *knew* him. I met him, was acquainted with him. I was not socially involved with him; the only time I ever saw him out beyond the dinner theatre was in Houston, Texas, where one night after the show, I happened to be at a bar and grill eating a sandwich with another member of the staff of the corporation, and Bob came in. And I watched him do his routine at a bar with a number of people with his magnanimous personality, and people gravitated to him and so forth. So my relationship at first with him was totally professional. He worked for us for a period of time at the five theatres. He worked across America in different other settings, and the only thing I knew about him before I met him was his professional career, plus, of course, the rumor that he was deeply involved in pornography and was quite a ladies' man.

Before the performance, they're in Equity; they have to be in a dressing room thirty minutes before the performance. They have to be ready to go ten minutes before with make up and all of that kind of thing. Bob was always punctual; never needed to worry about him being there, getting there; he was always on time.

The stars—it's like one of the cast members told me with Mickey Rooney one day: you work with these people like Mickey, you're on the stage with them, and something happens...you forget a line, or you forget a move. These people are such professionals that they are able to take whatever the situation is and use it positively and very creatively. I've seen situations with the Mickey Rooneys and the Van Johnsons and the Bob Cranes that that's what they did. They realized that live theatre is *live theatre*, and therefore, the unusual's going to happen; something's going to happen in the audience. Somebody is going to get sick, physically sick, have a heart attack or what have you. Didn't happen at our theatre, but those things can happen. Well, they've been around so long, the Bob Cranes and the Rooneys and so forth, they've seen everything, they've done everything, and so they handle those situations very, very well.

After the performance, depending upon if he had a date or something, then he was out pretty fast. But a lot of times, he would come out into the foyer area of the theatre and meet people afterwards. He loved children, so if there were younger people in the audience, or if there was a matinee and children were there, he just *loved* children. He would go out of his way to talk to children. I remember in particular seeing him go out of his way on every occasion he could to meet and greet children. If there were children in the audience or walking down a street, he would always make sure he introduced himself and would do a little magic trick to make them laugh. Though very masculine, he had a strong feminine side. Very sensitive, caring, and somewhat shy.

He understood the parameters of the work that he did and what was expected of him, and what his staff expected of him; his fellow cast members he had chosen to work with him, so that was sort of his professional family. And he was always professional with them and the people at the theatre. The people who worked in the theatre in the context of the waiters, the waitresses, the food personnel, and the people in the ticket areas—they liked him. He'd come by the theatre once in awhile during the day, talk to them. He generally liked people, and people instinctively liked him.

He *was* the star, but he wasn't a *prima donna*. I don't mean that he never communicated that, and I knew his staff very well—cast, staff. And they all liked him and felt he was fair in his dealings with them.

What you see on television—with the Crane movies and *Hogan's Heroes* and so forth, is who he was. I mean, Crane was Crane. He was not a complex individual. In no way was he a Johnny Carson, who would walk out on stage and be an extrovert and walk off stage and be an introvert. Crane was an extrovert. And in that sense, he was constantly "on stage." I don't mean that negatively; I just mean it descriptively. He liked the theatre. Of course he liked it because he liked the response of the audience—the *immediate* response of the audience. But he also realized that theatre—dinner theatre—was a step down from where he'd been. So he knew he was heading in the wrong direction career-wise. So he did not like that *about* it. But he liked the daily-ness of acting and the interviews with television; you know, they'd come and interview him and those kinds of things.

He wasn't in demand for another television series. He wasn't in demand for a movie position. His agent was working that, but that's what agents do, and they're constantly saying, "This is gonna happen, and that's gonna happen." But that had been going on for months and years, and it hadn't happened. Crane certainly needed success; he needed to be affirmed; he needed to be in the spotlight. That was his world—that was a form of his addiction. It was part of his addiction.

He played the audience, the audience played him, and he played *for* the audience, loved to do what he was doing, and he loved the adulation.

Of course, by the time that Bob approached me, I had been in and out of his presence from a business standpoint and a professional standpoint—in the sense that the executive vice president of the corporation he was working for, etc. And so I was not a friend of his, but I was basically acquainted, and he felt very much at ease.

We had an executive director of Windmil—Bill McHale, and Bill McHale apparently talked to Bob Crane one day, and Bob mentioned to him that he had a major problem and was trying to figure out what he needed to do in order to move away from it. And McHale mentioned my background. Bob was unaware that I was a clergy, unaware I was a professional counselor, and so he approached me. And so it was in that context, out of that referral, that I started my meetings with Bob, which were few in number, of course, before his death.

I felt fine counseling Bob. I counsel with a lot of people. Bob Crane was just Bob Crane. Happened to be well-known, and happened to have a very, very glaring problem, which at least with me he did not hide from in any way, and I felt him very sincere in his attitude to alleviate and get away from it.

He was very open with me. He had gotten into this film world of pornography. He had watched a lot of pornography, and with his background he realized that he could film it. And the interesting thing that he was able to do was to convince his partners, some whom he had only known for a few hours, met at a bar, or met after a play, or met in an office, or whatever it might be, and to convince them that he was going to [film them, and] that this was a part of him—film. His cameras were never hidden—we're not talking about any kind of subterfuge at this point; they were very apparent. He would get everything set and say, "Now it's gonna go, are you ready?" and apparently, all but a very few people said "Fine!" which was very, very interesting to me. I mean, I guess I had led a sheltered life. I just didn't believe people were that brazen or unconcerned about the future use of this film or how it might impact their life in the future. And after Bob's death, I received telephone calls from different women across this country, asking about what are they going to do with all those films, and what's going to happen to them? And some of these people—very prominent people—some I guess you might say at least well known in their communities, and all of a sudden it hit them that this was a part of their legacy. Now all of those films, and there were hundreds of them, so the possibility of personal identity soon [no longer became] a matter of concern of these people, so it kind of fell by the wayside.

He liked women, and he was always on the make. I don't care if the woman was thirty years of age or fifty years of age. Not that he was involved with anybody fifty, I don't mean that; what I'm saying is that his first focus with a woman was sexual conquest. Not that he would leap in bed with her, but whether he *thought* he could. And when he went to the bars at night, and they gathered around him, his selection process according to those who knew him a whole lot better than I did, was almost beyond belief. He had a way of deciphering out of a group of six or seven hanging around who he was going to be with that night. And he had a way of moving in, and he was a charmer, I mean, his personality was a charming, charming personality.

So, of course, the movie business and the television business is a business that surrounds these people. They're bigger than life; they have an aura about them; people are always hanging around them; people are always smiling when they walk into the room. It's a form of addiction in itself, and Bob was a very addictive personality. He was susceptible to all forms of addiction, and one form of addiction that took him was the world of entertainment, the constant need for affirmation and adulation and confirmation, and celebration in his performances, people just wanting to get to him and "gimme your autograph" and all of that. And so, this was a part of his background, he *grew up* in that. And so his addiction *emerged* out of that, out of his charming presence. He said to me on more than one occasion, "I like sex." Well, it was very available to him, very plentiful, and then that emerged into this whole idea of filmmaking… I think he justified it that he was one day he was going to be a director of films and this was just his beginning, but I think that was a form of subterfuge.

The average person walking down the street understanding the story of Bob Crane could understand that he needed a sex therapist. My counseling of Bob was a referral counseling only. And what that means was that he knew and I knew that we were not going to be seeing each other for an extended period of time. He knew that I was only going to do one thing, and that was evaluate in a non-professional way because I am *not* a professional sex therapist, but I could evaluate in a non-professional way the type of counselor he needed.

My relationship with Bob Crane was what it was. I mean, it was a professional relationship. Again I never was at a bar with him other than observing him the one night. I was not socially involved. I was at certain functions with him, but I was not buddy-buddy to him at all. And so when he came to see me, it basically was because I held these credentials, and he was seeking some aid. Now he knew I would not be able to help him for a long period of time because he wasn't going to be in Scottsdale. He was heading back to California, so what *I* was working on was—who were the best therapists in Southern California area when he is there that can start this process and surround him with the kind of support that he needs. And I was in the process of getting that data when he was murdered.

I had no contacts in California, and Bob's contacts—well, he didn't want people to know. But be that as it may, the research was being done by the psychiatrist at the Methodist Hospital in Louisville, Kentucky, for the *best* sex therapist in the southern California area. Now all that came to an abrupt end, of course, with the murder of Bob Crane. But that was the process.

I think Bob Crane literally liked people. I don't think he disliked very many people. That was one of his problems; he was not very discerning; he was not a good judge of character. But at least from all public appearances and the professional reports we had across his circuit, his treatment of people was most positive. If he had a temper, he certainly didn't express it, or was in control of it, or whatever you might say at that level.

He understood himself as a man that was *in control*. I mean, it's what made him a good actor. He was brilliant in many of the *Hogan's Heroes* episodes, but also in many of the films that he did. He was lauded as one of the up-and-coming leading men in film and screen and, of course, all of that started crumbling around him, and that shook him. And I think that impacted him.

But that was the *second* thing. His children were *number one*. Family was number one. But the second thing was that all these dreams and hopes that he was going to be the next whoever, Cary Grant, whoever, on stage and screen, never happened. It was devastating to him; he couldn't understand it. A part of it, not all of it, but a part of it had to do with his lifestyle and his dalliances, and other things.

Bob Crane battled his addiction for years. His second wife married him knowing. She was a very close friend of the first wife. So the [second wife] certainly got into the relationship with a whole lot of information. I think both of them were strong women. I think [the second wife] felt like she could change him. I think she just believed that she had all the ingredients to get him to turn around and fly right. Didn't happen, but I don't think it was because of her lack of effort.

Addiction is addiction. And he knew he had a tough addiction. And I made it very, very clear to him, though, that I was not the most competent therapist when it came to sexual addiction. Before I met with Bob, I had called a psychiatrist friend of mine in Louisville, Kentucky, who I considered at that time one of the foremost authorities in that world, and his emphasis on the sexual addiction did not give Bob Crane much hope. It's a tremendous addiction, especially when it comes to fetishes, like a foot fetish or a boob fetish or whatever kind of fetish. And of course, Crane had a *lot* of fetishes when it came to the sexual world. And his aberrations were most apparent in some of these films. And so you add just the sexual addiction to the aberrations *within* that addiction and you have a huge, huge problem. And so Crane had received not only this information from me, but apparently, he had received it from someone else that he had talked to, and others apparently.

He definitely wanted to change, and I think his confidence wavered from time to time. Because I think he said to himself, "I'm a strong man, and I can do this, and you know, I'm gonna be over here in this city, and I'm not gonna fool around—" Well, that lasted about five minutes. So that shook him because he saw that he could not handle this addiction. *Nobody can*—by themselves. And I've never heard of anyone with his kind of in-depth sexual aberrations and sexual addiction ever breaking it by himself. It's *possible* with psychiatric and surrounding support and group therapy and individual therapy, but we're talking about weeks and months, and probably even years. And once addicted, you're *always* an addict; it's like being an alcoholic, you're one drink away from being a *wet* alcoholic. And he was one woman away *always*, and he knew that. But he *did* want to change.

The primary reason that he wanted to move in a whole different direction was because of his family. He was losing his second wife. His children were growing up. He did not want to leave the legacy of all of these films and all of this type of lifestyle and so forth. So I think his goals and dreams were certainly to move in the new direction, get out of the lifestyle, whether he was going to destroy the films, we never had that discussion. There was an insinuation, and you make assumptions; that was probably what he was planning to do at a future time.

He understood himself as a strong person. He understood himself like most alcoholics understand themselves—"I can control this, I don't need to drink," you know—that was Crane, "I don't need this"—and so there were periods of time where he sort of removed himself from that world. Not for long, extended periods, but enough to give *him* at least the psychological understanding that, "Yeah, if I wanted to go on with my life and forget this area..." But he was addicted. And sexual addiction is one of the worst of all addictions.

Apparently he had been troubled about it over a number of years, whether it stretched back three or four or five years. His first divorce, of course, was caused by it, and his slight alienation from certain other people was caused by it. His agent was very concerned that it would impact his professional career, especially as he wanted to "get back into the movie world" and was working very hard to do that.

But I think what really got him thinking was his relationship with his children. His relationship with his children had somewhat deteriorated. They were growing older, they were now able to understand their father's idiosyncrasies, and if Bob Crane believed in *anything* about himself, he believed he was a wonderful father. And I think he was. I think he was a loving, caring father. But he was *absentee* a lot. That bothered him, but that's a part of his career, being on the road, he couldn't be with them. I will say he did *not* go out of his way to bring them to the sites where he was performing, and of course, he rationalized that it was better for them to stay at home, you know, not take these trips. But actually, he was just lying to himself. He wanted to be free, in his own lifestyle, yet he wanted to be this wonderful father.

He was open to people. Nobody came up to him and said "Tell me about your sexual addiction" as far as I know, but Bob was very open, and a very concerning, caring person, especially with children and young people. You know he was this wonderful, gregarious, warm, caring, magnanimous personality, people flocked to—male *and* female. He was always on the move, he was always on the make, with any woman who sort of fulfilled his feminine image, which of course was large bosoms, thin waist, and blondes. He was with redheads, brunettes and so forth, but blonde was his passion. Now he had this focus on women, don't misunderstand me, certain look of women, certain style of women, especially the big boobs, the blonde hair, or the heavy brunettes, or whatever it might be. And so it impacted his life negatively and started impacting his career negatively, and the family was basically down the tubes.

His whole life with his family at this time was a lie. He was lying to himself, but he was lying to them as well. Did he finally recognize this? Yes. I didn't have to point it out to him. I affirmed what he declared in one of the conversations, that he had built all of these sort of sand houses, and they had come crumbling down. So all of a sudden, I think it came tumbling down in upon him that he was a terrible father, and that the legacy he was leaving was not going to be positive at all. So the impact that all of this was having on his life was making him almost schizophrenic.

I think there is what I call functional schizophrenia. I'm not talking about clinical schizophrenia. I'm not talking about mental illness. I think there are a lot of people with two lives. I think there are wonderful business people who during the day make deals, are looked upon as wonderful, caring people, have your concerns in the heart and so forth, want to help you, and I think they get to five o'clock in the afternoon and never think of you again. And I think they can live all kinds of existences. We see this especially with sexual addictions.

So I don't mean it psychologically or mentally; I just mean it descriptively, that he was schizophrenic. He was two people: one heavily involved in this very dark and seedy and seamy world, and yet on the other, in this very open world of light and laughter and professional expressions, which were almost beyond belief.

I'm not sure *Bob* knew who he was. You play these characters so long and after awhile, it's difficult to separate them from who *you* are. I think that was his beginning process with me and with others. I think he was trying to figure out *who* he was, *what* he wanted, *why* he wanted to do *what* he wanted to do. Could he survive *not* doing what he wanted to do out on stage or whatever it might be, and so what motivated him? A *lot* of things motivated him—his family motivated him, but his career motivated him. So he was caught; he wanted to continue in the world that he knew, the world that he'd been a part of for years. He felt that his *role* in that world might be changing, and would he be able to adapt and change to it? Those are questions that he was dealing with.

Crane certainly needed success, he needed to be affirmed; he needed to be in the spotlight. That was his world, and that was a form of his addiction. But how do you need success too much? I think what Bob Crane was going through at the time of his death is he was trying to figure out what he was going to do for the future and what the future held for him. He knew that the world of addiction and the world of pornography is a dead end in every way, so he had to get out of that; he understood that. He was driven to see if he could get away from that world, he was driven to see if he could get back into the Hollywood good graces, to the television moguls, or whatever it was. Hollywood is a very, very small community, and it's a cutthroat business, and just because you've done it in the past does not mean a thing. And so he had his work cut out for him, and he knew it.

There was what you could call a traditional spiritual side to him. He had been a Roman Catholic, understood himself still to be a Roman Catholic. It was not necessarily a practicing in the church. It was a part of his tradition, but I wouldn't say it was overarching in importance. I really didn't talk to him much about it because it was only in the context that I'm a Protestant clergy, and he had come to see me, and it was a few minutes, "I grew up a Catholic, etc., etc." I think his value systems were traditional, which sounds oxymoron, I know, because of his problem with pornography and all of his sexual adventures, that kind of thing. But I think his value systems were shaped by his family.

He insinuated that the spiritual world was important, and when we talked about the context of addiction, I always use alcoholism and AA programs and the Higher Power that helps people through, not all, but most of them in that program. He was very in-tune to that, and I basically emphasized that in his therapy in the future, because I was going to refer him to a psychiatrist in the Los Angeles area, that no matter what happened in his future therapeutic sessions, he would have to rely on a power beyond himself, a presence beyond himself in order to battle the demons of his addiction, and he was quite in-tune to that. There was no dispute, no argument at all.

I told him I was getting him a couple of names or more [of psychiatrists] from my friend in Louisville, who was doing the networking for me and would be able to deal with him. He was concerned about the confidentiality of it, and of course, I was able to affirm to him that the psychiatrists are like clergy; they are bound to confidential expressions and able to deal with it.

One of the brief comments I had with him, in the context of Catholicism and Protestantism and so forth, was the understanding of the love of God. That you need this Presence and you need this Power and you need to recognize this Power, and that God's love is unconditional love. God's love accepts you even when you're unacceptable and loves you even when you're unlovable. And you have to respond to that. That is, you can choose to ignore it, you can choose to forget it, you can choose to live, as it makes no difference. Or it can be the power that can literally get you through whatever the challenges.

I guess we're all disappointed with ourselves in one way or another. He was certainly disappointed with himself that he had *allowed* this to become an addiction. People don't start out to get addicted, especially males, their self-image: "I can control this, I don't need this, etc., I can do whatever I want to do." Then all of a sudden, the appetites grew, and they were fed on by Bob, and he was strung out. I mean, it wasn't drugs he was strung out on. It was the pornographic addiction he was strung out on…he was sexually addicted.

There were all kinds of rumors; there were all kinds of questions about this "dark side of his life," but that was not in any way a part of his public expression or public relations. It was something he was struggling with individually. *And privately.* I'm sure he'd had conversations with his wives about it, especially his first wife because that was the reason for the divorce, and assuming that he was heading for divorce with his second wife and the same thing. So all of that lent itself to his self-evaluation and his self-awarenesses and self-concerns, and his desire to get unhooked from that addiction.

He was very trusting of me. I, of course, confided to him that counseling was confidential and that I was not an expert with sexual aberrations and sexual addiction. I would share with him what I knew and what I had learned from professionals beyond me, and, again, my whole stance with Bob was referral. He knew I was going to be referring him, or at least sharing with him certain options that he would have with other people. And so that was my process with him.

His main concern was his relationship with his children. That was his *modus operandi*; it is why he wanted to consider leaving this area. But like a true alcoholic, he knew that he couldn't do it on his own, and that's why he came to me, referred to me, and I was referring him out once he got out to California. The relationship *was* deteriorating. His children were getting old enough that at school, they heard things, you know children can be very cruel to other children, and so they were hearing things about Bob Crane's lifestyle, and so he had to answer certain questions that were not very nice to answer. He understood himself as a good father, but when the questions were coming: "Daddy is this true? Do you…?" Well, a good father is honest with his children, and everything was falling in, his house of sand was coming apart.

Alcoholics try to stop and *can't*. The addiction to alcohol and drugs, other than *certain* drugs, is nothing compared to sexual addiction. I mean, if Crane was going to pick an addiction that was almost impossible to extricate himself from, he did.

An alcoholic doesn't drink for a month, or three months, to show that they're in control, and then of course, they fall off the wagon. And I think that was Crane's situation. I think he was also *strongly* influenced by so-called male dirtbag friends. I mean these people were from the pits. They were lower than low. I mean squalor people. And you would see Crane with the professional people, whether it was his agent or so forth who came in from time to time, and then you would see him with these others who flew in for a night or two of whatever, and it was just so apparent. These people were strongly addicted, and they strongly influenced Crane. And I think Crane, like many actors, wanted everybody to like him. He personally hatred rejection, and he certainly didn't want to reject anyone or to put them down.

He had surrounded himself with weird people…I mean *weird*, weird people. And of course his closest associates…call them friends, call them whatever you want to call them…the hanger-ons, the ones who lived off of his leftovers, if you please, and the ones who lived in this very dark seedy, seamy world…his selection of people was *terrible*. And it [was] one of his problems, that he didn't want to hurt their feelings. And yet, he had to perform a "surgical procedure" in many ways to get out of the world of pornography. One is that he would have to destroy his work, and in the context of the films that he had hundreds of them, both in Arizona that he carried with him, and apparently a whole roomful of files in Los Angeles. That is what was really *wrong*. These *people*. And so they were the ones that he had to rid himself of, and I think he was in the process of doing that. I really do. I think that's what got him murdered. I personally believe that one of these people just would not say "no." They were not going to leave him, and they were not going in any way but kicking and screaming, and I think they probably had words and that was it.

Crane had befriended these people, these weirdos, or they had befriended him, whatever. They had a long-term relationship, and it was very, very difficult, when I was talking to him, that he had to get out of that situation. He had to say "No." I mean, he had to do surgery. Surgery is painful, but it's healing. He knew that they were negative in his life, and he had to make the decision to extricate himself from them.

I think that was the battle. I think that's personally why he was killed. I think one of them [John Carpenter] just said no, you're not getting out of this life; we live off your castoffs. I think on the night he was killed, he laid it out. "I no longer want you as a part of my life. I have to get back to my old life," and I think the guy just went berserk and killed him. He was certainly capable of it. I mean, he was just a weirdo, and it wasn't just *my* observation, it was the observation of my theatre staff at the front. These people would come in and get their free tickets, which Crane would leave up [at the theatre box office]. I mean it looked like some of them hadn't shaved, and you know, just scumbags. This was Crane's addiction which allowed him this dalliance with these weird, weird people.

Crane understood it as an addiction from way back. I think he understood it with his first wife, and their divorce. I think he understood that he couldn't control it. I think he still had this…call it whatever you call it—male complex of strength—but if I really have a good reason, and apparently the divorce wasn't a good enough reason, the children were small at that time, that wasn't a good enough reason—that's my summation of it all.

Fighting the addiction was probably at the core of his being, but what motivated him to change was the family situation. Then of course second was the recovery of the career. I mean for Bob Crane to work dinner theatre, at that day and time—dinner theatre in the United States in *this* day and time is huge. So it doesn't have the stigma. But back in *that* day and time it had the stigma of being *less* than quote-"professional" theatre. And if there's anything that Crane understood, he understood himself as a pro. And boy, that *was* hard for him. That the only place he could make money, the only place he could *get work*, was dinner theatre. Broadway didn't want him. Hollywood didn't want him. Even the classic summer theatres of which have very huge reputations, didn't want him. He was *persona non grata*. The reputation of the world of pornography was shunned even then.

Crane, I don't think, understood that what he was doing was eating him alive from inside out. I think he was outside in. In other words, what I mean by that was the family was inside and outside, and that was the main motivation to get out of the life, but the whole thing of acting was outside. I don't think he saw that "if I continue this, I'm gonna be a human derelict, I'm gonna lose meaning, purpose, fulfillment, direction." At least in my conversations with Bob Crane, he wasn't that philosophical.

He wanted to be liked—all actors want to be liked. They have these strange phobias; they *have* to be liked. Mickey Rooney used to say to me, "The worst nightmare I have is dreaming that I do something on stage and no one applauds me." Well, non-acceptance is the anathema, so I think actors are much more into…and I think that carries over into life. I mean, none of us wants to hurt people…well, there are some psychopaths that do, but the average person doesn't want to hurt people.

But again, the impetus to change…it was family and career. His career was coming to a dead end, and I think he wanted to change that, and I think his agent had pretty well got his attention on that. But I think it was his family. I think he wanted to not lose his family and not leave such a negative, negative legacy for his children.

He was vulnerable; he knew he was vulnerable. He understood the weaknesses of his addiction, and he knew he couldn't handle it by himself. But whether he was at the breaking point, I'm not sure. I think the impending divorce with his second wife grabbed his attention, but I really think the biggest problem that he was having at the time was the continuing relationship with his children, and he was afraid of marking their lives or losing them in the context of the relationship as a father that he loved and cared about so deeply.

He certainly didn't see himself as a "sick" person, although I used the word "sick" in front of him quite often, and of course, addiction is a sickness. He accepted that. He didn't see himself as a bad person because he really never understood that he was using or abusing people. He understood himself as a guy who was sharing his unbelievable components or whatever term you want to use, and apparently, he was a master at bringing satisfaction to his female partner or partners. He understood that that was positive, and when you sat down and tried to explain, you know, you don't know these people, you have no relationship with them except a physical relationship, and then you film them, and then you feed off of these films…

[I discussed the following with him:] What is the definition of good and bad? I mean…bad is the perversion of good. So how do you understand all of this? What is it that's eating on you? What is it that…? Is it just that you want to get by this to get back with the family, and so forth, or is it something that's at the very core of *your* being, and are you willing to tackle it? I mean, it's going to be a tough, tough road. And some therapists say you *can't* break it, you will always have this addiction at one level or another, and you will never be far away from it. Are you going to be willing to live as an alcoholic, knowing that you're one drink away from plunging yourself back in the addiction? Are you willing to go through detoxing? Are you willing to go through whatever process the therapist will send you through over a long period of time to break your addiction? Are you willing to destroy all your films? Are you willing to burn them? Are you willing to say that by destroying all that you have created, that it will never be used in any way to exploit people, and it will not be used in any way to enhance *you* in that world? Are you willing to do that? And these are the things that he was pondering, and I think that this is probably the reason he got murdered.

He didn't know his life was coming to an end. He had great dreams of his future. He was hoping that a break would come; his agent was always working on hopefully a movie part or something that would take him beyond the dinner theatre circuit. And this was his desire, this was his hope, this was his dream. But, again, I think his agent had gotten his attention that his reputation in the world of this sexual aberration and in the world of pornography was not a positive image. Because remember his projection was this fun-loving guy, cared for people, loved people, and all of a sudden he has this dark side of him. So I think that was also part of his motivation to get out of that world.

But the main motivation to get out of this world was his children.

What was right in his life was that he was still on top of his skills. He was an excellent, excellent actor. He had not lost any of his timing; he had not lost, at that time, much of his youthful appearance. He continued to like what he [did], he was obsessed with the world of entertainment. He wanted to be on screen, but he also was willing to work behind the screen as the director, that kind of thing.

He saw himself and his future as getting out of the world that he had become addicted to. He felt that this was going to help him, not only individually and personally, where he would get back to his old self and not be caught up in this strange world that he spent an inordinate amount of time in, but help him professionally. His agent said, "If you do certain things, we can get you back in the movies, maybe even back on television," and on and on and on. So he was highly motivated, and that was his image. His image was that he was going to return to his old positions, not his old shows, I don't mean that, but his old positions, and this was a part of his driving force.

But the main driving force was his family.

He understood he was addicted, he understood that this had certainly impacted his family and it impacted his professional world and was going to impact it more negatively. He understood it was not a quick fix; it was going to be a long, long arduous journey. He understood that. And so he was motivated, at least the last time I saw him. Well, from the first to the last time, that was his motivation.

Did he follow through? He didn't have a chance to follow. He was murdered. I think he would have followed through. Would he have been cured? Would he have started out different? I like to believe he would. His biggest problem was the seedy characters that were around him. I mean, these people are *sick*, and to extricate himself from their tentacles was going to be his biggest, biggest problem. But I think he was motivated to do it.

I remember him as just a wonderful, wonderful person. It's a tragedy that his legacy has to do with the pornography, and that we spend all of this time and all of the things that have come down, the writing, the movies, all deal with this side. Rather than what I think is the *real* side: the side of a very, very caring man, a man who understood himself as a wonderful father, as a lacking husband, he certainly confessed that, and wanted to change. The son who made the film about Crane…that would have broken Bob's heart. It certainly broke his daughter's heart.

Tremendous talent, in the sense of music, in the sense of drama, in the sense of comedy, any cast that worked with Bob will tell you that he was just an actor's actor. I think that he would have been a tremendous director. I think he was able to sense and see the scene in his mind that he would have been able to put that on film so I think he would have had a tremendous, tremendous future.

So I remember his potential. I remember what he contributed and *still* contributes—I mean his *Hogan's Heroes* is still shown every day. He brought *tremendous* humor to a lot of people. He was interesting in the sense that with all of this talent that he had, I mean God-given talent. He had worked very hard to hone the talent; he had spent a lot of time *becoming* the artist and *becoming* the musician and *becoming* the actor, I'm not discounting that, but he had just unbelievable gifts and graces, which the average actor did not possess. And yet on the other hand, this whole different world that he was addicted to, that obsessed him, and which I think in the beginning he thought was just a little dalliance every now and then, and then all of a sudden, it engulfed him.

I saw him the night he was murdered. I was at the theatre that night, did not talk to him professionally, don't misunderstand me, went to the back, to his dressing room, said hi, and so forth. But we had set up an appointment as I remember, for a couple of days, in passing probably referred to it, but had no discussion at all. The discussion that night… it was cheap talk, we were talking about the theatre and the play and life in general, that kind of thing. I did not bring up that he had requested a table for his friend because out of the previous conversation he said that the friend wasn't going to come there. So I didn't go into that because he was going on stage. You don't start talking about things that are going to distract actors before they go onstage. So I don't remember exactly what he said; it was just general talk.

He was the same at the end of his life. He didn't know his life was coming to an end. He had great dreams of his future, he had all kinds of hopes that his career was going to blossom—you know dinner theatre is sort of an interim station or a way station. Here actors have been on television or they've done movies, and then all of a sudden, the calls are not there yet, the monetary responsibilities are, which Bob had, they get a good cast, they go on the road, and they survive. They make quite a bit of money on the road, but it is a hard, hard life, and so he was hoping that he was coming to the end of this stage in his life. Mickey Rooney, of course, was very much like Bob Crane, not in the context of any sexual aberration, I don't mean that, but I'm talking about acting. Mickey had been big, of course, in radio, television, movies, then he wasn't on call. And all of a sudden he goes through dinner theatre and then *out* of the dinner theatre stint he's called to Broadway, and he's a smash hit on Broadway. And I think that's what Crane was hoping for. So, he was hopeful that that would happen; he was frightened that it would *never* happen. He was happy in the context that he brought happiness to people. He *loved* to perform, and all of these people did. I mean, once they were on stage, they were on stage and they were performing, and people were laughing and hollering and shouting, and at the end, standing ovations, and that's another form of addiction. And Crane had it, like many of them did in that day and time, and for that matter, many still do.

Bob Crane was a very sensitive and caring and warm human being, with weaknesses and foibles like all the rest of us. Bob's problem was he allowed one of those weaknesses to consume him. And he became extremely addicted into a very, very dark and a very, very sick world. But thank God for whatever reason, before he was murdered, he recognized that he needed to change, he was highly motivated to change, and he was heading in the right direction and just didn't have the time to get there.

His problem was that he had created an appetite from certain people in that dark world, who saw him as the chef, so to speak. And so, I think, when Bob said I'm through, I'm going back home, I'm going back to my family, I'm going back to my career and to hell with you, so to speak, I think this guy just said, "No you're not," and that was the end of Crane. Such a sad, sad commentary that we sometimes make very, very negative choices which impact us and impact those around us. Bob's children, bless their heart, especially his daughter, will never be able to get over she lost her father in such a tragic way. And of course, people like you, who have been impacted deeply.

That's the tragedy of it all. He had so much to give, and was unable to give it.

Clinical Perspectives on Bob Crane's Sex Addiction

In an effort to understand Bob's personal issues and addiction better, the authors interviewed several health care professionals in the field of psychology who specialize in addiction, sex addiction, and/or sex therapy. The authors shared the information they learned about Bob Crane with them, including all of his career and life accomplishments and setbacks, his values system, his lifestyle behaviors surrounding women and sex, and his brief yet insightful conversations with Reverend Edward Beck.

In no way is it the intention of the authors or interviewed specialists to psychoanalyze Bob in any great detail. He is not here to share his innermost thoughts and feelings, so no assumptions can be made. However, with the base information provided, these leading experts in the field of sex addiction and human sexuality were able to provide a professional analysis of Bob's behavior, allowing for a deeper understanding of who he was and how they believe he tried to cope with everyday life.

Portions of their responses are included here.

―――∞―――

Alexandra Katehakis, MFT, CSAT, CST

Alexandra Katehakis, MFT, CSAT, CST, is an award-winning certified sex addiction therapist; marriage and family therapist; and a certified sex therapist in Los Angeles, California. Further, she is the Founder and Clinical Director of the Center for Healthy Sex in West Los Angeles, California. She is a faculty member of the International Institute for Trauma and Addiction Professionals (IITAP) in Carefree, Arizona; and is a Senior Fellow at The Meadows addiction treatment center in Wickenburg, Arizona. The author of several prestigious works on sex addiction, she holds membership and/or certification with numerous professional organizations, including the Society for the Advancement of Sexual Health (SASH); the American Association of Sex Educators, Counselors and Therapists (AASECT); the American Association of Marriage and Family Therapists (AAMFT); and the California Association of Marriage and Family Therapists (CAMFT).

On Bob's Early Family Life

He had to subjugate what was really true and about what was going on in the household. So when there would be some kind of tension or some kind of problem with his father and the family, he couldn't really assert himself and say, "Hey, why are you talking to her like that?" or "That's not fair, I'm angry at you." Or to have a certain father that would say, "Okay, let's talk about why you're angry with me." The message was, "Shut up or you're gonna get in trouble." And so what happens to a person is their sense of agency [i.e., sense of control]—their sense of existing and mattering in the world—is [in reality], shamed. "You don't have the right to speak." "You don't matter." "You're in trouble." And then breaking up the tension by creating a joke is being a clown. It's not an *actual* description of what the person's really feeling; they're defusing it. So then the person's value becomes about how they clown around. It's like a false self that gets created. We've heard time and again about comedians—some of the best comedians are really unbelievable angry. They grew up in situations where they had to make fun of and dance and joke in order to endure the pain.

On How Bob Saw Himself as an Adult

Bob Crane was incredibly charismatic, which is true for most sex addicts. They're just incredibly likable and charming because they can adapt and create this false self. Bob was an actor, and he was handsome, so he had everything working against him in large part. He knew how to manipulate, control, and how to get what he wanted and needed. But it sounds like when he was on the set and didn't get what he wanted and needed, he started to act the way his father did. So often, people who are like that, who are sort of the life of the party and so personable, there's a superficiality to that—the old adage about the tears of a clown.

On Bob's Decision to Seek Help

The fact that he had some shame, guilt, and remorse means that he had a little bit of a heart. But when I talk about shame [in terms of being ashamed of his behavior], I talk about a shame-based sense of self, a shame-based sexuality where "I'm inherently dirty or bad." *People who feel that way engage in behavior that serves to actually validate that notion about themselves.* If a person doesn't feel good about him or herself, and they repeatedly go out and hire prostitutes, and then they feel bad about themselves afterwards, it keeps them stuck in this loop of, "I'm an icky person, and see? I just did something horrible, and I feel icky about it again." It's a repetition compulsion. They take care of the original wound or pain by engaging in the same behavior.

On How Bob Understood Women in General

He was truly dependent on his mother emotionally in a lot of ways, and he got all of his validation and needs met from her. And she never did anything to get him to launch or individuate, which is why he ran to women for soothing. But he sexualized it with other women. He didn't sexualize it with his mother; it wasn't a covert incest. But the way he treated women, he overtly eroticized all of his needs with them. When he married his first wife, he probably really did love her as best he could. I don't know how intimate he could actually ever be in terms of revealing himself to her because he couldn't really reveal himself to *himself*, and he probably also needed a *mom*. He needed a family. He needed some sort of base and sense of security so that he knew he existed in the world on some level. And then as he got older and more mature, as he also started to feel some power and control because of his looks and sexuality. That's when he started cheating on her and going out.

On Bob's Sex Addiction

Sex addiction, in large part, is a pathological relationship with a mood-altering experience. He was often going after the intensity, the high of what it feels like to be in love and be sexually attracted. And in pretty short order, he'd already be on to the next conquest because it made him feel good inside. So if he's always trying to pull himself out of numbness and depression, or self-loathing, then a beautiful woman is going to be the answer. Over time, it stops working, though, just like any other drug.

Sex addicts compartmentalize their behaviors. When he had a regular series—*Hogan's Heroes*—that was like having a marriage; he was with the same people over and over. Addiction requires novelty because that's what arouses the brain. Arlene Martel saw his pain and desperation, shame, guilt, and remorse which he couldn't admit to himself. I don't know that he was really enjoying it, especially toward the end. It sounds like there was a lot of desperation and pain. And I think if he could've found some help and a way out, he might have taken it.

On Bob's Need for Love

I think we have to assume that he *desperately* wanted to be loved, and so he couldn't get enough of that. And the more adoration he had, the more people that cared about him, the better for him. So he was seeking that kind of love and attachment and connection all the time.

On if Bob Could Have Received Treatment

Sex addicts cannot stop on their own. In fact, no addict can get sober on their own because addiction thrives in isolation. If someone came into my office today with this kind of sexual behavior and history asking for help, I would most likely recommend hospitalization for forty days.

Final Thoughts

I have often heard people say that sex addiction will kill you or have you losing everything that has any meaning to you. It's so tragic that he lived in a time when no one was paying attention to these issues. He clearly had a lot of early childhood trauma that never went treated. His sex addiction escalated until he was met with his horrible end.

Nancy Irwin, PsychD, C.Ht

Nancy Irwin, PsychD, C.Ht, is a certified practitioner of Neurolinguistic Programming, Time Line Therapy, and Emotion Free Therapy. She graduated with Honors from the Hypnosis Motivation Institute in Tarzana, California, and holds membership to the Hypnotists' Union, the California Psychological Association (APA, the American Academy for Experts in Traumatic Stress (AAETS), and the California Coalition on Sexual Offending (CCOSO). A popular keynote speaker, she says, "Change does not have to hurt!"

On Bob Crane's Addiction in General

It certainly seems that sex became a coping mechanism for Bob. In a highly stressful field, and blessed with such attractiveness and an ebullient personality, it was easy and "natural" for him to fall into this addiction. While many high-profile men have trouble resisting sexual temptation, many are able to manage it without it becoming an addiction. His childhood influences set him up for this addiction.

The Hallmarks of Addiction

The hallmarks of addiction are:
- Unable to stop even if they say that they want to.
- Need more of the "drug" to attain the "high" they are accustomed to.
- It interferes with their life.

On How Bob Understood Women

With his extremely religious upbringing, he suffered from the classic Madonna/Whore syndrome. This is the double standard (that the Catholic church, and many other religions, have exalted to an "art form") that disallows men from seeing women as whole sexual beings. Proof of this with Bob was that after Anne gave birth, he was unable to see her as his wife and sexual partner. Her role was Mother. Case closed. I'm not blaming the Church entirely for this; I'm sure his home environment supported this "good girl/bad girl" dichotomous thinking. Of course, men are allowed (under this philosophy) to be naughty *and* to be fathers and husbands. Bad girls are an open playing field for men, and good girls have an extremely short shelf life (after they lose their virginity and become mothers, they are done!). This was quite common in the era he grew up in [the 1930s/1940s].

On Bob's Compulsive Need to Document His Encounters

The fact that he needed to videotape his exploits highlights his inability to be intimate. When people need to preserve "proof," they are projecting their own fantasies, [their inability] to deal with a real person as a sexual partner. This is the height of objectifying women and distancing himself from relationships. "Look, but don't touch my soul."

On Bob's Recovery

It is clear that toward the end of his life he was able to see what this addiction had cost him and was ready to deal with it. I predict that, even with proper treatment, he might have relapsed several times. I say this because he was dealing with aging in Hollywood and had a lot to "prove" still. His sexuality was inexorably wrapped up in creativity. But had he been given the chance, I am sure he could have learned to be intimate as opposed to just sexual. As it was, he didn't have a clue what real intimacy was. He could have learned other coping skills to soothe himself when stressed (e.g., exercise, laughter, animals, creative pursuits) and to look outward to give to others instead of feeding his own needs.

Veronica Monet, ACS, SFSI, CAM

Veronica Money is a certified sexologist, certified sex educator and certified anger management specialist, an expert in empathy, and a spokesperson for sexual rights. The owner of Veronica Monet's Shame Free Zone, she has been featured prominently on all major U.S. networks and on CNN, FOX, CNBC, WE, A&E, as well as internationally. She is the author of several publications on the topic of sexuality and has lectured professionally at academic facilities, including Kent State, Stanford, and Yale Universities. She is included in popexpert's 2015 Top 20 Mindful Life Coaches to Watch, a list composed of distinguished professionals "on a mission to help the world live, work, and be more mindful in all aspects of life."

On Bob's Addiction to Love

I wonder, what about *love* addiction? One of the reasons he was able to take *no* from a woman was that he wasn't interested in sex so much as he was in this feeling of being *loved*. Look at the pattern here; he's got long-term relationships all over the place. If he has addiction problems, I'm much more leaning in the direction of it being about *love*. "I feel *so* empty inside that I *cannot* feel whole unless I've got *all* of these people loving and adoring me."

On Bob's Foundation of Coping

Being the family comedian, trying to deflect things, and being the peacemaker. That role really sets you up to read people well and to know what's really going on with people. When you feel that things are too dangerous at home—that you as a child have to go in and run interference to protect people in the family—you become a very intuitive, hypersensitive person. You're paying a lot of attention to what people's shifting moods are, and you can see that things are changing. And you go "Uh oh, how can I make that person feel better so they won't go do *this [upsetting behavior]*?"

On Bob's Actual Love of Women

This guy really loves *women*. He likes *their* opinions, he's interested in what *they* have to say, and he can find them attractive even though they may not conform to prevailing standards of beauty. Sounds like a man who loves women to me. It would be really shocking to me if a woman killed Bob because even the women who thought he was being inappropriate ended up liking him. Even his ex-wife was still friends with him. Women are thoroughly intuitive creatures, and if they like him even though they don't approve of what he's doing, then he must have *something* to recommend him.

On the Impact of Religion

The culture, the Catholic Church, his parents—whatever role his mother played, a good Catholic—she was probably aspiring to the Catholic icon for women, which is the Virgin Mary. It's very difficult to have sex and be the Virgin Mary. If you're a really good Catholic mom, you have to at some point disassociate yourself from sex. He probably got a thought in his head that "this is what mothers are like—they're like *my* mother; they're good Catholic women who hate sex." And if I want to respect a good Catholic woman, I wouldn't have sex with her.

On Bob's Shame and Guilt

He has huge shame and guilt and conflict around sex. And this to me is what is *glaring* about Bob Crane: that it was painful for him because of all this shame, and he's trying to *not* be this person. If you think that sex is basically evil, you try and keep it over *here* and not infect your family with it, to the point where you won't have sex with your wife. In a way I think he [was] more tortured because he [was] such an *honest* person. Here you've got this guy who is *incredibly* honest, and has a really low self-esteem, and so he's really sensitive to anyone not approving of him. I think it's sad that he absorbed so much of the judgment of the times.

On Good vs. Evil

[Society doesn't] think people who have addictions are evil. We just think people who do sex "the wrong way" [with multiple adult partners instead of exclusively within a marriage] are evil. Anybody who's doing sex the way *we* don't think they should do it is a bad person. It's really popular to hang the word sex addiction on any kind of sex we don't approve of.

Sometimes the fact that your behavior is considered shameful makes you a legitimate target for violence. Somebody else's shame comes up. "I'm feeling shame, and I am judging you." When people feel their own shame or self-contempt, they just project it out onto other people. I can't imagine that [the murderer] killed [Bob] *just* because [Bob] was trying to stop having sex with women.

David C. Bissette, PsyD

David C. Bissette, PsyD, is a clinical psychologist practicing in the Washington, D.C. area. He currently provides individual and group psychotherapy to adolescents and adults, and he specializes in substance abuse, adult attention-deficit hyperactivity disorder (ADHD), sexual compulsion, and trauma/sexual abuse.

What Is Addiction?

Addiction is all about mood management. By and large, it's a medication of the affects of post-traumatic stress. Anything that will medicate anxiety, and anything that will medicate pain, is addictive. Trauma doesn't have to be acute. It can be a slow eating away of something. But either way, there's an attempt to medicate it. When a person comes in to me, I tell them we need to get some support, we need to stop the behavior, but then we need to successfully treat the underlying trauma, or eventually, they're highly likely to collapse back to the behavior. Because no one can tolerate so much pain for so long without doing something about it.

On the Connection Between Sex and Attention

Sex and attention were both probably a drug to him. Attention [was] his most basic drug. Sexually [or otherwise]; any way he could get it. But it was all mood-altering. Everything he did was mood-altering. Everything he did would make him feel better about himself, but it would never last.

On Bob's Need for Attention

You're talking about a guy with a high level of stress; that sets him up for the possibility of some kind of addiction because he's going to want something to medicate away his emotions. You're also talking about a guy who's got all sorts of signs of being hypomanic. Hypomania is someone who doesn't need much sleep. They may be very outgoing, kind of grandiose. They may take lots of risks. They live life at a fast pace. You've got someone who just *feeds* off of attention. Because I don't think his stuff was just plain old sex addiction; there was something else going on here. He's got a "*mood*-something" going on here. And when you've got someone who's got a mood disorder, it makes it all the easier to deny all sorts of realities: "I'm a family man, I'm this, I'm that." Because they're pretty much not very connected with reality.

And you've got a guy who's been grandiose in the radio, who's got all these things to keep him going—I mean this guy is being stimulated *all the time.*

On Bob's Escalating Cycle of Addiction

Most of us can't become childlike enough to receive love where we're hurt. And that's where someone like Bob Crane gets stuck on repeat. The older he gets, the more desperate and unlovable he feels, and the more demeaning the situations, and therefore, more dangerous, he would get into.

On Bob's Recovery

Once a person is involved in [an addiction], then the only way they can get rid of the feelings of shame is to do more of the things that make them feel bad. Someone like Bob would not expect to be understood; he expects only to be judged, only to be told, "Stop it." And he knows he can't, so he doesn't bother to go for help.

On the Question of Morality

Real sex addiction is not about morality. It's not about values. It's about loss of control. The research shows it's more about trauma, not about morality. A real sex addiction isn't about being a sleazy person without values. That's not the issue. It's not about debauchery. It's about trying to get through the day. About trying to make it.

Chapter 12
Laughing All the Way to the Grave

Everybody has a dark side. Everybody thinks ugly thoughts. Everybody has a history to his or her life. Let's not paint Bob's life by—what shall we say?—the moments in his life. I say these things that are the flaws are like specks on the Parthenon. Let's look at the Parthenon and let's not look at the specks. Let's lift our eyes up to the man's eyes and soul and life, and not look down on the gutter.

—Joe Cosgrove, former staff announcer, KPOL, Los Angeles, and owner, KTHL, Lake Tahoe, CA; the first person to greet Bob when he arrived in Hollywood in August 1956.

Source: From the author's personal collection.

Source: Photo courtesy of Scott Crane. Used with permission.

Chapter 12

Laughing All the Way to the Grave

If ever I were to write my own autobiography, I would title it "Laughing All the Way to the Grave."
—Bob Crane, June 27, 1978

On June 27, 1978, in Scottsdale, Arizona, Bob Crane sat down with reporter Jimm Ingolio, and the two men began an interview. It was to be the last media interview Bob would give, but neither the reporter nor the star could have known what was to occur within the next forty-eight hours.

Typical of any interview, Ingolio had asked Bob a series of questions about his life and career, and Bob answered honestly. Bob joked about the funniest moments he remembered from *Hogan's Heroes*; he talked about his play *Beginner's Luck,* then being performed at the Windmill Dinner Theatre; he casually mentioned that he drove a station wagon rather than a Cadillac; he discussed his stalled movie career; and he became optimistic about the future, with a new television series on the horizon. He also openly remarked about his failing second marriage.

When discussing his impending divorce, Bob's tone changed from light to downhearted. "I wish we weren't going through with it," he said. "The *National Enquirer* did a scathing article about us based on my wife's complaint they got from courthouse records. I wish it were an amicable divorce. It's really a sad situation because we have a six-year-old son, and I have three older children from my first marriage who will be affected."

Otherwise, however, Bob was in good spirits and had a positive outlook, and according to Ingolio, his jovial wit and sunny personality came shining through. Despite his personal troubles, Bob had been hopeful about his future, and as was usually the case, he had laughed his way through much of their conversation. It was then that Bob mentioned if ever he should write his own autobiography, he would title it *Laughing All the Way to the Grave*.

"He was affable, humorous, and seemed to enjoy our conversation," said Ingolio. "I kept the questions light and let him cover the points he wanted to make. There was no hint of stress or anxiety. He didn't rush through my questions, and it ended quite cordially. He was looking forward to his next show and was eager to speak with me."

Two days later, in the early morning of June 29, 1978, the laughter stopped abruptly. By the cruel hand of another, Bob Crane was gone. On July 5, and at only forty-nine years of age—two weeks short of his birthday—Bob was in his grave, and no one was laughing.

Never again would Bob Crane have the chance to laugh or make others laugh. No longer would his boisterous and animated voice travel across hundreds of miles of radio airwaves to break into the wee morning hours, awakening a sleepy community. His children would, for the rest of their lives, be without their father, and they would grow into adulthood without him present to witness their life accomplishments. His grandchildren would never know him. His marriage with Patty would never be reconciled or dissolved. And Bob's own commitment to battling and overcoming his addiction would be lost—a journey only just started but never traveled nor completed.

That Bob Crane is not here to tell his own life story is *our* ultimate loss. This was a man rich with knowledge and talent. Bob had been a writer, and it is quite possible that later in life, he would have written his memoir.

If Bob had lived, just imagine the things we could have learned from him about radio and the entertainment industry: those first-hand accounts as told by Bob himself about the celebrities he interviewed; his landmark work in radio; his dedication as an actor and director—not to mention his time spent on *Hogan's Heroes*; and his music—all would have been nothing short of extraordinary.

Further, had he been successful in his attempt to overcome his addiction, what else could we have learned? Perhaps he would have written about his struggles, his setbacks, and his achievements, not only in the entertainment industry, but much more importantly, in living with, battling, and overcoming a powerful addiction. Maybe his words could have helped others—not only those suffering from addiction, but also their loved ones, who typically must endure the mental anguish and emotional roller coaster that comes with being the caring but helpless partner, parent, child, or friend of the addict.

But there would never be an autobiography written by Bob Crane. In its place would come the onslaught of a media blitz fueled by a curious public. As the facts of his private life were unveiled, without proper context and tainted with speculation, on the grand world stage during his murder investigation, nearly *everything* else Bob had ever done in his life—and practically *all* of the good—drifted further and further away from reach. Over time, Bob would become the target of media and public ridicule, his once good name becoming synonymous with humility and shame.

Today, what the public believes about Bob Crane is the media's creation: a washed-up sexual deviant who offered the world little else other than a starring role in a once-popular television series, a one-shot wonder who seemingly did not know how to handle his fame. He became an embarrassment to the industry, his memory shunned by the very institutions he helped establish. The legions of fans who once adored him in radio and on *Hogan's Heroes* found themselves shying away. To utter the name Bob Crane was to do so behind a cupped hand in a whisper so no one could hear.

Following his murder and the scandal that ensued, many of Bob's family and friends vowed not to discuss him with the media unless they could speak of his good points, the way *they* remembered him, not focusing on his addiction or murder. According to Tom Davis, brother of Larry Hovis, the main cast of *Hogan's Heroes* actually made a pact that if called upon by the media to talk about Bob, they would do so *only* if they could share the good he had done and not dwell on the negative.

But the media were not interested in anything good they—or anyone—had to say about Bob Crane. Only the scandal. The salacious details. The imperfections. *The specks.*

So the cast of *Hogan's Heroes* went silent. Some were happy to speak of the series and their role in it. But as for discussing Bob Crane, they would offer merely a casual mention, and then, usually only when pressed.

Talking about Bob Crane became taboo. It was impossible to stop the runaway train of media hype that picked up speed year after year. Although some continued to try to have their voices heard above the noise, they were often burned—their words being twisted or ending up on the cutting room floor. Thus, many of Bob's family and friends eventually decided they had no choice but to think of their own well-being. All trust gone, they opted to keep the cherished memories they held so dear to themselves. Cease and desist went into effect. Nearly all of them went silent.

Then, unchecked, every ounce of scandal came bubbling to the surface.

On June 29, 1978, a legacy was forced upon Bob Crane that he neither wanted nor deserved.

Legacy

It is a powerful word. In briefest of terms, it can be equated to one's thumbprint, or one's most important mark, left behind after death. More broadly, legacy can mean the actual memories others hold of a person, or how that person may have influenced others. A legacy is a universal, and yet uniquely personal, human experience.

What should Bob Crane's legacy be?

Cynthia Lynn, Actress, *Hogan's Heroes*

"I remember him for his kindness. His lovingness. Just…*all* of him. Just…what a waste of life, of a beautiful person. What a waste, what a waste, what a waste. Because he was a wonderful person inside. Not even his looks. It's him. His manner…His magnetism. He had something special, a magnetism, that drew people to him, like a magnet. He liked good things, he liked kindness, because he *was* kind. He didn't like bad stuff, so he didn't even talk about bad stuff. He would try to fix this world, I think. But he's not a god, so he couldn't do it. He tried in his own way to make people happy with his laughter. That's why he was in comedy. I think most comedians are comedians because they had a hard life growing up, and that's one way of getting it out, by laughter. Yes. I truly believe that he was trying to heal the world with laughter. Laughter can heal a lot of things. I am so *proud* of him for seeking help for his addiction. And I'm so happy you're doing this. I am so happy. I mean, really, from the bottom of my heart."

Arlene Martel, Actress, *Hogan's Heroes*

"I think he had a wonderful sense of comedy. He was a *good* actor. He could have done many other roles. He was an honest actor and very observant. I think he was observing people a great deal, rather than needing to *be* observed. He didn't seem like 'Mr. Showboat, push me in the spotlight and I'm happy.' Perhaps he could have written something really insightful and entertaining, and that would have helped people. He was troubled. Maybe his way of overcoming that was to make people laugh and entertain them and draw attention away and even distract himself away from his own pain."

Robert Butler, Director, *Hogan's Heroes*

"My strongest memory of Bob is that he was kind of honest. Kind of honest and direct. Fun-loving. Also his *joy*. His whole beard of joy was *immensely* genuine. I mean, he had a good time. That guy just *did* have a good time. He had to convey that on radio. He certainly *had* to convey that as Hogan. That might have been why that whole thing went together so well. Enjoyment, cavalierism, fearlessness. Coming to work—work wasn't work, it was play. There's a big factor there. It's all the same thing. The beard of joy or joyousness itself. He was a joyful guy. My recollection of Bob is *joyful*. A joyful guy."

Victoria Carroll, Actress, *Hogan's Heroes* and *The Love Boat*

"I think people should remember any actor, or any artist, for their work. Their personal life is their personal life. In his case, he was murdered, and that incredibly sensationalistic story is what brought attention to everything in his personal life. So had it been kept quiet—had he been able to get help and survive that addiction—it would've been a much different story, obviously. I think it's just this human condition that everyone wants to know *everything*. Personally, I don't. I'd just as soon not know about those things. It's personal! The whole 'who does what in their bedroom?' That's *their* business. It doesn't define the person. In his case, it was so severe that it did change the course of his life, and that was the tragic part of Bob Crane's life. It overwhelmed him. I think, in the 1960s, too, you didn't have the transparencies that we have now. He might have been able to get help rather than cover everything up and keep it very much his secret. Today, help might have been more forthcoming to him. I really think it's important. I think the whole idea of seeing anyone—and certainly a celebrity and an iconic figure—as a human being and not just a scandal, is a very important message to get out."

Donald Sappern, School Friend

"He developed a *great* sense of humor. I saw the beginnings of it, and he was *very* funny on the radio. He was *dynamite*. He developed such a *fabulous* sense of humor. I think he was a very courteous guy. Very ingratiated. I think that's a better word. He was an ingratiating person. Fun-loving. But his finish was grave. Nobody could have predicted that."

Albert S. Ruddy, Co-Creator, *Hogan's Heroes*
"He had that twinkle; he always had that look in his eye. He was *perfect* casting. The truth is, he always had his arsenal when we did the pilot. He didn't grow past that; we just accepted the plausibility of more outrageous situations as years went on. His character was very consistently played, and he was a very engrossing and attractive character."

Bruce Bilson, Director, *Hogan's Heroes*
"He was a good guy, a happy-go-lucky guy, and I felt very sad for him, that he got into all this stuff. I just thought he was a nice guy to be around. A nice guy to work with. And he made that character of Hogan great."

Jerry London, Director and Associate Producer, *Hogan's Heroes*
"Bob was a kind of a William Holden of television actor. He was a really handsome, good-looking guy that really knew how to have a good time in life. That's my feeling about him. I think what he did, he made a lot of people happy for a short period of time."

Tom Thornton, KNX Salesman
"He was wonderful. He was a delightful, charming, fun person who really seemed to be enjoying the position he found himself in. I never heard of him ever pulling an attitude. *Ever.* I mean, he was getting fan mail. He was getting mail from his audience. He read it. In performing his radio show, Bob kept within those 'boundaries.' He had a great deal of respect for that audience. I mean, a *great* respect for the audience. And he could see those Buicks and Oldsmobiles and Pontiacs just full of kids with a parent driving them all to school. He had respect for that. As wild and crazy as it was, there was dignity to it. And he did not cross a line. He did not say anything that was offensive to people. He went right to the edge, but he didn't do it. I would say that he was universally nice to *everyone.*"

Gary Owens, Friend, KMPC Radio Personality, Television Personality
"Bob Crane was a very talented young man. I have fond memories of those times because he was always bright, always a great conversationalist. We all loved great early movies that we would talk about. Bob was perky, as a personality. He was a good ad-libber. He had a wonderful sense of rhythm, of jokes. He was a fine interviewer. He was knowledge-

able. Bob read, I don't know how frequently, but he researched his people very well, who he would have on as guests. So he was knowledgeable, he was talented, and he had many things going for him. He did many things for charity also. So there are two sides to everything."

Pamela Hayes Thompson, Friend and Actress, *Beginner's Luck* and *The Bob Crane Show*
"He was a nice guy, and he wanted people to be happy because he *always* was. No matter what he was doing, I still can't imagine him as anything but a nice guy. He wouldn't hurt anyone. He gave to charity; he did free things all the time—he *was* a *good person*! And for them to paint him as a sleaze was not fair."

John Thompson, Friend and Actor, *Beginner's Luck*
"He was what you would call a 'man's man;' he really had a great time with other guys. He loved jokes, laughter, practical jokes...we had great fun together *all* the time. He was a joy to be around. It just came as a complete shock to both Pam and I when this [Bob's murder and scandal] happened because we couldn't believe it! We never saw any of it. We're not just loyal, we just loved Bob in anything he did. We were there. That's what we do."

Eliot Dober, Friend and Former Connecticut State Director for United Cerebral Palsy
"I want people to remember the good things about Bob. Bob gave of himself, that was very much who he was. And he was a *good* person. A *positive* person. He was positive—beyond words. With Bob, you've got to take Bob in two ways. The good and the bad. And nobody is all good or all bad."

Harvey Geller, Friend and Neighbor; Former Vice President and Editor, *Cash Box Magazine* (West Coast); Writer and Sales Executive, *Variety* and *Billboard* Magazines
"You could see his eyes would light up when the kids were around, sitting around the pool with them, playing games with them. His family was the most important. His children. Secondly, his career—his acting career was very important. And having a good time because he enjoyed life. He didn't try to impress people with the money he was making, and he was making considerably more than I was. What would Bob's true

legacy be? Talent. He would have been an important actor at some time if he had lived. A lot of people said he did about as well as he was ever going to do, that he had just enough talent to do what he did. But I think he would have eventually been a more important actor if he had stayed alive. Bob didn't get what he deserved. He should have been a big name. I think he should have been a major artist. A star."

Leo McElroy, Friend and KNX Booth Announcer

"I think his real legacy was unbinding the chains that bound radio personalities into a very tight little place. Bob, more than anybody else, was the guy who really said, 'For artistic freedom, I gotta do it my way. I'm doing it the way I know it works.' Bob did things in radio that opened doors and possibilities for other people. And he was a guy who quite obviously cared to make people's lives a little easier and a little nicer without intruding himself on them. And I really honor him for that. This was a friend who wanted nothing in return. If he had an opportunity to do something nice for someone, he would do it."

Joe Cosgrove, Friend, KPOL Staff Announcer, and KTHL Owner

"Bob's legacy should be a creative genius who brought laughter and good family entertainment to millions of people. And his legacy should be smile, smile, smile, no matter what happens in life."

Jack Coombe, Friend and Connecticut Radio Newscaster

"I had a reunion with Bob in March of 1977, while attending a Buddy Rich concert in Chicago. Almost all drummers idolized Buddy. Bob and I were no exceptions. It was a joyful reunion for Bob and myself. We chatted about old times, our individual lives, and those of colleagues since our days in radio. One incident remained in my memory bank: I remarked that I envied him because of his successful career and the big money he was getting. He looked at me for a moment, and his face grew serious. Then he replied, 'Don't envy me, Jack. Big money and a successful career aren't everything in life. You are happily freelancing and enjoying it. I envy you for your independence.' I have never forgotten that moment. It was time for the concert, and we bid farewell, both looking forward to when we could meet again. Little did I know that a year later, he would be brutally murdered, and that his case would never be solved, even to this day. Most of us who knew Bob enjoyed being with him. He possessed a sort of charisma, if you will, that attracted him to people and they to him. He was a highly talented and creative actor which no doubt contributed largely to the success of *Hogan's Heroes* and the sizeable amount of appearances on TV, film, and on the stage, during his long and brilliant career. Bob Crane will always be in my memory banks."

Tom Bernstein, KNX Salesman

"Bob was well liked by everyone in the [Columbia Square] building as far as I knew. He had no inflated ego, got along with everybody, and worked very hard for the radio station and at becoming a screen star. We had a small canteen on the ground floor run by an elderly couple who always looked down on their luck. I was told that one day, Bob bought out their entire stock of snacks and candy and distributed them to the programming staff. When Bob made personal appearances for clients, civic groups, my fifth college class reunion, etc., he had all his voices and effects recorded on a Wollensak tape deck, which he would take to these meetings, lunches, dinners. He would personalize each event, working the names of the people attending into his routine. He was never too busy to appear and was always a huge hit."

Jane Lippoth Golden, School Friend

I think everybody knew he was going to be successful. You know the way he looked on *Hogan's Heroes*, he looked that way his whole career. He just had a big smile on his face—all the time. I don't remember him being shy! No, that would be a complete turn for him. He was very witty. He had a great sense of humor and was very quick. He was one of those people who could come up with stuff, very funny most of the time, and he could work the room pretty well, I thought. And of course, everybody idolized him. When you go back to a high school reunion and you've become a quote-unquote celebrity—*everybody* was attracted to him, They all laughed and giggled and did all the usual stuff you do, I guess. I think they did treat him like a celebrity because he really was. *He really was*. He was a nice guy that everybody was very happy that made it. Bob was Bob. It was as if he'd never left us. He was still funny, witty, charming, and Mr. Nice Guy. We all had fun with him. I guess my favorite memory is he didn't change in our lives. He came home, and he was the same Bob he had been in high school, and that's a long time ago. He just was a happy guy. He was a witty and talented man, and he was trying to turn his life around. He would have had a fantastic career after *Hogan's Heroes*—as a Hollywood star."

Jon Cedar, Actor, *Hogan's Heroes*

"As far as *Auto Focus* is concerned, as far as I'm concerned, it is one of the ugliest movies I've ever seen. I pretty much have a positive memory of Bob. As far as I know, we all have some obsession or foible we'd rather people not know about."

Robert Hogan, Actor, *Hogan's Heroes*

"He was thrilled to be doing his job on *Hogan's Heroes*. He just was a very happy guy, a happy camper on that set. I didn't notice any disgruntled guy. This is a good guy, you know? None of us is perfect. I would consider him one of the good guys."

Tom Davis, Brother of Larry Hovis, Actor, *Hogan's Heroes*

"He should be remembered as a normal guy, who strayed. He was such a nice person to me. I never thought he was evil to anybody."

Maureen Arthur, Actress, *The Wicked Dreams of Paula Schultz*

"I love comics. If there is anybody who is more insecure than a comic, I don't know them. Because they're waiting for that laugh. And if they don't get that laugh...they work so hard at what they do. And they bring laughter to the world, and there's nothing better than that. I ran into him a couple of times, and it was always very friendly, and we'd have a few laughs. I want the parts of Bob Crane that I knew and respected to be known and have people think about it."

Rick Plastina, Actor, *Send Me No Flowers*

"I'd like people to remember him as being the nice guy and not the sleaze ball character that unfortunately is the image that lives on now."

Gordon Mason, KNX advertising salesman

I think Bob Crane was an incredible entertainer. I think he's up there with the other greats of radio. He had talent that was very rare, and he had a great personality to go with it—that would be his legacy.

Bob Maryon, KMPC Engineer

"I think his legacy should be a very talented, gifted performer on radio and on television. Because I think that was the maximum part of his life. He got caught up in this other thing, and I think unfortunately that's the legacy he has because his murder has never been solved. Instead, I think the legacy should be a very talented, gifted performer on radio and television. It's hard to negate the other things that happened *later*, but they *did* happen later, and he'd already demonstrated—to the world because of *Hogan's Heroes*—the ability that he had. I think that would be a much better legacy. You know everybody in the world makes mistakes, so he's not an isolated instance of people who have made serious mistakes in their life."

Victoria Berry Wells, Actress, *Beginner's Luck*

"He was very good. He could have had a future. He would have got more done in acting. He would have been a good director, too. What happened to him shouldn't happen to anybody. It breaks my heart. I felt a little sad this morning. I went and did a few errands, and I walked back, and I had a little tear in my eye. And I thought, Oh, God, this is making me remember that. And I prayed to God to be able to say the right thing to you. I was a little nervous. But he was not boisterous—he was just a normal guy. Normal, down to earth, very lovable guy. He had a sickness, and he was going through trials and tribulations, but he was a lovable man and a top professional, and he gave a lot to us as an actor and a person."

Charlie Zito, School Friend

"Bob...what a guy. We were close. Really close friends. You know, he never gossiped or talked bad about anybody, not if he thought it would hurt that person. He was a good guy. We would confide a lot in each other. I knew I could talk to him because I knew it wouldn't go any further. He would keep a confidence. Bob only ever played drums—never any other instrument. He would sit down at the piano at my house and pound out some tunes, and he'd ask my opinion of it. Now, when I say he pounded away at the piano, he *pounded* away at it. He'd sit there and peck at the keys like he was pecking away at a typewriter with one finger. Sometimes, I'd sit next to him on the bench and play the bass part, with him doing the one-finger melody. But that was about it. His idea of hitting the notes was to hit as many keys with one hand as he could! We were like brothers, especially in school. After graduation, we didn't see each other as much. But in school, when we were young adults, teenagers, we were brothers. We were brothers."

Scott Crane, Son

"I think the most important thing is that he didn't have a 'dark' side to him. He was really an up and chipper guy. No matter how bad his luck got, he always seemed to be able to see through into the humor of the situation. I think he was upset that he didn't get certain roles and stuff like that, but we all are. Or we lost a job. But I don't think he was a guy to sit around and be dark and depressed. He wasn't a real 'woe-is-me' guy. Obviously, what he was going to present to me was chipper and happy and excited because he was a good dad. He was a really fun, likable guy. He really, despite all the evidence or the exterior of the other lifestyle that people like to talk about, he was really a family guy. It was really important to him."

Karen Crane, Daughter

"Getting into his personal life challenges, people didn't want to hear that the boy next door, nice guy, liked porn, liked too many women, cheated on his wife. 'No, that's not the Bob Crane that we were sold on.' And a lot of people, to this day...I can't believe the things I read, whether it's on the Internet, or... 'Bob Crane was a creep.' Huh? Wait! No, no! Yes, he had personal struggles, but it didn't make him a creep. So many times, I will come up on some situation where I will think to myself, 'What would Dad be saying to me right now? What advice would he be saying right now?' And I swear there's an answer that comes into my head that is so much like I really truly feel he'd be saying to me. Looking at that gravestone, standing there, and just feeling this rage, I know that my dad would be saying, 'Ach! Get on with your life! It's just a hard thing that's put on the grass. Who cares?' I know that's what my dad would say. So, we don't put a whole lot of energy into the negative. We carry on his optimistic outlook."

Jim Senich, Cousin

"He was a big city guy. He loved excitement. Forget sexual stuff. He loved excitement and theatre and lights. He loved that. But he enjoyed coming back to Connecticut. He always said how he loved his uncles and aunts. He had to come back at least twice a year to re-energize again and be back with his people. When my dad was dying, he made sure he came up to see him before he died. He didn't have to do that. That's what you do for family. And he helped me in my career. He told me when I was starting my radio career, 'If you believe in what you're doing, don't let *anybody* change it. Don't let *anybody* change it; just do it. I don't care *who* they are.' He didn't say parents or whatever, but he said, 'Just *do* it. If the program director doesn't like it, then go somewhere else. If you're not different, you're not gonna make it. You've *gotta be different*. There are millions out there that sound alike. Develop something different, stay with it. Don't let anybody tell you it's wrong.' Bob once said to me, 'Look at it this way—when you get up to speak, and you look out at that audience, just remember one thing. *No one* out there can do what you're doing.' And that *really* stuck. *That really stuck*. And he said, 'They're going to be with you all the way. Usually an audience is sympathetic. If you're trying to tell a funny story, and you bomb, they're with you.' From that point on, I was all right. I was all right."

It is rare, nowadays, to hear someone laugh at a person seeking help to overcome addiction. Society has a better understanding of how psychological and physical traumas can drive a person to self-medicate, and how this attempt at self-healing can turn into full-blown addiction. But while it can seem obvious to those on the outside, the addict very often cannot see that the coping activity only masks the trauma; it does not heal it.

To understand this is to acknowledge the courage of an addict who says, "I need help," and to recognize that this person has finally reached the point where the cure is worse than the disease. Addicts who come forward know they are in for the fight *of* their lives—and *for* their lives. They understand that to be healed, they must face the painful demons that became so overwhelming that suppressing them was the only way they knew how to survive.

Bob knew this. And as a proud man, asking for help was not easy.
He asked anyway.

But then the unthinkable happened. Bob was murdered. People were intrigued. And because Bob was a celebrity, when the details of his private life spilled out, everything he had wanted to keep private—the addiction of which he had been most ashamed—was exposed to the entire world.

And the world mocked him.

"For some reason, those of us who work in the entertainment/arts industry seem to be dealt with differently by people for whatever reason," *Hogan's Heroes* actor Larry Hovis declared in 2001. "Let's absolutely get beyond that… My goodness, we're just people like you, with hopes and dreams and aches and pains and fears and foolishness and despair and hardship and reward and loss. All the things that make up living that we all endure."

Bob lived a full life. A life full of ups and downs, successes and failures, virtues and vices. He had tremendous talent and ambition, colleagues who respected and admired him, friends who cared about him, and a family who loved him—and who *still* love him today.

Like *all* human beings, Bob had feelings and emotions. He danced on the moon, jumped for joy, laughed in ecstasy, and leapt in triumph. He also cried in grief, mourned losses, threw his hands up to the sky in frustration, and felt desperate, scared, sad, and alone. Bob's flaws—the mistakes and bad choices he made, the most difficult moments he faced, and his descent into the jaws of a powerful addiction—were all but a *part* of his *whole* life journey. His flaws were merely the *specks,* like the specks on the Parthenon, that comprise *any* person's entire time on earth.

Whatever his struggles or disappointments, the compass of Bob's life always pointed toward the positive. *Hopefulness. Compassion. Excitement. Happiness. Courage.* He loved completely, supported unconditionally, worked untiringly, and remained "the guy that always assumes no matter what's in that room, there's a pony hidden underneath all of that stuff"—a rare optimism that wouldn't be snuffed out. He knew what he wanted in his work, and he figured out how to achieve it. Most of all, he wanted—*needed*—to be loved, liked, and accepted. And sometimes, in trying to meet that need, he was tripped up by human weakness.

At the end of our lives, do *we* want to be remembered and judged *only* for our flaws and imperfections? Do we want people to focus in on the specks that mar our heritage and blot out all the good we've done? Do we want our families to be reminded of our mishaps and struggles constantly? *No.* Bob was much more than his struggles and weaknesses. In spite of his flaws, he was a kind person, a joyful person, a talented person, a courageous person—*a whole person*.

Up until now, it has been way too easy to look at Bob and see only the specks.

It's time to look at Bob Crane and see the Parthenon.

Bob Crane publicity photograph (circa 1978).
Source: Courtesy of Scott Crane. Used with permission.

Resources

Original Research/Contributors (Research Phase: 2003-2015)

The following individuals have provided detailed recollections and information to the authors specifically for *Bob Crane: The Definitive Biography*. Some people wished to remain anonymous for various reasons, and therefore, they are not listed here. The authors are deeply indebted and profoundly grateful to *all* who contributed, not only for sharing their memories and thoughts about Bob Crane, but also for believing in the true purpose of this work.

Family and Close Friends

Karen Crane (daughter) – Ongoing conversations 2012-2015
Robert Scott Crane (son) – Recorded interview June 2010, ongoing conversations 2010-2015
Jim Senich (cousin) – Recorded interviews June 2007, ongoing conversations 2004-2015
Jane (Senich) Ryfun (cousin) – Ongoing conversations 2012-2015
Barbara Trembley (nee Senich) (cousin) – Ongoing conversations 2012-2015
Charles Zito (best school friend) – Recorded interview August 1, 2008, ongoing conversations 2008-2010 (d. February 5, 2010)
Donald Sappern (school friend) – Recorded interviews August 18, 2006 and June 4, 2007
Dr. Edwin Gordon (school friend) – Recorded interview March 2, 2007
Neil McGuinness (school friend) – Via letter Summer 2008
Dr. David Dugan (school friend) – Via letter Summer 2008
Jane Golden (nee Lippoth) (school friend) – Recorded interview September 20, 2008, ongoing conversations 2008-2015
Harvey Geller (friend and neighbor) – Recorded interview August 24, 2007, ongoing email correspondence 2007-2009 (d. March 12, 2009)
Salvatore ("Tootie") De Benedetto (friend and jazz band member) – Recorded interview November 30, 2007
Eliot Dober (friend, WICC, Exec. Dir. Cerebral Palsy Foundation – Connecticut) – Recorded interview June 20, 2009, ongoing conversations 2009-2010 (d. July 30, 2010)
Julius Bogdan (neighbor) – Conversation/statements only August 2009
John and Pamela (Hayes) Thompson (friends, theatre actors) – Recorded interviews August 23 and August 30, 2009, ongoing conversations 2009-2015

Friends and Classmates from Stamford High School, Stamford, CT

Edward Finney – Via letter Summer 2008
Raymond Gagliardi – Via letter Summer 2008
Louis Esposito – Via phone conversation Summer 2008
Aniello Casillo – Via phone conversation Summer 2008
Joe Delfino – Via phone conversation Summer 2008
Gloria Rosa (nee Di Sette) (also co-worker Finlay Straus Jewelers) – Recorded interview Summer 2008
Mary Anderson (nee Daly) – Via phone conversation Summer 2008
Patricia Mucci (nee De Angelis) Via phone conversation July 10, 2008

John Bell – Via phone conversation Summer 2008
Angelina Barcello (nee Moccia) – Via letter Summer 2008
Estelle Alterwitz (nee Silberman) – Via letter July 12, 2008
Nathan Gottfried – Via letter Summer 2008
Beatrice Wexler (nee Levinson) – Via phone conversation Summer 2008
Annalise Barrett (nee Biegler) – Via phone conversation Summer 2008
Ruth Lanyon (wife of Rodney Lanyon) – Via letter Summer 2008
Eric Ericson – Via letter Summer 2008
Catherine Dial (nee Kohores) – Via letter and phone conversation Summer 2008
Ed Caraszi – Via letter August 7, 2008
Jean Sempey (nee Packman) – Via phone conversation Summer 2008
John Mercede – Via phone conversation Summer 2008
Virginia Kristoff (nee Pendleton) – Via phone conversation Summer 2008
Martin Rosenblum – Via letter Summer 2008
Edward R. Martin – Via letter Summer 2008
Alice Jarrell (nee Peterson) – Via letter August 9, 2008
Cleante Pimpinella – Via letter Summer 2008
Frances C. Cassity (nee Maziuk) – Via letter Summer 2008
Anne Sessa (nee Lopiano) – Via conversation October 2011
Jackson A. Ransohoff (also brother of television producer Martin Ransohoff) – Via phone conversation Summer 2008
Doris Leidecker (nee Sidney) – Via letter Summer 2008
Phyllis Gallucci (nee Telesco) – Via letter Summer 2008
Audrey Ivanko (nee Swan) – Via letter Summer 2008
Additional members from the Stamford High School Class of 1946 who wished to remain anonymous but whose testimonies are on file with the authors.

Hornell, New York

Kevin P. Doran (WLEA, owner and on-air host) – Via phone conversation Spring 2014
John Sloggs (WLEA listener – 1950) – Via email correspondence 2014

Connecticut Radio

Frank Derak (WICC) – Ongoing conversations 2005-2015
Morgan Kaolian (WICC, Channel 43) – Via email correspondence, ongoing conversations 2007-2015
Wes Hobby (WICC) – Via email correspondence July 24, 2005
Al Warren (WICC) – Ongoing conversations 2005-2015
Jack Coombe (WNOC) – Via letter and ongoing conversations 2007-2015
Harry Luke (WICC, WNAB) – Via conversation August 2008
Bill Dillane (WADS, WICC) – Ongoing conversations 2007-2015
Gene Valentino (WATR) – Via email correspondence December 29, 2008
Martha Gross (WICC) – Via conversations 2007-2008
Rev. Tom Carten (WICC) – Via phone conversation May 18, 2009
Michael Collins (WICC, Connecticut Broadcasters Association Historian)
Bob Slugoski (WATR) – Via email correspondence
William Secor (participant, WICC Junior Achievement) – Via email correspondence February 3, 2013
John Ramsey (Connecticut Broadcasting History) – Ongoing conversations 2007-2015
Mark Ammann (nephew of Wayne Mitchell, WICC, Channel 43) – Phone conversation/email, February 26, 2015

California Radio

George Nicholaw (KNX) – Via letter and phone conversation June 13, 2007 (d. August 9, 2014)
Tom Bernstein (KNX) – Via email correspondence June 2007
Tom and Diane Thornton (KNX) – Recorded interviews July 13 and 14, 2007
Leo McElroy (KNX) – Recorded interview July 7, 2007
Gordon Mason (KNX) – Recorded interview August 16, 2007 (d. December 10, 2007)
Tom Kelly (KNX) (statement only) – Via phone conversation Summer 2007
John Hokom (KNX program director) – Via email correspondence
John Sutton (son of Robert P. Sutton, former KNX general manager) – Via phone conversation February 20, 2015
Geoff Edwards (KMPC) – Recorded interview June 28, 2007 (d. March 5, 2014)
Roger Carroll (KMPC) – Via email correspondence Summer 2007
Bob Maryon (KMPC) – Recorded interview August 11, 2007
Joe Cosgrove (KPOL-Los Angeles/KTHO-Lake Tahoe) – Recorded interview August 18, 2007
Gary Owens (KFNB/KMPC) – Recorded interview July 14, 2008 (d. February 12, 2015)
Bill Wolff (KNX) – Via phone conversation August 9, 2007 (d. December 2012)
Arlen Peters (KNX) – Via email correspondence August 2007
Alan Hall (KNX) – via phone and email correspondence (August 2012)
Tom Hatten (KNX) (statement only) – Via letter
Additional former KNX colleagues and Columbia Square alumni who wished to remain anonymous but whose testimonies are on file with the authors.

The Donna Reed Show

Eddie Foy, III (casting director) – Recorded interview March 30, 2008
Paul Petersen (actor) – Recorded interview April 15, 2008

Hogan's Heroes

Albert S. Ruddy (co-creator and producer) – Recorded interview April 15, 2008
Jerry London (associate producer, director) – Recorded interview August 17, 2007
Bruce Bilson (director) – Recorded interview February 6, 2008
Robert Butler (director) – Recorded interview April 13, 2009
Robert Clary (actor) – Via handwritten correspondence October 14, 2008
Cynthia Lynn (actress) – Recorded interview April 24, 2007 (d. March 11, 2014)
Arlene Martel (actress) – Recorded interview September 8, 2006 (d. August 12, 2014)
Victoria Carroll (actress, also *The Love Boat*) – Recorded interview June 20, 2009
Robert Hogan (actor) – Recorded interview October 28, 2008
Jon Cedar (actor) – Via email correspondence August 8, 2007 (d. April 14, 2011)
Inge Wegge (actress) – Via email correspondence March 31, 2005
Monte Markham (actor) – Recorded interview July 26, 2015
Ruta Lee (actress) – Via email correspondence October 14, 2014
Bernard Fox (actor; statement only) – Via email correspondence July 24, 2007
Alan Oppenheimer (actor; statement only) – Via email correspondence June 18, 2006
Stewart Moss (actor; statement only) – Via email correspondence September 9, 2006
Frank Marth (actor; statement only) – Via email correspondence September 2006

Bob Crane, His Drums and Orchestra Play the Funny Side of TV

Stu Phillips (music producer) – Recorded interview June 8, 2007

BOB CRANE The Definitive Biography

Wicked Dreams of Paula Schultz

Larry D. Mann (actor; statement only) – Via handwritten correspondence July 17, 2009
Maureen Arthur (actress) – Recorded interview August 1, 2009

Arsenic and Old Lace

Robert Scheerer (director; statement only) – Via handwritten correspondence September 2008

The Bob Crane Show

Norman S. Powell (creator/producer/director) – Recorded interview February 26, 2008
James Sutorius (actor) – Via email correspondence February 8, 2008
Bruce Kimmel (actor) – Via email correspondence July 27, 2006

Ellery Queen

Edward Abroms (director) – Via phone conversation September 2008

The Hawaii Experience

John Orland (director) – Recorded interview July 6, 2009

The Love Boat

Ted Lange (actor) – Via email correspondence August 18, 2009
Victoria Carroll (actress, also *Hogan's Heroes*) – Recorded interview June 20, 2009

Celebrity Cooks

Derek Smith (owner and producer) – Recorded interview June 19, 2009
Anne Kear (associate producer/talent agent) – Recorded interview June 27, 2009
Roger Packer (studio director) – Recorded interview June 19, 2009

The Flaw

Jim French (radio scriptwriter) – Via email correspondence June 20, 2006

Send Me No Flowers (1969)

Rick Plastina (actor) – Recorded interview June 3, 2009

Tunnel of Love (1959)
Who Was That Lady (1960)

Donald Freed (Director) – Recorded interview July 27, 2014

Beginner's Luck

Victoria Berry Wells (actress) – Recorded interview February 27, 2007
Donna (Siegfried) Goobic (lighting designer/stage manager, Beverly Dinner Playhouse, New Orleans [1972-76]) – Recorded interview August 16, 2009
Michael Cahill (The Cahill Archives, Beverly Dinner Playhouse, New Orleans) – Via email correspondence Summer 2009

Other Contributors

Dick Van Patten (actor) – Via email correspondence July 18, 2006
Monty Hall (television host) – Via email correspondence February 17, 2008
Tom Davis (brother of Larry Hovis, actor) – Recorded interview July 27, 2008
Richard Addrisi (musician, The Addrisi Brothers) – Via email correspondence July 25, 2007
Colonel Jerry Chipman, USAF (Retired) – Via email correspondence June 10, 2006
Pat Boone (musician) – Via email correspondence
Martin Ransohoff (television producer) – Via phone conversation October 2008
Marie Blesk (Stratford, CT, PAL Talent Unit) – Via letter August 2008
Ed Begley, Jr. (actor; statement only) – Via email correspondence July 21, 2008
Francine York (actress, The Red Skelton Hour) — via written correspondence May 8, 2015
Dr. Leo Finkelstein, Jr. (USAF film writer/producer/director) – Via email correspondence February 1, 2009
Frank and Marion Karas, owners, The Floor Covering Shop, Stamford, CT – June 2007
Ron Marcus (historian, Stamford Historical Society) – Ongoing correspondence 2004-2012

Therapy and Clinical Psychology Regarding Sex Addiction

Reverend Edward Beck (retired; vice president, Windmill Dinner Theatre, Scottsdale, Arizona; addiction counselor) – Via email correspondence and audio letters May 15, 2006, July 27, 2006, October 12, 2006, and July 7, 2009
Veronica Monet, ACS (sex addiction/human sexuality expert) – Recorded interview January 2009
Alexandra Katehakis, MFT, CSAT, CST (sex addiction expert) – Recorded interview January 2009
Nancy Irwin, PsyD, C.Ht. (sex addiction expert) – Recorded interview January 2009
David Bissette, PsyD (sex addiction expert) – Recorded interview January 2009

Print Resources

Many print resources included here were clippings Bob Crane saved in his scrapbooks. While he had written the date and publication on most of them, on some, he had not. Although every effort was made to locate the missing information, in some instances, we were unsuccessful. Digital versions of all articles and/or clippings are on file with the authors.

___. (1946, June 6). 537 receive diplomas at H.S. commencement. *Stamford Advocate* (Stamford, CT).
___. (1951, January 15). Variety show. *The Bridgeport Telegram*.
___. (1951, February 5). Air-casters. *Broadcasting-Telecasting*, p. 52.
___. (1951, April 19). New 'Town Crier.' *The Bridgeport Telegram*.
___. (1951, November 18). WICC control acquired by station WLIZ interests. *The Hartford Courant*, p. 16.
___. (1952, January 25). Playhouse will cast for 13 parts in Jerome Chodorov's 'Kind Lady.' *The Wilton Bulletin*. Retrieved from http://fultonhistory.com/Process%20small/Newspapers/Newspapers%20%20Out%20of%20NY/Wilton%20CT.%20Bulletin/Wilton%20CT%20Bulletin%201952%20Grayscale.pdf/Wilton%20CT%20Bulletin%201952%20Grayscale%20-%200054.pdf

___. (1952, July 21). Bridgeport fete: WICC ties in with parade. *Broadcasting-Telecasting*, p. 46.
___. (1952, December 8). Air-casters. *Broadcasting-Telecasting*, p. 58.
___. (1953). Back in your own back yard. WICC Bridgeport, Conn. Bob Crane. *Who's Who in TV and Radio, 1*(2), 92.
___. (1953, March 1). 1926 to 1953: WICC reflects epic of radio-TV. Local station history shows bold pioneering. *Sunday Herald* (Bridgeport, CT), p. 101.
___. (1953, March 6). "County members of the Connecticut Chiropractic Association…" *The Bridgeport Telegram* (Bridgeport, CT).
___. (1954, October 29). Campus notes: University of Bridgeport. *The Bridgeport Telegram* (Bridgeport, CT), p. 44.
___. (1955). Man of the morning. *TV Radio Mirror, 45*(1), 6.
___. (1955, January 15). Variety show. *The Bridgeport Telegram* (Bridgeport, CT), p. 5.
___. (1955, January 29). To address Kiwanis. *The Bridgeport Post* (Bridgeport, CT), p. 29.
___. (1955, March 6). "WICC's Bob Crane receiving fan mail…" *The Bridgeport Telegram* (Bridgeport, CT), p. B-1.
___. (1957, April 7). Former WICC disc jockey Bob Crane… *The Sunday Herald* (Bridgeport, CT), p. 80.
___. (1958, April 13). Rotary to hear Bob Crane, star of radio show. *Valley News* (Van Nuys, CA).
___. (1958, May). "'Oops' groans Bob Crane…" *TV Radio Life*.
___. (1958, May 1). Auxiliary sets moms' lunch. *Van Nuys News*, p. 38-A.
___. (1958, May 3). This week's television radio news in pictures. *TV Radio Life*, p. 7.
___. (1958, August 21). 'Man of 1000 Voices' guest of BP Rotarians. *Covina Argus Daily Tribune* (Covina, CA), p. 51.
___. (1958, October). Just plain Crane. *TV Radio Life*.
___. (1958, October 4). Along TV-radio row. *TV Radio Life*, p. 41.
___. (1959). A laugh in the morning: Bob Crane. *See/Hear, 1*(12), 10.
___. (1959, January 20). Kiwanians enjoy radio personality at Tuesday meet. *Van Nuys News* (Van Nuys, CA), p. 20.
___. (1959, May 20). Bob Crane goes on CBS network. *The Bridgeport Post* (Bridgeport, CT).
___. (1960, July 4). A stereo commercial. *Broadcasting*, p. 32.
___. (1960, October 6). Soroptimists set theater party Sunday. *Van Nuys News* (Van Nuys, CA), p. 28-C.
___. (1961, January 22). Disc jockey Crane guest of Valleyrama. *Valley News* (Van Nuys, CA).
___. (1961, April 27). Luncheon kicks off Realtor Week. *Valley News* (Van Nuys, CA).
___. (1962, March 22). Testimonial to erudition for Deejay Bob Crane. *Radio-Television Daily*, p. 5.
___. (1962, July 29). Candid TV week. *TV Sunday News*, p. 2.
___. (1962, August 7). "KNX's Bob Crane…" *Radio-Television Daily*, p. 8.
___. (1962, August 23). Bob Crane stars in comedy. *Pasadena Independent* (Pasadena, CA), p. 21.
___. (1962, August 27). Bob Crane to act in summer theatre. *Independent* (Long Beach, CA), p. 21.
___. (1962, December 27). It's slapstick to suspense for quick-change comic. *Radio-Television Daily*, p. 8.
___. (1963). It's the story of Bob Crane. *TV Radio Mirror, 61*(1), 64-65.
___. (1963, January 20). Being parent rough. *The Bridgeport Post* (Bridgeport, CT), p. 54.

___. (1963, April 14). Bob Crane stakes claim to TV fame. *Bridgeport Sunday Herald* (Bridgeport, CT), p. 17.

___. (1963, September 8). "It is interesting to note..." *The Bridgeport Post* (Bridgeport, CT), p. 93.

___. (1964, January 9). Tarzana Chamber. *Van Nuys News* (Van Nuys, CA).

___. (1964, February 18). Give $92,910 to aid fight on arthritis. *Van Nuys News* (Van Nuys, CA), p. 4B.

___. (1964, March 16). "This refreshing honest..." *Salt Lake Tribune* (Salt Lake City, UT), p. 23.

___. (1964, March 26). Bob Crane is full of it every morning. *Pasadena Independent* (Pasadena, CA), p. 28.

___. (1964, June 13). "A more domesticated 'doctor' Bob Crane..." *Standard-Speaker* (Hazleton, PA), p. 13.

___. (1965). *Critics' consensus – '65-'66.*

___. (1964, September 21). California query. *Broadcasting-Telecasting,* p. 103.

___. (1965). Deejay may have hit in Nazi POW series. *Cincinnati Post.*

___. (1965). First rating: Newcomer 'Hogan' 5th.

___. (1965). 'Hogan's Heroes' to premiere in black [and] white. *Longview News Journal* (Longview, TX).

___. (1965). Nielsen's new show numerology.

___. (1965, January 5). Crane on of Bing's TV pilot Heroes.'

___. (1965, January 5). 'Hogan's Heroes' rolling at Desilu this week.

___. (1965, January 9). Tarzan Chamber. *Van Nuys News* (Van Nuys, CA).

___. (1965, March 1). Award-winning commercials. *Broadcasting-Telecasting,* p. 36.

___. (1965, June 1). New comedy series added next season. *The Sandusky Register* (Sandusky, OH), p. 26.

___. (1965, June 4). Crane exits KNX for TV; Rege Cordic replaces him.

___. (1965, June 23). On all channels: 'Hogan's' humorous heroics; Brodkin's folktune pilot. *Variety.*

___. (1965, July 28). Rating the new television season. PiQ fates & fortunes on the new season. *Variety,* p. 53.

___. (1965, August 17). Bob Crane is star in upcoming series. *Progress Bulletin Entertainment,* p. 10.

___. (1965, August 30). Crane's rags Army vintage. *The Sandusky Register* (Sandusky, OH), p. 18.

___. (1965, September). Opening week top 20.

___. (1965, September 4-10). Two premieres in one: Lee's and Network's. *Chicago Tribune TV Week,* p. 8.

___. (1965, September 7). 'Survival kit' is promotion for CBS 'Hogan's Heroes.'

___. (1965, September 10). Taken for granted. *The Hawk-Eye Burlington News,* p. 13.

___. (1965, September 15). Radio and television. *The Virginian Pilot,* p. 28.

___. (1965, September 18). TV reviews: Mr. Roberts has to shape up or ship out. *The Los Angeles Times.*

___. (1965, September 20). Hogan's Heroes (review). *Variety.*

___. (1965, September 20). Looks like nip-and-tuck ratings race this season. *Variety.*

___. (1965, September 24). Show business: Television: The overstuffed tube.

___. (1965, September 27). Look: Networks turn to teen-agers. *Newsweek.*

___. (1965, October 2). Bob Crane. *TV Viewer* (Anchorage, AK).

___. (1965, October 12). 'Hogan's Heroes' TV's top NEW show! *Variety.*

___. (1965, October 24). Viewers apparently agree – POW camp can be funny. *Los Angeles Herald-Examiner TV Week,* pp. 4-5.

___. (1965, November 7). 'U.N.C.L.E.' No. 1 in J-A poll; 4 new shows in top 10. *New York Journal American,* p. 3-L.

___. (1965, November 14). TV poll. *Los Angeles Herald-Examiner,* p. H10.
___. (1965, November 22). Inside TV: Heroes to film 32 episodes. *Los Angeles Times.*
___. (1966). "Leader of 'Hogan's Heroes' attended school in city" (Hornell, NY).
___. (1966). The unlikeliest hero of them all. *TV Star Parade, 16*(6), 8, 70-71.
___. (1966). Who said that? Hogan's Heroes talk-a-thon. *TV Star Parade, 16*(9), 29-31, 71-72.
___. (1966, January 30). Cover close-up: 'Hogan's Heroes.' *Independent Star News* (Long Beach, CA), p. 9.
___. (1966, February 12). 'Hogan's Heroes': Bob (Hogan) Crane and Werner (Klink) Klemperer make it sound like 'a real fun war.' *TV News,* pp. 7-9.
___. (1966, February 27). Bob Crane names to headline show for Jewish home. *Van Nuys News* (Van Nuys, CA).
___. (1966, April 20). "Visitors to the set of 'Hogan's Heroes'…" *The Herald-Mail Company* (Hagerstown, MD), p. 3.
___. (1966, May 1). Ex-Waterburian served as 'Remington Raider.' *Waterbury Sunday Republican* (Waterbury, CT).
___. (1966, May 2). Letters help writers. *Valley Independent* (Monessen, PA), p. 21.
___. (1966, May 21). Kissing yes, smoking, no! *El Paso Herald Post* (El Paso, TX), p. 11.
___. (1966, June 5). Emmy off-guard. *Independent Star News* (Pasadena, CA).
___. (1966, June 5). TV talk: Emmy Awards a success. *Independent Star News* (Pasadena, CA), p. 69.
___. (1966, June 11). Actor Bob Crane an individualist. Hogan's Heroes won't do appearances as group. *Courier Times.*
___. (1966, June 25). Stars of 'Hogan's Heroes' to guest on John Gary Show. *Weekend Daily Reporter* (Dover, OH), p. 8.
___. (1966, June 26). Bob Crane and the dead fly caper. *Citizen News TV Week.*
___. (1966, June 26). Bob Crane's 'instant' success story. *Nashua Telegraph,* p. 3.
___. (1966, July 24). Bob Crane turns down Ed Sullivan. *The Times Recorder* (Zanesville, OH), p. 7-C.
___. (1966, September 12). Hogan's Heroes has new secretary to help befuddle Germans; rest of cast unchanged. *Montana Standard Post* (Butte, MT), p. 23.
___. (1966, September 24). 'Pleasant peasant' blouse: Hogan's girl sparks scenes. *El Paso Herald* (El Paso, TX), p. 31.
___. (1966, September 25). Crane makes comedy album. *Express and News,* p. 9.
___. (1966, September 26). Sigrid Valdis: She's there when needed or even sooner. *The Daily Herald* (Provo, UT), p. 24.
___. (1966, September 27). TV notes. *The Oil City Derrick* (Oil City, PA), p. 12.
___. (1966, November 8). "Werner Klemperer's father…" *Standard-Speaker* (Hazleton, PA).
___. (1966, December 3). Bob Crane wanted to be drummer. *Biddeford-Saco Journal* (Biddeford, ME), p. 11.
___. (1967). Bob Crane: 'How to be a hero in your own family!' *Photoplay, 71*(1), 38-41.
___. (1967, February 4). Tele-talk. *The Times* (San Mateo, CA), p. 62.
___. (1967, February 20). Bob Crane signed for first star role. *The Daily Herald,* p. 5.
___. (1967, April 1). When television stars have time, they make movies. *Alton Evening Telegraph,* p. B-2.
___. (1967, June 23). Model claims mod fashions make dolls resemble blimps. *The Kansas City Star,* p. 10.
___. (1967, August 5). Hunting for the brass ring: For Sigrid Valdis, it's a husband who'll buy her a carousel. *TV Guide,* p. 74.

___. (1967, August 19). POW cast moves into 3rd season. *The La Crosse Tribune* (La Crosse, WI), p. 19.

___. (1967, September 2). Hero's drumming dream finally becomes reality. *Simpson's Leader-Times* (Kittanning, PA), p. 19.

___. (1967, September 16). The sergeant' hard climb from the ranks. How Ivan Dixon made it from Harlem to 'Hogan's Heroes.' *TV Guide*, pp. 25-26.

___. (1967, October 27). "Bob Crane, star of 'Hogan's Heroes'…" *The Daily Reporter* (Dover, OH), p. 24.

___. (1967, November 26). Dad 'swiped' first drum for Hogan. *Express and News* (San Antonio, TX), p. 98.

___. (1968, February 1). Director suggests canned crying for sad TV shows. *The Van Nuys News* (Van Nuys, CA), p. 44-B.

___. (1968, February 13). "That Bob Crane is a very nice man…" *The Daily Reporter* (Dover, OH), p. 7.

___. (1968, February 14). Announce locations for pledges. *Oshkosh Daily Northwestern*, p. 17.

___. (1968, February 17). Local residents to appear on telethon. *Sheboygan Press* (Sheboygan, WI), p. 15.

___. (1968, March 13). Reviews of current movies. *The Sun*, p. B-7.

___. (1968, March 29). "Bob Crane, star of 'Hogan's Heroes'…" *The Luddington Daily News* (Luddington, MI), p. 12.

___. (1968, April 4). Key to urban health topic at luncheon. *Van Nuys News* (Van Nuys, CA), p. 43-B.

___. (1968, May 12). "'Operation Entertainment,' the ABC variety series…" *Bridgeport Post* (Bridgeport, CT).

___. (1968, July 26). World War II based 'Hogan's Heroes' returns to CBS for fourth season. *The Kokomo Tribune* (Kokomo, IN), p. 44.

___. (1968, October 20). "For Bob Crane of Hogan's Heroes: Do you think…" *Family Weekly, Daily Review* (Hayward, CA).

___. (1969, January 9). Bob Crane to star at 'Mesa's Heroes.' *The Arizona Republic* (Phoenix, AZ), p. F-9.

___. (1969, January 18). Bob Crane to appear in Drury Lane production. *The Jacksonville Daily Journal* (Jacksonville, IL), p. 13.

___. (1969, January 19). Lame brain of 'Hogan's Heroes' reveals considerable talent as writer in TV. *The Ogden Standard-Examiner* (Ogden, UT), p. 80.

___. (1969, January 26). Hogan role not frustrating. *San Antonio Express*, p. 130.

___. (1969, March 20). New rash of medicine shows set for television. *Kingsport Times*, p. 4-D.

___. (1969, March 21). Bob Crane not billed right for TV special. *The Bridgeport Telegram* (Bridgeport, CT), p. 27.

___. (1969, June 3). Mrs. Bob Crane sues actor for a divorce. *The Bridgeport Post* (Bridgeport, CT), p. 8.

___. (1969, June 5). TV's Col. Hogan coming to Albq. *Albuquerque Tribune*, p. B-3.

___. (1969, June 10). Bob Crane, Abby Dalton head 'Cactus Flower' cast in Warren. *Chronicle Telegram* (Elyria, OH), p. 11.

___. (1969, June 10). Crane at Kenley. *New Castle News* (New Castle, PA), p. 6.

___. (1969, June 20). TV series star in Kenley play. *The Times Recorder* (Zanesville, OH), p. 8.

___. (1969, August 24). Gaelic gambling instinct exploited. *Express News* (San Antonio, TX), p. 20.

___. (1970, February 4). Bob Crane hopes Chicago likes 'Beginner's Luck.' *The Hollywood Reporter*.

BOB CRANE The Definitive Biography

___. (1970, February 5). Bob Crane to join CP Telethon. *The Troy Record*, p. 34.
___. (1970, February 13). Glittering stars to appear on telethon. *Atlanta Enterprise*.
___. (1970, March 22). 'Beginner's Luck' show premiere. *News Journal* (Chicago, IL), p. 6.
___. (1970, March 28). Crane in comedy. *The Pantagraph* (Bloomington, IL), p. 20.
___. (1970, April 4). 'Beginner's Luck.' *Florence Morning News* (Florence, SC), p. 18.
___. (1970, August 14). Bob Crane in pre-Broadway play 'Beginner's Luck' at Playhouse. *The Ludington Daily News*, p. 25.
___. (1970, August 19). 20 years ago. *The Bridgeport Post* (Bridgeport, CT), p. 34.
___. (1970, August 19). Bob Crane sparks hilarious funfest at The Playhouse. *Traverse City Record-Eagle* (Traverse City, MI), p. 18.
___. (1970, August 23). New man stands guard. *The San Bernardino County Sun*, p. D-10.
___. (1970, September 18). Real POWs provide plots for Hogan's Heroes series. *The Anniston Star* (Anniston, AL), p. 7.
___. (1970, September 19). 'Col. Hogan' gets story ideas from real POWs. *The La Crosse Tribune* (La Crosse, WI), p. 15.
___. (1970, September 26). 'Hogan' gets new hero. *Pittsburgh Courier*, p. 13.
___. (1970, October 18). Bob Crane marries in ceremony on set. *The Kokomo Tribune* (Kokomo, IN), p. 23.
___. (1970, November 2). Broadcasting at 50: Can it adapt? *Broadcasting*, p. 70.
___. (1970, November 8). "Writer Laurence Marks based tonight's Hogan's Heroes on..." *The Anniston Star* (Anniston, AL), p. 28.
___. (1971, January 5). "Bit parts: Bob Crane, Werner Klemperer, and Richard Dawson..." *Daily Review* (Haywood, CA), p. 31.
___. (1971, March 5). Archie. *Independent* (Long Beach, CA), p. 2.
___. (1971, March 14). Bob Crane will star at Little Theatre-on-Square. *The Terre Haute Tribune-Star* (Terre-Haute, IN), p. 8.
___. (1971, April 5). Hogan gang is planning nightclub act. *The Coshocton Tribune*, p. 3.
___. (1971, May 4). "Bob Crane of TV's Hogan's Heroes..." *The Daily Reporter* (Dover, OH), p. 8.
___. (1971, June 29). Star of 'Hogan's Heroes' to appear at Playhouse. *Traverse City Record-Eagle* (Traverse City, MI), p. 3.
___. (1971, August 27). 'Send Me No Flowers' stars 'Hogan's Heroes' Bob Crane. *The Ludington Daily News* (Ludington, MI), p. 22.
___. (1971, October 2). Show in the making. *The Daily Times News* (Burlington, NC), p. 11.
___. (1971, December 5). Seven stars signed for San Diego stage. *The San Bernardino County Sun* (San Bernardino, CA), p. 53.
___. (1972, February 25). Beginner's Luck opens March 7. *The Vista Press* (Vista, CA), p. 8.
___. (1972, March 30). Bob Crane ducked TV personality bit. *The Lowell Sun* (Lowell, MA), p. 44.
___. (1972, April 12). Bob Crane is casting El Pasoans in comedy. *El Paso Herald-Post* (El Paso, TX), p. 5.
___. (1972, April 29). "Bob Crane in town..." *El Paso Herald-Post* (El Paso, TX), p. 35.
___. (1972, May 5). Autograph party planned at Bassett. *El Paso Herald-Post* (El Paso, TX), p. 28.
___. (1972, May 5). Lions' governor-elect seeks to strengthen clubs' goals. *El Paso Herald-Post* (El Paso, TX), p. 3.
___. (1972, May 6). 'Beginner's Luck' now at Marquee: Riotous comedy stars TV's Bob Crane. *El Paso Herald Post* (El Paso, TX), p. 35.

___. (1972, May 13). "One of El Paso's friendliest groups…" *El Paso Herald-Post* (El Paso, TX), p. 6.

___. (1972, May 26). El Paso memories cherished by military Mother of the Year. *El Paso Herald-Post* (El Paso, TX), p. 9.

___. (1972, July 22). "Bob Crane of television's 'Hogan's Heroes'…" *Freeport Journal-Standard* (Freeport, IL), p. 18.

___. (1972, August 9). "Bob Crane, starring in 'Who's That Lady I Saw You with?'…" *The Hoffman Estates Herald,* p. 3.

___. (1972, October 8). Bob Crane to star on stage in San Diego. *The San Bernardino County Sun* (San Bernardino, CA), p. 53.

___. (1972, October 27). "'Send Me No Flowers' comedy stars Bob Crane…" *Valley News* (Van Nuys, CA), p. 48.

___. (1972, November 16). Bob Crane in holiday special. *The San Bernardino County Sun,* p. 65.

___. (1972, November 26). Bob Crane makes return to radio in new specials. *Lubbock-Avalanche-Journal* (Lubbock, TX), p. 131.

___. (1972, November 27). Replacement. *Playground Daily News* (Fort Walton Beach, FL), p. 4B.

___. (1972, November 28). 'Hogan's Heroes' comedy star Bob Crane still waiting on money. *Playground Daily News* (Fort Walton Beach, FL), p. 8.

___. (1973, January 28). Arthritis telethon. *Progress Bulletin,* p. 13.

___. (1973, February 2). 'Hogan's Heroes' actor dead at 63 of hemorrhage. *Nevada Evening Gazette,* p. 2.

___. (1973, February 2). Sgt. Schultz of TV Hogan's Heroes, dies. *Progress Bulletin,* p. A-2.

___. (1973, April 12). Bob Crane returns to KMPC… *The Van Nuys News* (Van Nuys, CA), p. 96.

___. (1973, May 1). Crane set as star. *Grand Prairie Daily News,* p. 7.

___. (1973, June 28). Crane guffaw producer in Beginner's Luck.' *Arizona Republic,* p. 131.

___. (1973, July 26). "It looks like another sellout…" *Arizona Republic* (Phoenix, AZ), p. 139.

___. (1973, September 6). Hogan invades TWC. *Rambler, 48*(1), 1.

___. (1973, September 13). Crane explains problems of undressing on stage without special shorts. *Rambler, 48*(2). 3.

___. (1974, January 18). Bob Crane looks like a Disney dad. *Pittsburgh Post Gazette,* p. 11.

___. (1974, January 26). Prime Time rule to be relaxed in September. *The Los Angeles Times,* p. A2.

___. (1974, May 17). Stars set to entertain. *Valley News* (Van Nuys, CA), p. 30.

___. (1974, June 30). Actor Frank Sutton dies. *Abilene Reporter,* p. 68.

___. (1974, June 30). Heart attack kills actor Frank Sutton. *The Vernon Daily Record,* p. 2.

___. (1974, July 10). "Bob Crane—Hogan in the long-running, ever popular 'Hogan's Heroes'…" *Hope Star* (Hope, AR), p. 11.

___. (1974, July 12). Six new series are cancelled by networks. *The Gallup NM Independent,* p. 11.

___. (1974, October 3). "'Hogan's Heroes' star Bob Crane…" *News-Journal* (Mansfield, OH), p. 47.

___. (1974, December 29). TV time-line. *The Post Crescent Sun,* p. 16.

___. (1975, March 2). Bob Crane back on TV with Thursday night series. *Toledo Blade,* p. 79.

___. (1975, March 2). Cover close up: One more time. *Star News* (Pasadena, CA), p. 16.
___. (1975, March 3). Bob Crane returns with weekly TV series. *Victoria Advocate*.
___. (1975, May 23). Crane show may be heading for success. *The Sedalia Democrat (TV & Entertainment)*, p. 1.
___. (1975, July 25). "Bob Crane and wife…" *The Daily Herald* (Chicago, IL), p. 17.
___. (1975, July 31). "Opening next Wednesday at Drury Lane East…" *Suburbanite Economist* (Chicago, IL), p. 79.
___. (1976, January 29). Bob Crane hosts Cerebral Palsy Telethon Saturday on Channel 30. *The Hartford Courant*, p. 305.
___. (1976, February 8). "Bob Crane, who left WICC…" *The Bridgeport Post*, p. B-1.
___. (1976, March 20). Wayne Rogers to host Easter Seal Telethon. *The Independent Press Telegram*, p. B-8.
___. (1976, May 5). Gilberton area. *Evening Herald of Shenandoah-Ashland-Mahanoy City*, p. 15.
___. (1976, May 24). "Bob Crane, or as he is usually known: Hogan…" *The Newark Advocate* (Newark, OH), p. 14.
___. (1976, June 4). Bob Crane plays The Playhouse. *The Circleville Herald* (Circleville, OH), p. 3.
___. (1976, September 20). 30,000 watch Mum Parade. *The Hartford Courant*, p. 16.
___. (1976, September 20). 'Hogan's Heroes' star recalls job in Bristol. *The Hartford Courant*. p. 17A.
___. (1976, December 5). Bob Crane was inspired by Gig Young to act. *The Ledger*, p. 43.
___. (1977, June 23). Hogan's Hero stars at Country Dinner Playhouse. *The Seguin Gazette-Enterprise* (Seguin, TX), p. 37.
___. (1977, June 24). Bob Crane to appear at Country Dinner [Playhouse] [sic]. *The Taylor Daily Press*, p. 3.
___. (1977, August 11). "Actor Bob Crane, appearing…" *The Hearne Democrat* (Hearne, TX), p. 3.
___. (1977, November 10). Bob [Crane] [sic] to star at Beef 'n' Boards. *The Journal News*, p. 49.
___. (1977, November 11). "TV star to aid Medina fund drive."
___. (1978, April 25). 'Hogan' in 'Luck' at Windmill show. *Plano Daily Star-Courier* (Plano, TX), p. 2.
___. (1978, May 26). "Windmill Dinner Theatre Bob Crane in 'Beginner's Luck'…" *Irving Daily News*, p. 2.
Albert, D. (1967). The real-life 'Hogan's Heroes.' *Screen Stories, 66*(10), 32-33, 82.
Albert, L. (2003). Update with Jim French. *Air Check, 13*(2), 5. Retrieved from http://repsonline.homestead.com/AirCheck/Aircheck_V13_02May2003.pdf
Allman, K. (1987). *TV turkeys: An outrageous look at the most preposterous shows ever on television.* New York, NY: Author.
Alpert, D. (1968, March 3). Bob Crane sounds off: Ex-drummer beats the publicity drums. *Toledo Blade,* p. TV-11.
Anderson, J. (1965, August 23). Bob Crane is hoping for long POW term. *The Miami Herald*, p. 7B.
Anderson, J.E. (1971, September 3). Bob Crane plays final bill. *The Ludington Daily News*, p. 25.
Ardmore, J. (1967). Bob Crane: Daddy is the boss because mommy wants him to be! *Movie Mirror, 11*(4), 36-37, 63-64.
Ash, A. (1965, September). 5 new series blast off on land, sea, and air. *Miami News*.
Associated Press. (1964, March 25). Bob Crane is versatile showman. *Bennington Banner*, p. 7.

Associated Press. (1967, January 15). Bob Crane reflects his heroes.
Associated Press. (1967, January 29). Mock of authority, 'Hogan's Heroes' key. *The Bridgeport Sunday Post.*
Associated Press. (1967, February 23). Bob Crane on brink of movie stardom. *The Bridgeport Telegram.* p. 18.
Associated Press. (1967, June 23). Model claims mod fashions make dolls resemble blimps. *The Kansas City Star,* p. 10.
Associated Press. (1970, May 7). FCC limits network program ownership. *The Los Angeles Times,* G32.
Associated Press. (1970, June 18). Bob Crane ordered to pay $276,000.
Associated Press. (1970, October 18). Bob Crane marries in ceremony on set. *The Kokomo Tribune,* p. 23.
Associated Press. (1977, February 4). Crane hopes to break back into TV.
Associated Press. (1977, February 7). 'Col. Hogan' hopes show will capitalize on nostalgia. *Tri-City Herald,* p. 14.
Associated Press. (1978, June 30). 'Hogan's Heroes' star beaten to death. *The Eagle,* p. 1.
Austin, J. (1990). *Hollywood's unsolved mysteries.* New York, NY: Author.
Bacon, J., for Thomas, B. (1965, July 24). Crane gambles $150,000. *Newark Advocate,* p. 7.
Baer, A. (1965, September 1). Give new shows a chance—but be on guard. *New York Journal American,* p. 13.
Baer, A. (1965, October 16). War and little peace is video's Friday theme. *New York Journal American,* p. 24.
Baessler, P. (1965, August 22-28). Hogan's Heroes. *Los Angeles Herald Examiner,* pp. 4-7.
Barasch, N., & Moore, C. (1961). *Send me no flowers: A comedy in three acts.* New York, NY: Author.
Barasch, N., & Moore, C. (1973). *Beginner's luck: A comedy in two acts.* New York, NY: Author.
Barrett, R. (1964, May 3). Bob Crane hair was worry to producers. *The San Bernardino County Sun,* p. 56.
Batdorff, B. (1971, September 1). Playhouse capping banner 17th year with first-rate offering. *Traverse City Record-Eagle* (Traverse City, MI), p. 5.
Batdorff, R. (1970, August 19). Bob Crane sparks hilarious funfest at the Playhouse. *Traverse City Record-Eagle,* p. 18.
Bates, H. (1967, October 6). "'Hogan's Heroes' own Col. Hogan, Bob Crane, is one man…" *Valley News* (Van Nuys, CA), p. 32-A.
Bates, H. (1968, February 9). Top stars to aid Arthritis Telethon. *Van Nuys News,* p. 26-A.
Beck, E. (1983). *A love to live by: One couple's courageous fight for life.* San Bernardino, CA: Here's Life Publishers, Inc.
Beck, M. (1967, May 22). TV closeup. *The Daily Reporter,* p. 7.
Beck, M. (1974, January 9). Bob Crane's still waiting for windfall from 'Hogan.' *Miami News,* p. 10.
Beck, M. (1974, August 1). "Mary Tyler Moore and husband Grant Tinker…" *Albuquerque Tribune,* p. B-1.
Beck, M. (1975, May 27). Executive claims TV improving. *The San Bernardino County Sun,* p. 13.
Beck, R. (1967). Off the records: Celebrity of the month – Bob Crane. *TV Movie Screen, 14*(4), 15.
Berg, J. (1974, February 23). Echoes from entertainment. *Fond du Lac Commonwealth Reporter,* p. 10.

Biggers, B., & Stover, C. (1974, November 1). POW! *The San Bernardino County Sun*, p. 34.
Biggers, B., & Stover, C. (1974, November 22). Crane gets credit. *The Daily Times-News* (Burlington, NC), p. 4.
Bird, A. (1966). Bob Crane a TV hero. *The News American: Baltimore*.
Blank, E.L. (1970, December 30). Bob Crane: 'Hogan's Heroes' profits will come later. *The Pittsburgh Press*, p. 31.
Blinn, J. (1981). *Celebrity cookbook*. New York, NY: Author.
Boyle, H. (1967, June 14). Werner Klemperer has found niche, does not seek fame or riches. *The Plain Speaker* (Hazleton, PA).
Braithwaite, D. (1965). Mature comedy. Toronto, Canada.
Brock, B. (1965, May 7). Affiliates like Hogan's Heroes. *Dallas Times Herald*, p. 18-A.
Brock, B. (1965, September). Critically speaking: Stocks and bonds. *Dallas Times Herald*.
Brothers, J. (1965). Escapist fare on TV dwells far from reality.
Brown, B. (1965, August 27). Bob Crane 'Hogan's Heroes' star proves very amusing entertainer. *Oklahoma City Advertiser – TV Preview*, p. 1.
Brown, L. (1974, June 19) Court stay of Prime-Time rule to force shift in TV schedules. *New York Times*, 90.
Brown, S. (1970, August 18). Witty, humorous Bob Crane likes shows that are 'fun.' *Traverse City Record-Eagle* (Traverse City, MI), p. 12.
Brown, W.W. (1965). Hogan's Heroes a comic mixture. *The Dallas Times Herald*.
Brown, W.W. (1966, November 5). Actor Crane most happy when busy. *Dallas Times Herald*.
Browning, N.L. (1974, December 25). Mitzi Lures stars for TV 'Chorus.' *The Salt Lake Tribune*, p. B-2.
Bruner, A. (1966). "CBC affiliates laugh loudly at Gerda, Ouimet, 7 Days."
Burrows, A., Barillet, P., & Gredy, J-P. (1966). *Cactus flower: A comedy in two acts*. New York, NY: Author.
Busch, A. (1965, September 1). Drops radio for 'Chicken.' *Daily Signal*, p. C-7.
Calhoun, B. (2002, October 21). Family viewing. *Salon*. Retrieved from http://www.salon.com/2002/10/21/scotty_crane/
Campbell, G. (1972, July 24). 'That Lady' mediocre fare. *The Daily Herald* (Chicago, IL), p. 17.
Campbell, G. (1975, August 15). Bob Crane makes 'Luck' a summertime sizzler. *The Des Plaines Herald*, p. 13.
Carnes, D. (1965). On the air: Prisoner of war show to debut.
Cedrone, Jr., L. (1965, September 3). 'Hogan's Heroes is question mark. *Morning Sun Baltimore*.
Champlin, C. (1965, October 18). Crane on good side of fate. *Los Angeles Times*, p. D19.
Clary, R. (2001). *From the Holocaust to Hogan's Heroes: The autobiography of Robert Clary*. Lanham, MD: Author.
Coffey, J. (1965, August 11). Odd birds, gilded cage. *Fort Worth Star Telegram*.
Connoly, M. (1965, August 17). Rambling reporter. *The Hollywood Reporter*.
Crane, B. (1955, April). Disc jockey platter patter: Programming a DJ show. *Hit Parader*, p. 26.
Crane, B. (1966). School and the shy child. *TV Radio Mirror*, 66(3), 4.
Crane, B. (1968, February). How I avoid trouble. *Guideposts*, pp. 22-23.
Crane, B. (1970). "Bob Crane spurns 'Best Actor' prize."
Crane, B. (1970, September 6). My favorite jokes. *The Fresno Bee*.
Crane, B., for Lowry, C. (1967, July 21). Bob Crane's true love is drumming. *Indiana Evening Gazette*, p. 12.

Crane, B., for O'Brian, J. (1970, July 21). Bob Crane tells of student talk. *The Logansport Press* (Logansport, IN), p. 4.
Crane, B., for Rich, A. (1965, June 7). "It's been said repeatedly in different ways…" *Citizen News*, p. 18.
Crane, B., for Rich, A. (1966, June 11). TV week. *The Times*.
Crawford, L. (1967, January 1). Crane likes fun but not too much. *Chicago Tribune*.
Crawley, E.A. (1974). 'Hogan's Heroes' star Bob Crane confesses: 'I was a male chauvinist pig – until my new wife took me over!' *The National Tattler, 29*(2), 30.
Crosby, J. (1965, September). TV notebook. *Index Journal*, p. 10.
Crosby, J. (1966, March 27). Dawson's 'sole purpose' is to make people laugh. *The Corpus Christi Caller Times*, p. 21F.
Crosby, J. (1966, July 11). 'Hogan's' Crane can say no. *The Edwardsville Intelligencer*, p. 7.
Crosby, J. (1970, November 4). TV scout reports. *The Odessa American* (Odessa, TX). p. 21.
Crosby, J. (1970, November 13). TV scout reports. *The Odessa American* (Odessa, TX). p. 19.
Daley, F. (1968, February 17). Little more than leering in Paula's 'Wicked Dreams.' *The Ottawa Journal*, p. 39.
Dauphin, S., & King, L. (1974, April 18). Diversions. *The News*, p. 7.
de Vries, P. (1954). *The tunnel of love*. Boston: Little, Brown and Company.
de Waal, T. (2010). *The Caucasus: An introduction*. New York, NY: Oxford University Press.
Deeb, G. (1975, May 3). Bob Crane can't stand his own show. He prefers to watch 'Barney Miller.' *The TV Book. Detroit Free Press*, pp. 2-3.
Dern, M. (1965, February 27). Man in pursuit of himself. Bob Crane, actor and disc jockey, is running hard to catch up with a Jack Lemmon-Bob Cummings-Jack Benny image. *TV Guide*, pp. 15-17.
Dixon, C. (1976, April 18). Around Stamford. *The Bridgeport Post* (Bridgeport, CT), p. 90.
Doan, R.K. (1974, July 6). Networks curtail comedies after court decision. *TV Guide*, A-1.
DuBrow, R. (1965, September 20). Weekend premieres provided variety. *St. Louis-Post Dispatch*, p. 6D.
DuBrow, R. (1969, April 3). Critic slams updated 'Arsenic and Old Lace.' *Simpson's Leader Times* (Kittanning, PA), p. 21.
Dunn, B. (1970, November 12). TV cameos: Bob Crane – Bob's new role isn't written in the script. *The Kane Republican*, p. 7.
Efron, E. (1968, August 5). Think John Wayne! Hip, flip, cocky Bob Crane reveals his secret of playing a hero's role. *TV Guide*, pp. 25-27.
Ellison, B. (1970, May 1). Bob Crane, drummer 1st class. *Chicago Tribune*, p. B19.
Eres, G. (1968, February 10). A nice show, but let's not go gaga. *The Independent Press Telegram*, p. C-5.
Fanning, W. (1965). New season reviews for Thursday, Friday. *Post Gazette* (Pittsburgh, PA).
Feinstein, E.F., & Pendery, J.S. (1984). Stamford: An illustrated history. Chatsworth, CA: Windsor Publications, Inc.
Fetridge, A.E. (1965). 15 new programs. *Boston Herald*.
Fivaz, B. (1969). "I don't need you anymore!" The truth behind Bob Crane's separation. *TV Picture Life*, pp. 38-39, 72, 74, 76, 78.
Flaum, D. (1976, September 20). Actor leads parade. *The Hartford Courant*, p. 17A.
Foreman, B. (1956, April 1). Agency ad libs: Audience composition non-Nielsen style. *Sponsor*, p. 12.

Foster, B. (1974, November 21). It's back to a radio mike for Bob Crane. *The Times* (San Mateo, CA), p. 24.

Freberg, S. (1965, September 19). Confessions of a Trojan horse.

Freeman, D. (1965, September 21). 'The FBI' lauded in series debut. *San Diego Union Times.*

Freeman, D. (1965, October 31). Our hero, Bob Crane, was made in Bridgeport but reborn in Hollywood. *The Bridgeport Post.*

Freeman, D. (1972, April 20). Bob Crane ducks TV talk show. *Cape Girardeau Bulletin,* p. 3.

Freeman, D. (1975, January 25). Bob Crane tries 'hard comedy' in new show. *The Daily Review* (Hollywood, CA), p. 32.

Freeman, D. (1976, May 1). Can Bob Crane find another hit? *Beaver County Times,* p. 15.

Freeman, D. (1976, May 19). Quick-witted Bob Crane would like another TV series. *The Brownsville Herald,* p. 11-B.

Fuller, S. (1972, April 15). Looking ahead to a show with some guts. *Chicago Tribune,* p. 23.

Fultz, J. (1998). *In search of Donna Reed.* Iowa City, IA: University of Iowa Press.

Gaede, E. (1959, August 9). Pixyish KNX morning host seldom lets hearers know what's coming. *Los Angeles Times.*

Gardella, K. (1965, August 29). Who is Bob Crane? TV's next Sgt. Bilko. *Sunday News.*

Geller, H. (2002, October 13). Refocusing on Crane [Letter to the Editor]. *Los Angeles Times.* Retrieved from http://articles.latimes.com/2002/oct/13/entertainment/ca-letterslede13

Gerussi, B. (1979). *The new Celebrity Cooks cookbook.* Toronto: Initiative Productions Limited.

Gex, N.G. (1977). *The Beverly.* Baton Rouge, LA: Author.

Gioia, T. (1997). *The history of jazz.* New York, NY: Author.

Glazer, B. (1966, June 2). Barney Glazer's Hollywood hotline. *The Jewish Post: Winnipeg, Canada.*

Glenn, T. (1954, December 12). "WICC's Bob Crane steps out…" *The Bridgeport Telegram,* p. 3.

Goldberg, J. (1978). Crane visited city often. *Waterbury Republican* (Waterbury, CT).

Gordon, E.E. (2006). *Discovering music from the inside out: An autobiography.* Chicago: GIA Publications, Inc.

Gowran, C. (1965, September 18). Hogan's Heroes best of zany new shows. *Chicago Tribune.*

Grant, H. (1964, December 22). On the air with Hank Grant. *The Hollywood Reporter.*
Grant, H. (1965, September 1). On the air with Hank Grant. *The Hollywood Reporter.*
Grant, H. (1965, September 10). On the air with Hank Grant. *The Hollywood Reporter.*
Grant, H. (1965, September 20). On the air with Hank Grant. *The Hollywood Reporter.*

Graysmith, R. (1993). *The murder of Bob Crane: Who killed the star of Hogan's Heroes?* New York, NY: Crown Publishers, Inc.

Grimaldi, L. (1993). *Only in Bridgeport: An illustrated history of the Park City* (2nd ed.). Bridgeport, CT: Harbor Publishing.

Gris, H. (1966). Bob Crane of 'Hogan's Heroes' talks about…'My biggest break.' *The Enquirer.*

Haise, J. (2013). *Dr. Robert Steadham Hogan: Was he the real Hogan's hero?* Retrieved from http://www.jeffcohistory.com/newsletter_Apr_13_pg3.html

Hamilton, J. (1967). The making of a very fast woman. *Pageant, 23*(4), 134-143.

Hamlin, C. (2012, July 4). Kiwi lad's novelty woos KNX kingpins. *The Napier Mail,* p. 6.

Harris, H. (1965, September). Screening TV. *Philadelphia Inquirer.*
Harrison, B. (1965, September 18). A long night for TV comedy. *The Evening Star* (Washington, DC).
Heimer, M. (1970, April 27). TV cameos: Bob Crane. Intrepid 'Hogan's Hero' loves his work. *The Daily Notes* (Canonsburg, PA), p. 3.
Heisner, J. (1965, August 29-September 4). A talk with Bob Crane: From Hornell to 'Hogan's Heroes.' *TV Tag Magazine,* p. 5.
Hellman, J. (1966, May 31). Light and airy. *Variety.*
Henniger, P. (1976, December 5). 'Feather and Father' get sneak preview. *The Journal News,* p. C-12.
Hobson, D. (1966, November 19). The strange history of A-5714. He is Robert Clary, who has moved from Buchenwald (in Germany) to Stalag 13 (in Hollywood). *TV Guide,* pp. 23-26.
Hobson, D. (1967, May 6). Achtung!...please. John Banner plays the most huggable Nazi on TV. *TV Guide,* pp. 16-17.
Hobson, D. (1967, July 1). How the other half lives: The case histories of eight women widowed by the TV camera. *TV Guide,* pp. 6-11.
Hogan's Heroes Fan Club. (n.d.). *The Hogan's Heroes Herald, 1.*
Hogan's Heroes Fan Club. (n.d.). *The Hogan's Heroes Herald, 2.*
Hogan's Heroes Fan Club. (n.d.). *The Hogan's Heroes Herald, 3.*
Hogan's Heroes Fan Club. (n.d.). *The Hogan's Heroes Herald, 4.*
Hogan's Heroes Fan Club. (n.d.). *The Hogan's Heroes Herald, 5.*
Hogan's Heroes Fan Club. (n.d.). *The Hogan's Heroes Herald, 6.*
Hogan's Heroes Fan Club. (n.d.). *The Hogan's Heroes Herald, 7.*
Hogan's Heroes Fan Club. (n.d.). *The Hogan's Heroes Herald, 8.*
Hogan's Heroes Fan Club. (n.d.). *The Hogan's Heroes Herald, 9.*
Hogan's Heroes Fan Club. (n.d.). *The Hogan's Heroes Herald, 10.*
Holley, T. (1976, January 30). He's a super guy – Bob Crane back in town for WICC's 50th anniversary. *The Bridgeport Post.*
Houston, R. (1965, October 17). Fly caper helped boost Crane's career. *Sunday World Herald* (Omaha, NE), p. 1.
Hoyland, R.J. (965). Hogan's Heroes may be a comedy sleeper. *The Star.*
Hull, B. (1965). TV talk: Crane comments on critical blasts of 'Hogan's Heroes.'
Hull, B. (1965). TV talk: New shows survival list includes many surprises.
Hull, B. (1965, August 10). Bob Crane exits radio 'forever' to be TV star. *Los Angeles Herald Examiner,* p. B-5.
Hull, B. (1965, September 20). TV talk: Early predictions. *Los Angeles Herald Examiner,* p. B6.
Humphrey, H. (1963, December 1). Nielsen rating heady stuff for Donna Reed. *The Kansas City Star,* p. 166.
Humphrey, H. (1968, June 12). Foreign countries ask TV performers to visit. *Beckley Post Herald* (Beckley, WV), p. 4.
Humphrey, H. (1968, June 12). They love Hogan south of border. *Toledo Blade,* p. 43.
Ingolio, J. (1978, June 27). [Untitled, unpublished article.]
Inman, J. (1965). Real Bob Crane will emerge in Hogan's Heroes. *Indianapolis Star.*
Irvin, B. (1965, May 11). Bob Crane finally captured by TV. *Chicago American.*
Johnson, E. (1965). Meet Bob Crane: What's new, copycat [raw article].
Johnson, E. (1965, August 13). Shades of Bilko in 'Hogan's Heroes.' *Abilene Reporter News,* p. 51.
Johnson, E. (1966, May 14). Crane of 'Hogan's Heroes' is individualist POW. *The North Adams Transcript,* p. 5.
Johnson, E. (1966, June 18). Ivan Dixon plays Kinchloe role in Hogan's Heroes. *The North Adams Transcript* (North Adams, MA), p. 15.

Jones, D. (1965, August). Networks are oozing with confidence over new shows. *The Tulsa Tribune.*
Judge, F. (1965, September). Last 15 new programs are topped by 7 hits. *Detroit News.*
Judge, F. (1965, November 7). Why Col. Hogan bets a fortune he can make a million. *The Sunday Star TV Magazine* (Washington, DC), pp. 2-5.
Judge, F. (1969, March 30). What's Sue Lyon doing? *The Sunday Star* (Washington, DC), pp. 2-4.
Kane, M. (1973, December 11). 'Hogan's Heroes' star visits his relatives. *The Waterbury Republican.*
Kaufman, D. (1966, December 14). Reluctant 'Heroes': Rich finds ratings 'deceptive.' *Variety.*
Kaufman, D. (1970). On all channels: Bob Crane spurns 5-Yr. CBS pact; protests book plugs. *Variety.*
Kaufman, D. (1971). On all channels: 'Hogan's' demise no surprise to Bob Crane, sorry for crew. *Variety.*
Kellogg, L. (1965, September 19). Bob Crane: A name with a future. *TV-Radio Dial,* p. 5.
Kieffer, J. (1976, May 24). Happenings. *The Newark Advocate,* p. 14.
Kleiner, D. (1965). Crane bets on Hogan's Heroes.
Kleiner, D. (1965, August 23). Hollywood today: Crane on the five-year plan. *Standard Speaker* (Hazleton, PA), p. 15.
Kleiner, D. (1965, September 16). Bob Crane believes 'Hogan's Heroes' is best for him. *The Manhattan Mercury,* p. 5.
Kleiner, D. (1967, February 26). Howie Morris: He's own boss now. *Independent Press Telegram,* p. 17.
Kleiner, D. (1967, April 16). Family film for adults only. *Santa Cruz Sentinel Sun,* p. 31.
Kleiner, D. (1967, May 7). Show beat. *The Danville Register* (Danville, VA), p. 10.
Kleiner, D. (1968, August 11). To be a leading man takes real bravery. *The Corpus Christi Caller Times,* p. 19F.
Kleiner, D. (1969, January 19). Television's Negro stars agree on one thing: Situation better than before. *The Kokomo Tribune* (Kokomo, IN), p. 21.
Kleiner, D. (1970, September 20). TV scout report. *The Abilene Reporter,* p. 7-B.
Kleiner, D. (1971, September 26). Star of police stations and mailboxes. *The Corpus Christi Caller Times,* p. 83.
Kleiner, D. (1972, March 25). Larry had his cake and ate it too. *The Ottawa Journal* (Ottawa, Ontario, Canada), p. 119.
Kleiner, D. (1976, September 20). TV scout report. *Abilene Reporter News,* p. 30.
Kogiones, P. (1975). *Petros' famous recipes (an adventure in Greek cooking).* Chicago: Author.
Krasna, N. (1958). *Who was that lady I saw you with?* New York, NY: Author.
Kreiling, E. (1965, May 25). A closer look: All signs show Bob Crane, 'Hogan's Heroes' as comer. *San Gabriel Valley Daily Tribune,* p. C-8.
Kreiling, E. (1965, October 19). A closer look. *Valley Greensheet.*
Kreiling, E. (1973, April 12). A closer look. *Van Nuys News,* p. 19-C.
Laine, G. (1965, September 20). Television view & review. *Evening Outlook,* p. 22.
Larkin, L. (1966). Meet 'Hogan's Heroes.' *Modern Screen, February,* 42-43, 68-70.
Laurent, L. (1965, September 18). Radio and television: 9 new TV programs offer good, bad and indifferent. *The Washington Post,* p. C14.
Leonard, V. (1965, June 2). He has the courage of a hero. *The Pittsburgh Press.*
Leonard, V. (1965, September 18). Five shows in search of an audience—Hogan, Hank deserve it. *The Pittsburgh Press,* p. 22.

Leonard, V. (1965, October 8). Quartet heroes to the cause: 'Hogan' cast in tune over merits of hit show. *Pittsburgh Press.*

Ligon, B. (1972, May 13). 'Beginner's Luck' star charms El Pasoans: Bob Crane's likeability apparent. *El Paso Herald-Post*, p. 33.

Lowry, C. (1962, January 18). Carson's anxious to leave ABC for Paar's job on NBC. *Sheboygan Press*, p. 17.

Lowry, C. (1965). Critic concludes TV producers accident-prone.

Lowry, C. (1966, February 6). TV programs portray WWII as full of mirth and frolic. *The Bridgeport Sunday Post*, p. C-15, C-14.

Lowry, C. (1969). Hogan's hero is perfect as occasional TV host. *Star Ledger*, p. 248.

Lowry, C. (1969, April 3). Reviews of 'Arsenic and Old Lace': They should have rerun the movie. *The Anniston Star*, p. 6B.

Lowry, C. (1969, April 12). Television's Bob Crane: 'I want to be an actor.' *The Pottstown Mercury*, p. 7.

Lowry, C. (1969, April 18). Crane still hunting that movie role. *The Daily Telegram*, p. 27.

Lowry, C. (1969, April 20). Bob Crane is among stellar elite by new TV standards of stardom. *Tri-City Herald*, p. 10.

Lowry, C. (1970, October 19). 'Hogan's Heroes' still a winner in world of fantasy. *Long Island Press.*

Lycan, G. (1978, July 13). Bob Crane's KNX DJ days recalled. *The Register*, pp. E11-E12.

Lynn, C., with Ansara, E. (1992). *Escape to freedom: An autobiography of Cynthia Lynn.* Los Angeles: Authors.

MacKenzie, B. (1965, October 4). On television. *Oakland Tribune*, p. 20.

MacKenzie, B. (1969, April 3). Old Wine 'updated.' *Oakland Tribune*, p. 16.

Mackin, T. (1965, July 26). Comedy in POW camp. *Newark Evening News.*

MacMinn, A. (1964, June 7-13). Raising Crane on 'Reed' show. *TV Weekly Magazine—The Dallas Morning News*, p. 2.

Maddox, T. (1967). Nanna makes the world go round. *TV Radio Mirror, 67*(11), 32, 76-77, 79.

Majerus, J. (2011). All aboard for fun: Mum Fest riding in style. *The Bristol Press.* Retrieved from http://www.bristolpress.com/articles/2011/09/24/news/doc4e7e8527e8f8c919622580.txt

Manners, D. (1969, December 3). Dorothy Manners' Hollywood. *The Alexandria Times-Tribune* (Elwood, IN), p. 12.

Martin, B. (1972, July 6). Tele-vues: Driving along with Bob Crane. *Independent* (Long Beach, CA), p. 44.

Martin, B. (1975, February 1). Stars will be out tonight. *The Independent Press Telegram*, p. B-12.

Martin, B.K. (1970, October 29). Daisies won't tell but I will! *The Courier Express*, p. 5.

Martin, D. (1967). How Bob Crane puts the fun in fatherhood! *TV Radio Mirror, 67*(4), 52-53.

McElroy, L. (2011). *...But you can't report that! A journalist goes on the record...* Lexington, KY: Author.

McGrath, R. (1963). A [blur] of motion.

McQueen, M. (1979, April 4). 'Hogan's Heroes': Klemperer stands behind his character. *Indiana Gazette* (Indiana, PA), p. 52.

Meyers, R. (1975). Bob Crane: The nice guy who's always getting dumped on. *TV Show People*, 46-48.

Misurell, E. (1966, July 3). TV cameos: Werner Klemperer: His family keeps him in line. *The Eagle*, p. 24.

Moore, H. (1970). "'Chit chat': Editor Hank Moore interviews Bob Crane."
Morris, L. (1965, September 18). Hogan and his hot-shot heroes. *TeeVee* (Phoenix), pp. 4-5.
Mosby, W.H. (1965, July 18). A funny P.O.W. camp? Bob Crane & Co. hope they'll have one on CBS-TV's 'Hogan's Heroes.' *The Milwaukee Journal*, p. 4.
Mulr, F. (1968, September 29). Hogan's Hero swapped for Mantle. *The Abilene Reporter*, p. 7-B.
Nakken, C. (1996). *The addictive personality: Understanding the addictive process and compulsive behavior.* Center City, MN: Hazelden Foundation.
Newton, D. (1965, September 18). Pandemonium night on TV. *The San Francisco Examiner*, p. 9.
Nash, L.W. (1957, September 18). New radio twist. *Pasadena Independent*, p. 11.
Nisbet, F. (1965, July 17). 'Hogan's Heroes' play for laughs. *The Dallas Morning News*, p. 8-B.
Nisbet, F. (1966, November 5). Col. Hogan visits Dallas. *The Dallas Morning News*, p. 12-A.
O'Brian, J. (1965, June 7). On the air: Jumpin' Gemini! *New York Journal American*, p. 20.
O'Brian, J. (1965, August 4). On the air: Six more new ones. *New York Journal American*, p. 24.
O'Brian, J. (1971, May 17). On Broadway. *News Journal* (Mansfield, OH), p. 25.
O'Brian, J. (1973, October 19). Voice of Broadway. *The Daily Bulletin* (Anderson, IN), p. 5.
Ochoa, S. (2014). *Stella! Mother of modern acting.* Milwaukee, WI: Author.
Oppenheimer, P.J. (1969, August 31). The not-so-happy life of Bob Crane. *Family Weekly*, p. 43.
Otnes, M. (2001). *The final interview with beloved actor/singer and educator Larry Hovis; best remembered as 'Sergeant Carter' from TV's 'Hogan's Heroes.'* Retrieved from http://patchesofpride.wordpress.com/2013/07/30/the-final-interview-with-beloved-actorsinger-and-educator-larry-hovis-best-remembered-as-sergeant-carter-from-tvs-hogans-heroes/
Owens, D.L. (1965). Bob Crane happy with hero's role. *Daily News*.
Page, D. (1963, December 8). The radio beat: The sun also rises. *Los Angeles Times*, p. B30.
Page, D. (1965, June 13). The radio beat: Farewell (sob!) to Bob Crane. *Los Angeles Times*, p. N38.
Parker, C. (1966, May 17). Charles Parker's television pictures. *Evening Outlook*, p. 21.
Parker, C. (1977, September 29). Emmy Awards follow Ali fight tonight. *Valley News*, p. 7.
Paul, Jr., J. (1965, May 31). Prediction for viewers. *Star Free Press* (Ventura City, CA).
Pearson, R. (1965, August 20). Three new comedies. *Desert News*, p. 4B.
Peterson, B. (1965). New one for Donna's 'Dave' (and a few parting shots). *The Detroit Press*.
Petoskey, T. (1975). Bob Crane reminisces old days of Stalag 13. *VN Entertainment*.
Phillips, S. (2003). *'Stu who?' Forty years of navigating the minefields of the music business.* Studio City, CA: Author.
Pullen, G.C. (1969, June 8). Hogan's hero has eye on future. *Plain Dealer*.
Quallich, S.A. (2014). A historical perspective on the male sexual case history. *Urologic Nursing, 34*(4), 187-192.
Quarm, J. (1972, May 12). Two of 'Hogan's Heroes' make Marquee comedy among the funniest. *El Paso Herald-Post* (El Paso, TX), p. 20.

R.A. [No full name given.] (1969, February 9). Hogan's a hero at home, too. *Seattle Post-Intelligencer,* pp. 50-51.

Raddatz, L. (1966, November 27). World War II with a Laugh Track: With an improbable premise and an unlikely star, 'Hogan's Heroes' is marching to TV popularity. *TV Guide,* pp. 22-24.

Randall, B. (1973). *6 rms riv vu: A comedy in two acts.* New York, NY: Author.

Rhiner, K. (1965). 'Hogan's Heroes' will debut from German POW camp. *San Diego Tribune.*

Rich, A. (1965, August 9). "Bob Crane, KNX radio's talented morning man…" *Citizen News,* p. B-12.

Rich, A. (1965, September 8). "If laughter doesn't ring out…" *Citizen News,* p. D-10.

Rich, A. (1965, September 17). "Tonight is the night that the networks' policy…"

Rich, A. (1965, September 21). "Hogan's Heroes Friday nights…" *Citizen News,* p. A8.

Rich, A. (1965, September 30). "It is expected that the National Academy of Television Arts and Sciences…"

Rich, A. (1965, October 6). "A visitor to Gene Autry's…" *Citizen News,* p. B12.

Robbins, R. (1966). Tape to type. Fred Robbins interviews Bob Crane. *Photoplay, 70*(2), 14.

Roberts, E. (1965). After week of debuts. *Boston Traveler.*

Ronnie, A. (1965, June 5). Bob Crane leaves radio for TV prison. *Los Angeles Herald Examiner,* C-4.

Royce, B.S. (1993). *Hogan's Heroes: A comprehensive reference to the 1965-1971 television comedy series, with cast biographies and an episode guide.* Jefferson, NC: Author.

Royce, B.S. (1998). *Hogan's Heroes: Behind the scenes at Stalag 13!* Jefferson, NC: Author.

Royce, B.S. (n.d.). *Hogan's Heroes episode guide.* Los Angeles: Author.

Ruddy, A.S., & Fein, B. (1964, December 22). The informer (1st draft). *The Heroes.*

Russell, F.H. (1957, December 12). Crane on record. *The Bridgeport Post,* p. 38.

Salerno, A. (1965, December 10). Politics makes staunch TV fellows. *New York World Telegram and Sun.*

Saunders, W. (1965). Laughs from a prisoner of war camp? That's what 'Hogan's Heroes' is seeking.

Schlaerth, D. (1965). Finding fun in PW camp. *Buffalo Evening News.*

Schull, R.K. (n.d.). He flew to fame on a fly. *Indianapolis Times.*

Scott, B. (1965, December 18). 'Hogan's Heroes' star lives good, plush life off screen. *Chronicle Telegram* (Elyria, OH), p. 12.

Scott, V. (1965, October 25). Life can be funny in POW camp. *The San Bernardino County Sun* (San Bernardino, CA), p. 18.

Scott, V. (1965, December 18). Bob Crane gave up $75,000 a year as disk jockey; now doing better. *The Dispatch,* p. 3.

Scott, V. (1966, April 30). Television in review. *New Castle News,* p. 17.

Scott, V. (1966, December 3). 'Hogan's Heroes' accurately cast. *Simpson's Leader-Times,* p. 18.

Scott, V. (1967, February 23). Bob Crane: A successful throwback. *The Kokomo Morning Times,* p. 13.

Scott, V. (1967, February 27). Bob Crane is moving to big movie screen. *Great Bend Tribune,* p. 6.

Scott, V. (1967, March 1). TV muddles progression for comics. *Kingsport Times* (Kingsport, TN), p. 18.

Scott, V. (1967, March 31). [Elke] shines as track ace. *The Odessa American,* p. 5-B.

Scott, V. (1967, June 19). Larry Hovis likes backyards better than nightclubs. *The Daily Herald* (Provo, UT), p. 20.
Scott, V. (1967, July 8). Blonde beauty enjoys 'Hogan's Heroes' role. *Leader-Times*, pp. 1-2.
Scott, V. (1971, March 12). 'Hogan's Heroes' taking their show to Las Vegas. *The Brownsville Herald*, p. 2.
Scott, V. (1971, March 13). 'Hogan's Heroes' leave Stalag 13 for Vegas stage. *Seattle Post-Intelligencer*, p. 22.
Scott, V. (1972, February 12). Larry Hovis lives on bread, meat. *The Times* (San Mateo, CA), p. 43.
Scott, V. (1972, November 27). Bob Crane is left with percentage bag; series in red. *Denton Record Chronicle*, p. 11.
Scott, V. (1975, April 2). Crane Show 'poser.' *The Times Recorder* (Zanesville, OH), p. 8-A.
Scott, V. (1975, April 25). Crane bounces back into new comedy role. *Denton Record Chronicle*, p. 35.
Scott, V. (1975, May 25). Bob Crane's lifestyle same with new wife, baby, show. *The Bridgeport Post*, p. 13.
Scott, V., & DuBrow, R. (1966, April 30). Television in review. *New Castle News*, p. 17.
Shaw, J. (1969). Bob Crane: The "perfect" marriage that cracked apart at the seams. *TV Radio Mirror, 69*(9), 74, 95-96.
Shayon, R.L. (1965). TV and radio: The history game. *Saturday Review Magazine*.
Shervey, B.C. (2000). *The Little Theatre on the Square: Four decades of a small-town equity theatre*. Carbondale, IL: Board of Trustees Southern Illinois University.
Sisul, J. (1969, October). Bob Crane's wife's bitter cry - "I thought my husband was different!" *TV Radio Show, 4*(1), 32-33, 58-60.
Smith, B. (1965, September 18). Friday night shows. *Chicago Daily News*.
Stamford High School. (1944). *Spirit of '44: Class of 1944 yearbook*. Stamford, CT: Author.
Stamford High School. (1945). *Spirit of '45: Class of 1945 yearbook*. Stamford, CT: Author.
Stamford High School. (1946). *Spirit of '46: Class of 1946 yearbook*. Stamford, CT: Author.
Stamford High School. (1946, April 18). Interesting personalities. *The Siren*, p. 1.
Stang, J. (1965, October 31). Con man to the Wehrmacht. *New York Times*.
Stang, J. (1965, November 7). A dream show without a dream. *San Diego Union*.
Starr, E. (1965, August 5). Inside television. *Pottstown Mercury*, p. 4.
Stars, T. (1966). God spoke to us: Bob Crane. *TV Radio Mirror, 66*(5), 52-55, 78-82.
Steger, P. (1976). "A Hogan junkie who never remembers a repeat show."
Stone, L. (1973, September 22). Celebrity spotlight: Breakfast with Bob. *News Record*, p. 37.
Sylos, M. (1963, February 28). Mad chatter. *Valley News* (Van Nuys, CA), p. 24-A.
Syse, G. (1970, March 27). 'Luck' was poor, audience wasn't. *Chicago Sun Times*, p. 33.
Television Obscurities. (2013). *The Fall 1974 that wasn't*. Retrieved from http://www.tvobscurities.com/articles/fall_1974_that_wasnt/
Terry, P. (1966). 'Hogan's' hero Bob Crane confesses all! 'I struck out on my honeymoon.' *TV Radio Mirror, 65*(3), 42-45, 88-90.
Texas Wesleyan College. (1974). *Texas Wesleyan College 1974 yearbook* (p. 16). Fort Worth, TX: Author.
Thackrey, Jr., T. (1978, June 30). Actor Bob Crane found beaten to death. *Los Angeles Times*, p. SD-A1.

Thomas, B. (1964, February 1). Bob Crane has radio, movie and TV jobs, specializes in wackiness. *The Bee* (Danville, VA), p. 13.
Thomas, B. (1964, February 1). Bob Crane is kept busy by comedy roles. *Corsicana Daily Sun,* p. 10.
Thomas, B. (1964, February 3). Bob Crane is an active man. *Daytona Beach Morning Journal,* p. 13.
Thomas, B. (1965, November 27). Bob Crane fulfilling own vision of TV destiny. *Reading Eagle,* p. 8.
Thomas, B. (1965, November 27). Bob Crane likes role in 'Heroes.' *Indiana Evening Gazette,* p. 7.
Thomas, B. (1965, December 23). Donna Reed feels just like college graduation. *Indiana Evening Gazette,* p. 7.
Thomas, B. (1968, July 17). 'Hogan's Heroes' conquer monumental problem. *Reno Evening Gazette,* p. 36.
Thomas, B. (1968, July 23). Hogan's Heroes survives the test. *The Ogden-Standard Examiner,* p. 13.
Thomas, B. (1977, June 25). Blacks soon can identify with WWII. *The San Bernardino County Sun,* p. 10.
Thompson, R. (1968, May 14). 'Hogan's Heroes' – An acting triumph for Bob Crane. *Gettysburg Times.*
Thornhill, B. (1965, August 25). Bob Crane finds a new life in 'Stalag 13.' *The Macon News,* p. 17.
Tusher, W. (1978). The story behind the whispers that sex was the bait in his death trap: Who really murdered Bob Crane? *Photoplay, 92*(9), 48-51, 66, 68.
TV Scout. (1972, March 6). "Best bet – Don't miss 'The Delphi Bureau'..." *Odessa American,* p. 5-B.
Twyford, W. (1965). A happy hero is Hogan.
Vernon, T. (1965, February 11). Tele-vues. *The Independent* (Long Beach, CA). p. 44.
Vernon, T. (1966, June 10). Tele-vues. *The Independent* (Long Beach, CA), p. D-1.
Vernon, T. (1966, December 2). Tele-vues. *The Independent* (Long Beach, CA), p. C-4.
Vote For Bob Crane. (n.d.). *Home page.* Retrieved from www.vote4bobcrane.org
Vowell, D. (1957, October 5). What's so funny? Well, mostly it's the commercials, which really become a laughing matter when presented by KNX Radio's early morning man, Bob Crane. *TV Radio Life,* p. 50.
Walsh, D. (1965, September 5). You, me and TV. *Sunday Herald.*
Waterbury, R. (1966). Eva Gabor: 'I wanted to meet Bob Crane.' *TV Radio Mirror, 66*(1), 30-33, 75-77.
Waterbury, R. (1966). My big mouth gets me in trouble. *Modern Screen, 60*(10), 36-37, 86, 88-90.
Whitney, D. (1966, January 22). His podium is a prison camp: Werner Klemperer, son of the conductor, finds himself in a comedy hit but still wonders about the concert hall. *TV Guide,* pp. 22-25.
WICC. (1985). *WICC Annual Report: 1984-1985.* Bridgeport, CT: Author.
Williams, K. (1977, November 29). Bob Crane excels in 'Beginner's Luck.' *The Journal News* (Hamilton & Fairfield, OH), p. 19.
Williamson, C. (1971, October 6). Hogan's Heroes rate a 'superb.' *Alton Evening Telegraph* (Alton, IL), p. 8.
Wilson, E. (1970, February 24). It happened...last night. *The Times-Reporter,* p. B-5.
Wilson, E. (1970, October 28). Maybe they never had marriage proposed. *The Galveston Daily News* (Galveston, TX), p. 17.
Wilson, W. (1968, January 25). Capsule reviews of current movies. *Van Nuys News,* p. 36-B.

Witbeck, C. (1964, August 26). Donna's doctor's head and image trimmed. *The Evening Independent,* p. 6-B.
Witbeck, C. (1965, July 12). Set in World War II prison camp, new comedy reaches deep. *News-Journal,* p. 14.
Witbeck, C. (1971, June 16). 2 of 'Hogan's Heroes' move to 'Laugh-In.' *News-Journal* (Mansfield, OH), p. 12.
Witbeck, C. (1975, February 28). Bob Crane hoisting a new series. *The Daily Reporter* (Dover, OH), p. 27.
Wolfe, M. (1966). Bob Crane: Our 16 years have been heaven…but for 1 year it was hell! *TV Picture Life, 11*(3), 46-47, 69-70, 72.
Wright, S. (2015). *Initial airing of Jim French shows on Seattle Radio: 1965-present.* Retrieved from http://www.old-time.com/otrlogs2/jimfrench_sw.log.pdf

Audio

Crane, B. (1962). *Unpublished audio letter to cousin Jim Senich.*
Crane, B. (1963). *Unpublished presentation to LA College broadcasting students.*
Crane, B. (1976). *Unpublished audio compilations to friend Charlie Zito.*
Crane, B., for KAYO Radio. (1977, January). *Bob Crane guest host* [aircheck]. Seattle, WA: Author.
Crane, B., for KMPC Radio. (1972, July 5). *The Bob Crane Show* [aircheck]. Los Angeles, CA: Author.
Crane, B., for KMPC Radio. (1972, September 15). *The Bob Crane Show* [aircheck]. Los Angeles, CA: Author.
Crane, B., for KMPC Radio. (1972, November 23). *The Bob Crane Show* [aircheck]. Los Angeles, CA: Author.
Crane, B., for KMPC Radio. (1972, December 31). *The Bob Crane Show* [aircheck]. Los Angeles, CA: Author.
Crane, B., for KMPC Radio. (1973, April 13). *The Bob Crane Show* [aircheck]. Los Angeles, CA: Author.
Crane, B., for KNX-CBS Radio. (1957, March 27). *The Bob Crane Show* [aircheck]. Hollywood, CA: Author.
Crane, B., for KNX-CBS Radio. (1957, November 13). *The Bob Crane Show* [aircheck]. Hollywood, CA: Author.
Crane, B., for KNX-CBS Radio. (1960). *The effervescent humor of KNX-trovert Bob Crane.* Hollywood, CA: Author.
Crane, B., for KNX-CBS Radio. (1960, February 24). *The Bob Crane Show* [aircheck].. Hollywood, CA: Author.
Crane, B., for KNX-CBS Radio. (1961, June 6). *The Bob Crane Show* [aircheck]. Hollywood, CA: Author.
Crane, B., for KNX-CBS Radio. (1961, December 11). *The Bob Crane Show* [aircheck]. Hollywood, CA: Author.
Crane, B., for KNX-CBS Radio. (1962). *Lafftter, sweet and profane: Bob Crane* [plus liner notes]. Hollywood, CA: Author.
Crane, B., for KNX-CBS Radio. (1962, March 9). *The Bob Crane Show* [aircheck]. Hollywood, CA: Author.
Crane, B., for KNX-CBS Radio. (1962, April). *The Bob Crane Show* [aircheck]. Hollywood, CA: Author.
Crane, B., for KNX-CBS Radio. (1964, January 1). *The Bob Crane Show* [aircheck]. Hollywood, CA: Author.
Crane, B., for KNX-CBS Radio. (1964, May 22). *The Bob Crane Show: 8th anniversary special.* Hollywood, CA: Author.

Crane, B., for KNX-CBS Radio. (1964, December 11). *The Bob Crane Show* [aircheck]. Hollywood, CA: Author.
Crane, B., for the United States Armed Forces Radio Network. (1968, July). *Bob Crane, host; Ruth Waterbury and Cecil Barker, guests; various performers*. Los Angeles, CA: United States Armed Forces Radio Network.
Crane, B., for WICC Radio. (1976, January 29). *Bob Crane guest – WICC's 50th anniversary special*. Bridgeport, CT: Author.
Crane, B., for WICC-600 AM. (1976, January 29). *WICC 50th anniversary show*. Bridgeport, CT: Author.
Epic Records. (1966). *Bob Crane, his drums and orchestra play the funny side of TV*. Santa Monica, CA: Author.
McMann, S. (1970). *Bob Crane interview from 1971* [incorrect date: actual year of interview is 1970]. Retrieved from https://www.youtube.com/watch?v=ohFWIbovqw8
Radio Kidnappers. (2012). *Radio Kidnappers presents: The Bob Crane show*. Napier, New Zealand: Author.
Robertson, E. (2013, November). *Interview with Karen Crane*. Los Angeles, CA: TV Confidential.
WCFL Radio. (1972). *Bob Crane – Local radio interview – August 4, 1972*. Retrieved from https://www.youtube.com/watch?v=gkocHRV6fCY

Video

A&E Network. (1999). *Cold Case Files: The Bob Crane Murder* [pilot episode]. New York, NY: Author.
A&E Network. (2000). *A&E Biography: Bob Crane. A Double Life*. New York, NY: Author.
CBS/Rysher Entertainment. (1965-1971). *Hogan's Heroes: Kommandant's Kollection* (seasons 1-6). [Interviews with Patricia Olson Crane, Richard Dawson.] Santa Monica, CA: Author.
Connecticut Public Broadcasting Network. (2012). *You're on the Air! The Early Years of Connecticut Television*. Hartford, CT: Author.
Crime and Investigation Network. (2000). *Murder in Scottsdale: The Death of Bob Crane*. New York, NY: A&E Networks. Retrieved from https://www.youtube.com/watch?v=YKsOtIBdvEk
NBCUniversal. (1998). *E! True Hollywood Story: Bob Crane*. New York, NY: Author.
Reelin' in the Years Productions/The Griffin Group. (1966, January 10). *The Merv Griffin Show: Bob Crane, guest*. El Cajon, CA: The Griffin Group.

Index

Note: Page numbers followed by f indicate figures.

A

Abroms, Edward, 398
Ackerman, Harry, 172
Acting career, 147–183. *See also Hogan's Heroes;* Television shows; Theatre performances
 and Stella Adler acting course, 178–180, 181–182
 adlibbed skit with Jonathan Winters on, 158–160
 on *The Alfred Hitchcock Hour,* 163
 on Channel 43, 150
 in community theatre, 153–156, 157, 167, 184f
 desire to start, 147, 150–152
 on *The Dick Van Dyke Show,* 168–169
 on *The Donna Reed Show,* 148f, 169–178, 183
 on *General Electric Theatre,* 163
 in high school, 149–150
 and KNX contract, 156–157, 161–162
 parts as DJ in, 161, 162
 in *Picture Window* pilot, 157–161
 in promo of *Superfun,* 161
 on *Return to Peyton Place,* 162–163
 and talk show circuit, 163–166
 on *The Twilight Zone,* 161
Adams, Don, 256, 328
Addiction. *See also* Sex addiction
 in 1970s, 373
 breakdown due to, 545
 breaking process of, 551
 defined, 517, 521–522, 581
 delusion system of, 537
 early warning signs of, 531
 escalating cycle of, 582
 foundations of, 521
 hallmarks of, 577
 and manipulation, 543
 pain of, 531
 shame and emotional withdrawal due to, 526, 576, 580
 susceptibility to, 521

Addictive personality, 517–522
The Addictive Personality (Nakken), 517, 521–522, 525–526, 531, 537, 543, 545, 551
Addrisi, Don, 124
Addrisi, Richard (Dick), 7, 124
The Addrisi Brothers, 124
Adler, Stella
 Bob's acting course with, 15, 178–180, 181–182, 534
 and *The Love Boat,* 429
 Patty's acting classes with, 347
Adler Drum Studio, 40
Adopted daughter, 375
Advertisers
 on "The Bob Crane Show" (KNX-CBS Radio), 111–112, 114–115, 119, 121–122
 poking fun at, 65, 66–67, 68
Album collection, 378–379, 519
Alcohol, 334, 342
Alda, Alan, 385, 412
Alexander, Dick, 84–85, 91
The Alfred Hitchcock Hour (TV show), 163
Alimony
 for Anne, 354–355, 389
 for Patty, 471
Allen, Steve, 164, 165, 223
All in the Family (TV show), 374
Amendole, John, 475
Amsterdam, Morey, 169, 312
Angie the Antenna Man, 89–90, 102f
Archivist, Bob as, 520–521
Arsenic and Old Lace (film), 302–304
Arthritis Foundation Telethons, 312
Arthur, Maureen, 5, 295, 298, 595
Artistic control on "The Bob Crane Show" (KNX-CBS Radio), 109–111
Art Linkletter's House Party (TV show), 393–394
Askin, Leon, 200, 263f, 295, 297
Asner, Ed, 392
Astaire, Fred, 209, 414
Astin, John, 378
Ateyeh, George Gilbert, 347
Ateyeh, Melissa (Mitsu, Mits), 347, 375
Attention and sex addiction, 581–582

627

Aubrey, James (Jim), 202–203
Audio tape recording, 379–380, 519, 520
Auto Focus (film), 243, 437, 595

B

Backus, Jim, 328
Baer, Arthur "Bugs," 78
Bailey, Jack, 152, 312
Ball, Lucille, 211
Banner, John
    on *Bob Crane, His Drums and Orchestra Play the Funny Side of TV* (album), 292
    and camaraderie, 237
    cancellation letter to, 258, 274
    casting of, 195–196, 200, 203
    cast photos of, 188f, 263f, 266f, 268f
    death of, 248, 385
    declining health of, 384–385
    and *"Hogan's Heroes" Revue,* 366
    Jerry London on, 241
    muffing lines by, 228
    nickname for, 244
    on promotional tours, 208–210, 269f, 271f
    and sex addiction, 540
    tension between Werner and, 247
    on *The Wicked Dreams of Paula Schultz* (film), 295
    working with, 251
Barasch, Norman, 508f, 509f
    Beginner's Luck written by, 473–476
    and Bob's known performances of *Beginner's Luck,* 461
    and Bob's revisions, 478
    production rights secured from, 389, 477
    Send Me No Flowers by, 465–466
Barney Miller (TV show), 412
Barnum, P.T., 78, 93–94
Barnum Festival, 93–94
Barrett, Rona, 357–358
Beck, Edward L. (Ed)
    on Bob's character, 513
    as Bob's counselor, 17, 551, 552–553
    on impact of Bob's death, 505–506
    professional background and credentials of, 554–555
    remembrance by, 8
    testimony provided by, 556–573
Beck, Marilyn, 405
Bedtime Story (film), 337–338
Beginner's Luck (play), 473–491
    agent insisting on commission for, 389–390
    Victoria Ann Berry on, 484–490
    cast photos of, 458f, 493–495f
    directing of, 460, 464, 476–477, 483, 486–487
    and divorce papers from Patty, 423, 471, 489
    as feature film, 477
    and filling in for Frank Sutton, 490–491, 494f
    first run of, 476–478
    and insistence on live audience for *Second Start,* 406
    interaction with audience after, 479
    known performances of, 460, 461–463
    plot of, 473–476
    predictions and reviews of, 459, 460, 463–465, 469
    preparation for performances of, 460, 473
    pride in, 473
    prop placement for, 496f
    and radio appearances, 418–420
    and relationship of John and Pam Thompson, 384, 479–480
    rewriting and restructuring of, 477, 478–479, 497f
    second run of, 477
    securing rights to, 477
    sex addiction during, 548–549
    John Thompson on, 388–389, 389–390, 458f, 478–479, 480–482
    Pam Thompson on, 389, 458f, 477–478, 479, 480, 481
    writers of, 473–476
Belltown Braves, 36
Belltown Commandos, 36
Benny, Jack, 215, 406
Berle, Milton, 406
Berman, Shelley, 128, 131–133, 163, 209
Bernstein, Tom, 109–110, 111, 119, 594
Berry, Victoria Ann, 484–490, 546
The Best of Times (song), 395
Betz, Carl, 176

Bevan, Donald, 215
Beverly Hills house, 389–390
Biggers, Buck, 410
Bilko (TV show), 224
Bilson, Bruce
    on cancellation of *Hogan's Heroes*, 257
    cast photo with, 266f
    on communality, 237
    on Ivan Dixon's departure from show, 256
    on Edward Feldman, 237
    on Forty Acres, 221, 227
    on funny moments during filming, 244
    on legacy of Bob Crane, 591
    on POW camp, 221
    on props, 225
    remembrance by, 6
    on sex addiction, 540–541
    on shaping characters, 232
    on tensions between actors, 247
    on working with Bob Crane, 243, 250, 252
Bing Crosby Productions, 204, 207, 215, 354, 357–358, 388
Bisa, Anna, 336
Bissette, David C., 581–582
Blackman, A. Lee, 472
Blaine, Hal, 291
Blanc, Mel, 113–114, 161
Blinn, Johna, 330, 334
Bob and Ray, 152
Bob Crane, His Drums and Orchestra Play the Funny Side of TV (album), 287–293, 314f
"The Bob Crane Show" (KMPC Radio), 414–418
"The Bob Crane Show" (KNX-CBS Radio), 105–135
    advertisers on, 111–112, 114–115, 119, 121–122
    artistic control on, 109–111
    and Sonny Bono, 125–128
    career growth on, 130–135
    contract for, 156–157, 161–162
    and *The Donna Reed Show*, 175
    drumming on, 115, 137f
    and *Hogan's Heroes*, 205–207
    innovations at, 124
    live celebrity interviews on, 123, 126–127, 128, 136f, 144f
    music on, 119–120, 124
    news on, 121
    personal appearances and charity events on, 112–114
    photos of, 106f, 143–145f
    prep work for, 120–121
    and private family life, 123–124, 128–130
    professional adversary of, 125
    promotional albums for, 138–139
    promotional campaign for, 142f
    promotional flyer for, 105
    seamless program of, 114
    self-deprecating humor on, 131–133
    "Send Dead Flies" gimmick on, 117–118
    sense of humor on, 125–128
    sex addiction while working at, 531–537
    start of, 107–112
    studio of, 119
    turntables at, 111
    voice impersonations on, 115–116
"The Bob Crane Show" (WICC), 84–86, 92
The Bob Crane Show (TV show), 399–401, 407–413, 546
Bodge, David, 420, 456f
Bogart, Humphrey, 224
Bono, Sonny, 125–128
Boone, Pat, 136f, 137
Braeden, Eric, 357, 382
Brando, Lisa, 338
Brando, Marlon, 179, 200, 337–338
Bridgeport, Conn., 78, 83
Bridgeport Symphony Orchestra, 41
Brooks, Dinah, 312
Brooks, Mel, 115, 219
Brown, James Harvey, 359
Brown, Ted, 96
Burdick Junior High School (Stamford, Conn.), 29
Burrows, Abe, 465
Butler, Robert
    on controversy over prison camp plot, 224
    on Bob Crane, 240
    on Crane-Dawson rivalry, 246–247
    on Edward Feldman, 237–239
    on Leonid Kinskey, 203
    on legacy of Bob Crane, 590
    and Jerry London, 194
    on male communality, 212, 236

on persona of actor and character, 230–231
on pilot, 201–202
on romance, 227
on working with Bob on set, 232
Butterfield, Bobby, 91

C

Cactus Flower (play)
cast photos from, 492f
and divorce from Anne, 351, 354
Patty acting in, 349, 355, 470
production details for, 465
Caine, Howard, 200
Caine, Michael, 235
Campo 44 (TV show), 214–215
Camp Pendleton, Calif., 320f
Can You Top This (TV show), 391
Capra, Frank, 303
"Captain Traffic" (WICC), 89
Car(s), 382
Caricature, 26f, 31
Carpenter, John Henry, 18, 499, 502–503, 520, 549, 568
Carroll, Victoria, 233, 247, 251, 336, 429, 590
Carson, Johnny
and Cindy Lee, 337
hard comedy of, 406
as host of *Tonight Show,* 163
interviewing, 128
off-camera personality of, 235, 558
subbing for, 166, 391
on *Who Do You Trust?,* 166
Casey, Larry, 328
Casillo, Aniello, 42
Catholic Church. *See* Roman Catholicism
Catino, Teddy, 51
Cedar, Jon, 200, 234–235, 245–246, 595
Celebrity, 279–321
and *Arsenic and Old Lace* (film), 302–304
and charity, 307–313, 316–321f
and desire for more challenges, 305–306
and fan mail, 283
hometown friends on, 282–283
patience and, 281
and record of television themes, 287–293, 314f

Jim Senich on, 283–284
and television guest appearances, 293–294, 296–297, 315f
and *The Wicked Dreams of Paula Schultz* (film), 294–302
Celebrity Cooks (TV show), 429–430, 433–448, 455f
Celebrity interviews on "The Bob Crane Show" (KNX-CBS Radio), 123, 126–127, 128, 136f, 144f
Channel 43 (television station), 88–91, 102f, 103f
Chaplin, Charlie, 219
Chapman, Jack, 119, 141f, 145f
Charisma
on *Celebrity Cooks,* 445, 446
Jack Coombe on, 593–594
and drumming, 33–34
in high school, 22
on *Hogan's Heroes,* 230–231, 234, 251
Rick Plastina on, 7, 468
sex addiction and, 560, 575
Pam Thompson on, 479
at WICC, 87–88
Charity events on "The Bob Crane Show" (KNX-CBS Radio), 112–114
Charity work, 307–313, 316–321f
Charles, Larry, 220
Charles, Ray, 289
Chatham Oaks, 60
Cherrystone (record), 124
Chicken rating new records (stunt), 82, 85, 86, 102f
Child, Julia, 430
Childhood of Bob Crane, 27–47
early moves during, 27–29
friends during, 34–35
meeting of Anne Terzian during, 36–38
nickname during, 34
Children
child support for, 354, 355, 375, 389, 471
devotion to, 331, 332, 353, 380–381, 503, 561
and divorce, 325, 339, 352, 354–355, 355–356, 516
from first marriage, 375, 382, 482–483
photos of, 12f, 13f, 363f, 370f, 449f, 450f, 500f
protectiveness of, 283–284

Index

and sex addiction, 561, 564, 566–567
spending time with, 129–130
Child support
for Anne, 354–355, 355–356, 375, 389
for Patty, 471
Chipman, Jerry, 309, 316f, 317f
Chrysanthemum Festival (Bristol, Conn.), 311–312, 319f
Cigarette smoking, 334, 342
Clary, Robert
album by, 292
background of, 197, 220
on John Banner, 196
cancellation letter to, 258, 274, 387
casting of, 197, 200, 203
cast photos of, 188f, 264f, 266f, 268f, 273f
on drumming, 242
on Edward Feldman, 237
at first outdoor shoot, 214
and *"Hogan's Heroes" Revue*, 366
on learning of Bob Crane's death, 509
on male communality, 236, 241
in military films, 310
nickname for, 244
on politics, 245
popularity of, 219
on POW camp vs. concentration camp, 220–221
on promotion of *Hogan's Heroes*, 210
remembrance by, 7
singing by, 287
working with, 253
"Class A" time, 121
The Classic Cat (topless bar), 484
Cleary, Richard, 154, 466
Cobb, Lee J., 347
Coburn, James, 347
Cody, Kathleen (Kathy), 392, 395, 397
Cohan, Martin (Marty), 401–402, 409, 410
Cold War, 373–374
Cole, Cozy, 22, 40
Cole, Nat, 90
Coleman, Ronald, 90
Collector, Bob as, 520
Collins, Dorothy, 294
Colonari, Ray, 420, 456f

Commercials on "The Bob Crane Show" (KNX-CBS Radio), 112, 114–115, 119, 121–122
Community service at WICC, 93
Community theatre, 153–156, 157, 167, 184f
Como, Perry, 125, 388
Concentration camp vs. prisoner of war camp, 219, 220–221, 223
Connecticut Symphony Orchestra, 41, 87
Connolly, Mike, 209
Conrad, Robert, 347
Control, 518–521, 561, 563
Conway, Tim, 130, 392
Coombe, Jack, 88, 94, 282, 593–594
Cooper, Gary, 235
Cooper, Jackie, 400, 402, 412
Coppola, Francis Ford, 390
Cordic, Rege, 204, 209
Correspondence, archiving of, 519
Cosgrove, Joe
on Bob at KNX, 108, 112
on death of Bob Crane, 509
on legacy of Bob Crane, 583, 593
on move to California, 129, 135
remembrance by, 3
The Courtship of Eddie's Father (TV show), 162
Cowlicks, 249
Crane, Alfred John (Al Jr.) (brother)
as alcoholic, 520
during childhood, 30, 32, 34
financial help to, 393
move to California, 192
photographs of, 10f, 49f, 50f
during World War II, 44–45, 191–192
Crane, Alfred Thomas (Al Sr.) (father)
background of, 29–30
death of, 422
on first radio job, 62–64
marriage of, 30
move to California, 284
on offer to inherit jewelry store, 59
personality of, 32
photographs of, 10f, 49f, 50f
and Scotty, 376, 378
and sex addiction, 522–523, 524
work of, 31
during World War II, 44
Crane, Ana Marie, 375

631

Crane, Anne Margit Terzian
   and acting career, 150–151
   alimony and child support to, 354–355, 355–356, 389
   and Bob's affair with Cindy Lynn, 341, 343
   Bob's devotion to, 514, 516
   on Bob's popularity with women, 330–331, 335
   and Bob's work on set with women, 335
   and *Cactus Flower,* 349, 355
   Cindy Lynn on, 341, 539–540
   divorce from, 259, 325, 351–356, 353–356, 360–361
   and early radio career, 56
   in family photographs, 362f, 363f
   as Hollywood "widow," 328, 330–331
   illness of, 325–328
   on Karen's shyness, 332–333
   marriage to Bob of, 59–61, 71f
   and Patty Olson, 349, 352
   pets with, 380
   photographs of Bob with, 12f, 324f, 362f, 364f
   restraining order by, 354
   second marriage of, 361, 375
   sex addiction during marriage to, 513–516, 527–530, 544
   supporting parents after marriage, 65, 68
   as teenager, 37–38, 52f, 523, 524–525
   transition to Los Angeles, 128–129
   travel to Sweden, 62
Crane, Deborah Ann (Debbie), 12f, 129, 154, 329, 332, 361, 363f, 364f
Crane, Karen Leslie
   and Anne's second husband, 361
   birth of, 129
   on Bob's devotion to Anne, 516
   childhood photographs, 12f, 363f, 364f, 449f
   and Cindy Lynn, 343
   on Richard Dawson, 248
   graduation from high school, 501f
   on learning of Bob Crane's death, 505
   on legacy of Bob Crane, 597
   on *The Love Boat,* 428
   on parents' divorce, 350–351
   on sex addiction, 547
   shyness of, 329, 332–333
   on *Superdad* (film), 395
Crane, Patricia (Patty) Olson
   affair with, 258–259, 350–357, 365f, 514, 540
   attempted reconciliation with, 516
   and Beverly Hills house, 389–390
   birth of Scott to, 361, 370f, 482
   on *Bob Crane, His Drums and Orchestra Play the Funny Side of TV* (album), 292
   Bob's devotion to, 516
   Bob's proposal to, 356–357
   in *Cactus Flower,* 470, 492f
   in cast photos, 13f, 266f, 324f, 365f
   and children from first marriage, 482–483
   and Anne Crane, 349, 352
   early acting career of, 347, 365f
   early life of, 346
   education of, 347
   and embezzlement by Lloyd Vaughan, 472
   first marriage of, 347
   as Fräulein Hilda, 254–255, 348–349
   guest appearance on season one of *Hogan's Heroes* by, 347
   hair color and wig of, 348–349, 358–359
   handling of finances by, 382–383
   hiring of, 347
   as homemaker, 382–383, 470
   honeymoon with, 359
   impending divorce from, 423, 471, 489
   last visit by, 500f
   love letters to, 358
   marriage to, 259, 324f, 357–359, 361, 366–368f
   pets with, 369f, 380
   photographed at home with Bob, 368–370f, 450f
   reactions of Bob's friends and family to, 376–377
   sex addiction during marriage to, 516–517, 544, 548–549, 561–562
   and visit to topless bar, 484
   wardrobe of, 348
   Westwood home with, 378–379, 380, 381, 382

Crane, Robert David (Bobby, Jr.)
    and Anne's second husband, 361
    birth of, 83
    childhood photographs of, 12f, 363f
    help getting into industry for, 393–394
    on KMPC, 418
    on KNX, 129, 329
    in Little League, 97–98, 129–130
    move to California, 83–87
    on-set at *Hogan's Heroes,* 393–394
    on set of *The Hawaii Experience,* 424, 550
Crane, Robert Edward (Bob)
    affair with Cynthia Lynn, 258–259, 336–346, 359–360, 514, 539–540
    affair with Patty, 258–259, 350–357, 365f, 514, 540
    and Anne's illness, 325–328
    in *Beginner's Luck,* 473–491
    birth of, 30
    caricature of, 26f, 31
    celebrity of, 279–321
    childhood of, 27–47
    children and stepchildren of, 375
    death of, 502–509
    dinner theatre by, 470–472, 568–569
    divorce from Anne, 259, 325, 351–356, 353–356, 360–361
    early acting career of, 147–183
    enlistment in National Guard by, 59–60
    extended family of, 31–32
    on first vs. second marriage, 377–378
    high school graduation of, 26f, 41, 45–46
    on *Hogan's Heroes,* 187–277
    at KNX-CBS Radio (Los Angeles), 107–135, 136–145f
    last interview with, 585–586
    legacy of, 583–600
    marriage to Anne of, 59–61, 71f
    marriage to Patty, 259, 324f, 357–359, 361, 366–368f
    during 1970s, 371–456, 457–509
    not taken seriously as actor, 163, 167, 178, 180, 254, 394–399, 460
    parents of, 29–31
    relationship and family life with Anne, 328–335
    remembrances of, 3–8
    sex addiction of, 511–582
    start in radio by, 61–70
    at WLIZ/WICC (Connecticut), 69–70, 77–99
Crane, Robert Scott (Scott, Scotty)
    birth of, 259, 361, 370f
    on Bob as workaholic, 120, 520
    Bob Crane as biological father of, 482
    on Bob helping others, 394
    on Bob's devotion to Patty, 516
    and Bob's parents, 376, 378
    childhood memories of, 380–382
    childhood photographs of, 13f, 449f, 450f
    on Richard Dawson, 248
    on death of grandfather, 422
    on fans, 545–546
    on journaling, 519–520
    last note to, 499f
    last visit by, 500f
    on legacy of Bob Crane, 597
    on *Superdad* (film), 395
Crane, Rosemary (Rose) Senich
    background of, 30
    on first radio job, 64
    marriage of, 30
    move to California, 284
    and Patty Olson, 376, 378
    personality of, 31
    photographs of, 10f, 49f
    and Scotty, 378
    and Mike Senich, 78
Crane and Friends, 92
Crane-Catino Jazz Band, 33, 38–39, 42, 51f
The Crane Little Theatre Players, 157
Crean, Mary Hogan, 30
Crean, Patrick, 30
Crenna, Richard, 194–195
Crisis (radio series), 474–475
Crosby, Bing, 293–294
Crowley, Pat, 190
Cruise, Tom, 490
Cullen, Bill, 152
Cummings, Robert (Bob), 190–191, 399

D

Daley, Frank, 297–298
Dalton, Abby, 349, 470, 471
Daly, Frank, Jr., 51
Daly, Maggie, 471
Dane, Jim. *See* Senich, Jim
Dann, Mike, 197–198
Date book, 519–520
Davenport, Bill, 277
Davis, Luther, 303
Davis, Sammy, 291
Davis, Tom, 6, 228, 244–245, 542, 587, 595
Davis Monthan Air Force Base (Tucson, Ariz.), 309, 316f
Dawson, Richard (Dickie)
   album by, 292
   background of, 197–198
   on John Banner, 196
   cancellation letter to, 258, 275, 387
   casting of, 193–194, 197–198, 200, 203
   cast photos of, 188f, 263f, 264f, 268f
   character played by, 238
   on *Family Feud*, 394
   at first outdoor shoot, 214
   German accent by, 228–229
   on *Hogan's Heroes* as parody, 220
   and *"Hogan's Heroes" Revue,* 366
   on *The New Dick Van Dyke Show,* 399
   on nicknames, 243–244
   popularity of, 219
   pranks by, 244
   rivalry between Crane and, 246–250
   and sex addiction, 541
Day, Doris, 150, 285, 391
DeBenedetto, Salvatore "Tootie," 92, 527, 530
Deeb, Gary, 411
Dehner, John, 391
Delfino, Frank, 91, 392, 527
The Delphi Bureau (TV show), 391
Derak, Frank, 81–82
Desilu Cahuenga Studios, 201, 225
The Devil's Advocate (film), 521
DeVries, Peter, 466
Dickenson, Angie, 391

The Dick Van Dyke Show, 168–169, 172, 256, 405–406
The Dictator (film), 220
Diller, Phyllis, 415
Dinner theatre, 471–473, 568–569
Disc jockey
   creation of term, 128
   and musical acts, 124
   typecasting as, 161, 162
Divorce
   from Anne, 259, 325, 351–356, 353–356, 360–361
   impending from Patty, 423, 471, 489
   reactions of friends and family to, 376–377
Dixon, Ivan
   album by, 292
   cancellation letter to, 258, 275
   casting of, 199–200, 203
   cast photos of, 188f, 264f, 266f
   departure from show of, 255–256
   German accent by, 228–229
   and Ted Lange, 428–429
   on line muffing, 228
   nickname for, 244
   racial anecdote on, 238–239
   on work atmosphere, 243
   on working with Bob Crane, 245
Dixon, Nomathande, 199
Dober, Eliot
   on air with Bob, 93, 94
   on death of Bob's father, 422
   on legacy of Bob Crane, 592
   remembrance by, 3
   on sex addiction, 528–529, 530
   at United Cerebral Palsy Telethon, 313, 420, 451f
Documentation, Bob's need for, 518–520, 578
Donlevy, Brian, 388
The Donna Reed Show
   Bob as regular on, 170–178
   cast photos, 148f
   departure from, 183
   guest starring on, 169–170
   vs. *Hogan's Heroes,* 205–206
   and KNX-CBS Radio show, 175
   sex addiction during, 535–536
The Doris Day Show (TV show), 391
Dorsey, Tommy, 23f, 32, 329, 379
Douglas, Michael, 350–351
Downey, Harry, 527

Downs, Hugh, 166
Dramatic roles, Bob's desire for, 383–384
Dramedy, 374, 402
Drums and drumming
  on *Bob Crane, His Drums and Orchestra Play the Funny Side of TV* (album), 287–293, 314f
  on "The Bob Crane Show" (KNX-CBS Radio), 115, 137f
  with Connecticut Symphony Orchestra, 41
  in Crane-Catino Jazz Band, 33, 38–39, 42, 51f
  Karen Crane on, 329–330
  with Tommy Dorsey Orchestra, 23f
  during early school years, 32–35
  earning money for, 34
  finding teacher for, 39–40
  first drum set, 33
  in high school, 22, 27, 33–35, 39–42
  on *Hogan's Heroes* set, 242
  with Harry James Orchestra, 22
  with Stan Kenton Orchestra, 21
  by Scott, 381
  during wedding reception with Patty, 367f
  while at WICC, 91–92
Duffy, Frank, 48f
Dugan, Dave, 43, 282
Duke, Patty, 378
Dukoff, Bobby, 91
Dunlap, Wallace (Wallie, Wally)
  background of, 79
  and Channel 43, 90, 91
  course on radio technique by, 62, 75
  at WICC, 76f, 102f
  and WLIZ job, 69–70, 79, 80

E

Ebsen, Buddy, 328
The Ed Sullivan Show (TV show), 164–165
Edwards, Geoff, 123, 508
Efron, Edith, 187, 236
Ego(s)
  in Stella Adler's class, 181
  in community theatre, 155
  of Bob Crane, 6, 8
  on *Hogan's Heroes*, 212, 236–241
  Anthony Hopkins on, 246–247
  at WICC, 98
Eglin Air Force Base (Fort Walton Beach, Fla.), 308, 319f
Ellery Queen (TV show), 391, 398
Ellington, Duke, 32, 91
Ellis, Raymond C., 59
Embezzlement, 472
Enarc Week, 81, 85, 86
Energy crisis, 374
Erdel, Jeff, 433–436, 444
Ericson, Eric, 149
Evans, Art, 311
Evans, Jerry, 167

F

Fabares, Shelley, 170, 287
Family Feud (TV show), 394
Fan(s), 331, 479, 545–546
Fan mail, 283
Fatal Attraction (film), 350–351
Federson, Don, 165, 166
Fein, Bernard (Bernie)
  casting by, 191, 193–194, 196, 216
  at first day of shooting, 214
  naming of character by, 218
  writing pilot script by, 213–214, 215–216
Fein, Kay, 193, 216
Feldman, Edward H. (Ed, Eddie)
  as associate producer, 217
  and John Banner's declining health, 384–385
  and *Beginner's Luck*, 477
  casting by, 191–200
  on character of Hogan, 233
  choice of name by, 218
  and Cindy Lynn's departure, 344–345, 346, 359
  on Bob Crane, 240
  on hiring of Patty Olson, 347–348
  at marriage of Bob and Patty, 357–359
  and pilot, 202–204, 214
  on props, 225
  and rumor on reactivation of *Hogan's Heroes*, 422
  on set design, 226–227
  and success of *Hogan's Heroes*, 237–240

Feller, Sid, 289
Feminist movement, 373–374
Fetishes, 562
Fields, Joseph, 466
Finch, Rayburn A., 152
Finkelstein, Leo, Jr., 310, 321f
Finlay Straus Jewelers, 57–59, 62
First Methodist Church (Pueblo, Colo.), 555
Fisher, Eddie, 201
Fitzgerald, Ella, 128
"The Flaw" (radio theatre show), 474–475
Fletcher, Jack, 401, 409, 412
The Floor Covering Shop, 31, 523
Flynn, Joe, 392, 395
Ford, Glenn, 128
Ford, Tennessee Ernie, 418
Forman, Joey, 295, 298
Forty Acres Backlot, 201, 221, 226–227
Fotine, Larry, 91
Fox, Bernard, 11f, 200, 391, 463, 471, 479, 483
Foy, Eddie, III, 170–172, 174, 175–176
Francis, Connie, 289
Fraser, Elisabeth, 150
Frasier (television show), 17
Freberg, Stan, 220
Freed, Donald (Don), 8, 153–156, 466, 535
Freeman, Ernie, 289
Freeman, Kathleen, 200
French, Jim, 474–475
French, Pat, 475
French, Samuel, 474
Fultz, Jay, 174
Functional schizophrenia, 564
"Funds for Dinah," 312

G

Gabor, Eva, 256, 294, 306, 325
Gaede, Elmer, 115–116
Gambling, John B., 152
Garner, James, 219–220
Gaynor, Mitzi, 312
Geller, Harvey
    on acting career, 157, 161, 163
    on Crane as Hogan, 234
    on fame, 285
    on family life, 129
    on improvising, 81
    on legacy of Bob Crane, 592–593
    on naming of children, 361
    remembrance by, 5
    on sex addiction, 529–530, 543–544
    on success at KNX, 125
    on wanting to work in New York, 96
    on watch collection, 519
General Electric Theatre (TV show), 163
German accent, 228–229
German viewers of *Hogan's Heroes*, 219, 223
Gerussi, Bruno, 429, 430, 439, 442, 444, 446, 447, 455f
Ghostley, Alice, 200
Gibbsville (TV show), 391
Gilford, Jack, 303
Gilman, Ken, 467
Gimmicks
    artistic control over, 109–110, 110–111
    in *Hogan's Heroes*, 223, 224, 287, 346
    at KNX, 109–110, 110–111
    of Henry Morgan, 67
    "Send Dead Flies," 117–118
    Valentine's Day kisses, 81–82
    at WICC, 80, 92
    at WLEA, 65
Gish, Lillian, 303, 304–305
Gleason, Jackie, 337
Glendale Elementary School (Stamford, Conn.), 29
Glen Island Casino (New Rochelle, N.Y.), 91
The Godfather (film), 390–391
Godfrey, Arthur, 67, 198
Golden, Jane Lippoth
    on Anne's personality, 330–331
    on Bob and Anne's marriage, 60
    at Class Reunion, 98
    on divorce and remarriage, 377
    on drumming, 40
    on hometown roots, 46
    on legacy of Bob Crane, 594
    on move to California, 129
    photograph of, 72f
Golden, John, 60, 72f
Goldman, Roy, 242, 267f
Goldsboro, Bobby, 395
Goobic, Donna, 490–491
Goodman, Benny, 34, 40, 329, 379

Good Morning America (TV show), 399
Good vs. evil, 569–570, 580, 582
Gordon, Edwin (Eddy), 39–40
  on Bob's father, 32, 33
  on drumming, 41, 48f
  on sex addiction, 522–525, 550
Gottfried, Nathan, 6
Gould, Harold, 401, 409
Graham, Ronny, 401, 412
Graham, Virginia, 391
Grammer, Kelsey, 17
Grandy, Fred, 427
Grant, Cary, 224, 235, 303, 304
Gray, Dennis, 242, 267f
Graysmith, Robert, 437
The Great Coogamooga, 138–139
The Great Dictator (film), 219
The Great Escape (film), 219
Griffith, Andy, 400
Grimaldi, Lennie, 78
Griswold, Deborah, 93
Gross, Martha, 420, 456f
Groundwater, Linda, 476
Gudegast, Dale, 357
Guest appearances
  after *Hogan's Heroes,* 391–392
  during *Hogan's Heroes,* 293–294, 296–297, 315f
Guiliani, Joe, 48f
Guilt about sex addiction, 526, 576, 580
Gus (film), 392, 547
Gwynne, Fred, 303

H

Hagman, Larry, 402, 408
Hall, Alan, 128, 136f
Hall, Monty, 3, 451f, 476
Hard comedy, 406
The Hardy Boys/Nancy Drew Mysteries (TV show), 392
Harper, Phil, 475
The Harry James Orchestra, 379
Hart, Tricia, 401, 412
Hartley, David, 319f
Harty, Patricia, 401, 412
Haskell, Jimmie, 295
Hatten, Tom, 154, 155, 167, 353
The Hawaii Experience (TV show), 423–427, 453f, 454f, 489, 549–550
Hayes, Helen, 303, 304–305

Hayes, Pamela. *See* Thompson, Pamela (Pam) Hayes
Haygan, Sam, 242, 267f
Hendrix, Jimi, 374
Henning, Paul, 237, 399
Herman, Woody, 32, 39
High school
  acting in, 149–150
  drumming in, 22, 27, 33–35, 39–42
  sex addiction during, 522–525
  tenth Class reunion, 98–99
  thirtieth Class reunion, 547–548
Hillerman, John, 401
Hitchcock, Alfred, 163
Hlavaty, Ed, 48f
Hobby, Wes, 530
Hogan, Margret, 30
Hogan, Richard, 218, 270f
Hogan, Robert (actor), 212, 213–214, 216, 239, 242–243, 595
Hogan, Robert E. (great-grandfather), 30, 218
Hogan, Robert Steadham (physician), 218, 270f
Hogan's Heroes (TV show), 187–277
  ad libbing on, 249–250
  aloofness on, 251–252
  award nominations for, 256–257
  behind-the-scenes photographs of, 273f
  cancellation of, 257–258, 274–277, 387
  cast and characters' personas on, 230–231, 233–236
  cast changes on, 254–256
  casting of, 189–203
  cast photographs of, 188f, 263–268f
  changes in personal life during, 258–259
  color filming of, 203–204
  comedy style of, 224
  congratulatory telegrams and letters on, 210–211
  controversy over, 189–190, 219–223
  debut of, 210–212
  directing Bob on, 231–232
  drumming on set of, 242
  ensemble acting on, 212–213, 229
  fear and romance on, 227
  first press about, 204

637

funny moments during filming of, 244
German accents on, 228–229
idea for, 213–215
and job at KNX, 205–207, 209
lightness vs. realism of, 223
male communality on, 212, 236–245, 252–254
muffing lines on, 227–228
name changes on, 215–216, 218
original drawing by Mike Senich of, 262f
as parody, 219–221
photographs of Crane in, 188f, 261f, 272f
pilot episode of, 201–203
pitching idea for, 216–217
plagiarism suit against, 215–216
popularity of, 217–219, 223
preparation for scene on, 228
profit participants in, 207, 388
promotional tag line for, 220
public appearances to promote, 208–210, 269–271f
recurring but unnamed extras on, 242
residuals from, 388
rivalries on, 246–250
rumor on reactivation of, 420–422
schedule for filming of, 225–227
scrapbooks on, 204, 214, 292f
sex addiction during, 537–544
vulgarity or rudeness on, 250–251
worldwide audience of, 282
"Hogan's Heroes" Revue, 385–387
"Hogan's Heroes" Sing the Best of World War II (album), 292
Hogan's Horde, 207
Holden, William, 591
Holley, Tim, 421
Hollywood Radio Theatre, 474
Hollywood Squares (TV show), 391
Holy Childhood Association, 310–311
Honeymoon
with Anne, 60–61
with Patty, 359
The Honeymoon Game (TV show), 391
Hope, Bob, 305–306, 406, 418
Hopkins, Anthony, 246–247
Horne, Lena, 128
Hornell, N.Y., 54f, 62–68, 73f, 74f
Hotel Tap Room (Bridgeport, Conn.), 91
"Housewives' Time," 121

Hovis, Larry
album by, 292
cancellation letter to, 258, 276, 387
casting of, 198, 203
cast photos of, 188f, 264f, 266f, 268f
Tom Davis and, 228
German accent by, 228–229
and *"Hogan's Heroes" Revue*, 366
on legacy of Bob Crane, 598–599
nickname for, 243–244
on sex addiction, 542
Humor
in *Beginner's Luck,* 478
on *Bob Crane, His Drums and Orchestra Play the Funny Side of TV* (album), 287–293, 314f
on *The Donna Reed Show,* 170
on *Hogan's Heroes,* 212–213, 220, 222, 242–243, 245–246
inoffensive, 353
on KMPC, 373
on KNX, 120, 122, 125–128, 138, 154
on "Laffter Sweet and Profane" (promotional album), 138–139
and laugh track, 298–299
about Nazis, 191–193, 196–197, 214–215, 219–221, 222, 236
off-color, 546
self-deprecating, 41, 55, 67, 131–133, 298, 534
sense of, 7, 40, 125–128
on WICC, 81–83
Hutton, Jim, 193

I

I Love Lucy (TV show), 202
Imagination Theatre, 474–475
Imus, Don, 124
Ingolio, Jimm, 585–586
In Search of Donna Reed (Fultz), 174
The Interlude (nightclub), 131
Intermission Riff (song), 21
The Interview (film), 220
Interviews on "The Bob Crane Show" (KNX-CBS Radio), 123, 126–127, 128, 136f, 144f
Irvin, Bill, 204

Irwin, Nancy, 577–578
I Spy (TV show), 224
Ivanko, Audrey, 42
I Witness (TV show), 400

J

The Jackie Gleason Show (TV show), 337
James, Harry, 22, 379
Jarecki, Dave, 119, 141f
Jarrell, Alice, 42
Jarvis, Al, 128
Jessel, George, 139
Jewish background of cast members of *Hogan's Heroes*, 195, 197–198
Jewish viewers of *Hogan's Heroes*, 219–224
Jim French Productions, 474–475
Jimmie Haskell Orchestra, 295
Joe Forrester (TV show), 391–392
Johnson, Edgar, 242, 267f
Johnson, Erskine, 329
Johnson, Van, 193, 556, 557
Jokes on radio, 68
Joplin, Janis, 374
Journals, 519–520
June Taylor Dancers, 337
Junior Achievement program (Bridgeport, Conn.), 93, 103f, 307

K

Kaolian, Morgan, 3, 89–91, 102f, 150, 290, 529
Karas, Frank, 31
Karas, Marion, 31
Katehakis, Alexandra, 574–577
Kaye, Danny, 147
KAYO-1150 AM, 418
Kear, Anne, 4, 430, 433, 436, 438, 440, 444–448
Keaton, Buster, 130
Kelley, DeForest, 477
Kenney, David, 103f
Kenton, Stan, 21, 91, 379
Kesselring, Joseph, 302
Kimmel, Bruce, 401
"King of the LA Airwaves," 114
King Rat (film), 193
Kinskey, Leonid, 200, 203, 214, 236
Kleiner, Dick, 227–228, 297

Klemperer, Otto, 195
Klemperer, Victor, 195
Klemperer, Werner
  on *Bob Crane, His Drums and Orchestra Play the Funny Side of TV* (album), 292
  Robert Butler on, 231
  cancellation letter to, 258, 276, 387
  casting of, 194–195, 200, 203
  cast photos of, 188f, 263f, 266f, 268f
  on comedy about Nazis, 221
  on communality, 237
  Emmys won by, 256, 257
  on filming in color, 203–204
  on filming schedule, 226
  and *"Hogan's Heroes" Revue*, 366
  Jerry London on, 241
  in military films, 310, 321f
  nickname for, 243
  promotional tour by, 208, 269f, 271f
  on sex addiction, 542–543
  tension between John Banner and, 247
  on *The Wicked Dreams of Paula Schultz* (film), 295, 298
  on work after *Hogan's Heroes*, 431
  working with, 253–254
  on working with Bob Crane, 251
KMPC Radio, 372f, 373, 414–418, 452f
Knotts, Don, 392, 490
KNX-CBS Radio, "The Bob Crane Show" on. *See* "The Bob Crane Show" (KNX-CBS Radio)
Kopell, Bernie, 427
Kovacs, Ernie, 89, 152
Krasva, Norman, 155
Krupa, Gene
  on "The Bob Crane Show" (KNX-CBS Radio), 106f
  Edwin Gordon and, 41
  as idol, 46
  at New York World's Fair, 27, 32, 286
  radio exposure for, 34

L

Laddin's Terrace, 38, 72f, 98
Lafferty, Perry, 205

"Laffter Sweet and Profane" (promotional album), 138–139
Lamm, Richard, 555
Lane, Priscilla, 303
Lange, Ted, 7, 427, 428
Laugh-In (TV show), 198
Laugh track, 298–299
Lee, Gypsy Rose, 209
Lee, Michele, 414
Lee, Peggy, 128
Lee, Ruta, 229, 233, 240, 475
Legacy, 583–600
Leidecker, Doris Sidney, 46
Lemmon, Jack
    and becoming a star, 173
    and Colonel Hogan character, 233
    on KNX radio show, 144f, 156
    and typecasting, 162, 164
    and *The Wicked Dreams of Paula Schultz*, 295
Leonard, Sheldon, 168, 237
Levy, Mike, 216, 217
Lewis, Jerry
    childhood of, 305
    interviews with, 128, 156, 209, 418
    on success of *Hogan's Heroes*, 210, 211
Lind, Alisa, 337
Linden, Hal, 412
Linkletter, Art, 152, 164, 286, 315f, 393–394
Lippoth, Jane. *See* Golden, Jane Lippoth
Lipson, Larry, 466
Little Theatre, 157, 160
Live audience, filming in front of, 405–406
Lloyd, Harold, Jr., 167
London, Jerry
    on camaraderie, 247–248
    on Crane as Hogan, 235
    on Crane-Dawson rivalry, 246
    on Edward Feldman, 238, 240
    on German accent, 229
    on learning of Bob Crane's death, 507
    on legacy of Bob Crane, 591
    photo of, 265f
    on pilot, 194, 202
    on production schedule, 225
    remembrance by, 6
    on set design, 226–227
    on sex addiction, 541
    on working with Bob Crane, 231–232, 241, 242
Loren, Sophia, 536
Lorne, Marion, 256
Love, American Style (TV show), 391
Love addiction, 579
The Love Boat (TV show), 392, 427–429
Loverde, Frank, 469
Lucey, Matt, 91, 337, 338
Lucky Platt Department Store, 29
Lynn, Cynthia (Cindy)
    affair with, 258–259, 336–346, 359–360, 514, 539–540
    background of, 220, 222
    on Bob and Anne, 341
    on Bob's childhood, 342
    on Bob's need for feminine understanding, 343
    casting of, 200
    cast photos of, 188f, 324f
    on character of Hogan, 233–234
    on communality, 237
    on controversy over *Hogan's Heroes*, 223
    on Crane-Dawson rivalry, 247
    departure from show of, 254
    on filming schedule, 225
    immigration and childhood of, 336–337
    on learning of Bob Crane's death, 506–507
    on legacy of Bob Crane, 589
    marriages of, 337, 339, 344–346
    move to Hollywood, 337
    remembrance by, 4
    return to *Hogan's Heroes* of, 359–360
    screen romance with, 230, 338
    television debut of, 337
    on working with Bob Crane, 250
Lyon, Sue, 303

M

MacLeod, Gavin, 427
Macy, Bill, 475
Madonna/Whore syndrome, 578
Make Mine Red, White, and Blue (TV show), 414
Male communality *on Hogan's Heroes*, 212, 236–245, 252–254
Mann, Shelly, 21

Index

"Man of a Thousand Voices," 115–116
Man-Trap (film), 162–163
Marching band, 33, 35
Markham, Monte, 235, 253–254, 394
Marks, Larry, 225
Marriage, 323–370
  and affair with Cynthia Lynn, 324f, 336–346, 359–360
  and affair with Patty Olson, 258–259, 346–357, 365f, 383f
  to Anne, 324f, 325–336, 362–364f
  and divorce from Anne, 259, 325, 351–356, 353–356, 360–361
  and impending divorce from Patty, 423, 471, 489
  to Patty Olson, 259, 324f, 357–359, 361, 366–368f
Marriage on the Rocks (film), 347
Marshall, George, 295, 297–299
Martel, Arlene
  on Bob's aloofness, 252
  on Bob's need for feminine understanding, 343
  on Bob's personality, 518
  on Bob's relationship with women, 336
  casting of, 200
  on Ed Feldman, 238
  on legacy of Bob Crane, 589
  remembrance by, 6
  on sex addiction, 538–539, 543, 576
  on working with Bob Crane, 229, 239–240, 250–251
Martin, Bob, 373
Martin, Dean, 128, 289, 305–306, 347
Martin, Ross, 347
Martino, Teddy, 51
Maryon, Bob, 414–418, 595–596
Mary Tyler Moore (MTM) Productions, 400–401
The Mary Tyler Moore Show (TV show), 374
Marzano, Janice, 282
M*A*S*H (TV show), 374
Mason, Gordon
  on artistic freedom, 111
  on getting started in television, 166–167
  on legacy of Bob Crane, 595
  on popularity of Crane at KNX, 120
  on prep work, 121
  on sex addiction, 534–535
  on sponsors, 111–112, 112–114, 119, 121–122
Matthau, Walter, 193
May, Elaine, 138
McCormack, Val, 311
McCrea, Ann, 172, 174–175, 535
McElroy, Leo
  on artistic control, 110
  on Crane's personality, 123, 245
  on *The Donna Reed Show,* 173
  on getting into acting, 162, 166
  helped by Bob, 393
  on *Hogan's Heroes,* 283
  on learning of Bob Crane's death, 508–509
  on legacy of Bob Crane, 593
  remembrance by, 4
  on sex addiction, 532
  on spontaneity, 120
  on theatre performances, 472–473
  on transition to acting, 156
  on voice tracks and drum solos, 114, 116–118
  on WEEI, 108, 111
McEveety, Vincent, 395
McGowan, Mary K., 60
McGuinness, Neil, 5, 34, 42, 282
McHale, Bill, 559
McHale's Navy (TV show), 224
Merryman, Phillip, 80, 88, 90
Miller, Glenn, 32, 38, 379
C.O. Miller's Department Store, 31
Miritello, Kathy, 244
Mitchell, Guy, 81, 125
Mitchell, Shirley, 168
Mitzi and a Hundred Guys, 312
Mobile One (TV show), 400
Mona Lisa (song), 90
Monet, Veronica, 578–580
Monroe, Marilyn, 139
Moore, Carroll, 508f
  Beginner's Luck written by, 473–476
  and Bob's known performances of *Beginner's Luck,* 461
  and Bob's revisions, 478
  production rights secured from, 389, 477
  Send Me No Flowers by, 465–466
Moore, Clayton, 285
Moore, Mary Tyler, 168, 169, 374
Morality, 569–570, 580, 582
Morgan, Hal, 133

Morgan, Henry, 67
Morris, Howard, 227–228
Moses, Horace A., 93
Moss, Stuart, 203, 250
MTM (Mary Tyler Moore) Productions, 400–401
Mucci, Patrick, 42
Multiple-camera set, 405–406, 406–407
Music. *See also* Drums and drumming
    in 1970s, 374
    on "The Bob Crane Show" (KNX-CBS Radio), 119–120, 124
    Bob's love of, 22
    on KMPC, 373
    on KNX-CBS Radio, 105, 108, 109, 115, 116–118, 119–120
    and radio, 56, 68
    on WICC, 92
Musical entertainer, Bob as, 41
Music videos, 90
My Living Doll (TV show), 190–191

N

Nakken, Craig, 517, 521–522, 525–526, 531, 537, 543, 545, 551
Nazis, comedy about, 191–193, 196–197, 214–215, 219–221, 222, 236
Nelson, Gene, 175
Never My Love (song), 124
Never Too Late (film), 193
The New Dick Van Dyke Show (TV show), 399
New Life Ministries, 554
Newman, Paul, 302
News on "The Bob Crane Show" (KNX-CBS Radio), 121
The New Tommy Dorsey Orchestra, 379
Nichols, Mike, 138
Nichols, Red, 40
Nicholson, Jack, 392
Night Gallery (TV show), 391
Nimoy, Leonard, 285, 378
1970s, 371–456, 457–509
    Beginner's Luck (play) in. *See Beginner's Luck* (play)
    The Bob Crane Show (TV show) in, 399–401, 407–413
    Celebrity Cooks (TV show) in, 429–430, 433–448, 455f
    charity events in, 451f
    death of Bob Crane in, 502–509
    death of father in, 422
    divorce papers from Patty in, 423, 471, 489
    drug and alcohol abuse in, 373
    embezzlement from Bob in, 472
    family life in, 375–383, 449f, 450f
    The Godfather (film) in, 390–391
    guest-starring roles on television in, 391–392
    The Hawaii Experience (TV show) in, 423–427, 453f, 454f
    helping others in, 392–394
    Hogan's Heroes in, 384–385
    "Hogan's Heroes" Revue in, 385–387
    hope for future in, 498–499, 499–501f
    KMPC Radio in, 372f, 373, 414–418, 452f
    The Love Boat (TV show) in, 392, 427–429
    music in, 374
    profit participation program in, 388
    Second Start (TV show) in, 401–407
    steady work during, 472
    Superdad (film) in, 392, 395–398
    technology in, 374
    television programs in, 374
    typecasting in, 390–391, 394–399
    Vietnam War in, 373
    WICC in, 420, 421, 456f
Nixon, Richard, 374
No-acting clause, 156–157, 161–162
Norton Air Force Base (San Bernardino, Calif.), 310
Norwalk Symphony Orchestra, 41
"Novel Orchestra," 312

O

O'Brien, Edmond, 163
Obsessive-compulsive behavior, 518–521
O'Connor, Carroll, 378, 451f
Olson, Patricia (Patty). *See* Crane, Patricia (Patty) Olson
On-air promotions at WICC, 81
Operation Entertainment (TV show), 308, 319f
Oppenheimer, Peer J., 361

Orland, John, 423–427, 507–508, 549–550
Orland, Marcia, 453f
O'Sullivan, Colleen, 154, 155, 466
Our Man Flint (film), 347
Owen, Tony
    on Anne's illness, 327
    on *The Donna Reed Show,* 169–170, 170–171, 172, 178
    on release of Crane from *The Donna Reed Show,* 180–183
    support for *Hogan's Heroes* by, 210
Owens, Gary, 4, 128, 130, 307, 544, 591–592

P

Paar, Jack, 164, 165, 166
Pacino, Al, 521
Pack, Dick, 95
Packer, Roger, 430, 433, 436, 437, 438, 440–444
Page, Don, 209
Page, Patti, 66–67, 84, 125
Paley, William S. (Bill), 216–217
Palmer, Earl, 291
Paradise Point, 382
Parenti, Tony, 91
Parents, 29–31. *See* also, Crane, Alfred Thomas (Al Sr.) (father); Crane, Rosemary (Rose) Senich
Parker, Fess, 328
Pasternak, Joe, 162
Patience, 281
Patriotism (film), 311
Pepper, Dick, 515
Perrin, Nat, 297
Persky, Bill, 256
Personal appearances on "The Bob Crane Show" (KNX-CBS Radio), 112–114
Personality, addictive, 517–522
Pet(s), 369f, 380, 391
Peterfy, Richard, 482
Petersen, Patty, 170
Petersen, Paul
    on Bob's personality, 518
    and Bob's work on set with women, 336
    on *The Donna Reed Show,* 170, 174, 175–177, 178, 180
    on ensemble acting, 229

on KNX show, 122
and Stu Phillips, 287
on sex addiction, 535–536
Pet Set (TV show), 391
Pettet, Joanne, 330
Pheasant Run Dinner Playhouse (Elk Grove Village, Ill.), 418
Philbin, Regis, 171–172, 174
Phillips, Stu, 7, 287–293, 314f
Photography, Bob's interest in, 340, 379, 520, 543–544
Picture Window (TV show pilot), 157–161
Plastina, Rick, 7, 467–470, 541–542, 595
Playboy magazine, 533, 547
Please Don't Eat the Daisies (TV show), 190
Pocono Mountains, 60–61
Poitier, Sidney, 199
Police Woman (TV show), 374, 391
Poller, Arnold, 282
Pornography
    Edward Beck on, 557, 559–560, 567
    Edwin Gordon on, 550
    in Hollywood, 544
    Jerry London on, 541
    and obsessive-compulsive ways, 520–521
    and *Playboy,* 533, 547
Porter, Cole, 40
Poughkeepsie, N.Y., 29
POW(s) (prisoners of war)
    meeting with, 309–310
    as viewers of *Hogan's Heroes,* 222–223
POW (prisoner of war) camp vs. concentration camp, 219, 220–221, 223
Powell, Norman S.
    on *Beginner's Luck,* 473
    on casting of Bob, 408–410
    on concept for *Second Start,* 401–402
    on multiple-camera set, 405–406, 406–407
    on sex addiction, 546
    on show failing, 413
    on starting show in March, 404
Powell, Richard M., 196, 212
Prima, Louis (Lou), 87, 91
Prime Time Access Rule, 403–404

Prisoner(s) of war (POWs)
  meeting with, 309–310
  as viewers of *Hogan's Heroes,* 222–223
Prisoner of war (POW) camp vs. concentration camp, 219, 220–221, 223
The Producers, 219, 243
Profit participation program, 207, 388
Promotional films, 310–311
Public service announcements (PSAs), 310–311, 455f

Q

Quallich, Susanne A., 511
Queen for a Day (TV show), 152
Quincy M.E. (TV show), 250, 392

R

Radio and Television Engineers Union (IBEW), 111
Radio career
  desire for, 55–57
  hard work in early, 95–96
  jokes in, 68
  at KMPC, 372f, 373, 414–418, 452f
  at KNX-CBS Radio, 107–135, 136–145f
  lack of success breaking into New York City market, 94–98
  poking fun at advertisers in, 65, 66–67, 68
  recording and cataloging of, 519
  short stories in, 68
  spontaneity in, 56
  training for, 62
  at WBIS, 68–69, 77
  at WICC, 76f, 79–99, 101–104f
  at WLEA, 54f, 62–68, 73f, 74f
  at WLIZ, 69–70, 77
  and WVPO, 61
Radio theatre, 477–478
Radio TV Mirror (magazine), 98
Randall, Bob, 461
Randall, Tony, 162, 164
Ransohoff, Jack, 28
Ransohoff, Martin, 28, 35

Rayburn, Gene, 95
Record collection, 378–379, 519
Record of television themes, 287–293, 314f
Redgrave, Vanessa, 330
Reed, Donna
  on Crane's release from *The Donna Reed Show,* 180–183
  on *The Donna Reed Show,* 169–178, 190, 229
  and sex addiction, 535, 536
  support for *Hogan's Heroes* by, 210, 254
Reeves, Keanu, 521
Reiner, Carl, 168–169
Religion and sex addiction, 522–523, 538–539, 565–566, 578, 580
Remembrances, 3–8
"Remington Raider," 60
Residuals, 388
Restlessness, 153
Return to Peyton Place (film), 162–163
Reynolds, John T., 289f
Rich, Buddy, 329, 593
Rich, John, 168, 183
Richards, Ronni, 475
Ritter, John, 401
Ritz Ballroom (Bridgeport, Conn.), 91
Rivers, Fred, 337
Robbins, Fred, 36
Robertson, Dale, 328
Robertson, Ed, 329, 428, 547
Rod Serling's Zero Hour (radio show), 474
Roman Catholicism
  of Bob's parents, 29–30, 31
  after marriage to Anne, 65
  and marriage to Anne, 60, 71f
  and move to California, 107–108
  and plot involving struggling priest, 383–384
  and sex addiction, 522–523, 530, 544, 565–566, 578, 580
Romero, Caesar, 556
Rommel, Ronnie, 91
Rooney, Mickey, 22, 152–153, 415, 557, 569, 572
Rosa, Gloria, 57
Rose, Robert L., 405
Royce, Brenda Scott, 193, 194–195, 210, 216, 237, 251
Rubin, Stan, 132, 163

Ruddy, Albert S. (Al), 193, 213–217, 222, 390–391, 591
The Rural Purge, 258
Rush, Barbara, 392, 395
Russell, Kurt, 392, 395
Ryan, Dick, 242, 267f
Ryfun, Jane Senich, 77, 248, 257, 378

S

Safranski, Eddie, 91
Sales, Soupy, 233, 418
Sands, Lee, 337, 344–346
Sandwich shop commercial, 82
Sanford and Son (TV show), 374
Sappern, Donald (Don)
    on character of Hogan, 234
    on Crane-Catino Jazz Band, 38–39
    on divorce and remarriage, 377
    on drumming, 33, 40–41
    graduation of, 45
    at High School reunion, 98
    on legacy of Bob Crane, 590
    on sex addiction, 523
Scheerer, Robert, 303–304
Schigliampaglia, Vito, 33
Schizophrenia, functional, 564
Schneider, John A. (Jack), 202, 205
Schwab, Bill, 311
Schwartz, Milton, 57, 58
Schwartz, Vernon, 468–469, 476
Scott, Vernon, 547
Scrapbooks, 204, 214, 519
Second Chance (TV show). *See Second Start* (TV show)
Second Start (TV show), 401–407, 409, 411, 412–413, 473
Secor, William B., 93
Self-deprecating humor, 41, 55, 67, 131–133, 298, 534
Seltzer, Wil, 401
"Send Dead Flies" gimmick, 117–118
Send Me No Flowers (play), 167, 351, 467–470, 541–542
Senich, Anna Walko, 30
Senich, Jane Ryfun, 30
Senich, Jim
    on Bob as non-drinker, 334
    on "The Bob Crane Show" (KNX-CBS Radio), 112, 124
    on Bob's parents, 31, 32
    on Bob's work at WICC, 83, 87
    on career after *Hogan's Heroes*, 392, 431
    on desire for dramatic roles, 383
    on divorce and remarriage, 376
    on *The Donna Reed Show*, 169
    on early radio career, 56, 59, 61, 64, 67, 95–96, 96–97
    on fame, 283–284
    on *Frasier* episode, 17–18
    on getting into acting, 164
    on *Hogan's Heroes*, 192
    on legacy of Bob Crane, 597–598
    remembrance by, 8
    on residuals, 388
    on sensitivity to feelings of others, 174
    on sex addiction, 526–527, 533–534
    on Ellen Terzian, 331–333
    at WICC, 392, 420
Senich, Michael (Mike)
    during Bob's childhood, 26f, 30–31
    caricatures by, 26f, 31, 262f
    deathbed of, 286
    influence on Bob of, 77–78
    visit to California by, 378
    and WICC, 96
    in World War II, 191
Senich, Onnifer, 30
Senich, Rosemary. *See* Crane, Rosemary (Rose) Senich
Sennes, Frank, 387
Serling, Rod, 161, 391, 474
"The Seven Lively Arts of Cole Porter" (musical revue), 40
Sex addiction, 511–582. *See also* Addiction
    addictive personality and, 517–522, 560
    and attention, 581–582
    Edward Beck on, 513, 551, 552–573
    to blondes, 563
    Bob's decision to seek help for, 559–563, 566, 568–569, 575, 578, 582
    and Bob's early life, 574–575
    Bob's view of, 568–571
    and Bob's view of self as adult, 575
    and charisma, 575
    and children, 561, 564, 566–567
    clinical perspectives on, 574–582

compartmentalization of behaviors with, 576
as coping mechanism, 577, 579
counseling on, 551, 552–573
and dinner theatre, 568–569
during *The Donna Reed Show*, 535–536
escalating cycle of, 582
and fans, 545–546
and fetishes, 562
and functional schizophrenia, 564
and good vs. evil, 569–570, 580, 582
vs. love addiction, 579
and "male dirtbag friends," 567–568
and marriage with Anne, 513–516, 527–530, 544
and marriage with Patty, 516–517, 544, 548–549
movie business and, 560
Craig Nakken on, 517, 521–522, 525–526, 531, 537, 543, 545, 551
and need for control, 518–521, 561, 563
in 1970s, 547–551
and pornography, 520–521, 543–544, 550
religion and, 522–523, 538–539, 565–566, 578, 580
shame and guilt about, 526, 576, 580
as teenager, 522–525
understanding of women and, 576–577, 578, 579
while doing *Hogan's Heroes*, 537–544
while working at KNX-CBS Radio, 539–544
while working at WICC, 526–530
Sex therapist, 560, 574–577
Shame about sex addiction, 526, 576, 580
Shaw, Artie, 379
Shaw, Jim, 353–356
Shepard, Huey, 355, 356
Sherwin, Wally, 423–424, 426, 453f
Shipley, Jeff, 337
Short stories on radio, 68
Short-Term Evangelistic Mission (S.T.E.M. project), 554
Shriner, Herb, 312
Shulman, Max, 157–160
Sikorsky, Igor, 78
Silvers, Phil, 213–214
Sinatra, Frank, 128, 198, 289, 347
Sintay, Joseph, 451f
Sisul, Joanne, 352
6 Rms Riv Vu (play), 461, 470
Slater, Manning, 79, 80, 418
Sloan, Charles W. (Chuck), 361, 375
Smith, Derek, 4, 430, 433, 437–440
Smith, Walter, 242, 267f
Smothers, Tom, 475
Snader Telescriptions, 90
Sommer, Elke, 295, 298, 300, 397
Sound effects
    artistic control over, 110–111
    on KNX, 110–111, 115, 118–119, 120
    on WICC, 82
    on WLEA, 65, 67, 68
Spector, Phil, 125
Spencer's Pilots (TV show), 391
Spirituality and sex addiction, 538–539, 565–566
Sponsors on "The Bob Crane Show" (KNX-CBS Radio), 111–112, 114–115, 119, 121–122
St. Ann's Catholic Church (Hornell, N.Y.), 65
St. Maurice Roman Catholic Church (Stamford, Conn.), 60, 61
Stalag 13, 218, 219
Stalag 17 (play), 192–193, 215, 219
Stamford, Conn., 27–29
Stamford High School, 22, 38, 42–43, 45–47, 547–548
Stamford National Guard, 59–60
The Stan Kenton Orchestra, 379
Stark, Art, 166
Julia Stark School (Stamford, Conn.), 29, 42
Star Wars (film), 374
Stein, Julie, 128
S.T.E.M. project (Short-Term Evangelistic Mission), 554
Sterling, Jack, 152
Story, Ralph, 107, 109, 111, 114, 129
Stover, Chet, 410
String of Pearls (song), 38
Strout, Dick, 298, 396–398
Stunts. *See* Gimmicks
Sullivan, Ed, 164–165

Summer stock, *Cactus Flower* in, 349, 351, 354, 355
Superdad (film), 392, 395–398, 547
Superfun (radio show), 161
Susman, Todd, 401, 412
Sutorius, James, 401, 546–547
Sutton, Frank, 462, 490–491, 494f
Sutton, John, 145f
Sutton, Robert P., 109, 145f, 161, 206

T

Talbot, Nita, 200, 256
Talk show host, 163–166
Tarzana, Calif., 128–130, 284–285, 307
Taylor, June, 337
Technical savvy, 87
Television shows
  in 1970s, 374
  The Alfred Hitchcock Hour, 163
  The Bob Crane Show, 399–401, 407–413
  on Channel 43, 88–91, 102f, 103f
  The Dick Van Dyke Show, 168–169, 172
  The Donna Reed Show, 148f, 169–178, 180–183
  General Electric Theatre, 163
  guest appearances after *Hogan's Heroes,* 391–392
  guest appearances while on *Hogan's Heroes,* 293–294, 296–297, 315f
  Hogan's Heroes. See Hogan's Heroes (TV show)
  Second Start, 401–407
  The Twilight Zone, 161
Television themes record, 287–293, 314f
Tenafly (TV show), 391
Terry, Polly, 36
Terzian, Alexander, 37, 68
Terzian, Anne Margit. *See* Crane, Anne Margit Terzian
Terzian, Ellen, 37, 60, 83–87, 331–333, 363f
Terzian, Victoria Ellen, 37
Tewes, Lauren, 427
Theatre performances, 457–501
  of *Beginner's Luck. See Beginner's Luck* (play)
  of *Cactus Flower,* 349, 351, 354, 355, 465, 470, 492f
  Bob Crane's known, 461–466
  mishaps in, 469, 488–489
  preparation for, 460
  of *Send Me No Flowers,* 167, 351, 467–470
  of *6 Rms Riv Vu,* 461, 470
  of *Tunnel of Love,* 153–154, 164, 184f, 459, 466
  of *Who Was That Lady I Saw You With?,* 155, 167, 418, 459, 466, 470
Thomas, Danny, 168
Thompson, John
  in *Beginner's Luck,* 388–389, 458f, 478, 480–482
  on Bob as father, 482–483
  on Bob as private person, 483
  Bob confiding in, 481–482
  cast photos of, 493f
  on Crane-Dawson feud, 248
  on *Hogan's Heroes,* 384
  on *"Hogan's Heroes" Revue,* 366
  on learning of Bob Crane's death, 507
  on legacy of Bob Crane, 592
  meeting future wife, 384, 479
  on Patty's pregnancy, 482
  remembrance by, 4
  on *Second Start,* 412
  on sex addiction, 548–549, 553
  on working with Bob, 478–482, 483–484
Thompson, Pamela (Pam) Hayes
  in *Beginner's Luck,* 389, 458f, 477–478, 479, 480, 481
  on Bob as private person, 483
  cast photos of, 493–495f
  on Crane-Dawson feud, 248
  on *Hogan's Heroes,* 384
  on learning of Bob Crane's death, 507
  on legacy of Bob Crane, 592
  meeting future husband, 384, 479
  remembrance by, 4
  on *Second Start,* 412
  on sex addiction, 548–549, 553
  on working with Bob, 477–479, 480, 481, 483–484
Thornton, Diane, 5, 119–120, 123–124, 532–533
Thornton, Tom, 114–115, 119, 121, 122, 533, 591
Thorpe, Bud, 75, 79

Thorpe, Jerry, 190, 191
Tinker, Grant, 401, 402, 404, 405, 406, 410
Tin Pan Alley, 40
To Be or Not to Be (film), 215
Tommy Dorsey Orchestra, 23f
Tom Thumb and Lavinia Warren Contest, 93–94
The Tonight Show (TV show), 163, 164, 166, 391
Topless bar, 484
Tormé, Mel, 22
"Town Crier," 75, 80
Tracy, Spencer, 20, 235
Trump, Donald, 29
Trzcinski, Edmund, 215
Tucker, Forrest, 302
Tunnel of Love (film), 150–151, 515
Tunnel of Love (play), 153–154, 164, 184f, 459, 466, 535
Turntables at "The Bob Crane Show" (KNX-CBS Radio), 111
Tusher, Will, 433, 434–436
The Twilight Zone (TV show), 161
Two O'Clock Jump (song), 22
Typecasting, 162, 390–391, 394–399

UHF television, 90
United Cerebral Palsy Telethon, 313, 318f, 420, 451f
United States Armed Forces Radio Network, 308
United States National Guard, 59–60, 307
Uritis, Visvalds, 337
U.S. Air Force films, 310–311
USS Bunker Hill (aircraft carrier), 44

Vacations with children, 382
Vacation Village (San Diego), 382
Valdis, Sigrid. *See* Crane, Patricia (Patty) Olson
Valentine's Day kisses stunt, 81–82
Valley Playhouse, 153–156, 184f
Van Dyke, Dick
    on *The Dick Van Dyke Show*, 168–169
    Emmy awarded to, 256, 257
    filming in front of live audience by, 405–406
    naming of shows starring, 407
    on *The New Dick Van Dyke Show*, 399
    as radios show guest, 156, 209
Van Patten, Dick, 392, 395–396
Variety Club of Southern California, 451f
Vasectomy, 482
Vaughan, Lloyd, 472
Vaughn, Robert, 347
The Venetian (film), 347
Veterans, meeting with, 309–310
Video engineer, Crane as, 88
Video taping
    of Victoria Ann Berry, 485
    of family life, 379, 381
    and need for control and organization, 519, 520
    of pornography, 520–521, 540–541, 543–544, 546, 550, 557, 559–560, 567
    at topless bar, 484
Vietnam War, 373
The Virginia Graham Show (TV show), 391
Voice impersonations
    on "The Bob Crane Show" (KNX-CBS Radio), 115–116
    on WICC, 80–81, 85
Voice talent opportunities, 161

W

Wald, Jerry, 106f, 162–163
Walt Disney Productions, 392, 395, 547
Waring, Fred, 294
Warner, H.B., 90
Warren, Al, 420
Warren United Methodist Church (Denver), 554–555
Warren Village (Denver), 555, 556
Washington, Kenneth, 255, 258, 268f, 277
Watch collection, 519
Wayne, David, 303
Wayne, John, 233, 389
WBIS (radio station), 68–69, 77
WCFL-1000 Radio, 418
Weedin, Harfield, 161
WEEI (radio station), 108–109

Wegge, Inger, 251–252, 264f, 336, 540
Weiss, Sid, 40
Welch, Raquel, 536
Wells, Alan, 484
Wells, Victoria Ann Berry (Vicky)
- on divorce papers from Patty, 423
- on legacy of Bob Crane, 596
- on murder of Bob Crane, 18, 498–499, 504–505
- remembrance by, 5
- on sex addiction, 549, 550–551, 553

West, Paul, 171, 211
The Westner (Westport, Conn.), 91
Westwood home, 378–379, 380, 381, 382
Whatever Became Of? (TV show), 425–426
White, Larry, 404, 407
Whittinghill, Dick
- filling in for, 373, 414–415
- interview with, 209
- photographs of, 372f
- as rival, 125, 372f

Who Do You Trust? (TV show), 166, 337
Who's Who in TV and Radio, 87
Who Was That Lady I Saw You With? (play), 155, 167, 418, 459, 466, 470
WICC (radio station), 79–99
- and Channel 43 (television station), 88–91
- chicken rating new records stunt at, 82, 85, 86, 102f
- community service at, 93
- enhancement of commercials on, 82–83
- 50th anniversary celebration at, 420, 421, 456f
- hiring of Crane by, 79
- idea of learning at, 97–98
- merger with WLIZ of, 79–80
- move to Booth Hill by, 88
- on-air promotions at, 81
- photographs of Bob at, 76f, 101–104f
- popularity of Crane at, 87–88
- promotions at, 80
- salary at, 83
- Jim Senich at, 392
- sex addiction while working at, 526–530
- technical sharpness at, 87
- typical morning at, 84–86
- Valentine's Day antic at, 81–82
- voice impersonations at, 80–81

The Wicked Dreams of Paula Schultz (film), 294–302, 397
Widmark, Richard, 150
The Wild, Wild West (film), 347
Williams, Guy, 328
Williams, Jack, 35, 282
Williams, Ken, 457
Williams, Robin, 236
Wilson, Edith, 467–468
Wilson, Teddy, 40
Winchell, Walter, 388
Windmill Dinner Theatre
- Ed Beck at, 17, 505–506, 513, 552, 556
- *Beginner's Luck* at, 461, 463, 585
- history and mission of, 555, 556
- John and Pam Thompson on, 507

Winquist, Ralph, 85
Winters, Jonathan, 144f, 156, 158–160, 173
WLEA (radio station), 54f, 62–68, 73f, 74f
WLIZ (radio station), 69–70, 77
Wolfe, Marjorie, 327
Wolff, Bill, 536–537
Woodward, Joanne, 302
Workaholic, 120, 520
World War II, 29, 43–45, 191–192
WVPO (radio station), 61
Wynn, Keenan, 475

Y

York, Francine, 540
Young, Dee, 420
Young, Doug, 475
Young, Gig
- and becoming a star, 173
- and *Superdad* (film), 395
- in *Tunnel of Love* (film), 150–151, 515
- and typecasting of Bob, 162
- and *The Wicked Dreams of Paula Schultz* (film), 295

Young Tom Edison (film), 152–153

Z

Ziemelis, Alisa, 336–337
Ziemelis, Zinta Valda. *See* Lynn, Cynthia (Cindy)
Zito, Charlie
    on Anne's life in Hollywood, 331
    audio recordings sent to, 379–380
    with Bob and Anne, 364f
    on character of Hogan, 234
    on "color blindness" of Crane, 199–200
    on divorce, 349–350, 351–352
    on drumming, 33–34, 36, 40
    on early marital troubles, 65–67, 514
    and early radio career, 56–57
    on hairstyle, 178
    high school graduation of, 45
    at high school reunion, 98
    on legacy of Bob Crane, 596
    remembrance by, 8
    on sensitivity to feelings of others, 174
    on sex addiction, 514, 522, 541, 547–548
    at wedding to Anne, 60
    during World War II, 44
Zito, Yvonne, 60, 331, 350, 351–352, 364f, 541
Zukowski, Chester, 218

Carol M. Ford has twenty years of experience in the publishing industry. She earned her BA degree with Honors in English/Liberal Arts from Glassboro State College (now Rowan University) in Glassboro, New Jersey. She is currently the Director of Editorial Services, an editor, and a managing editor for Anthony J. Jannetti, Inc., a health care association management, marketing, and publishing firm located near Philadelphia. Working with leaders in the nursing community, she oversees the production of several clinical peer-reviewed nursing publications, including scholarly journals, as well as nursing textbooks and specialty health care publications.

Carol has authored and published several articles on writing and publishing, has self-published two short stories, has written one fiction novel now under review, and has co-authored a two-part teleplay. In addition to her deep understanding of Bob Crane and her writing skills, her extensive knowledge of publishing for the health sciences has equipped her with keen investigative and research skills, ensuring the final publication of the book, which was thoroughly researched for twelve years, is evidence-based.

In 2011, Carol also nominated Bob for the National Radio Hall of Fame on behalf of his family, friends, and colleagues, and has resubmitted his nomination every year since. She will continue to spearhead the efforts for his recognition in the National Radio Hall of Fame and on the Hollywood Walk of Fame as well.

Strong in her faith, her spare time is filled with writing, reading, photography, drawing, music, traveling, hiking and fitness, enjoying the company of friends, her pets (a cat named Charley and a Golden Retriever named Copper), and spending time with family. Carol has traveled extensively across the United States, as well as around the world, including to England, Ireland, Scotland, and Australia. She has tutored with Literacy Volunteers of America, teaching adults how to read and write, and has also assisted young children in developing their reading and writing skills.

Dee Young has maintained an impressive career in radio and at WICC-600 AM for nearly forty years. She is currently the Assistant Business Manager for WICC 600-AM and WEBE-108 FM, in Bridgeport, Connecticut. In January 1976, Dee was fortunate to have had the opportunity to meet Bob Crane on the day he was in Bridgeport to help WICC celebrate the station's 50th anniversary. She remembers him and the overall experience of his visit fondly. Dee has been instrumental in the research and development of *Bob Crane: The Definitive Biography*. She brought a wealth of radio knowledge and history spanning several decades to the book, and her network of radio colleagues, including several key individuals who worked alongside of Bob at WICC and/or knew him well, has allowed for a rich illustration of Bob's early career in broadcasting.

Since 2011, Dee has also assisted Carol Ford with Bob's nomination for the National Radio Hall of Fame. WICC is an official sponsor of the nomination.

BOB CRANE The Definitive Biography

Linda J. Groundwater is a former freelance writer and American radio news journalist. She has worked as a news reporter and anchor for WSMN in Nashua, New Hampshire, and the now-defunct WKBR in Manchester, New Hampshire, where she also acted as News Director. She was also employed with WCAP in Lowell, Massachusetts, doing their morning drive news reporting. She earned her BA degree with Honors in Communications/English in Rivier College (now Rivier University), Nashua, New Hampshire.

Linda relocated to Australia with her husband Paul in 1994, and following the birth of their son Andrew in 1996, she began working in banking and finance. She is currently a Retail Lending Specialist for the Bank of Queensland, Capalaba, and has nearly twenty years of experience in banking management.

In 2003, Linda took an interest in learning more about Bob Crane. She believed there had to be more to his story than his starring role on Hogan's Heroes, or his murder and the scandal that grew from it. Using her journalism skills, she began to reach out to people from Bob's life with the intent to gather information to produce a more balanced biography. Early contributors/supporters included Bob's cousin Jim Senich and Reverend Edward Beck, who applauded the effort. From there, the list began to grow steadily. Dee Young and Carol Ford became involved in the project in 2005 and early 2006, respectively, and together, they amassed a collection of interviews and memories from close to 200 people from Bob's life specifically for *Bob Crane: The Definitive Biography* (then with the working title *Flipside: The True Story of Bob Crane*).

Also an actress, Linda performs professionally as well as in local community theatre in the Queensland area. She is also Vice President and Publicity Officer for the Mount Cotton Drama Group. Linda's faith, her family, loyal friends, and her German Shepherd named Midnight are all most important to her. She is especially proud of her son Andrew, who is pursuing his professional acting career in both Australia and the United States.

www.ingramcontent.com/pod-product-compliance
Lightning Source LLC
Chambersburg PA
CBHW021303240426
43669CB00041B/48